IN THE SERVICE OF STALIN

In the Service of Stalin

The Spanish Communists in Exile, 1939–1945

DAVID WINGEATE PIKE

CLARENDON PRESS · OXFORD
1993

Oxford University Press, Walton Street, Oxford OX2 6DP
Oxford New York Toronto
Delhi Bombay Calcutta Madras Karachi
Kuala Lumpur Singapore Hong Kong Tokyo
Nairobi Dar es Salaam Cape Town
Melbourne Auckland Madrid
and associated companies in
Berlin Ibadan

Oxford is a trade mark of Oxford University Press

Published in the United States
by Oxford University Press Inc., New York

British Library Cataloguing in Publication Data
Data available

Library of Congress Cataloging in Publication Data
Pike, David Wingeate.
In the service of Stalin : the Spanish Communists in exile,
1939–1945 / David Wingeate Pike.
p. cm.
Includes bibliographical references.
1. World War, 1939–1945—Refugees. 2. Refugees, Political—Spain—
History—20th century. 3. Refugees, Political—Europe—
History—20th century. 4. Communists—Spain—History—20th
century. 5. Communists—Europe—History—20th century. 6. Spain—
History—Civil War, 1936–1939—Refugees. 7. Spaniards—Soviet
Union—History—20th century. 8. Spaniards—Europe—History—20th
century. I. Title.
D808.P55 1993 325ʹ.21ʹ0946—dc20 92–42791

ISBN 0–19–820315–2

1 3 5 7 9 10 8 6 4 2

Typeset by Graphicraft Typesetters Ltd., Hong Kong
Printed in Great Britain
on acid-free paper by
Biddles Ltd., Guildford and King's Lynn

In memory of my father

PREFACE

This is the story of a large group of Spaniards, numbering tens of thousands, who left Spain for the most part in the great Republican exodus of January to February 1939. It traces their experiences in the period of the Second World War, focusing on what they did in the struggle against fascism. Their story is in many points and places no different from that of any other Spanish Republican in exile, for Spanish communists were everywhere that Spanish exiles could be found. They languished in the detention camps in south-western France, emigrated to the Americas, enlisted in French war factories and pioneer units, served in the French and British Armies, fought in the Resistance, suffered in the Nazi concentration camps. In such experiences no rigid distinction is drawn between those of communists and those of non-communists. Most survivors of Mauthausen, for example, insist that political ideology was subordinated to comradeship, and ultimately to the tie that binds humanity. Similarly, in the guerrilla war in France, units might be ideologically mixed as long as survival was more important than ideological purity. In such cases, the reader should not take every account as an exclusively communist experience. On the other hand, in the case of Spaniards in the Soviet Union, the experience was peculiar to communists or to those deemed sufficiently loyal to Stalin to be admitted into the country.

If, then, this book recounts the experience of the Spanish communists in exile, it describes not merely what they did but what they witnessed and recorded. In some cases, as at Mauthausen, the only evidence that remains, including the photographic evidence, is uniquely the work of Spanish communists. For that reason some material included here was the experience of non-Spaniards, but only Spaniards survived to record it.

Another feature of this book is the material it provides on the Spanish communists' closest ally (the French Communist Party) and their common enemy. The Spanish communists came out of Spain both revered and hated: revered by those who argued that only the communists and their friends were ready to fight fascism to the death; hated by those fellow-Republicans who saw in the communists' treatment of their Republican allies a glimpse of a New Spain no freer than the fascist one they fought and fled. In France, as outcasts among the outcast, they depended heavily on the French communists for help and for information. Lacking a press of their own they read the French communist press, legal or clandestine. Lacking a politburo and even a central committee, they kept abreast of the initiatives taken by the French Communist Party. As for the Nazi enemy, this book also sets out to provide the information they could not know, whether it be the identity and background of the SS staff in Mauthausen or the composition and organization of the German occupation forces in France.

This book, then, is a saga, of the kind that traverses not generations but continents, and each sector of their experience poses a different challenge to the historian. The first of these to consider is the story of the Resistance in France. Henri Noguères, one of the leading historians of the genre, has said that 'it is almost impossible to provide dates in writing on the Resistance', giving the impression that he considers it pretty hopeless, and that it is best not to try.[1] But without dates, history is reduced to cherished legend. It is no reflection on the integrity of the *guerrilleros* who have written their memoirs or provided their testimony to say that they are of very limited use to the historian. It was not their fault that they could not and dared not keep diaries. But the fact remains that their accounts only occasionally provide specific details of an action, such as place and date, and the identity of the enemy unit or its commander.[2] It was obvious that the only acceptable way to examine the claims of the Resistance was to begin with the surviving German records and to build on those. Fortunately, the records of the Wehrmacht's Army Group G are reasonably intact, and those of its LVIIIth Panzerkorps are complete, at least for the key months leading up to the retreat of the German forces. The historian of the Spanish Resistance is nevertheless at an even greater disadvantage than the historian of the French Resistance. Forty-one years went by before the French universities began a systematic attempt to co-ordinate their investigations,[3] and attempts by Spanish historians in France have produced virtually no results at all.[4] The silence of the heroes is matched by the verbosity of the poseurs. Even more harmful to the good name of the Resistance has been the success of former collaborators, especially of Vichy police officers, in passing themselves off, after the Liberation, as members of the Resistance.[5]

If the Resistance in France is a major theme of this book, no less so is the agony of the Spaniards in Mauthausen. How does one describe life in Mauthausen? Historians have been warned incessantly to approach the subject of the *KZ* with dispassion. John Colville, before he became Churchill's private secretary, no doubt expressed the sentiment better than anyone when he referred to a British Government white paper on the Nazi concentration camps as 'a sordid document calculated to appeal to people's lowest instincts. . . . After all, most of the evidence is produced from prejudiced sources, and it is in any case undesirable to arouse passions.'[6] The account given here is admittedly based upon the testimony of prejudiced sources (the surviving inmates), but it does not suppress any counter-claims (of the Nazis) that the SS were bringing joy to the world. If passions are aroused, it may be the fault of the evidence more than of the author, who knows well enough that Spaniards are capable of exaggeration. Indeed, some statistics read and heard belong only in the tales of Munchausen. The tales of Mauthausen need no adornment, and any attempt by the film industry to portray the reality of *KZ* life ends up ineluctably as fiction.

The plight of the Spaniards in the Soviet Union presents its own set of difficulties. The report in August 1987 that Soviet judicial archives covering the 1930s, 1940s, and 1950s were being burnt at the rate of 5,000 dossiers a month[7] seemed to ring the knell for the future full disclosure of Stalin's crimes. Unlike Nazi Germany, which kept its archives to the last in the hope of final victory, the USSR was proceeding without haste in the destruction of its records. Nor is it likely that the leaders of the Spanish Communist Party, whether they spent the war in Moscow or in Mexico City, will ever tell the truth about the Party or themselves. They fill their memoirs with vainglory and vain flattery, using the same phrases translated into a hundred tongues, the English model being provided by Harry Pollitt, secretary-general of the British Communist Party, when he marked the death of Stalin with an obituary in the *Daily Worker*: 'Never since my first meeting with him in 1921, together with Comrade Lenin, have I met anyone so kindly and so considerate, so easy to talk to and exchange views, and one so obviously only actuated by the desire to help. Never the dictator; never [one] to lay the law down—always eager and willing to listen, to understand another's point of view, and then to express in the most simple way his own thoughts about the matter under discussion.'[8]

There lies, in that blind unquestioning loyalty to Stalin and the cause, the common thread that runs through this book. Fascism, Stalin could handle in his erratic way, but dissidents (real or imagined) and left-wing alternatives to Stalinism sent him berserk. Hence the purges, and the assassinations, and the quiet little murders of Trotskyists, Poumists, and anarchists that the Second World War was not allowed to interrupt. Oceans of lies were then released to drown the evidence, and Stalin could die with the happy thought that, in the main, the lie had prevailed. His triumph was due largely to the sheer tenacity of his followers. They deserved their success, as a prominent member of the Republican centre said after the war, even though she scorned them, for their refusal to be discouraged by failure. They try every window in the house, Churchill once said, and when they find nothing open they break in the back door. The back door for the PCE, even more than for the PCF, meant setting up the screens and the fronts, in which the communist party was supposedly only a modest member in a whole range of ideologies running from anarchist and socialist to monarchist and Catholic. One of the purposes of this work has been to investigate the Party's claims that all the delegates to such fronts were the bona-fide representatives of their parties. So successful were the communists in this ploy that it is possible, forty years later, to find anarchists, active at that time, who still believe that Stalin's Unión nacional española was a force representing every political sector of the Republic in exile, with every delegate duly accredited. A similar challenge is posed by the need to identify the Spanish communist leadership in all times and places. I am reminded here of a remark made to me by Julio Carrasco, a socialist with experience of communist methods. Look behind the mask, he said, and what you may find is only another mask; the true identity may be carried to the grave.

It was precisely in the Soviet Union that the Spanish communists could see for themselves the difference between the reality and the dream, and it was there that all three of the leading Spanish communist dissidents (Jesús Hernández, el Campesino, and Castro Delgado) honed their contempt for the cause they served. To serve the cause and then abandon it is of course to play into the hands of quite another coterie, about whom Arthur Koestler wrote that it comes as a shock to those who do it to find out in the morning who has jumped into bed with them in the night. That in turn provides more work for the lock-step Stalinists, among whom none has laboured harder than the French Hispanist Pierre Vilar, who looks back to the death of Stalin as the beginning of Soviet decline, and who continues to speak as if anticommunism does not figure on the list of human rights. Antifascism or anticapitalism is good French or whatever, but anticommunism is a profanity that true scholars do not express.

Time has finally taken care of the truth, and communism, like the Christian Church at its base, has suffered massive losses to secular humanism. The process has been slow but steady. It goes back at least to the Kravchenko trial, and, for the discerning observer, to the first Moscow show trial in 1936. What happened after that was rearguard action. The forces of Stalinist obscurantism could be seen in terms of a gallant holding operation, never surrendering their cities without a fight, retreating, under the blows of overwhelming evidence, to the towns, thence withdrawing in the face of relentless logic to the villages, regaining a town here and a city there as a result of the ignorance or imprudence of some of their pursuers, and then driven back again into the hills and mountains, and ultimately to the last redoubt of their remaining credibility, until they succumb at last to the damage inflicted on the mind by speaking only to themselves.

Paris,   D.W.P.
April 1990

ACKNOWLEDGEMENTS

My thanks go first to the archivists who allowed me access to official documents: in France, to Mme Chantal Bonazzi, head archivist of the contemporary division of the Archives nationales; to M. Pierre Gerard, head of the Archives départementales in Toulouse; to the late Henri Michel, president of the Comité international d'histoire de la Deuxième Guerre mondiale and founder-director of the quarterly now renamed *Guerres mondiales et Conflits contemporains*, who created a library with its own primary sources (since transferred to the Archives nationales); to M. Marcel Spivak, of the Service historique de l'armée de Terre in Vincennes; in Germany, to Manfred Kehrig and Klaus Meyer of the Bundesarchiv-Militärarchiv, and Oberst Dr Rohde of the Militärgeschichtliches Forschungsamt, both in Freiburg-im-Breisgau; in the United States, to Robert Wolfe and Robin Cookson of the National Archives in Washington, DC; and to Carol A. Leadenham of the Hoover Institution on War, Revolution, and Peace, at Stanford, Calif. I am also grateful to those who allowed me the use of their private collections: the late Pierre Bertaux, in Le Pellay en Yvelines, and Daniel Latapie, in Toulouse; and to those in libraries and institutes with equally important collections, especially Jordi Planes, director of the CEHI/FIEHS centre at the University of Barcelona, Mme Geneviève Dreyfus-Armand at the Bibliothèque de documentation internationale contemporaine, in Nanterre, and the librarians of the Institut d'histoire du Temps présent, in Paris, which inherited the library created by Henri Michel.

Some others to whom I owe much have died since 1984 when I began this work: in first place, my father, who gave me enormous help; my good friends Burnett Bolloten and Colonel John Nicolétis, whom I had known for decades; Julián Gorkin, Arthur London, and Mme la générale Riquelme. Among the living to whom I am indebted: Ronald Hilton (Professor Emeritus, Stanford University), Eduardo Pons Prades (Barcelona), Jorge Semprún (survivor of Buchenwald and recently the Spanish Minister of Culture), and Charles Tillon (Paris). My gratitude also goes to the Spanish *guerrillero* leaders who received me, whether with warmth (Vicente López Tovar), suspicion (Luis Bermejo), hostility (Tomás Ortega Guerrero), or embarrassment (the late Miguel Angel Sanz). I am also grateful to M. Jacques Bellay for arranging, at his home in Montrouge in April 1992, a memorable private session in which a number of survivors of escapes from death-trains discussed the nightmare reality of these train-rides and the techniques of escape; not least among the revelations was this, that the guards, in spite of all that has been said and written, were not necessarily in the SS at all, with everything that that means to the Wehrmacht and to Germany.

For the illustrations I express my thanks to a survivor of Mauthausen who figures prominently in this book, Antonio García Alonso; to the Ministerialrat DDr Peter Fischer, in Vienna; to Max Hastings, in London; and especially to the Mauthausen survivor Dr Přemysl Dobiáš, in London, who also provided useful information and contact with Hofrat Hans Maršálek in Vienna, Vilém Stašek in Mariánské Lázně, Czechoslovakia, and Col. Richard R. Seibel (retd.) in Defiance, Ohio.

My thanks also go to the Fédération espagnole de déportés et internés politiques, in Paris, and especially to the editor of its journal *Hispania*, the Mauthausen survivor Lázaro Nates; and to the Amicale de Mauthausen in Paris and to all those survivors who talked to me on pilgrimage to Austria; to the survivors Sir Robert Sheppard and Dr Paul Le Caër, who, even in the setting of the Deauville Golf Club, struck the note of reverence for their comrades who died, and the determination never to forget; and above all to Juan de Diego Herranz, the greatest single source of information in this book, for his constant willingness over many years to answer endless questions—especially in Limoges in 1986, when, after three days and nights as my host, he told a friend, in respect of the arguments over detail which he had undergone, that I was 'worse than the SS'. (He was joking, of course.) If this book, the chief inspiration of which has been the courage displayed by the Spaniards at Mauthausen, can now hold up on Mauthausen under the toughest scrutiny, it is due to him more than to anyone.

Finally, I extend my thanks to the team at Oxford University Press who produced this work: Anne Gelling, Dorothy McCarthy, and my copy editor, Sylvia Jaffrey; and to my indexer in Paris Tomaž Lovrenčič.

CONTENTS

LIST OF PLATES

(between pages 203 and 204)

ABBREVIATIONS, ACRONYMS, AND PORTMANTEAU WORDS

AG	*Aktiengesellschaft*
AGE	Agrupación de guerrilleros españoles
AMI	Appareil militaire international (Mauthausen)
ANFD	Alianza nacional de fuerzas democráticas
AS	Armée secrète
BdS	Befehlshaber der Sicherheitspolizei und des Sicherheitsdienstes
CEDA	Confederación española de derechas autónomas (Catholic bloc)
CGT	Confédération générale du travail (communist)
CNR	Conseil national de la Résistance
CNT	Confederación nacional del trabajo (anarchist)
CPSU	Communist Party of the Soviet Union
CTE	Compagnies de travailleurs étrangers
FEDIP	Fédération espagnole de déportés et internés politiques
FFI	Forces françaises de l'intérieur
FTP	Francs-tireurs et partisans
GE	Guerrilleros españoles
Gestapo	Geheime Staatspolizei (Heinrich Müller)
GFP	Geheime Feldpolizei
GPU or OGPU	Gosudarstvennoe politischeskoe upravlenie (Soviet secret police, replaced in 1934 by the NKVD)
GTE	Groupes de travailleurs étrangers
Gulag	Glavnoe upravlenie lagerey
HSSPF	Höhere SS-und-Polizeiführer
HVS	*Hauptverbindungsstäbe*
IRC	International Red Cross
JARE	Junta de auxilio a los republicanos españoles (socialist)
JEL	Junta española de liberación
JLE	Junta de liberación española
JSU	Juventudes socialistas unificadas
JSUN	Junta suprema de unión nacional
KdS	Kommandeure der Sipo und des SD
KIM	Kommunisticheskiy international molodyozhi (Communist Youth International)

KL or *KZ*	*Konzentrationslager*
KM	Kriegsmarine
Komsomol	Kommunisticheskaya molodyozh (Communist Youth)
KPD	Kommunistische Partei Deutschlands
KTB	*Kriegstagebuch*
Lw	Luftwaffe
MBF	Militärbefehlshaber in Frankreich
MOI	Main-d'œuvre immigré
Narkomindel	Narodnyy kommissariat inostrannykh del (People's Commissariat for Foreign Affairs)
NKVD	Narodnyy kommissariat vnutrennikh del (People's Commissariat for Internal Affairs), Soviet secret police
ObW	Oberbefehlshaber West (von Rundstedt, then von Kluge, then Model)
ODESSA	Organisation der ehemaligen SS-Angehörigen
OKH	Oberkommando des Heeres (von Brauchitsch, then Hitler)
OKL	Oberkommando der Luftwaffe (Goering)
OKM	Oberkommando der Kriegsmarine (Raeder, then Dönitz)
OKW	Oberkommando der Wehrmacht (Hitler, Keitel)
OME	Organización militar española
OSS	Office of Strategic Services (US)
OT	Organisation Todt
PCE	Partido comunista de España
PCF	Parti communiste français
PCI	Partito communista italiana
POUM	Partido obrero de unificación marxista (semi-Trotskyist)
PSOE	Partido socialista obrero español (socialist)
PSUC	Partit socialista unificat de Catalunya (communist)
Pz. K.	Panzerkorps
RSHA	Reichssicherheitshauptamt (Heydrich, then Kaltenbrunner)
SA	Sturmabteilung (Roehm, then Lutze)
SAS	Special Air Service (British)
SD	Sicherheitsdienst
SERE	Servicio de evacuación de refugiados españoles (communist)
SFIO	Section française de l'Internationale ouvrière (socialist)

SIM	Servicio de investigación militar (communist)
Sipo	Sicherheitspolizei
SOE	Special Operations Executive (British)
SS	Schutzstaffel (Himmler)
Stalag	Stammlager
STO	Service du travail obligatoire
UGT	Unión general de trabajadores (socialist)
UNE	Unión nacional española (communist)
V1, V2	Vergeltungswaffe
WVHA	Wirtschafts Verwaltungshauptamt

AUTHOR'S NOTES

Until 11 November 1942, the terms Vichy Zone, Unoccupied Zone, and Southern Zone were used interchangeably. After that date, what was formerly known as the Occupied Zone became known as the Northern Zone; the other was generally known as the Southern Zone, though the term Vichy Zone was still in use on the grounds that the Vichy Government still existed.

German Army units are presented in accordance with the numbering system of the Wehrmacht: letters for army group, arabic numbers for armies, divisions, and regiments (brigades), and roman numbers for army corps and battalions.

At Mauthausen (and elsewhere), the term *Revier*, or surgery, was commonly used as a synonym for the *Sanitätslager*, or hospital camp. The terms *Krankenlager* and especially *Russenlager* (named after the Soviet prisoners who built it) were also used for the same compound.

In the Endnotes, when more than one source is cited in the reference, the order in which the sources appear corresponds to the chronological order of their publication, with primary sources nevertheless taking precedence.

In the Index, military and SS ranks correspond to those held by the individual at the end of the war.

COMPARATIVE RANKS

GERMAN ARMY	SCHUTZSTAFFEL	BRITISH ARMY
	Reichsführer-SS (Himmler)	
Generalfeldmarschall	SS-Oberstgruppenführer	Field Marshal
Generaloberst	SS-Obergruppenführer	General
General der Infanterie (etc.)	SS-Gruppenführer	Lieutenant-General
Generalleutnant	SS-Brigadeführer	Major-General
Generalmajor	SS-Oberführer	Brigadier
Oberst	SS-Standartenführer	Colonel
Oberstleutnant	SS-Obersturmbannführer	Lieutenant-Colonel
Major	SS-Sturmbannführer	Major
Hauptmann	SS-Hauptsturmführer	Captain
Oberleutnant	SS-Obersturmführer	Lieutenant
Leutnant	SS-Untersturmführer	Second Lieutenant
Stabsfeldwebel	SS-Sturmscharführer	Warrant Officer 1st Class (Regimental Sergeant-Major)
Hauptfeldwebel	SS-Stabsscharführer SS-Hauptscharführer	Warrant Officer 2nd Class (Company Sergeant-Major)
Oberfeldwebel	SS-Oberscharführer	Staff Sergeant
Feldwebel	SS-Scharführer	Sergeant
Unterfeldwebel Unteroffizier		
Stabsgefreiter	SS-Unterscharführer	Corporal or Bombardier
Obergefreiter	SS-Rottenführer	
Gefreiter	SS-Sturmmann	Lance Corporal
Obergrenadier or Oberschütze	SS-Oberschütze or SS-Mann	Private, Trooper, or Gunner
Grenadier or Schütze	SS-Schütze or SS-Mann	

Note: On questions of authority between Wehrmacht officers and SS officers of equal rank, SS officers automatically rose by one rank.

INTRODUCTION
The Spanish Republicans in their Defeat

The Spanish refugees in the French camps—President Lebrun's order in council of 12 April 1939—The status of the Spanish refugees—Enlistment of Spaniards into French units and war industries —The residual population in the camps—Organizations assisting the Spaniards in their evacuation to the Americas—Last attempts by Republican leaders to escape from France—Further disunity in the Republican camp

¡Ay de los vencidos!

This history opens with a defeat that was glorious, and a humiliation that was pitiful. Battered and exhausted, the remnants of the Spanish Republican Army finally surrendered at the end of March 1939 to the Nationalist forces and their Axis allies. Accompanied by hundreds of thousands of civilian refugees, they crossed the French border in February 1939 to find themselves facing the misery of the concentration camps. The story has already been recounted in *Vae Victis*.[1] The suffering may well have been understated.[2]

Little by little the population of the camps declined. A programme of heavy propaganda was implemented from the start to persuade as many refugees as possible to return to Spain; to this end, loudspeakers mounted on trucks blared out the message in every camp. The effort was rewarded: of the 460,000 Spanish refugees in France in mid-February 1939, 70,000 had agreed to return by the end of March.[3] On 12 April, President Lebrun signed an order in council, drawn up by the Prime Minister, Edouard Daladier, and the Minister of the Interior, Albert Sarraut, concerning the status of foreigners residing in France. In its article 1, he authorized all foreigners between the ages of 18 and 40 to enlist in peacetime in the French Armed Forces. Article 2 imposed on all stateless persons and other foreigners holding the right of asylum the same liability to enlistment in wartime as that governing French citizens (pursuant to the law of 11 July 1938). Article 3 authorized the recruitment—even in peacetime and for projects which were clearly paramilitary—of all male stateless persons and other foreigners holding the right of asylum, from the ages of 20 to 40.[4] The Spanish exiles quickly remarked that such a decree was in violation of international law.[5]

Although the decree of 12 April placed the Spanish refugees theoretically on the same level as the stateless, in fact they fell into a special category. France had recognized the Franco Government on 27 February in exchange for an agreement guaranteeing the neutrality of Spain in the event of a European conflict. If the French Government were to recruit Spanish Republicans into these military units, the Spanish Government might well consider it a violation of the spirit, if not the letter, of the Burgos agreements.[6]

It seems that, at the beginning, the French Government avoided any action which might offend Franco. It preferred to send the Spaniards home rather than use them in national defence.[7] Besides, the French authorities were apprehensive about the morale of the Spanish refugees and tended to consider them a danger to national security. As a result, the Spaniards who volunteered had the choice of only three services: the Foreign Legion, the Bataillons de marche, and the Compagnies de travailleurs. At least 2,000 chose the Legion, for the statutory term of five years.[8] Between 5,000 and 8,000, including a number of Republican Army officers, joined (for the duration of the war) the Bataillons de marche, forming its first regiment.[9] The great majority (between 40,000 and 50,000) preferred to serve in the Compagnies de travailleurs, on the basis that it was the least military of the three. This attitude of recalcitrance to military discipline should not be interpreted as pacifism: the Spanish Republicans were as antifascist as ever they were, but they were reluctant to serve as cannon fodder in a foreign army. Indeed, with the defeat of 1940, the descendents of Viriatus who gave the word guerrilla to military science finally came into their own.

Within a few weeks of the decree of 12 April the first Compagnies de travailleurs were placed at the disposal of the generals commanding the military regions. They were used in a variety of ways: camp maintenance, the construction of arms factories and hydro-electric plants, and especially the fortification of the German and Belgian frontiers. Following the declaration of war, these units were reconstituted on 17 October as Compagnies de travailleurs étrangers (CTE) and came under the authority of the French Army; the men wore military uniforms with sky-blue caps.[10] At their peak in May 1940 these companies numbered 226, each one composed of some 250 men and commanded by a Spaniard.[11] The CTE were included in the thirty-four battalions of foreign workers which the Ministry of War dispatched to the Alps (to build roads), and to North Africa (to build airfields).[12] Most of the Spaniards, however, whether enlisted in the Bataillons de marche or in the Compagnies de travailleurs étrangers, were sent to the French north-east, where they were used to fortify the Maginot Line, especially in the region of Puttelange in Lorraine, or to the area between the Maginot Line and the Loire.[13]

The employment of Spanish refugees in war factories was another obvious way to reduce the number of internees in the camps, and there was no question of the government's need for skilled labour. Senator Eugène Hénaff announced, on 3 May 1939, that national defence could employ some 40,000 Spanish workers, and Albert Forcinal, the *député* from Eure, stressed how valuable the Catalan technicians could be to the French war industry. In the same way, the Ligue internationale des amis des Basques, under the direction of Cardinal Verdier, François Mauriac, and Jacques Maritain, pointed out to Daladier how useful the Basque refugees could be to France as naval officers, pilots, aircraft technicians, and skilled workers.[14]

The French Communist Party also had its part to play. André Marty, unfazed by the parliamentary hearing held in March on his role in Spain (a hearing which in fact humiliated him),[15] spoke up at an international conference held in Paris on 15–16 July. Calling for 'a human French solution' to the internment of the Spaniards and the veterans of the International Brigades, he demanded the immediate release of 3,000 severely wounded, and of 20,000 Spaniards and 1,200 International Brigaders who, he claimed, had been resident in France before the Spanish Civil War. It was intolerable, he added (to thunderous applause), that the French Government should punish any of them for having fought against fascism in Spain.[16]

On the eve of the Second World War, there were still 77,133 Spanish workers and some 48,000 peasants interned in the camps; the former group comprised 32,870 skilled workers, 26,387 artisans, and 17,876 manual workers.[17] Even with the declaration of war, the French Government still did not appreciate the services they could render. On the contrary, on 19 September the Minister of the Interior instructed his prefects and the Governor of Algeria to use 'active persuasion', arguing the state of war and the shortage of housing, to induce all Spaniards who had not found employment to return to Spain.[18]

If Albert Sarraut, as Minister of the Interior, took this attitude towards the Spanish exiles, other members of the government saw things differently. The Ministry of National Defence and War took the decision on 17 October to form new Compagnies de travailleurs.

Spaniards would thus be used in war industries, allowing Frenchmen who had been mobilized for the factories to join the army or to return to work on the land.[19] This amounted to a reversal of the policy of encouraging the Spaniards to return to Spain, but it still failed to make the best use of the 48,000 Spanish peasants who would have been better employed on the land if the war in France had continued through the summer of 1940. In the particular circumstances, the Daladier Government could say with hindsight that it made the best use of the Spanish peasants.[20]

There were also reports that Spaniards who volunteered to serve were turned away. From the moment that war was declared, all political refugees in France were suspect. The soldiers of the Spanish Republican Army were not excepted. Of the 230,000 Spaniards who could have been mobilized in late 1939 under the decree of 12 April, only 52,000, or 23 per cent, were in fact enlisted.[21] In the camp of Le Vernet (Ariége), more than two-thirds of the volunteers were rejected, even in September 1939.[22] In fact the movement was now in the other direction. By virtue of the laws of 17 September regarding suspects, and of 26 October concerning security measures to be taken against 'refugee extremists'—particularly communists, Trotskyists, and anarchists (without distinction)—many former soldiers of the Republican Army found themselves back in the camps, especially in Le Vernet and Gurs, which by now had been transformed into veritable concentration camps.[23] The French extreme right turned the situation inside out. Jean Ybarnegaray, *député* of Mauléon in Basses-Pyrénées, who was soon to serve as Minister of Family and Youth in the first Vichy Government, set an example in an address he gave to the National Assembly in December 1939. Addressing the Minister of the Interior, Ybarnegaray declared: 'On the day war was declared, Minister, 17,800 Spanish militiamen in the camp at Gurs stood shouting, for hours on end, "Long live Hitler". The camp commandant finally brought machine-guns into position to calm them down.' Sarraut called the accusation 'false as a dicer's oath'.[24] Not only was it highly improbable on the grounds of logic, but the story is not supported by a single mention in the Press or a single archival document.

Meanwhile, the task of emptying the camps was being completed by General Jean Ménard, commanding the 17th Military Region (Toulouse), whom the government had appointed Superintendent of Camps on 23 February. By April 1940 there were no more than 6,000 Spaniards left in the camps, most of them unfit either to serve or to work. At least 55,000 Spaniards had been incorporated into the CTE, 40,000 into industry and agriculture, and perhaps 15,000 into the Foreign Legion and the Bataillons de marche.[25] Spanish Republicans in these last two services were to participate in some of the hardest fighting in the war, and numerous memoirs have recounted the role of the Spaniards in the expedition to Narvik, in Flanders, in the Battle of France, in Syria, in North Africa, in the Italian campaign, in Normandy, and especially in the Resistance. Between 1940 and 1944 some 6,000 Spanish Republicans fell in battle.[26]

At the moment of the French capitulation in 1940 there was no Spanish Republican organization in France, but two such organizations, the SERE and the JARE, had provided important services to the Spanish refugees in the preceding year. The Junta de auxilio a los republicanos españoles (JARE) was a socialist organization financed and controlled by Indalecio Prieto, the former Republican minister of war. Under the presidency of Luis Nicolau d'Olwer, the former governor of the Bank of Spain, it served the interests of the socialists supporting Prieto, the left-wing republicans, and even the libertarians. The Servicio de evacuación de refugiados españoles (SERE) was also at its birth at the service of several exile groups, but under the honorary presidency of the former socialist prime minister Juan Negrín it came to serve the exclusive interests of his left-wing faction of the Socialist Party and its sole ally, the Communist Party. This meant that priority in the evacuation of Republicans to the Americas, especially to Mexico, always went to the communists.[27]

The conflict, first within the SERE and then between the communist-dominated SERE and the socialist-dominated JARE, did nothing to heal the schism which had racked the Republic. The two leading figures in the SERE, after Negrín, were Pablo de Azcárate (president) and Bibiano Fernández Ossorio y Tafall (secretary-general). Pablo de Azcárate was the Republic's former ambassador to London, and the father of the communist leader Manuel Azcárate. Ossorio y Tafall was a former professor at the University of Madrid; though formally a left republican, the communists had found him sufficiently malleable for them to arrange his appointment as commissar-general.[28] Negrín had subsequently chosen him as Secretary-General of the SERE. This organization, created in Paris on 20 March 1939, was well financed: its head office, at 94 rue Saint-Lazare, included all the first and second floors and employed a staff of fifty; it had an annexe that occupied the entire building at 11 rue Tronchet, a fashionable street next to the Madeleine. A credit in the amount of 300 million francs was deposited by Negrín into Ossorio's account at the Banque commerciale pour l'Europe du nord, at 26 avenue de l'Opéra.[29] The activities of this bank were of deep concern to the French authorities. An official report refers to a sum of 200 million francs which the Comintern had deposited into the account of the French Communist

Party, for the purpose (ran the report) of promoting French intervention in Spain and preparing revolution in France. The bank's president and vice-president, Nicolas Vassilied and Ivan Sedykh, were Soviet citizens who lived inside the bank, and the capital transfers and other operations of the bank lay entirely outside any official auditing.[30]

With the crack-down by the French Government on all communist organizations, following the signing of the Molotov–Ribbentrop Pact, the SERE soon found itself out of business, despite the fact that it enjoyed the patronage of the Mexican Government. Interrogated by the French police on 20 September, Ossorio claimed that 400,000 Spaniards had sought help from the SERE. While this was a deliberate exaggeration, Commissaire Julien Meneret, who inspected the premises of the SERE, reported that there were at least 100,000 cards in the card index. The funds to defray the expenses of the SERE, according to Ossorio's testimony, derived almost entirely from the Solidarité internationale. While the attempt had indeed been made to form a coordinating committee to group the various committees operating world-wide in support of the Spanish Republicans, the particular organization to which Ossorio referred was an unimaginative invention.

In the same month of September 1939, even before the summons issued to Ossorio, the Communist Party realized that the Sûreté nationale had infiltrated the SERE. It therefore instructed the SERE to vacate its premises and move to Clermont-Ferrand.[31] Although it has been said that the SERE had run out of money,[32] Ossorio made arrangements to transfer the SERE's funds out of the Paris bank into banks in Belgium and Holland.[33] Soon afterwards he left France for South America.[34] The work of the SERE and the JARE was now in the hands of the Mexican and Chilean authorities. The sympathy thus shown by the Chilean Government towards the Spanish refugees resulted in Franco's suspension of diplomatic relations with Chile in June 1940. In the case of Mexico, there were no such relations to break off.[35] From the moment that the Vichy Government was established, the subsidies to the Spanish refugees were handled by the Mexican Legation, and all matters concerning emigration were entrusted to the Mexican Consulate-General in Marseilles.[36]

Marseilles had become the favourite city of those Republican leaders who had not yet succeeded in fleeing from France. In theory, the Vichy Government permitted all foreigners to leave, unless they were wanted for questioning by the police.[37] In practice, all Spaniards were wanted for questioning, and the Vichy authorities began to refuse exit visas even to those who had obtained visas to enter Mexico. At the same time, the authorities were poorly informed: a secret order went out to prefects on 20 July instructing them to prevent Juan Negrín and

Indalecio Prieto from crossing the frontier with false papers.[38] In fact, both had already left. Prieto was in exile before the Civil War ended: he had agreed in late 1938 to serve as Negrín's 'special ambassador' at the inauguration of President Pedro Aguirre Cerda of Chile, and afterwards toured Latin America, writing in the Press. In the case of Negrín, the former prime minister had beaten the Germans by only two days, making use of a Mexican passport and a false identity[39] to leave Paris for London on 12 June.[40]

Apart from the communist leaders, two other Republican leaders had also left in time. Diego Martínez Barrio, Speaker of the Cortes, had sailed for Cuba on 16 May 1939, and then on to Mexico. The former foreign minister Julio Álvarez del Vayo had left for New York; up to that time he lived in Montgeron (Seine-et-Oise), where several Cabinet meetings were held, the Cabinet continuing to consider itself the legitimate government of Spain.[41] That still left a number of Republican leaders in France after the capitulation, including the former president of the Republic Manuel Azaña, the former prime ministers Manuel Portela Valladares and Francisco Largo Caballero, the former ministers Julián Zugazagoitia, Federica Montseny, and Juan Peiró, the former presidents of the Catalan and Basque Governments, Lluis Companys and José Antonio Aguirre, and the former ambassadors to Paris and London, Luis Araquistáin and Pablo de Azcárate.

In the case of President Azaña, on his arrival in France in February 1939 he stopped first at the Spanish Consulate in Perpignan before moving into the Spanish Embassy in Paris. On 27 February the British and French Governments granted recognition to Franco. Azaña left Paris the same day to take up residence in the village of Collonges-sous-Saléve near the Swiss frontier, where he resigned the presidency the following morning. He then moved to the Atlantic seaside resort of Pyla-sur-Mer, near Arcachon, his health getting steadily worse. Negrín visited him there, urging him to leave with him for London, but Azaña replied that he was too weak to undertake the journey. In June 1940, as the Germans approached Bordeaux, he made his way to Montauban, where he finally put up at the Grand Hôtel du Midi. The Mexican Minister in Vichy tried to persuade the Swiss authorities to allow the former president to enter Switzerland; they refused, arguing Switzerland's status as a neutral. The Vichy authorities gave orders that he be prevented even from leaving Montauban. Meanwhile, at the Spanish Embassy in Paris, Ambassador José Félix de Lequerica was at the centre of a plot to kidnap Azaña and force his return to Spain. The mission was assigned to a certain Urraca, an official at the Embassy, who with a group of Falange henchmen arrived in Montauban in late August, only to be recognized by some Spanish Republicans as they alighted from the train. But the plot was unnecessary: Azaña died at the hotel on 3 November. The burial was almost surreptitious, and the coffin was draped in the Mexican flag.[42]

Nothing prevented the Vichy authorities from arresting other Republican leaders, and if they refrained from handing them directly to Franco[43] they still handed them to the Gestapo, which amounted to the same thing when the Gestapo delivered them to Franco. Companys, Zugazagoitia, and Peiró were arrested, deported to Spain, and duly executed in October 1940.[44]

A different fate awaited Largo Caballero. When the former socialist prime minister arrived in France as a refugee in late January 1939, he was already in poor health and sought a quiet anonymous life. The French police reported that he took the train from Cerbère to Paris on 1 February, and put up at 9 rue Roy.[45] The police were mistaken. Largo Caballero was in fact staying with President Azaña in the Spanish Consulate in Perpignan.[46] By the time Azaña resigned the presidency, Largo Caballero had moved to the tiny village of Trébas, 30 kilometres east of Albi, where he lived with his daughter Carmen in total seclusion. Only once in this period of his life did he break his silence, to write a letter to the Toulouse daily *La Dépêche* to repudiate the various statements that had been published in his name.[47] The French capitulation did not lead to his immediate arrest, but on 7 August 1941 Franco requested his extradition; the Vichy Government ordered him to move to the village of Crocq, in Creuse, and subsequently imprisoned him in Limoges while it debated Franco's request. This was not the quiet life he had envisioned. He was released from Limoges only to be interned in Vals-les-Bains (Ardèche), and was under house arrest in Nyons (Drôme) when the Gestapo, with or without the approval of Vichy, arrived in September 1942 to grab him. He was driven to Paris and delivered to the Kriminalkommissar Karl Boemelburg. Boemelburg had the responsibility for safeguarding celebrities, and for this purpose he had requisitioned a large private house in Neuilly, at the corner of boulevard Victor-Hugo and rue de Rouvray. It was an elegant house, with its façade of white columns, its ten bedrooms, a lawn at the front and a kitchen garden at the back. Monsieur Prod'homme served as concierge, tending the garden and taking care of the cooking with the help of his two daughters. The house now served as home to Boemelburg's distinguished guests, including the former president of the Republic Albert Lebrun, the former French ambassador to Berlin André François-Poncet, Colonel François de La Rocque of the far-right Parti social français,[48] the brother of General de Gaulle, and Prince Napoléon. This unusual company was to end soon enough for Largo Caballero, but in his memoirs he attributes the collapse of his health not only to the twenty-one days he had spent in a Gestapo cell in Paris, but to the four and a half months he was kept in Neuilly, without the proper medical attention being given to his infected leg. The Gestapo now transported him, not to Spain but to Germany, and on 20 February 1943 he entered the concentration camp at Oranienburg as *KL*-O 69040.[49]

Largo Caballero had been at the epicentre of the quarrel which had split the socialists and which, perhaps more than anything else, had cost the Republic the war. It is a truism nowadays to say that victory in the Civil War went to the camp which was the least divided. It is not the purpose here to re-examine the causes of disunity on the Republican side, but the Republican refugees had arrived in France attached for the most part to either of the other two socialist leaders: Negrín, who had received the support of the communists, and Prieto, who had opposed the communists and in so doing had become the arch-enemy of the communist leader Dolores Ibarruri, better known as Pasionaria.[50] This conflict was transferred to Mexico, and in time a new animosity developed between the exiles in Mexico and the exiles in France. This animosity was partly socio-cultural in origin: the Spanish manual workers ultimately found employment in France, while the professional class, including the intellectuals, whether they wanted to or not, found themselves in America. Most of the members of the anarchist CNT and the socialist UGT (the latter dominated by Largo Caballero) remained in France. As a general rule, the leaders moved to Mexico and their supporters stayed in France. This situation was not dictated by Mexico. The Mexican Government of General Lázaro Cardenas accepted more Spanish refugees from France than any other country, 10,000 having entered before the summer of 1940. The readiness of Mexico to accept Spaniards and the eagerness of Vichy to drive them out of France explains the agreement of 23 August 1940 under which all Spanish refugees in France who so wished could leave for Mexico. This could well have meant the departure from France of 150,000 Spaniards. The fear that a considerable number of these could finish up as recruits for the British Army led to German intervention, and the Vichy Government reversed itself. In March 1941 the Minister of the Interior published a decree prohibiting all male Spaniards of military age (18 to 48) from leaving France, and on 27 June 1941 the German Commission informed the Vichy Government that with immediate effect no refugees at all could leave for America, whether singly or in groups.[51]

The Spaniards in France now lacked even a newspaper. Their principal journal, the Paris weekly *Voz de Madrid*, founded in July 1938, had been forced to close as early as April 1939, and no journal would

replace it before the Liberation. The disappearance of the last remaining organ of the Frente Popular at the hands of the last government
of the Front populaire was one more symbol of the disintegration of
the Third Republic.

The Spanish Communist Party itself moved into exile under the
weight of all the resentment and suspicion it had engendered among
its allies in the Frente Popular, not so much on account of its objectives as on account of its methods. The Party had become an outcast
in the midst of outcasts. In such circumstances it is understandable
that, from the moment of its arrival in France, the PCE was closely
tied to its only friend, the PCF.

1
The Communists in Isolation

The 'Antwerp Conference': the PSUC versus the PCE—The PSUC applies to the Comintern for admission—Following the Casado coup, the Politburo meets in Toulouse—The Cortes meets in Paris: the Negrín government discredited—The communists forced to withdraw from Cortes—The evacuation of communists from the French concentration camps—The selection of refugees to the USSR—The refugees depart for Russia and America—Carrillo and the JSU prepare for the Sixth Congress of the Socialist Youth International—Tagüeña returns from Moscow to help Carrillo—The Congress expels the JSU—Carrillo leaves for Moscow—The Spanish communists left behind in the French camps

The bitterness of defeat, and the humiliating suddenness of the collapse in Catalonia, were too much for a totalitarian party to endure in silence. Blame had to be apportioned. The Politburo of the Spanish Communist Party spread the word that the chief culprit was Catalonia itself. But to attack Catalonia, or more precisely its government, the Generalitat, for not pulling its weight in the war effort, when the dominant political party in Catalonia since May 1937 had been the PSUC (the Catalan Communist Party),[1] was tantamount to calling the PSUC a party of selfish petty nationalists. It was to counter this innuendo that a meeting of the PSUC's Central Committee was held on 2–3 March 1939 on the outskirts of Paris,[2] though for reasons of security it was given the code-name of Antwerp.

The inspiration for the Antwerp Conference came from a group of PSUC Central Committee members detained in the concentration camp at Saint-Cyprien, the most notable of whom were José del Barrio and Felipe García, the former commander and political commissar respectively of the XVIIIth Army Corps in the Republic's Army of the Ebro. These PSUC leaders wrote to their secretary-general, Joan Comorera, proposing that the Central Committee meet to debate the issue. Comorera agreed, and sixty members of the Central Committee and forty other delegates attended the meeting; many of them were in the same situation as del Barrio and García, and the PCF had to arrange their escape and their conveyance, in closed trucks, to the place of meeting.

The meeting was also attended by some delegates of the PCE, notably Jesús Hernández and Vicente Uribe, and three from the Comintern: the Argentine Vittorio Codovila, the Hungarian Ernö Gerö, and the Bulgarian Vanini Stepanov.[3] Hernández and Uribe were present precisely because both were under attack: the PSUC's report, written by del Barrio and read to the conference by Comorera, criticized the Republican Government's precipitate flight from Madrid to Valencia in 1936, at a time when Hernández and Uribe were government ministers, and it raised the delicate matter of the relationship between the two communist parties. This relationship suffered mainly from the envy and resentment felt by the Spanish party towards the Catalan: the PCE envied the PSUC's meteoric rise, and it resented the fact that the PSUC had applied for membership in the Comintern without even consulting the PCE. The task of presenting the case for the Politburo of the PCE, and thus for the Comintern, was given to Wenceslao Colomer, head of the Catalan communist youth organization; Colomer could be trusted though he was Catalan, because his organization was federated in the national JSU and thus derived its authority not from the PSUC but from the PCE. His task was unenviable, and Colomer found himself in virtual isolation.

On the second day of the conference, at the moment when rebuke had reached the danger point, a telegram arrived from Moscow. It proposed that the debate be immediately suspended and that a delegation be sent to the Soviet Union where the discussion could be continued, in the presence of the PCE and Comintern leaders, 'and in much more suitable conditions'. Reluctantly and resentfully, the assembly complied, but before it dissolved, it adopted Comorera's report by a strong majority, while Colomer found himself expelled from the Central Committee and a new Executive Committee (the PSUC's equivalent of a Politburo) was elected. The report as adopted rejected the accusation that Catalonia and the PSUC were responsible for the defeat of the Republic, and it called on the government and certain parties (meaning the PCE) to show more understanding toward the PSUC. The Antwerp Conference also adopted a formal resolution to solicit the recognition of the PSUC as the Catalan section of the Comintern. The resolution was unusual in that, under the statutes of the Comintern drawn up by Lenin, only one communist party could be admitted for each state. The petition of the Catalan party amounted almost to a declaration of Catalonia's national independence and certainly to an act of defiance of the PCE's claim to hegemony. A delegation of nine members was appointed to present the petition to the Comintern in Moscow. A month later Moscow replied, ignoring the delegation of nine and inviting Comorera alone to report to Moscow. It was to end, in the summer of 1939, in a spectacular personal triumph for Comorera, for the Kremlin agreed to change the very statutes of the Comintern to allow the PSUC to enter, and thus become the first communist party ever to be admitted into that body without representing an independent country. Meanwhile, the delegates to the Antwerp Conference who had come from the concentration camps were returned there as surreptitiously as they had been taken out.[4]

In Madrid on the night of 5–6 March, Colonel Casado staged his coup against the Republican Government, and especially its communist leadership. This resulted in the immediate flight of the Communist leaders in the capital, who now made their way to France by plane or ship. Dolores Ibarruri ('Pasionaria') reached Marseilles on 8 March, travelling via Oran.[5] Most of the other PCE leaders arrived that day or the next. A meeting of the Politburo was held in Toulouse on 12 March. The purpose of the meeting was to examine the causes of the Republican collapse. The resolutions of the meeting have never been disclosed, nor is it known for sure which members attended, but it is understood that the causes invoked to explain the collapse were the unfavourable international situation, the disunity within the Frente Popular, and 'the weakness of the PCE leadership, which had under-estimated its enemies and allowed itself to be taken by surprise by the Casado coup d'état'.[6]

The Republican Government, now exiled in France, no longer had any legal standing in the eyes of the French Government, but its existence, and even its activities, were tolerated. Accordingly, in March 1939, the Cortes held three memorable sessions: on 6 and 7 March and 31 March to 1 April, Martínez Barrio still officiating as its Speaker. At the last of these three sessions, held in Paris in the building oc-cupied by the Comité France–Espagne at 26 rue de la Pépinière, Prime Minister Negrín made his first appearance before the Cortes in France and was summoned to report upon his activities since the last meet-ing he attended: that of 1 February, in the castle of Figueras, the last held in Spain. Negrín responded with a call for the condemnation of the Casado junta. Prieto, leading the centre and right-wing segments of the Socialist Party, retorted that the resignation of President Azaña on 27 February invalidated the Negrín Government. The commun-ists, led by Pasionaria and Antonio Mije, rallied to Negrín's defence, but they were the only ones who did. In the end a vague compromise was worked out, to the effect that the government was legitimate but Negrín was no longer its head. As for the Casado junta, it was not condemned. Whatever remained of Negrín's authority evaporated in July when the Cortes met again; at the urging of Prieto, the Negrín Government was declared null and void and the communists were forced to withdraw from the Cortes. In the absence of a president and of a recognized government, the Cortes now considered itself to be the only legitimate instrument of Spanish government.

Apart from justifying its actions in public and in apportioning blame in private, the first task of the Party in exile was to organize the evacuation to Paris, and thence to their respective homelands, of all communist officers and officials who had served the Republic. These included a certain number of Soviet citizens left behind when Stalin began withdrawing his senior advisers in late 1938.[7] The French Communist Party sent more than half of its members of parliament to the frontier to assist in the arrangements.[8] As a result, the PCE leaders did not have to share the sufferings of their comrades in the concentration camps.[9] Instead, accommodation was quickly found for them in Paris. The Party's secretary–general, José Díaz, had already benefited from the help of the PCF when he was evacuated from Spain four months before the Civil War ended: he was given a place to stay at 32 boulevard Pasteur, and soon afterwards received a Soviet passport and left for Russia. Pasionaria, on her arrival in March 1939, was hidden in the home of the PCF *député* Prosper Mocquet. Her son, Rubén Ruiz Ibarruri, was still detained in the concentration camp at Saint-Cyprien, but she now quickly arranged his release.[10] As for General Líster, who was also sheltered by Prosper Mocquet, he was to remember this moment, among others, with deep and lasting resentment. His character was complex. His animal energy was admired by all, but he has been variously described by associates as warm and human, or fault-finding and cantankerous. He was in fact volatile, even cyclothymic, better adapted to battle conditions than to peace in exile, and unforgiving towards those who he felt had wronged him.

Líster, the former commander of the Republic's vth Army Corps, is one of the few Spanish leaders to give any detailed account of his life in exile. He had arrived in France on 10 February 1939 in the retreat from Barcelona, and at that time had been saved from the concentration camps by French communists who took advantage of the general confusion by picking him up in Banyuls and driving him to the Spanish Consulate in Perpignan. Líster describes the Consul, who was obviously still the Republic's nominee, as a reactionary who refused to see him. Líster nevertheless stayed overnight in the Consulate,[11] and in the morning Constancia de la Mora, the communist wife of Hidalgo de Cisneros, commander-in-chief of the Republic's air forces, came to see him, and with her help he was able to rejoin his wife Carmen and their 3-month-old daughter. The Lísters had been separated in the evacuation, and Carmen, with her mother as well as her infant, had been directed to the women's camp at Le Boulou. Since Carmen's mother spoke French, they were able to avoid internment in the camp, and with the wife of General Juan Modesto and their two daughters they too had been able to reach Perpignan.

The next morning the Lísters left for Toulouse. Constancia de la Mora had given them the name of the Hotel Regina, opposite the station, as the rendezvous of the Spanish Politburo. They found Antonio Mije ensconced in a magnificent suite. After a broad discussion, they agreed to meet at noon in the hotel restaurant. Entering the restaurant at the appointed hour the Lísters found, seated around the table, a group composed of Mije with his wife and son, Francisco Antón, Luis Cabo Giorla and his wife, and Santiago Carrillo and his wife.[12] The first three were all members of the Politburo, while Carrillo controlled the socialist youth organization (JSU). None of them let the fate of the Republic spoil their party. The food and the wine were of the highest quality, paid for, it would seem, out of the funds made available by General Rojo, chief of staff of the Republican Army; those funds were set aside to provide every Republican soldier entering France with a severance of at least one month's pay. As for the conversation, Líster adds, 'it was a planet removed from the war and the concentration camps.'[13] Not wanting to stay at the hotel, the Lísters accepted the invitation of a friend in the PCF (presumably Mocquet). Two days later, on the night of 13/14 February, Líster left by air for Alicante, leaving his wife and child with their friends in Toulouse. The plane had thirty-three seats, and most of them had been reserved for the PCE. Despite that, there were only thirteen passengers. Obviously, those at the Regina preferred to remain in Toulouse, oblivious to the fact that the communist youth organization had its base in the still uninvaded south-east.[14] Líster in his memoirs reminded Mije that he was an Andalusian, but he reserved his deepest scorn for Carrillo, challenging this self-promoted war hero to reveal, with dates, names, and numbers, the units and the battles in which he claimed he had fought.[15]

In his second departure from Spain, following the Casado coup, Líster left the Monóvar aerodrome near Alicante in the early morning of 7 March, landing in Toulouse. His wife and daughter were now in Paris. Dodging a group of reporters at the station, he took the train for the capital, where another group of reporters was awaiting him. Líster offered them nothing, but he was still suspect in the eyes of the French police; the Líster family was put under surveillance in a house in Gien, 30 miles south of Paris, then moved to nearby Châtillon-sur-Loire. What altered this situation was the arrest in Alicante, as Franco's troops entered the city, of the French communist *député* Charles Tillon, who had been sent by the PCF with 700,000 francs to aid in the evacuation of the PCE. There was talk of a prisoner exchange: Líster for Tillon. The Soviet Embassy in Paris took the report seriously, and it was decided that Líster had to be evacuated from France at once. A Soviet vessel lying in Le Havre and about to sail for Leningrad was ordered not to leave. The Soviet Embassy found a way to pick up Líster and drive him to Le Havre, while the PCF succeeded in snatching his wife and infant daughter from impending arrest and driving them to the Soviet Embassy, where another embassy car conveyed them to the same ship. The Líster family thus left France together, arriving in Leningrad on 13 April.[16]

Meanwhile, in March, the PCE leaders in Paris, in liaison with the Comintern, established a committee responsible for selecting the communist militants and International Brigaders to be admitted as refugees into the Soviet Union. About half the Spanish communists wished to be admitted, but the USSR had no intention of accepting more than a minimal proportion. The selection committee was composed of six representatives of the PCE and five from the Comintern. The PCE's six consisted of Dolores Ibarruri, Jesús Hernández, Juan Modesto, Enrique Líster (despite his difficulties), Martínez Cartón, and Irene Falcón (Pasionaria's secretary). The Comintern's five comprised Palmiro Togliatti (who chaired the committee), Maurice Thorez, André Marty, Antonio Mije, and Santiago Carrillo. Martínez Cartón, though a member of the Politburo, was replaced in April by Pasionaria's favourite, Francisco Antón. Martínez Cartón, called to Moscow, was to become the first Spanish victim of the purge. The reasons are not clear, but the former *diputado* from Badajoz seems to have lost his standing from the moment he married the German representative in the KIM, the international communist youth organization; she was hated in the JSU for her dogmatism and was best known to Spaniards as Carmen the Fat (Carmen la gorda). Although Martínez Cartón had a second chance when he was sent to Mexico, he found himself further and further removed from the Party centre.[17]

In view of the Soviet Union's determination to accept only a small number of refugees, the committee adopted rigorous methods of selection. The order of priority was as follows: Soviet military and civilian advisers, members of the Soviet secret services, delegates and officials of the Comintern, top-ranking leaders of the PCE, senior non-Soviet veterans of the International Brigades, and Spanish communist militants, together with the families of all those selected.[18]

Altogether, from the end of the Spanish Civil War to the beginning of the Second World War, six sailings were organized to convey the selected groups from Le Havre to Leningrad. The first vessel to leave was the *Smolny*, which set sail on 10 April, and the largest contingent of Spanish leaders left on the *Siberia* on 14 May. Togliatti and Ibarruri left on 4 May aboard the *Maria Ulianova*.[19] Among the other Spanish communists who sailed for Russia at the time, to join Secretary-General José Díaz, were the five generals, Juan Modesto, Hidalgo de Cisneros, Manuel Tagüeña, El Campesino, and Antonio Cordón; Colonel Martínez Cartón, Vicente Uribe, Joan Comorera, José del Barrio, Rafael Vidiella, and Irene Falcón. Jesús Hernández also sailed from Le Havre to Leningrad but in his memoirs could not remember when,[20] nor do the memoirs of the others mention his presence. Hernández says merely that, on his release from prison in Oran, he made his way to Marseilles and Paris with the intention of sailing for Mexico or living illegally in France. However, Vittorio Codovila, the former Comintern representative in Spain, was waiting for him in Paris with a telegram from Moscow instructing him to report there and explain 'how the war had ended so suddenly and badly'. Hernández left at once for Le Havre, and sailed with no other Spanish company than a hundred communist boys and girls.[21] The total number of Spaniards admitted into the USSR, including 3,000–4,000 children[22] and the group of teachers and air-force personnel who arrived mainly in 1937–8, together with the merchant seamen who found themselves in Soviet ports at the end of the Civil War, is estimated at 6,000.[23]

Another 2,000 Spanish communists left for the Americas,[24] concentrating in Mexico, Argentina, Brazil, Uruguay, and Cuba; and in smaller numbers in Venezuela, Dominican Republic, Costa Rica, Paraguay, and Chile.[25] Mexico City and Buenos Aires became the two centres of their activities and attracted most of the top PCE leaders, even though several of these reported first to Moscow and crossed to America later, between late 1939 and mid-1940. These leaders included Pedro Fernández Checa, Vicente Uribe, Antonio Mije, Francisco Antón, Santiago Carrillo, Fernando Claudín, and Joan Comorera. Mije was one who took care not to pass through Moscow, following a mishap suffered in the course of the retreat from Barcelona: he had lost some important files on the history of the Party, which had been entrusted to him and had fallen into the hands of the French police. The thought of explaining that to his superiors in Moscow terrified him.[26] As it happened, he and Francisco Antón were selected to stay behind in France after the others left to direct the operations of the SERE up until the service was closed in June 1940. As for Santiago

Carrillo, he remained secretly in France in the summer of 1939 trying to the last to prevent his youth organization, the JSU, from being expelled from the Socialist Youth International.

The departure of almost all the PCE leadership left the rank-and-file in France with no direction. Their press was minimal.[27] In the tense summer of 1939 the isolation of the communists increased. On 31 July the Sixth Congress of the Socialist Youth International was to open in Lille. It was decided in Moscow that General Tagüeña should make a special trip back to France to map the best strategy with Carrillo. Tagüeña handed in to the Russian authorities his Soviet identity card, and received a Cuban passport under the name José Sandoval Fernández; his visa allowing him to return to the USSR was mailed to the Soviet Embassy in Paris. On 10 June he took the train from Moscow to Odessa, finding himself seated behind Pedro Checa, the PCE's secretary of organization, who with his wife was also returning to France on a separate mission. In Odessa they boarded a vessel owned by France-Navigation, the shipping company created by the PCF in 1938 with part of the gold of the Spanish Republic. The ship did not reach Marseilles until 27 July. There was little time left for preparation. In Paris Tagüeña was met by Vittorio Codovila and Francisco Antón, and together they left by car for Lille. Putting up at a hotel in Lille which was known to Codovila and where identity papers were not required, they arranged at once to meet secretly with Carrillo. On the following day, 30 July, the French Socialist Party (SFIO) held an impressive rally in Lille in which Léon Blum was the guest of honour. The meeting was clearly intended to focus upon the congress scheduled for the following day. Bitter attacks were made upon the Spanish JSU. To the consternation of the Spaniards, the speeches were greeted with frenzied applause by an audience made up largely of miners.

It was a harbinger of the day that followed. Only Carrillo, as secretary-general, was permitted to speak for the JSU, though at the end of the day the rules were relaxed and Tagüeña took the risk, in his borrowed identity, of speaking too. He was greeted in silence, but he was unlikely to succeed where Carrillo failed. All Carrillo's eloquence that day was to no avail. All his tributes to the valour of Spanish youth in the antifascist struggle, all his references to the JSU as the vanguard of that youth, fell on deaf ears. His fate was sealed when the French socialists distributed to the assembly copies of the letter Carrillo had sent his father, in which he called him a traitor for siding with Casado, and renounced all his filial ties. The vote came, and the JSU was expelled from the Socialist Youth International, for the reason that the communists themselves could not deny: the

Spanish socialist youth organization had fallen into the control of the communists.

Tagüeña left Lille at once, fearful of being denounced to the police. Carrillo invited him to stay at his house in Créteil, a suburb to the south-east of Paris, where the JSU had its secret headquarters. The house was surrounded by high walls which gave it privacy from prying eyes, an important asset for a building which was intended to serve as a departure point for young communists assigned to secret missions in Spain. However, in Moscow, where the decisions were made, it was decided that the JSU's future activities were to have a safer base, and Mexico City was the choice. Mexico, therefore, was to be the land of exile of Carrillo, still the JSU's secretary-general. The Comintern instructed him in September 1939 to leave Paris for Brussels, where he was given a Chilean diplomatic passport. But before he could leave for Mexico the plans were changed, and he was told to report to Moscow. With his Chilean passport and the protection of the Nazi–Soviet pact, he passed through Nazi Germany, now at war. He reached the Baltic, took ship for Leningrad, and arrived in Moscow on 26 December. In the Soviet capital he was to receive the full recompense for his loyal service, especially his readiness to call his father and his former friends the tools of fascist agents and traitors to their class. At the age of 25 he was to find himself at the highest level of international communism, for Dimitrov took him under his wing, made him secretary of the KIM—replacing the Frenchman Raymond Guyot—and invited him to attend meetings of the Comintern secretariat. After six months in Moscow, he would finally leave for Mexico. As for Tagüeña, he returned to Moscow to stay, but by that time he had already formed a very clear and unfavourable impression of Carrillo. Carrillo's letter to his father, thought Tagüeña, was merely that part of Carrillo's cynicism that showed: everything in him carried the stamp of a man ready to sacrifice anything and anyone to his personal ambition.[28]

With the PCE leadership now established in Moscow and other leaders installed in Mexico and Argentina, a certain opportunity for self-advancement presented itself to younger leaders in France. While the PCE's Politburo in the USSR did its best to transmit its orders in the normal way, the PCE's rank-and-file, whether in France or in any other country where Spaniards had taken up exile, reorganized itself with a speed and efficiency that was the wonder of all other parties and groups. This could be seen particularly in camps in south-western France, where the vast majority of Spanish communists, unable to emigrate, were forced to remain. Since the French authorities ceded

to the inmates the responsibility for a number of camp services—
kitchen, mess, mail, infirmary—it was not long before the communists,
with their unique discipline and knack for organization, secured these
key positions for themselves, and once in control they set out to
favour their fellow-members and penalize the political groups they
hated most: the Trotskyists, the POUM, and the libertarians.[29] Certain communist writers later boasted of the power communists held
in the camps, while others have found it an embarrassment.[30] At
Septfonds, for example, in the summer of 1939 the communists held
almost complete control of the camp, and not merely in the matter
of its infrastructure: 'We controlled all the demonstrations against the
French authorities. We organized the strikes. We imposed the camp's
internal discipline.' Even when all the PCE leaders in the camp were
arrested in a raid at 5 o'clock in the morning and sent off to the prison
at Fort-Collioure, the Spanish communists were still able to continue
their activities as before. Part of these activities was to prevent other
Spaniards from volunteering (or being forced) to serve in French units:
on one occasion, when 1,200 inmates were assigned to the Compagnies
de travailleurs and were about to leave for Montmédy, the communists succeeded in preventing the departure of 400.[31] Miguel Celma, of
the anarchist CNT, describes the situation at Septfonds when he arrived
there in 1939: 'At the time of our arrival we were surprised to find the
Bolshevik police wearing uniforms. They wore colonial topees and
armbands, and carried clubs. They were the masters of everything.'
He adds that from the moment the Molotov–Ribbentrop Pact was
signed, they were the masters of nothing.[32]

2

In the Shadow of the Pact

Impact of the Pact on the Spanish communists—The initial reaction of Thorez and the French communists—The Daladier Government decrees the abolition of all communist organizations—The French and Catalan communists continue the patriotic line—The new orders of the Kremlin—The communists vilify the socialists: the 'imperialist war'—Pasionaria turns on Negrín—The Comintern and the blitzkrieg in the West—Thorez deserts in the field—Suppression and repression of the communists in France—Axis and communist sabotage—Spaniards in the line—The Germans close the exits—The Mexican and Chilean legations continue their help to the Spanish refugees in France—PCE members attempt to regroup

No event in the history of the Soviet Union was more grievous to its reputation, more jarring to its friends, and more onerous to its later supporters than the signing, on 23 August 1939, of the Molotov–Ribbentrop Pact. So great was the shock that some Party members believed the document to be a forgery.[1] In time a number of standard explanations were developed: it was a justified response to Munich, it was never more than a pact of non-aggression, it was the key to ultimate victory over Nazism. Our purpose here is to examine the immediate effect of that sensational event, not only upon the Spanish communists but also upon the French Communist Party with which the great majority of Spanish communists were closely associated.

The French communists were more affected by the Pact than anyone else in the West, and their efforts in recent years to explain it have consumed their energies.[2] As for the Spanish communists, they have relied more on their leaders than on their intellectuals for an explanation. Santiago Carrillo, in later years much more ready than Pasionaria to discuss the events of that period, has never wavered in his viewpoint. In 1948 he wrote that the Pact 'ensured the later victory of the forces of democracy over fascism'.[3] In 1974 he insisted that it posed no problem to any member of his party:

To a Spanish communist of that time, the Pact presented no difficulty; not simply because we had total confidence in Stalin, but especially because we had left Spain filled with hatred for the European powers which called themselves 'democratic' and which had sold us down the river. It was because of those European powers that we had lost the war. . . . Among the Spanish communists, not one, as far as I can remember, suffered any twinge of conscience, neither among the intellectuals nor among the workers. It was said at the time: 'Those swine are getting just what they deserve'.[4]

That, as Carrillo put it in his conversations with Régis Debray and Max Gallo, was as far as he could remember. It is unlikely that he heard, during his stay in Moscow in the winter of 1939–40, anything similar from General Tagüeña, who writes that the majority of Spanish communist emigrants found the pact with fascism 'shameful'.[5] Carrillo forgets to mention those communists who left the Party, especially the four PSUC leaders in Mexico who resigned in disgust not only with the Pact but with Stalin's policy in general, and the forty leading members of the PSUC's labour union who were expelled for their hostility to the Pact.[6]

For those Spanish communists in France, without leaders and almost without a press, the statements of the PCF leaders and their press was of special significance. The immediate reaction of the PCF to the Pact was expressed by its secretary-general, Maurice Thorez, at a meeting of the communist parliamentary group on 25 August. The words became famous: 'But if Hitler, in spite of everything, unleashes war, then let him know that he will find the French people ranged against him in their entirety, the communists in the front rank in the defence of the nation.'[7] *L'Humanité*, the organ of the party, carried a similar message in its issue of the following day: 'If Hitler dares to carry out the action he is contemplating, the French communists . . . will be in the front rank of those defending Republican France against its enemies.'[8] A similar message, though with a much more limited circulation, was published the same day both in *La Voz de los españoles* and in *Catalunya*. The former asked what the Soviet Union had given away by signing the Pact, and provided the answer: 'Nothing. . . . Today we are closer to peace than we were a week ago.'[9] The latter saw in the Pact the guarantee of Soviet assistance: 'Germany will know that [the USSR] will come to the help of the Western democracies if they are the victims of aggression, just as it will come to the help of any nation so guaranteed. In no sense, then, can it be said that the Pact leaves Germany a free hand in the West.'[10]

Sincere or sham (but let us assume it sincere), the patriotic asseveration of *L'Humanité* did not spare the Party from the fury of the Daladier Government, which promptly on 25 August suppressed its two leading journals (the morning *L'Humanité* and the evening *Ce Soir*);[11] even the communist bookshop Éditions sociales internationales, at 24 rue Racine, was closed down.[12] In spite of the government's action, the PCF maintained its position. On 1 September, the day Hitler unleashed the Wehrmacht on Poland, the communist parliamentary group, now severely weakened by defections,[13] published a similar resolution: 'The communists will prove themselves the best defenders of the nation's democracy and independence.' And on 6 September, Marcel Cachin, editor-in-chief of *L'Humanité*, circulated a letter to all his colleagues in the Senate: 'We repeat that the communists will be in the front rank to crush the perpetrators of this criminal violation of peace. . . . Communist members of parliament who are liable for call-up, with Maurice Thorez in the lead, have joined their units.'

The Spanish communist press in France had never been legalized. Nor, for that matter, had the Spanish non-communist press. Up until now, however, both had benefited from that particularly Gallic tolerance of things illegal. Now the Spanish communist press was to share the fate of its French counterpart, just as the PCE was to share the fate of the PCF. But even in these circumstances, *Catalunya*, which was the unofficial voice of the Catalan communist party, reappeared on schedule on 2 September, with its position in perfect alignment with the PCF's: 'If war should break out, we Catalans have a clear understanding of our duty. . . . If the fascist aggressor forces France to defend herself, we shall fight, die and ultimately prevail with France.'[14]

This patriotic and democratic reaction of the PCF, backed by the PSUC if not by the PCE, was very quickly denounced by the Comintern. The French and Catalan communists had not understood the Pact's real meaning. On 20 September, three days after Stalin had invaded eastern Poland in accordance with a secret protocol in the Pact, Raymond Guyot, while still secretary-general of the KIM, arrived from Moscow with precise instructions: the Party was to oppose the 'imperialist war' and demand that the government make peace with Hitler.[15] Instead, on 26 September, the government suppressed the Party, with the rest of its press. Whatever the French Government gained by its actions of 25 August and 26 September, the communists found respite, first from the obligation to justify the Pact and then from the duty to transmit the new orders from Moscow. The Party in France could now present itself as the victim of the Daladier Government; its prestige was safeguarded.[16] The new policy, readily adopted by the French Communist Party, continued, with various nuances, from 20 September 1939 to the magic day of 22 June 1941, when the Wehrmacht struck against the Soviet Union. The policy passed, however, through four time-periods, each worse than the precedent for the cause of freedom: the death agony of Poland in the second half of September, when the Soviet Union's actions were visible and the Soviet

Union vulnerable to rebuke; the Phoney War; the blitzkrieg in the West; and the first year of Nazi occupation. It will be seen that the communist underground press did introduce certain changes of tone in the course of these four periods, but the basic substance, 'revolutionary defeatism', was constant until the war finally became holy. There were few references to Hitler. The term Nazi was stricken from use. Fascist, when used, was applied to the French Government. The war was merely a struggle between two imperialist camps. A pamphlet distributed in February 1940 in the region of Nord-Pas-de-Calais, near where half a million British and Empire troops had left their bones some twenty years earlier, summed up the sentiments of the Communist Party: 'This is England's war, England the vampire of the world! If the British want to fight, let them go and land on the German coast. Since they rule the waves that shouldn't be difficult. And let us rid the soil of France as fast as possible of their unwanted presence.'[17]

The capitulation of Poland at the end of September 1939 introduced a period in which the large group of conservative appeasers in France and the small group of conservative appeasers in Britain hoped that a way could still be found to placate Hitler and Stalin with Poland and leave Western Europe in peace. The appeasers on the right were thus in harmony with the revolutionary defeatists on the left. Those in the middle, especially the socialists, were in the firing line, for Stalin's return to a revolutionary policy meant the end of his interest in any popular front.

The principal targets of the communist press were Léon Blum, the French socialist leader, leader of the Front populaire, and former prime minister; Léon Jouhaux, leader of the French socialist labour union, the CGT; Sir Walter Citrine, secretary-general of the Trades Union Congress in Britain, and Clement Attlee, leader of the British Labour Party. All four were vilified not only in France but also in Mexico, where the Spanish communists, with considerably more freedom than in France, published two political manifestos in this period of the Phoney War.

The first of these carried the date of 1 November 1939, and was distributed mainly in the colonies of Spanish refugees in the Americas, its content preventing it from being distributed, publicly at least, in France. Entitled 'La socialdemocracia y la actual guerra imperialista', the pamphlet did not actually bear the endorsement of the PCE but its author was none other than Pasionaria. It contained not a single word of denunciation of the Nazi invasion of Poland. On the contrary, the martyred victim, one of Europe's oldest nations, was referred to as 'a state artificially created', and its political system, authoritarian at worst betwixt two totalitarianisms, was described as 'the concentration-camp republic'. While the pamphlet included the standard attack on Blum, Jouhaux, Citrine, and Attlee, it also included a denunciation of Negrín. This was indeed a novelty. Pasionaria had defended Negrín, as we have seen, at the meeting of the Cortes in Paris only a few months earlier, and since then Negrín had refused to denounce the Pact, which delighted her and predictably infuriated his fellow-socialist Prieto. But Negrín had committed the crime of not following up with a denunciation of the imperialist war, expressing instead his support of French mobilization and the French combatants. On top of that, Negrín seemed to be planning to settle in London. It was all too much for Pasionaria, who now accused her erstwhile ally of being the servant of the French bourgeoisie and the British imperialists. 'Let not a single Spaniard', proclaimed her manifesto, 'lend himself to the sordid game now being played by the French and British Governments.'[18]

The second manifesto bore no date, but it appeared in the same autumn and was published in Mexico City in the December 1939 issue of *La Voz de México*, under the title 'España y la guerra imperialista', and in Buenos Aires, in 1940, under the title 'España hoy'. This time the manifesto was signed, not only by Dolores Ibarruri, but also by José Díaz, though there is reason to think that Pasionaria wrote it herself and added the secretary-general's name. Very similar in content and tone to the preceding pamphlet, it denounced the treacherous leaders—never the rank-and-file—of the socialist and republican parties and of the anarchist movement, and of course the treasonous entirety of the POUM. It also called on all Spaniards 'not to shed a single drop of Spanish blood in defence of foreign imperialist interests. Down with the imperialist war!'[19]

In February 1940, the PCE in Mexico produced its own denunciation of the Daladier Government, accusing it of forcing the Spanish refugees into the Foreign Legion, 'in order to use them as cannon fodder in the shadowy service of the warlike birds of prey of Anglo-French imperialism'.[20] This was followed by a manifesto issued by the Comintern on May Day of that year, and published in Mexico if not in France.[21] This represented the Comintern's first reaction to the opening of the blitzkrieg in the West, with the German invasion of Denmark and Norway. The manifesto stood history on its head: 'In reply to the brutal violation of Scandinavian neutrality by Britain and France, Germany sent its troops to Denmark and occupied strategic positions in Norway.' German fascism, it was made clear, was no longer the imperialist aggressor.[22] As the blitzkrieg was unleashed on France and the Low Countries, *Nuestra bandera*, which was soon to become the Party's most influential organ, devoted its first issue to the same denunciations. The unsigned editorial vilified every other party or movement in the Republican camp and ended with the ludicrous call: 'Now more than ever, we appeal to the Spanish people to unite.' The issue included articles by Antonio Mije and Maurice Thorez. In the best tradition of his colleagues, never using one word when two would do, Mije announced that 'the triumphant victory [*sic*] of the worker-peasant class hinges entirely upon the total annihilation of anarchist ideology in the workers' movement.' Thorez collaborated with a diatribe against Léon Blum, whom he described as a 'spy, traitor, and police agent', and ended with an appeal for immediate peace.[23]

In calling Blum a traitor, Thorez was speaking as a recognized expert in the field. The army unit to which he had been assigned was stationed at Chauny, to the north-east of Paris. Under Stalin's strong and constant pressure, Thorez deserted his post and fled to Belgium.[24] On 2 November 1939, the court martial of the 3rd Military Region sentenced Thorez *in absentia* to six years' imprisonment for desertion in time of war, and on 17 February 1940, he was stripped, again *in absentia*, of his French citizenship. This was the same Thorez who, before the Kremlin changed its signals, issued his warning to Hitler as to where the French communists would be if he were foolish enough to unleash war. Where Thorez finished up was as far from the front line as he could get. During his brief stay in Belgium Thorez was interviewed by Sam Russell of the *Daily Worker*, the organ of the British Communist Party. The interview appeared in the *Daily Worker* of 3 November and the clandestine *Humanité* (no. 7) of 17 November. Russell reported that the interview took place 'somewhere in France', but the Party has since conceded that the rendezvous was Brussels.[25] The purpose of the interview was to present the desertion of Thorez as an example for all true communists.[26] With that mission accomplished Thorez made his way to the Soviet Union.[27] The clandestine *Humanité* continued along the new orthodox lines, even when France itself was in the front line of the blitzkrieg. In its first issue after the opening of the brief Battle of France, *L'Humanité* ran a new Comintern manifesto: 'When two gangsters fight, honest men are not obliged to go to the help of one simply because the other has dealt him a blow below the belt.'[28] Again denouncing the 'Anglo-French imperialism responsible for the war', the manifesto avoided any other criticism of Nazi Germany. Nothing was said about the fact that the war endangered the traditional values of France, including freedom itself.

Quite logically, the French Government had increased its repression of the PCF and the PCE, both illegal ever since the decree of 26

September announced the dissolution of all communist organizations. The treatment meted out to the PCE was particularly severe, because the Pact made all Spanish Republicans suspect. Fear and uncertainty increased the government's distrust of the Spaniards, especially the Spanish communists. In early December, the SERE's offices were raided by the police, and France-Navigation, the merchant fleet administered by the PCF, was attacked. Several PCE members thus found themselves back in the concentration camps, notably Argelès and Le Vernet. Following these actions, the communists dispersed their archives in the south-west, and the police checks carried out in Paris were all to no purpose.

Official circles in France were more and more concerned that the communists, whether French or Spanish, were engaged in sabotage. If the Minister of the Interior was opposed to the Minister of Labour in so far as the employment of Spanish refugees was concerned, it was because he feared that the Axis might infiltrate its agents into their midst. In the fortnight that followed the declaration of war, the Minister of the Interior reported the arrival in Pamplona of two officers of the Abwehr, Colonel Hans von Funck and Major Hans Wilhelmi.[29] The Minister had reason to believe that their visit to Pamplona was part of a plan to sabotage the Dewoitine factory in Toulouse and the important hydro-electric plant at Marignac (Haute-Garonne) near the Spanish frontier.[30] In October he was informed that the Germans had sent agents of Franco into France with the mission of carrying out sabotage or at least of obtaining information. The Minister consequently gave instructions to the Prefect of Haute-Garonne to transfer all Spaniards who had arrived in France in recent weeks to the camp at Le Vernet, and to send back to Spain under escort all Spanish refugees who should enter France in the future. In November, the same Prefect received a report from the Chief of Police in Toulouse that the presence of 249 Spanish ex-militiamen in the gunpowder factory in that city, and of others in similar factories, constituted a danger to national security.[31]

With or without the complicity of the Spanish authorities, German activities continued in the region of the Pyrenees. In January 1940, according to information from the headquarters of the French Army, German agents were extensively engaged in smuggling very large sums of money across the Spanish frontier into France; the money was to be used to finance communist and defeatist propaganda.[32] In the same month, the Superintendent of Special Police learned that German agents in Spain had asked their superiors to order the torpedoing of all Spanish vessels sailing from Bilbao to French ports.[33] Other information revealed that German agents in Spain were secretly slipping poisoned oranges into the consignments shipped to Saint-Jean-de-Luz and in the same transaction sending messages to other Nazi agents in France. The reports added that the Spanish Government was doing all it could do to put an end to this traffic.[34] In early March, French Army headquarters reported that German agents in Spain had recruited several Spaniards, most of them veterans of the Civil War, for the task of placing small delayed-action bombs in French rivers and canals used for hydro-electric plants.[35] The danger from sabotage, however, was not limited to the action of Axis agents. Even in early October 1939, a telegram from the Minister of the Interior gave warning of the imminent arrival from Belgium of four Soviet agents, whose names were supplied, and whose mission it was to place bombs in French merchant vessels.[36]

At the end of February 1940, the Comintern called upon all workers employed in French national defence to present multiple claims to their employers, and if these were rejected, to engage in go-slow tactics, sit-down and wild-cat strikes, and even acts of sabotage.[37] The end of the Finno-Russian war on 12 March changed nothing in this regard. As a result, an appreciable quantity of war weapons manufactured in Paris factories by workers under communist influence proved unusable. Planes were fixed so as to result in fatal accidents. The technique consisted of cutting the brass wire holding down the screw on the fuel supply pipe. The vibrations of the engine in flight would do the rest: after the plane had been flying for a certain number of hours the screw would work loose and allow the fuel to escape, at first drop by drop, then in a flow, on to the white-hot exhaust pipe, producing steam which would cause the plane to explode in mid-flight, with the certain loss of its crew. Hundreds of planes built in the Farman factories at Boulogne-Billancourt[38] blew up in mid-air as a result. The Spanish communist press in Mexico even boasted of the sabotage carried out by comrades in the important ammunition factory in Toulouse, where daily production had fallen from 4 million to 1 million rounds as a result.[39] Such acts of sabotage led, at the end of May 1940, to the execution of three young communists in the fortress of Le Hâ in Bordeaux.[40] The first communists to be executed in France during the war were thus shot for treason.

By mid-May 1940, the collapse of the military front seemed imminent, but certain isolated reports attested to the stalwart action of Spaniards in the line. Dr Antonio Ros recounts that on 16 May, the day after the fall of Sedan, he heard Prime Minister Paul Reynaud declare on radio: 'The only unit to have acquitted itself well in the action was the Spanish contingent in the Foreign Legion.'[41] Several historians have described the role of Spaniards in a company of Travailleurs étrangers stationed near Tourcoing who took up the arms abandoned by retreating French troops and braved the enemy.[42] Such incidents give an ironic meaning to the later boast of Carrillo: 'Throughout the period of armed resistance to Hitlerism, the communists fought in the vanguard, as always when it is a question of fighting for freedom.'[43] It is quite true that Spanish communists were in the vanguard of the struggle, but it was no thanks whatever to the instructions they received from their Politburo in Moscow.[44]

By the end of May, the remaining leaders of the PCE in Paris had packed their bags. When the Germans arrived, all had left the capital. The identity of the PCE members of Cortes remaining in France was not known to the French authorities, who knew only that they had set up their centre in Marseilles. Liaison between the PCE and the PCF was said to be entrusted to Lieut.-Col. José Vila Cuenca, operating under the name of René. But there is every reason to believe that Vila Cuenca was being used. He was not a communist but a socialist. He had served as deputy-director of the security services in Barcelona, which placed him in a position of knowing all kinds of secrets about the communist role in Catalonia. The French authorities formally considered him no danger to security. The report of the special police in Toulouse showed that, as a captain of Carabineros, he had refused to submit to the authority of a Soviet agent. As a result of his refusal, he had twice been the target of an assassination attempt and both times wounded. The report added that the first attempt was perpetrated by a communist, and the second by an anarchist.[45] While this is theoretically possible, the odds against a socialist surviving a communist assassination attempt only to be targeted by an anarchist are simply overwhelming. The role of Vila Cuenca in this period is undoubtedly important, but nothing yet is certain. The last heard of him is that he left Marseilles for Toulouse in early January 1941, and that he returned to Marseilles to request a visa at the Venezuelan consulate.[46] Meanwhile, the last vessel to leave France for England sailed from Bordeaux on 15 June. From that moment the Spaniards no longer had the chance to flee.

What the communists did in France in the period between the Junes is still hotly disputed. The French and Spanish Communist Parties insist, with ever greater stridency, that communist resistance to the Nazi invaders began on the first day of the Occupation. In fact, it was the paucity of attacks by communists on the occupying forces during the first twelve months of the Occupation—or the last twelve months of the Pact—that is established by the German reports that survive.[47]

Certainly no Spanish communist could have drawn inspiration from the messages of his leaders. In an article published in Mexico in October 1940, Santiago Carrillo concentrated his fire on 'British imperialism' with barely a mention of the Italo-German variety, and without any mention at all of fascism.[48] This was clearly intended as a disincentive to Spanish communists to engage in resistance. It was as if Santa Teresa of Avila had become the patron saint of the Party. But if quietism was the Party's new policy it was openly defied by individual communists, Spanish as well as French. Besides, the Spanish Communist Party faced growing difficulties with the Catalans. Antonio Mije, who still headed the PCE in France, did all he could to conceal the news that the PSUC, the Catalan communist party, had been admitted into the Comintern as the Catalan section. Mije, of course, feared a decline in the PCE's influence, as well he might: after the French capitulation the two parties were entirely reintegrated in both zones, but most of the leadership posts fell into the hands of the Catalan militants. The reason was that, at the end of the Civil War, the intermediate-level leaders of the Catalan party had crossed the frontier _en masse_, while most of their counterparts in the PCE had been trapped in the central zone.[49]

Meanwhile in Vichy France, the Spanish communists were reported by the authorities to be active in Toulouse, Montauban, Perpignan, and Sète, which remained the largest centres of Spanish immigration. Marshal Pétain even thought it appropriate to visit Toulouse on 5 November 1940. A massive publicity campaign preceded him. The Marshal might well have pondered on the admonition he himself had launched, just five months earlier, after the worst defeat in French history: 'The French have a short memory!' Despite the Press accounts of mass enthusiasm everywhere he went, not everyone in Toulouse engaged in adulation. Some young communists had mounted an ingenious device on the roofs which scattered leaflets over Pétain's motorcade. The police, ordered to the roofs, found no one.

Although the Spanish social services[50] had been dissolved, the Mexican and Chilean legations continued to help the refugees to emigrate to Latin America, and were currently distributing several million francs a month.[51] The Catalan communist Josep Moix took charge of the funds received from both legations, but it seems that the PCE leaders were already trying to prevent all further emigration.[52] On this matter at least they had the support of the Vichy Government, following its decree in March 1941 prohibiting all male Spaniards of military age from leaving France. Vichy furthermore gave its assurance to Madrid that no Spanish Republican leader would be allowed to leave. General José Riquelme, who had been the ranking Spanish general on either side during the Spanish Civil War, had been engaged until June 1940 in recruiting Spanish regular officers for service in the French Army. Refusing the chance to embark for England, he made contact with Resistance elements in Montauban. When now the Gestapo and the Vichy authorities began their round-up of Spanish Republican leaders, Riquelme was rescued only by an invitation from General Aguilar, the Mexican Minister in Vichy, to take refuge in the Mexican Legation.[53]

The reason for the authorities' interest in General Riquelme was that he had shown favour to the communists during the Civil War in Spain.[54] Among other names included in the list of Vichy's most wanted Spaniards[55] was that of Joaquín Olaso Piera, who had served during the Civil War in the separate functions of inspector-general of public order in Catalonia and agent of the dreaded secret police, the Servicio de Investigación Militar.[56] The man who had earned the nickname of 'the eye of Moscow' was now directing action groups in France, but it is certain that they were aimed primarily at Trotskyists and members of the POUM. Both these parties were strongly opposed to Vichy: the Fourth International published *La Vérité*,[57] and members of the POUM were active in Toulouse and Montauban. A number of Poumistas were seized by the Vichy police in February 1941, and one of their leaders, Juan Andrade, was arrested in Seix (Ariège) while serving in a Groupe de travailleurs étrangers. Their trial came up in Montauban on 17–18 November. Accused of 'engaging in communist activity', fifteen of the defendants were sentenced to prison, to terms ranging from five months to twenty years' forced labour.[58]

The first attempt by PCE members to regroup was made in late October 1940 in the most unlikely place: inside the concentration camp at Argelès. Two Spanish colonels (Miguel Angel Sanz and Vicente López Tovar) have confirmed that the meeting was held, though López Tovar, who was invited, thought the idea foolhardy and refused to participate.[59] The garrison was in fact very much under strength, and it was easy to move in and out of the camp, as was the case at the time of the youth meeting in Brussels. The purpose of the meeting being to find a way to replenish the senior ranks of the PCE in France, it was decided that they should take advantage of the low level of security in the camps to arrange the escape of certain militants. The meeting ended with a resolution 'to fight Nazism at the side of the French people'.[60]

If those at the meeting at Argelès had been in contact with the PCE leaders in Moscow, it is unlikely in 1940 that they would have adopted a resolution to fight Nazism. The view from Moscow was simply different.

3
Arrival in Russia and America

*The problem of sources—The Spanish refugees in Russia by category—
Committee meetings with the Comintern—The fate of the children
and their teachers—The reassignment of the rest—The PCE leaders—
The Spanish refugees in the Americas—The transfer to Mexico of
Spanish and Catalan communist leaders—Opposition to Stalin's
policy: desertions and expulsions—Spanish officers in Moscow ad-
mitted to the Frunze Academy, the Voroshilov Academy, and the
Planiernaya School of Leninism—Stalin's assassination team in
Mexico—The assassination of Trotsky, Krivitsky, and Tresca—Gorkin
and Sala escape*

It is not certain, even in the age of *glasnost,* that we shall be alive on
the day that the Soviet archives are thrown open to the public. Nor
is it certain that the documents needed here still survive, for we have
noted in the Preface the destruction observed in Moscow in August
1987 of thousands of dossiers pertaining to Stalin's terror. In the
absence of the official Soviet records we must rely on four other
sources of information for our knowledge of events pertaining to the
Spaniards in Russia.

First of all, there are the memoirs of the orthodox communists.
They are not useful. Pasionaria glides over everything, whether in her
own account or in the interview she granted to Jaime Camino in the
1970s.[1] In describing the life of the Spaniards in Russia, she insisted
that 'Stalin was ever ready to help. He was never authoritarian. We
never heard about the Soviets' internal problems'—adding innocently,
'we had links with all the Soviet organizations'. The Spaniards,
Pasionaria went on, 'were always a closely knit group. Our only concern was bringing up our children and making sure they didn't lose
their command of Spanish.' For the Spanish children, she concluded,
'every help was given'.[2] Similar in style and content is the account by
José Gros, a Catalan from Tarragona, who, as a perfect Party member,
avoids every embarrassing question, whether it be the fate of the
Spanish children, the leadership of the Party, or the effect of the Titoist
heresy. Santiago Carrillo is equally evasive, and equally well served

by his interviewers. Carrillo reached Moscow on 26 December 1939, crossing Germany with a Chilean diplomatic passport issued in France. He too had been in Moscow before, arriving in 1936 to work on the unification of the communist and socialist youth organizations. This time he was to work as secretary to the KIM, and was able to attend meetings of the Comintern secretariat and its executive committee. It is easy to understand why Carrillo allowed himself to be interviewed by Lilly Marcou. She is the perfect sympathizer who never asks a hard question and who describes Carrillo on her cover as 'one of the founding fathers of Spanish democracy, one of the last of the Great'. Her book she describes as 'a document of value', since the recollections of those who made history 'have always been a precious source, a living archive'. Lilly Marcou then sets out to serve as the devil's advocate, as she puts it, while in fact she allows Carrillo to repeat what he has made public already and to pass over every point of embarrassment. 'If there was any fear of Stalin in the Soviet Union', Carrillo told Marcou, 'I did not see it. For many years only a minority knew about the trials and the purges. Outside that circle, the families of the victims certainly knew about them, but I didn't meet any of them. I had entered a world which did not talk about such matters.' It would have been easy enough at this point for Lilly Marcou to ask her interviewee how the members of the Comintern could not have been among the minority that knew, but instead she allows him to repeat his story about the indignation he felt that night when he left the Hotel Lux without his *propiska*, and the concierge refused at first to let him back in. Carrillo then describes how difficult it was for him, when he first entered the Party, to participate in singing Stalin's praises: not that he thought Stalin undeserving of the praise, but because it was not in his character to show such reverence. Anyway, he adds, 'in Moscow I was able to breathe freely for the first time in years. . . . I was never conscious in Stalin's time of what people call his oppression.' As for what Stalin did to Zinoviev, Kamenev, Bukharin, and others (Carrillo does not include Tukhachevsky or Trotsky), 'he did not need to do it. I think that that was one of the negative aspects of Stalin's personality. . . . But Stalin considered the internal opposition within the Soviet party to be a very serious danger. In the face of foreign aggression . . . it could have divided the Party and the people. I can imagine that, and I can understand why he had to get rid of these people politically. What I cannot understand is why he had to shoot them. . . . Stalin could have eliminated them politically while sparing them physically, as Castro has done more or less in Cuba.'[3]

Then we have the testimony of the renegades, especially Jesús Hernández, Valentín González ('el Campesino'), and Castro Delgado.

It is true they have nothing kind to say about the Party leaders, but the evidence they adduce has never been rebutted. The Kremlin and the Party found it easier to respond with threats and insults. They could say with truth that Castro Delgado went over to Franco's camp, but the fact remains that he was the only one who did. To the memoirs of the renegades we should add the accounts of the surviving children, whose testimony is useful but limited.

Then there are the pro-Franco historians, writing exclusively for their public. Among them is Comín Colomer, whose messianic approach leads him to refer to the greatest Spanish philosopher of this century as 'the shameless Unamuno' and to hurl anathemas at all who fought Franco and thereby 'offended the Divine Artisan'.[4] As for Ruiz Ayúcar, he is proud to have fought with the Blue Division alongside the Nazis in Russia, but objects (half rightly, half wrongly) to the term 'fascist' in reference to his Spain.[5]

In the category of eyewitness accounts, limited in scope but not ideologically motivated, we should mention the testimony of the surviving pilots such as Juan Blasco Lobo (*Un piloto español en la URSS*) and Juan Lario Sánchez (*Habla un aviador*). Writing many years later (1969 and 1973, respectively), they rely on their not-infallible memories. In the case of Lario Sánchez especially, vagueness pervades the book, but the publisher's blurb tells us that the author was among a group of some fifty Spanish aircrew who sailed from France in June 1939. After a 'lengthy period of physical recuperation' he settled down in Kharkov where he worked and studied until early 1941. Mobilized by the Soviet authorities in July 1941 with other Spanish pilots, he was called upon to fly German planes in special guerrilla actions. In 1946 he married a Russian woman and remained in the Soviet Armed Forces until the end of May 1948. After that he worked as a translator of technical books and teaching manuals for the Spanish-American market, and in January 1957 returned home to Madrid with his wife and two daughters.[6]

Finally, there are the accounts written by Spanish-speaking diplomats and others who happened to be in the Soviet Union at that time and who were in contact with the Spanish exiles. Their field of knowledge is also quite limited, but in certain areas they provide the most detailed accounts we have. Among these writers is Rafael Miralles Bravo, a Cuban diplomat who served for ten months, beginning in July 1944, as press attaché at his country's legation in Moscow. Miralles was a wounded veteran of the war in Spain; he had served as a major, in the 11th (Líster) Division, and in January 1939 he was given command of the 710th battalion in Líster's 5th Army Corps.[7] The account by the Argentine Pedro Conde Magdaleno (*En busca de la verdad soviética*) falls into the same category. At the beginning of the Civil War, when he was 23, Conde had tried to enlist as a volunteer for the Republic; he enrolled in the Spanish Embassy in Buenos Aires, but lacked the means to cross the Atlantic. In 1947, as a Peronist, he was sent to Moscow to serve as labour attaché at the Argentine Embassy in order to study the communist system. A third such account is provided by José Antonio Rico Martínez, a young Spanish Republican teacher attached to no specific party. His book (*En los dominios del Kremlin*) is in a narrative style that reads almost like a novel, but his experiences leave him vehemently anti-Soviet and even anti-Russian. His feelings toward communism are inferred rather than expressed by his account of the conversation he had with Ramón Alvarez Builla, son of a distinguished Spanish diplomat, who told him on one occasion: 'All right, all right. But to be a communist has its advantages. Almost all members of the Party are workers without any education. That's why an educated person cannot fail to reach the top of the Party hierarchy; that kind of thing simply doesn't happen in other political organizations.'[8]

We have seen that the total number of Spaniards who entered the Soviet Union amounted to some 6,000. Up to two-thirds of these were children, most of whom arrived before 1939, the six expeditions from Le Havre in that year carrying fewer than 2,000 passengers (wives and children included).[9] Included among the 6,000 were 102 teachers and 20 nurses who accompanied the children in 1937–8; about 150 trainee pilots who were sent to the USSR in that period, and another 50 aircrew who arrived in 1939; 234 Spanish seamen who found themselves in Odessa and other Soviet Black Sea ports at the end of the Civil War and who were prevented by the Soviet authorities from leaving; and the officials of the Bank of Spain who had accompanied the consignments of gold sent by the Spanish Republic to the USSR in 1936.[10]

To administer these Spanish refugees, a committee was set up in Moscow in May 1939. Unlike the committee formed in Paris in March to select the emigrants, this committee included only three Spaniards, headed by Dolores Ibarruri.[11] They were thus outnumbered by the representatives of the Comintern: Dimitrov (chairman), Togliatti, Marty, the Soviet Andreï Bielov, and the Bulgarian Stella D. Blagoyeva of the NKVD.

The committee proceeded to divide up the 2,000 adults into four groups: the political leaders, who were given posts commensurate with their quality, to the extent that this was possible in the Soviet Union; the military leaders, who were sent to the Soviet military academies; the second-rank political leaders, who were sent to the Planiernaya political school to take courses in Marxism-Leninism; and the remainder, who were broken up into eighteen subgroups and sent to various regions of the USSR to work in the factories. No doubt the monolithic character of the Soviet system made it incapable of absorbing foreign contingents into its structure, but the Spaniards had all been assured, before leaving France, that they were going to take courses in political science. No one had said anything about working in industry, at levels far below their competence and under ignorant and boorish supervisors. This they deeply resented, and if José Gros chooses to describe factory life in the best possible light ('work in the factories was a new experience for us, but little by little we got used to it'),[12] Jesús Hernández and others paint it in the darkest colours.

Meanwhile the Comintern, in its headquarters at 6 Mokhovaya Ulitza, opposite the Kremlin, was concerned with a different question. In the tranquillity of Moscow, Stalin brooded over the causes of the Republic's defeat, dropping the artless question to the leaders of the Comintern: 'Why did the struggle of the Spanish people end in such a tragic and unexpected way?' Fearful that Stalin might repeat the question, the Comintern met in two sessions, the first in the summer of 1939 and the second in February 1940, to find a satisfactory answer. Five delegates of the Comintern (Dimitrov, Manuilski, Togliatti, Stepanov, and Gerö) were joined at the start by all five members of the PCE Politburo in Russia (Díaz, Ibarruri, Fernández Checa, Hernández, and Uribe), together with the generals Modesto and Líster and the PSUC leader Comorera.[13] The debates served only to deepen the feelings of frustration and resentment. Blame fell on the Secretary-General, José Díaz, despite the fact that he had been sent to Russia at least four months before the end of the Civil War.[14] There had been talk since May 1937 that Díaz was in poor physical condition, brought on by overwork, and that Codovila had wrily suggested at that time that he take a holiday. Some said that he had contracted tuberculosis; others, that he was suffering from a stomach ulcer that forced him often to stay in bed, and at other times to leave in the middle of meetings and stroll outside until the pain had eased.[15] But the intensive care unit to which the Secretary-General was consigned may have had nothing to do with therapeutics; there is evidence that Díaz was sufficiently independent of mind for a summons to Moscow to be necessary. Whatever the truth, Díaz dropped out of the Comintern's meetings, which ended in no public announcement but instead in an agreement that each PCE leader would submit an individual report on the position and action he had taken in response to the Casado coup.[16] This solution allowed the Comintern to emerge blameless, while the PCE leaders would inevitably damage one another in their individual accounts. As for Díaz, the ailing Díaz, he was now inexplicably given responsibility for the whole of Latin America, and India to boot![17]

The responsibility idly or cynically conferred upon Díaz was part of a range of appointments decided upon by the Comintern and the PCE leaders at this series of meetings which were concerned with the future as well as the past. Even before France fell to Nazi Germany in June 1940, it was agreed that communications with the communists in Spain were to be developed from bases in Latin America. Mexico was to serve as the trampoline, on the basis that there were more Spanish refugees in Mexico than anywhere else in the hemisphere. Five members of the PCE Politburo (Uribe, Hernández, Carrillo, Mije, Antón) were assigned to the region. The Comintern also decided, in November 1939, that the top leadership of the Catalan communist party (the PSUC) should also leave France and the USSR for the Americas, concentrating in Mexico. The main exception was Josep Miret who was instructed to remain in France. As for the PSUC's secretary-general, Joan Comorera, after the defeat of February 1939 he had made his way directly to Latin America, whereupon he had been promptly summoned to Moscow. Stalin had not forgotten that, in the internal conflict in Republican Spain in August 1938, Comorera had sided with Catalonia's President Companys against Prime Minister Negrín, and Comorera was known to share the desire of the Catalan communists for independence from the PCE.[18] It was nevertheless agreed that Comorera should return to America. Stalin had an interest in separating this popular leader of a troublesome party from his followers in the USSR,[19] and the Comintern's investigative committee was now satisfied with his performance in Spain. The PSUC had achieved what the PCE had failed to achieve, an amalgamation of the socialists in an alliance controlled by the communists. The PSUC thus stood as a model for the PCE to emulate.

Of the six top leaders thus selected to head the PCE and the PSUC in the Americas, Uribe was already there before the end of 1939. Mije crossed directly from France, after staying behind to direct the evacuation service known as the SERE up to the moment it closed in June 1940. Carrillo and Comorera crossed in the same year. As for Hernández and Antón, their departure would be delayed, as a result of the war and other difficulties, until late 1943. One other top PCE leader left Moscow for Mexico without officially being assigned to the PCE in Mexico. Pedro Fernández Checa, the PCE secretary of organization, outranked all the others, but his purpose in Mexico remains obscure. It is known that he arrived in 1940 and took the name Pedro

Fernández Izquierdo, but it is uncertain whether his assignment was to observe the work of the others in reorganizing the Spanish communists or to plan the murder of Trotsky.

For the Spaniards left in the Soviet Union, it was matter of adjusting to a new life. We have seen that the first to take up residence there were the children and their guardians who arrived in 1937. Those who arrived in Leningrad were taken to Moscow, where they were housed in a magnificent building, set amid spacious gardens, on Bolshaya Pirogovskaya Ulitza.[20] Those who disembarked in Odessa were accommodated in a summer camp in the Crimea, ordinarily used by Komsomol (Young Pioneers), the organization which was Stalin's answer to the Hitlerjugend.[21] In both cases the children enjoyed a separate and favoured life. The idea was presumably to train them to become the leaders of a Soviet Spain of the future. The privileged life ended soon enough. The change seems to have come from the moment the Spanish Republic collapsed, when the Soviets realized that a Soviet Spain was further off than they had thought.[22] The teachers fared worse. When el Campesino arrived in Russia in 1939, he found that three-fifths of the teachers, accused of Trotskyism, had already been removed. Most of them were republican or socialist by affiliation or sentiment, and they were inclined to resist Soviet demands that they adapt themselves to the Soviet system of education. Some were arrested and thrown into Lubianka prison. Others were sent to factories or sentenced to hard labour in the correctional camps. The most outspoken of them were shot.[23] The children were now scattered in several of the leading cities but continued their school-work in preparation for university or technical school.[24]

As far as the Basque children were concerned, the Basque Government in exile began, as early as 1938, to express its anxiety over the future of its Catholic sons and daughters in a country dedicated to atheism. President Aguirre consequently sent a personal letter to Stalin, asking him to allow children to return when their parents so requested.[25] Stalin never replied, and it would not be until after the Second World War that any Basque child would be repatriated. Having terminated his recognition of the Spanish Republic, Stalin obviously felt that he did not have to account to anyone for what happened to the children, two-fifths of whom would be dead within five years.[26]

That the Soviet authorities were heartless towards the children is corroborated on all sides. What the Basques had first experienced was now the lot of others. As long as the Molotov–Ribbentrop Pact remained in effect, the Spanish Government continued to transmit, via

Berlin, the requests of parents in Spain for the return of their children. The Soviet authorities turned a deaf ear to the requests until some official in the bureaucracy hit upon the idea of imposing Soviet citizenship on all who reached the age of 16, thus making them subject at once to laws forbidding Soviet citizens from leaving Soviet territory.[27] Santiago Carrillo, as head of the youth organization JSU, played his part in this miserable affair by 'persuading' the Spanish children that they should not return home, even if their parents begged them to.[28]

It was the treatment of the children and their teachers, together with employment in the factories and enslavement in Karaganda, that provided the dissidents with their strongest accusations against the Soviet system. The historian Antonio Vilanova imputes the blame for the maltreatment of the children equally to the Soviet authorities and to certain Spanish leaders.[29] El Campesino reproaches Pasionaria for making it impossible for the Spanish teachers to continue to teach unless they took out Soviet citizenship.[30] Manuel Tagüeña, a former army corps commander in Spain (at the age of 25) and the only Spanish refugee in Russia to hold a university degree, denounces the way in which the children, from the age of 12 and after a brief apprenticeship, were separated from their compatriots and from everything which could remind them of their homeland and their families, the better to exploit them in the factories.[31] Jesús Hernández also decries the indifference shown towards the children, insisting that even before the German attack half of them had contracted tuberculosis and another third were in imminent danger of doing so. As a result, some 750 had already died, either of tuberculosis or malnutrition.[32] At least one child was driven to suicide. Florentino Meana Carrillo and his brother had asked permission to return to Spain. Pasionaria, the only PCE leader empowered to grant it, had refused. Florentino wrote out a death note expressing his despair of ever leaving 'this vast camp of hunger called the USSR',[33] then swallowed a glassful of sulphuric acid. When the news reached his brother, he took a knife and made his way to the Hotel Lux in Moscow where he thought Pasionaria was staying. Finding her absent, he vented his fury on her assistant José Antonio Uribes, the former communist *diputado* for Valencia, who escaped by the skin of his teeth. The boy finished up in prison.[34] Five young girls, at a school in Kaluga to the south-west of Moscow, were the victims of a celebrated incident recounted by el Campesino in which Líster allegedly got drunk one day and raped all five, justifying his conduct on the absurd ground that they were fascist. 'Armed with a deposition signed by the victims,' writes el Campesino, 'I appeared before a special commission of the Comintern and demanded that action be taken against the criminal. I received a promise that such action would be taken, provided that I handed over the incriminating document. After much hesitation I handed it over. No action was taken.'[35]

In 1940 the PCE's top leadership rested in the hands of José Díaz, Dolores Ibarruri, and Pedro Fernández Checa; when Checa left for Mexico, his place was taken by Francisco Antón, the last to arrive from France. Jesús Hernández was assigned to the Comintern as the Party's official representative. Enrique Castro Delgado served as Díaz's private secretary and the PCE's representative on the Comintern's executive committee.[36]

Díaz being now terminally sick, Pasionaria's power continued to rise. While both were poorly educated—Díaz as an Andalusian would even spell 'certain' (*cierto*) with an s—their characters stood in strong contrast. The Secretary-General, a former baker from Seville and an ex-anarchist, had a vast capacity for work and organization. His demeanour was modest, even shy; his comportment, honest.[37] Pasionaria, for her part, had arrived in the Party from further afield. The black-haired young beauty who roamed the villages outside Bilbao, carrying a basket of sardines on her head and crying out her wares, was a fervent and practising Catholic, deeply devoted to the virgin of Begoña. It was not easy for the modest and simple labourer Julián Ruiz, one of the obscure founders, in 1921, of the communist party in Vizcaya, to wrest her from her fanatical devotion.[38] Having thus married and converted, Dolores la Sardinera brought a passionate simplicity to the Party, but a certain artificiality went with it too. Her spell-binding oratory was rehearsed, her appearance studied. Dressed always in black, her face ever grave, she freely accepted the role bestowed upon her of revolutionary saint. No PCE leader could vie with her for the veneration of the masses, but the respect of peers that Díaz enjoyed was never to be hers.

Pasionaria certainly won no admiration from the two Spaniards attached to the Comintern. Jesús Hernández was himself outgoing and well liked. Daring and dynamic, he had been a member of the PCE since its inception in 1921, when he was only 14. Suspected in 1931 of the killing of two socialists in Bilbao, he had fled to the USSR, returning a year later to become a member of the Politburo and editor of *Mundo obrero*. He remained as editor until 1936, when his powers as an orator in Cordova won him a seat in Cortes. He was subsequently appointed Minister of Education in the Largo Caballero Government, a remarkable promotion for a man of 29 who had learned to read and write while sentenced to prison under Primo de Rivera. He had retained the Education portfolio, and added that of Health, in the Negrín Government, then served, from 1938 until the Casado coup, as Commissar-General of the Army of the Centre-South. His ability was never in question. Nor was his fanatical devotion. His attack in the *Communist International* on the socialists, the POUM, and the anarchists ('poisonous reptiles', 'the scum of Spain') was a paradigm of Stalinist vilification.[39] As for the cause he had adopted, and the leaders he had befriended, their claim to his loyalty was a matter over which he reserved the fullest control. Jesús Hernández was a man who would not be cowed into submission by anyone.[40] Enrique Castro, a former metal-worker from Madrid, had also served as editor of *Mundo obrero*, replacing Hernández in 1936 before taking charge of the Institute of Agrarian Reform. A good organizer and a man of some aptitude in political theory, in the arts, and in languages, Castro had served in the Central Committee since 1937.[41] As senior officials of the Comintern, Hernández and Castro were now lodged in Kuntsevo, the residential park outside Moscow where Stalin had his dacha, while the Comintern's second- and third-level officials were put up in the Hotel Lux at 10 Gorky Ulitza. This antiquated relic of the Romanovs had been used since 1919 to house distinguished communist visitors. It had slowly deteriorated to the point that rats and cockroaches were now permanently installed. Guests cooked in their bedrooms, in turn and collectively, so that the building smelled of every gastronomy in the world. This did not dishearten the residents, who were more than grateful to be the guests of Stalin.[42]

Meanwhile, some thirty officers of the Spanish militia were admitted in autumn 1939 to the Frunze Academy, the Red Army's training school for officers up to the rank of major-general.[43] Among these officers were Modesto, Líster, Tagüeña, el Campesino, Francisco Romero Marín, and Marcelino Usatorre. All these men had commanded military units in Spain larger than those to which they were actually entitled by their ranks. Modesto, for example, had been appointed to command the Army of the Ebro without receiving the corresponding promotion. If the Spanish Republic had been reluctant to promote these men on the grounds that they were not, after all, regular army officers, it was certain that they would not receive greater recognition from the Soviet authorities. Only Modesto was given the rank of *Kombrig* (brigadier-general); none of the others received a higher rank than that of colonel, and five who had held the rank of lieutenant-colonel (a rank not in use in the Red Army at that time) found themselves demoted to major.[44] All were given Russified names. Modesto received the name of Morozov, apparently from Stalin. The name was already a household word. Pavlik Morozov had been a youngster in a remote village when he denounced his kulak father to the authorities. His deed was commemorated by a monument in marble. Songs were composed in his honour, and Pavlik Morozov was to stand as a model for future generations of Komsomol.[45] Líster too, it was said, received his new name from Stalin, but the name is in dispute.[46]

The Frunze Academy was designed, the students were told, to produce Red Army leaders in the cause of world revolution. That explains the presence of the forty-eight Chinese generals mentioned by el Campesino.[47] Modesto and Líster were trained for action specifically in France, though Spain was not overlooked.[48] Lectures were given in simultaneous translation by four interpreters whose main job, el Campesino tells us, was to spy for the NKVD.[49] Tagüeña relates that Modesto and Líster were sufficiently intelligent to follow the course but they preferred, for demagogic reasons, to join the less-gifted students.[50] In any event, out of the thirty-odd students, all passed except two. One of them was el Campesino.

El Campesino, whose real name was Valentín González, is the subject of an even greater legend than is Líster. As a result, the facts are not always easy to separate from the fantasies. His associate Julián Gorkin warns against the distortions of his character bequeathed by Ernest Hemingway and particularly by Ilya Ehrenburg. Gorkin was originally el Campesino's ideological enemy, and when Gorkin was imprisoned by the NKVD in Madrid, it was el Campesino who was to take charge of his execution; Gorkin was saved only because el Campesino was held up on the Estremadura front, and because the Republican Government transferred him under strong escort and in all haste to Valencia. When the virtually illiterate el Campesino finally broke with Stalin, Gorkin offered his services as ghost-writer of his autobiography, signing only the introduction.[51] In the introduction, Gorkin describes how el Campesino's anarchist father, in his native Estremadura, became a guerrilla leader in the Civil War until, with one of his daughters, he was taken prisoner by the Falange towards the end of 1936. They were hanged together from a tree, their bodies left dangling for a week with signs indicating that they were the father and sister of el Campesino. El Campesino, for his part, had been a communist since 1929, when he joined the PCE in Madrid. In the Civil War he built first a battalion, then a brigade, and finally the 46th Shock Division which bore his name until the end. Despite his thick beard and uncouth manner, el Campesino was simple, charming, even shy.[52] More importantly, for the value of the account he gave, he had what Gorkin called a 'truly astonishing memory'.[53]

Gorkin's own phenomenal memory no doubt played a part in el Campesino's autobiography, for Gorkin knew Stalin as he knew all the members of Lenin's Politburo. El Campesino describes the first time he saw the Soviet leader, at an event held in the Bolshoi Theatre in Moscow. Stalin came on stage with his short and rather heavy steps, as if wrapped in heavy worries. The ovation went on three, four, five minutes; Stalin made no effort to stop it, accepting it as gods accept incense. Three weeks after el Campesino arrived in Moscow, he received an invitation to a Kremlin banquet from General Gregoriy Shtern, who under the name of Grigorovich had served in Spain as the chief Soviet military adviser. Shtern, his face glowing with servility towards the leader who two years later would have him shot, introduced el Campesino to Stalin. He was uglier than he looked in photographs, thought el Campesino. His head was fleshy, almost square, his forehead low, his hair and moustache thick, his eyes small and half-closed. The whole gave him a look of vulgarity, but also of a man apparently good-natured and easygoing. For el Campesino Stalin had only a knowing look and a single phrase: 'You look like a promising lad.' Everybody laughed politely. The Spaniard's heart sank. He had fought in the Civil War from the first day to the last, sustaining eleven wounds and incurring on Stalin's behalf a reputation for savagery. His sole recompense now was a tasteless jibe.[54]

El Campesino had left a companion and three children behind in Spain. In Russia, where he received the name Piotr Antonovich, he had no sooner arrived than he married a Russian girl barely out of her teens and twenty years younger than he. She was also beautiful, refined, intelligent—and the daughter of a distinguished general in the Red Army. Not unnaturally, the bride's parents were opposed to the marriage. They would have opposed it more had they understood the Spanish expletives which their gentle daughter was learning in all innocence from the only tutors she had: her husband, and his crapulous comrades. Early in 1940 she gave birth to a boy. Meanwhile, el Campesino had entered the Frunze Academy, but in January 1941 he got into a violent argument in class with its elderly director, Boris Shaposhnikov. This breach of discipline, coupled with his poor academic performance, was all that Líster, on behalf of the PCE, needed to arrange his expulsion from the Academy. A longstanding and bitter quarrel was thus resolved in Líster's favour. El Campesino insists that during the Civil War Líster and his friends had tried to murder him several times, and that in the battle for Teruel in 1938 Líster, in collusion with Modesto and Grigorovich, had betrayed him, ordering his division not to evacuate the town and then refusing him the reinforcements that were close at hand. El Campesino had subsequently demanded that Líster be executed for his action, but the latter had the protection of the Soviets.[55] The humiliation of expulsion from the Academy, however, did not teach el Campesino humility. 'I could have been a general in the Red Army,' he writes, 'I preferred to be sentenced as rebel to hard labour in the Moscow Metro.'[56] In fact, el Campesino appealed against the decision, first to Stalin, and later to Kalinin, but to no avail.[57] Not even the German invasion of June 1941 was to bring him better fortune, as we shall see.

Six officers who were indeed career men were admitted to the Voroshilov Academy, the centre of higher studies for officers above the rank of two-star general. Among these were Vice-Admiral Pedro Prados, the former chief of staff of the Navy, and Antonio Cordón, the former under-secretary of defence. Cordón had been promoted to general rank by the Republican Government on 1 March 1939, but he was among those now forced to revert to the rank of colonel.

As for the Planiernaya School of Leninism, situated some ten miles north-west of Moscow, it was directed by Mikhaïl Koltzov, the former *Pravda* correspondent in Spain, and initially by a committee made up of Pedro Fernández Checa, Vicente Uribe, and Castro Delgado. Francisco Antón was given responsibility for the instruction, the purpose of which was to prepare students for leadership positions in the PCE.

The leadership of the PCE was now so mired in jealousy and intrigue that the whole colony took on the look of a Byzantine palace. Ever since 1939 the question had been asked why José Díaz had been summoned before Stalin. Had his star fallen?[58] At a meeting of the Comintern in late 1940, Pasionaria launched a savage attack on the secretary-general, accusing him of nepotism and jobbery. The ensuing commotion was so great that Dimitrov had to suspend the session and order the Spanish delegation to get its house in order.[59] Pasionaria subsequently apologized to Díaz, but the quarrel marked the end for the secretary-general. It now seemed certain that he was really ill, perhaps the victim of cancer.[60] His private life remained above reproach, and so rare was this among the PCE leaders that his household received the nickname of the 'Holy Family'.[61] Such respect was certainly not shown to Pasionaria, whose character and private life had the effect of separating her and her lover Antón from the other Party leaders. Her personal followers strove to turn her into some Immaculate Mother, and panegyrics to the divine Dolores continued when later she returned to France. But in fact she was not exempt from criticism within the Party, even if the criticism was never direct. As for Francisco Antón, the former commissar-general of the Republican Army, we have seen that he and Antonio Mije, who was responsible for the SERE evacuation service, were the only PCE leaders still in France in June 1940. He was therefore at that moment at the mercy of the Nazi invaders. Pasionaria's plea to Stalin to work her lover's release was unique in the annals of the Molotov–Ribbentrop

Pact. No doubt Stalin was puzzled that such a request by a member of the Comintern could be motivated by passion and not by politics. But he agreed. The Soviet Foreign Ministry arranged the rest, and Antón was given a Soviet passport and allowed to walk out of the concentration camp at Le Vernet, now under the jurisdiction of Pétain; with the help of Otto Abetz, Hitler's Ambassador to France, he crossed Germany and reached Moscow.[62] There was to be no embarrassing scene in the Soviet capital: Pasionaria's husband, Julián Ruiz, was packed off to a factory in Rostov-on-Don, and later to Ufa, while their daughter Amaya Ruiz was ordered by her mother to break all contact with her father. Antón's privileged life now continued: in Moscow he was given the coveted post of inspector of the Spanish military groups. Antón could not resist confiding the secret of his success, admitting to Manuel Tagüeña the nature of his relationship with Pasionaria. Antón was twenty years younger than she. For the Spaniards, and especially for the young militants who had indeed felt a profound respect for her, it seemed like a sacrilege. They began to call him Godoy, after the favourite of Charles IV, and similar epithets were used in reference to Pasionaria.[63]

Variations of nepotism worked to the advantage of other Spaniards. The marriage of Ignacio Gallego to Pasionaria's daughter Amaya certainly did not harm his career, and an obscure brother of Santiago Carrillo had been able, through his family connections, to travel in style (while the opportunity existed) all over Eastern Europe.[64] Irene Levi de Falcón, Pasionaria's quadrilingual private secretary, also took advantage of the circles in which she moved by remarrying, to a senior official of the Comintern.[65]

Castro Delgado was among those who frowned upon the behaviour of the Spanish leaders. Castro had come to Russia with his wife Esperanza Abascal, and although he treated her as a woman who simply cooked and sewed and waited ready for a chat whenever he came home, he did not look elsewhere for company.[66] He was therefore ready to pass judgement on his colleagues, noting that it was common among the Spanish communists to leave their wives and children in Spain or France. This was the case of Antonio Cordón, Juan Modesto, and Enrique Líster,[67] who had all remarried. If Modesto liked to beat his new wife, Castro added, the crime in his case was venial. Cordón was the only one who refrained from insulting others. If he was intoxicated with big words, at least he did not drink. The others never stopped drinking. If Dolores deserved the opprobrium in which she was held, he concluded, it still did not mean that any of the others had set an example in their private lives that qualified them to take her place.[68]

Since Díaz was incapacitated and Uribe and Mije were in Mexico, the PCE's Politburo in Moscow was dominated by Pasionaria, Jesús Hernández, and Pedro Fernández Checa. When Checa also left for Mexico in 1940, the top leadership was further reduced. Hernández, though living in Kuntsevo, kept his apartment in the Hotel Lux which remained permanently open to those who needed his help no less than to those whose help he needed. He owed a great deal to his wife. Pilar Boves was not only strikingly beautiful but also endowed with a generosity of heart and a gift for getting on with people that placed her beyond the reach of the gossip-mongers.[69] In the struggle between Hernández and Antón, Modesto and Líster were in Hernández's corner. The two generals usually acted in unison, but their partnership was forced by circumstances. Their opinions sometimes collided, and they remained essentially rivals. Modesto had the habit of never trusting anyone, while Líster went out of his way to retain the loyalty of those who owed their admission to the USSR to him.[70] Hernández also had a close friend in Castro Delgado. Like Hernández, Castro was a close associate of Jose Díaz, working as he did as secretary to the general secretariat. Castro too nursed a deep and growing antipathy for Pasionaria, and he and Líster, in the presence of Tagüeña, would freely vent their criticism of Dolores and Antón, and of Modesto too.[71]

The house of Dmitri Manuilski, Second Secretary of the Comintern, provided another den of intrigue. The nominal head of the Comintern was Georgi Dimitrov, the hero of the Leipzig Trial. But Dimitrov was a Bulgarian, and he never gave an order which was not first approved by Manuilski, the representative of the Soviet Politburo, who was totally dependent upon Zhdanov, the Comintern's Director for Foreign Affairs.[72] The house was home to many Spaniards, but not apparently to Santiago Carrillo. Togliatti and José Díaz refused to allow Carrillo to live there, or even to attend the meetings there during his brief stay in Moscow.[73]

In propagating this story, Líster has his personal reasons for discrediting Carrillo: in 1939 Carrillo had ousted him from the Historical Commission of the Spanish Civil War which had been established in Moscow, and to which Líster had been elected.[74] Líster was a man who knew how to nurse a grudge, but his denunciation of Carrillo was supported by others. Manuel Tagüeña, a much more balanced observer, makes it clear that he never liked or trusted Carrillo and considers him a man capable of subordinating everything to political ambition. The famous letter in which he denounced his father, Wenceslao Carrillo, provides an example. 'Nobody', writes Tagüeña, 'doubted that he wrote it in order to prove to the PCE leaders that here was a true party member, ready to sacrifice his own family to the

cause.'[75] Finally, to complete the turn of this sombre carousel, Carrillo
—even if he denies ever having had a serious difference with Pasionaria,
and even though he joined Antón in 1945 in a new attack on the
POUM—contended in 1971 that Antón was 'the mirror image of
everything that was wrong with the Party leadership'.[76]

In America at this time, the Spanish communists were concentrated
in Mexico, Argentina, Brazil, Uruguay, and Cuba, and to a lesser extent in Chile, Venezuela, Dominican Republic, Costa Rica, and Paraguay. In his report to a plenary meeting of the PCE in 1945, Fernando
Claudín estimated that some 2,000 Party members had crossed the
Atlantic, most of them directly from the French concentration camps.
Mexico remained the centre of their activities.[77] But there, as elsewhere, the communists were isolated. Even the entry of the Soviet
Union into the war was not going to change this situation. Many of
the Spanish social clubs, especially the Catalan centres, were divided
between their communist and non-communist cliques. As a result,
communist activities were circumscribed, even though it was to
Mexico that the largest number of PCE and PSUC leaders were sent.
Most of these arrived from Moscow between the end of 1939 and the
middle of 1940. Among them were three of the members of the PCE
Politburo selected by the Comintern: Pedro Fernández Checa, Vicente
Uribe, and Antonio Mije. Checa, as we have seen, was playing a
special role, and he was sick. Uribe and Mije were not sick, but they
were soon installed in the capital's residential sector of Cuernavaca,
in villas staffed by domestic servants and private chauffeurs.[78] For the
two men with responsibility for the PCE throughout Latin America,
the opulence of their lifestyle was a grievous error.
   Meanwhile in Moscow it was decided that Jesús Hernández, his
wife Pilar Boves, and the PSUC leader Comorera, before they left for
America, would go to Oslo to build a new communication link between Moscow and France. Hernández, for one, was overjoyed at the
chance to leave the Soviet Union. At the beginning, his reasons were
not even political. As he writes in his memoirs, 'I did not like the
Soviet Union as a land of exile, even though at the time I felt no
political hostility toward the regime'.[79] In Norway, Hernández and
Comorera found their mission impossible, and soon moved back to
Stockholm, where they tried in vain to persuade the Kremlin to furnish
them with passports so that they could get to Mexico. When, on 8
April 1940, Norway was invaded, the Kremlin ordered them to return
to Russia at once. All three complied. Hernández returned to find that
in his absence Pasionaria had removed Enrique Castro from his post
as private secretary to Díaz and replaced him with Keti Levi Rodríguez,

the sister of her own secretary Irene Falcón. Again Hernández and Comorera insisted on leaving for Mexico. Pasionaria responded by arranging for the Comintern to give Hernández a new assignment in Russia: writing a book on the role of the anarchists in the Spanish Civil War. Comorera, on the other hand, was more fortunate, taking advantage of the situation in Mexico to obtain the Kremlin's final agreement to his departure. This left Rafael Vidiella, a former minister in the Generalitat, in charge of the PSUC in Moscow and the permanent representative of the Catalan party in the Comintern.

Communist groups everywhere had suffered heavy losses as a result of the Molotov–Ribbentrop Pact, with many former militants leaving political life entirely and devoting themselves to their professional life. Only in Mexico, however, did the dissidents form an alternative political group, and the Catalans were at the heart of it. Within the Catalan communist party, two currents were now of major concern to the Kremlin. One was the PSUC's traditional desire to be a party independent from the PCE. The second was the tide of opposition not only to the Pact but to the whole range of Stalin's policies. In Mexico some leaders had left the Party in protest. Some forty others in America were soon to be expelled. These included Serra Pàmies who, with José del Barrio and the Basque Luis Cabo Giorla, arrived in Chile in May 1940 via Vladivostok, Yokohama, and Vancouver.[80] Comorera reached Mexico in August, following the same itinerary. When José del Barrio asked to be transferred to Mexico, Comorera sent him (again with Cabo Giorla) to Buenos Aires instead, with instructions to organize the dispatch of propaganda materials to Spain. Comorera's reasons for keeping an influential leader like del Barrio out of Mexico and in seclusion in Argentina soon became clear. Del Barrio was a supporter of the so-called Antwerp initiative, and in Moscow, in conversations with Manuilski, he had criticized the Pact. Comorera's first action was to abolish the executive committee of the PSUC which had been elected at the Antwerp meeting and replace it with a troika headed by himself.[81]

The result was the Stalinization of the PSUC, but the dissidents did not lie down. In November 1940 they published a manifesto protesting against four specific items of Stalin's rule: the promotion of Party members on no other basis than their willingness to accept orders from above; the failure to implement the agreement making the PSUC a member of the Comintern, independent of the PCE; the Hitler–Stalin Pact, and the use of the Comintern as a mere instrument of Soviet policy; and the abandonment by the USSR of the Spanish refugees in France, while it was still possible to evacuate them. Comorera's men responded by denouncing the dissidents as Trotskyists and counter-revolutionaries, whose treason was proven by the mere fact that they wanted to distinguish between the interests of the Soviet Union and the interests of the world revolutionary movement.[82]

However small the Spanish communist numbers, they were not without their press. For fewer than a thousand Spanish communists in Mexico there was the weekly *España popular* and the monthly *Nuestra bandera*, together with the PSUC journal *Catalunya*. The Basque communists, led by Sebastián Zapirain, also had their *Alkartu* and *Euzkadi roja*. In Havana, the PSUC produced *Per Catalunya*.[83] Finally, in Santiago de Chile, José del Barrio launched the Catalan monthly *Retorn*.

In Moscow, the Comintern had been contemplating the establishment in neutral and strategic Switzerland of a European centre for KIM activities. The expansion of Nazi control in Eastern Europe caused the plan to be abandoned, but the man whom Dimitrov had in mind for that mission was to receive an equally attractive reassignment. Santiago Carrillo had caught Stalin's attention from the moment he passed the Morozov test: readiness to denounce one's own father. 'Between a communist and a traitor there can be no relations of any kind', wrote the young Carrillo to his father Wenceslao after the latter had given his support to the Casado coup.[84] The germ of heresy, in Stalin's eyes transmissible through the blood, had not in this case infected the son. For six months Carrillo remained in Moscow, staying at the Hotel Lux and attending the meetings of the Comintern secretariat and of its executive committee.[85] During that time Dimitrov decided to establish in the Americas a triumvirate directly responsible to the Comintern, to consist of Earl Browder in the United States, Vittorio Codovila in Argentina, and a third man to be sent now from Moscow. The Hungarian Mikhail Wolf, second highest in rank among the non-Soviet members of the Comintern, wanted the assignment, but Dimitrov's choice was Carrillo, whose function in the triumvirate was again to organize communist youth.

In June 1940 Carrillo left for New York, via Vladivostok, Tokyo, Vancouver and Montreal. Carrillo found New York no more to his taste than he found Earl Browder. There was too little of the cosmopolitan, too much of the country bumpkin about Santiago Carrillo for him to adapt to North American life. Culturally limited, and unable to learn the language, he was soon discouraged. The whole United States political setting was alien to him, weighed down as he was with all the dogmatic baggage he carried. Earl Browder did nothing to make him feel at home. The secretary of the US Communist Party, and long-time representative in the Comintern for all the communist parties in the Americas, showed no interest in sharing the role with anybody. As a result, the projected committee of three never functioned, and at the end of six months Carrillo decided to leave for Cuba.[86] There he felt no better, since the Cuban Communist Party was following a policy of alliance with Batista, and Batista was following the foreign policy of Roosevelt. After a few more months, with the approval of the PCE but without asking the advice of Moscow, Carrillo left Cuba for Mexico. In so far as the primary purpose of Spanish communist leaders in America was to develop communications with the PCE in Spain, this was a bad move: the chances of succeeding in Mexico were even slimmer than they were in Cuba, for unlike Cuba Mexico had almost no shipping links with Spain. Besides that, the Mexican Communist Party had been rent as much as any by the Molotov–Ribbentrop Pact, with many of its leaders, including its secretary-general Hernán Laborde, expelled from the Party for their criticism of Stalin's policy. The murder of Trotsky made a bad situation worse.[87] As a result, Carrillo achieved little in Mexico except to launch a magazine entitled *La lucha por la juventud*, for distribution throughout the hemisphere. Carrillo admits that his work as the KIM's delegate in the Americas was a failure, especially when in 1943 the Comintern was dissolved. After two or three months in Mexico, he began working again directly for the PCE, but being an illegal immigrant he kept apart from the other leaders, confining his efforts to communicating with the Party in Spain. To this end it was decided that he would move to Buenos Aires, since that was the only city in America with direct links to the Peninsula. José del Barrio and Cabo Giorla, we have seen, had preceded him, and Vittorio Codovila was busy trying to expand his control over all communist operations in the Southern Cone.[88] In Argentina Carrillo was again an illegal immigrant, but so were the others, and the Argentine Communist Party was itself illegal. Carrillo describes his relations with the Argentine communists as perpetually cordial, but his silence on the rest is eloquent. With his deputy Fernando Claudín, and with the help of Spanish, Portuguese, Greek, and Swedish seamen—motivated in some cases by ideology, in others by monetary gain—he developed the communications network with Spain, maintaining the flow of propaganda, transmitting messages, dispatching agents, and trying to establish the same links with Spanish communists in France. Carrillo was to remain in Buenos Aires until 1942.[89] During that time he revealed his un-Marxist weakness for dalliance; no sooner had he arrived than he was entranced by a certain Lidia, the sister of Claudín's inamorata Angela. The tryst ended when Consuelo, whom Carrillo had married in Spain, arrived in Buenos Aires.[90]

The assassination team which Stalin dispatched to Mexico in 1939 or 1940 remains shrouded in mystery. It has been said that the overall operation was entrusted to Vittorio Vidali, the Italian communist leader from Trieste who operated under the name of Carlos J. Contreras,[91] and that the team consisted of three Spanish communists: Pedro Martínez Cartón, Santiago Alvarez, and a certain Jiménez.[92] These three were allegedly chosen from a group of eight Spaniards who had been selected, on their arrival in Moscow in 1939, for training in a secret school within the Frunze Academy and therefore under the direction of General Ivan Stepanovich Koniev. Of these three, perhaps only Santiago Alvarez, the former political commissar of the Líster Division, actually took part. The third man was identified by el Campesino, many years later, as a certain Puentes from Santander, who had been Líster's political commissar before Santiago Alvarez.[93] As for the role of Martínez Cartón, the plot thickens. A former representative of Bajadoz in the Cortes, he had served in the Civil War as a lieutenant-colonel, commanding the 64th Division in the Battle of Teruel in December 1937. In the course of the war he had also been promoted to the PCE Politburo. In exile in Moscow, however, he had been singled out for special rebuke in the purge of the PCE in 1939–40.[94] He seems to have set out to make amends, for in the same period as the purge he joined the NKVD.[95] Even if he was in Mexico in September 1939,[96] it seems certain that he was in Russia at the time of the murder of Trotsky.[97] But if the identity of the murderers remains in dispute, their targets are not. Apart from Trotsky they included the former Red Army general Walter G. Krivitsky, the elderly Italian anarchist Carlo Tresca, and Julián Gorkin of the POUM.[98]

Trotsky had reached Mexico from Norway in a Norwegian tanker, landing in Tampico on 9 January 1937. The compound in which he now lived, at 45 Avenida Viena, on the outskirts of Coyoacán, was a veritable fortress, for Trotsky knew only too well, from the systematic elimination of his family and his staff by Stalin,[99] the tenacity of Stalin's vengeance. His assassination no doubt required a special organization, and Robert Conquest tells us that it was assigned to Leonid Eitingon, a senior officer in the NKVD who had served under Orlov in the Civil War, when he used the name 'Kotov'; he now received the name 'Leonov' for his assignment in Mexico.[100] The first attempt was carried out at early dawn on the night of 24–5 May 1940. Trotsky escaped almost by a miracle. The attack was led by the great Mexican muralist David Alfaro Siqueiros, a founder of the Mexican Communist Party who had entered the OGPU in 1929; in the Civil War in Spain he had commanded the Mexican volunteers, and was made a colonel—the circumstances are obscure—in the Spanish Republican

Army. He and his men (who may have numbered as many as twenty) found their way into Trotsky's house in the guise of policemen, Alfaro dressed as an officer. As they entered the bedroom where Trotsky was sleeping with his second wife, the little golden-haired Natalia Ivanovna Sedova, the two intended victims sprang for their very lives, hurling themselves under the bed as the assassination team poured as many as 300 rounds from their sub-machine-guns into the bedclothes and the wooden bedstead. But the bedstead was not of wood alone; a steel plate allowed the couple to emerge unharmed. But Trotsky's American secretary and bodyguard, Robert Sheldon Harte, was kidnapped. His corpse was found in a shallow well filled with lime in the garden of a little house rented by the brother-in-law of Alfaro Siqueiros. He was the seventh of Trotsky's secretaries to be murdered.[101] Alfaro Siqueiros was charged with complicity in his murder and with attempted murder in the case of Trotsky. The Mexican police set him free on bail, but forbade him to leave the country. It was at this point that the Chilean poet Pablo Neruda came to his rescue. Neruda, who was attached to the Chilean Consulate in Mexico City in 1940–1, issued him with either a visa or a passport, and thanks to that Alfaro Siqueiros was able to leave Mexico on 5 March 1941, bound for Chile.[102]

The assassination of Trotsky on 20 August 1940—after 37 vain attempts dating from 1927—has been too well reconstituted, and the personality of his assassin too well analysed, especially by Julián Gorkin, Jorge Semprún, and Pierre Broué, for any further study to be needed here. The key role was played by Caridad del Río Mercader, who, Robert Conquest tells us, 'had been sexually entangled with Eitingon during the Spanish Civil War, when she herself worked in the liquidation squad'.[103] With her will of iron, she had persuaded her son Ramón to work for the NKVD, probably from 1938. When Trotsky's bodyguards caught him and began smashing his head, Ramón screamed out: 'They forced me to do it! They forced me to do it!'[104] According to one authoritative version, he added: 'They've imprisoned my mother.' Whatever the circumstances, Caridad Mercader survived and received no less a reward than the Order of Lenin, while her son was awarded the highest possible sentence under Mexican law: 20 years' imprisonment. It is said that in 1945 she went to Mexico on a Cuban passport to plead for the release of her son, and to this end approached Lázaro Cárdenas, who had been President of Mexico at the time of Trotsky's death, and who now refused to see her. If the story is true, it is astonishing that the identity of the assassin should continue to be concealed, for the assassin had given his name to the Mexican police as Jacques Mornard, a Belgian, and throughout hundreds of hours of questioning he steadfastly maintained it, insisting that his motives were personal. It was only in 1952 that his persona came apart: his prison warders heard him humming a lullaby in Catalan. The tip led the investigators to Spain, where Franco's police duly discovered a thick dossier on Mercader, including his photo and fingerprints. In 1961 he was released on the completion of his term. He took a plane to Prague, and from there to Moscow. In early 1977, terminally ill with cancer, he flew to Havana, where he died on 17 October of the following year. His ashes were flown to Moscow and buried in a place of honour, though the Soviet Union still did not publicly acknowledge that Mercader was acting on Stalin's orders. With his death, the writer Teresa Pàmies, who had known Mercader during the Civil War, threw another shaft of light on the affair. She revealed that with other Spanish communists she had believed Stalin when he asserted that Trotsky was a fascist agent. That was why, she said, they kept silent when they recognized the assassin in the photographs. To raise the veil, she added, would have done harm to the Party, and especially to the Soviet Union.[105] At the time, in any event, the communist press studiously avoided mention of the death of Trotsky.[106]

Among the other enemies of Stalin targeted for assassination, General Krivitsky had served as head of Soviet military intelligence in Western Europe up until November 1937, when he broke with the regime as a result of the Moscow trials. He reached the West and went into hiding in Washington, DC, but there, on 10 February 1941, his bullet-ridden body was found in a room in the Bellevue Hotel. The assassin was never caught, but Julián Gorkin and others saw evidence of Stalin's hand at work. With three other fugitives from Stalin's vengeance (Marceau Pivert, Victor Serge, and Gustave Regler), Gorkin published an appeal referring to the fate of Krivitsky and revealing the mortal danger to which they were exposed. The appeal was addressed to Manuel Avila Camacho, the new President of Mexico, and ran: 'We solemnly declare, in response to whatever may befall us, that none of us suffers from a weak heart and none of us has any intention of committing suicide.'[107] Gorkin was to be the target of five successive attempts on his life, the worst of which, at a public meeting in Mexico City in 1943, left him with a fractured skull and a permanent crease in his head. But he survived, and returned to Europe in 1948.[108] As for Carlo Tresca, he was currently the director of the New York anarchist weekly *Il Martello*, in which he systematically revealed the misdeeds of Vittorio Vidali and denounced him repeatedly as the murderer of the Italian anarchist philosopher Camillo Berneri. He also accused him of the murder of his own mistress, the young communist Tina Modotti. On 9 January 1943, Tresca told some friends in New York:

'Vidali has arrived. He is here to carry out some job. I smell death in the air.' Two days later, on the evening of 11 January, Tresca was leaving his office on the corner of Fifth Avenue and 15th Street when he was shot dead. Vidali was arrested by the FBI and interrogated, but nothing could be proved against him and he was released.[109] Vidali then returned to Mexico.[110]

A similar fate could well have befallen Victorio Sala. During the May Days in Barcelona in 1937, Sala had been chief of police, taking his orders from Ernö Gerö.[111] The PCE then sent him to Mexico. Sala ran the mortal risk of knowing too much, especially about certain secrets relating to the activities of the NKVD in Barcelona during the Civil War. He had also been one of the officials responsible for evacuating to France the top archives of the PCE and the PSUC,[112] and as such could be chosen as a scapegoat for the ensuing debacle. He also knew too much about relations between the PCE and the PCF. In Mexico, however, nothing happened to him, other than that he was quietly evicted from the Party,[113] which he then proceeded to accuse of hideous crimes.[114]

By 1941 a 'delegation of the PCE Politburo' had been created, its seat in Mexico and its jurisdiction covering Latin America. Checa was the ranking member, but in March of that year he was so sick he could hardly get out of bed. This advanced the position of Uribe, the half-Castillian, half-Basque metal-worker who had served as an early editor of *Mundo obrero*. Uribe was known as a party theoretician, but he was also known for intellectual mediocrity, vulgarity, and a brutality that won him the nickname of 'Herod' among communist youth. Unlike Checa, who was a simple, unambitious man who worked hard for the cause he believed in, Uribe was self-centred, had no capacity for organization, and was lazy into the bargain. If Uribe respected Carrillo, the feeling was not reciprocated: both Checa and Carrillo were unhappy with Uribe's leadership in Mexico, especially the abusive way he treated others.[115] Mije, who was responsible for communications with the rest of the hemisphere, was an Andalusian and an ex-anarchist just like the PCE secretary-general. The similarity ended there, for Mije was no more like José Díaz than Uribe was like Checa. Somewhat feminine in appearance, lively and talkative in manner, even demagogic in style, Mije was as inept as Uribe, and the two leaders symbolized the comfortable Latin-American exile described by Claudín[116] which stood in such contrast with the sufferings of the exiles in France, Russia, and Germany.

4

In the Hands of the Nazis

Experiences of the Spaniards following the collapse of France—
The Travailleurs étrangers in the hands of Vichy and of Germany—
Captives in the Channel Islands—The march to Germany: Trier,
Nuremberg, Munich, Mauthausen—Distribution of the Spaniards in
Germany—The KZ universe—The special character of Mauthausen
—The historical sources—The records compiled by the inmates

> Es gibt einen Weg in die Freiheit.
> Seine Meilensteine sind:
> Gehorsam, Fleiss, Ordnung, Sauberkeit,
> Ehrlichkeit, Opfermut, und Liebe zum Vaterland.[1]

The Spanish refugees were among the first to suffer the consequences
of the disaster of June 1940. More than 10,000 Spaniards were taken
prisoner by the Germans, and the Vichy Government made no attempt to protect them under international agreements pertaining to
prisoners of war. Many of them thus found themselves back where
they started, in the concentration camps of the south-west. In September Argelès-sur-Mer was again the largest: swollen by the influx
of Spaniards transferred from the camp at Bram, and of Jews and
former members of the International Brigades transferred from the
camp at Gurs, it accommodated some 20,000 people. Hicem, a Jewish
migration agency which the Vichy authorities tolerated at that time,
managed to evacuate some 600 Spaniards to Mexico towards the end
of 1941.[2]

On 27 September 1940, René Belin, the Vichy Minister of Labour
and Industrial Production, introduced a law whereby all male foreigners
aged 19 to 54 who were a burden on the French economy and who
could not return to their country of origin were subject to enlistment
in the Groupes de travailleurs étrangers; they would receive no salary,
but their families were entitled to aid according to rates fixed by the
government.[3] Perhaps as many as 15,000 Spaniards who were enlisted
in this way found themselves employed by the Organisation Todt
(OT) in the construction of the Atlantic Wall.[4] Their work included

the construction of the submarine bases at Lorient, La Pallice, and in the Gironde estuary, and of an airfield at La Rochelle, despite frequent bombing attacks by the Royal Air Force. A considerable number of these workers were transferred in late 1941 to Vigo, in north-western Spain, where they were employed in the construction of another submarine base, probably intended for German use.[5]

Other contingents of Spaniards, estimated at 4,000, were sent to the German-occupied Channel Islands. When the Islands fell under Nazi rule in June 1940, they were at first administered by a military government, but in October 1941 Hitler issued his Directive on the Fortification and Defence of the Channel Islands, requiring immediate and intensive work on strong concrete fortifications. This was to be carried out by foreign labour, 'especially Russian and Spanish'. Very large stocks of cement and steel reinforcement arrived in the same month, and responsibility for the construction was given to the OT. The Catalan lieutenant Joan Dalmau, who later became a British subject, was among the first batch of 2,000 workers (mainly Spaniards, but including Frenchmen, Belgians, Dutch, Poles, and Czechs) who were transported from Saint-Malo to St Helier, Jersey. There they worked on the construction of the sea-wall in St Brelade's Bay, and when that was completed, in the summer of 1942, on the building of tunnels underneath Fort Regent. By that time, by one estimate, 18,000 foreign workers had arrived in Jersey. A curious feature of camp life on that island was that the workers were allowed, even forced, to leave the camp in order to seek food outside, thus reducing the cost of their upkeep. The people of Jersey did not lack in generosity, even when the local Feldkommandant, a certain Schultz, ordered them to stop providing any food to foreign workers. Despite the help of the islanders general starvation set in and many prisoners, especially those not accustomed to rural life, died as a result of eating poisonous plants. Those causing trouble were sent to Elizabeth Castle, where a prisoner could find himself in a cell with 0.2 square metres of floorspace, forcing him to sleep standing. In August 1942, 2,000 Russians arrived, having been marched across Europe. In January 1943, Dalmau and his Catalan friend Vidal were part of a small group taken by boat from Jersey to Saint-Servan on the French mainland. Schultz himself was in the escort. An opportunity arose: Vidal knocked out the commandant, Dalmau strangled him, and the body was tossed into the sea. The Germans, oddly enough, came to the conclusion that Schultz has been swept overboard, but Dalmau and Vidal still finished up in the island-prison of Alderney.[6]

Alderney had the distinction of housing the only SS camp erected on British soil. In this island, the OT began by evacuating almost all the civilian population; a Spanish prisoner, Francisco Font, made the observation that all the birds left with them. Four separate camps were established: Helgoland, Nordeney, Borkum, and Sylt—the last being reserved for political prisoners. In March 1943 Sylt was taken over by the SS, to be administered by *KL*-Neuengamme, near Hamburg; its command was given to SS-Hauptsturmführer Maximilian List. Most of the Spaniards were sent to Nordeney, whose first Commandant, OT-Haupttruppführer Karl Tietz, had previously served as Commandant at Sylt; he was replaced early in 1943 by OT-Haupttruppführer Adam Adler, who held simultaneously the SS rank of Untersturmführer. The principal firms in Germany to which the OT labour in Nordeney was contracted were Fuchs of Koblenz and Sager und Wörner of Munich. The first prisoners to arrive there were a convoy of 297 Spaniards; they were joined by Soviet prisoners of war and Jewish prisoners transported from the sorting camp at Drancy.[7] No drinking water was available in the camp, and prisoners would suck the grass on the road to and from the quarry where they worked. Dalmau recounts that in his group seven prisoners collapsed on the first day, whereupon they were thrown, still alive, over the cliffs into the sea.[8] Many died of disease. An incident on Christmas Eve 1943 was particularly destructive to the prisoners' morale. OT-Meister Heinrich Evers, Nordeney's Unterlagerführer, whom the Spaniards nicknamed 'Mucos' on account of his perennially runny nose, summoned the prisoners to the *Appellplatz* where a bonfire had been lit. Evers announced jubilantly that he bore tidings of great joy. He carried in his hand a stack of letters, and began reading off the names. Minutes passed, while the expectation of the prisoners reached fever-pitch. At last a letter from home. Evers then walked over to the bonfire, and whooping with laughter threw the whole stack in. Despite such torments, the Spanish communists claim that in the Channel Islands they succeeded in assembling a radio on which they were able to listen to the BBC and even Radio Moscow, and that they even circulated a news-sheet entitled *Acero*.[9] As for escape, there was no chance at all, and of the estimated 4,000 Spaniards sent to the Channel Islands, only fifty-nine survived.[10]

Without taking into account those Spanish workers who later volunteered, over 30,000 Spanish refugees were deported from France to Germany,[11] and of these perhaps 15,000 entered Nazi camps.[12] The great majority of these had served in the Travailleurs étrangers units. If, as we have seen, some of these were at first sent back into the French camps or into the Vichy forced-labour groups, most of them shared the initial experience described by Amadeo Cinca Vendrell and Juan de Diego Herranz, both of whom were former internees in the French concentration camp at Septfonds (Tarn-et-Garonne) and then volunteers in the 103rd Compagnie de travailleurs étrangers. This company, under the command of the French Lieutenant Simon, consisted of some 250 Spaniards, and Cinca Vendrell, a captain in the Republican Army, was given subordinate command. The unit had been assigned to the extension of the Maginot Line to the west, and had been stationed at Saint-Hilaire, near Cambrai. Simon was a courageous officer, but he was a retired veteran of the First World War who understood nothing of Guderian's concept of blitzkrieg. Cinca's pleas that the unit be allowed to retreat were brushed aside, and on 20 May 1940, in the forest of Amiens, Simon saw his whole company taken prisoner. The character of their captors was soon in evidence. The prisoners were marched 25 miles a day in the summer heat almost without food or water, with four to five hours of rest. Several Frenchwomen tried to give the prisoners water, apples, or eggs, but were driven away by the Germans at bayonet point. The Spaniards were also witnesses to the way the Wehrmacht treated their British prisoners of war. Perhaps because the British, unlike the French, did not allow defeat to destroy their morale—'they whistled all the way'—they were treated, as Captain Cinca reported it, worse than the others. Whenever the convoy encountered dead Germans on the side of the road, it was exclusively the British prisoners who were forced to dig the graves and bury the corpses, at the same time forfeiting whatever rations the Germans made available.

At a crossroads near the German frontier, the British contingent was separated from the Spanish contingent and the two continued in different directions, the Spaniards marching to Trier. On the way the convoy came across two cows in a field. The Wehrmacht officers saw an opportunity for some amusement. Killing the cows with their pistols, they then left the animals to the starving Spaniards, watching with glee as the prisoners tore the cows apart like cannibals. After a brief stop in Stalag XII-D in Trier, the Spaniards proceeded to Nuremberg. There, in the holy city of National Socialism, they were marched through the streets, the German populace spitting at them and making signs with their forefingers slicing their throats, as if to say they were as good as dead already. From Nuremberg they were taken in sealed cattle-cars to Stalag VII-A in Moosburg, north-east of Munich, where to their surprise they were interrogated by the Gestapo. A group of 392, all of them Spaniards, was now assembled for a final destination. Still carrying their meagre possessions, at most a small suitcase, they reboarded the cattle-cars, but in leaving Munich they could at least take one happy memory: the German railroad workers were dismayed at the condition of the Spaniards and showed their compassion, with some even giving the clenched fist salute, a rare and risky tribute. The worst of the journey was still ahead. They had received food and water before they left Nuremberg, but no more during the eighteen hours they spent in the train. It was the heat of August, some of the men were suffering from dysentery, all physical functions took place within the wagon, and the air was Augean. At 8 o'clock on the morning of 6 August 1940, the Spanish contingent arrived at Mauthausen—one of the first non-German groups to do so—and discovered the full meaning of the Nazi concentration camp universe.[13]

Most of the Spaniards who entered Nazi concentration camps passed first through a Stalag, though not necessarily Stalag VII-A at Moosburg.[14] The German High Command took the decision to refuse the status of prisoner of war to the Spaniards, even if they were captured in French uniform. The belief, prevalent in Spanish Republican circles for the last forty years, that the German decision was the result of a request by Serrano Súñer to Himmler, has no documentary support whatever, and the evidence on which it rests is a demonstrable fiction.[15] The decision was undoubtedly taken on the harsh but legal basis that Germany was not at war with Spain, that these Spaniards had no passports, and that their status was stateless. The German purpose, however, in sending them to concentration camps went further: the Spaniards were dedicated antifascists who had fought the Germans and Italians in Spain, and as inveterate enemies of Nazi Germany their proper place was Mauthausen. Although Spaniards were sent to several other camps, probably nine-tenths of all Spanish prisoners were sent to Mauthausen and its various Aussenkommandos throughout Ostmark, the land once called Austria.

Only in the case of Mauthausen and some of its Aussenkommandos can accurate statistics be presented. The fact that accurate statistics can be given at all is remarkable, and we shall examine later the fortune that came even in such adversity. The monument at Mauthausen to the Spanish dead gives the figure of 7,000. The following tableau presents the most authoritative estimates of the number of Spaniards who entered the camps and died there. Preference should be given to the figures of Casimir Climent Sarrión.[16] Not only was he in a most privileged post, as we shall see, but he was also a man of patience and painstaking care. Razola, on the other hand, does not explain his sources, and they surely come from a number of personal and unfounded estimates, based on memory.[17] As for Borrás, his figures are based on an amalgam of sources, among which Climent remains the most reliable.[18]

1. Mauthausen, including Aussenkommandos and Schloss Hartheim

	Climent	Razola	Borrás
Entering	7,186	9,067	7,189
Exterminated	4,765[19]	6,784[20]	4,761
Transferred to other camps or returned to Spain	238		
Liberated	2,183	2,283	2,428

2. Other Camps

Dachau	
Entering, August 1940	500[21]
Liberated	267[22]
Buchenwald and Dora-Mittelbau	
Liberated	200[23]
Flossenburg	
Exterminated	14
Liberated	86[24]
Auschwitz[25]	
Gross-Rosen	
Neuengamme, including Alderney[26]	
Ravensbrück	
Sachsenhausen, including Oranienburg[27]	
Estimated totals:[28]	
Entering	1,000
Exterminated	200
Liberated	800

3. Died from Other Causes

In transit, victims of Allied air-raids, in Gestapo and Vichy prisons	1,000[29]

A number of observations should be made. The figures for Mauthausen (or at least Climent's) omit those who arrived at the station dead, or who were murdered on the road and taken straight to the crematorium without receiving a number. They also omit those who died during the last days prior to liberation, when no records were kept, and when the mortality rate was highest. Nor do we have accurate figures for such Aussenkommandos in Austria as Ebensee, where the proportion of Spaniards was very high; or Schlier, near Salzburg, where the 400 Spaniards interned made up almost the entire penal colony;[30] or Steyr-Münichholz, the munitions factory 30 kilometres south of Mauthausen, where the Spaniards were also in a heavy majority from spring 1941 onwards.[31] Vilanova adds that Spaniards were in the majority in all three Gusen Kommandos as well as in Ternberg.

A final general observation concerns the manner of their dying. Razola considers that more Spaniards were murdered by the SS than were killed off by cold, hunger, or forced labour.[32] Vilanova estimates that 95 per cent of all the Spaniards who died were exterminated in the period 1940–2.[33] The reason for this, as we shall see, was the shortage of manpower that the Third Reich faced from 1943. In calculating the proportion of deaths to the number detained, Vilanova takes the figure of 8,189 Spaniards interned in Nazi camps and that of 5,015 exterminated, and presents the figure of 61 per cent, the highest percentage among all the national groups. In fact the mortality rate is even higher when it is remembered that 50 per cent of the survivors died in their first year of freedom.[34] But in the story we are about to tell, freedom is a long way off.

In the first week of 1941, Himmler decided to classify the *Konzentrationslager*. On 2 January, Reinhard Heydrich, as head of the Reichssicherheitshauptamt (RSHA), issued a secret circular (later produced at the Nuremberg Tribunal) which divided the camps into three principal categories. The first category (known as *Stufe* I) included Dachau, Sachsenhausen, and Auschwitz I; its prisoners were considered rehabilitable. *Stufe* II included Buchenwald, Auschwitz II, Flossenburg, and Neuengamme; although charged with more serious crimes, the prisoners in these camps were still considered capable of redemption. *Stufe* III (or *Ausmergungslager*) included only Mauthausen and Auschwitz III (Birkenau); this category was reserved for 'hardened criminals and antisocial elements incapable of rehabilitation'. This classification was later modified, as we shall see, when the Economic Administration Office (Wirtschafts Verwaltungshauptamt, or SS-WVHA) established three new categories, but the classification *Stufe* III continued to denote a camp where prisoners were never to be released.[35]

Mauthausen never lost this classification of *Stufe* III, the worst. In the offices of the RSHA it was referred to by its nickname *Knochenmühle*, the bone-grinder. One way to punish prisoners at Auschwitz was to send them to work in the quarry at Mauthausen. Buchenwald too had its quarry, but the prisoners there knew what Mauthausen meant, and dreaded the thought of being transferred.[36] Suzanne Busson, who was evacuated from Ravensbrück to Mauthausen, remarked that 'Ravensbrück in hindsight seemed like paradise'.[37] It should be noted here that the *KL* were different in kind from the extermination camps (*Vernichtungslager*) which is what Auschwitz III

(Birkenau) became. All six of the *Vernichtungslager* were located outside Germany, in a great circle in Poland. Though the fate of the inmates could be the same, the difference lies in the essential purpose of the two systems. What distinguished *Stufe* III was the long-drawn-out agony of those condemned to it. The purpose was to make the inmate suffer the maximum before death came as a merciful release.

None of this implies that a camp classified *Stufe* I was less technologically advanced than others. Even lowly Dachau had its gas chamber and its crematorium, and camps of every category were engaged in medical experiments. Like medieval universities they had their specialities. For typhus, it was Buchenwald and Auschwitz; for sterilization, Auschwitz, Ravensbrück, Flossenburg, and Buchenwald; for experiments on twins, Auschwitz; for the effects of freezing temperatures and high altitude, Dachau; for surgical operations, Gusen and Dachau; for tuberculosis, Gusen and Dachau; for cancer, Auschwitz; for bone transplants, Ravensbrück; and for malaria, Dachau.[38] At the centre of all this scientific research was the SS medical academy in Graz.

When an SS physician was not engaged in such experiments, there was always some other work to do, or services to render. Lieutenant-Colonel Eleuterio Díaz Tendero, of the Spanish Republican Army, was in an advanced state of tuberculosis when he arrived in Sachsenhausen. He was transferred to Dachau, where he was at once given a fatal injection of phenol in the heart.[39] At Flossenburg, Dr Schmidt had a mania for operating. Any prisoner who asked for an aspirin or complained of pain in any part of the body would discover that Dr Schmidt's remedy in all cases was to open the patient's stomach, to practise his hand, as he put it.[40] The anaesthetic used for such operations was called, by the SS and the prisoners alike, the *Holznarkose*, or wood narcotic. It consisted of the prisoners who served as hospital orderlies beating the patient on the head with his own wooden clog or similar object. When the patient had lost consciousness, the operation was ready to begin.[41] What the SS doctors never did was care for the sick.

The charts below describe the administrative structure of a *KL*, and the identification colours worn by all *Kazettler*.[42] Every prisoner, on his arrival in a camp, received a classification by the Politische Abteilung in the form of a coloured triangle, which he wore, point downwards, on his camp jacket and trousers.

Lagerführer	Camp commandant
Verwaltungsführer	Chief of staff
Schutzhaftlagerführer	Chief security officer

Rapportführer	Inspector, responsible to the Schutzhaftlagerführer
Blockführer	Officer in charge of a housing unit of 250–500 prisoners, responsible to the Rapportführer
Kommandoführer	Officer commanding a work detail
Lagerälteste	Senior prisoner, or prefect, selected by the SS and responsible for discipline in the entire camp
Blockälteste	Prisoner responsible for the unit
Oberkapo	Senior prisoner responsible for discipline in a Kommando
Lagerschreiber	Prisoner serving as administrative clerk for the entire camp
Blockschreiber	Prisoner clerk, responsible to the Blockälteste
Friseur	Prisoner responsible for unit hygiene

Triangle insignia worn by prisoner:

Red	Political[43]	1933 on
Green	Common criminal[44]	1933 on
Pink	Homosexual[45]	1934 on
Purple	Conscientious objector[46]	1935 on
Yellow	Jewish[47]	1938 on
Brown	Gypsy	1938–40; thereafter black
Black	Antisocial[48]	1938 on
Blue	Stateless	1940 on

In some camps, certain categories predominated. Before the war, Sachsenhausen, Flossenburg, Gross-Rosen, and Mauthausen were all used primarily for Greens, and Sachsenhausen (with Neuengamme) continued in this role. But in general, the classifications were mixed. Although the classification Blue was intended for all stateless prisoners, in fact it was worn only by the Spanish Republicans and some stateless Russians. In selecting prisoners to fill the Kapo positions, the SS looked to the Greens and the Blacks, in that order, giving priority to Germans and Austrians.[49] This was the situation in Mauthausen when the Spaniards arrived, though some of the Kapos were Poles.[50]

Triangles could even be exchanged. The shoemaker Joseph Schwaiger, with 18 previous convictions, entered Mauthausen with a Black triangle, but the shoes he made for Karl Schulz, the handicapped Gestapo chief, won him such favour that Schulz rewarded him with a Green. Once he could sport the proud emblem of a criminal on his vest, Schwaiger later declared, everyone showed him respect and left him in peace.[51]

Schwaiger the shoemaker belonged to the corps of service personnel known as the *Prominenten*, representing some 10 per cent or more of the prisoner population. While they did not enjoy all the privileges of the Kapos, they shared the most important: they were safe, however precariously, from extermination, and they were free to move about the camp. They were also in direct contact with the SS officers, and in a position to identify them closely and to observe their conduct. These *Prominenten* included all those working in the offices, in the workshops, in the kitchens, in the stores, in the tailor's shop, and in the shoeshop; servants of the SS and of the senior Kapos; assistants to the SS doctors, dentists, and pharmacists; barbers, Block orderlies, painters, chimney-sweeps, firemen, garage mechanics, and electricity and hydraulic workers.[52] Like the Kapos, the *Prominenten* were drawn at first exclusively from the Greens and Blacks. But murderers, thieves, and vagabonds were not likely to give satisfaction in such jobs; nor were surgeons, engineers, or skilled workers, who could serve as specialized assistants, to be found among the Blacks and Greens. Reluctantly, the administration turned to the Red triangles to fill the posts: first to the Germans and Austrians, and then to other nationals who understood German.[53]

The rest of the *KZ* universe, over 85 per cent, were slaves condemned to die. Among the quickest to die were those placed in a *Strafkompanie*, and for the Jews there was virtually no hope of survival. A change in the character of *KZ* life could indeed be seen at about mid-point in the war, but overall it did not affect the chances of survival. In the early years the Nazis did not consider the use of their slaves in scientific terms; at the same time, they were prone, in the flush of victory, to express their sense of racial superiority more readily. Then came the German defeats at El Alamein and Stalingrad, and arrogance gave way to rage.

Even before El Alamein, the failure, in 1941, to take Moscow before winter set in had altered the character of the war. The German High Command saw that it would not be so simple a matter after all. This was evident in the decision taken on 30 April 1942 to establish a new organization, the SS-WVHA, headquartered at Berlin-Lichterfelde, with overall responsibility for the *KL*. Its command went to SS-Obergruppenführer Oswald Pohl, and his decisions were thereafter enforced on every *KL* commandant by SS-Gruppenführer Richard Glücks who, as head of Amt D, served as inspector-general of the camps.[54] On the day of his appointment Pohl wrote to his superior, Himmler: 'The war has quite clearly changed the purpose of the *KZ*. Our task is now to redirect its functions towards the economic side.' To the camp commandants Pohl wrote:

The camp commandant is the sole person responsible for the employment of the work-force. This employment must be total in the true sense of the word, in order to obtain the maximum output. There are to be no limits to working hours. The limits are to depend upon the type of work, and the hours are to be fixed by the commandant. All factors tending to reduce the work schedule must be limited to the maximum. The break for food at noon must be reduced to the very shortest period possible.

The industrialization programme of the WVHA accelerated a development already under way: the creation of a constellation of subsidiary camps, known as Aussenkommandos. In the case of Mauthausen, the Aussenkommandos extended throughout all of Austria except the Tyrol. These subsidiary camps, still administered by the mother camp, were attached to one or other of the major industrial groups. In order to make these factories invulnerable to Allied bombing, the prisoners were put to excavating hundred of subterraneans tunnels. The result was that most prisoners arriving in Mauthausen stayed there only for the quarantine period and what the SS called basic education. They would then be sent to any of the Kommandos: the quarries at Gusen and Ebensee, the mines at Eisenerz, the oil refinery at Moosbierbaum, the agricultural factory at St Lambrecht, the SS school at Klagenfurt, the construction of dikes at Gross-Raming, of a tunnel into Jugoslavia at Loibl-Pass, of a railroad at Amstetten, and of an industrial park at St Ägyd; and above all, the arms factories: the Hermann Goering Works at Linz, the Messerchmitt factory at Gusen, the Siemens plant at Ebensee, the Heinkel aircraft factories at Floridsdorf and Schwechat, the Daimler factory at Steyr, the Florians factory at Peggau, the tank factories at St Valentin, and the V1/V2 factory at Schlier.[55]

The camp commandants thus received a new title, Betriebsleiter, or industrial manager, and earned as such a second stipend, supplementary to the pay they received as camp commandant. But the new policy was not without its critics. If the WVHA represented the policy of realism, there were still the idealists in the RSHA who resented this interference in the policy of programmed extermination, especially where the Jews were concerned. It was, after all, only three months earlier, on 20 January 1942, that the top-level meeting at Grossen-Wannsee had decided upon the *Endlösung*, or final solution to the Jewish question. To those in the SS administration who thought it more important to liquidate the Jews and other enemies than to fight for victory (and by 1945 this faction would predominate), Pohl's programme sounded like betrayal. But for the moment the realists had the upper hand over the idealists, and the Jews able to work would be allowed to work, and to work themselves to death.

Pohl's directives meant that the Reich was no longer to be denied the maximum output of every prisoner by the premature termination of his life. The average life expectancy of the *KL Häftling* was now calculated, in the carefully compiled tables of the central offices, at nine months. In actual practice, the various camp commandants intensified or attenuated the directives according to their individual temperament. An example of the wide range of their temperaments can be seen in the vivid contrast between the commandant of Mauthausen and the commandant of Dachau. Though operating under the same orders, the commandant at Dachau actually punished a Kapo in 1940 for savagely beating a Jewish prisoner. At Mauthausen, in the words of Karl Schulz, the Gestapo officer who was finally brought to trial, 'such a proceeding was unthinkable'.[56] Let it be said that in most cases the camp commandants intensified rather that attenuated the directives, and in most of the camps life expectancy was less than the prescribed nine months.

The reasons for this are not hard to find. The SS and the Kapos continued to murder the prisoners, whether by beating them to death with their clubs, hurling them to death from the cliffs, or seizing their berets and throwing them on the wire, then forcing the prisoners to recover them, and be electrocuted or shot from the watchtowers in the process. To try to put an end to this regrettable violation of the rules, the Gestapo moved in with a solution. The Gestapo office in every camp now included an officer responsible for investigating every case of 'unnatural death', for opening proceedings against any-one charged with misconduct, and for submitting a report to the SS courts in Vienna (in the case of Mauthausen) and to the RSHA in Berlin.

Such reports were indeed filed, and many escaped destruction at the end of the war. In every case, of course, they absolve the SS of respons-ibility in what is described as an attempt at escape, or an accident at work, or an act of suicide. Since the falsification of these reports was admitted to the Cologne Tribunal in 1966–7 by SS-Rottenführer Erich Walter Kruger,[57] the reports serve only to reveal the bizarre workings of the SS mind, incapable even of taking pride in achievement.

Where the WVHA showed genuine concern was the discovery, at the end of 1942, that the mortality rate showed no sign of decreasing. It responded with a letter to the senior medical officer of each *Lager* (with a copy for the information of the respective commandant), de-ploring the fact that of the 156,000 prisoners who had so far arrived in the camps, over 70,000 were already dead. At that rate, ran the letter, the total prison population would never reach the level desired by the Reichsführer-SS. It should be remembered, the letter concluded, that the best doctor is not the one who distinguishes himself for his severity, but the one who preserves the working capacity of the prisoner for the longest possible time.

Sound medical opinion at this point would have proposed an increase in the food supply. Occasionally this desperate remedy was adopted, but with little or no effect, since the supplementary rations usually fell victim to the rapacity of the SS or the Kapos. Well might it be said that the *Lager* by now was a mechanism that functioned according to its own logic.

The Reichsführer-SS himself seems to have taken a middle position between the 'realists' and the 'idealists'. In 1943 he still raged against the high mortality rates, but in 1944 he showed indifference, no doubt consoled by then by the apparently inexhaustible supply of slave labour from every corner of Europe. This explains why he allowed his underling, the Gestapo chief Heinrich Müller, to issue a decree on 4 March 1944 in defiance of the WVHA. All military personnel who escaped and were recaptured were to be sent in the strictest secrecy (not therefore by train) to Mauthausen, and only Mauthausen, there to be executed on arrival by a bullet in the back of the neck. It was the birth of the *Kugel-Aktion*, the practice of stamping the prisoner's papers with the letter K; when he arrived at Mauthausen, he was not entered in the registry or given a number but promptly murdered. Müller's directive was endorsed four months later by none other than Generalfeldmarschall Wilhelm Keitel, the timocratic chief of staff of the honour-loving Wehrmacht. In the '*Kugel Erlass*' of 27 July 1944, Keitel ordered that, with the exception of Britons and Americans, any prisoner of war, whatever his rank, who was recaptured after attempting to escape was to be handed over to the Sicherheitsdienst. Total silence was to be maintained, and the Wehrmacht records were to show that the escaped prisoner was not recaptured.[58]

If Himmler could contemplate an ever-increasing supply of manpower, it was a very different matter for Keitel. In 1943 the Wehrmacht faced a shortage in the ranks that grew steadily worse. This meant among other things a reduction in the number of SS guards and ultimately their replacement by Luftwaffe and other elements. The manpower shortage gave the Greens (and even the Blues) the opportunity to serve in the Wehrmacht. The vast majority of the prisoners remained in the camps, and for them, in the final year of the war, the pace of construction moved to breakneck even by the standards of the SS. The Nazis knew that their last hope was to build superior weapons, and this race against time meant a staggering increase in the death rate, but not, ironically, for the Spaniards, who paid most heavily in the first two years.

Conditions were made worse by overcrowding. Mauthausen, intended originally for 3,000 inmates,[59] came to house 70,000, and Buchenwald, designed for 7,000, accommodated up to 60,000. This meant that a Block with accommodation for 200 might house 1,600—especially in the case of the quarantine Blocks—with no provision for additional washing or toilet facilities. Even the water ran short.[60] Overcrowding, of course, did not mean squalor. '*Eine Laus, dein Tod*' was still the slogan that ruled, right up until the end when the SS cared only about killing. Until then, the SS operated in accordance with their paradox: a mania for hygiene, coupled with the delight in humiliation. Toilet paper was a commodity unknown in the latrines, and the carts carrying the bread and dragged by the inmates were the same that were used for the refuse.[61]

Much has been said of the impact on the prisoner's mind of the day of arrival, when he passed through the *Effektenkammer* on his way to the disinfection room and the quarantine Block. The SS would sit behind a long row of tables, with prisoners serving as their assistants. At the first table the incoming prisoner would surrender his identity cards; then at the next his money; then his ring, watch, medals, and other valuables; then the rest of the contents of his pockets, including letters and photos; then the contents of his bags; then his clothes and his shoes. Clothing included all bandages; if a man was wearing a hernia bandage he might also be told to jump.[62] He had now reached the end of the line, naked and bereft of everything. Next came the *Scherraum*.[63] Then the showers, with the Kapos as well as the SS on hand to administer the first breaking-in. The water would alternate from scalding to freezing, and if a prisoner were to break away the Kapos would beat him on the skull with their cudgels. After this he would enter the quarantine Block, where there were no bunks but only palliasses on the ground. These were filled with wood cuttings which were rarely changed, so that the cuttings were reduced to dust. Rations in the quarantine Block were reduced by half, in accordance with three principles: that those who do not work have less need to eat; that it helped to instil despair; and that the reduction helped to accelerate death's progress among the dying. The quarantine period generally lasted a week to ten days. The prisoner would then enter his prescribed Block. Accommodation consisted of wooden cots on three and sometimes four levels, with less than half a metre between levels. The lower bunks were infected with the dirt and dust from the palliasses above, which fell into the mouth and eyes of those below. Those above had to clamber up over the others, and at reveille, when the prisoners lingered in sleep, those at the top were more likely to receive the blows of the Kapos than those at the bottom. Those at the top had the advantage that their bunks were inspected less thoroughly than those below, but they also suffered the disadvantage that in winter the cracks in the wood allowed the melting snow to enter from the roof, and the blanket was always damp. A prisoner dying in an upper bunk might well soil the bunks below; at such times it was not uncommon for the others to bang his head against the bedpost until he succumbed.[64]

The prisoners woke to the sound of a gong. This *Weckruf* came at 4.45 a.m., the winter schedule being thirty minutes in arrears. Roll-call followed at 5.15 a.m., and work began at 6 o'clock. Michel de Boüard remembers that most of the prisoners at Mauthausen working in the local or daily Kommandos, notably the quarry, did not leave the inner camp until 7 a.m.[65] The truth of the matter is that the hour varied with the season and the weather: the SS were afraid of the dark, and only the inner camp was floodlit.[66] Work then continued to 5.30 p.m., with thirty minutes to one hour at noon for roll-call and *Eintopf*, the midday meal consisting of a soup containing turnips and potatoes. Roll-call followed at 6 p.m. and soup at 7 p.m. Prisoners had to eat either standing up or on their bunks; they could never sit at a table or on a bench or stool, nor could they approach a stove, for these were the exclusive privileges of the Kapos and the *Prominenten*. Lights out followed at 8 o'clock.

The daily food ration was set by Berlin at 2,300–2,400 calories. The Czech professor Josef Podlaha, who as a *Prominenter* survived Mauthausen, observed that to survive in that camp a minimum of 3,000 calories was necessary. Instead of that, the actual ration distributed was between 1,000 and 1,500, and in the *Revier*, the antechamber of death, between 700 and 900. Toward the end of the war, the daily calorie intake did not exceed 500.[67] At its best then, the daily food ration represented barely 60 per cent of the daily physical expenditure. The gnawing, mind-consuming pain of hunger was at its greatest for the first hour after a meal, for the stomach had secreted too much gastric juice for the little sustenance it took in return. Such extreme hunger could lead to some bizarre excesses. Paul Tillard describes the feat of a Spaniard who, one Saturday afternoon, obtained access to the kitchen and in front of Tillard drank 11 litres of soup. The following day he drank another 17. There was of course nothing in the soup that filled.[68] Hunger would drive prisoners to suck on charcoal or chew on the tar-lined paper which they tore from the roofs of the Blocks, if only to have the sensation that they were eating something.[69] Hunger did indeed consume the mind. Once again, everything had been carefully thought out at the highest level. Programmed hunger was to serve as the means to destroy not just intellectual ability but the reasoning faculty itself.

The number of dead at the evening roll-call was generally greater than at the morning muster. It was common for those who had been carried back by two comrades from a daily Kommando to fall dead during the roll-call. This muster was as much a strain on the mind as on the body, since it consisted of a seemingly endless succession of orders on the same theme: *Mützen ab, Mützen auf*, the prisoners having to doff and don their caps with each order. Mauthausen, in this regard alone, was lenient: the average roll-call took only thirty minutes. But there were exceptions: sometimes the evening muster went on all night, and even the following day and night. The record at Mauthausen was forty hours. On two such occasions the death toll reached 500. Food and water were denied, and the second time the temperature fell to −25°C.[70] The effect on the legs of standing at attention for so long a period was to induce oedema. A survivor has described how his legs swelled to three times their normal size, and how he lost sight of his knees as the swelling mounted to his thighs.[71]

There was always the *Revier* for those who wished to report sick. The first step towards it would be for the Blockälteste and the Blockschreiber to decide that a particular prisoner was not in a fit state to leave with the work detail. What the prisoner risked, whether he knew it or not, was the decree issued by Himmler in March 1941 which extended his euthanasia programme (first introduced in September 1939) to those *KL* prisoners who were ill for more than three months and those who were generally unfit to work.[72] The Reichsführer's solution to this problem was the practice known to the SS as the *Himbeerpflücken* or raspberry picking: the sick and disabled would be assembled, issued with tin-cans, taken to the periphery of the camp, ordered to pick the berries, and then shot 'while attempting to escape'.[73] The first lesson of survival in a *KL* was to avoid reporting sick.

Sundays normally gave prisoners a day of rest,[74] except those in the punishment squad (*Strafkompanie*) who worked as usual. If religion had been a reason, the SS would have picked Wotansday. The fact is simply that the SS were loath to forgo their own day off the job, and the SS guarding the *Strafkompanie* could be expected to be in a particularly ugly mood.

Prisoners who attempted to escape were relentlessly pursued. The SS called the pursuit the *Hasenjagd*, or hare-hunt, betraying their relish for the event. It was hard enough to break out, but to survive in the alien countryside, amid a hostile people, was harder still: only ten Spaniards succeeded in escaping from Mauthausen, six in 1941 and four in 1942.[75] Those who were recaptured were whipped or hanged or, more commonly, both.

An escape and the subsequent recapture was not an everyday affair, and the SS thus turned the event into a spectacle, with orchestra and choir. The music varied according to the tastes of the Lagerführer. Among the favourites were Johann Strauss waltzes, an old German ballad ('Alle Vöglein sind schon da'), and the contemporary French song made famous by Charles Trenet, 'Je vous attendrai'.[76] Goethe once said that you can tell any man's character by what he laughs at. The SS found hilarity in what was a whole litany of lampoons—of diabolical invention. A particular spectacle which took place at Mauthausen one evening in June 1941 has been recorded in detail, but similar executions occurred anywhere in the *KZ* universe. The prisoners had had to re-enter the camp, as usual, on their knees. As the local Kommandos returned to the fortress that day, they found three gallows mounted in the *Appellplatz*. After the usual muster, the camp orchestra entered through the gates playing a lively march. Behind the orchestra came a tumbrel, drawn by prisoners. Standing on the platform, bare-chested, were three prisoners who had escaped the previous day. They bore the marks of the tortures they had undergone. The little platform was adorned with brightly coloured ribbons and a placard on each side: 'Warum in die Ferne schweifen, wenn das Gute doch so nah' ist?' ('Why stray so far from home, when things are so good so close?'), and 'Hurra, wir sind schon wieder da!' ('Hurrah! We're back home again!'). The procession went around the square, then stopped in front of the gallows. More than 10,000 men stood watching, as the condemned men were strapped to a wooden horse. Each received twenty-five strokes. They then mounted the platform. The second to die placed the noose around the first, then knocked away the stool supporting him. The third then did the same to the second, and the Lagerälteste then did the same to the third. The orchestra was still playing. The entire parade then had to march around the gallows, one by one, with each man raising his eyes to the corpses. The SS watched intently, and if any man dipped his eyes he was made to go around again, this time under the whip.[77]

Himmler's orders were that hangings were to be carried out by prisoners who would receive three cigarettes in payment.[78] Whipping consisted of 25, 50, or 75 strokes. Sentences of 50 or 75 strokes were divided into sessions of 25 strokes each, to allow the prisoner to recuperate for a day or two while he contemplated the next session. A single beating would leave a prisoner marked for life and incapacitated for any manual work. This in turn would expose him to the charge of idleness, punishable by sentence to a *Strafkompanie*, or of uselessness, punishable by instant death in the gas chamber.

Many prisoners simply lost the will to survive. Even men of great intellectual vigour and moral integrity lost interest in everything except food. A certain class, rejected by all Kommandos, went around the camp in rags, unshaven, filthy and sick, begging for food, stealing where they could, indifferent to everything, waiting for the freedom of death; death that never tarried, whether it took the form of the gas chamber, or came from a beating by some Kapo, or from inanition in some dark corner. What marked them as a class was the blanket they carried over their heads or shoulders. It earned them the name of Mohammedans (*Muselmänner*), a name invented in Auschwitz which then spread throughout the *KZ* universe.[79] Juan de Diego points out that at Mauthausen these vagabond derelicts were few indeed: they might be seen on Sundays, but not in any number, and not for long, for the gas chamber clamoured for its fill.[80]

On the matter of survival, Michel de Boüard, himself a very distinguished survivor, writes of the prisoner's sudden realization of the difference between social standing and the sense of personal worth. Those who had the first and not the second were quickly thrown into the deepest despair, and very few survived. Often the filthiest and most wretched were those who had lost their social standing and their privileges. Boüard considers it a class reaction: most members of the business bourgeoisie, the military, and the intelligentsia adopted this passive attitude, awaiting liberation from the outside: the fight was over for them. The individualist was equally one of the great losers in this ultimate test of character, in which the truly strong instinctively inclined to community life and organized action.[81] Montserrat Roig points out that, in the French camps, the worker had held a natural advantage over the petit bourgeois, and the agricultural worker over the urban. In the Nazi camps, there was no such advantage. Fate was determined by morale, and morale depended upon solidarity and collective defence.[82] A Spanish survivor writes that the only way to survive was not to let the mind dwell on the atrocities of the day and to keep calm and vigilant.[83]

To keep calm and vigilant in the face of this daily horror was indeed the supreme test of character. The back-breaking work continued whether it rained or snowed, in scorching sun or icy wind. The purpose was to exterminate through work, on the logical basis that the system enjoyed a virtually inexhaustible supply of slaves.

Fear and anxiety, perpetual anguish, solitude in a world of hostile elements. The prisoner denied the dearest thing of all: a letter from home. 'No one knew anything of us,' remarks a survivor, 'nor we of them.'[84] These were the forces at work in this universe at once terrifying and absurd, in which all civilized norms were uprooted. In his physical and moral degradation, each prisoner was intended to represent for all others a figure of loathsomeness; each was meant to see himself as an object of pure disgust, for which he could feel he was justly punished. Thus reduced to docile servitude, deprived of all personal identity, the prisoner would accept with animal indifference whatever fate lay in store for him. It is this that explains why 2,000 desperate prisoners working in a quarry did not at a given signal rush the SS guards. It would require organization. Any such plan would become known to those passive prisoners who would willingly betray the plan to the Kapos in exchange for a Kapo post or some other privilege. The very idea of a revolt was at variance with the nature of an SS camp. The prisoner on his arrival had lost everything he had, down to the hair on his body. Nothing was left to him but his gold teeth, and these would be removed from his body on the way from the gas chamber to the crematorium. Everything was done to make him feel he was worth nothing, less even than the rock he carried. And like the rock, it crushed him into mindless passivity.

The Italian survivor Primo Levi presented, just before his suicide in 1987, a harrowing thesis that the survivors were in the main not the best but the worst: the selfish, the violent, the insensitive.[85] Such extreme pessimism on Levi's part was no doubt linked to the depression that killed him; the evidence is fortunately stronger on the other side. Perhaps the secret of survival in this implacable world was this: to concentrate upon one tiny act of resistance, or if that were impossible, to construct some little corner—if not of tangible form, then a corner of the mind—where nothing could intrude upon human dignity, a corner proof against all pressures to conform, all efforts to degrade. Certainly those who fought to survive felt less isolated, and not feeling isolated was the key to everything. Hence the vital importance of the sense of community. The supreme human virtue may well be cheerfulness in adversity. A smile, a kind word at morning, the sharing of a piece of bread, could have a significance far beyond the gesture, and could well make the difference to donor and recipient alike between bowing to fate and fighting it through another day.

What we have said could apply to almost any of the sixteen *Konzentrationslager*. What remains is to examine the specific camps to which the Spanish prisoners were sent, ranging from Oranienburg to Mauthausen. In any comparison with the rest of the system, *KL*-Oranienburg was a dream; a survivor called it 'a model camp, human and gentle',[86] but strictly in reference to the others. Its most famous Spanish inmate, the former socialist prime minister Largo Caballero, survived it, but died a premature death. Buchenwald too had its Spanish inmate of renown, the future novelist and Minister of Culture Jorge

Semprún.[87] Like others, Semprún was to remark on the camp's peculiar setting. The hill surrounding it, known as the Ettersberg, is situated only a few miles north of Goethe's Weimar. The oaks that covered it, all but one, had been cut down. The great oak they chose to spare was none other than the famous tree in whose shade Goethe used to rest in his walks with Eckermann, sitting and reflecting, perchance, on the future of Germany. Now it stood inside *KL*-Buchenwald, 'forest of oaks', on the esplanade between the *Effektenkammer* and the kitchens. Here amid Thuringia's greenery, which could be taken for the heart of Germany itself, source of the life-affirming philosophy of its greatest poetic genius, even here nature was uprooted and overturned. As the entering prisoners passed through the main gate, and saw the hills of their lost freedom stretching for miles in front of them, two monuments were there to greet them, to which every prisoner had to turn eyes left in salute. There, on a lofty plinth, stood a giant statue in stone of the German eagle, its wings outstretched. Then, on similar supports, two groups of statues that stood face to face: on the right, a priest, a monk, and a Jew in vulgar caricature, and on the left, four SS taking aim.[88] Buchenwald had other particularities. A feature of its everyday life was the sound of the 'singing horses', the four-man teams of prisoners dragging the rock-filled carts and forced to sing as they pulled. These were not the only sounds. Ettersberg became known as 'the hill which the birds forsook', for the shouts, shrieks, groans, and screams emanating from the camp forced even the birds to change their habitat. Neither were there birds where the Spaniards worked at Dora, which was set up in September 1943 as a Buchenwald subsidiary. Set in the Harz Mountains a few miles from Nordhausen, Dora was an underground factory for the production of Hitler's *Vergeltungswaffen* (Vls and V2s). Working from twelve to fourteen hours a day in damp, dark tunnels, and sleeping there, the prisoners did not see the sky or breathe fresh air for months on end.

It was nevertheless Mauthausen to which 90 per cent of the Spanish prisoners were sent and which will be for ever associated with the cause of the Spanish Republic. Mauthausen has been called the most mysterious of Nazi camps, on the grounds that not even in Germany, and still less by the Allies, was its reality suspected.[89] The thesis is questionable: the same source tells us that Austrian civilians called it *Totenberg* and *Mordhausen*, and that its system of watch-tower lights was never turned off, not even during Allied air attacks.[90] But the matter lies outside our purview. It was certainly intended to be a model camp, a depository for the incorrigible enemies of National Socialism, and it was the only camp to be built in stone. It was also the first camp to be built outside Germany, the first to receive non-Germans, and the very last to be liberated. This was the logical result of its geographical position, at the farthest point from the invading armies.

The place that has been called by a survivor and author 'unimaginable to Dante' sits on a hill that bathes its feet in the Danube, 25 kilometres downstream from Linz. The little village to the east, almost at the confluence of the Danube and the Enns, was noted for its calm and its little inns. Mozart himself remarked on its beauty, when with his parents he stayed there overnight on the way to Vienna. Another of Austria's sons looked at the region through different eyes, seeing Linz, close to his birthplace in Braunau, as the future industrial capital of the thousand-year Reich.

Halfway up the hill at Mauthausen lies the largest granite quarry in Austria. Originally it belonged to the city of Vienna, hence its name Wienergraben, but in the wake of the *Anschluss* a law transferred its entire ownership to the SS, under the name of Deutsche Erd- und Steinwerke (DEST) in Berlin; the little Messerschmitt factory built on the site in 1943 was to be the only industrial unit established at Mauthausen proper. Immediately following the transfer, a labour Kommando was sent to the quarry from *KL*-Dachau, made up almost entirely of common criminals (Greens),[91] and in April Himmler and Pohl inspected the quarries and decided they were suited to the creation of a *KL*.[92] The particular climate of Mauthausen was no doubt also a favourable factor: in less than two hours it can pass from scorching sun to rain and cold.[93]

The first mention of *KL*-Mauthausen in operation came in July 1938. Its first inmates were Austrians,[94] soon followed by Czechs, and it is they who began the construction of the fortress. With the water system functioning at the end of 1942, *KL*-Mauthausen was by then essentially completed. But by that time the flood of new arrivals was far more than the camp could house, or use. In spite of the rising mortality, the population in 1943 doubled, then tripled, and in 1945 it was six times the population of 1942.[95] The camp registry shows that the total number of prisoners who had entered up until April 1945 was about 139,000,[96] and by the very end, 156,000.[97] But these figures are in no way comprehensive. In the early years, incoming prisoners received the same registration numbers as those who had died. Those who arrived bearing the code letter K (for *Kugel*) in their transit papers were executed on arrival, as we have seen, and if their name was entered in error in the registry, the name was erased and the number was given to the next prisoner to enter.[98] In the last weeks countless thousands arrived in the evacuation convoys from east, north, and west. Hans Maršálek gives the figure of 206,000 (of whom 110,000 died).[99] Vilanova estimates the number who entered Mauthausen between 8 August 1938 and 5 May 1945 at 350,000 (of whom 285,000 died, including 11,525 in April 1945 alone).[100] A commission of ex-prisoners tried to calculate the exact number of dead, but was unable to offer sure conclusions. An official Austrian study arrived at a total of 127,767.[101] Finally, a study of life expectancy of all categories of prisoners in Mauthausen came up with the following approximate estimates:[102]

August 1938 to autumn 1939	15 months
Winter 1939–40 to summer 1943	6 months
Autumn 1943 to winter 1944	9 months
1945	5 months

Though the number of SS assigned to Mauthausen and its Kom-mandos increased with the rise of the inmate population, proportion-ately it declined. In February 1940 there were 1,250 SS, including 460 in Mauthausen proper and 600 in Gusen, or one SS for every ten prisoners.[103] By the summer of 1944 the proportion had widened to one SS for every fifteen prisoners. On 1 January 1945, there were 5,562 SS to guard 72,392 male prisoners, and 65 SS women to guard 959 women prisoners. It should be mentioned that at that time there were more prisoners—and more SS—at Mauthausen than in all but two camps in the *KL* archipelago.[104] In April 1945, at its apogee, the SS garrison stood at 5,984.[105] The total number of SS who served in the Mauthausen complex at some time or other during its existence, according to the SS administrators who survived and were interrog-ated, was about 15,000.[106] While it is often assumed that camp garri-sons were staffed only by Allgemeine SS, it should be borne in mind that an indeterminate number were on loan from Waffen SS units.[107] In the case of Mauthausen, its commandant Franz Ziereis stated on his deathbed that between 4,000 and 5,000 of his guards belonged to the Totenkopfverbände, with the remainder made up of former Wehrmacht and Luftwaffe personnel.[108]

In 1985, on the occasion of the fortieth anniversary of the liberation of Mauthausen, the University of Vienna began issuing questionnaires to survivors who attended any of the remembrance ceremonies held throughout Austria. The question could be asked, 'Why did the Uni-versity wait forty years to begin?' The bigger question, though it finds a facile answer, is why the Western world went to sleep after Nurem-berg on the question of Nazi crimes.

If we consider first the studies written on Mauthausen in general, and not primarily on the Spaniards in that camp, one of the best is the article by the survivor Michel de Boüard, published in 1954. Boüard is not a communist, but he pays warm tribute to the communists: unlike the bourgeoisie and intellectuals who turned passive, he writes, the communists, most of them workers, turned instinctively towards collective action. He goes further: except for the Poles, whose organized resistance was led by former reserve officers who were antisemitic and anticommunist, no resistance movement at Mauthausen was formed outside the communist group.[109] Four other noteworthy accounts by French survivors had already appeared. Those of Paul Tillard and Jean Laffitte, both communists, came out in 1945 and 1947. In 1946 Dr François Wetterwald, a surgeon who was allowed to practise for a time in Mauthausen and Ebensee, produced a work of literature critical of his fellow-countrymen. Most distinguished of all was the 1947 work of Roger Heim, a member of the Institut de France, who reflected upon the implications of Mauthausen to German history and German character. These early accounts have two things in common: the survivors are ill-informed about the organization that enslaved them and the personal identity of their enslavers, but able and willing to write judgements on their fellow-prisoners. A recurrent theme in these accounts is the admiration felt for the Spaniards. This admiration is summed up in a later work, published in 1955, by the non-communist Edmond Michelet, who rendered a special tribute:

The prisoners might have varying opinions regarding the worth of each foreign national group. But all were in agreement that the Spaniards deserved the utmost sympathy and admiration. . . . In their very adversity they found a source of pride which forced respect. Never did we hear them pine. A sense of modesty held them in check. Despite their political differences . . . they had the good manners to keep the matter to themselves. . . . Their behaviour was at all times exemplary. They would neither take too long in the washstands nor take more than their fair share of the rations. Their proud stoicism had a grandeur to it that derives perhaps from their country's history.[110]

Among the Spaniards, the first published author was probably Amadeo Cinca Vendrell, a captain in the Spanish Republican Army who spoke sufficient English for the Nazis to make him an interpreter, English being apparently a lingua franca for a certain number of their prisoners; Cinca's work is undated, but in any event it contains few points of detail. Amat Piniella followed in 1963 with a work that can be read only as a novel, with fictitious names and events that lack even a partial connection with the facts.[111] Vilanova and Razola-Constante appeared together in 1969. Unlike Razola and Constante, Vilanova was not himself a prisoner, and he compiled his book in Mexico, far from the main body of survivors. His work certainly contains a mass of information, but it lacks an orderly presentation, and it almost never provides any reference to the source. Razola and Constante, both of them survivors, present a useful collection of separate testimonies, but it tilts towards communist propaganda, exaggerating the importance of the secret organization.[112] Javier Alfaya produced a scholarly contribution in the form of a chapter to a general work, but like the general work itself, it is short in primary-level research. José Borrás Lluch, another survivor, arrived in 1989 with a useful addition. The best account of the Spaniards, though it is limited to the Catalans, is the 1977 work by Montserrat Roig in Catalan (*Els Catalans als camps nazis*), which appeared in Spanish as *Noche y Niebla* in 1978, though in an abridged version.

Among the German contributors, the communist Bruno Baum in 1965 produced a useful work concentrating on the last phase in the history of Mauthausen. His account suffers from the same limitations as those of other survivors, but it adds to our knowledge of *KZ* life and the resistance movement. It reminds us of Michel de Boüard's warning, pertinent to all contemporary history: 'The definitive study of the *KZ* system will be produced by our generation, or it will never be produced.'[113]

The three most useful works on Mauthausen are by Evelyn Le Chêne, Hans Maršálek, and the two Pappalettera. The first two are the only book-length scholarly studies published in any language. Le Chêne is an Englishwoman, not herself a survivor but married to one, the British special agent Pierre Le Chêne. Her book, published in 1971, represents twelve years of research. While an excellent study of Mauthausen in general, it says almost nothing of the prisoners themselves, and mentions only two Spaniards, Casimir Climent and Antonio García, whose important role we shall discuss later. Maršálek, an Austrian communist turned social-democrat, was one of the most active members of the resistance in Mauthausen, and has since served as historian for the Österreichische Lagergemeinschaft. His 1974 publication *Die Geschichte des Konzentrationslagers Mauthausen* is remarkably well documented. Vincenzo and Luigi Pappalettera are an Italian team of father and son, the former a survivor of Mauthausen and the son a political scientist. Their 1969 publication *La parola agli aguzzini* is a compilation of the evidence against the SS at Mauthausen as it emerged from the trials at Dachau (29 March to 13 May 1946) and Cologne (21 November 1966 to 30 October 1967).

The most complete records, of course, were once in existence. An index card was made out on every single new arrival in camp, with the exception of the K prisoners, but even here their transit papers would still have been filed. After the capture of Vienna by the Red

Army on 13 April 1945, the SS used the last fires of the crematorium to burn their archives, and for a whole day, fragments of burned paper rained down on the camp.[114] Then, on 2 May, one day before companies of municipal police arrived from Vienna to mount guard outside the camp, the gas chamber was dismantled and partly destroyed, together with the crematorium and the instruments of torture, while those who had worked in the crematorium (the *'Kohlenfahrer'*) were shot.[115] The SS could thereby expect what their colleagues expected everywhere else, that no precise historical record could ever be put together on the crimes committed in their camp.[116] What chance was there of putting together any accurate account, when most prisoners were known to others only by their first name or nickname, when each prisoner moved only in his own unit, and when none ever had a pencil and paper available to make notes on this constant and enormous flux? To be perfect, however, the SS needed to shoot three prisoners, all Spaniards, who held the keys to reassembling an important part of the records of the camp. They failed to do this, and as a result, in the words of Vilanova, 'all accounts regarding the prison population of the *KL* are merely guesses, except in the case of the Spaniards in Mauthausen.'[117]

The SS in Mauthausen, as elsewhere, kept two separate sets of records. One of these were the general camp records housed in the *Lagerschreibstube* in Block 1. This collection included a card on each prisoner, with basic data and his record in the camp. To maintain this collection the SS employed two prisoners (later three) as Lagerschreiber, or clerks. No secret copy of any part of this collection was made, and the entire collection was destroyed by the SS in the days before the Liberation. The other set of records was housed in the offices of the Politische Abteilung (Gestapo), which had a compound outside the fortress consisting of eight or nine rooms. This collection also included a card on every prisoner; while it duplicated the basic data it excluded the prisoner's current camp record but included his earlier history, notably the reasons for his being in Mauthausen and his address in the country where he was arrested. Here too the SS employed prisoners to assist in the work.[118] Fate ordained that the choice of the SS, on 16 March 1941, was a Spaniard from Catalonia, Casimiro Climent Sarrión.

The choice was not haphazard: Climent had a working knowledge of German, and had been an officer in the Spanish Republican Army. In France he had been conscripted into a Compagnie de travailleurs, and was taken prisoner on 20 June 1940. Sent first to Stalag XI-B, he was transferred to Mauthausen on 23–25 November 1940, in the company of forty-six other Spaniards.[119] In his post as clerk in the Politische

Abteilung, Climent was engaged with others in maintaining the vast catalogue that amounted finally to 180,000 cards.[120] It is quite possible that the real reason Climent was selected was the realization by the SS that the Spanish entries in the catalogue were in serious disorder: the Spanish use of both parents' surnames and the arbitrary omission of a weak patronym by the bearer (a common practice in Spain) had created real confusion. In any event, Climent was put in exclusive charge of the Spanish card index, which was now kept separate from the general catalogue. In this work he was later assisted by another Catalan, Josep Bailina, of no political affiliation. Climent's own political affiliation was centrist, which explains his later actions. His work allowed him considerable independence, and as a result he could, and did, make a complete second set of cards for himself, as well as a copy of other lists of incoming convoys and transfers to the Kommandos. Moreover, Climent was responsible for filing the Gestapo's correspondence with whatever organization might inquire about a Spaniard who it believed was interned in Mauthausen. Such organizations included the International Red Cross, the Spanish Embassy in Berlin, the Spanish consulates in Vienna, Munich, Paris, and elsewhere, and the Falange Exterior in Berlin, Paris, and its many branch offices.

Climent then faced the stupendous problem of preserving a collection that ultimately weighed about 14 kilos. He could not get it out of the Gestapo compound, nor hide it in a cellar, on the roof, or in the furniture. His solution was marvellously simple. He hid it in the boxes of paper and index cards in the stockroom. When, on 2 May 1945, Karl Schulz, the Gestapo officer responsible for the Politische Abteilung, ordered all documents to be burned, none of the SS thought that the stores of paper and index cards could be in any way incriminating, and while all else was destroyed, Climent's collection, with its precise record of 4,765 Spanish dead,[121] was saved.

Among the first Allied troops to reach Mauthausen was Benjamin B. Ferencz, a war crimes investigator for the US Army. Writing in 1979, Ferencz described his meeting with an inmate registrar ('whose name I shall never know') who greeted him with joy, then left the barrack and returned a few minutes later with a soiled box. The box contained a complete record and picture of every SS man who had ever been in Mauthausen, a gift of inestimable value to a war crimes prosecutor at Nuremberg. The former prisoner explained that one of his jobs had been to type identification cards for the SS guards. When the guards were reassigned, the card was to be destroyed, but the prisoner had found a way to save the cards from destruction, putting them in a box and burying it carefully in a field. 'I was moved', writes

Ferencz, 'by the blind faith which inspired the unknown prisoner to risk his life in the conviction there would come a day of reckoning.'[122] It is remarkable that Ferencz did not later identify his benefactor, who was none other than Climent Sarrión.[123] Ferencz thus brings to light an aspect of Climent's work that is not recorded elsewhere.

Apart from the two sets of prisoner records of the SS (one destroyed, one saved), there was a third and secret record, compiled as a hand-written list by Climent with the help of his compatriot Juan de Diego, from the time he became the Dritte Lagerschreiber. Both men moved around the camp, between Block 1 inside the fortress and the Politische Abteilung outside, and thus were in a position to collaborate. What they drew up between them was a list of every Spanish inmate, with information that neither of the SS collections contained: the address in Spain of every prisoner, compiled by asking the information from each inmate or his companions. This list was concealed by Climent with the rest of his treasures,[124] and after the Liberation was to be of vital help in the task of informing the families of those who did not return. As for Climent's duplicate card index, it filled suitcases, but Climent took them with him when he left Mauthausen, and with the help of Juan de Diego and others, a list was typed up (original and seven copies) that ran to 360 sheets.[125] The list was finally published in the 1977 work of Montserrat Roig.

Juan de Diego had a further contribution to make, both to historiography and to the cause of justice. The Politische Abteilung kept a register called the *Unnatürliches Todesfalles* (Of Unnatural Deaths). However commonplace such deaths might be, it did not alter the SS mania for tidy records; in every case of violent death, a report was entered and signed by the SS member responsible, or by a witness to the deed. In the closing days when the SS records were being burnt, the German Red Gerhard Kanthack, who had once been a government official and now worked in the Politische Abteilung, managed to remove the book and wedged it inside a cupboard. Not daring to remove it from the compound, Kanthack begged de Diego, who had free access to the compound, to take it out himself. De Diego did so, concealing it in his jacket and then hiding it in the *Lagerschreibstube*, where there were more possibilities for concealment. On the day of liberation, de Diego handed the book to an American officer and asked for his name. He still retains the piece of paper which the American gave him, on which was written: 'General commanding 3rd US Army, Judge Advocate Section, War Crimes Commission (APO 403, US Army)'. Later the book apparently fell into oblivion, because at the time that the Cologne trial of 1966–7 was in preparation, de Diego wrote to the prosecuting attorney in Cologne drawing his attention to the existence of the book.[126] It was retrieved, and for saving it, de Diego later received a letter of gratitude from Michael S. Bernstein of the US Department of Justice.[127]

The third self-made archivist was an assistant in the photographic laboratory who owed much to the compatriot who trained him. Every *KL* had a laboratory as part of an office of identification, but its services were restricted to official business, such as the occasional visits by celebrities and the daily incidents in the camp, including every killing. Schinlauer, the non-commissioned officer in charge of the laboratory, needed help in the work of developing, printing, and filing the photographs, and in May 1941 he was given the Spanish inmate Antonio García Alonso. Schinlauer, however, was deep in personal graft. The SS guards were not permitted to take their own photographs of the camp or the prisoners, and they ran the risk of becoming instant prisoners themselves if they were caught. But a few of them found the temptation too great, even if the results were disappointing: the photos they received were always small in format and usually poor in quality. For Schinlauer it meant personal profit, but it also meant the danger of exposure, and for his Spanish assistant it meant an opportunity for subtle blackmail and the chance to move a comrade into the new post of second assistant. At the end of 1942 García was thus joined by another Spaniard, the Catalan Francesc Boix Campo, who had worked during the Civil War as a photo reporter for *Juventud*.[128] From the very beginning García realized the supreme importance of conserving this photographic material as proof of Nazi crimes. For three and a half years he risked his life, and more than his life, in making a copy of the most descriptive of the photographs he handled, until at the end of 1944 he fell sick and was sent to the hospital. This left Boix in charge. Both Boix and García were communists, but they had little else in common. Boix was unstable, and he and Climent even fell to blows.[129] Boix now began to transfer the photos from their hiding place in the laboratory, which lay outside the fortress, to another inside the fortress. Boix's supporters claim that he did this with the agreement of García and in accordance with a plan devised by the Spanish resistance organization. Juan de Diego calls this false, together with the claim that the hiding place was— of all places—the *Arrest*, or camp prison.[130] The hiding place was probably the carpentry shop, but the action certainly entailed an enormous risk, since it meant passing the main gate several times with the hidden material. For the sake of precaution some prints were sewn into the shoulder lining of certain jackets, and others hidden in mattresses. Early in 1945 it was decided that the material would be safer if most of it were transferred to the Poschacher youth Kommando, made up exclusively of Spanish children. Although the Kommando worked, like any other, under SS guard, the children circulated in Mauthausen village and in the neighbouring granges. It was one of these children who conveyed the precious photographs to the house of Anna Pointner in Mauthausen, where they remained until the day of liberation, when Boix called at the house to retrieve them.[131] Meanwhile, the SS had given the order to burn every last piece of material in the laboratory. The order was scrupulously enforced, and when the Allied investigators arrived they found not a single trace of evidence. Thanks to the courage of Antonio García and Francesc Boix, the evidence remained.[132]

5

Birth of the Spanish Resistance in France

Problems of documentation—The contribution of the Spaniards be-littled—Earliest Spanish Resistance activities—Communist reaction to the invasion of Russia—Response of the Spaniards in Russia and Mexico—The Spaniards in France regroup—The MOI—The Bertaux network—The south-west, cradle of the Spanish Resistance—Development of the Spanish communist Resistance: two conflicting theories —Creation of the 'Delegation of the Central Committee of the PCE'— A Spanish communist committee formed in Paris—Creation of the XIVth Army Corps—The Gestapo strikes at the leadership in Paris— The guerrilleros of the south-west combat-ready

> Five and twenty barbarians
> perched on a rock.[1]

The history of the Spanish Resistance will never be written. The problem goes beyond the normal difficulties of recording resistance activity: the absence of operational plans, of marching orders, and of unit records. Unlike the French Resistance, which at least had a general staff in London and later Algiers to assemble information and record radio transmissions, the Spanish Resistance had no outside controlling body anywhere. All that is left to the historian are the memoirs and the memories, the memoirs written in point of fact long after the memories have faded; three or four memoirs at most, plus half a dozen published or unpublished studies, often repeating the same oral accounts or embellishing them with each new edition. This approach to history, based as it is on memory, has produced a kind of Islamic hadith, or chain of authority, which may sometimes be difficult to refute, but which is no more scientific for that. As for documents, all that are available to the historian are those of the Wehrmacht, and these are fragmentary—a large part of the Wehrmacht archives at Potsdam were lost in a fire in April 1945—but it is against these documents that the Spanish Resistance 'tradition' must be tested, and not the opposite.

Nor is it certain, even now, how the central organization of the Spanish communist Resistance in France formed and functioned. Most of its members are dead, having died intestate as it were, and those who survive choose neither to speak nor write about the past, determined no doubt to take their secrets with them to the grave. As a result, there is still no answer to the most basic of questions: did the Spanish communist Resistance develop centrifugally, outwards from a Central Committee with an effective organization, or centripetally, from the slow integration of originally isolated units of resistance? In normal circumstances, a Communist Party would insist on the centrifugal answer, and in presenting its official history would extol the leaders of the Party who had inspired the mass. But these circumstances were not normal: the leaders were in Moscow, or Mexico, or Buenos Aires, but not anywhere in France. Those who in the absence of the leaders became the leaders would pay, as we shall see, a very heavy price.

The geographic distribution of the Spanish refugees being what it was, it is safe to assume that it was in Vichy France, and not in the Occupied Zone, that the Spanish communists made their earliest progress in organization. We have seen that their first initiative took the form of a resolution decided at Argelès in October 1940. The framers of that resolution constituted the *de facto* leadership of the PCE in France. The resolution places them historically in a much more favourable position than their French counterparts, not only on the matter of the date but also in the matter of the provision: the Spanish communists set out to arrange the escape of their most valuable comrades from the French detention camps, at a time when the PCF was enjoining its members not to attempt escape.[2] In spite of that, or perhaps because of that, the French communists have never paid proper tribute to the role of the Spanish communists in the Resistance, and the French non-communists have paid virtually no tribute at all. The same holds true, with perhaps only one exception, for the historians of the Resistance, whether French or foreign, from the earliest (General Adeline) to the most recent (David Schoenbrun).[3] This oversight may explain the tendency among the Spanish writers to exaggerate the role of the Spaniards. By a curious irony, it is the Spanish pro-Franco writers who are the most generous towards the Spanish *guerrilleros*, and their accounts betray a secret pride in the exploits of their compatriots. An example of such writers is the propagandist Bravo-Tellado who, though devoid of pity for the suffering of the Republicans, is nevertheless sensitive to the humiliations they endured as Spaniards, not least of which was the attitude of Pétain expressed by Laval concerning deportation to Germany: 'For

every Spaniard, one Frenchman less!'[4] For an unforced appreciation of
the qualities of the Spanish *guerrillero* it is necessary to consult the
more modest accounts, such as that of Lucien Maury, who writes:
'They do not behave like regular troops, they always look as if they
need a shave . . . but they make damn fine soldiers.'[5]

Can it be said that Spaniards, communist or non-communist, engaged in guerrilla warfare before the invasion of Russia? In the way
that France was divided into its two principal zones (Occupied and
Vichy), most of the terrain suitable for guerrilla activity, and most of
the Spaniards, were to be found in Vichy. In Vichy, apart from the
presence of the ubiquitous Gestapo, there was no opportunity for
direct action (in the sense of attacking the Germans) before the German
invasion of Vichy in November 1942. The idea of Spaniards attacking
the representatives of Vichy posed a real problem: it was unlikely to
win them any support from the French, and as long as Pétain enjoyed
nearly unanimous support it was certain to win them rebuke. There
is nevertheless some evidence that a Spanish Resistance group was
operational at the end of 1940, and thus achieved the honour of being
the first such group ready to fight on French soil in the Second World
War. Any such claim is admittedly invidious to the French, but the
counter-claims are not compelling.[6] The incontrovertible fact is that
the number of Spaniards entering the Resistance, proportionate to
population, was markedly higher than the number of French.

The nucleus of Spanish resistance was the Organización militar
española, whose origins go back to the period prior to the collapse of
June 1940. The organization, directed by General José Riquelme, began as a recruitment office for Spanish regular officers who wished to
serve in the French Army under the command of General Henri Dentz.[7]
Having no political character, the OME was open to communists and
non-communists alike. It remained like this for a time after June
1940, but the communists soon moved into a position of control.[8]

Hitler's attack on the Soviet Union, on 22 June 1941, finally put an
end to the division in the French communist camp and enabled the
French and Spanish communist Resistance groups to collaborate. On
3 July an order from Stalin was transmitted by radio to every communist party in Nazi-controlled Europe: communists everywhere were to
attack the Germans in any way they could. The fact that Stalin waited
eleven days before issuing his order reflects his state of shock at
learning that the honeymoon was over. *L'Humanité* had already, the
day before, called on all communists in France to resist the enemy,
but there is a curious absence of alacrity in it all.[9] A call for sabotage
and armed combat does not appear until 29 July. It is as if *L'Humanité*

too is in a state of shock at Stalin's total lack of preparedness, and now has to explain to its readers, conditioned to believe in the visionary genius of the Vozhd, how the Soviet front has melted like the snows of yesteryear. 'Soviet troops had to be mobilized and transported to the front line,' it offered lamely.[10] Just six weeks after the invasion its headlines ran: 'HITLER HAS LOST 1,500,000 MEN IN RUSSIA.'[11] Its readers would have been better informed if those losses had been attributed to the other side, but *L'Humanité* never wrote of Soviet disasters, only stupendous victories that moved none the less eastwards. The credulity of its readers rose to the occasion. A 'special issue' of *L'Humanité* appeared with the simple date of July 1941. A special issue of *L'Humanité* is always suspect, since it carries no number and could always have been interpolated into the series at a later date. If Stalin had been removed from power by rivals blaming him for the disaster, a different special issue would have been necessary. Indeed, the removal of Stalin for the disaster of June 1941 would have been as logical as the earlier removal of Daladier and Chamberlain. If Stalin survived, it was the very magnitude of the disaster that explains it. But in surviving, Stalin retained the power to write and unwrite history according to his fancy. It is to the further advantage of a special issue that it can also be repudiated later as a counterfeit. In this particular special issue, which may or may not have been authentic, Stalin is exonerated from all charges that the Soviet Union was militarily unprepared. The issue goes on to describe the role which the USSR has just assumed: 'The Soviet Union [is fighting] for the freedom of all the peoples of Europe who groan under the yoke of German fascism.' Most of these peoples, of course, had been groaning under the fascist yoke for more than a year without any of that disturbing the conscience of a government proud of the treaties it had signed 'in the cause of peace'. In any event, ran the special issue, the war would be of short duration: 'We have the peoples of Europe and America at our side. That includes the Germans.'[12]

The Germans of 1941 remaining, in reality, true to their Führer, communists would need more than propaganda to impress the forces of occupation. Violence, on the other hand, carried an awesome price, especially for the communists. Keitel's decree of 16 September 1941 fixed the policy to be followed throughout Occupied Europe: 'In every instance of rebellion against the German occupation forces, whatever the circumstances might be, the action is to be laid at the door of the communists. For every German soldier killed, from fifty to one hundred communists are to be executed. The method of execution must be such that it too contributes to the effect of intimidation.'[13] Accordingly, Stalin's order of 3 July, calling on communists to attack the Nazis in any way they could, resulted in massive reprisals and an announcement by General de Gaulle over the BBC on the evening of 23 October: 'The order I give for Occupied France at the present time is to desist from killing Germans.' The French communist leadership followed suit. Marcel Cachin himself wrote to Major Walter Beumelburg, liaison officer for the German military administration in Paris, disclaiming responsibility for the attacks on German personnel.[14]

The total confusion into which Stalin was thrown by Operation *Barbarossa* is reflected in the communist press not only in France but in Mexico and elsewhere. In Mexico the Spanish communists reacted within two days, with a manifesto blasting Hitler's act of aggression, but it reflected Stalin's fears in its warning against the 'reactionary manœuvres' in Britain and the United States aimed at reaching agreement with Hitler and leaving the Soviet Union alone in the struggle.[15] *España popular*, the principal organ of the PCE in Mexico, refrained from taking any ideological position other than a condemnation of the Nazi attack, and *Nuestra bandera*, the Party's monthly ideological review, solved the problem by not appearing that month at all.[16] Nearly a month went by before Stalin, reassured by the signing of the Anglo-Soviet Pact of 12 July, passed word through the Comintern that the ideological position taken in the Molotov–Ribbentrop Pact was now reversed: the bourgeoisie was no longer the enemy, and the war had changed from an inter-imperialist struggle into a fascist–antifascist conflict. In line with that new definition of the struggle, the PCE leaders in Moscow (Díaz, Pasionaria, Hernández), with the necessary support from the Comintern, issued their manifesto of July 1941. This manifesto, inspired by the fear that Franco might indeed now enter the war on Hitler's side, appealed for a national union of Spaniards of all classes in the struggle against fascism. The PCE's treatment of the socialists was reversed overnight. No longer were they the lackeys of imperialism. They were now fellow-warriors in the fight to build a happy and prosperous Spain. In Mexico the manifesto, known as the Appeal of 1 August 1941, appeared in the next issue of *Nuestra bandera* and included an 'open letter' to the PSOE.[17] By way of introduction, the PCE insisted that the communists had never left the antifascist struggle for a single day, 'and only those suffering from insuperable ignorance could argue the contrary'. Not every socialist, and not every anarchist, was included in the amnesty. There was to be no forgiveness for the 'traitors' who had rallied in March 1939 to Colonel Casado, no redemption for socialists like Prieto or Araquistáin, or anarchists like Abad de Santillán, who had worked, 'like shameless fascist agents and Trotskyist provocateurs, for the triumph of reaction and the downfall of the people'. Negrín, on the other hand, was restored to full favour; his speech in London of 20 July was carried verbatim, and the Appeal of 1 August 1941 ended in the slogan: 'We want a government of national union, with Negrín at its head.' The same national union which spurned reconciliation with those on the left who had opposed communist policy now opened its arms to every monarchist, Catholic, and conservative in Spain who was willing to abandon Franco.[18] The political misjudgement in all this was palpable. No Republican unity was in sight, and the PCE thought it could create a national union headed by Negrín. Its failure was inevitable.

In what condition did Hitler's attack on the Soviet Union find the Spanish communists in France? There are many differing answers to the question. The story of the Spanish Resistance is not a simple one. Not all Spaniards who joined the Resistance were communists, but most were.[19] Not all Spaniards who joined joined Spanish units, but most did. The Spanish Resistance leaders, overwhelmingly communist, did all they could to enlist other Spaniards, but the fact remains that even at the time of the Liberation Spaniards could still be found in non-Spanish units. The two other organizations in which Spaniards enrolled were the Francs-tireurs et partisans (FTP), controlled by the French communists, and the Main-d'œuvre immigrée (MOI), which consisted of foreigners, most of whom were communists.

If the FTP could draw its strength from almost anywhere in France, the MOI tended to draw its strength from the cities and the Midi, and the Spanish units from the south-west. The demographic pattern of the foreign elements in France explains the development of the MOI and the Spanish Resistance. Apart from the Spaniards, who were the predominant foreign group also in Gard and Aveyron (especially in the industrial region of Decazeville), certain other national groups were prominent in the south-west. The mass exodus of Belgians in April 1940 was estimated by the Belgian Embassy in Paris at 2,200,000;[20] they made up the first wave of the flood heading towards the south-west. Though later ordered home, many hid. The Polish refugees formed important colonies in Tarn, especially in the mining communities of the Carmaux region; at Cagnac-les-Mines they constituted 48.5 per cent of the total population.[21] Some Polish airmen who fought in the French Air Force in the Battle of France were demobilized in Toulouse, where they subsequently organized the 'Famille' Resistance network, making contact with British intelligence and becoming the first in France to establish radio contact with London.[22] The

Italians were spread across the countryside of Gers, Lot-et-Garonne, and Tarn-et-Garonne (where the Germans and Austrians were also concentrated).[23] The future president of Italy, Giuseppe Saragat, had taken refuge in Saint-Gaudens; under tight guard, he could hardly take part in Resistance activities. It was another matter for Professor Silvio Trentin and Francesco Fausto Nitti, both members of the Bertaux network, and Trentin's bookshop at 10 rue de Languedoc in Toulouse served from the very first as an important meeting place of the Resistance in Haute-Garonne, especially for students and teachers.[24] These included the university professors Soula and Ducuing in medicine, and Bertaux in German literature.[25] Finally, the Jewish population: there had been very few Jews in Toulouse for a very long time, but their numbers had swollen with the arrival of refugees and fugitives from the camps.[26] They were to move into the MOI in great numbers, but as Arthur London has said, membership in the MOI has always been discussed in terms of national groups, and the role of the Jews in the Resistance has been ignored.[27]

The Main-d'œuvre immigré, or MOI, had been founded in 1919 as an organization for foreign workers in France, with its members grouped according to their language. Communist in the ideology of its leaders and the great majority of its members, it responded to the capitulation of 1940 by establishing an underground organization in Paris within six weeks. For reasons of security, Annie Kriegel tells us, it was attached to the PCF only at the very top.[28] The PCF leader Jacques Duclos maintained control,[29] but its best-known leaders were, like the majority of the rank-and-file, veterans of the International Brigades in Spain: Arthur London, Jacques Kaminski ('Hervé'), and Louis Grojnowski ('Brunot' or 'Bruno' to the MOI, 'Michel' to the Party).[30]

London had left Spain, where he fought under the name of Captain Singer, without anyone knowing his real name. In Paris he went into hiding under the name of Gérard before reverting to the name of Singer. Fearing that Vichy might deliver into Hitler's hands his former comrades in the Brigades and other political exiles who were detained in the concentration camps at Le Vernet and Argelès, London decided in early October 1940 to make his way to Toulouse and Marseilles to arrange their escape. At the same time he acquired emigration visas for them from the consulates of Mexico, Central America, Dominican Republic, Venezuela, Argentina, Chile, and the Soviet Union.[31] After the German attack on 22 June 1941,[32] London took charge of organizing the section known as Travail Allemand (TA) whose work consisted of trying to sap the morale of the German forces. A journal appeared in German in September 1941 under the title *Der Soldat im*

Westen, and continued to appear as a monthly until 1944, even after London himself was arrested and deported to Mauthausen.[33] Spaniards too participated in this work. Mercedes de la Iglesia has described how she, her husband, and a woman comrade helped first in locating the barracks and buildings occupied by the Germans, especially in Pont-de-Sèvres outside Paris, and then distributing the propaganda in the dead of night.[34]

It was in the Unoccupied Zone, however, that the MOI was most active and effective. As in the Occupied Zone, the communists predominated, especially in the leadership, but socialists and others also played a part. In national affiliation it was the Spaniards who were predominant, but the MOI was cosmopolitan by definition and its forces included Frenchmen, Italians, Poles, Germans, Austrians, Czechs, and Hungarians. The more significant fact is that over half the MOI was Jewish.[35] Its essential centre was cosmopolitan Toulouse, where the German antifascists in Vichy France kept their headquarters until September 1943, when they moved to Lyons. Though the MOI's forces never had the strength of the *guerrilleros*, they were highly disciplined and motivated. Ideological training was given high priority. The MOI's first chief delegate in the Unoccupied Zone was the Italian Teresa Nocce ('Estella'), the first wife of Luigi Longo who served as Palmiro Togliatti's chief aide in the leadership of the PCI. Her arrest at the end of 1942 unsettled the MOI in the Southern Zone, but not for long: it was already an organization in arms, and the Pole Edouard Kowalski was to assume its leadership from the beginning of 1943 up to the time of the Liberation.[36]

The Spaniards, for their part, while scattered over almost every *département* of France, had remained concentrated in the south-west. It is there, in the forested foothills and mountains of the Pyrenees and in the region to the south of the Massif Central, that we find the first elements of a Spanish Resistance. Very quickly and very early, before the end of 1940, Spaniards employed as woodcutters and charcoal-workers,[37] in mines and dam construction, and in certain large towns, especially Toulouse and Carcassonne, banded together in the cause both of antifascism and of self-protection. As antifascists they already had three years of battle experience in Spain, and they had more reason than the French to protect themselves from a summons by Vichy's Service du travail obligatoire, for they had more reason than the French to fear being selected as forced labourers for Nazi Germany. Many a Spaniard finished up in the Maquis precisely as a result of avoiding a summons or escaping from a draft; fleeing to the hills, he would find himself without work or work papers, and wanted by the police. The Spanish Resistance member was thus different in kind from his French counterpart who, if he resisted from the very beginning, was expressing (in Jean Cassou's phrase) 'an absurd refusal'.[38] The Spaniard's decision to resist was quite logical. Most Spaniards had nothing to lose. The forest was their natural refuge, the Maquis their natural home.

Every factor was thus propitious for the development of the groups of Spanish *guerrilleros* in the south-west: the terrain, their occupations, their experience of fighting in such a terrain against a better equipped enemy, and even, in many cases, their experience of guerrilla warfare itself. They already knew how to make bombs out of scraps, how to set traps, how to lay an ambush, and how to derail a train without the help of explosives.[39] Forest workers by day would transform themselves into saboteurs and Pyrenees guides at night. The only factor missing (except in Basses-Pyrénées) was the German enemy. But whatever hesitation Spaniards might have felt about fighting Frenchmen on the soil of France, we shall see that they were fully engaged against the forces of Vichy long before the German invasion of the south in November 1942.

Although it has been said that the Spanish Resistance did not exist before July 1941, that is to say before the German invasion of Russia,[40] there is enough evidence that it did. It seems to have begun without contact with the French Resistance, and with no concern for the latter's objectives: making and maintaining contact with London, providing London with military, economic, and psychological data, providing an escape route across the Pyrenees, and obtaining from London weapons, ammunition, and financial assistance, all of which were the objectives of the Bertaux network formed in Toulouse in March 1941.[41] Jean Cassou ('Alain') arrived in Toulouse from Paris[42] and joined the Bertaux group in the same month. The group, small but active, comprised a score of refugees and intellectuals, with Trentin's bookshop continuing to serve as a rendezvous. Another meeting place was the Viadieu bicycle shop on the rue de Metz.[43] The group's propaganda section was entrusted to Cassou. Jean-Maurice Herrmann, a socialist journalist who had covered the Spanish Civil War, was made responsible for recruitment. The sabotage section was given to the Italian socialist Nitti, and military organization to the Toulouse communist Bernard. In November 1941 Bernard was arrested while carrying a notebook with the names of the network members in clear. This astonishing blunder spelled the arrest, on the night of 12–13 December, of all the leaders. The sentences were light,[44] but the network was totally destroyed.[45] Its leaders lacked neither intelligence nor courage, but they certainly lacked experience in underground operations.

Unbeknown to Bertaux's group—or it would have probably shared its fate—a Spanish underground organization had also formed in Toulouse, consisting of over 250 members, with cells in several factories including the Breguet and Dewoitine aircraft plants. The Hôtel de Paris, at that time at 58–66 rue Gambetta near the Place du Capitole, served from 1940 as a centre for Ponzán's group until the moment on 20 February 1943 when its proprietors, François Stanislas Mongelard and his wife, were arrested; he was sent to Nordhausen and she to Ravensbrück.[46] One of the Spaniards' earlier exploits was to organize a food supply which delivered some 400 kilos of food a month to certain inmates in the Saint-Michel Prison in Toulouse and in the camp at Le Vernet in Ariège. This action was uncovered and the Spaniards responsible were sent to a camp at Clairefonds where the treatment was particularly harsh.[47]

The two branches of the Resistance, urban and guerrilla, led very different lives, but the work of sabotage was common to both from the beginning. The earliest recorded Spanish guerrilla activity dates from September 1940, in the Alpine *département* of Haute-Savoie, where Miguel Vera laid the foundation of an action group; it began by distributing pamphlets and from the winter of 1940–1 provided help to fugitives, especially to Jews. In the same first winter of defeat, a sabotage group was organized by Armando Castillo in the central *département* of Haute-Vienne, in the region of Limoges.[48] And in January 1942, in the region of Annecy in the Alps, a unit was formed which later claimed to be the very first Maquis.[49]

Nevertheless, it is in the south-west, and in the region known to the Resistance later as R4, an area rather larger than the group of *départements* known as the Midi-Pyrénées and in which the Spanish population was densest, that we find the cradle of the Spanish Resistance. We have seen that in Pyrénées-Orientales a resistance group had its birth inside the camp at Argelès; they soon afterwards escaped, and proceeded to form the first organized Spanish Resistance movement. Known as the 'Reconquista de España', communist in inspiration and leadership, it was active in the *départements* of Pyrénées-Orientales, Aude, Ariège, and Haute-Garonne. Its purpose was to print and distribute pamphlets urging direct action against the German forces and the Vichy administration, in such ways as sabotaging factories and destroying railway installations.[50] In Aude, the first resistance units were organized in the isolated mining companies of the Montagne Noire, at Salsigne, Villanière, and Laubatière, grouping together a hundred Spaniards of all political factions. In the region of Limoux and Quillan, several other groups were formed among the woodsmen and charcoal-workers, who had no difficulty in finding dynamite: on one occasion, they came away with a haul of 40 kilos.[51] It was in Aude, on 5 May 1942, that the 234th Brigade (later renamed the 5th) was formed and the command given to Antonio Molina. By July 1942 it included several hundred *guerrilleros* in lumber camps throughout Aude. Its first activities were sabotage, which provided field training and combat experience. The brigade thus set out to train future leaders. The *guerrilleros* of Aude were proud later to say that they produced the future brigade commanders of several other *départements*, including, as we shall see, Jesús Ríos and Luis Fernández.[52]

The other engine of the Spanish Resistance was in Ariège, and it kept pace with the one in Aude. With its mountains and forests and the large number of lumber enterprises operating in the area, it offered the best possible refuge for those on the run from other regions. The nucleus of its guerrilla force was to be found in the region of Varilhes-Dalou. Resistance groups in Ariège even created their own lumber enterprises which later served as bases for the guerrilla units. It was a log cabin in the Col de Py, in the centre of the quadrilateral Foix–Pamiers–Mirepoix–Lavelanet, that served as the first headquarters of their guerrilla activities.

Colonel José Antonio Paz, who like General Riquelme was a republican sympathetic to the communists, has described how very difficult it was in the early days: 'We were nothing. We got together to look for men. Sometimes a unit consisted of a single *guerrillero*.' Weapons were obtained by raiding the police stations, or attacking Vichy (and later German) patrols. There was no choice, because the Spaniards had had no chance to retain and bury their arms at the time they entered France, and because they were excluded from the distribution of supplies flown in from England.[53] A Spanish chronicler has written: 'At the beginning, the number of those enlisted in the *guerrilleros* was tiny. This was understandable, since so many of the able-bodied men had been deported. Suffice it to say that, in one small town in the Midi, one of the first brigades was made up of seven men. They were all captains or lieutenants, without any troops to command.'[54] If now they adopted the term of brigade, and later division and army corps, it is obviously not in the strict military sense of the term. The term brigade was applied to the number of *guerrilleros* operating in a single *département*, with a division responsible for a group of *départements*. Even in 1942 the *guerrilleros* numbered only in the hundreds, but by mid-1943 (with the arrival of the Germans in the south) they had increased to three thousand,[55] and would continue to grow. Built up primarily by communists, these units remained under communist control. The Spanish Communist

Party had meanwhile spun its web over the entire Midi, and by the autumn of 1942 the PCE had a bureau in every *département* of Vichy France. The standing orders were: 'Work less and worse. Sabotage more and better.' Thousands of little acts of sabotage were the result.[56]

Among such little acts, the efforts to subvert the Blue Division earned their place. Franco's contribution to the Russian Front was not an all-volunteer force, and its communications line ran on the rail between Hendaye and Paris. Here was an opportunity for Spaniards of the south-west, and some arranged to be present as the troop trains passed. In the verbal brawl that would ensue, Franco's volunteers would scream their faith in their cause, but there was always a conscript, and sometimes as many as three, who could be persuaded to leave the train, whereupon the exiles would hide them in their homes while they found them clothes and would then show them the way to refuge in the hills. While they never attempted to entice away a Spanish officer, they did on one ocasion persuade a Wehrmacht soldier to desert with his rifle, and as a result of their success with members of the Blue Division the Germans gave orders prohibiting anyone from approaching a railway station when the Blue Division was passing through.[57]

The question remains: did the Spanish communist Resistance develop centrifugally or centripetally? We have noted the natural preference of the Party for the centrifugal answer. The Party seeks exclusive credit. It does not take kindly to the action of a Party member which anticipates the decision of the Party. Members can err, but the wisdom of the Party is infinite because it is guided by the infallible. It is loyalty to that principle that inspires the account of Miguel Angel Sanz, the PCE's chief chronicler of the Spanish Resistance in France. Sanz gives credit to the Party without describing the leadership. The insuperable problem he faced, as a loyal Party member, was that after the departure of Francisco Antón there was not a single member of the Politburo and hardly a member of the Central Committee[58] left behind in France. The only way Sanz had to credit the Party without embarrassing it was to refrain from describing its wartime leadership at all, and in this way he did not have to explain how these same leaders mysteriously disappeared before the end of the war, when the conquering heroes returned from Russia and America. Even here Sanz could not be certain how the Party would regard his book, so that even from the safety of Havana in 1971 Sanz chose to write under the pseudonym of his forenames Miguel Angel. Sanz faced another problem. While he avoided discussion of the overall Party leadership (which, as we shall see, had its centre in the Southern Zone), Sanz was quite ready to discuss the operations of the subordinate committee in Paris, which took responsibility for the Occupied, or Northern, Zone. This Zone included the Atlantic coast southwards to the Pyrenees. In order to exalt the prestige of the Paris committee at the expense of the PCE leadership in the Southern Zone, Sanz offers the blithe remark: 'The Bordeaux region was the centre of Spanish resistance in the south-west.'[59]

From the moment the Germans arrived, the French police had been hard at work, especially in Paris, tracking down Spanish communist officials, and had soon arrested some two hundred of them and interned them in a concentration camp in Seine-et-Oise. The French authorities even appealed to the German authorities 'to deal more harshly with the communists'.[60] The resulting vacuum in the PCE leadership was filled by a perfect unknown, Carmen de Pedro ('Maria Luisa'). Short, a little plump—she was better known as 'Mari la gorda'—with a low, authoritative, even masculine voice, de Pedro was still in her early twenties. She had never held a post during the Civil War other than that of typist or secretary to Togliatti or the Central Committee of the PCE, but she had enjoyed the confidence of her employers, and it is reasonable to suppose that she was appointed to the post by Francisco Antón before he left for Moscow.[61] In initiating the work of regrouping she was quickly joined by Jesús Monzón Reparaz, who became both her lover and the uncontested brain of the PCE in France. Although he was not a member of the Central Committee and belonged only to the third level of leadership in the Party, he had already achieved much in his thirty years. Born into a wealthy middle-class Navarrese family, he was a lawyer by profession and had risen to some important posts in the course of the Civil War; Civil Governor of Alicante in 1937–8, Civil Governor of Cuenca in 1938–9, he had been appointed Secretary-General at the Ministry of War at the moment in March 1939 that the Casado rebellion ousted the communists. As a result he had left Spain on 5 March, travelling by air from Monóvar (Alicante) in the same plane as Pasionaria and Stepanov of the Comintern. By the time that Monzón and Carmen de Pedro began to live together he had already separated from his wife Aurora Urritia; their son Sergio, sent to the Soviet Union at the age of 4, was to disappear later when his father fell into disgrace. Not that Monzón ever stood in Stalin's grace, for he did not fit into the Stalinist mould of puritanism, self-discipline, and blind obedience. An extreme individualist and bon vivant, he was more at home at the gaming tables of a casino, surrounded by women, than in the quiet and anonymous role he was now called upon to assume, once Carmen showed that she lacked the political savvy to be a leader. No one questioned his valour, his daring, or his powers to persuade, but discretion was not his suit at all. He could be even flamboyantly defiant, as he showed in his secret visits to Spain, when he would attend the bull-fights with long cape, wide-brimmed hat, and walking cane, puffing on a cigarillo and posing as a doctor. All of this would serve the Party later, when it came time to brand him a dissolute bourgeois reprobate, but for the moment it served Monzón, winning him a certain charisma. If contact with the Comintern was maintained up until November 1940, the difficulties of communications after that meant that the PCE in France, while never completely disconnected from Moscow and Mexico City, and while holding to the general guidelines established by the Comintern, operated with great autonomy. As a result, Monzón was free to put his stamp, his style, his personal touch on everything he did.[62]

De Pedro and Monzón were in turn joined by two other communists, both as young as Carmen and not much better known: Manuel Azcárate ('Juan') and Manuel Gimeno ('Raúl'), both of them in the JSU, the communist-dominated youth organization.[63] While Gimeno held solid proletarian credentials—he was a tailor—Azcárate was the son of Pablo de Azcárate, the Spanish Republican Ambassador to London during the Civil War, and like Monzón had received a university education. These four young communists decided to call themselves the Delegation of the Central Committee of the Spanish Communist Party in France.[64] Its purpose was to amalgamate all the communist organizations created in both Zones, with Azcárate acting as liaison with the Occupied Zone. The delegation continued to expand with the entry of Eduardo Sánchez Biezma ('Torres') and Gabriel León Trilla.[65] While Sánchez Biezma had no particular background—he was working in the Dewoitine factory in Toulouse—Trilla certainly had. Intellectually inclined, he had been a founding member of the PCE in 1920 and a member of its Politburo in 1927, but in 1932 he had been removed from his post by the Comintern.[66] Trilla, now very much Monzón's man, was given responsibility for setting up a new centre in Aix-en-Provence, while Monzón continued to direct the Delegation from the base in Marseilles.[67]

There is controversy whether this Delegation was formed before the famous meeting in October 1940 inside the concentration camp at Argelès.[68] The point is not a minor one, since extermination was so often the reward later for those who gave birth to an idea. If the Delegation already existed, then Pelayo Tortajada represented it at Argelès.[69] Other communist militants attending that meeting now formed a task force of the Delegation, each responsible for organizing the PCE in a given *département* of Vichy France. These included in particular Sixto Agudo ('Andrés'), Angel Celadas ('Paco'), Jaime Nieto ('Bolados'), and Manuel Sánchez Esteban.[70] The principal area of their operations was the region of the south-west known as R4. Its centre was Toulouse. Dr Aguasca became prominent in its local PCE committee, and José Linares emerged as its guerrilla leader. Antonio Nuñez was given responsibility for the PCE in Lyons, where the Spaniards worked in association with the MOI.[71]

We have seen that this Delegation and its subcommittee had been formed without any contact with the Party's Politburo or its Central Committee, which were thousands of miles away. It has been said that the Delegation received (and faithfully executed) orders from Moscow which were transmitted by Radio España Independiente (in operation from autumn 1941) and even (up until the German occupation of the Midi in November 1942) by mail.[72] While the Kremlin was no doubt able to maintain its communications with communist leaders in Paris through the use of diplomatic channels, it is highly unlikely that it was able to maintain such links with the leaders in the Midi, and the same author reveals that Azcárate and Carmen de Pedro had to leave for Switzerland, even in 1943, in order to pick up their instructions.[73] The Delegation, which considered itself responsible for the PCE in the whole of France, found communications difficult even across the demarcation line.

Independently of the meeting at Argelès, but in the same month of October 1940, some Spanish communist militants living in the Paris area joined to form a provisional committee. The three prominent names in the formation of this committee are Captain Daniel Sánchez Vizcaino ('Roger'), Juan Montero ('Domínguez'), and Chacón.[74] These three proceeded to form cells in almost every *arrondissement* and suburb of Paris. Shortly afterwards they made contact with Louis Grojnowski ('Brunot') of the MOI, and with the help of the MOI they obtained a duplicating machine and sufficient paper to produce an issue of *Mundo obrero* on 7 November 1940.[75] In mid-December 1940 the Delegation in the Midi sent Angel Celadas to Paris to make contact with its provisional committee, and to report on the possibilities of combat in the Occupied Zone.[76] What he learned is unfortunately not recorded. At the end of that month a new man, Emilio Gómez Nadal ('Henri'), arrived in Paris from Brittany to take charge of reorganizing the PCE in the Occupied Zone, and with the agreement of the provisional committee he assumed the title of Secretary-General of the PCE in Occupied France. The ascent of Gómez Nadal was accompanied by the transfer to Brittany of two of the three members of the provisional committee in Paris, Montero and Chacón, who were now assigned to organize the PCE in Rennes. In January 1941 Gómez Nadal formed a co-ordinating committee for the Occupied Zone with Josep Miret Musté of the PSUC (the Catalan communist party), and Grojnowski of the MOI. With the German attack on the USSR, the Delegation of the Central Committee appointed Manuel Azcárate to take Nadal's place as leader in the Occupied Zone, Nadal receiving the subordinate responsibility for Unión nacional.

It should never be overlooked that the Delegation of the Central Committee of the Spanish Communist Party was self-appointed. Independent actions of this kind were not customary in an organization as monolithic and hierarchical as a Communist Party, and those who showed such initiative, if they survived, might rue it later. A document in the hands of the English historian George Hills adds a whole new dimension to this question. If authentic, it exonerates the members of the Delegation from having taken an arbitrary or ill-advised decision, since the message comes from the Kremlin and calls for the immediate creation in France of a Politburo of the PCE. The document is typed in Spanish, dated 7 August 1941, but is unsigned. The authenticity of this document, however, will not be easy to establish, since it is necessary to show that it was typed on a Soviet typewriter manufactured in or before 1941.

Whether the message was authentic or counterfeit, the Delegation did not proceed to call itself the Politburo but continued to act as if it were. In the autumn of 1941, it instructed its branches to select a certain number of their militants to form the first guerrilla groups. The strongest forces were created in the *départements* of Aude, Ariège, Tarn, and Haute-Garonne. When sufficient men were mobilized, a military command of the Unoccupied Zone was established. The choice fell on Jesús Ríos, a former staff officer of the xivth Army Corps of Guerrilleros, which had covered the retreat from Madrid of the last Republicans at the end of the Civil War.[77] Since 1939 Ríos had been employed in a team of charcoal-workers in the region of Majou, near Montréal in Aude. Ríos continued in his job, and continued also to live with his wife and little daughter in the Villa Odette in Carcassonne. But Majou soon proved to be a vulnerable base of operations, and Ríos had to flee into Ariège. At the same time in Cantal, a group of Spaniards employed in dam construction at Laroquebrou organized themselves into a unit under the command of Silvestre Gómez ('Margallo'), a former brigade commander in the Civil War. Their first orders from the Delegation were to purloin all the dynamite they could.[78]

The man now giving the orders in the name of the Delegation, and who travelled to Cantal himself to instruct Silvestre Gómez, was Jaime Nieto, who had thus emerged as the leader in the Unoccupied

Zone. It was he who now presided, in April 1942, at a meeting held in Toulouse in the house of Francisco Sentenero. The twelve men present[79] decided to form a unit to be known as the xIVth Army Corps of Spanish Guerrilleros, thus reviving the name of the unit already famous for its exploits in Spain. The purpose was to group together all Spanish guerrilla units operating both in the Occupied and the Unoccupied Zones. Ríos was confirmed in the command, while the post of chief of staff went to one of those obscure and unsung heroes who might easily have disappeared entirely from the record.

Little is known about the background of Major Antonio Buitrago except that he came from Madrid and that he had fought in the xIVth Army Corps in Spain in the final retreat. Under the German occupation he travelled all over France, including the Restricted Zone in the north where he helped to evacuate escaped prisoners of war. In mid-1942 he arrived in Paris from Bordeaux with both the French police and the Gestapo hard on his heels. His mission was to take command of the PCE action groups in the capital, at a time when the communists had suffered their first major setback. The French police had received information from the friend of an imprudent Spanish woman militant. They had set up a full-scale surveillance of the Spanish communists, especially in the suburb of Issy-les-Moulineaux, with shadowing operations beginning on 9 April. On 27 June they struck, seizing 119 Spanish communists in various parts of France. Although no top leaders were involved, it was a very hard blow to the Spanish communists and their network was temporarily paralysed.[80]

Buitrago found a hiding place in the apartment of María Aucejo de Llena, at 75 rue Quincampoix in the 3e *arrondissement*. It was a dangerous choice of sanctuary. María Llena's companion, Andrés Borrás, had been active in the Resistance from the moment the capital fell, and in September 1940 he had been arrested by the French authorities. Borrás was taken to the *'dépôt'*, the cellars below the Sainte-Chapelle on the Île de la Cité which descend to a level lower than the Seine and whose sinister history dates back beyond the Revolution. It was there under the German occupation that many a Spaniard was tortured by a Frenchman, and almost always by the same Frenchman—a certain Jordan, who was not to escape execution at the time of the Liberation. Why the Germans permitted his companion María Llena and their 8-year-old daughter not only to attend his trial in 1940 but also to visit him in no fewer than three prisons (La Santé, Fresnes, and Clairvaux) is a question that still surprises the survivors of his family. But permit it they did, and in Clairvaux María Llena and her daughter could see for themselves that the Gestapo had indeed, as he said, taken out every tooth in his head, one by one, at intervals. He also told them how they liked to hang him upside down, and that is how he died, on 4 April 1942, when it went on too long and the blood coagulated in his lungs. Up until this time María Llena, a fervent Catholic from Valencia, had taken no part in politics or the Resistance, but this experience changed her world. She was now in both the Resistance and the Party, but the Gestapo had not maintained its surveillance of her apartment, which is why Pierre Maillot (who after the Liberation was to become the local mayor) would come there to hide, and it was Maillot who first brought Buitrago to those premises. Buitrago, however, soon fell into a police trap which Maillot was able to evade. The Spanish leader died four days after his arrest.

It was now María Llena's turn. Under the *nom de guerre* of Victoria López, she belonged to a group of Spaniards, led by Sandalio Puerto, that formed part of the FTP group headed by René Camphin. Her apartment was again used, as it had been by Andrés Borrás, for the production of all kinds of material. But the group was infiltrated by a traitor, the Jewess Edith Kache, who hoped to save herself from the current round-up of the Jews by serving the Gestapo as a double-agent; the treachery was not to save her, for she was arrested in 1943 and died in the sorting camp at Drancy before she could be sent to Germany. Her perfidy nevertheless resulted, on 3 September 1942, in the arrest of both Sandalio Puerto and María Llena. Puerto was sent to Mauthausen, but survived. María Llena was taken to the same dungeon below the Sainte-Chapelle that her poor husband had known, and there, for ten weeks, she shared his experience at the hands of Jordan. Jordan wanted the names of the members of the group, and María Llena replied each time that she would say anything he wanted her to say but that it would all be lies. Jordan's favourite method was to stand on a stool and lift the woman by the hair, and María Llena still groans at the remembrance of it, but the police photograph of herself that she still holds, taken at the time she arrived in the '*dépôt*', shows her smiling in defiance, and her daughter says that she was still smiling when she visited her mother in prison: 'She liked to smile.' From the '*dépôt*' María Llena was sent to the Caserne des Tourelles, a barracks in eastern Paris which the Germans had converted into another sorting centre for prisoners prior to their transportation to Germany. María had the good fortune to be sent instead to the nearby Hospital Tenon, where the Resistance had organized a method of escape. An Italian male nurse by the name of Panico told her that if she did not get out at once she would surely die: a new convoy to Germany was about to be assembled. With his help she slipped away in the early morning, then went into hiding until the Liberation.[81] Meanwhile, Buitrago's branch also survived, and its contacts with other PCE branches were maintained. Juan Montero returned from Rennes to take Buitrago's place, and when he too was caught, in the round-up of November 1942, he was replaced in turn by the Catalan brothers Miret Musté.[82]

The name of Miret was well known in *émigré* circles. Josep, the younger brother, had served during the Civil War as a minister (Councillor of Supplies) in the Catalan Government. He had entered France in the flood of February 1939, and he had been interned. After escaping from the camp he had settled in Montpellier, where he launched the first journal in Catalan published by the exiles in France. When this was suppressed by the French Government he moved to Paris, where he launched a new journal, *Catalunya*,[83] equally short-lived. As a member of the Catalan communist party he had also been elected, as we have seen, to its Central committee at the Antwerp Conference in March 1939. He had subsequently remained behind to direct the PSUC in France. His reaction to the arrival of the Germans in France, however, was not dictated by the Party leaders. On the contrary, it ran counter to the Comintern's policy. Once again Miret launched a journal in Catalan, the underground *Butlletí d'informació radiada*, in which he lampooned German propaganda and urged resistance with the theme: 'Defeat, Combat, Revolution'. His action at once put him at the top of the Gestapo's wanted list, but they had difficulty in catching him. The French authorities knew him under the name of Musté, for he had used his mother's name when he entered France in order not to be identified, and he was now living under the name of Jean Regnier.[84] It was not until 30 November 1942 (when he directed the PCE as well as the PSUC in the Occupied Zone) that the Gestapo tracked him down to his address at 26 rue Menilmontant. All indications point to the treachery of the Stalinist agent Olaso Piera.[85] Miret was tortured and, whether or not he talked, the whole network fell into the Gestapo's hands. He was then held in the prison at Fresnes until, with Montero and forty other Spaniards, he was sent to Mauthausen, arriving there on 27 August 1943. It was in the Mauthausen Aussenkommando at Floridsdorf, to the north-west of Vienna, that he died, ironically the victim of an Allied air raid in November 1944.[86] As for his brother Conrad, who used the names 'Lucien' and 'Alonso', he too was arrested in Paris, but not before 1943. An artist friend of his, who was summoned for questioning at Gestapo headquarters, was the last to see him alive; the artist, when allowed to return home, reported to his friends that Conrad Miret's face was no longer recognizable.[87]

This time the entire network in the Occupied Zone had been dismantled,[88] but another Spanish communist, José Barón Carreño

('Robert'), took on the task of rebuilding it. Barón, who came from Melilla in North Africa, travelled constantly between the Occupied Zone and Vichy, trying to reduce the tension which continued to bedevil relations between the Spanish communists and the rest of the Spanish antifascist groups. But what the Spanish communists had achieved in the south could not be repeated in the north. In the Occupied Zone (or Northern Zone, as it was called after November 1942), the PCE never succeeded in forming a military staff—and the non-communists were not likely to succeed where the communists failed. As a result, the PCE Committee in Paris continued to direct the armed movement in the north as best it could, appointing Barón (as earlier it had appointed his predecessors) as a delegate to the committee, with the title of Chief of Staff (Northern Zone).

The PCE leadership in Paris in 1943 faced a difficult situation. Nadal, now secretary-general of the Party, was back in the Southern Zone. Montero, Miret, and Perramón were dead or in Nazi hands. Only Sánchez Vizcaino ('Roger') remained, and only precariously. He had been caught in a round-up in early 1941. Since the Gestapo failed to identify him as the communist leader that he was, he was merely sent to work on the airfield at Beauvais, 80 kilometres north of Paris. He soon escaped, and rejoined the Paris Committee,[89] but in 1943 he was caught again, and this time imprisoned in La Santé. Transferred to the Tourelles barracks, Sánchez Vizcaino again escaped, and now set about restructuring the PCE organization in the Northern Zone. The new leadership consisted of a new troika: himself, Sánchez Biezma ('Torres'), and José Ramón Alvarez.[90] It was to the lasting glory of the Resistance that, like the phoenix, it could regenerate itself every time it seemed destroyed. Each one who fell, as the hymn of the Resistance says, found another in the shadows ready to take his place.[91]

The reason why Juan Montero and Chacón had gone to Rennes was that Brittany had become the centre of Spanish communist activity in the Northern Zone. Combat groups had been formed in that region before the end of 1942. Some Spaniards were working for the commercial enterprise Pyrotechnie Saint-Nicolas, in Rennes and Lorient, and there and elsewhere they obtained dynamite which they made available to the FTP. The Catalan communists were particularly active. In May 1943 the PCF in that area was decapitated, and the FTP requested the Catalan communists to operate in its place and give the impression that the PCF was still functioning. Early in 1944 the Spaniards were themselves the target of the Gestapo. Under their leader Pedro Flores Cano, they carried out a number of acts of sabotage between January and March on the rail routes linking Rennes with Saint-Malo, Brest, and Saint-Nazaire. On 10 February 1944 Flores assassinated a German officer in Rennes. Dressed in the dead man's uniform, he entered the Cinéma Royal, which was reserved for German troops, and left a bomb. A few days later, a similar operation was carried out in the Cinéma Paris. Even more spectacular was the blowing up of the restaurant on the Avenue Janvier used by the German railway technicians.[92] As a result, the Gestapo hunted for Flores and his group with more than usual fury. A traitor came to their aid. One of their number, Josep Borrás Guach from Barcelona, was persuaded by his mistress, who was in the pay of the Gestapo, to make contact with the Abwehr in Angers. He subsequently worked as a double-agent. As a result, the Nazis were able to penetrate the entire Catalan communist network in the region: its cells in Saint-Malo, Brest, and Le Mans fell one after the other. The worst for the Spaniards occurred in Rennes, where their leader Flores had his headquarters at 91 boulevard Cartier in the Colombier district. Several Spaniards were caught when the Gestapo raided the building. A few days later the Gestapo staged a round-up in the city by closing all the streets surrounding place Sainte-Anne and arresting all the Spaniards found in the area. Another sixty-five Spaniards were arrested on the rue Saint-Malo. Nine were shot on 8 June in the Colombier barracks, and the rest were deported to Germany. Flores was among those shot, but not before the Gestapo burned out both his eyes. As for the traitor Borrás Guach, after the war he fled for his life to South America, but vengeance pursued him and he was shot to death in Caracas in 1960.[93]

It was so rare for anyone in the hands of the Gestapo to make an escape that an incident at that moment should be recorded. Vicente Fillol had arrived in Paris from Montpellier and promptly joined the Resistance. He made it a rule never to go anywhere without a pistol. The Gestapo set an ambush for him in a darkened corridor, and Fillol was overpowered before he could even draw his weapon. Taken to the prison on the rue du Cherche-Midi, where he had every finger-nail extracted, he was sentenced to be executed at 6:30 a.m. on 13 April. On 31 March, however, he was driven to a building on the rue Boissy-d'Anglas, near the place de la Concorde. The reasons for this are unknown, but presumably the Gestapo wanted to place him beside another prisoner too weak to be moved. He was about to be taken back to the rue du Cherche-Midi when he flung himself from a balcony, and as luck would have it found a parked, unlocked bicycle. Fillol made his escape.[94]

April 1944 found the PCE committee in Paris reinvigorated. While José Barón was in Gironde trying to co-ordinate the activities of the various units of the south-west Atlantic coast, which still came under the jurisdiction of the Northern Zone,[95] the political leaders were strengthening their ties with the MOI: Sánchez Vizcaino with the MOI's political leaders, and Sánchez Biezma with Ljubomir Ilic ('Louis'),[96] of the MOI's military branch. In May a guerrilla training school was opened in the attic of a dilapidated building in the 2ᵉ *arrondissement*, which served not only as a school but as the students' home. Sánchez Biezma provided the training. Barón and Ilic would on occasion be there to greet the trainees; the reputation of Ilic in particular created a certain awe. When the students had completed the course they were sent out to command guerrilla groups. Barón himself now stayed in Paris as military commander of the Spanish groups in the Northern Zone; he was to die at the moment of liberation.[97] As for the new *guerrillero* officers, none as far as is known was sent inside the Southern Zone. It is unlikely that the battle-hardened *guerrilleros* of the Southern Zone, where men rose in rank by virtue of their feats in arms, would have taken kindly to the notion of a new and unknown commander imposed upon them from without. Nor were the posts of much importance. Enrique Corachán ('Vicente'), for example, took the course in Paris and was sent to Bordeaux,[98] but the command he received was only of a group in the local brigade.[99] The question that remains is why the school took men away from the battlefield to learn guerrilla tactics which could surely be better learnt *in situ*, unless of course the purpose of the training was not so much military as political.

Did the Spanish *guerrilleros* move into action before the occupation of Vichy France by the Wehrmacht in November 1942 (Operation *Attila*), and did their earliest actions anticipate those of the French Maquis? The answers are obscured by prejudice and pride, but the general lines are clear. The French Maquis was not organized before the end of 1942 and did not launch its first attacks before July 1943.[100] Moreover, the first Maquis units, organized by the French communists in Seine-et-Marne and in Doubs in 1942, were quickly annihilated.[101] It is therefore reasonable to call the Spanish *guerrillero* unit operating in Haute-Savoie from June 1942 the first resistance unit in France to enter combat. Early that month in Haute-Garonne, Spanish saboteurs blew up the Toulouse–Saint Gaudens railway line at Cazères.[102] In July some Spaniards living in Toulouse formed a commando which, though it trained for street fighting, had to content itself for the present with sabotage and attacks on personnel. Under the command of José Linares, the commando evolved into the 2nd Brigade of Spanish Guerrilleros.[103] The situation facing this commando is symbolic of the predicament of all the Spanish *guerrilleros* in Vichy France who in a sense were all dressed up with no one to fight. The prestige of Pétain was still too high for a guerrilla action not to be interpreted as provocation. As a result, there was no authentic guerrilla action before the arrival of the Wehrmacht in the Midi in November 1942.[104] On the other hand, the communists, Spanish as French, now benefited from the Vichy and German news bulletins, since in both the zones entire blame for 'terrorist attacks' was thrown on the communists.[105] The next recorded attempt at sabotage was staged in Lot on 11 August 1942, when sticks of dynamite were found on the railway. The blame was duly laid on the large number of Spanish Republicans in the *département*, and especially on the communists.[106]

The Spanish guerrilla units continued to grow, from the fifty men at their inception to some 10,000 well-armed troops at the time of the Liberation.[107] Recruitment had suffered at the beginning because so many Spaniards of military age had been mobilized by the French Government and subsequently caught by the Germans, or interned by the French and similarly trapped by the Germans. But by 1942 more young Spaniards had come of age, and no youth in the world matures earlier than the Spanish. As for the Spaniards who had been pressed into the Groupes de travailleurs étrangers by Vichy,[108] by 1942 most of these were hired out to private employers. The subsequent decentralization was of assistance to the guerrilla movement, because the Spaniards were then loosely supervised and could escape. When, on 4 September 1942, Vichy introduced the system of Service du travail obligatoire, meaning servitude in Germany, there was an added incentive to dodge the draft.[109] The hills and mountains looked more inviting every day. The young Spaniard of no political persuasion could make contact with anarchist or socialist groups, but one party only was fully organized by the time the Wehrmacht invaded the Midi, and one party only was ready with tactics that would make the Wehrmacht wince.

No one in the Resistance could know what Mauthausen meant, but no one was unfamiliar either with the real nature of Nazi Germany and the price of falling into its hands. The true resistant and the innocent suspect would share the same ordeal. The journey to Compiègne, north of Paris, where the red-brick cavalry barracks at Royallieu were now used as a sorting centre. The daily crowd that milled around outside, of parents looking for a son, of women and children looking for a father or a brother. The sweets thrown at random into a departing group. The shouting of the guards, the thud of their falling batons, adding to the anguish of the observers. The cattle-cars intended for loading forty but used for sixty, and with the help of the batons roomy enough for twenty more; the sound of the bolt driven home, then the clatter of the chain, and the huge padlock snapping shut. The last farewells are called, beloved names resound, and the cries of the children drift for a moment in the air and then are lost for ever.

6

Mauthausen, Subsidiary of Hell

The arrival—The prisoner's circle of acquaintance—The SS officer and NCO staff—The Kapos and their role—The first contingent of Spaniards—International friction among the prisoners—The Spaniards as seen by others—The Revier, antechamber of death—The quarry and the 186 steps—Growing solidarity among the Spaniards—Gusen, Ebensee, and other Aussenkommandos—Schloss Hartheim

Ob Tag, ob Nacht,
stets bedacht.
Der Glocke Ruf erklingt.
—Ein Zeichen,
Deine Pflicht beginnt.[1]

The train clanked to a bumping halt in an unknown place. It was half past one in the morning. The long nightmare, we thought, was at an end. We had sat, crouched, sprawled, or stood, 140 to a freight-car, without food or water, shivering in a temperature of twenty degrees below freezing. The train had barely stopped when the bolts of the doors were pulled out, the doors pulled back, and there before us were the SS, a hundred of them, with huge snarling dogs. '*Kanaken, 'raus!*' came the screams of the guards, who at once sent us back to drag out the sick and the dead. Then they began to strike us with their cudgels and rifle butts as they pulled us to the ground. We dropped on to snow which reached our knees, pressing it to our mouths. Some of us had no shoes. Carrying the few possessions we had, we ran the gauntlet through the blows and the bites until we reached the assembly point on the station platform. '*Hijos de puta*', '*Maricones*', the Spaniards were saying. The Germans did not understand, but now let loose a barrage of insults at the Spaniards, who replied, unseen by the SS, with the forearm signal. '*Angetreten!*' We formed up in fives. There we were counted and recounted. Then, '*Im Gleichschritt, marsch!*' We set off in quick march, a row of SS on each pavement, the dogs behind, down the road that leads from the station to the village. The dogs went on baying and nipping at the ankles of the two outer ranks, who soon envied those in the middle three. We stopped. Alberto the interpreter announced: 'We are crossing the village. Anyone who stops or mounts the pavement will be shot on the spot.' We crossed the silent village. The pace now quickened. '*Dalli, dalli!*'[2] The formation had broken from fives into twos. The SS, who seemed to bark more ferociously than the dogs, began to beat those who lagged. We stopped again as Alberto announced: 'We have 3 kilometres to go. Anyone not keeping up will be shot. Anyone who tries to escape will be eaten alive by the dogs.' Jaime, with some view of the road ahead, noticed an apple in the gutter and bent down quickly to scoop it up. A guard saw him, pulled him from the file, and beat him brutally before shoving him back into the ranks. We reached a hill, but the pace did not slacken. *'Wollt ihr laufen, ihr faulen Hunde! ihr Drecksäcke!'* We were indeed running. Paco staggered and dropped the package he was carrying. Two guards fell on him, pulled him from the ranks and began to beat him by the side of the road, in full view of the prisoners behind, as though they would beat him to death. We were gripped in fear now. Would we all die here on the road? We reached a turn and saw the silhouette of a massive fortress above us. We continued to climb, passing a crucifix, and beside it, a post with a skull and crossbones painted in white on its dark base. Finally we arrived at the top of the hill, and caught a glimpse in the moonlight of rails and tip-trucks. The SS ordered us back into fives. In front of us stood the main gate, Mongol in style, with its huge wooden doors which opened as we approached. We passed between the granite pagoda-like towers, under the arch. We had arrived in Mauthausen. All of us but seven: the seven who had died in the four kilometres between the station and the camp.[3]

As we passed through the gates, we had some notion to our right of a granite wall with iron rings. We would learn soon enough what it meant. For those prisoners whose interrogation went badly, their first experience of Mauthausen was to be chained there at the *Klagemauer* for 24 or 48 hours without food or water. In front of us was the parade ground, covered with ice. The searchlights from the perimeter made it bright as day. The SS barked their orders, followed again by *'Dalli, dalli!'*, and we lined up in tens on the square. Men in striped suits, their head shaved, counted and recounted us. They were the Kapos, all of them wearing a green or black triangle. At the order of an SS officer, a Kapo asked, 'Are there any Jews?' One Jew stepped forward. The Kapos rushed to beat him to the ground with their cudgels, while the SS smiled. Then another interpreter, a Spanish-speaking German called Enriquito, came toward us. *'Mariconas!'*[4] he began. We were all exhausted, but his first word left us open-mouthed with astonishment. It was not in the normal run of malapropisms, and it sounded the more idiotic in the mouth of a man so effeminate in speech and manner. In spite of our sufferings, or perhaps because of them, we felt like laughing, and we did. 'Little Spanish Reds,' Enriquito went on, more irate than before, 'you have just entered Mauthausen. You have come to work and obey. There will be no protests of the kind you're used to. Don't ask for anything. Everything here is forbidden. And here you're going to pay me back for everything. You kept me in prison in Montjuich for two years, and now you're going to pay dearly for it, because not one of you—do you hear that?—not one of you is going to get out of here alive.' He lifted his arm, and with his index finger pointed to the chimney of the crematorium. 'You see that smoke? That's what we're going to turn you into!'[5]

We were ordered to undress. Even in the bitter cold, we were still sweating from the climb up the hill with our bags—and the bodies of the seven dead prisoners. For half an hour we stood waiting naked in the snow. Then we were herded into the first building on the right. The SS relieved us of whatever possessions we had brought. A clerk made a note of every item taken. Those were the orders. Every item was to be returned to us when we left. Only we were also told that we would never leave. It was to be our first lesson in the way the system contradicted itself. Every detail had to be in order, if only to observe the principle.[6] We were then jabbed, shoved, or kicked towards the enormous shower-room, sparkling in cleanness and light, where we showered with buckets.[7] Then came the shaving of all our body hair: skull, beard, moustache, armpits, chest, groin, and legs, with a razor that scraped rather than cut. The shaven parts were doused with phenol. A disinfectant, they called it, but it caused such pain in the armpits and the groin that we had to walk with our arms held up and our legs splayed. The same carbolic acid was daubed on open wounds, causing the men to scream or faint. Next came the medical examination. A prisoner pointed out to a clerk that he had a wound in the lung, no doubt hoping that he would be given light work. A veteran whispered never to say that here: it was the quickest route to the gas chamber. We would find out later, to our astonishment, that we were never sick in the normal way.[8]

After the shower and the medical, another wait: for half an hour we again stood barefoot in the snow. Then we were issued our blue and white striped uniform, or *Drillich* as they called it. Some of the uniforms bore the holes traced by the bullets that had put an end to the lives of the last men to wear them. Then two clogs, not necessarily a pair, and many of them with projecting nails: we were given no socks. It was up to us to find rags to put around our feet, and the paper of the cement bags to use as underwear.

We were then sent off to the quarantine blocks, to a musical accompaniment: two German prisoners, one on violin, the other on accordion, playing 'Addio alla vita' from *Tosca*. The SS never missed a chance for amusement. We found the quarantine blocks completely isolated not only from the main camp but also from one another. On our arrival a Kapo known as Popeye, who was not a Spaniard and spoke to us through an interpreter, gave us the Block greeting: 'If you smoke, we'll kill you. If you drink at the wrong time, we'll kill you. If you talk too loud, or make a noise, twenty-five strokes with the bullwhip. Anyone not German who puts the blame on a German, we'll kill you. You are here to die.' The whole thing was so ridiculous that at the end, despite our misery and our fatigue, we again began to laugh, whereupon Popeye drove us all outside the Block, and we found ourselves stamping our clogs in the snow.

At last came the moment of rest. The quarantine blocks, however, had no bunks. We lay on worn-out palliasses, in rows of five, packed on our right sides like spoons, unable after that to move our position. A single blanket covered the five of us, thrown over us by the Block Kapo when we had taken our position. In some cases a Block Kapo would walk across the bodies, stopping to dance upon us and crushing our ribs with his boots.

So ended our first day. Everything we had had been taken from us. We had the feeling that the we were nothing, simply *Stücke*. It was to foster that sentiment that the whole system had been invented.

No man or woman or child who survived Mauthausen remembers his arrival there in quite the same way. The above description is a composite of various accounts by survivors of the convoy of 849 men which reached Mauthausen from Strasbourg on the night of 12–13 December 1940.[9] In no sense does it capitalize upon the most dramatic elements from each. On the contrary, the picture it gives is banal and run-of-the-mill. A consignment of prisoners might be kept standing in the *Appellplatz* right through a freezing night.[10] Vilanova points out that the arrival at Mauthausen was possibly worse than anywhere else, since almost all convoys reached Mauthausen by train,[11] and the prisoners had to march more than 4 kilometres from the station to the camp, with a steep and often slippery hill which they had to take at a run.[12] Conditions were proportionately better in spring or autumn, but the heat of summer provided a different agony. Charles Renaud, who arrived in Mauthausen in April, when the main preoccupation was thirst, describes how his convoy entered the main gate to see, instead of prisoners chained to the *Klagemauer* on the right, a prisoner left hanging from the chain on the left, his arms behind his back in that most agonizing of positions known as the *Pfahlbinden*. He adds that it was the Kapos, not the SS, who helped themselves to the incomers' watches and wedding rings in exchange for some spoonfuls of water.[13] Finally, not all prisoners arrived in the dead of night, unseen by any. Others describe how they passed through the village of Mauthausen in broad daylight, the villagers showing 'prodigious indifference'[14] or the children throwing stones at them and shouting, 'You'll soon be on *Totenberg* and up the chimney!'[15] In daylight the prisoners would have glimpsed the Danube and noticed how very grey it was, like everything else in front of them. Shades of the prison-house began to close before the prisoner had even stepped inside.

Arriving in Mauthausen has been described as landing on another planet. The life, to call it a life, to which the prisoners had to adapt revolved around a small number of men in authority whose personalities, if not always their names, remain engraved in the memories of the survivors. There were the SS officers, most of whom remained in their posts throughout their internment. There were the sentries and the guards, who were transient and faceless. And there were the Kapos, fellow-captives turned into captors, wielding the instrument of authority closest at hand to the hapless inmate. It was usually the Kapos whom the prisoners knew best. No SS slept in the fortress, and few SS ever entered it apart from the Rapportführer and his team of

NCOs. Each NCO was responsible for a Block, and it was the responsibility of the Rapportführer to collect and check the reports of the NCOs. As for the SS guards in the watchtowers, they entered and left by steps mounted on the outside, not the inside, of the walls. The result was that only a few prisoners, notably the *Prominenten* who worked in the offices and services, came to know in detail the personalities of their tormentors. Other facts would emerge later, when some of those tormentors stood trial for their lives.

In the case of the SS officers, two impressions were generally shared: they were young, well built, and physically attractive, but mentally of very limited grasp. Until National Socialism lifted them out of obscurity, Ziereis was a carpenter, Bachmayer a cobbler, Schulz a blacksmith, and Streitwieser an unsuccessful mechanic. As for their moral sense, the more depraved they were, the faster they would be advanced.

Franz Ziereis, born in Munich in 1907, remained in command of Mauthausen, and of all its dependencies throughout Austria, for almost the entire period of the war, rising from the rank of SS-Sturmbannführer to Obersturmbannführer in 1943 and to Standartenführer in 1944. Blond, blue-eyed, and tall, he had served as a corporal in the Reichswehr of the Weimar Republic, later became an instructor at *KL*-Oranienburg, and was only 34 when Himmler picked him for the top post at Mauthausen. He owed his promotion to his energy. He had few other virtues. He impressed others mainly by his lack of education, so marked that he could barely read and write. Nor did he ever take part in a military action, despite the rank he reached of full colonel. He countered this with a swagger and a high degree of affectation, with his hands constantly on his hips, so that the Spaniards dubbed him *el Pavo* (the Peacock).[16] But there was a darker side to his nature than mere arrogance. He was emotionally unbalanced. So for that matter was his wife Ida, whose testimony at the 1967 trial in Cologne was merely self-serving.[17] The whole Ziereis family, living in their massive chalet overlooking the Danube and the Linz-Perg road, was a model of correct SS behaviour. The Spaniard Mariano Constante, assigned as orderly to the Oberscharführer in Ziereis's office, found himself on occasion in Ziereis's house. Ida's bestiality, he says, matched her husband's. Hairy as a witch, and robust and strong, she could not even pass Constante and his fellow-prisoners without kicking them. Their three male children, the oldest of whom was 10 and wore the uniform of the Hitlerjugend, treated the prisoners like dogs, tripping them up or kicking them in the ankles, whereupon their mother would scream with laughter.[18] But Ziereis was hard to please. Three sons were not enough, he would tell her, for an SS officer to achieve his full ambition. It was an unfounded accusation: Ziereis received promotions as fast as he could expect them. But receiving no higher appointment, in self-pity and resentment he found solace in drink, both in private with his fellow-officers at home,[19] and in public in front of his prisoners.[20] The prisoners had special cause to fear his celebrations. One of his own sons admitted, in a sworn statement after the Liberation, that on his birthday his father would instruct him in the art of shooting at live targets. Lining up forty prisoners in front of his son, and loading the pistol himself, Ziereis watched while his son shot down all forty, one after the other, as if at a fair.[21]

The second-in-command, responsible for the Mauthausen garrison, was SS-Hauptsturmführer Georg Bachmayer. Dark of complexion, with nervous eyes and furtive looks, he trembled at the lips when enraged. He was none the less a cold-blooded killer. As the officer in charge of security (Schutzhaftlagerführer), he was responsible for discipline, including capital punishment. All Spanish survivors remembered him as one of the most savage tormentors of their group, but in time he seemed to soften a little towards them, out of involuntary respect, and began to appoint some of them *Prominenten*. The key to his character, like that of Ziereis, is to be found in the poverty of his early life and the rapidity of his rise, but the sense of grievance of this young officer may have run deeper than most. One of his hands was crippled: its middle finger was permanently bent, and the first phalanx of the index finger was missing.[22] The SS tended to avoid him. They considered him of partly gypsy stock, and they passed the word that his body smelled.[23] Since he was eager to pass himself off as a man of breeding, and chased women shamelessly, it can be understood that his personality was more excitable and volatile than most. He adored his wife and children, as well he might. Frau Bachmayer stood out from all the other SS wives. Again it was a detail of Spanish prisoners, including Mariano Constante, who attested to it. She received the prisoners with a smile and even a shy '*guten Tag*', calling them 'men' and telling them gently the jobs they had to do. The two little Bachmayer daughters were, like their mother, gentle and charming, and the smiles of these three were the only smiles that the prisoners had seen, or would see, for years.[24] If her husband, the 'bloody gypsy' (*gitano sanguinario*), adored her, he also adored the prostitutes in the officers' brothel, and bestowed his free time equally on both his homes. He would return to his house with his uniform spattered with the blood of his last victim, hand it to his servant, the Red triangle Karl Oliva, and re-emerge in a fresh uniform, with every stain removed, to receive the adulation of the girls in the home away from home.[25]

It was the consensus, however, that the most powerful man in

Mauthausen after Ziereis was not Bachmayer but SS-Obersturmführer Karl Schulz, head of the Politische Abteilung. This was the branch office which the Gestapo maintained in every camp, with a permanent representative acting as a political counsellor and answering directly to the regional Gestapo authorities as well as to the camp commandant. The representative was responsible for seeing that the orders received for the extermination of a particular prisoner or group of prisoners were duly carried out—by the SS in uniform or by the prisoners whom they designated. In the case of Schulz, like Ziereis and Bachmayer he held his post at Mauthausen for virtually the entire period of the war, from 1 September 1939 to 3 May 1945, when the SS fled. Throughout that time, he served in the capacities of registrar, civil magistrate, and director of the crematorium, and no prisoner, from the moment he arrived, lived outside the clutch of the man known as 'the Bird of Death'.

The son of a postal clerk, Schulz was born with a misshapen foot, which forced him to wear special shoes. Starting out as a railroad metal-worker, he was ambitious enough to find a post with the criminal police (*Kripo*) in Cologne. He was not lacking in intelligence, and taught himself fluent French. He then obtained a post in *KL*-Dachau and was promoted to SS-Hauptsturmführer. For reasons that were not explained even at his trial in 1966–7, Schulz was demoted in 1939 to SS-Hauptscharführer and sent to Mauthausen. The Politische Abteilung's office was just opening, and Schulz at once applied for, and obtained, its top position. He later described how Ziereis introduced him to his responsibilities: 'When you get up, tear the day off the calendar; the rest of the day is yours.' Schulz found it a labour of love: he ran the office from 6 a.m. to 6 p.m. He built a reputation for himself as the *Lager*'s *éminence grise*, and lived like a little king, his fingers manicured and toes pedicured by the inmate servants, and his huge hound Hasso at his feet. His home—he lived with his wife and son in the house of the village pharmacist, close by the station—was fitted with furniture made by the prisoners, using the finest wood. It was a case of what the SS called corruption, and when Bachmayer intercepted a delivery, it led to a violent quarrel between the two. Schulz's character has been called superficial but inscrutable. At least parts of it are known, and alcoholism helps to explain his violent rages.

Schulz's principal aides, in the nine-room compound that made up the Politische Abteilung, were SS-Oberscharführer Werner Fassel, SS-Unterscharführer Wilhelm Mueller, and SS-Unterscharführer Hans Prellberg von Brunswick.[26] He also had, at some time or other, twenty German, Czech, and Spanish prisoners, and, late in the war, twelve female civilian employees. The women, who were probably all local Austrians, were introduced in 1943 so as to release the SS men for service in the front line. The men, however, were not sent, and the twelve women were the cause of very frequent quarrels. Schulz's marriage was already in ruins before they arrived, so Schulz was especially pleased to have the women around him.

Since Climent Sarrión was among those who worked in the compound, as we have seen, he was asked to testify at Schulz's trial in Cologne. So was Francesc Boix, since the photographic laboratory in which he worked was housed in the front of the same building. It was in the office of Schulz's subordinate Wilhelm Mueller that the prisoners were usually interrogated and tortured, but all Schulz's SS staff did their part, and the only precaution taken to conceal the evidence was to stop at the approach of a visitor. Bloodstains were visible all over the furniture. The shelves contained reports and bullwhips side by side. Climent Sarrión described how Schulz remained relatively correct towards those who worked with him in the compound but became insanely violent toward those he interrogated. A hackneyed phrase became his favourite, and he repeated it like the catechism: 'The road out of the *Lager* passes through the crematorium.' He had no oven in his office but he had a little stove. Whether mid-winter or mid-summer he would yell to his subordinate Hans Prellberg, 'Prellberg, light the stove!' That was Schulz imperious. There was also Schulz exultant, at which times he would call, 'Light the stove, Prellberg!' The Spaniard Climent recalled how in February 1942 a group of elderly Jews stood waiting naked in the snow outside the compound. Schulz beckoned to two small rabbis to enter his office, asking them if they were cold. The stove glowed with heat. They moved towards it. Schulz then seized one of them and seated him on top of it. The burns were intense. When lifted off—he was unable to move—pieces of his flesh stuck to the stove. Two days later the rabbi died in the *Revier*. Another favourite game for Schulz was to force prisoners into narrow holes dug in the ground, which he sealed with wooden lids.[27]

Mauthausen was hell in the sense that it was man's finest attempt to create a subsidiary on earth. From the devil's point of view, it was spoilt by sporadic human weakness. Schulz's behaviour could exceed what the civilian staff could endure. Many a time Frau Steinman and Frau Steiner left the office in tears. Even Frau Neugebauer, who was Schulz's mistress, broke down, but it was Fräulein Brigitte Sombeck who provided the sensation. Stunningly beautiful, refined, well groomed, she was from her arrival the cynosure of all eyes. There could not have been an SS who did not look for some excuse to drop by the compound to get a peek at her. All tried to date her, and certainly Schulz. Schulz decided that prisoners would no longer be brutalized while the secretaries were present, but it was asking much of the SS always to restrain their instincts. One day in the autumn of 1944, Werner Fassel began beating a prisoner in front of her. Brigitte Sombeck broke down in tears. Fassel went up to her to console her. She punched him in the face.[28]

At the lower levels of command, five names remained prominent in the collective memories of the survivors, not least the Spaniards. SS-Obersturmführer Heinrich Hans Eisenhöfer was generally the first officer they set eyes on; as the officer responsible for the *Effekten-kammer* and the expropriation of the prisoners' belongings, he was always present at the moment that new inmates arrived.[29] Anton Streitwieser, who served under Bachmayer, came from a working-class family and had almost no education. He had arrived from *KL-*Dachau as an Unterscharführer in 1938, when he was only 22. He was soon appointed commandant at Gusen, but in May 1940 he was dismissed from his post for setting up his own pig farm, using as pig food the rations he embezzled from the prisoners' supplies. He was later sent to fight on the Russian front, and after being wounded four times he was reassigned to Mauthausen. Late in the war he was promoted to Obersturmführer and given command of the Aussen-kommando at Schwechat, then Floridsdorf, and finally Mödling-Hinterbrühl, where he would direct the final evacuation.[30] Energetic, ambitious, arrogant—he would on occasion parade before the prisoners dressed in his fencing costume—he was most remembered for the hideous hound, a bitch named Asta,[31] which he trained to mutilate the prisoners. The French survivor René-Jean Demanche, who was himself its victim, has described how the dog would savage a prisoner for three or four minutes while Streitwieser calmly observed. Another prisoner, Franz Wessely, died in Floridsdorf in the autumn of 1944 when Streitwieser loosed the hound and it ripped off his penis.[32] More than once, in Mauthausen's Block 16 in the quarantine section, four inmates were taken out and thrown to the SS dogs for training. The shrieks and the groans continued for half an hour. The next morning the mortality Kommando picked up four corpses alongside the Block.[33] Such incidents have been recorded only because they were witnessed by survivors. Most horrors were not witnessed, or witnessed only by those who were next in line as victims.

The command of Mauthausen's infamous quarry was entrusted to SS-Obersturmführer Johannes Bernhard Grimm, whom the Spaniards knew as el Seco.[34] Grimm entered the Allgemeine SS on 8 October 1941, and the Waffen SS on 10 April 1942, and was assigned to

Mauthausen that year. With startling candour, cynicism, or naïveté, he admitted later at his trial at Dachau that some 10,000 prisoners died in the quarry during the three years of his mandate, 'some of them as a result of the work load, which was too heavy for anyone in their weak physical condition'. He added, however, that most of the prisoners were murdered in one of three or four conventional ways.[35] Grimm found time to set up a kitchen garden beside the quarry for his personal use, fertilizing it with the ashes from the crematorium.[36] Sometimes the Spaniards were able to steal a tomato, or a beetroot, or a potato, but they risked their lives even in trying.[37] Grimm's immediate subordinate was Otto Drabek, but the man most remembered by the Spaniards in the quarry was SS-Hauptscharführer Johann Spatzenegger. So fanatical a Nazi was Hans Spatzenegger that his own comrades labelled him 'the Nazi'.[38] 'Spatz' was the name the inmates gave him,[39] but it was never said except in fear and loathing.

The two others were staff-sergeants and their reputation no less fearful. Michel de Boüard considers them on a par with Bachmayer and Spatzenegger as the top four in brutality.[40] SS-Oberscharführer Andreas Trum,[41] tall, thick-lipped, with a long pale face, had entered the SS in 1940 at the age of 19; he arrived in Mauthausen in 1943 to assume the post of Arbeitsdienstführer, responsible for all the work details, and remained there until the end. Finally, SS-Oberscharführer Josef Niedermayer, an Austrian from nearby Linz,[42] joined the SS in 1938 at 17 and arrived in Mauthausen in April 1942, also staying until the end. There he was placed in charge of the *Bunker* and (from November 1944) of Block 20, where some of the worst horrors were committed.[43] He was also responsible (under Eisenhöfer) for collecting the personal effects of the 4,000 prisoners[44] who were assigned to the gas chamber,[45] which was connected to the *Bunker*. The *Bunker* consisted of thirty-three cells (*Kastenhofen*) measuring 5.4 square metres and one cell of 8.4 square metres, and was used for special prisoners and for further interrogation of others. The special prisoners included British, American, and other Allied airmen[46] who had fallen into German hands, and in the final months of the war, many prominent European politicians were incarcerated here under false names.[47] Of the 4,600 prisoners who were thrown into these cells, only 400 survived.[48] Niedermayer himself admitted at his trial that he had carried out some 400 executions in the *Bunker*.[49]

'Over 4,000 died in the *Bunker*' is history's terse conclusion. How did they die? Some clues are available. SS-Hauptscharführer Hans Michael Killermann would sit on a stool in one of the cells. In front of him would dangle the body of a naked man, his feet bound to the top bolts of the cell door, his head brushing the ground. A cord was attached to his testicles. Killermann would draw the cord slowly, then give a sharp pull and let the writhing body crash against the iron door like a hammer against a gong.[50]

Such were the men, to call them men, who held in their hands the lives of the 7,000 Spaniards who arrived in Mauthausen and to whom each prisoner, whenever summoned, would incant the ritualistic phrase of abject submission: '*Häftling* (and his number) *gehorsam zur Stelle.*' It would be unwise to suggest that others were less bestial; they were simply less visible, or there a shorter time. Such a one was SS-Oberscharführer Johann Müller, who was at Mauthausen (as Rapportführer) only from 1942 to 1943. Tall, strong, and totally without feeling, he was dubbed 'Boxer' by the prisoners, both for his gait (he rolled from side to side in a prize-fighter's swagger), and for his custom, after first putting on a glove, of knocking prisoners to the ground with a single punch in the face. Mariano Constante apparently attracted Müller's attention, since Müller liked to call the Spaniard '*Nonneschlächter*'—in fun, obviously, since the SS were hardly concerned about the slaughter of nuns.[51] But despite everything the SS could do, the more immediate threat to the inmates' survival came from the class of prisoners selected by the SS to serve as Kapos. The essential idea of delegating power to prisoners was to destroy all sense of honour and human compassion among *KZ* inmates. The Kapos were victims and executioners at the same time. Morally weak, and faced with the choice of dying or killing, they were content to murder others in the hope of saving themselves. Some of these myrmidons were murderers already. The first step in building up a Kapo class at Mauthausen had come in the very first week of the *Anschluss*: every prison and penitentiary in Austria was emptied of its criminals, those with suspended sentences were placed under arrest, and all were sent to Dachau, and from there, later in 1938, to the new camp at Mauthausen. It was these holders of the Green triangle, 'the founding members', as they grotesquely called themselves, who became the first Kapos and enjoyed all the privileges pertaining to club membership: alcohol, tobacco, free access to the '*Puff*' (the camp brothel),[52] and the right to steal with impunity the rations and clothing of the inmates.[53] The very first Kapo of all at Mauthausen was the Green triangle August Adam, who made it a habit to ask the incoming prisoners what their profession was. Whenever he found a lawyer, priest, magistrate, or professor—'*ein Eierschädel*' in the parlance of the SS—he informed him with delight that here in the *Lager* the world stood downside up, and if they had any trouble in understanding that, the translator—he tapped his *gummi*—was there to help; whereupon he made free use of the translator, and when he was satisfied, lined up the chosen group into a *Scheissekompanie* and marched them off to clean the latrines.[54]

Much was said, during the trials of SS officers after the war, about the regulations from Berlin strictly forbidding the Kapos to strike the prisoners. In the case of Mauthausen, it was admitted, by Ziereis's adjutant Viktor Zoller, that Ziereis allowed and even encouraged Kapos to strike.[55] Such regulations, of course, had no more to do with reality than the famous report that even an SS member could be arrested for ill-treating a prisoner, and that at Mauthausen one wing of the *Bunker* was permanently reserved for naughty SS who were caught red-handed. At the trial at Dachau an SS corporal announced with a straight face that a fellow-member had been sentenced to five years' imprisonment at Mauthausen for killing a Polish Jew without reason.[56]

Up to March 1945, all the top Kapo posts, with some notable exceptions, were held by Greens, and often by the worst of Greens. The highest post of all (Lagerälteste I) was held for a time by the German Schöps, who wore Red, but for no known reason. Brutal, and servile to the SS, he was always ready to volunteer to hang his own comrades. Under him, the Lagerälteste II was the Austrian Green Franz Unek, from Vienna, who was considered by some to be the worst sadist in the entire *Lager*. He had moved up from Kapo of Block 12, which housed the Spaniards and French, and his victims numbered in the hundreds.[57]

The best known Kapo in the history of Mauthausen was not Schöps, however, but Magnus Keller, whom everyone in the *Lager* knew as King Kong,[58] on account of his enormous size, his ambling gait, and his simian rages. A Munich motor mechanic, ruddy, often drunk, he had entered the *KZ* (Dachau) as a Red triangle, and was probably a follower of the fallen Ernst Röhm. Transferred to Mauthausen on 27 September 1939, he launched himself on a highly successful career that took him through the ranks of the Kapos until in 1941 he was appointed Lagerälteste I. Thereafter he selected the subordinate Kapos, and they obeyed him blindly. Keller was a man who inspired real horror, and many a prisoner was strangled in a his enormous hands.[59] Sometimes a mere frown from Keller, puffing perennially on his long-stemmed porcelain pipe, his pearl-grey eyes set in a Buddha-like head, was all the indication given that a prisoner was to die, or suffer worse than a quick death. It was to the refinement of his tortures that he owed the astounding privileges he enjoyed: not only a bedroom, radio, servants, and the like, but liberty to go into town by himself, go fishing on the lake, and hunting in the woods.[60] To the millions of *KL* prisoners whose thoughts were concentrated on getting through the day, or the minute, such freedom was beyond their dreams.

It is most unlikely that a history of the Kapos of the *KZ* will ever be written. It is surprising how imprecise all accounts have been in their regard. The reason for this may well be that while the SS had the opportunity to flee in May 1945, and took it, the Kapos could not follow them, and in the Liberation many of the worst were beaten to death before their identity and background had been properly established. Most of them are known only by their nickname: Popeye, for example, or Rudi el Gitano.[61] The Spaniards and all others could remember the German Green Johann Zaremba, the Kapo of the quarry Kommando, who had a little hut in the quarry in which to take refuge from the rain and snow,[62] and whose brutality made him the natural choice of his superior Spatzenegger;[63] and another German Green, Josef Pelzer, the Kapo of the *Steinträger* as they mounted the 186 steps.[64] There was also Karl Maierhofer, a German gypsy Black and the self-important leader of the band, whose knowledge of music was limited to beating time, and who relished the public hangings for the chance they gave him to perform—as the strutting drum-major with the white kepi decorated with double gold bars. Karl, as he was known to everyone except the Spaniards, who called him Llup, was equally proud of his second hat, that of semi-official night executioner. Ganz would say to him, 'I don't want to see this man around here tomorrow morning,' and that night Karl, with two acolytes, would hang, strangle, or drown him in the latrines.[65] Other prisoners could remember Indalecio González González and 'el Negro', both Spaniards, both at Gusen, who were as brutal as any Green.[66] Another Spanish Kapo, José Palleja ('el Negus'), enjoyed a reputation that travelled far beyond the Aussenkommandos at Schwechat, Floridsdorf, and Mödling where he worked. A notorious pederast, he beat his fellow-prisoners, especially the French and including the sick, for the sheer love of it; more than one died from the beating.[67] The French captain Billotte, though marked for life by blows inflicted by Palleja, lived to see the day when he would confront the Spaniard before a military tribunal in Toulouse. He described him as the 'most terrible of Kapos: Kapos in other camps would threaten prisoners with a transfer to the care of "el Negus" if they caused trouble, and we knew what that meant.'[68] Such documented cases were the exceptions: the general picture of the Kapos at Mauthausen, as elsewhere, remains extremely blurred.

We have seen that the first contingent of Spaniards entered Mauthausen on 6 August 1940.[69] The train ride in summer was a terrible ordeal, and some Spaniards had died from suffocation and dehydration. Frédéric

Ricol, of Paris, testified in court that he had gone three days and three nights without food or water,[70] and José Escobedo, an anarchist turned socialist from Teruel, who had been taken prisoner by the Germans at Dunkirk and sent first to Stalag I-B in East Prussia, attests that the 169 men in his convoy who arrived at Mauthausen on 9 August travelled for four days without food or water.[71] Thirst drove some to the point of madness, whereupon others killed them.[72] Mariano Constante writes that his Compagnie de travailleurs numbered 350 when taken prisoner in June 1940, and that the Gestapo records show that only 300 of them reached Mauthausen.[73] Roger Heim writes that of the 450 Frenchmen in his group, 130 were dead either on arrival or within a few days of arrival.[74]

If other contingents arrived in the dead of night, without the villagers of Mauthausen seeing them as they passed through from the station on the way westward to the camp, the first Spanish contingent on 6 August arrived at 8 o'clock in the morning, in full view of the villagers.[75] No prisoner died on the road in that particular convoy, despite the fact that many Spaniards had not been able to replace the boots they had worn out in the forced march from France to Germany. It was a testimony to the endurance of the Spaniards, whose long experience of deprivation worked in their favour.

At the time of the arrival of the first Spanish contingents, the camp was not yet a fortress. It was surrounded only by electrified wire. Escobedo recalls arriving through the quarry and the 186 steps.[76] His group climbed the steps in ranks of five, passing other Spaniards carrying rocks who indicated that they had arrived there three days earlier. The great gates to the fortress were not quite completed, and 1,500 prisoners were engaged in the Baukommando, building—at enormous human cost—the main road leading up to the garage entrance, the *Appellplatz*, and the massive granite ramparts. The only other inmates they found were Germans, Austrians, Czechs, and Poles, with some stateless Russians, to a total of some 6,000.[77]

On 24 August, a further contingent of 430 Spaniards arrived from Angoulême, via Colmar and Strasbourg. It consisted of Spanish families which had been interned at Angoulême by the French Vichy Government. Sending them as families to Mauthausen was an administrative error, since Mauthausen was not built to cater for women and children. But the matter of sending Spanish women and children to any place in Germany, when Angoulême is so much closer to Spain, raises a broader question: which government—Vichy, Berlin, or Madrid—was responsible for the decision? The answer is probably all three, Madrid and Vichy sharing the desire to be rid of these unwanted elements, and Berlin always happy to assist. The situation on the Mauthausen platform on 24 August attests to the lack of preparation. Usually a convoy was cleared from the station within minutes. This one remained there for two or three hours, while the Mauthausen commandant was reportedly in phone contact with the Spanish Embassy in Berlin. At the end of that time it was decided that the men and boys over 12 would enter *KL*-Mauthausen while the women and children would remain on the train, to be transported to Spain.[78]

The experience of Lázaro Nates provides a useful case-study. He arrived on 24 August at the age of 16, with his mother, and younger brother aged 12. Although his mother lied about Lázaro's age by reducing it by four years, it made no difference, since the SS judged the children on the basis of height and build. She and her younger son were subsequently returned to Laredo, her home town in Spain, where she suffered the fate of any wife or widow of a Republican. In her case she was thrown into prison as proxy for her husband, a centrist who had served in the Civil War as a village mayor and who was then working, and dying, in railroad construction in the Sahara. Their son Lázaro meanwhile was witness to the fate of those veterans in the convoy who had been disabled in the Civil War: they were liquidated on arrival, without their names being entered in the camp registry.[79] He himself was assigned to Block 17, but other children were housed in Block 16[80] and Block 18, the latter under the command of 'Al Capone', one of the most degenerate of the Kapos.[81] Block 16 gave the children a quick insight into life at Mauthausen, since it was kept for food experiments: the prisoners there were fed a diet abundant in barley, with the result that they became fat but had less strength than ever.[82]

The fate of the Spanish children, forty-two boys between the ages of 12 and 17, is in some dispute. It has been said that some of the children worked in the quarry, where they were shown no more favour than the adults and where they could literally watch their fathers die.[83] The testimony of Lázaro Nates, as a survivor, must however take precedence. He had the good fortune to be selected as a Stubendiener, or Block orderly, a post of privilege that usually went to youths of 15–18 years of age;[84] as such he was in a good position to know every detail of his compatriots' work assignments, though it is still possible that some of the Spanish children were given assignments without his knowledge. According to Nates, all the Spanish youths were enrolled, from the beginning, in a special unit organized by Bachmayer and known as the Kommando Poschacher, Poschacher being the name of the Austrian firm which derived the benefit from this unremunerated labour.[85] The unit was exclusively Spanish, and the youths remained in it only until they reached the age of 18, at which time they were assigned to another Kommando as adults. The Kommando Poschacher was assigned to a different quarry, the firm's own small quarry near Mauthausen station, which employed Austrian civilians (all of them over 60 years of age) as skilled workers to operate the machines. At first the boys were marched there each day along a hill road that skirted the village, but later the SS lost interest in guarding their secret and the boys subsequently marched through Mauthausen. The Poschacher unit, wherever it was assigned,[86] enjoyed blessings unknown to those they left behind: however hesitant and isolated, expressions of sympathy and consideration were shown to them by the local Austrian villagers—and when this chapter of their lives was closed some of these same Spanish boys would choose to marry girls from the village of Mauthausen.[87] One such was Manuel Gutiérrez. He and Lázaro Nates found themselves in a detail scheduled for transfer to Gusen. In discussing the matter they agreed that whatever Mauthausen was, it was a known factor, while Gusen was an unknown, but under the same management. At the moment that they assembled in the *Appellplatz*, they decided to try the impossible. In front stood the snub-nosed Rapportführer whom they knew as 'el Chato'. Beside him towered 'King Kong'. Nates suddenly called out, ungrammatically but in the only language permitted: '*Wir wollen bleiben hier, da hier sind unsere Väter!*' A prisoner of Mauthausen was calling out from the ranks with a plea to stay in the place he was because he liked to be close to his father! The whole idea was so totally unexpected that 'el Chato' and 'King Kong' stood looking at each other for a moment in silent wonder and then broke out in uncontrollable laughter. The Rapportführer forgot even to check the matter out, thinking no doubt that the request was so outlandish that the facts had to be true. Perhaps he was grateful for the amusement. In any event, the upshot of the incident was that both Nates and Gutiérrez remained in their places in Mauthausen, and both survived. The same Gutiérrez, after the Liberation, returned to France and married a French girl, but his heart remained with the Austrian girl whose house they used to pass on the way to the quarry and who was always there to smile to him. In the end Gutiérrez returned to Mauthausen and married the Austrian. Today they live in Savoie, and return occasionally to Mauthausen to visit friends in the village.[88]

Razola considers the Spanish contingent of 849 that arrived on the night of 12–13 December 1940 to be the largest of all. At that time the only camps in operation in Austria were Mauthausen and Gusen. These large-scale convoys continued up to the summer of 1941,[89] and that year, according to Hans Maršálek's records, no fewer than 8,000 Spaniards arrived.[90]

The Spaniards had by now moved into the unenviable position of replacing the Poles as the national group with the highest death rate, at least at Gusen. In June 1941 one in every four mortalities was a Spaniard; in October 1941, the ratio was three in every four, and in December 1941, four in every five.[91]

The Spaniards, like other national groups, were housed together, but they soon came into contact with other national groups, and they discovered what all discovered: international solidarity faced all kinds of obstacles, because the national groups in general were unable to free themselves from national prejudice and animosity.[92] The Czechs did not forget Munich, and were bitter against the French; they would have been equally bitter against the British, except that there were not yet any Britons in Mauthausen to be bitter against, and besides, that bitterness was assuaged by the fact that Britain was showing no sign of surrendering. The Poles remembered the Phony War, and shared the feelings of the Czechs. The Germans and the Austrians blamed the French for allowing themselves to be defeated. The Russians, when they began to arrive in late 1941, shared most of these sentiments. As for the Spaniards, with their experience of France limited to the concentration camps and indented service, the bitterness was profound. The ignominy of the French collapse, and the reality of Vichy, made francophobia the one camp passion in which almost all the prisoners could indulge. Razola and Constante write that in the eyes of many national groups the French symbolized 'non-intervention in Spain, the abandonment of Poland, the repudiation of treaty obligations, and the spirit of collaboration.'[93] The resentment was directed not just at France in the abstract but at the French individually. The Frenchman Jean Laffitte attests to this: 'Generally speaking, everybody hated France. We found nothing around us but indifference, contempt, and hatred. In the opinion of most of the Spaniards, we were a bunch of bastards.'[94] Another Frenchman, the journalist Paul Tillard, writes of the brutal and imbecilic Spanish Kapo called 'el Negus', who terrorized the French prisoners out of rancour for everything he had gone through in a concentration camp in France.[95] What tended to dilute this rancour was the growth of other animosities, and the realization that the SS derived their deepest satisfaction from such animus, which they and their agents encouraged wherever they could.[96]

It was not easy to admit, but Amat Piniella and Alfaya have admitted it, that Spaniards of differing backgrounds (presumably political rather than social) came to blows in futile quarrels.[97] At the same time, the Spaniards felt a common distaste for the Poles, who in 1940 were the only group, apart from the Germans and the Austrians, to be included among the Kapos. As we have seen, these Kapos were at first drawn entirely from the holders of the Green and Black triangles, who together formed a sort of international gang, and the selected Poles were Green.[98] Even among the Poles who wore Red triangles, there were many who should have received Green; they received Red only because they had been arrested outside Poland.[99] The antagonism towards the Poles was widespread among the Western Europeans, whose nickname for them was 'cholera', and even in 1985, at the time of the fortieth anniversary of the Liberation, these feelings had not been forgotten. Père Michel Riquet attests to the anti-Polish sentiment in the camp.[100] Razola describes the Polish Kapos as reactionaries who showed a strong animosity towards the Spaniards.[101] Cinca Vendrell writes of the selfish behaviour of the Poles in general, who treated the Spaniards as if they were their worst enemies.[102] Michel de Boüard refers to them in even harsher terms: 'Some sort of divine egoism seems to have led them into isolation. They wanted to keep all the major posts they had acquired. Their leaders, mostly reserve officers, retained that haughty self-complacency which had in fact already cost them dearly. On the question of anti-Semitism, many of them matched the SS.'[103]

The SS, ever on the watch for some amusement, saw the uses they could make of the *'Puff'*, or camp brothel, to inspire sexual jealousy along national lines. The prostitutes were German, Austrian, or Polish prisoners who had fallen into the trap of volunteering to serve a fixed term in exchange for a promise of freedom.[104] Some Spaniards were issued with tickets,[105] allowing them access to certain prostitutes.[106] Paul Tillard describes how an incident, which might have remained in the realm of the burlesque, degenerated into violent conflict. The German Kapos and *Prominenten*,[107] whose Nazi education had not all been wasted, winced at the idea that prostitutes of German racial purity should be defiled by *Untermenschen*, and persuaded the prostitutes to refuse to cater to the Spaniards. When the Spaniards remonstrated, the two sides fell to blows. The SS stepped in, six ticket-holders were dragged out and hanged, and the brothel returned to normal.[108]

There was nothing normal, of course, about a brothel in the *KZ* universe. It functioned mainly as one more privilege for the Kapos and the *Prominenten*. Only a very few others entered it: only a very few obtained tickets, and only a very few had the strength or inclination to indulge. Those who had the inclination were not usually driven by sexual desire, even though, at Mauthausen at least, the prostitutes were young and pretty. Sexual desire was for most prisoners one of the first things they learned to live without. The idea of a woman was so far from everyday reality that the whole gender seemed to belong to a different genus, one which was on loan to earth from some other planet. What the prisoner wanted most was to be physically in a woman's arms, no more than that, to enjoy, if only for a fleeting moment, the illusion of tenderness, and to relive in his memory the central experience of his life.

It was the Spaniards, and the Czechs, who restored a sense of proportion to these international resentments.[109] No national group had been tested as the Spaniards had been. 'We all knew, on the journey from France, that we were going to be sent to Nazi camps,' says the survivor Juan de Diego, 'but we understood that we were going to work, not to be relentlessly beaten into exhaustion.'[110] The majority of the Spaniards who died at Mauthausen were merely survivors of the Spanish Civil War, not members of the Spanish Resistance in France. But whether they came to Mauthausen in the first category or the second, they were never in doubt about their feelings on Germany. Nor did the Czechs ever lose sight of who the enemy was, and the Greens had good reason to fear them. After the assassination of Reinhard Heydrich, the Czechs in Mauthausen fell victim to terrible reprisals, and of the 3,000 still alive in 1942 there were barely 300 still living in 1944.[111]

As for the Soviets, no group at Mauthausen was larger and none more disparate. Most wore the letter R on their Red triangle, and the rest SU. The R prisoners were civilians, the SU former Red Army soldiers. Few of the R prisoners deserved the Red triangle. Many of them were Ukrainians whom the Soviet authorities had sent to prison in Kiev and Kharkov for various felonies, and who were subsequently prisoners of the Nazis. The Germans offered them their freedom if they agreed to work in Germany. They agreed. But many were accustomed to stealing, and in Germany they continued their usual business; it was for that they were thrown into Mauthausen, whether they were individually guilty or not. These youths were for the most part healthy and robust, but years of concentration camp life would degenerate them. The SU captives were prisoners of war who had been given the choice of starving to death or enlisting in the army of General Vlasov. When in Vlasov's ranks they subsequently deserted or failed to carry out orders, they too were sent to Mauthausen.[112]

It was the Spaniards—the '*Spaniak*', as the SS and the other prisoners called them—who, in the opinion of all observers, came out of this supreme ordeal the best. '*Spanier gut, Niemic nix gut*' was the pidgin German expression frequently heard in praise of the Spanish *Prominenten* and in contempt of the German and Austrian *Prominenten*.[113] Unlike the Poles, the Russians, and many Germans and Austrians, every one of the Spaniards was there because he was an antifascist. Almost all were veterans of the Spanish Civil War. Their youth—the average age of the Spaniards was 27 on their arrival—their military discipline, and their previous experience of concentration-camp life, are factors that help to explain how they coped with *KZ* life better than any other national group.[114] But there is more to it than that. Whether they expressed the libertarian recalcitrance to authority or accepted the iron discipline of the Communist Party, they understood the vital need for solidarity. Christopher Burney, who in Buchenwald formed such adverse impressions of the French, had nothing but admiration for the small group of Spaniards 'who were models of what prisoners should be. . . . They were always polite, helped each other and . . . never allowed a sign of flagging courage to escape them. . . . He who thinks ill of Spaniards should think again. Whatever their faults, they behave like men of dignity.'[115] At Dachau it was the same: a Frenchman writes of their 'exemplary dignity', of their 'great capacity for order and discipline.'[116] The Spaniards also understood the vital need for vigilance. The expression '*immer gucken*', though German, was of Spanish coinage,[117] and the remarkable organization they developed was soon recognized by other groups who often owed their very survival to the Spaniards.[118] The Austrian Hans Maršálek calls them 'masters of organization, moving with cat-like speed'. He adds that they made use of another vital attribute: when they were caught out, their tactic of playing upon a certain innocent oafishness more than once earned them impunity.[119] A man of Czech descent thus recognized in the Spaniards a whole brigade of Good Soldier Svejks.

French survivors in particular have attested to the valour of the Spaniards. Dr Jean Benech writes: 'The Spaniards distrusted us, rightly so, after what had happened in 1938 and 1939. Long before the liberation of the camp, these Spaniards won our admiration by their valour and nobility.'[120] Jean Germaneau goes out of his way to pay tribute to the courage shown by the Spaniards in the Mauthausen Kommando at Hinterberg-bei-Peggau: 'Thanks to them, we were able to obtain weapons, and with our Soviet comrades they were the impetus of our military organization.'[121] Dr François Wetterwald refers to the Spanish colony as 'the most united, the most harmonious. . . . They do not give their friendship freely. But when they give it, the value of it is felt at once. . . . They do not go in for killing, nor denouncing others.'[122] Père Michel Riquet pays equal tribute to the Spaniards, and especially the Spanish communists.[123] The French communist Jean Laffitte, who probably owed his own survival to the help of the Spaniards, pays his tribute to all the Spaniards, irrespective of political affiliation:

The friendship of a Spaniard is a thing of supreme worth. . . . The Spanish collective is admirably organized. One of the most striking paradoxes of Mauthausen is to see a people so individualistic in temperament provide every other national group with a model of perfect organization. Such an organization obeys very simple laws. A Spaniard placed in a good post has the duty to use it at all costs to obtain food for his comrades. A Spaniard in need, whatever his need, must be able to count upon the help of the other Spaniards. All Spaniards owe one another aid and assistance, according to the principle that whoever attacks a Spaniard attacks all Spaniards. . . . The German prisoners do not dare to attack them. As for the Spaniard who is cast out of the collective—and I know only one such case—it is the equivalent of a death sentence. If, on the other hand, the Spaniards undertake to protect a non-Spaniard, that man is saved, provided that he remains worthy of their respect. There are only two sorts of men whose death a Spaniard can watch with indifference, and indeed with satisfaction: cowards and traitors.[124]

What better example of this than the case of Enrique García, who was chosen by the Kapos of Block 13 to be their Stubendiener. When ordered by the Kapos to strike one of his compatriots, he explained to those around him: 'I know it means my death, but I would rather die a thousand deaths than raise my hand against a comrade.' The language is ornate; the sentiment was sincere. He was murdered on the spot.[125]

Laffitte also describes what it meant for a French prisoner to be protected by a Spaniard: 'I have seen Spaniards go up to one of their compatriots, a Kapo in the quarry, and give him this little warning: "You touch a French antifascist, and we'll beat you into pulp".'[126] Sir Robert Sheppard, big, strong, and in the prime of life, was on his way to death from exhaustion after ten days on the Steps. What saved him was the action of the Spaniards, who like others showed great respect for the presence of an Englishman in the camp. Knowing that he would die in the normal way if he stayed on the Steps, they decided to turn him into a stonemason, teaching him the craft virtually overnight.[127] Michel de Boüard writes that in time even the SS came to respect the Spaniards: 'Their courage and esprit, and the cohesion of the group, in spite of so much suffering, earned them what was perhaps the only consideration ever shown by the SS. The Spaniards in Block 12 were allowed to keep a little library, made up of books saved from the fire to which the worthless possessions of every *Zugang* were normally consigned. The library, incidentally, was open to all prisoners.'[128] A library at Mauthausen! The paradox again at work. There was more. There was even, in August 1944, a Spanish theatrical production: a revue, with Spanish music and dances.[129] There was even football on Sunday afternoons, with just three national teams:

German, Polish, and Spanish.[130] There was even a Catalan pugilist, Paulino Espallargas, who occasionally volunteered on Sunday afternoons to box on the *Appellplatz*. Since his opponents were usually German inmates, Paulino could count on the support of most of the crowd.[131]

In what surrealist setting could these things happen, when virtually the entire camp was starving to death, and men relied on Sunday for the chance to husband their strength to survive another week? There are some simple answers: the SS could make up teams with newly arrived prisoners who were still in reasonable health, or they could favour someone like Paulino who offered them the boon of entertainment.[132] The inmates, on the other hand, took part because it was in their own interest. Luis Gil, who arrived in Mauthausen on 8 September 1940, and became Stubendiener to 'King Kong' himself, sums up the secret of their survival: 'In the early period, we Spaniards did not have title to a single privileged post, but we knew from experience that the worst fatigue comes from letting oneself go.'[133]

Those who let themselves go doomed themselves to the care of the SS doctors in the *Revier*. This infirmary was situated, up until 1943, next door to the crematorium. It served as its antechamber, and every prisoner soon learned never to go near it, unless absolutely unable to stand up, at which point the choice was made for him anyway. The SS doctors who supervised the *Revier* made their visits for the sole purpose of selecting the patients for liquidation.[134] Three out of every four were selected.[135]

Our knowledge of what happened in the *Revier* derives from the testimony of the inmate Austrian engineer Ernst Martin, who was made secretary to the chief medical officer, SS-Sturmbannführer Dr Eduard Krebsbach and his successors. He was responsible for keeping the records, making out the death certificates, and handling the correspondence with Berlin and the other camps. On 20 April 1945, Martin was ordered to burn all the archives, but he succeeded in hiding thirteen dossiers in a cupboard in the pharmacy, and at the time of the Liberation he handed these over to the US military authorities. On pages 568–82 of register 5, the term 'heart failure' was given as the cause of death of 203 persons all dying on the same day, 19 March 1945.[136]

Krebsbach was simply the most celebrated of seven physicians who served as SS-Standortarzt at Mauthausen. Four had preceded him when he assumed the post in October 1941. Up to then he had enjoyed a solid reputation as a pediatrician in Cologne. In Mauthausen his fondness for injections earned him the name of 'Spritzbach', and among the Spaniards, 'el Banderillo'.[137] His assignment ended abruptly in June 1943 after he killed a drunken Wehrmacht soldier who had entered his garden. The Gestapo stepped in to prevent an inquest, but Krebsbach was none the less reassigned to *KL*-Kaiserwald, near Riga.[138] Those who replaced Krebsbach, SS-Hauptsturmführer Dr Hermann Friedrich Entress and SS-Sturmbannführer Dr Waldemar Wolter, had already served as his assistants.[139] Another member of the team was a dentist, SS-Hauptsturmführer Dr Wilhelm Henkel, who clearly enjoyed putting on a white gown and entering the operating room as a surrogate surgeon; Henkel was also responsible for extracting the gold teeth from the corpses.

The work of Krebsbach's team consisted of both lethal injections and non-lethal tests. Camp commandant Ziereis, on his death-bed, told Allied interrogators that the injections consisted of intravenous doses of benzene, hydrogen, calcium sulphide, Eumarcon, or Evipan-Natrium.[140] In April 1942 a group of thirty Spaniards and Russians, working in the quarry, were taken to the subsidiary infirmary in Block 5 and given an injection in the region of the heart. The injections produced an inflammation which spread slowly up to the shoulder like a blue pencil mark. For the next few days the victims were half paralysed in the head and shoulders and for two weeks even the strongest had to walk more or less on hands and knees. Every afternoon they had to report to the infirmary, where an SS doctor stuck his fingers into the painful region. Those who were too weak were taken to Block 20 where they were finished off with an intracardiac injection of benzene. Among the victims was the Spaniard Pere Vives.[141] At the end of two weeks, Krebsbach asked the survivors if they still felt pain. No, they wisely replied. Apparently delighted with the success of the experiment, he gave each of them two slaps in the face and sent them out. Only seven of the thirty survived the test.[142]

Another doctor who served under Krebsbach at Mauthausen was Heribert Ferdinand Heim, who in 1992 was one of the leading Nazi war criminals still at large. An Austrian and graduate of the University of Graz, Heim arrived in Mauthausen on 8 October 1941, when he was 27, and stayed only until 29 November of that year. Seven weeks were enough for him to establish a reputation. Benzene injections and mock operations kept him busy, but Heim is especially remembered for a case concerning two Dutch Jews, aged 18–20, whom he selected from among an incoming contingent for their perfect teeth. Forced to undergo appendectomies that they knew to be unnecessary, the two youths died in agony, whereupon their heads were cut off and their skulls boiled and cleaned. Heim gave one of the skulls to a colleague to decorate his desk, and kept the other as a paperweight on his own.[143]

As Mauthausen grew, so did the *Revier*. In 1944 its population reached 5,000, housed in eight Blocks, with each Block crammed with at least 500 patients sleeping up to twelve to a bed, or four to each of the three bunks making up the bed. They were packed head to foot, like sardines, and only patients on the top bunk had the space to sit up. Since many were too weak to move, they lived in one another's excrement. Hunger might drive them to bite the feet of their neighbour. This could result in a fight in which the bunk collapsed and then the bed, with predictable consequences. Those suffering from contagious diseases, including dysentery, scabies, pneumonia, bronchitis, diphtheria, and tuberculosis, were all assigned to the same Block. On 21 March 1945, when a new compound known as Lager III was opened, the total sick amounted to 18 per cent of the total population of the camp: 16,201 out of 83,249 men and 2,295 women.[144]

Another survivor, the Spaniard Lázaro Nates, describes his predicament when he contracted gastric hernia. He was told by the Czech inmate Professor Podlaha that he would die if he did not undergo an operation. Nates did not want an operation: he knew all about the SS doctors and the *Holznarkose*. But Podlaha insisted, saying that he could perform the operation himself. Podlaha had already operated on the wife of Commandant Ziereis in 1942 and saved her life; this success won him the respect of the SS and the permission to perform other operations. Nates therefore agreed. He was given only a local anaesthetic but he knew he had to be grateful for that. Since the anaesthetic was only local he had the rare opportunity to assist at his own major operation, watching the SS doctors as they watched the professor. On another occasion Nates was suffering from tonsillitis. Again he was reluctant to report to the *Revier*, but he did so, and was treated by an Austrian prisoner working as a nurse. The nurse extracted his tonsils with an instrument more appropriate for picking up coke for the fire, but Nates nevertheless survived.[145]

As for Mauthausen's gas chamber, it was designed and installed on Krebsbach's orders by SS-Hauptsturmführer Dr Erich Wasitzky, who served as the camp's pharmacist from 1941 to 1945. It was not, however, well designed. At the time it was first used the doors opened inwards. As a result, when the victims rushed to the doors they clogged up the entrance as they died, and the SS had difficulty in getting in to clear the corpses. This happened only once: the SS ordered the door hinges to be changed so that the doors opened outwards. The Spaniard Juan Gil was among those who worked on the alterations.[146] The supply and administration of the gas were also personally supervised by Dr Wasitzky, with SS-Hauptscharführer Martin Roth (in charge of the crematorium) assisting him, and with either Niedermayer or Trum responsible for marshalling the victims into the chamber.[147] Vilanova gives, without proof, a total of 499 Spaniards gassed at Mauthausen (and as many more shot in the back of the neck).[148]

Roth's crematorium was conveniently next door, though Roth took his orders not from Bachmayer but from the Gestapo chief Schulz.[149] Since a single crematorium could not keep pace with the supply of corpses, two more were added. 'The acrid odour of burnt roast', as the nose-witness Paul Tillard called it,[150] could now be picked up as far away as Linz.[151] But all three crematoria were considerably smaller than those in the killing factories of Treblinka and the like, and many thousands of corpses were buried in mass graves.[152]

Each morning, at the appointed hour, the Kommandos marched out of the fortress, or inner camp. By far the largest of these was the Kommando assigned to the granite quarry owned by the Deutsche Erd- und Steinwerke (DEST), which was now in the hands of the SS. This quarry (Steinbruck DEST), situated about a kilometre from the fortress, forms an enormous circle, or well, some 350 metres in diameter, partly surrounded by walls 40–75 metres in height. In summer, the sun is reflected by the granite cliff; in winter, the cliff serves to turn the wind into a cyclone.[153] What is today the quarry base was in 1940 a hill of granite at a level with the surrounding cliff, and what is today the granite staircase was at first a ramp. Each morning, at the appointed hour, the quarry echoed to the rhythmic beat of thousands of wooden clogs on the granite steps, as the army of slaves began a new day's descent into hell. That staircase has become, more than any other single travail imposed by the Nazi system, the symbol of its martyrs' path to Calvary.[154]

The staircase of the 186 steps consisted thereafter, and up until 1942, of randomly placed, loosely piled rocks or boulders of uneven height, so that all the steps were irregular and some of them were 40 cm. in height. Simply to climb them at a military pace, under the bludgeons of the SS and the Kapos, required an immense effort; no halts were permitted. Add to that ordeal the effect of a diet of programmed starvation. Add to that the fatigue of working through the day, whatever the climate, under the blows, dragging the granite rocks, loading them into the tip trucks, without a moment's pause except at noon. Imagine then what strength remained for the march back to the fortress up the 186 steps, each prisoner weighed down by a rock of 20 kilos, or the corpse of a comrade (since nothing was left behind), or the lunchtime soup tureens (the *Kessel* which carried 50 litres and weighed over 35 kilos empty). The agonizing climb, seeing nothing but the legs of the prisoners in the three rows ahead, staggering desperately to keep in line, and expecting to be singled out at any moment by the SS, being tripped, perhaps, and sent tumbling to the bottom with one's rock, there to be beaten to death—this was the experience that lay behind the cold inanimate statistics which report that 'thousands died'.

The inhuman work that the quarry represented was reserved from 1944 for those in the *Strafkompanie*. The year 1943 was a period of transition, but in 1940–2 almost all the prisoners were assigned to it.[155] There were two types of workers: the skilled and the manual. The former were employed on the dynamite, the hydraulic rock crushers, and the pneumatic drills; they were not struck or harshly treated unless they made errors or failed to maintain the pace. The latter, which made up the mass, were put to loading and unloading. On an average, over 2,000 prisoners were at work on the quarry every day, and these were at the mercy, as we have seen, of Grimm and Spatzenegger.

There was always an element of blind chance. To survive Mauthausen it was essential to avoid assignment to the quarry, mainly on account of the 186 steps. Most prisoners climbed the staircase once a day, but many climbed it more: at least two Spanish survivors, Juan de Diego and Sebastián Mena, attest that their groups climbed it daily ten to twelve times, five or six times in the morning and five or six in the afternoon.[156] The SS would sometimes find amusement in staging a version of the travail of Sisyphus, ordering the prisoners to take down the same rock which, at such cost, they had carried up.[157]

The historian yearns to know, the humanitarian shrinks from knowing, how big, how heavy was the rock. We have seen that there was a standard size weighing 20 kilos, which is to say that in most cases there was no selection to make.[158] The rocks were cut in the quarry, of the same size, but some of smaller size might also be needed and available. In so far as logic had a place in Mauthausen, the smaller rocks would go to the smaller prisoners. Spaniards in particular, then if not now, were physically small, however sturdy. But to select a rock the SS might think too small would be a most dangerous gamble. If a prisoner's rock was deemed too small, he was given first a beating and then a supplementary rock. The trick was to try to make the r look biggest from the outside.[159] What then might the minim Juan de Diego gave this eloquent answer to the brutal qu

I cannot say. It is impossible to make an accurate estimate to lift one of them, it seemed bigger than a house. But s carry up a 50 kilo sack of cement. You know what tha weight is written on it. And unlike a rock, which shoulder trestle, there is no easy way to carry

The British SOE officer Pierre Le Chêne describes how he also had to carry these sacks, which weighed as much as he did (since he had lost half his original weight); and when it rained, the sack split.[161] The all-time record was a rock weighing 140 kilos which a Polish Jew was forced to carry the entire kilometre from the quarry to the camp. The man died, of course, as he reached the gates, but the SS thought it marvellous: they threw the corpse into the crematorium and placed the rock in the museum.[162]

Physical condition and morale are the only factors to explain how some survived the quarry. The Frenchman André Morel says that he had no employable skill and did nothing but work in the quarry,[163] but Morel is a superb athlete who, barely two years after the Liberation, was selected to play in the French national rugby team. Juan de Diego attributes his own survival in part to never trading his soup for cigarettes, as many Spaniards were tempted into doing. Those who laboured in the quarry with the *Strafkompanie*, of course, were in a different category, for they were simply under sentence of death, labour being a mere alternative to death by hanging or the gas chamber. Death for these rarely took more than a few days: of the sixty men in the company who started out on a certain Sunday, only two were left alive on the following Saturday.[164] To be assigned to the *Strafkompanie* it was sufficient to break a rule, fall victim to a Kapo's whim, or be Jewish, though for the 20,000 Jews who entered Mauthausen and Gusen, there was a special Judenkommando. The SS were hard put to think out any further humiliations. Working naked in the cesspits was one device, though the 'Scheisserkolonne' was not exclusively for Jews.[165] Another was to require the Jews to join in the chant that the SA had launched twenty years earlier in the *Bierkeller* of Bavaria: in marching out or in passing an SS, the Kapo would call, '*Wer ist an unserem Unglück schuld?*' to which the Jews would shout ⌐⌐⌐⌐⌐!'[166] By July 1944 there were only twenty-two left ⌐⌐⌐⌐ was murdered in August 1944

⌐⌐mber of the SS as more brutal ⌐⌐parison, when the gentlest ⌐thing his imagination might ⌐to watch the 'parachutists'. ⌐d off the cliff by the SS, to ⌐e pond. They also included ⌐the steps, and put an end ⌐A number of Dutch Jews ⌐o survive, an example to any group, was crushed, and they decided to emulate their ancestors at Masada in AD 73 by committing group suicide, in the same collective leap.[168] The SS were therefore used to suicides, when on 13 December 1943, two French Jews, the brothers Schwartzenberg, made what was to be their last climb up the steps. The brothers were still schoolboys, too young to be, as their 19-year-old brother Léon was, in the French Resistance, but Schulz made it known he wanted to see them dead. How they died has been told in two quite different accounts. Jo Attia, a gangster from Marseilles who, after the Liberation, returned to criminal life, but at Mauthausen won the respect of many, has given what has been accepted as an eyewitness account. The brothers are mounting with their rocks at close of day when Raymond, the older but smaller and weaker of the two, realizes, at precisely the 144th step, that he can go no further. He veers to the right on to the ledge, 20 metres long and 2 metres wide, which had been hewn into the granite cliff; letting the rock drop into the abyss, he remains standing there, with his hands on his hips, in a posture of defiance. The human chain stops its climb. Jacques slowly lowers his own rock to the ground, then joins his brother on the ledge. Even for Mauthausen this is a moment of drama. The Kapos pause in their brutal swings and eye the SS with malign curiosity. The SS are just for an instant taken aback by this act of rebellion. Now they move in unison. SS-Unterscharführer Johann Vinzenz Gogl, in command of the steps, cannot believe his luck. Two Jewish brothers can be made to fight on the ledge, with survival the reward for the stronger. The brothers respond to the challenge by stripping off their *Drillich* tunics. It promises well. 'Fight, fight!' roars the Unterscharführer. The brothers stand facing each other, motionless. The SS, impatient for action, begin stoning them. 'Fight, dogs, fight!' The brothers, insensible to the stones, move slowly towards each other, meet in a last embrace, then, locked together not in combat but in a love that defies hate, step from the ledge into the void, from life into death.

Was that all that happened on that December night? Attia's account is contradicted by another, which is more than an account, more even than a myth. If a myth is a public dream, a symbol that stirs psychological energy and reflects a people's sorrows, joys, and hopes, then a collective hallucination is a myth made flesh. For only collective hallucination can explain the strength of another belief, that the brothers somehow enticed two of the SS onto the ledge, that they offered the SS their hands as if in a final act of forgiveness, that the SS thought it amusing to shake hands with a Jew about to kill his brother or be killed by him; and that the brothers held on to the Nazis with all the strength they had, lurching backwards, somersaulting almost as all four hurtled into space, suspended so it seemed in air before they plunged into the yawning gulf below.[169]

Apart from the quarry, there were two other local Kommandos in which the first contingents of Spaniards were employed. In spring 1941, the SS established the Siedlungsbau, a Kommando whose task it was to build villas for the SS officers on a picturesque site overlooking the Danube: on the hill near the fork of the road running from Mauthausen to Gusen. Some 350 Spaniards were employed in it, including many skilled workers. The conditions were particularly harsh, and the majority of the Spaniards died. The other was the Kommando Donaulinde, located in the village of Mauthausen. The work consisted of unloading granite rocks brought in by truck from the quarry; the rocks then had to be lifted on to a *Trage*, or stretcher, which the men, working in pairs, carried up the narrow gangplank to the barges moored on the riverside, loading the rocks inside. On one particularly cold day in early 1941, with the Spaniards forced to work barefoot, the work proved too much for many of them. They slipped and fell into the water. The SS opened fire, and the Danube carried off the corpses.[170] All of this took place in full view of the worthy villagers of Mauthausen.

The prestige of the Spaniards at Mauthausen was never in question. No national group had a stronger sense of solidarity. This was shown in the very first month, when on 28 August 1940 José Marfil Escabona became the first Spaniard to die there. Julián Mur Sánchez, of the anarchist CNT, promptly asked Bachmeyer for permission to pay the respect of a minute's silence. No such request had ever been made before. It amounted to a protest, and it left Bachmayer astonished, but he silently consented. That evening at roll-call, Mur Sánchez broke from the ranks to address the Spaniards. While some survivors reported later that the SS jeered, others described the SS reaction as silent amazement: an SS officer who was standing there with his arms crossed and a cigarette in his fingers allowed his arms to drop and his cigarette to fall. As for Mur Sánchez, he was transferred to Gusen, where he died.[171]

An incident that affected the Spaniards in particular involved a group of Romanians who were former members of the International Brigades. Arriving one morning in the quarry, they began to hug one another and then, singing The Internationale, they moved towards the watch-tower. The SS guards screamed at them to halt. They continued forward, singing with all their might. The sound of The Internationale was heard by all in the quarry, until the machine-guns mowed the last of them down. Because the men had fought for the Republic, the Spaniards were deeply moved. That evening when they returned to their Block, they formed a group and paid the Romanians the same tribute of a minute's silence. Such a gesture of honouring the dead was unknown, and it astonished the Kapos. It was not lost on the rest of the camp, and it served to enhance even further the Spaniards' prestige.[172]

Such a solidarity on the part of the Spaniards required the willing suspension of the party quarrels which had racked the Republic so short a time before. An example of this could be seen in the case of Joaquín Olaso Piera, the 'eye of Moscow' who, as we have seen, was widely held responsible for the betrayal of Josep Miret Musté and his resistance group into the hands of the Gestapo; Miret and his group were sent to Mauthausen, but so no less was Olaso Piera. As Juan de Diego describes it, 'we knew the charges against Olaso, but we had no proof, so we let the matter go'. The result of all this, as the commission chaired by Jean Laffitte later confirmed, was that the Spaniards were the first to give an organized form to the Resistance.[173]

Can the mind conceive anything more monstrous than Mauthausen *Mutterlager*? The contender is *Mutter* Mauthausen's even uglier daughter Gusen. Razola has written of Mauthausen-Gusen, that nothing can be said about *KZ* life elsewhere that is not gentle in comparison,[174] and he describes the shock of those sent from Mauthausen when they found conditions at Gusen even worse.[175] Since Ziereis controlled every one of the ninety or more Aussenkommandos in Austria from his base in Mauthausen, there was no reason why any particular camp should have a worse reputation than another, or why an external Kommando should be worse than the mother camp. All prisoners assigned to Gusen were under the direct command of Bachmayer, as they were at Mauthausen. From survivors who knew both, however, the story that emerges is that most of what happened at Gusen happened at Mauthausen too, but the tempo at Gusen was speeded up, and the cruelty, in some respects, refined.

The village of Gusen is situated only 6 kilometres from Mauthausen on the main road from Linz to Vienna. The construction of the first camp at Gusen was begun in December 1939, by German and Austrian prisoners under the command of Streitwieser. The original purpose of the camp was the exploitation of the quarry to the north of the camp; the quarry, and the brick factory attached to it, were, as at Mauthausen, in the ownership of the Deutsche Erd- und Steinwerke. The original panorama of Gusen, then, was no different from that elsewhere: quarries attacked with dynamite, and rocks transported by columns of slaves. But Gusen was Mauthausen at higher speed. Those at Mauthausen too weak or sick to work were told that they were being sent to Gusen to be looked after.[176] This was part of the SS play on words, such as rest-home and convalescence. From their arrival in Gusen, all prisoners were tested for their strength. The prisoners were made to run, and the weakest eliminated at once. Of the first 10,000 men sent to Gusen, 3,000 were selected for instant liquidation. It was the forms of liquidation that Gusen adopted that made it so well remembered.

The local commandant responsible for Gusen was SS-Hauptsturm-führer Karl Chmielewski, who arrived there from Mauthausen in March 1940 and stayed until February 1942, when he was transferred to *KL*-Herzogebusch in Holland. Described as a warrior type, he was tall, lean, deep-voiced—and usually drunk.[177] His successor in 1942 was SS-Hauptsturmführer Fritz Seidler, who replaced the random brutality of his predecessor with something closer to the Prussian model.[178] The results are impressive: a survivor as authoritative as Roger Heim attests that Seidler took a personal part in the killing of 6,000 prisoners.[179] In his private hobbies, Seidler shared the taste of Chmielewski: Ziereis himself admitted, on his death-bed, that both had screens and book covers made from human skin, a preference being given to skin tattooed in attractive designs.[180]

The precise details that are available regarding most of the SS officers at Mauthausen *Mutterlager* are absent in the case of those in the Kommandos, Gusen included,[181] but one appointment speaks volumes: Hans Killermann, the man who used to sit on the stool in Mauthausen's *Bunker*, was transferred to Gusen in 1942 with a promotion to Arbeitsdienstführer.[182] As for the Kapos, in every camp in Austria, without exception, they remain mere shadows. It is rare to find a Kapo referred to by more than a nickname, and there may well have been more than one nickname for the same Kapo. We know only that the general principle remains the same: the posts of privilege were in the hands of the Greens, and at Gusen the Block Kapos were all German Greens.[183] What distinguished Gusen in this regard was the emergence of two Spaniards, 'el Negro' and Indalecio González, who won a reputation for brutality second to none.[184] There was also the case of the Spaniard Tomás who, as we shall see, became a killer of his fellow-Spaniards.

The first contingent of Spaniards arrived at Gusen on 24 January 1941.[185] The first Spaniard to die there succumbed two days later.[186] At that time Gusen, like Mauthausen proper, was not yet complete, and the Spaniards were used to build a wall around the electrified barbed-wire perimeter.[187] Since Gusen stood on the edge of the main road, the primary purpose of the wall was to provide the SS with the privacy they needed. As long as the wall was still under construction, logic required that the SS modify their treatment of the prisoners, but this was in no way apparent. Santiago Raga, who worked on the construction of the wall, saw Austrian children passing every morning on their way to school. They were eyewitnesses to the daily crimes. Never once did Raga see a child or anyone else stop or show the slightest emotion or the smallest sign of indignation at the sight of prisoners mercilessly beaten or electrocuted on the wire.[188]

Among the forms of liquidation employed at Gusen, the method known to the SS as *Badeaktion* was unknown in any other camp. The idea was probably born in the brain of SS-Hauptscharführer Heinz Jentzsch, since he became known as the '*Bademeister* of Gusen', but it was readily endorsed by commandant Chmielewski. Unlike those at Mauthausen, the showers at Gusen had a protective wall which allowed the water, when the drains were blocked, to rise to a level of 20 cm. One night in December, a group of tuberculosis victims and other sick were driven or dragged out of the *Revier* and into the showers. They were held for at least thirty minutes under the icy water. An SS-Oberscharführer known only as 'Dracula' stood in his shirt-sleeves, holding a branch, flailing those who fell until they drowned, then flailing those still standing until they fell too. Two of the victims were Spaniards, of whom one was a youth of 21 whose last cries were '*Justicia! Justicia! Jus . . .*'. Most of those who did not drown froze to death. Those who were stronger and survived the night succumbed soon afterwards to collapse of the lungs. This method of eliminating the sick and the exhausted was then continued with other groups, of 100 at a time.[189]

The legendary showers of Gusen were still considered, by the camp's actuarial wizards, to be too time-consuming. Other methods were tried. Night after night in winter, 150 men were left outside Block 32, naked and starving. The cold did the work: more than half died in the night, the rest, the following day. It was in Block 32 that a group of a dozen Spaniards were murdered by Chmielewski and his adjutants in the course of a routine inspection. To the disgust of the Spaniards, their fellow countryman Tomás, who was a Stubekapo, served as an accomplice.[190]

Of the 3,846 Spaniards who arrived in Gusen in 1941, only 444 were still alive in January 1944.[191] Life expectancy in the period 1940–1 was about six months from the date of arrival, and the average weight of prisoners for the period 1940–2 (these being the only periods for which such statistics are available) was about 40 kilos.[192]

A later and alternative method of liquidation was introduced by

SS-Hauptsturmführer Dr Helmuth Vetter, whose previous research in the fields of sulfa drugs and typhus had been conducted in the laboratories of Dachau and Auschwitz, respectively. On his arrival in Gusen in 1944, he made tuberculosis his principal study. The experiments, which he recorded and which have been preserved, consisted of injecting phlegmonic pus into the lungs of healthy prisoners and observing the reaction. Each experiment ended with Vetter forcing his victim to run until he dropped from exhaustion, whereupon Vetter dispatched him with an injection of benzene.[193] Such injections were given also to sick Spaniards from Blocks 13 and 31. Injecting the benzene into the lung rather than into the heart or stomach prolonged and intensified the agony, but if death took too long and Vetter grew impatient, he or a Kapo would finish off the victim by strangling him or by crushing his skull.[194]

The economic needs of Nazi Germany from 1942, and the massive arrival of prisoners in Mauthausen from that same year, made Himmler decide to build a new camp, Gusen II, 3 kilometres away at St Georgen, on the other side of the road towards Linz; and then another, the much smaller Gusen III, 8 kilometres away at Lungitz. The prisoners assigned to Gusen I's Kellerbau Kommando, or the 'death group' as it was known, travelled there each day in a train and on a track specially built for the purpose; each wagon held 100. Their initial work was to build vast underground tunnels, invulnerable to Allied air attack, in which workshops and assembly lines were then set up to produce sub-machine-guns and aircraft parts for Steyr-Werke and Messerschmitt. As we shall see, Gusen II was not the only Kommando designed for underground factories, but the softness of the soil at St Georgen explains why Gusen II was by far the most ambitious: no less than 50 kilometres of underground factories were projected, against merely 12 kilometres at Ebensee. Most of the prisoners in Gusen II were Soviets and Italians, but Spaniards were also present, and José Sanz describes his animus with the Spanish Kapo Asturias. What distinguished Gusen II was its unbreathable air. The dust never dispersed or settled, and was so thick that the men operating the pneumatic drills had to use headlamps. The deafening roar of the drills reverberating in the tunnel and the lack of oxygen meant that the prisoners were quickly exhausted.[195] The SS themselves decided that no man could work effectively in the tunnel for more than eight hours, so the schedule operated on three teams working round the clock. But the sixteen hours of 'repose' were spent in the tunnel, in that air and noise, so that the prisoners' usefulness as slaves was soon used up.[196] There was one other factor about Gusen II that distinguished it, and Roger Heim of the Institut de France attended a tribunal after the war to insist upon this single point: if the SS guarded Gusen II like any other camp, its financial management was in the hands not of the SS but of the honour-loving Wehrmacht and Luftwaffe.[197]

Spaniards, in fact, were to be found virtually everywhere in the Austrian *KZ* constellation, which comprised not merely Aussenkommandos like Gusen I, the biggest, but units as small and sophisticated as Redl-Zipf, engaged in the production of counterfeit money, or Schloss Mittersill, an SS research institute which made use of no more than fifteen women.[198] The next Kommando to open after Gusen I was at Steyr, 30 kilometres south of Mauthausen, beginning operations in the spring of 1941 and serving the Steyr-Werke munitions industry; it was composed of 49 Spaniards and one Romanian (a certain Mirón, who had fought in the International Brigades). At first the men were transported there and back to Mauthausen in trucks, but in 1942 the Kommando was enlarged, with 300 more Spaniards sent there on 6 January under a certain SS officer Müller and nine German green-triangle Kapos.[199] Their task was to build a factory for Steyr-Daimler-Puch *AG*, to be used for the production of aircraft engines, aircraft cockpits, ball-bearings, trucks, caterpillar tracks for tanks, and sub-machine-guns. The Steyr Kommando was thus the first to use prisoners in war industries, and the Spaniards were the first to be so employed. The Commandant, Müller, was young, good-looking, and robust, but at 25 he was already a pale shadow of his earlier life when he served as a model for Hitlerjugend. Only his fanatical hatred had stayed with him, and this he directed at the Spaniards. During that first hard winter of 1941–2, he would give up his own Sundays at home with his wife for the pleasure of tormenting them further. In April 1944 the workshops were finally moved to other centres, including Ebensee, as a result of heavy damage by Allied bombers.[200]

Another Aussenkommando that opened at Ternberg to the south-west in September 1941 was made up exclusively of 350 Spaniards.[201] In late 1942, the SS revived a project that was 200 years old: the construction of a tunnel at Loibl-Pass to provide Germany with a strategic route linking Klagenfurt with Ljubljana. The situation at Loibl-Pass, however, was different from that anywhere else: the Kommando was situated in hostile territory, with Tito's partisans masters of the region, and the project was finally abandoned.[202] The Kommando at Schwechat, south-east of Vienna, was engaged in the construction of Heinkel aircraft, and was a natural target for Allied air attacks. On 14 July 1944 almost every prisoner in Schwechat was transferred to Floridsdorf, to the north-west of the capital. In the course of an Allied raid on this Kommando on 17 November 1944, two Spaniards, José Miret Musté and José Juncosa Escoda, were seriously wounded. Not wanting to be inconvenienced, the local SS commandant ordered his men to fire a bullet into the neck of each.[203]

It was precisely the vulnerability of these Kommandos to air attack that induced the Nazi chiefs to order the construction of vast underground factories like those of Gusen II. The decision was actually taken too late for this enormous project to be of any practical use to Germany, but the more the project seemed hopeless, the more the Nazis pursued it with frenzy. The organizational work was entrusted to Bachmayer, who, on 25 September 1943, accompanied the first convoy of prisoners to a site 45 kilometres from Salzburg on the road to Linz; between the villages of Zipf and Redl, 6 kilometres north of the road, stands the famous Zipfer brewery. The Kommando established here took its official name of Schlier from the enterprise it was to serve. Its purpose was to convert methanol and oxygen into liquid fuel for use in V1s and V2s, and the Kommando's first task was to build underground tunnels to house the factories.

Bachmayer's first contingent consisted of twenty prisoners, all of them Spaniards.[204] Bachmayer also brought Hans Killermann, whose reputation in the *Bunker* at Mauthausen and as Arbeitsdienstführer at Gusen had won him promotion to Rapportführer at Schlier. He was now known to the Spaniards as 'Fernandel' or 'the Grin'. What made him grin most was his practice—he boasted of 'holding the patent'—of placing matchsticks in the eyes of the prisoners so that they could not close them or even blink in the sunlight. The Kommando was officially opened on 11 October 1943. Once a week a truck arrived from Mauthausen with provisions, and since Schlier lacked an incinerator it returned with the corpses for incineration in the *Mutterlager*. It is possible that other bodies lie forever buried in the cement, into which they fell or were pushed. Schlier remained to the end of special significance to Spaniards: there were more Spaniards there at the time of evacuation in May 1945 than all other nationalities combined.[205]

Meanwhile, the success of Allied bombing raids on the factory at Wiener-Neustadt, built by a Kommando in 1943 for the production of V2s, precipitated the decision to transfer all such factories underground. Wiener-Neustadt was bombed twice in August of that year and again on 2 November, the third attack demolishing the factory. It was not rebuilt. Three weeks later, Bachmayer again left Mauthausen on a mission, this time to organize, on the southern tip of Lake Traunsee 80 kilometres to the south-west, a new secret Kommando with the code-name *Zement*. It would be hard to find a more exquisite setting for *Zement*. Nearby lies the village of Ebensee, where the violets, roses, and green hills are reflected in the still water of the lake. There, at the base of a mountain, and taking its name from the village, a Kommando was set up to provide the Siemens *AG* with an industrial complex which was immune to bombing and which it was hoped could even now turn the tide of war in Hitler's favour.

This time Bachmayer brought with him his trusted Magnus Keller, 'King Kong' himself, together with sixty-two other Kapos and 500 red-triangle prisoners of various nationalities. Their job was to build the *Lager*, situated at a distance of 3 kilometres from the projected central tunnel. Since Bachmayer had to return to the *Mutterlager*, he handed over command, first to two commandants who were replaced for incompetence,[206] and finally (in May 1944) to SS-Hauptsturmführer Julius Anton Ganz. Though affected and even effeminate,[207] Ganz gave his superiors the fullest satisfaction.[208] So too did 'King Kong'. Even Ganz treated him with circumspection, and he held his post of Lagerälteste-Ebensee right to the end.

With construction of the *Lager* completed, more than 10,000 prisoners and another 250 Kapos arrived in Ebensee in the first months of 1944 to begin boring into the mountain. Since most came from Mauthausen *Mutterlager* they found themselves in some familiar company: 'King Kong', with his enormous shoulders and swaggering walk, and his own Great Dane presented to him by the grateful SS; and Karl the Kapellmeister, whose sadistic pleasure it still was to drown prisoners with his own hands by plunging their heads into a pail of water or a latrine bucket.[209] The camp soon grew into a little town, from fewer than 600 at the start to over 16,000 at the end, the dead being constantly replaced.

The prisoners worked in three shifts: 7 a.m. to 3 p.m., 3 p.m. to 11 p.m., and 11 p.m. to 7 a.m. Fourteen tunnels were projected, with several hundred men employed in each. The crews consisted of four categories: those operating the drills, those erecting the scaffolding for the drillers, those clearing the fallen rocks from the tunnel, and those outside the tunnel loading the rocks on to tip trucks. When it snowed or rained, there was an advantage to being employed inside the tunnel: it was impossible to dry a *Drillich* overnight, the material being of a fibre that did not dry, and such prisoners were forced to put on clothes the following day that were still wet. There were no other advantages. The drilling team consisted of ten prisoners moving forward in a line against the rock, with drills operated by compressed air supplied by generators parked outside the tunnel. When the rock was dry, the dust from the drills formed a white cloud of such density that the drillers could see no more than a yard or two. In the initial stage of boring a tunnel, when the explosives were set all those in the tunnel were evacuated, but once the tunnel had progressed to a depth of some 25 metres the evacuations were regarded as a waste of time and discontinued. For at least half an hour after every detonation the tunnel was filled with gas as well as dust and the air became virtually unbreathable, but the work continued.

Everywhere it was a frantic race against time. By May 1945, of the fourteen projected tunnels, ten had been completed, to a length of 428 metres, together with transversals. The entrances were deliberately kept small: 2 metres wide and 2 metres high, the plans providing for the installation of a pivoting steel door. To pass through the modest entrance into the interior gave the impression of entering the nave of a cathedral, 20 metres in width and 15 metres in height, and that breathtaking length. Some galleries were in perfect readiness, with machines in place on the lower floor, and dormitories, refectory, and other services on the upper floor. In one workshop the production of synthetic fuel from charcoal had already begun, and in two tunnels the production of aircraft or V-weapons was about to begin. In another few weeks, the Nazi war industry would have been able to produce such weapons with the assurance that no Allied bomber could ever reach them through a thousand feet of rock. And once the project was complete, the prisoners would never leave the tunnels nor ever again see the light of day, the pivoting steel door sealing them off from the world. They would be the forgotten men in the mountain, the prisoners in the cave.

If the Allied invasion of Austria was to rob the Nazis of this dream, the prisoners of Ebensee were nevertheless subject to a mortality rate which was among the highest. The soup was often made from grass, and in February 1944 no bread was distributed to any prisoner for an entire week.[210] It was impossible to convey all the corpses to the *Mutterlager*, so in August 1944 Ebensee received its own crematorium. The post of crematorium Kapo went to Franz Susok, better known as 'Franz Krema', a Green who was brought in from the *Mutterlager* where he had served in the same capacity. On his arrival at Ebensee, Ganz told him: 'Here you can let your hair grow, you can dress anyhow you want, you can eat and drink anything you feel like, but you don't leave this place alive.' This, as we shall see, was the basic SS plan for all Kapos in such posts. It is only surprising that Ganz warned him in advance. After the liberation of Ebensee, Susok was found near the barbed wire, a bullet in his head.[211]

The role of the Spaniards at Ebensee was unusual. Up until the last weeks, when more reached Ebensee in the evacuation of other camps, there were very few, between 100 and 150,[212] but several were very well placed: two were Block Kapos, several were Stubekapos, five were Friseurs, and many more were subordinate Kapos, Stubendiener, and kitchen and store personnel.[213] This attests to the success of the Spanish prisoners in obtaining the removal of several Greens and Blacks and in replacing them in their privileged posts. As such, they were observers and surviving witnesses to many a dreadful scene.

The mass worked on the mountain. We have seen what concern the SS attached to their lives, but there was still the fear of contagion. As a result, the prisoners received regular showers, though with a difference. Four or five prisoners were grouped under a single jet, first hot, then cold, their bodies rubbing, with only occasionally a little piece of soap, and never a towel to dry with. They then returned, as always in ranks of five, to the barracks, wet and naked, in temperatures that could fall to −20 °C, made even worse when the wind was blowing. A convoy that reached Ebensee on foot in the particularly cold winter of 1944–5 was directed as usual to the showers, the hot being followed by the glacial. But this time the prisoners were forced out into the snow and the icy wind, then returned to the showers, then to the snow and wind. This continued several times throughout the night. Those who fell were beaten until they got up or until they never got up again. By the morning few were still alive.[214]

Dysentery was a perennial problem, at Ebensee as elsewhere. Prisoners looked for remedies by chewing on turf, charcoal, or fir-tree shoots. But it was a disease that in a *KL* was impossible to cure. The worst error in its early stages was to stop eating, for no prisoner could afford to miss any calorie at all. Dysentery was often the prelude to other misfortunes. It was impossible for a prisoner to change his soiled clothes, and to smell dirty in the Block was to be subjected to twenty-five lashes from the Kapo.

The latrines at Ebensee, as elsewhere, were always the secret meeting place, the only spot where it was safe to meet a prisoner from another Block and exchange information. It was also the exchange market where left-over soup and morsels of bread were traded for cigarettes. At night the latrines were off limits: the curfew went into effect one hour after evening muster, after which it was forbidden for a prisoner to leave his Block unless he was accompanied by a Kapo. At the door of each Block stood a large wooden tub for those who needed it. With 300 to a Block and dysentery rife, the tub was soon filled to overflowing. The next morning the Block Kapo would assign, at random or according to his whim, four men to carry it. Each carried an end of one of two wooden rods that were placed in the two handles of the tub. Their walk might be several hundred yards over sometimes difficult ground.[215]

A distinctive feature of Ebensee was the genial cynicism of making Block 23 a convalescence centre, or *Schonungsblock*. Here again prisoners were piled five and often six to a straw mattress 80 cm. wide, virtually unable to move, with the living sometimes wedged for hours between the dead, until the Stubendiener arrived to remove the corpses and make room for others. Three times a day all prisoners would be turned out of their bunks, producing an indescribable uproar. At most other times the prisoners sank into silence. It was not just that men were thrown together here without any common language. There was no exchange of signs either. Everyone had retreated into himself, thinking of nothing, unable to hear even a death rattle or offer a glance of sympathy, physically and morally spent. The few who survived this could not afterwards remember anything about it, not even the position of the latrine tub. They were living like somnambulists, no longer in the world.[216]

On 21 April 1944 Streitwieser inaugurated an Aussenkommando similar to Ebensee at Melk, 60 kilometres to the east of Mauthausen, and two weeks later SS-Hauptsturmführer Julius Ludolf, who had served as commandant at Loibl-Pass, took over its command. Up to this time Melk had been known chiefly for the beautiful Benedictine abbey where, in 1767, the boy Mozart stopped to play the organ. The abbey was now a school run by monks, who showed neither concern nor curiosity about what was being built next door.[217] The population of *KL*-Melk grew rapidly, to over 10,000. In a single year, up to the moment the Kommando was evacuated to Ebensee on 11 April 1945, the prisoners excavated seven main tunnels, 8 metres high, 25 metres wide, linked with transversals, to a total length of 3,000 metres. The first machines were installed, but Melk, like Ebensee, had produced nothing by the time it was abandoned.[218]

We have seen that Mauthausen *Mutterlager* had a gas chamber in use from autumn 1941 and at full performance from May 1942, and that its capacity (65–70 persons) was negligible in comparison with that of the killing factories of the Vernichtungslager in Poland. Only some 4,000 people died in the Mauthausen *Gaskammer*, most of them towards the end of the war, especially in the final weeks; at that time large numbers of prisoners were being transported from Gusen to the *Mutterlager* because of the inadequate gassing facilities at Gusen, where a mere 800 would be liquidated, all in the closing months of the war, in barracks crudely converted into gas chambers. The impact of the gas chamber on *KZ* life, however, is not to be measured in terms of the number of its victims. It should be seen rather in terms of the fear haunting every prisoner that, if he should become too weak or sick to work, the *Gaskammer* gaped for him.

To the west of Linz, and in a direct line between Mauthausen and

Dachau, stands the forbidding castle of Hartheim, its towers giving it a Byzantine appearance. Built in 1898 as an asylum for the mentally retarded, it was requisitioned by the SS and refitted, with a crematorium chimney that rose to a height of 25 metres but which was concealed from outside view by walls three storeys high.[219] At the time Hartheim stood isolated,[220] and the approach was forbidden to outsiders. From May 1940 until 1941, the SS used the castle for their euthanasia programme, and gave it the nicknames of *Erholungsheim* (convalescent home) and *Bad Ischl*, the therapeutic baths being the gas chamber. Hartheim also contained an electric bone mill.[221] A staff of thirty Nazi doctors and assistants, under the direction of SS-Hauptsturmführer Rudolf Lohnauer, worked there on medical experiments and in the greatest secrecy.[222] From 1941 it was used for the liquidation of those crippled by *KZ* life, especially in Mauthausen and Dachau, and from April 1944 the castle came under the jurisdiction of *KL*-Mauthausen.

Once again, the survival of Juan de Diego allows us to know how the victims were transported from Mauthausen to Hartheim. A shipment consisted of forty to fifty men, and in certain periods the shipments left with great regularity. The selection was made by Schulz's Politische Abteilung, which then informed the *Lagerschreibstube*. Juan de Diego thereupon made out the death certificates even before the men left. At first every case was entered, both in the SS registry and in the card index under the word Hartheim. Then orders were given not to mention Hartheim at all and to discontinue the practice of making out death certificates. Secrecy was now considered even more important than order and precision, which is to say a great deal. The registry and the index cards were now to carry the word Escaped (*Entlassen*), accompanied by a mark in green crayon, the code for extermination.[223] At least 30,000 prisoners died there, including 11,000 from Mauthausen. Of these 449 were Spaniards, twelve of them murdered in a single day (12 August 1941).[224] Schloss Hartheim was unique in that not a single prisoner who entered it came out alive. Before the end of 1944 the SS took the very early precaution of dismantling this chamber of horrors, and on 13 December twenty prisoners arrived from Mauthausen to transform it not merely back into a château, but into a château charitably converted into a school. To this end, in January 1945, after first taking care to murder the prisoners brought in to work on the reconstruction,[225] the SS brought in thirty-five German children, six nurses, and a teacher. Such was the happy house of Hartheim when the Allied forces reached it.[226]

One other method of liquidation remains to be recounted: the killing in the trucks. The mobile gas chamber, code-named *Phantom*, and better known as 'Black Raven', was the invention of SS-Standartenführer Walter Rauff.[227] The operation was quite simple: after the prisoners were loaded into the back of the truck, the driver and two other SS mounted the cabin, which was sealed off, and on the journey to Hartheim or elsewhere, the driver released the carbon monoxide from the exhaust into a pipe running directly into the back. In the case of Mauthausen a bus was converted into what looked like a mail truck. Ziereis admitted on his deathbed that the vehicle served as a shuttle between Mauthausen and Gusen in the period from mid-1942 to mid-1943. All its passengers arrived dead, and went straight to the ovens. At other times, the vehicle left Mauthausen with live prisoners and came back with the same prisoners dead; it was so recorded in the camp records by Juan de Diego, using always the same green crayon. The total number of prisoners who died in this way is estimated at 1,500. Among them were a considerable number of Spaniards, including the air force major Busquets, who had commanded the airfield in Barcelona during the Civil War, and Emilio Andrés, who had served as commissar of an army corps in the Spanish Republican Army. Another Spaniard, Lieutenant-Colonel León Luengo Muñoz, died in the same way in Dachau.[228] If more prisoners were not liquidated in the trucks, it was because the system was slow and cumbersome.[229] And as the war progressed, and victory receded, the pace of killing quickened.

7

In Russia, from Honeymoon to Holy War

War and its opportunities—Exploits of the Spaniards: the case and cult of Rubén Ruiz—The PCE leadership rent by scandal—The Politburo reduced to a troika—The death of Díaz—The problem of the succession: Hernández versus Pasionaria—The departure of Hernández for Mexico—Hernández expelled from the Party—The fate of the Republican pilots and seamen—Rendezvous at Karaganda

On 22 June 1941, Hitler launched his invasion to the east. The PCE leaders in their memoirs do not describe the scene around the Vozhd as the awful truth of his gullibility began to emerge. Castro Delgado, however, as a delegate to the Comintern, was in a good position to observe the effect. As the Anglo-Soviet alliance came into being and the promise of British supplies was announced, he describes how eight members of the Comintern huddled around the radio tuned to the BBC. '*Horosho!*' they cried again and again; '*Slava Bogoo!*'. Never in Churchill's long political life were his words received with more rapt attention.[1] Meanwhile, in a pamphlet entitled *¡Guerra implacable al fascismo!*, published in Moscow in September, Pasionaria rediscovered the nature of Nazism.

Below the top leadership, it seemed to Spaniards everywhere that their moment for revenge had come. No one, surely, would want to deprive them of the chance to throw themselves once again into the antifascist struggle. It was not only zeal they offered. Whether their expertise lay in tank warfare, air warfare, or infantry warfare, they had what no Soviet had: three years of front-line experience in the hardest of struggles, and familiarity with the best and most modern weapons, including the Wehrmacht's. No one doubted that some of the Spanish officers were fit to take command of Soviet units. The courses they were taking at the Frunze Academy were almost completed at the moment that Hitler struck. Despite this, hardly a Spaniard was given the chance to fight in a regular unit; none received a command. Even the disasters of the summer, autumn, or early winter of 1941 did not lead to any real change in the picture. The Frunze Academy was evacuated to Tashkent in late October, and the Spaniards enrolled there either went with it or received insignificant teaching assignments elsewhere.

In the factories, in the barracks, on the farms, groups of Spaniards gathered to hear the announcers on Radio Moscow declare over and over again: 'Our cause is just. Victory will be ours!' 'And ours, you blockhead! And ours!' shouted the Spaniards at the box. The Soviet officials paid them no more attention than did the box. Alfredo Francisco Villalón, working in the Molotov automobile factory in Gorki, wrote to the authorities on 28 June 1941 to say that in 1938, as a squadron leader in Spain, he had piloted Soviet I–16 fighters and had fought in seventy-three air battles.[2] Villalón was among those whose application was accepted,[3] but they were the small minority. The answer they habitually received was this: 'You've fought in your war. Now you have to contribute to ours, by working in our factories and making ready so that you can be best in everything by the time you return to Spain.' According to Dimitrov, it was on Stalin's direct instructions that the Spaniards were not to take part in battle: their place was Spain and they had to save their strength for the future struggle.[4] Many a Spaniard saw in it rather the hand of the PCE leaders. Either way, it gave them one more reason to be embittered.

As a result, only two Spanish combat units were formed. One of these was the group of 120 men selected from among those studying at the Planiernaya School of Leninism. At a moment when the Wehrmacht was approaching the outskirts of Moscow, and a German tank unit had crashed its way through to reach the suburban terminus of a city tramline,[5] these Spaniards were enrolled in a unit known as the 4th Special Company, which formed part of the 1st Regiment of the Special Motorized Division of the NKVD. Command of the company was given to Peregrín Pérez Galarza, who up to that moment had been employed in a Moscow automobile factory. The post of commissar went to Celestino Alonso, the two men having served together in the 5th Regiment defending Madrid in the autumn of 1936. The company enjoyed such trust that it shared the honour of guarding the Kremlin, for which it duly received the award of the Red Star.[6] In the desperate defence of Leningrad, too, several Spaniards had the chance to take part. Prominent among these was Maria Pardina Ramos, known as Marusia, who up until then had worked in a textile factory in that city. As a nurse in the 3rd Volunteer Division, she twice won the Order of the Red Flag, the second time posthumously.[7]

Everywhere Spaniards tried to enlist for front-line battle, and almost everywhere they were rejected. The only combat unit open to them served in the only role they were allowed: guerrilla warfare. The idea came from Jesús Hernández, who in July 1941 proposed the creation of a Spanish infantry brigade to save the Spaniards from starving.[8] It took concrete form in May 1942 when the Soviets launched the Kharkov offensive and two old friends met in a chance encounter. Domingo Ungría, of Valencia, had formerly commanded the xivth Army Corps of guerrilleros in Spain; Colonel Ilia G. Starinov had served as the corps' instructor.[9] Ungría had been refused admission to the Frunze Academy and had been forced to work in a factory.[10] The new unit, known as the Ungría guerrilla brigade,[11] shared in the new Soviet military disasters, with 75 per cent of its members killed in battle.[12] This expense of Spanish blood explains Pasionaria's rage at Ungría, who may have owed his survival to the fact that Starinov helped him to enter Soviet military intelligence.[13] The brigade was thus dissolved, but a new guerrilla unit, known as the NKVD Special Battalion, was formed out of the nucleus of the 4th Special Company and of survivors from the brigade. This battalion, which was the only unit of that size in the Soviet Union to be formed exclusively of Spaniards, was put together by Caridad del Río de Mercader. A Cuban communist who had served in the OGPU even before the Spanish Civil War, this tall, white-haired woman with the Catalan accent was the mother, no less, of the man who murdered Trotsky. Many of the Spaniards owed their lives to the formation of the battalion, since from the moment they entered it they were entitled to medical attention. After fighting in various guerrilla operations, the battalion was nevertheless dissolved in its turn in October 1944, and those in it were then transferred to the aircraft factories in Moscow.[14]

Spaniards were to be found in several similar units all operating behind German lines. Prominent among these was the force of over 50,000 men commanded by Sidor Kovpak, which set out westwards from the Ukraine towards the Carpathians, to operate in territory sparsely occupied by the fascist invaders. Another group, consisting of only eight Spaniards and four Soviets, was commanded by José Fusimaña Fábregas and ordered in March 1943 to parachute into an area in the Crimea. They miscalculated their jump and landed on a beach near the village of Shubino. The inhabitants promptly betrayed them to the Nazis. Hounded and cornered, the twelve men took up a defensive position in an area of rocks and for two days held out against the enemy until all were killed. A monument to the twelve who died now stands in Shubino.[15]

Spaniards were also among the seventy who gathered at Tuchino airfield in Moscow on the evening of 20 June 1942. Under the command of Colonel Dmitri Medvedev, they climbed aboard a plane which flew them to the forests near Lvov, 600 kilometres behind German lines. The Spanish group was led by José Gros, from Tarragona, who had already won a singular honour earlier that year when he was invited to the Kremlin to receive the Medal of Valour from Mikhail Kalinin, President of the Supreme Soviet.[16] The group's radio operator was a young woman, África de las Heras, who was to receive the Order of the Patriotic War, First Class.[17] Gros and his group continued their guerrilla activities until the advancing Soviet forces reached them in 1944.

The largest of the Spanish guerrilla groups, however, was that of Francisco Gullón, who was also the most celebrated of the Spanish *guerrilleros* in Russia. For his actions in the Ukraine, he was awarded the Order of Lenin, the second highest military decoration in the USSR. He was then sent into the forest between Smolensk and Bryansk, to the south-west of Moscow, where huge numbers of Red Army troops had been surrounded by the Germans. In late August 1942 Gullón was withdrawn and summoned to the office of the Chief of Staff of guerrilla warfare in Leningrad. His mission was to take command of a special force of Soviet and Spanish guerrillas, all of them with long experience, and to fly into the Luga area, 80 miles to the south, again behind German lines, where the Spanish Blue Division (renamed the 250th Division) was among the Wehrmacht units in action. The mission took off on 29 September. Badly wounded in March 1943 while following orders to cross back into the Soviet lines, Gullón was unable after that to take any further part in combat, and became an announcer on Radio Moscow. When in September 1944 he died from a pulmonary abscess, he received the highest decoration of all, Hero of the Soviet Union, an honour conferred upon only 5,901 combatants out of the 32 million men and women enlisted in the Soviet Armed Forces.[18]

The most dramatic of all such missions was the attempt to rescue Stalin's son Jakov, a Red Army officer who had been taken prisoner during the siege of Smolensk in 1941 and was interned in *KL*-Sachsenhausen. The operation was planned, under the greatest secrecy, by the Soviet High Command. A special commando was assembled from among the most élite troops available, but the key role was entrusted to José Parra Moya, known to his comrades as 'Parrita'. Given a false identity, that of Lieutenant Luis Mendoza Peña, and a German uniform with the red and gold shield of the Blue Division on the right arm, Parra was parachuted behind German lines, and though stopped continually for identity checks he travelled through the Baltic Republics. The attempt to penetrate *KL*-Sachsenhausen, however, was cancelled. Parra succeeded in returning to Soviet lines and resumed his normal place in the Red Army.[19]

Altogether, some 700 Spaniards fought in the defence of the Soviet Union, with 300 of them dying in battle, or reported missing.[20] Two (including Gullón) received the Order of Lenin, and seventy received other awards (the Red Flag, the Red Star, the Great Patriotic War, and the Guerrilla Medal). However, it was not Gullón who emerged pre-eminent among the Spanish heroes who died in Russia. That honour went, not haphazardly, to the sons of two famous women: Rubén Ruiz Ibarruri and Santiago de Paúl Nelken. Unlike so many of their compatriots they had no difficulty in obtaining commissions as officers in the Red Army.

Rubén Ruiz, Pasionaria's only son,[21] was serving as a lieutenant commanding a machine-gun company in a Guards unit when he first saw action at Borisov, in September 1941. Badly wounded in the shoulder, he was evacuated to a hospital in Ufa, conveniently close to his mother. There he received the award of the Red Flag. So determined was he to return to the front—or as Pasionaria's detractors have put it, so disgusted was he by his mother's treatment of his father[22]—that he slipped out of the hospital before his wounds were healed. In July 1942 he was given command of a company at Scholkobo near the capital. He later took part, as a captain in the 35th Guards Division, in the opening stage of the Battle of Stalingrad, in which he was mortally wounded on 3 September 1942, while leading a counter-attack; transported to the nearby village of Srednaya Ajtuve on the left bank of the Volga, he died the same day.[23] As for Santiago de Paúl Nelken, he was the son of Margarita Nelken, the Catalan writer and art critic who had been a Socialist representative for Bajadoz in the Cortes.[24] A graduate of the Red Army's engineering school in Moscow, he too served in the defence of the capital, as a captain in a trench-mortar unit. After taking part in various engagements in the Ukraine, his body was found blown to bits by a shell in January 1944. The remains of both men lie buried in Volgograd (ex-Stalingrad), in the Square of the Fallen Heroes.[25]

The German invasion obviously made things worse for the Spanish children. Their centres were transferred to Tbilisi and Samarkand, and to remote and distant points in and beyond the Urals. There they were put to work in the factories and the collective farms, especially in Aircraft Factory 31 in Tbilisi. Other children, abandoned in the chaos of the Soviet retreat, joined the ranks of the *besprizorni*, vagabonds and delinquents who might well finish up in penitentiaries in Siberia.[26] Prison and death did not deter them. Hunger and cold, which were to take the lives of 1,500 of the Spanish children in Russia, drove the children in Tashkent and Kokand to form highway gangs that engaged in armed robberies and worse against the local inhabitants.

In Kazan, a gang held up a baker's shop. Among those arrested was the son of Colonel Carrasco, a former officer of the Republican Army who had been admitted to the Frunze Academy in Moscow; the boy died of tuberculosis in prison. As for the young girls, in Tbilisi and in Samarkand they were driven by hunger to prostitute themselves to army officers or government officials. Some fifteen Spanish children fell into German hands. The Germans normally returned such prisoners to Franco, but an exception was made in the case of the daughter of Virgilio Llanos, a former commissar of the Republican Army. She was 18 when she was taken prisoner near Stalingrad, and the Nazis persuaded her to take part in propaganda broadcasts beamed to the Soviets.[27]

Meanwhile, the senior Spanish officers, who had naturally expected to be given major assignments, received to their astonishment and chagrin only menial tasks and empty honours. Modesto, Líster, and Cordón, who deserved most, were given insignificant posts or were made instructors on the general staff. All three were made generals of the Red Army in November 1944, but they were still not given any command. Even when the Red Army re-entered Poland, and the three were given the uniform of colonel or higher in the so-called Polish Liberation Army, they were still not put in command of a unit nor did they participate in any military action.[28] All of this could have given some satisfaction to el Campesino, had he not so many troubles of his own. The machinations of Líster had left him stripped of his rank of general, dismissed from the Frunze Academy, and expelled from the Party. In late 1941, he, his beautiful Russian wife, and their infant son were sent to Tashkent, where there were at that time several hundred Spanish women and children. The boy was among those who died of hunger, while el Campesino was showing the initial symptoms of tuberculosis. Rather than allow his wife and himself to share the fate of their son, el Campesino began his career as a highway robber, distributing his spoils among the Spanish mothers and their starving children and thus saving several lives. The Soviet authorities now ordered his wife to return to Moscow, forbidding him to accompany her. If the PCE leaders hoped he would now kill himself out of loneliness, they were disappointed. At the head of a band of robbers, el Campesino made his way across the 1,500 miles to the capital, selling on the black market what they stole *en route*. His reunion with his wife was brief. Arrested by the police, he escaped the firing squad only through the intervention of some friends in the Party who invoked his exploits in Spain. He was sentenced instead to forced labour in the Moscow Metro. In prison or out, he still had Líster to worry about. On one occasion Líster and two of his cronies[29] burst into el

Campesino's room where he and his wife were sitting on the sofa. 'Not dead yet, you dog?' snarled Líster, and with the aid of the other two, who held el Campesino down, Líster began hitting him with his fists, then with a chair, until el Campesino broke loose, darted to the window, and yelled for help.

Tired of his life as a robber, fearful of Líster's malice, el Campesino made up his mind, in mid-1944 when his wife was in the seventh month of her second pregnancy, that he could regain his reputation only by getting out of the Soviet Union and that he must leave at once. One evening as she returned from a visit to her parents, his wife found a farewell note on the table; if her husband already had a plan of escape he was keeping it to himself. El Campesino worked out his plan with two friends (Major Román Lorente and Lieutenant Salvador Campillo), both of them experienced pilots from the school in Kirovabad who had enlisted as officers in the Polish Liberation Army. This Army, formed in Moscow in 1941, contained almost no Poles and was merely a propaganda device. In 1944 the two Spanish officers were discharged and returned to Moscow in their Polish uniforms. Their clothing kits enabled them to fit out el Campesino too in Polish uniform, and with safe-conduct passes and forged documents showing them to be on a special assignment, they arrived by train at the Caspian Sea, where they took a boat to Iran. In Teheran they were arrested as suspects by a British patrol and held in a camp where they pleaded for asylum. The British gave them only a light guard and asked London for instructions. Fearful that the British authorities might hand them over to Franco, the three Spaniards did not wait, knocking out the sentry and making their escape, only to be picked up down the road by a Soviet patrol. While they had dumped their Polish uniforms, the Soviet documents and medals they still carried were their undoing. The NKVD took them back to the Soviet Union, where all three were sentenced to forced labour in the coal mines of Pechora. El Campesino insists that up to this moment he was still a Stalinist.[30] If so, the Gulag system now gave him fresh insight and made him more determined than ever to escape. He did, and again he was caught. He tried a third time, and this time Stalin was to pay most dearly for his failure to silence a key witness, for if the Spaniard's wife and the infant daughter he never saw became the surrogate victims of Stalin's rage for revenge,[31] it served to stoke his own.

Since the top Spanish officers were exempted from military action, they were free to observe and take part in all the devious operations of the politicians. On 18 October 1941, while the 4th Special Company was engaged in the defence of Moscow, every official in the

Comintern Secretariat (numbering between 2,000 and 2,500) and every member of the Comintern Executive Committee (some 200) was ordered to appear at the capital's Kazan station between 6 and 8 p.m. for departure to Ufa, carrying only a suitcase. The PCE leaders went with them.[32] The train took ten days to reach Kuibyshev, the new Soviet capital on the Volga, where Hernández got out,[33] but only another day to reach Ufa. There the Comintern's Executive Committee was housed in a school, while Pasionaria was given two rooms in the Hotel Bashkiria on Leninski Prospekt, one for herself and Antón and one for her children. Although the PCE leaders did not remain long in Ufa before returning to Moscow, it was in Ufa that Radio España Independiente: Estación Pirenaica began to broadcast on 22 July 1941. While the radio station was directed by Castro Delgado, its policy was set by Togliatti, the overall supervisor for all broadcasts and foreign printed material.[34] That policy was to further the Anglo-Soviet alliance and avoid alienating the Spanish conservative class. As a result, there were to be no further references to communism, class struggle, or revolution; the terms now in vogue were patriotism, democracy, and co-existence. The only elements around Franco now under attack were the 'Germanized' generals such as Muñoz Grandes and Yagüe. Even the Falange was no longer denounced in its entirety but a distinction made between its native and its 'Germanized' elements. As for Pasionaria, every Sunday she made a special broadcast to Catholics, written entirely by her, in which she invoked Christian humanism, its sense of social justice, and love for all men of goodwill.[35]

At the time the Nazis struck, José Díaz was well removed from the centre of Party and Comintern affairs, shut away as he was in Pushkin, near Leningrad. Accompanied only by his NKVD escort, he was now transferred to Tbilisi. On the eve of his third operation since arriving in the Soviet Union, Díaz received a message from Stalin asking if there was anything the Spanish secretary-general might wish before passing under the knife. Díaz replied that his only wish was 'to squeeze the hand of Stalin'. His wish was granted: for the first and only time, Stalin came to his bedside, accompanied by a large number of Soviet officials of the Comintern.[36] While recuperating from the operation on 19 March 1942, Díaz fell to his death from his balcony on the fourth floor. He was only 47. There is no known witness to the death scene. The principal accounts attribute his death to suicide or defenestration.[37] It is certain that his doctor, Josep Bonifaci, knows the truth, but he has changed his story. Dr Bonifaci told both Castro Delgado[38] and Jorge Semprún[39] (when both Bonifaci and Semprún were members of the

PCE Central Committee) that Díaz had committed suicide, that his death was premeditated, and that he had left five letters on his table, which were then picked up by the NKVD. Castro describes how Bonifaci, who came to see him in his hotel room in Moscow, betrayed his fear when he spoke of the five letters. El Campesino, arguing the case that Díaz was pushed, mentions that the adjacent room was reserved for the doctors, and accompanying them, two NKVD agents.[40] But when Bonifaci was confronted by the author, without warning, on a staircase in a suburb of Barcelona, he declared that at the moment Díaz died he himself was 1,000 kilometres from Tiflis, and that he did not sign the death certificate or examine the body. His testimony was not convincing.[41] Díaz's wife Teresa Márquez and daughter Teresita were in the Hotel Bashkiria in Ufa, as was Pasionaria, when they received the news from Dimitrov by phone from Moscow.[42] As for the corpse, it was customary to honour communist party leaders who died in the Soviet Union by burying them in the wall of the Kremlin. Díaz was given nothing. He was buried without a stone.[43]

The death of Díaz left open the problem of his successor. There were two possible contenders: Jesús Hernández, who was then working as a foreign correspondent and radio commentator in Kuibyshev, the provisional capital, in the company of Dimitrov; and Pasionaria, in Ufa with the rest of the Comintern. Among the PCE delegates in Russia, the preference ran overwhelmingly for Hernández. He had a reputation for helping those in need and especially those who wanted to leave the Soviet Union. Líster and Modesto were firmly in his camp. As for Pasionaria, her indifference to the fate of the Spanish rank-and-file in Russia, together with the arrogance of her clique, left her with very few diehard supporters at the higher levels of the Party other than her lover Antón, her secretary Irene de Falcón, and her disciples Gallego and Carrillo. Gallego was now her son-in-law and was also indebted to her for finding him a seat on the PCE delegation to the Comintern. Carrillo was in América, where he could do little to help. The thought of the PCE leadership going to a woman led the Soviets at first to favour Hernández. Both Dimitrov and Manuilski gave him their support. But if the Kremlin felt no enthusiasm for the candidacy of Pasionaria, certain Soviet leaders were even less ready to see the Party fall into the hands of Hernández, who was guilty of two serious crimes: independence of spirit, and excessive popularity. They might have worried more had they known about Hernández's inner deliberations about the possibilities of assassinating Stalin.[44] As for the friendship that had developed between his wife Pilar Boves and Stalin's daughter Svetlana, it could not have improved his stock in Stalin's eye. The young and rather unattractive redhead who was bored to frenzy by her ever-present nurse certainly preferred the company of Pilar, who talked to her about fashion and bourgeois soirées and taught her how to knit sweaters. Svetlana's sweaters soon became Stalin's aversion. He hated them to be tight, and it drove him to violence.[45]

Months went by and the PCE still did not have a secretary-general. In September 1942, when Pasionaria lost her only son, she won a certain sympathy, but her grief threw her for a time into even greater isolation.[46] Hernández, meanwhile, was subjected to increasing criticism. Several of his closest supporters, including Modesto and Líster, were deserting him in favour of Pasionaria. But if Hernández was losing the contest for the leadership, he was about to gain something he valued more: the chance to leave the USSR.

In the early summer of 1942, while Hernández was in Kuibyshev, he received a phone call from Dimitrov in Moscow, summoning him at once to his office. The first thing he was told when he arrived was that Antonio Mije, co-leader of the PCE delegation in Mexico, was a *provocateur*. The more substantial charge was that he had made contact with American agents. Dimitrov showed him the copy of the cable he had sent Mije ordering him to desist, and the cable he had subsequently received from Soviet secret agents in Mexico describing Mije's reaction to the order. 'What the hell does Dimitrov know about any of this?' was how Mije was quoted. Dimitrov was still fuming with rage. Mije had to be removed from the leadership in Mexico at the earliest moment. Hernández had been selected to take his place.[47]

There was surely more to Mije's disgrace than what Dimitrov told Hernández. His decision to take his family from France to New York, and from there to Mexico, rather than move to the Soviet Union which had been so often the object of his praise, might have raised some suspicions. It is also possible that the Kremlin had offered him control of the International Red Help, and that he had declined the offer. Or again, that Mije could not exonerate himself in the Kremlin's eyes for the loss of the PCE archives which disappeared during the crossing into France and finished up in the hands of the French police. But whatever mistakes Mije might have made—and he survived them—they were nothing compared with those made by Hernández. On hearing the news of his departure, it was as much as he could do to conceal his joy. Yet despite his frantic efforts, months went by and still he lacked the necessary visas. The arrival in Moscow in May 1943 of his good friend Luis Quintanilla as Mexico's ambassador settled the question of the Mexican visa in eight days, but the transit visa from the United States authorities still eluded him. As a result, he was still in the Soviet Union on 22 May 1943 when he learned, from the newspapers, that the Comintern had been dissolved.[48]

The dissolution of the Comintern served to show how tightly wrapped the organization was. Castro Delgado, who was a member of its executive committee, writes that it changed its name to Scientific Institute 205 when it moved to Ufa,[49] and that this changed again, after the supposed dissolution, to Scientific Institute 301.[50] But Castro himself admits that he knew little about what was happening in the Comintern; the only ones who knew were Dimitrov, Manuilski, and Togliatti,[51] and Castro learned of its dissolution as Hernández did, only by reading about it in the Press.[52]

The question of the succession had still not been resolved when in autumn 1943 Hernández finally received his marching orders. He was to leave with Francisco Antón for Vladivostok, in the hope that their United States visas would by then have arrived. But in Vladivostok they waited two months in vain. Hernández wrote to Dimitrov that it was useless to wait longer and obtained his permission to leave without the visa. On arrival in Vancouver, the Canadian police were waiting. He was ordered to return to his port of departure, but with the help of lawyers engaged by Earl Browder, the leader of the American Communist Party, he was transferred to a prison in Seattle. As Hernández describes it, a storm of protest in the American Press persuaded the US Department of State to allow him free transit into Mexico, where he arrived in January 1944.[53]

In letting him go, the Kremlin was making sure that it would be the arbiter of the succession, and that its choice of Pasionaria would not be contested. With Hernández gone, Pasionaria had no serious rival in the Soviet Union, and if the leadership of the Party were to be decided in Mexico, now the home of the majority of its Politburo, Pasionaria's supporters there were much stronger than those of Hernández.[54] That was obvious soon enough to Hernández, who now discovered that Mexico City could match Moscow as a centre for Byzantine intrigue. Fernández Checa had died on 2 August 1942, following an appendectomy. Uribe had suggested that Carrillo take Checa's place, if only to stop Mije from taking it. Carrillo had left for Argentina instead, just before Hernández arrived in Mexico. As for Hernández, Uribe loathed him, and Hernández loathed him right back. He arrived in Mexico City with pneumonia, and was promptly shut up in the Hotel Roosevelt where Uribe forbade anyone to visit him. The reason why Antón had accompanied him from Moscow was now apparent. Officially, all members of the Politburo had a distinct assignment; Hernández was responsible for propaganda, and Antón for organization.[55] But Antón had loftier ambitions: he hoped to become the new Checa. Since the far more gifted Hernández stood in his way, and since Hernández's ideas were much more contagious than his germs, he was now sent off to a convalescent home in Cuernavaca while Antón could instruct the Party members in the danger he represented. By the time Hernández returned to the capital, opinion in the rank-and-file had turned from cordial to glacial.[56]

None of this made much difference to Hernández. He never missed a chance to denounce the incompetence of Uribe and Mije in their management of the Party in Latin America. At the same time he went right on criticizing life in the Soviet Union, revealing to his compatriots the frightful conditions under which the Spanish immigrants were living. He even accused Pasionaria of having brought about the death of Díaz in order to replace him in the leadership.[57] It was little wonder that the Central Committee in Moscow met, on 7 April 1944, to consider the case of Hernández. He was accused of wanting to gain control of the Party in order to withdraw it from the Comintern, of acting out of spite when he lost the succession to Pasionaria, and of anti-Soviet activity for proposing that the Spanish emigrants be free to leave.[58] Not only was Hernández removed from his seat on the PCE delegation to the Comintern—proof that the Comintern still existed—but he was expelled from the Party as a traitor and an enemy of the people.

Hernández had left Russia despite his fear for the safety of his family[59] and especially for his friend Castro Delgado, who was on no better terms than he with Pasionaria. Castro, for his part, could not forgive Hernández for leaving. 'I saw him off,' he wrote, 'without rancour or hatred. . . . What he did was human, but it was also criminal.'[60] Castro's memoirs were to appear before Hernández's, and the depth of Hernández's disillusionment was clearly not known to Castro when he wrote, in his assessment of the PCE leaders in Moscow: 'Neither does Hernández count for much. He will never draw the conclusion that we were cheated, that socialism does not exist, that the concept of power to the working class has been replaced by a system of castes.'[61] To Hernández, of course, and to the other dissidents, Castro was the renegade who finished up in the Franco camp.[62]

Hernández's fears were well founded. On 5 May 1944, Castro went on trial in Moscow, in front of the PCE Central Committee members resident in the USSR and Stepanov as representative of the Comintern. Castro was expelled from the delegation to the Comintern, from the Central Committee, and from the directorship of Radio España Independiente,[63] but not from the Party, and he took the initiative of writing to Stalin and Molotov. Almost certainly his close friendship with Caridad del Río Mercader, the mother of Trotsky's killer, saved him, and in the early winter of 1945 he and his wife were allowed to leave for Mexico. If Castro had counted on the PCE, Tagüeña remarks, he could have spent the rest of his life in the Soviet Union.[64] Such was now the fate of those in Hernández's family whom he had left behind in Moscow, and who were now deported to a forced labour camp. One of these camps had become a rendezvous for Spaniards of all kinds.

The name of Karaganda has come to symbolize the sufferings and the disillusionment of so many Spanish antifascists who arrived in the Soviet Union unaware of what lay in store. It was not the only camp the victims knew,[65] but it was the camp where almost all the survivors from the other camps finished up.

Most of the 6,000 Spanish refugees in Russia were communists or the children of communists, but two other groups were not refugees at all but visitors who found themselves in the Soviet Union at the end of the Civil war by mere chance. These groups, composed of aircrew and merchant seamen, had tried to leave Russia in 1939, but were prevented from doing so by the Soviet authorities.[66]

The aircrew, 210 in all, most of them pilots, had arrived in Russia in various contingents, one at the end of 1937 and others in 1938 and 1939,[67] for the purpose of receiving further training. Many of them had already had battle experience in Spain. Only a fifth of them were communists.[68] They were sent first to a training school in Baku, on the Caspian Sea, where they were warmly received by the young Caucasian women who regarded them as heroes of the Spanish Revolution. From Baku they were directed in March 1939 to the training school at Kirovabad, where they distinguished themselves as fine pupils and received excellent treatment. Then later—the moment is in question[69]—the situation abruptly changed. Colonel Pedro Martínez Cartón arrived in Kirovabad with the authority to act in the name of the leaders of the PCE. He had once held a seat in the Cortes and had served in the Politburo; he was now a member of the NKVD. His purpose in Kirovabad was to conduct a questionnaire asking the airmen whether they preferred to return to Spain, leave for America, or remain in the Soviet Union. The names of those who expressed a preference to leave the USSR—all but sixty-five—were handed over to the Soviet authorities at the base.[70] The next day the mood of the Russians changed from friendly to sullen or hostile, and all the airmen were recalled, to be housed in a residence in Moscow.[71] A woman survivor of Karaganda reported that the airmen received a series of visits from two PCE delegates: the wife of General Manuel Tagüeña and the commissar José Sébil, an inseparable companion of Enrique Líster. They suggested to the airmen that they participate in a spectacular act of homage to Stalin. When the airmen showed little interest in the proposal, they were arrested. Twelve of them were taken away in a NKVD truck and were never seen again.[72] Twenty-six were sent on such an odyssey of camps and prisons that it is difficult to record it precisely, but the route lay through Tobolsk, Tomsk, and Novosibirsk to Yakut in eastern Siberia; there they worked on the construction of a railroad running along the river Lema, on the rim of the Arctic circle, where the cold reached −70 °C. They remained there for two months, during which time many died. All the rest would have died in another two months had they not been transferred to Krasnoyarsk, where they were employed in a giant sawmill whose lack of elementary safeguards caused the death or mutilation of many. From there they were sent back to Novosibirsk,[73] and finally, in November 1942, to Karaganda. Only half a dozen of the airmen survived.[74]

As for the 274 merchant seamen, they were crew members of at least four vessels[75] of which the largest was the *Cabo San Agustín*, a three-funnelled steamer owned by the Compañía Ibarra and commissioned by the Spanish Republican Government to ply between the Republic's ports in Levante and Soviet ports in the Black Sea. As the Civil War proceeded, this vessel was used to evacuate from Spain large quantities of gold and valuables. Towards the end of 1938 the vessel was in Odessa and preparing to return to Spain when the Soviet authorities prevented it from sailing. It was a time when Stalin, convinced that the Republic had lost the war, was eager to withdraw his advisers and specialists from Spain while there was still time. He was equally eager to prevent the Spanish seamen, who knew more than a few secrets about Soviet trade with the Spanish Republic, from revealing what they knew, and the fact that the anarchist movement had a strong following in the Spanish navy and merchant navy gave him extra reason to fear them.

The Spanish seamen soon had fears of their own. Russian girls were now sent from Moscow to Odessa with the mission of befriending them. They offered the Spaniards the choice between a free ticket to any country they preferred and an excellent job in Soviet industry if they chose to stay in Russia. The great majority of the seamen expressed a preference to leave. A few of these asked to return to Spain; these were given their tickets at once and returned to their homeland in August and September 1939 via Turkey or, when the moment came, via Germany. But of those who expressed the wish to move to other countries—Mexico, Argentina, Chile, the United States, Australia, and France were the favourites—not one received a visa. Heavy pressure was then applied to these Spaniards in the hope that they would agree to enter Soviet factories, but again the majority refused to submit. Those who did were incorporated into the collectives for political exiles, especially those in Vorochilovgrad and Taganrog. Many of the seamen sent to Vorochilovgrad arrived there with the Russian wives they had married in Odessa and Feodosiya. Some of these wives may have been among the agents whom Stalin sent from Moscow to 'befriend' the Spaniards, for the Spaniards soon learned to avoid like the plague any Russian girl who could speak Spanish, on the grounds that these girls were invariably NKVD agents. But not before many a Spaniard, in his forlorn loneliness, and with passionate sincerity, succumbed to the wiles of these enchanters who wrung from them the secrets of their very souls.[76]

The seamen now experienced, in June 1941, the same odyssey as the airmen. From the prisons of Odessa and Feodosiya they followed the route that led to Yakut, and finally, for the twenty still alive in November 1942, to the camp of Karaganda. Eugenio Mostilla, captain of the *Cabo San Agustín*, died in the railway station in Tashkent, stretched out like a dog, famished, before the Spaniards in that city could bring him food.[77] The ship's doctor died in Yakut, while the first mate, the socialist Ramón Sánchez Gómez, and the political commissar, the anarchist Secundino Rodríguez de la Fuente, who was highly popular among the crew, died in Karaganda.

It was to Karaganda, by the winter of 1942, that all the surviving Spanish Republican prisoners were transferred. This camp, sometimes known as Spassk, was located to the north of Lake Balkhash in Kazakhstan, between the coal- and tungsten-producing city of Karaganda and the little town of Spassk; the area, known as Bet Pakdala ('the steppe of famine'), is twice the size of Denmark. Up to the end of the 1920s there was no permanent construction anywhere on the entire steppe, for the Kazaks were nomadic. The prisoners began to arrive there in 1932, and it was they who built the camp, which was originally called the Karaganda State Farm of the OGPU. It became the Karaganda Special Regime Corrective Labour camp of the Ministry of International Affairs and was known as Camp 99; its postal address was consequently 99/22 Spassk, but the commandant Serikov took care that no letter so addressed by any relative or international agency ever reached a prisoner.[78]

It is difficult to estimate the prison population of Karaganda, precisely because of its vast extent and of the apparent confusion between the centre at Dolinskoi and the huge outer complex. The press of the semi-Trotskyist POUM reported a total population of 150,000 prisoners of both sexes, employed in the copper, coal, iron, and silver mines of the region, and referred to Area 26, a unit situated in Akmolinsk and popularly known as the 'widows' camp' since it contained a sizeable number of wives and widows of Soviet leaders who had been imprisoned or executed during the various purges.[79] None of this was exaggerated. In 1988 *Kazakhstanskaya Pravda* revealed that Karaganda at that time included 'hundreds of thousands' of prisoners, and that Area 26 was 'the Akmolinsk camp for wives of traitors to the Homeland.'[80]

Dolinskoi itself was only 300 yards square. At the time the Spaniards arrived in 1942, the total number of prisoners—men, women, and children—was no more than 800, and though it increased shortly afterwards to 1,400 it remained microscopic in terms of the Gulag archipelago. By 1946 the population had fallen to 700; most of these were Austrian Jews,[81] but the rest were of a very wide range of nationalities and included sixty Spaniards. The sexes were separated in their barracks, but otherwise their life was collective. In the universe of Stalin's penal colonies their sufferings were no different from the main. Pulmonary tuberculosis was rife. The daily food ration corresponded to the minimum necessary to maintain life: 600 grams of black bread, 10 grams of margarine, a concoction called soup served at midday and evening, and 17 grams of sugar which was not regularly distributed. Inmates of the camp prison were fed only once every three days, when they received the soup and 100 grams of bread. But even amid the general suffering there was room for the individual human tragedy. There was the case of Dr Juan Boté García, interned in Karaganda from 1942, admired by everyone, and loved by the orphans who looked upon him as their father. For refusing to teach the children Marxist doctrine (and perhaps just for teaching them reading, writing, and arithmetic instead),[82] he was seized and transferred to Siberia, where he disappeared without a trace.[83]

The story of the Gulag archipelago remained virtually unknown (or unproven) in the West until 1948, when it fell to the press of the POUM and the anarchists to take the lead in the exposure. The weekly *Batalla*, organ of the POUM, published the following estimates on the growth of the Soviet penal system:[84]

	Number of prisoners	Number of camps
1928	30,000	unknown
1930	662,257	6
1932	2,000,000	unknown
1937	5–6,000,000	35
1942	2,000,000	38
1947	>20,000,000	125

To the 1947 figure of 125 should be added several other camps not located. The largest camp of all was the Sevostlag, meaning Camp of the North-East, but better known as Kolyma. Situated mid-distant from Yakoutsk, the Bay of Nogaev, and the estuary of the river Kolyma, this enormous complex had its administrative centre at Magadan, on the coast of the Sea of Okhotsk. Kolyma had a slave population in 1940 of over 3,000,000.[85] But statistics, however horrendous, can never describe the reality of a concentration camp. What emerged in the studies that followed, especially in the inquiry undertaken by the Commission internationale contre le régime concentrationnaire, based in Brussels, was the remarkable similarity (even though the Commission made no such comparison) between the Soviet Gulag and the Nazi *Konzentrationslager*, which had been obliterated only two years earlier. This similarity was confirmed by the most authoritative sources imaginable: the wretched victims who had passed through both systems and survived.

A few examples may suffice to illustrate this similarity. The first concerns the choice of site. Just as Himmler chose to build a camp at Buchenwald near Weimar, around the tree where Goethe used to sit with Eckermann, so Yezhov picked Taganrog, the birthplace of Chekhov. Second, the NKVD derived the same direct benefit from the camps as did the SS, living off the proceeds of the labour of the prisoners. Third, the camps themselves were subdivided. Just as Mauthausen, for example, had its Aussenkommandos, grouped around the central camp but set as far afield as Vienna and Wiener Neustadt, so the Soviet concentration camp included annexes at distances of tens and sometimes hundreds of kilometres from the administrative centre. In the case of Karaganda, the centre was at Dolinskoi, 48 kilometres from the city of Karaganda, while its annexes were located as far away as Vatyk (201 kilometres), Akmolinsk (282 kilometres), Djaltass (483 kilometres), and even Balcache (483 kilometres).[86] Fourth, in the classification of prisoners, a class existed, no different in effect from the *Zigeuner Asoziale* segment bearing the black triangle under the SS, which the NKVD called the *Sotsialno Opasni* Element. This socially dangerous element was the category, Solzhenitsyn tells us, that was given to the Spanish children; he adds that the international camp at Kharkov was full of Spaniards.[87] Whenever such a prisoner was called upon to do so, he had to call out his name (Russified wherever necessary to make the matter simpler), his prisoner number, his classification, and his sentence. (There it might be said that the situation of the prisoner of the SS was worse, since he no longer had a name, nor did he have a sentence, and his whole condition was indicated by the emblems on his clothes.) Fifth, discipline in the Soviet camps was entrusted to the *nachalniki*, who were drawn from the same criminal class of prisoners, enjoyed the same privileges, and exercised the same local tyranny as the green-triangle Kapos chosen by the SS. Finally, even the form of punishment might find its reflection in the other system, and anyone who knew Mauthausen and its infernal 186 steps might be surprised to see, in the punishment camp in the Solovetski Islands, a model of strangely parallel invention. There the steps numbered 273, and were always covered with ice. The prisoner, barefoot and carrying two buckets, had to clamber down the steps to the lake at the bottom, and then fill the buckets through a hole cut in the ice. He then began the climb back. By that time his feet were stiff with cold and he could not keep his balance. As he tottered, the water spilled from the buckets. The guard at the top of the steps would scream to him to go back and refill the buckets. Needless to say, most of those who were subjected to this punishment ended their lives at the bottom of the steps, frozen solid.[88]

Were the similarities between *Konzentrationslager* and Gulag mere coincidence? One is reminded of the testimony of the French journalist Bertrand de Jouvenel, who was in Moscow in 1935 in the press group accompanying Pierre Laval. The group was staying at the Hotel Nazional on Manejnaya Ploschad which was set aside for foreign dignitaries. De Jouvenel was walking down the staircase when a young man walking up stopped and greeted him. He was one of the Hitlerjugend leaders whom he had met in Berlin in January 1934. De Jouvenel asked the Nazi what he was doing in Moscow. He replied that he had been sent to study the Soviet camp system.[89]

The sense of despair for prisoners of the two camp systems was different in kind. A loyal communist in a Stalinist camp could not comprehend his fate as could an antifascist in a camp of Hitler's. It is also true that the sense of being transported thousands of kilometres into a desert of ice made the prisoner of the Gulag feel he had left the world. But it is equally true that the prisoner of the SS who could hear the birds and glimpse the ineffable beauty of the lake at Ebensee as he went to work in its underground tunnels was conscious that nothing but a miracle could keep him alive for three months. The only real difference between the two camp systems, which struck all those who experienced both, is that the NKVD system provided for collective servitude, with the sexes mixed, living in savage promiscuity, indescribable filth, and rank disorder. The SS system was order personified. No *Zek* in the Gulag, and no *Kazettler* in the *Konzentrationslager*, could ever have preferred the one over the other.

8

In France, Inside the Two Camps

Structure of the German military and civil administration in France—Structure of Army Group G—Hitler's strategic priorities—Operation Attila and the reaction of the Spanish guerrilleros—Jesús Ríos assumes general command—Ríos captured; Silvestre Gómez succeeds—The Kremlin's appeal for unity, and the Conference of Grenoble—Formation of the UNE—Growth of a communist journal: Reconquista de España—*The PCE controlling committee, centred in Toulouse—Elimination and replacement of the PCE leadership: Monzón and 'Mariano'—Relations with the MOI and the FTP—The Spanish xivth Army Corps of Guerrilleros integrated into the FTP-MOI—Guerrilla activity in Toulouse—The Manouchian group*

> The roving Spanish Bands are reached at last,
> Charged, and dispersed like foam: but as a flight
> Of scattered quails by signs do reunite,
> So these,[1]

Just 8 kilometres north-east of Toulouse lies a hamlet called Rouffiac-Tolosan. It is less than a kilometre from the railway and highway to Albi, being linked to the latter by two narrow roads; to the south it is bounded by a forest. The château in the centre is today a home for the aged. The name Rouffiac-Tolosan remains virtually unknown, even to those who passed the war in Toulouse, even to historians of the Resistance, and even to historians from Toulouse. Madame Sastre, the director of the present establishment, does not answer questions or reply to letters of inquiry regarding its occupants of 1944, and no doubt she has her reasons; but this hamlet, ideally located, sitting just off the direct escape route to Germany if such were needed, was in 1944 the headquarters of Generaloberst Johannes von Blaskowitz, Commander-in-Chief of the Wehrmacht's Army Group G, responsible for the entire southern half of France.

The German occupation of France consisted of two separate structures, or three if we consider that the SS operated virtually independently and answered to the other two only when it pleased them to do so. The first of these structures was the Wehrmacht's chain of command, the second the organization headed by the military governor (Militärbefehlshaber in Frankreich), resident in Paris.

In the spring of 1944, the forces at the disposal of the Supreme Commander in the West (OB West), Generalfeldmarschall Gerd von Rundstedt,[2] consisted of two army groups. Army Group B, commanded by Generalfeldmarschall Erwin Rommel, was responsible for north-west France, Belgium, and the southern Netherlands.[3] Army Group G, created in May 1944 and placed under the command of Generaloberst Johannes von Blaskowitz, included all forces south of the Loire. At the time of D-Day, the Wehrmacht's strength in France amounted to fifty-nine divisions, of which ten were Panzer, though certain deficiencies were evident: several divisions were below strength, supplies were inadequate, and air support was virtually non-existent.[4]

Von Blaskowitz had come to his eminent post from a position of some obscurity. In 1939 he had commanded the German 8th Army in the invasion of Poland, and it was he who received the surrender of Warsaw on 27 September of that year. But soon afterwards it seemed his star had fallen, and in May 1940 he found himself transferred to an insignificant command. The story ran that he had protested vehemently against the vicious measures introduced into Poland by the SS. The story has its importance, since it established the legend that von Blaskowitz was an anti-Nazi, but it nevertheless runs counter to the evidence, examined later here, that he was responsible for war crimes committed in France.

The army group he now commanded (AG Gustav) amounted to approximately 250,000 men and was responsible for an area stretching from the Bay of Biscay to the Italian frontier, including the Western Mediterranean. From his headquarters outside Toulouse he controlled two armies and a sizeable reserve, with the bulk of his forces positioned to the west of Avignon. The 1st Army, under General Kurt von der Chevallerie, had its headquarters in Bordeaux,[5] while the 19th Army, under General Georg von Sodenstern, was based in Marseilles.

On 7 January 1944, Hitler had concluded that the chances of an Allied landing in Portugal were remote,[6] and the last of his schemes for the Peninsula—Operation *Nürnberg* (the cordoning off of the Spanish frontier)—was thus abandoned.[7] The supreme command in Berlin (OKW) concerned itself next with the fear of an Allied invasion on the Atlantic coast of the French south-west, combined with a second invasion on the Mediterranean coast, which could result in cutting Germany off from Spain and depriving the Reich of its vital supplies of Spanish wolfram. OKW quickly reassured itself on that score. 'Such an undertaking', ran the minutes of that meeting, 'pre-supposes, on the part of the enemy, a greater strategic audacity than has been demonstrated so far. He would have to proceed without the protection of his single-engine fighter aircraft, and would be exposed to the German U-boat reserves and airfields on his left flank.'[8] But nothing was left to chance. Construction had begun on a Mediter-ranean Wall in the late summer of 1943.[9] In reviewing the situation on 1 February, OB West reported to Berlin that barriers were being erected on the Garonne and the Canal du Midi, and plans were under way for the construction of concrete dug-outs.[10] The major strategic task of Army Group G was now to keep open the land bridge between the Atlantic and the Mediterranean.

The other German organization in France, headed by the Militärbefehl-shaber in Frankreich (MBF), had been responsible since June 1940 for all matters pertaining to the military and civil administration. For most of the first two years the post had been held by Otto von Stülpnagel, a monocled Prussian who established his residence in the capital's most elegant hotel, the Raphael (a Turner original hung in the foyer), and his headquarters in the adjacent Hôtel Majestic. Directly behind it he constructed a concrete bunker of such prodigious durability that as late as 1970 the French authorities had still not found a way to demolish it.[11] Under Stülpnagel the Occupied Zone was subdivided into four districts (*Bezirke*), centred in Paris, Saint-Germain-en-Laye (north-west), Angers (south-west), and Dijon (north-east). Each *Bezirk* was responsible for a number of local headquarters (*Kommandanturen*), with a *Kommandantur* for every French prefecture and a *Kreis-kommandantur* for the most important subprefectures.

The most striking feature of the German administration was the rivalry that existed among its organizations. Several of them made use of the French police, placed at first under the control of SS-Brigadeführer Dr Werner Best, and where repression was concerned they even competed. The Army also had its own intelligence service, the Abwehr; from his headquarters in the Hotel Lutétia Colonel Rudolf answered directly to its chief, Admiral Canaris, in Berlin. It was the Abwehr that first gave chase to the Resistance, using for this purpose the Geheimefeldpolizei (GFP) and the Feldgendarmerie. While the latter concerned itself mainly with traffic and curfew enforcement, the GFP, similarly headquartered in the Hotel Lutétia, was responsible for carrying out the executions ordered by the Abwehr.

In April 1942 the struggle between the Wehrmacht and the Reichsführer-SS for the control of all police work in France was re-solved in Himmler's favour. Hitler gave him full responsibility, and

Himmler responded by sending to France, with the title Höhere SS-und-Polizeiführer (HSSPF-Frankreich), his trusted associate SS-Gruppenführer Karl Albrecht Oberg. Oberg's mission was to set up in France the same system that existed in Germany, with the police virtually independent of, and superior to, the military. To this end Himmler made Oberg his personal representative in every branch of administration in France: the Supreme Commander West (von Rundstedt), the German occupation forces in France (von Stülpnagel), the German ambassador (Abetz), and the French Government. His function was part of Himmler's plan gradually to eliminate the Wehrmacht from the administration of the Occupied Territories, prior to the final goal of putting the SS in command of the Wehrmacht.[12]

To succeed in his mission, Oberg could hardly rely on his charm. Bald and stout, he knew nothing about France; he spoke appalling French, and with difficulty. Laval said that to speak to him was like talking to a block of cement.[13] He was none the less a dedicated Nazi, hardworking and meticulous, and these qualities were sufficient to win him the name of 'the Butcher of Paris'. Oberg set up his headquarters at 57 boulevard Lannes, and appointed as his deputy, with the title Befehlshaber der Sicherheitspolizei und des Sicherheitsdienstes (BdS-Frankreich), the SS-Sturmbannführer Helmut Knochen, a young man of 28 who, like Best, held a doctorate of philosophy.[14] Knochen chose as his headquarters the building at 72 avenue Foch, the fashionable boulevard which had served in the 1930s as the parade ground for the reactionary demonstrations of Colonel de La Rocque. Knochen was assisted in turn by deputies known as Kommandeure der Sipo und des SD, abbreviated to KdS. These officers, directly involved in the work of the Gestapo proper, included Karl Boemelburg and Kurt Lischka. The former was relatively old, but spoke excellent French and knew every detail of the French police organization, which (after the departure of Dr Best) he then controlled; the latter, another doctor of philosophy, was responsible for Paris and installed himself in the building of the French Ministry of the Interior, at 11 rue des Saussaies.

It should be noted that the term 'Gestapo' has been grossly over-used in historical accounts. If the Sipo-SD personnel in France totalled about 2,000, most of them working in their offices on the avenue Foch, its Amt IV (Gestapo) barely exceeded a hundred for the whole of France, and the Gestapo only went calling when they were in possession of an important lead. They did have the help, however, of the Selbstschütz, the action units made up of French volunteers under the Alsatian Bickler.[15] These in turn had the help of the informers, whose pay scale is on record: 5,000 francs to a woman agent providing pillow talk, 5,000–10,000 francs for an average-size assignment, and 20,000 francs a month for an agent regularly employed.[16]

Meanwhile, the growing influence exerted by the SS in France induced Otto von Stülpnagel to resign, and on 20 February 1942 Hitler appointed Otto's younger cousin, Karl-Heinrich von Stülpnagel, to replace him. Since orders displayed in the streets and elsewhere carried no other signature than that of von Stülpnagel, it was some time before the French populace realized that there had been a change of command. The change, in fact, carried major possibilities. While Otto was to be arrested by the French in 1946 and tried in Paris for crimes against humanity—he committed suicide in his prison cell in 1948—the tall, slim, cultured Karl-Heinrich was secretly opposed to Nazism and had been associated with the cabal which tried to overthrow Hitler in 1938. In his desire to avoid responsibility for the repression he knew to be inevitable, he sought, and acquired, a division of authority between the military responsibility which he retained and the political responsibility, including police operations, which he now gladly delegated to Oberg.

Knochen's deputies, the KdS, were installed from the beginning in Rouen, Dijon, and especially Bordeaux, where the assignment went to SS-Sturmbannführer Herbert-Martin Hagen. Hagen arrived in Bordeaux in late August 1940 with five men and two women, setting up his discreet little group on board the abandoned yacht of the King of the Belgians. In May 1942 Hagen was succeeded by SS-Hauptsturmführer Dr Hans Luther, and he in turn, in October 1942, by SS-Sturmbannführer Dr Walther Machule, but the man most steeped in villainy was their subordinate, Friedrich-Wilhelm Dhose. Dhose was a mere sergeant when Boemelburg sent him from Paris, but he would soon win promotion for his success in dismantling the Bordeaux Resistance. Communist suspects were interned in the building at 24 quai de Bacalan, in a camp erected at Mérignac-Beaudésert, or in the Boudet Prison entrusted to SS-Hauptsturmführer Hortman. There as elsewhere, elements of the French police assisted the Gestapo in its hell-born work, Commissaire Poinsot and his team contributing to the Nazi cause with the capture of nearly 1,000 members of the Resistance. Treason, too, explains the difficulties facing the Bordeaux Resistance in the period from July 1943 to March 1944.

It would be wrong to say that the SS waited until the invasion of the Unoccupied Zone in November 1942 before extending its activities to the whole of France, but with the invasion of 11 November six new branches were formally established in the Midi: in Vichy (Geissler), Limoges (Jessen), Lyons (Dr Knab), Marseilles (Rolf Mühler), Montpellier (Dr Tanzmann), and Toulouse (Retzek). SS-Hauptsturmführer Helmut Retzek obtained the KdS post in Toulouse as a result of his diligence in Bordeaux, and his authority now ran from the Demarcation Line in the west[17] to Marseilles in the east; his only superiors in

France were SS-Hauptsturmführer Kurt Geissler in Vichy and Oberg in Paris.[18] His first premises in Toulouse were a building on the rue Rivals. He later set up shop in the Hôtel de l'Ours Blanc on the rue d'Austerlitz, a mere hundred yards from place Wilson and the centre of the city's social life.[19] The strength of the Resistance in the Toulouse area explains why Retzek had jumped the gun on the invasion of November 1942, opening his operations not only in Toulouse but in Pau, Carcassonne, Cahors, and Caussade.

The southern zone, like the northern, was now divided into military districts, the only difference being the name given to them: instead of *Bezirke* they were called *Hauptverbindungsstäbe* (*HVS*), of which the most important to the Resistance were *HVS* 564 (Toulouse), *HVS* 588 (Clermont-Ferrand), and *HVS* 590 (Lyons).[20] Vichy's authority was still recognized by Germany, but in practical matters that authority was much diminished, and to the Resistance the two zones were known simply as North and South. As for the new Militärbefehlshaber, he had no jurisdiction whatever in the South, with the result that Oberg, whose SS-SD now operated as openly there as in the North, was responsible in the South only to Himmler and to OB West. Where Karl-Heinrich von Stülpnagel did indeed maintain control was in the originally occupied sector of the south-west along the Atlantic coast (known to the Resistance as Interregion B), with the result that 1st Army, stationed in Bordeaux, continued to come under his jurisdiction right up until D-Day.[21] Another aspect of this curious arrangement was that MBF came under the orders of OB West where military operations were concerned, but under the direct orders of OKW in Berlin where administration was concerned.[22] It may well have been in Germany's interest to avoid this division of authority in the Supreme Command on the Western front.

Toulouse had now become the centre of all SS-SD operations in the south-west, and a growing number of premises in the city became associated with the day-to-day abominations of the Gestapo. The elegant building on the corner of the allées Frédéric-Mistral and rue Maignac (now rue des Martyrs) became its headquarters, but it also requisitioned numbers 4, 13, and 15 on the same rue Maignac, with annexes in half a dozen other places.[23] The Gestapo (or Section IV) in Toulouse was headed by SS-Obersturmführer Karl Heinz Müller, who answered to Retzek, the KdS. Müller's subordinate Karl Scheid was responsible for the repression of sabotage and resistance activities (or Section IV-2). But the work soon proved too much for Retzek, who often preferred his tennis, and at the end of May 1943[24] he was reassigned (to Nice, then to Albania) and replaced by SS-Obersturmbannführer Dr Rudolf Bilfinger. A lawyer by profession, Bilfinger had made his reputation in the Gestapo in Berlin, and retained excellent relations with Himmler, but his habit of not passing through the proper channels did not sit well with his superiors in Paris. Though harsher than his predecessor, he was not considered harsh enough, and in April 1944 he in turn was reassigned (to Cracow). His place was taken by SS-Obersturmbannführer Friedrich Suhr, whose reputation for severity was such that after the German retreat from the south-west Himmler would name him to replace the disgraced Helmut Knochen as BdS Frankreich, too late in the war for Suhr to apply his energies in the French capital.[25] In Toulouse Suhr and his adjutant Bolle were assisted by an assault force (*Stosstrupp*) made up of French volunteers headed by Pujol and Dedieu.[26]

Theoretically, the Wehrmacht and the Sicherheitsdienst were concerned in the south-west with different enemies, the former preparing to repel invasion on either or both of the coasts, and the latter intent on extirpating the cancer of 'terrorism', this being the word habitually used in German reports with reference to the *maquisards* or the *guerrilleros*. In the disposition of the Wehrmacht forces, we have seen that an army had been allocated to each coast. The 1st Army was responsible primarily for the defence of the Atlantic coast from the Loire to the Pyrenees, but it had further responsibility for protecting communications and suppressing the Maquis through the vast inhospitable hinterland of the Massif Central. For this task it was quite inadequate, being the weakest of the four German armies in France. To the east, 19th Army, with eight divisions, not one of which was armoured, was responsible for the area between Pyrénées-Orientales and the Italian frontier. The south-eastern zone from the frontier westwards nearly to Marseilles[27] had been entrusted, from the time that Vichy was invaded, to the Italian 4th Army,[28] but with the capitulation of Italy on 8 September 1943, the army was called home without ever having fought a battle. The Wehrmacht at once began moving in to take its place, entering Nice on 11 September.

The 19th Army's three corps included the IVth Luftwaffen-Feldkorps under General Petersen, headquartered at Capendu on the main road between Carcassonne and Narbonne, beside the ruins of the Château de Miramont. The existence of such heavy Luftwaffe ground forces is explained by the fact that most German paratroop units had been incorporated by 1939 into the Luftwaffe, which also included such units as tank crews for the defence of airfields. Heinkel and Junker repair shops were set up in the aircraft factories at Blagnac and Colomiers outside Toulouse. Runways were lengthened, and plans were drawn up in 1944 to store V1s and V2s.[29] Another Luftwaffe unit, the Hermann Goering Division, had been withdrawn from the Russian front to recuperate in 1943 and had been assigned to the coastal defences south of Bordeaux.[30]

Stationed between the two German armies of the south stood von Blaskowitz's headquarters force centred in Toulouse, covering the entire region from the Rhône to the Demarcation Line in the west, and from the Pyrenees northwards through the wild Cévennes and the wilder Massif as far as the Loire. The headquarters force, however, had the strength of another army. It comprised the LVIIIth Panzerkorps, the LXVIth Reserve Corps, and a curious unit known as the Ost Legion. As a communications centre linking the German forces on the Atlantic with those on the Mediterranean, Toulouse was considered vital to German strategy. Hence the importance of protecting Highway N 113, linking Bordeaux, Toulouse, and Narbonne. Another vital link was the train route Toulouse–Tarbes–Bayonne: on a single day in 1943 no fewer than fifty munitions trains were counted rolling westwards to the Atlantic Wall; after the landings in Sicily in July 1943 the movement ran in the opposite direction.[31] While this route was a favourite target of the Resistance, Highway N 113, in the Garonne valley, was not advantageous to guerrillas, and attacks on German convoys using the road had to wait until D-Day. But thereafter much of the guerrilla activity of the south-west was directed at that highway, and no less a unit than 'Das Reich' was assigned to its protection: the dreaded division was frequently in operation in towns along the route, especially in Marmande, Tonneins, Aiguillon, and Port-Sainte-Marie.

The golden rule of guerrilla warfare was always the same: avoid combat with a superior force. De Gaulle's injunctions were clear: no guerrilla action was to be undertaken until the signal was given. But this rule and these injunctions ran counter to a certain political expediency. The FTP defied them, deliberately provoking the Germans, as in the case of Jean-Jacques Chapou in the area of Tulle. If the Germans retaliated by shooting hostages, the reasoning went, the more the French would rally to the FTP. In this, the communists in France acted like the communists in Yugoslavia, where Tito, unlike Mihailovic, pressed the attacks regardless of the losses sustained. But whereas Tito was rewarded by dispatches of British arms which earlier had gone to his Cetnik rival, the communists in France found themselves denied supplies from England until as late as the Normandy invasion. In Toulouse and its immediate vicinity, the Resistance in general had few men and fewer weapons,[32] but elsewhere, where the terrain provided the best cover and where German strength was weakest, guerrilla strength was strongest. Even so, the difficulties facing the Maquis should not be underestimated. Living for months and years in the bush raised its own problems of physical and mental health. The basic questions of supply, not only of arms but also of food, had to be solved by intercepting trucks, stealing ration cards from town halls, robbing collaborators, or finding civilians who would support the Resistance with food or money. Beyond that, the secret of survival for a guerrilla group was to maintain constant vigilance and rigid discipline. Hence the vital importance of good leaders.

Six weeks after the Germans invaded the previously unoccupied zone, several commanders of the Spanish *guerrillero* groups convened in Ariège, in a log cabin in the Col de Py, 7 kilometres to the east of Foix. Jesús Ríos had been hunted by the gendarmerie in Aude since 10 September, and had crossed into the adjacent *département* of Ariège with the police in hot pursuit. Under his new name of Mario Martín he had rebuilt his base of operations in the quadrilateral formed by Foix–Pamiers–Mirepoix–Lavelanet. The log cabin in the Col de Py thus served as the first headquarters of xivth Corps. It was now decided to redesign the command structure. Ríos remained commander-in-chief. His wife, Libertad Rocafull, served from the first in liaison. To replace Buitrago, who as we have seen had fallen into the hands of the Gestapo and had died under torture, the post of chief of staff went to Silvestre Gómez. The new post of political commissar went to Modesto Vallador. It was also decided to transfer corps headquarters to the hamlet of Dalou, near Varilhes, while at the same time decentralizing the command in order to facilitate operations on the local level. Of the units so far formed, only four had brigade commanders.[33] The new structure provided for the units in each *département* to form a single brigade, and for the brigades to group regionally into divisions, with one division for three or more *départements*.[34] Each brigade was to be made up of three or four battalions, and each battalion of three companies, with each company operating autonomously in its *département*. Since the strength of a company was between twenty and thirty men, and a battalion between sixty and eighty, it goes without saying that the *guerrillero* divisions did not correspond in size to those of a regular army. Even at the time of the Liberation, the average *guerrillero* division amounted to only 500 men, except in the Haute-Garonne, where the division numbered 1,000.[35] A special battalion of forty *guerrilleros* was placed directly under Corps Command as a protective force. Antonio Molina, who had built the 5th Brigade in Aude, was chosen to lead it and set up his post in a remote area of mountain and forest near Les Cabannes, in the forest of Aston.

Such is the version of those adhering to the centrifugal doctrine. It does not go unchallenged. Eduardo Pons Prades, a member of the anarchist CNT who fought in Aude and Ariège, insists that the guerrilla movement first developed on the local level, with a minimum of liaison among units. The communist *guerrillero* leader Miguel Angel Sanz confirms this: 'The constitution of a general staff was a totally arbitrary action, taken without any prior discussion with the leaders in other *départements*.'[36] Sanz's centripetalist doctrine would inevitably place him at odds with the Party and its chosen heroes.

Whatever the top command was in terms of legitimacy and authority, disaster struck it on 22 April 1943. A traitor by the name of José Ávila Peña had given the gendarmerie in Foix the exact position of two *guerrillero* units, without which they would never have been located: the unit at Rieux-de-Pelleport, between Pamiers and Foix, and the headquarters force itself. The mission was entrusted to Vichy's new and already dreaded Milice, the organization created by Louis Darnand on 30 January precisely for actions such as this. Launching their attack at dawn, the Milice succeeded in overpowering thirty-four of the forty *guerrilleros* in the headquarters force; the six that escaped, including their Commander Molina, managed to reach Andorra. Ríos, the Commander-in-Chief, was also captured, with (according to Maury) no fewer than thirty-two bullets in his body.[37] Miraculously, he survived. A week later, on 29 April, José Linares, the guerrilla leader in Toulouse, was arrested in the railway station in Foix. All the captives were taken to the Foix prison, and presumably interrogated by SS-Obersturmbannführer Kutschmann of the Sipo (or by his assistant and successor Stickler) who were installed in the Villa Lauquier 2 kilometres from the town.[38] After a summary trial, all but one were deported to Germany.

The exception was Ríos, whose fate is wrapped in mystery. Why should the Commander-in-Chief have been exempted? According to one account, at the time of his trial the Vichy authorities admitted that in searching his home neither weapons nor any other incriminating evidence had been found.[39] According to Miguel Angel Sanz, who remains a loyal communist, the Vichy police did not realize that they held the Spanish Commander-in-Chief.[40] If that is so, if indeed they were deceived by his double identity, it is hard to imagine why they would have taken so much trouble to nurse him back to health, then submit him to special bouts of torture, and finally, at the beginning of 1944, after holding him in the camp of Noé in Haute-Garonne, send him under guard to the Northern Zone by train. It is equally curious that Ríos had the opportunity and the physical strength to escape from the train.[41] What happened next is something the loyal communist Sanz prefers to gloss over, recounting simply that some time later Ríos joined a guerrilla unit organized by the Spanish communist youth organization.[42] Sanz obviously does not think it to be a matter worthy of comment that a commander-in-chief should escape from enemy hands, return to his forces, and be greeted, not by his subordinate officers on the general staff, but by the rank-and-file of a youth platoon. For that was now his fate: suspect in the eyes of the other *guerrilleros*, he was readmitted into the organization only as a common soldier. What happened to him after that has been described by an eyewitness. On 23 May 1944 Ríos appeared at the door of Elvira Veleta, at her home near Dalou. The Veleta family, consisting of Elvira and her two nieces, the sisters María and Conchita Ramos Veleta, had served in the local 3rd Brigade of Guerrilleros since it was formed, and the two girls had begun serving as liaison agents even before Conchita had reached 18. The family had provided Ríos with a hiding place when he first arrived as a fugitive in Ariège, and now he begged them to hide him again. The family already had in the house two or three mountain guides who were to leave the next morning for the frontier, to take some Allied airmen across the Pyrenees, but they took Ríos in at once. The next morning the Milice arrived in force and surrounded the house. Suddenly shooting broke out. The guides broke through the cordon and escaped, but Ríos was caught in the stomach with a burst of machine-gun fire. He might have survived had not the Milice deliberately waited six hours before taking him to the nearby hospital in Foix. The Milice were more interested in the three women; before passing them over to the Gestapo in the Villa Lauquier they submitted them to their own interrogation. For all three it was the beginning of a journey which would take them to Oranienburg and Ravensbrück, but neither the Milice nor the Gestapo obtained any information from them on the Col de Py Maquis.[43]

The treason of Ávila provoked a desire for revenge which was perhaps more damaging to the *guerrilleros* than the capture of Ríos or of Linares. Summary executions were reported of those suspected of having entered the ranks of the *guerrilleros* as spies and informers.[44] Meanwhile, Ríos's place was taken by his Chief of Staff, Silvestre Gómez, who transferred corps headquarters to Bagnères-de-Bigorre in Hautes-Pyrénées. The new site was no better for the Spaniards than the old. No sooner was Carlos Mera installed as the new chief political commissar than he was arrested by the Sipo in Tarbes,[45] and never seen again.[46] By August 1943 Silvestre Gómez had moved his headquarters once more, this time to Gaillac in Tarn, where he set himself up in the house of a young Spanish couple, Andrés and Josefa Ramos, and later in a country house on the outskirts of the town.[47] While Gómez remained commander-in-chief, a new communist political organization had come into existence with an authority superior to his. This was the Union Nacional Española, whose origins we shall next examine. Gómez continued in his post until May 1944, when he was entrusted with 'an important mission to Spain'.[48] The term was to take on a fearful meaning.

The house in Gaillac, at 40 rue de la Madeleine, belonged, curiously enough, to members of the anarchist CNT, Andrés Ramos being an accountant in the local wine co-operative, but when it came to choosing a safe house for the new corps headquarters his wife Pepita offered theirs without the slightest hesitation. Pepita Ramos is an example, among many, of the quiet unassuming heroine of the Resistance, whose husband would have us think he did it all himself, and who smiles and lets it go at that. The house in Gaillac, frequented by the future generals Luis Fernández and Juan Blázquez, was well known to the Spanish women, many of them very young, who served in the work of liaison. This work was unsung, but it was also vital. The smooth, unbroken transmission of orders, assignments, information, and especially warnings often meant the difference between the success and failure of an operation, and between life and death for a *guerrillero*. Aurora Segría Doménech, from Tarragona, served in that capacity between Pepita Ramos in Gaillac and her own guerrilla group operating near Villefranche-de-Rouergue, close to the railway line to Toulouse.[49] Another was María Martínez, from Valencia, whose family owned the farm in the Col de Py which served as headquarters of the 3rd Brigade of Guerrilleros; in combat she served as a front-line nurse. Rosa 'la Asturiana', the wife of Alfonso Soto Herrera, was responsible for acquiring information on the Milice and the Germans in the area around Foix. One day she saw a German patrol approach their farmhouse. She had just enough time to help her husband into the backyard, then went out to the front to begin calmly feeding the chickens. By the time the Germans entered the backyard Alfonso Soto was ready with hand grenades, killing two Germans and making his escape. Alfonso Soto was later to be awarded the Croix de Guerre, but Rosa's reward was Ravensbrück.

The Basque girl Serafina Vélez was another who received no award but who won the admiration of all who knew her, whether bringing ammunition and food to guerrilla units or providing first aid and evacuating the wounded. Her strongest suit was a perfect calm. When travelling by train, she was always dressed as for a wedding, on the sound basis that no one that conspicuous could ever be taken for a secret agent. On one occasion she arrived in Toulouse by train with two suitcases full of documents and money. Unknown to her, she was accompanied by a comrade, a certain Marín; at Matabiau Station she was to be met by another comrade. At the station there was the usual tight control. Marín went first, and with proper documents, was allowed through. Fearing that her own could be questioned, Serafina Vélez went straight up to an officer of the Garde Mobile: '*Monsieur l'agent*, look, I can't go on. I have a sick baby girl staying at a neighbour's home, and I have to feed her. If you'd be kind enough to carry the suitcases outside where a friend of mine is waiting...' Serafina was young and pretty, the Garde Mobile was not invulnerable to poise and charm, and Serafina found herself escorted through the outer German ring to her comrade sent to pick her up. (Marín's function was apparently to watch the money, but not to share Serafina's fate if the police arrested her.) On another occasion, early in 1944, Serafina Vélez was assigned, with a socialist teacher from Galicia named Pláceres Castellano, to take a train with some suitcases filled with small arms. The suitcases were old, and the jolting of the train caused one of them placed on the seat beside them to fly open. The other passengers could see the weapons in the case, but at once looked the other way. Serafina Vélez, elegant as always, calmly took off her hat, placed it and a magazine over the weapons, and then tied up the case with some cord. Getting out of the train at a halt outside Toulouse, the two girls escaped detection.[50]

Ever since the German invasion of Russia, the Kremlin had been making frantic appeals for antifascist unity. In August 1941, and again on 22 September 1942, the Spanish Politburo in Moscow, urged on by Dimitrov, called upon all anti-Franco forces to form a single bloc.[51] Such a bloc would do for the Spanish communists what the Front national was intended to do for the French: provide them with a multi-party front behind which the Kremlin would make every decision. In Mexico, the PCE launched a manifesto calling on all Spaniards to unite in a vast national front, whose goal was to constitute a government of national unity. Another manifesto called for a government of all Spaniards under the presidency of Juan Negrín, and added: 'We must help the Soviet Union, the United Kingdom and the peoples of Europe to conquer German fascism! We must help Russia and England to liberate the peoples who live under Hitler's yoke!' England could be grateful for the first moral support it had received from the PCE or the PCF. But in view of what was to come, the most ironic aspect of the manifesto was the part which read: 'Neither hunger for power nor personal intrigue can prevail over this magnificent task.'[52]

In point of fact, the animosities that had developed between communists and other antifascists in the course of the Civil War would not dissolve by the Liberation, nor after it. Instead they would result in the formation of two organizations fundamentally opposed. On 7 November 1942, the PCE announced the creation of the Unión nacional española, or UNE.[53] It was founded in the course of a meeting attended by eleven Spanish political figures, of whom only the PCE and the PSUC delegates could be called true representatives of their parties.[54] The name it went by, the Grenoble Conference, was a ploy used to deceive the police, for in actual fact it opened in a large rambling house near Montauban and closed in Toulouse (in the home of the young Catalan Cros,[55] at 13 rue Cujette).[56] It was there that the UNE set up its administration, and it was there that Manuel Azcárate, on the run from both the Gestapo and the Vichy police, shortly afterwards went into hiding.

There is no doubt that the appeal launched at the Grenoble Conference found a receptive public. 'Spaniards, wherever you may be, your duty is to seize arms and to place yourselves in the front line, at the side of the French people, against the common enemy, until the day of victory and liberation!' was a slogan that arrived at the right moment, for even without the visible presence of the Wehrmacht it offered Spaniards a new perspective: combat against fascists in a French civil war. At UNE's founding meeting the communists fixed two priorities: to prevent the deportation of Spaniards to Germany, whether as volunteers or as forced labourers, and to find a means to print and distribute the PCE's underground journal, *Reconquista de España*, whose title expressed its hopes and imminent plans.

The first issues of *Reconquista de España* were written by hand.[57] Issues from August 1941 were typed and reproduced on a small hand-operated duplicator in a charcoal workers' log cabin in the mountains of Vaucluse.[58] Later, at the beginning of 1942, a printing shop was set up in nearby Cavaillon, using an abandoned factory whose electricity had been disconnected. From that time on, the journal appeared on a more regular basis.[59] Meanwhile in Toulouse, Aquilino Gómez, living on the rue du Caillou Gris, had with the help of his friend Francisco Sentenero obtained a mimeograph machine. The machine was admittedly in a sad state of repair: Sentenero had acquired it from its French owner in exchange for a pair of shoes. But the machine was made to work, and even before the Unión nacional was created Gómez had begun to publish leaflets, not regularly perhaps but none the less tenaciously.

After the creation of the UNE in November 1942, *Reconquista de España* was to serve as its organ and as an important means of co-ordination. To extend its circulation to the whole of France, a distribution centre was set up in Toulouse. Women especially were assigned to the work of distribution. While Gómez gave up his activity in Toulouse for other services, Antonio Pomares took charge of liaison between Toulouse and Cavaillon as well as the distribution of the journal. Pomares set up his office at 16 rue Berthelot, near the cemetery. Accompanied by one or two comrades he made regular trips to Cavaillon, carrying large suitcases which were empty on the outward journey and filled on the return. From Toulouse, in smaller cases, copies of *Reconquista de España* were conveyed, very often by bicycle, to various railway station left-luggage offices throughout Haute-Garonne, Ariège, and several other *départements* of the southwest. Other comrades to whom the tickets were passed collected the cases and proceeded in turn to distribute the journal to the *guerrilleros*. This operation, which continued until the Liberation, required a continual purchase of new cases, to the amazement of the salesgirls working in the Galeries Saint-Étienne on the rue de Metz, who took care to ask no questions.[60]

From 1943 the journal, with its various supplements, appeared on a regular basis. Certain supplements were distributed even inside camps and prisons: one such appeared at Argelès from 1941,[61] and another, usually of four pages handwritten by a bank employee named Díaz, from Madrid, appeared regularly for an entire year, beginning in mid-1943, inside the main prison in Foix, where a large number of Spaniards were held in preventive custody. During the Battle of Stalingrad and from D-Day to the Liberation, the supplement appeared every day and was read by every inmate.[62] The number of supplements of this kind, whether handwritten, typed, mimeographed, or printed, exceeded 300.[63] To these should be added the PCE's semi-official *España popular*, which was published in Mexico from 1940 to 1945[64] and which circulated to some small extent in France up until the time that the PCE began publication of its official weekly, *Mundo obrero*.[65]

The importance that the PCE gave to publishing under the name of the UNE became clear after the Liberation. A report submitted to the UNE Conference held in Toulouse estimated the total number of copies produced, including copies of a few hundred manifestos issued immediately after the Liberation, at approximately half a million.[66] It must be remembered that copies were not discarded but instead circulated by hand. As for radio, the UNE's own station, Radio-Pyrénées, broadcast to both Zones, even before November 1942. Its location has never been revealed. It was probably Toulouse, but it ran a grave risk of detection by the Gestapo if it was not mobile.

The UNE was to serve the PCE as a perfect screen, as long as it faced no challenge. It could claim the support of the majority of the *guerrilleros* and 15,000 others.[67] A year later it announced the creation in Spain of the Junta suprema de unión nacional. The truth as to how, when, and even whether this organization came into being will probably never be known. Conflicting versions proliferate,[68] and to little avail when one considers how small its impact was. The purpose at least was clear: the UNE, more euphoric than clearheaded, hoped to achieve the unification of all Spanish antifascists, including the Catholics of Gil Robles, the monarchists, and the military.[69]

The urban Resistance, more politicized than the *guerrilleros*, suffered serious reverses even before the Germans reached the Unoccupied Zone. In Ariège, for example, the majority of the local French and Spanish leaders, twenty-four in number, were arrested in a police raid on 12 July 1942.[70] Another raid, launched the following September, had far worse consequences for the Spanish urban Resistance.

At that time, in September 1942, the PCE controlling committee (or Delegation of the Central Committee, as it called itself) still consisted of Jaime Nieto (secretary-general), Angel Celadas, and Manolo Sánchez Esteban. This committee operated throughout the Unoccupied Zone, while the committee in the Occupied Zone (made up of Sánchez Biezma, Sánchez Vizcaino, and José Ramón Alvarez) remained subordinate but autonomous. On 6 September, the three members of the controlling committee had arranged to meet in Toulouse in the home of the Udave sisters. Nieto and Sánchez Esteban were awaiting the arrival of Celadas from Perpignan when the police suddenly burst through the door. The police belonged merely to criminal investigation; they had suspected that the house was being used by black marketeers. But the sight of copies of *Reconquista de España* piled up on the table led to the immediate arrest of the two Spanish leaders, together with the Udave sisters. The security police at once took the matter in hand.[71] Knowing that Celadas was due to arrive in Toulouse by train from Perpignan, they sent a squad to Matabiau Station. Celadas, of such dark complexion that his comrades knew him as 'el Negro', had no chance to slip through the barrier. All three PCE leaders were subjected to the usual barbaric horrors,[72] and Nieto and Celadas were later deported to Buchenwald; both would survive. A different fate awaited Manolo Sánchez. Since the torture he had undergone had left no traces on his face, the police escorted him to the station every time a train from Dordogne was due to arrive; they knew, from a notebook they had found, that a certain Bermejo, active in the Resistance, was visiting Toulouse. Bermejo arrived, spotted Sánchez where he had been placed, and despite all the subtle gestures that Sánchez used to try to warn him, Bermejo went up to him, only to be grabbed. Even worse, when the police searched him, they found a list of names in one of his pockets.[73] This unexpected boon—and unforgivable blunder—furnished the Gestapo with the material for a massive round-up, which netted 200 Spaniards, most of them in the *départements* of Lot, Lot-et-Garonne, and Tarn-et-Garonne. As for Manolo Sánchez, he was not to die at the hands of the Gestapo, nor in France. The treatment he suffered in Saint-Michel Prison in Toulouse left him in such a state that he required brain surgery. He was moved to the nearby Hôtel-Dieu Hospital, where he recovered to such an extent that in early October 1943 he succeeded, with the help of others, in making his escape. Nothing is known of him in the nine months that followed. Then, a week or two after D-Day, at the very moment that the guerrilla forces were engaging in open battle with the Wehrmacht, he was ordered by the Party's new leader to cross over into Spain, in order to help the leadership in Madrid. He had got as far as Perpignan when he was again arrested by the Germans, and again he escaped. Eschewing the two major roads into Catalonia he climbed the mountains to the Vallespir, and from there, escorted by a group, he crossed the frontier on 1 July. The group had not advanced 20 kilometres when, near the village of San Juan de las Abadesas, they found themselves facing the Guardia Civil. The communist leader who had twice defied the Nazis fell in the shoot-out, and was buried in Ripoll.[74]

The PCE leadership in France was thus wiped out, and in 1943 a new committee had to be formed. Logically, Manolo Sánchez served on it from his first escape from the Germans to his departure for Spain, but for obscure reasons very little is known about the leadership that followed. Miguel Angel Sanz, the best placed of those who survived to write, says merely that a new committee was formed, but that almost all the leaders of the period from late 1943 to early 1944 moved into Spain, presumably to prepare for the imminent overthrow of Franco. Sanz adds that from early 1944 up until the Liberation the leadership was in the hands of a 'working commission' headed by Manuel Gimeno ('Raúl'), now head of the Spanish communist youth organization in France.[75] Sanz thus studiously avoids even mentioning the man at the centre of the deepest mystery of the Spanish Resistance, Jesús Monzón Reparaz, whose name has been linked to the *nom de guerre* 'Mariano'.

For the first thirty years after the Liberation, the only fact known about the leadership of the PCE in France in the last year of the Occupation was that the man at the top went by the name of 'Mariano'. Tomás Cossías describes him as a former petty officer in the Republican

Navy who as a communist was both a mediocrity and a fanatic, forcing his subordinates into absolute obedience to his commands. Cossías adds, however, that 'Mariano' had a capacity for organization which could serve as a model in both the political and the military domaines.[76] In 1976, Angel Ruiz Ayúcar, a colonel in the Guardia Civil who was the first to use its archives for a book, announced that 'Mariano' was in fact no other than Jesús Monzón, the former civil governor in Spain, who, as we have seen, was one of the very first in France to organize resistance. That did not, however, put an end to the mystery of 'Mariano'.[77]

By the time the Germans invaded Vichy France, the PCE was in liaison with all sectors of the communist or communist-dominated Resistance: the MOI, the PCF, and the FTP. Homogeneity was extremely rare in Resistance units. An exception might be made for the Spanish *guerrilleros* operating in Haute-Savoie from June 1942, but few Spanish units failed to include outsiders, and that tended to lessen the political and historical impact of the Spanish contribution.[78] Similarly many Spaniards, instead of joining the Guerrilleros or the MOI, joined one or other of the French organizations, in particular the FTP.[79] The MOI accepted the FTP as the superior national organization,[80] communist ideology being the binding force, and most of its units were incorporated into it, but here again the Spaniards were an exception: even in the MOI they enjoyed a certain autonomy.[81] Spaniards everywhere continued to celebrate their national feast-days, and 14 April,[82] 1 May, and 11 November were regularly marked by an increase in their activities. The *guerrillero* organization, for its part, operated on the margin of the FTP but in more or less close collaboration with the MOI. The overall picture of the Resistance in France until February 1944 shows that no unified command existed, the communists remaining apart from the Gaullists. If we look at the picture in detail, we might find a sergeant who could not give the name of the organization to which his unit belonged![83]

We have seen that, in the Occupied Zone in January 1941, Nadal of the PCE had formed a co-ordinating committee with Josep Miret Musté of the PSUC and Louis Grojnowski ('Brunot') of the MOI. In the Southern Zone the MOI was led by the Yugoslav Ljubomir Ilic, who had fought in Spain as a major in the International Brigades. Once the PCE had formed its political front, the UNE, in November 1942, its liaison with the MOI and with the FTP became stronger. The arrangement was for Ilic to command all FTP-MOI forces in the Lyons region from his base in that city, while the MOI forces in the south-west would be integrated into the FTP centred in Toulouse.

The Guerrilleros would collaborate with both, and Luis Fernández (who had earlier worked under Ríos to establish contact among the *guerrillero* groups) was now appointed commissar for liaison with the leaders in Lyons. By serving in this capacity, he laid the groundwork for his later claim to the leadership of the entire Spanish *guerrillero* movement.[84]

As for the FTP, in which Spaniards also served, it was the military arm of the PCF, but in the vital Toulouse region the role of the PCF remains in almost total darkness from 1940 to 1944, when the metal-worker Henri Dupont ('Maxime') emerged as its head.[85] Until the invasion of the Southern Zone in November 1942, the PCF confined itself almost entirely to organization and propaganda, but by that time the FTP had created its own military structure. Meanwhile the PCE shared certain PCF facilities, and it is probable that it made use of the Imprimerie Lion, the printing shop run by the brothers Henri and Raoul Lion at 23 rue Croix-Baragnon in Toulouse, because from 1941 it provided several parties and movements not only with printed pamphlets but also with false papers. It was there that Raymond Naves produced his journal *Le Populaire du sud-ouest*, and it was there that Georges Seguy (the future secretary-general of the communist CGT) worked as an office boy. All four were arrested when the Gestapo, responding to a denunciation, raided the premises on 4 February 1944. By turning the shop into a trap, they netted over forty more, including a girl of 13. All were deported to Germany, and Naves and the Lion brothers died in Mauthausen.[86]

We have also seen that the Spaniards' own organization in the Toulouse region was hard hit in April 1943 by the capture and deportation of José Linares. His place was taken by Joachim Ramos,[87] who went on to command, to the end of the Liberation, both the 2nd Brigade of Guerrilleros and the 35th Brigade FTP-MOI, the latter taking the name 'Marcel Langer Brigade' in honour of the MOI's most famous hero. The 2nd Brigade confined its operations to Haute-Garonne, especially the woods and forests of Bouconne-Lévignac, Loures-Barbazan, and Luchon-Bourg d'Oueil.[88] The 35th Brigade used Toulouse as its base, but its detachments extended as far afield as Lot-et-Garonne, Gers, and Tarn-et-Garonne, especially the vicinities of Montauban and Castelsarrasin.[89]

A further step toward integration came in the period September to November 1943, at a time when the Spaniards' xivth Army Corps claimed to have extended its organization over thirty-one *départements* in the Southern Zone.[90] The PCE, PCF, and FTP agreed to incorporate the xivth Corps into the FTP-MOI. The command centre that the MOI had established in Lyons was now reorganized. The new integrated command consisted of Ilic, Luis Fernández, a German named 'Albert' (in charge of operations), and three other former officers of the International Brigades. The meeting also resulted in the reorganization of the Spanish *guerrilleros*. That was not difficult. The base structure of the xivth Army Corps was very similar to that of the FTP-MOI, and it was decided to link the two parallel organizations at every level of command. Further meetings between the leaders of the Spanish *guerrilleros* and the French Resistance took place in the Toulouse region at the end of 1943 and early in 1944.[91] The theoretical result of all this was the coalition of the French and Spanish resistance forces. But Miguel Angel Sanz is almost certainly right in saying that, in reality, the xivth Corps even now retained its independence; all that really changed was that, in certain *départements*, action was co-ordinated.[92] The reason for this is not hard to find. The Spaniards fought as if this was the last campaign but one. When it was won, they would need all their unity for the final campaign south of the Pyrenees.

It is clear that Spaniards could be found in virtually any Resistance organization, especially in the south. In Angoulême, Francisco López emerged in the winter of 1941–2 as leader of the regional PCE. His fame as the undisputed leader of the Spanish activists travelled far beyond his city, and indeed to the Gestapo headquarters in Limoges. The prevalence of sabotage in the Angoulême region in 1943 explains its decision to send a team to track him down. Francisco López was arrested in a hotel in Angoulême in January 1944, and the Gestapo went to work. The evidence suggests that López gave nothing away on the membership of his group, but the question must be asked why the Gestapo did not execute him. Instead they sent him to the Royallieu sorting centre in Compiègne prior to transportation to Germany, but before they could do so, in early 1944 López escaped, and was back in Angoulême in time to take part in its liberation.[93]

In the urban resistance, the MOI was especially prominent. Again Spaniards were involved, though not as prominently as the Jews. The MOI faced the same first concern as the PCE: the protection of those comrades who were most vulnerable to arrest and deportation. In the case of the Jews, all were vulnerable, but several Spanish *guerrillero* leaders, including it is said Tomás Ortega Guerrero, also owed their escape from internment to members of the MOI. The urban MOI no doubt faced greater psychological pressure than any other Resistance organization since most of its members were already three times on the wanted list: as Jews, as communists, and as foreigners. Precisely because the urban Resistance was more nerve-racking, discipline was rigid and security precautions tight. The MOI was an underground army but members lived very much in isolation. Liaison was handled by the women, who were no less exposed to the stress.

The MOI's principal unit was the 35th Brigade, which was always international and always integrated into the FTP. From the moment the Wehrmacht arrived in Vichy France, it was busy in sabotage and in isolated attacks on German military personnel, soldiers as well as officers, and especially on the French and German security forces. It was equally busy in efforts to undermine German morale. No study has yet been made on the effectiveness of this propaganda, but it is certain that this work, which Arthur London had originated in the Occupied Zone in 1941, was more successful in the south-west precisely because of the large and growing number of non-Germans in the Wehrmacht, in particular Georgians, Ukrainians, Armenians, and Yugoslavs. It was for them that Clara Malraux and Madeleine Lagrange, who had taken refuge in Montauban, began the publication of *La Victoire* in late September 1943, producing it in both French and German. In Toulouse the Freies Deutschland movement went a stage further in December 1943 by arranging the escape of Soviet prisoners employed on the airfields at Francazal and Balma.[94]

The exploits of the MOI took on greater vigour with the arrest, in February 1943, of Marcel Langer, the founder and commander of the 35th Brigade. A Polish Jew whose real name was Langer Mendel, he had fought as a captain in the International Brigades in Spain. His Spanish wife, Cecilia Molina, was still living there. Since 1942 Colonel Langer had commanded all FTP forces in the Toulouse region. On 6 February 1943, Langer was on the platform of the little station of Saint-Agne in Toulouse as a train arrived from the Pyrenees. A passenger opened a door and handed Langer a heavy suitcase. It was filled with explosives stolen by Spanish workers in Ariège. Cabanac, a police agent who simply happened to be there, pounced on the suspect. Langer was taken to the building on the rue du Rempart-Saint-Étienne which served as headquarters of Vichy's 8th Brigade of Security Police. There he found himself in the hands of Chief Inspector Caussié, who gloated over his prize and personally participated in his torture.[95] He was then transferred to Saint-Michel Prison. Vilified and sentenced to death by Pierre Lespinasse, the local magistrate, he was guillotined in the prison yard on 23 July, but not before crying out: 'I am certain to be avenged!'[96]

Indeed he was. On Sunday, 10 October, Lespinasse and his wife left their house to walk as usual down the Allée Pont-des-Demoiselles on their way to mass in the church of Notre-Dame de Lourdes. They were accompanied on this occasion by the sister of Madame Lespinasse, the magistrate walking between the two women. A cyclist drew slowly up to them, then stopped. It was Boris Frenkel, a medical student. Drawing a 9 mm. Mauser from his pocket, he fired four times. Lespinasse fell mortally wounded, while Frenkel rode off on the bicycle. A large reward was immediately offered in *La Dépêche* to anyone who could identify the assassin. Since no trace of him was found, a number of suspects were arrested. Meanwhile Cheneaux de Leyritz, the Prefect of Haute-Garonne, paid a collaborator's tribute to a colleague: 'He enjoyed the respect and the affection of everyone. . . . He was nobility itself.'[97]

Similar attacks continued. The rue d'Austerlitz in the very centre of Toulouse includes two hotels which had been requisitioned by the Germans: the Hôtel de l'Ours Blanc, on the corner, used by the Sicherheitsdienst, and the Hôtel de France, halfway down the street, used by the Feldgendarmerie. On 3 March a bomb exploded in the restaurant of the Ours Blanc, and on 13 June an attack on the Feldgendarmerie left several dead. On 19 December the *guerrilleros* and the 35th Brigade, armed with sub-machine-guns and grenades, joined in an attack on a requisitioned tramcar running along the avenue de Muret. The Resistance communiqué announced that fifty Germans had been killed and as many wounded. Two days later the abbot Sorel, an enthusiastic collaborator with a seat on the National Council, was also shot dead. On 1 April 1944 the *guerrilleros* and the 35th Brigade staged another attack on a German tram, this time near the Purpan Hospital in Toulouse, leaving many dead and wounded.

They also had their failures. On 1 March 1944 the MOI planned an attack on the Cinéma les Variétés on the grounds that it was showing Nazi propaganda films. The bomb, detonated at 6.30 p.m. in the second balcony, close to the projector, went off too soon, killing the man and the girl who were placing it. The FTP accused the MOI of unruly, reckless, and provocative action. It was the low point in the fortunes of the MOI. Not only had it strained its relations with the FTP but in April the police dragnet succeeded in decapitating the Brigade: over thirty were killed or captured. The captives would be executed or deported to Dachau on the famous 'ghost train' that left Toulouse on 2 July.[98]

The accusation by the FTP that the MOI had engaged in reckless action opened rather than closed the affair, which transcended the place and time. Marcel Langer was only the second most famous member of the MOI. The most famous was the Armenian poet Missak Manouchian, in Paris, and it would be another forty years before his widow Mélinée would expose the story to the Press and a documentary would be shown on French television.[99] Manouchian had entered the FTP-MOI at the beginning of 1943, at a time when seven successive administrations of the organization fell into Nazi hands in little more than a year. Its military commander in the Paris region was then Boris Holban, a Romanian Jew who had served in the Comintern in the 1930s. It was Holban who, in the spring of 1943, selected Manouchian to command the 4th (Mixed) detachment, made up mainly of Armenians and Spaniards. When in May and June the Gestapo dealt the MOI another shattering blow, arresting over eighty members, the PCF, as its controlling body, decided that its best hope of recovering its prestige was to commit the remnants of the MOI in Paris to spectacular action at whatever price. To this end a new, mixed group was formed, again under the command of Manouchian,[100] combining Armenians, Spaniards, Italians, and others. Among these was a Spaniard from Salamanca named Celestino Alfonso Mates.

Alfonso had served in the Spanish Civil War as a tank lieutenant, and hitherto in the Spanish detachment of the FTP-MOI in the Paris region. In the celebrated 'Red poster' which the Nazis in April 1944 affixed in hundreds to the walls of Paris, Alfonso is given pride of place beside Manouchian, and he enjoyed a reputation second to none.[101] He was given responsibility for the assassination of a German colonel who took regular walks in the Parc Monceau. On 19 August 1943 he walked up to the Nazi as he sat on a bench reading a newspaper, and at a distance of one foot shot him in the face.[102] On 28 September Alfonso and the Pole Marcel Rayman were assigned to the assassination of an SS general, Dr Julius Ritter, whom Sauckel had personally selected as his representative in France and who thus headed the STO. Ritter's office was in the Maison de la Chimie at 28 rue Saint Dominique, but the group preferred to trace him to his home at 18 rue Pétrarque, a quiet little street behind the Trocadéro, and there plan the assassination to the second. This was possible because Ritter always left his house in the morning on the stroke of 8.30 a.m. Alfonso and Rayman were thus walking down the street on the morning of 29 September at precisely the moment that Ritter strode outside, and the instant that Ritter stepped into his limousine Alfonso fired two shots into the back of his head; Rayman, $4\frac{1}{2}$ metres behind Alfonso, fired two more into the slumped figure of Ritter.[103] On another occasion the plot went sadly awry. The target was none other than General Ernst von Schaumburg, commander of the garrison of Greater Paris. At 9.30 a.m. on the morning of 28 July 1943, Schaumburg's staff car, its hood rolled back, was turning the corner on the avenue Paul-Doumer and rue Nicolo when it was attacked by the Special Team of four, armed with grenades and pistols. A grenade allegedly landed inside the car, killing the chauffeur and the two passengers. For the remainder of the war and for the next forty years it was said by many that the Resistance had assassinated the German

Commander of Greater Paris. But von Schaumburg was no longer in France—he had been replaced on 1 May 1943 and died in Hamburg in 1947—and his replacement, Lieutenant-General Hans von Boinelburg-Langsfeld, was not in the car either. The man in the car was indeed a member of the general's staff, but the grenade landed harmlessly in the road.[104]

Manouchian's immediate superior in the FTP-MOI structure was Joseph Dawidowicz, a communist from the 11ᵉ arrondissement in Paris who served as political commissar and who went by the name of Albert. In October 1943 he disappeared. The records that survive of the Brigades spéciales, the French equivalent of the Gestapo, show that they had arrested him. The Manouchian group immediately asked the FTP command (that is to say the PCF) to allow them to take refuge in the provinces. The PCF refused. Manouchian bowed to the higher authority, but demanded arms, food, and money. All three were denied. Their operations became more and more risky, and they experienced their first serious reverses. Then, a month after he disappeared, Albert returned. The members of the group were told that a meeting was to be held on 16 November near the station of Evry-Petit-Bourg, on the Seine south of Paris. Manouchian confided to Mélinée his fears of a trap: 'I truly believe that they [the Party] want to send us to our death.' He decided to go to Evry early, to try to alert the others. Outside the tunnel by the station, Albert was there to meet him. He signalled to the police, who pounced on Manouchian. Sixty-five others fell in turn into the trap.

In the prison at Fresnes, the Gestapo went unhurriedly about its work. It was the Gestapo who would decide the membership of the most celebrated ring in the French Resistance: the Manouchian group of twenty-two men and a woman, immortalized in the 'Red poster'. The composition was arranged as a mosaic, with as many nationalities as possible included and the Jews the centre of attraction. A trial was held on 19–21 February 1944 in the Hôtel Continental on the rue Rivoli.[105] Alfonso was described in the collaborationist press as having 'the classic face of the terrorist: sallow complexion, raven hair, and a furtive, evil look'.[106] All were condemned to death. No sooner was the verdict read than all but one were taken to Mont-Valérien and executed. The exception was the Romanian Olga Bancic, who was held for further interrogation and beheaded in Stuttgart on 10 May, her birthday.

A few hours before their execution, the prisoners were allowed to write a last letter. 'I don't regret my past,' wrote Alfonso, in faulty French. 'If I had to do it again, I would still want to be the first. . . . I die for France.'[107] Manouchian wrote his last lines to Mélinée, who still holds them.[108] They include a startling sentence: 'I forgive all those who have done me harm or who have tried to do me harm, except him who betrayed us to save his own skin and those who sold us out.' No one doubts any longer that the betrayer was the Commissar Albert. A policeman who was secretly in the Resistance identified him as the traitor. The MOI had its suspicions anyway, from the moment that Albert returned after his disappearance. The time now came to settle accounts. A rendezvous was arranged in a house in Bourg-la-Reine. Albert arrived and was executed, by unknown communists. All that is in dispute are the reasons why Albert went to the rendezvous, and why the Gestapo failed to follow him. The graver question concerns the way the sacrifices of the Manouchian group and the Marcel Langer group were treated by the Party. We have seen that the MOI in Toulouse had been incited to the same frenzy of dangerous and even suicidal activities, and then rebuked for its frenzy. After the Liberation the Party set out to efface the memory of both groups. Year after year the anniversaries passed unnoticed in the pages of *L'Humanité*. Worse still, the Party rewrote its history to give French names to the non-French heroes. Worst of all, the PCF twice published (in 1946 and 1966) the last letter of Manouchian and both times omitted the key sentence referring to the group's betrayers.[109]

Here lies the clue to understanding why the MOI, like so many other groups before and after, was sacrificed at the altar of Stalin. Stalin needed for the time of the Liberation a PCF which appeared to the French people to be irreducibly antifascist and unmistakably French. Who were to be its heroes? Surely not Armenian Jews or Spanish *guerrilleros*. The orders to the MOI thus came down from Jacques Duclos, the ranking leader of the PCF in France, through his aide Jean Jérôme,[110] who as treasurer of the Party had already confiscated from the PCE whatever the PCE had confiscated and evacuated from Spain. Jérôme transmitted the orders through Boris Holban to the man he had imposed as the MOI's political commissar, Albert. Those orders were to involve the MOI to the fullest possible extent, maximizing its casualties and letting the survivors fall into Nazi hands, so that no one in it would be left. This would remove the main obstacle to creating an image of a French communist party which was patriotic and nationalist. The sacrifices of the MOI, like those of the Spanish *guerrilleros*, had brought enormous credit to the communists precisely because the Nazis themselves had made the matter clear in their public bulletins, especially the 'Red poster'. Had there been no 'Red poster', it seems probable that the names of Manouchian, Alfonso, and Rayman would have disappeared from history, buried under the weight of antihistory.[111]

9
War to the Knife

Creation of the FFI by General de Gaulle—The Spaniards, fearful of being assimilated, create the AGE—The Spanish guerrilla leaders: Generals Fernández and Blázquez—The failure of the insurrection at Eysses—The disasters of Glières and Vercors—Creation and structure of the role of the German LVIIIth Panzerkorps—Role of the 2nd SS-Panzerdivision ('Das Reich'): Tulle and Oradour—Further anti-guerrilla activities—Hitler's deteriorating position in France—Role of the Ostlegion and Freies Indien Legion—The Spanish volunteers for Hitler

> Back to the struggle, baffled in the strife,
> War, war is still the cry, 'War even to the knife!'[1]

The final act of amalgamation of all Resistance forces in France came on 1 February 1944, when the Comité français de liberation nationale, based in Algiers and headed by General de Gaulle, announced the creation of the Forces françaises de l'intérieur, or FFI. The FTP, the MOI, and the Spanish Guerrilleros were thus all absorbed. Up until now, the *guerrilleros* had relied for their arms on the difficult method of seizing them from police stations, the Milice, or the Germans. They were now entitled to receive them from the Allies by parachute drops.[2] For this they were grateful, but the prospect of losing their identity in the amorphous mass of the FFI was not pleasing at all. This fear of being submerged explains why, in May 1944, their organization's name was changed from XIVth Army Corps to the Agrupación de guerrilleros españoles, or AGE. This did not affect the structure of the organization, but it coincided with a change in the leadership which could hardly be unrelated. It was precisely at this moment that Silvestre Gómez, the commander-in-chief, resigned to prepare for a suicide mission to Spain. The new leadership consisted of General Luis Fernández (Commander-in-Chief), General Juan Blázquez (Political Commissar), and Colonel Miguel Angel Sanz (Chief of Staff).[3] Colonel José Antonio Paz held the post of liaison officer, and headquarters remained at Gaillac, in the country house outside the town.[4]

It was Fernández and Blázquez, and not their predecessors, who would ultimately receive the laurels of victory, or whatever laurels the PCE leaders in Moscow wanted to confer upon those who fought and led in their absence. Fernández's origins are obscure. Sergeant or private soldier in Spain,[5] lumberjack in Ariège or muleteer in Aude, he had risen in 1943 to command, in theory at least, the guerrilla forces of three *départements*: Ariège, Aude, and Pyrénées-Orientales.[6] It has also been said that in 1943 Fernández co-ordinated the Maquis not only in those *départements* but also in Haute-Garonne[7] and the *départements* of Central France. After the Liberation a communist newspaper described him as 'a quiet, modest man from the working class'.[8] The FTP leader Ravanel met him twice during the Liberation and several times afterwards, and considers him 'a man of integrity who does not mince matters'.[9] General Chevance-Bertin met him once, and describes him as 'a fine man, quite charming, and most respectful: he addressed me as his superior general'.[10] Their subordinate Jean-Pierre Vernant remembers having excellent relations with him, and Dr Claude Levy found him 'pleasant and cordial'.[11] Carmen de Pedro continues to hold him in high esteem, and insists on the noble ideal that inspired him and the others in the top group.[12] But Fernández also has his critics, and some would call him an impostor. Claude Urman, while commanding the MOI's 35th Brigade, met Fernández several times in the period of the Liberation (August 1944) and found him pretentious: 'He wanted to pass very much like the leader. He even wore the uniform of a general of the French Army, with full insignia.'[13] Eduardo Pons Prades, who fought in the Aude-Ariège region, denies that Fernández ever commanded any of the brigades formed in those *départements* and which constituted, from April 1943, the 4th Division.[14] Lieutenant-Colonel Vicente López Tovar, a division commander in the Civil War,[15] calls him 'the phantom general, the man who went to bed a private soldier and woke up a brigadier'.[16] In his unpublished autobiography he writes of the guerrilla leaders:

Neither Guerrero in Gers, nor Redondo in Basses-Pyrénées, nor Cristino García in Lozère, nor Castro, nor López, nor Pinocho in the north of Dordogne, nor Perera at Limoges, nor Navas at Dijon, nor myself ever once received an operational order from Fernández. In reality, apart from Ariège and a few lumber camps in Aude and Haute-Garonne, the Fernández group never controlled anything. . . . General Fernández never took part in a single operation, . . . nor had any regular force under his orders.[17]

It was Monzón, he adds, not without bitterness, who gave both Fernández and Blázquez the rank of general.[18]

As for General Blázquez, who served up to April 1944 as commissar in the lst Division, he had been arrested on 29 December 1942 and thrown into Saint-Michel Prison in Toulouse, to be transferred later to the camp at Le Vernet. To escape from the camps, so easy in 1940, had become extremely difficult now that the Germans had arrived. The Germans did not take direct control of Le Vernet until 9 June 1944, that is to say three days after D-Day, at the time they disarmed the French gendarmerie. But in the interim it was no less difficult to break out, and López Tovar considers that Blázquez's spectacular escape under fire in October 1943, in the company of two Romanians,[19] was in a class of its own.[20]

De Gaulle's purpose in creating the FFI was to fuse all the Resistance forces operating in France into a single command under General Pierre Koenig, who remained in London until the invasion of Normandy. The centre and south-west, however, was a special case. The objective of the Anglo-Americans in Normandy was not primarily the liberation of France; they were concerned about getting to Germany and smashing it. The Allied landing in Provence, in the south-east of France, would have a similar mission: to drive up the Rhône and link up with the Allied forces driving south-east before advancing into Germany. This left a box, roughly one-third of the whole of France, stretching from the Loire to the Pyrenees and from the Atlantic to the Rhône which would be left to liberate itself and, as some saw it, establish afterwards the government of its choice.

The Southern Zone was split up into six 'military regions', numbered clockwise and starting with Lyons.[21] The twenty-six *départements* of the south-west made up four of these: R3 (Montpellier), R4 (Toulouse), R5 (Limoges), R6 (Clermont-Ferrand and its north-east region), plus Interregion B (Bordeaux) which was never under Vichy administration. Among these regions, only R6 came into direct contact with an Allied army, that of General de Lattre de Tassigny in the force advancing from Provence. The rest came, theoretically at least, under the command of General Chevance-Bertin, appointed by de Gaulle in Algiers. The Spaniards were especially active in R3 (Pyrénées-Orientales, Aude, Hérault, Aveyron, Lozére, and Gard) and, as we have already seen, in R4, centred on Toulouse.

We have also seen that the Spaniards converted their xɪvth Army Corps into the Agrupación de guerrilleros españoles precisely to maintain their unity and their autonomy. Some *guerrilleros* went so far as to call it independence, and Miguel Angel Sanz calls it 'absolute independence', even in regard to the two other communist-dominated organizations, the FTP and the MOI which remained linked. If Sanz is right, it amounts to a stubborn refusal on the part of the Spanish communist leaders to accept the decision taken by the Allied Supreme Command. There was a price to pay, however. The communists might sometimes need help and find it denied to them. This seems to be the cause of the tragic failure, early in 1944, to liberate the inmates of the penitentiary at Eysses, near Villeneuve-sur-Lot, where prisoners were sent from other prisons if they were considered dangerous.

For the Spanish *guerrilleros*, the fortress at Eysses carried a meaning which only three other prisons shared: Fort Montluc in Lyons, Nontron in Dordogne, and the Central Prison in Nîmes.[22] Impregnability was part of it: Eysses had served as a fortress since 1266. At the end of 1943 it contained about 1,200 political prisoners, including at least eighty-two Spaniards.[23] If any break were to succeed, it had to be co-ordinated perfectly with an assault from the outside. A plan was drawn up for an attack to be launched in the week beginning 25 December. The operation was aborted, however, for political reasons: a French Resistance unit would not co-operate with communists.[24] The French authorities suspected anyway that a plan had been drawn up, and decided to replace the Commandant with a certain Colonel Schivo. The inmates meanwhile decided to try to break out by themselves, though they knew the heavy odds against them and the dire penalties that would accrue from failure. The day selected for the uprising was 19 February 1944, a Saturday. The rebels had prepared by infiltrating twelve sub-machine-guns and thirty-five grenades into the camp, partly with the complicity of the guards. By coincidence, Schivo happened at that moment to be inspecting that particular part of the prison. As the signal for the insurrection was given, Schivo was grabbed as a hostage while several guards were disarmed. The prisoners then ran into the unforeseeable event: a work detail made up of common criminals and employed outside returned to the fortress two hours earlier than usual. As the prisoners filed past the camp chapel they saw some rebels inside dressed in the uniforms of the guards. Surprised and frightened, they started to shout and run away. The rebels, in their desperation, pursued and quickly silenced them, but not before the noise had attracted the attention of the other guards. The vital element of surprise had now been lost. The only prospect left was a frontal attack on the north-east machine-gun tower. The Spaniard Félix Llanos, who had organized resistance in the Loire region as early as 1941,[25] volunteered to lead a 'death commando' of twelve men whose mission was to seize the tower. All was in vain; they were cut down as they approached. After seven hours of combat, the rebels were still not masters of the situation: the main gate was still closed.

Llanos, badly wounded, watched the rebellion collapse. A court met. On 23 February, twelve of the rebels were executed, among them two Spaniards: Doménec Serveto Bertrán and Jaume Serot. In early April the Germans decided to transfer all the political prisoners in Eysses, now numbering 1,500, to camps in Germany, and on 30 May an SS detachment from 'Das Reich' arrived to take command from the French. On 17 June, on the eve of their departure, Félix Llanos died of his wounds, humming to the end happy songs from the Civil War. The next day the prisoners were put in trucks, only for the sake of security, and driven to the station of Penne-d'Agenais 7 kilometres away. But there were not enough trucks for the last eighty. A group of thirty-eight set out, jabbed with rifle butts. Frenchwomen, seeing them, strewed red carnations across the road. To make certain that did not happen twice, the local authorities prohibited the sale of flowers. In the last group, the Spaniard Angel Huerga Fierro could not keep up; the SS shot him on the road. At Penne-d'Agenais they were all forced into the customary wagons, 120 to each, without water or food, and almost without air. Such was the intensity of the Allied air attacks that it took them five days to reach the SS sorting centre in Compiégne. A few days later they were put on a train for Dachau. An attempt was made to escape. The SS replied that for every one who escaped they would shoot five. Heavy machine-guns were set up at every stop. This transfer, like every other, took a very heavy toll of life. Of the 2,521 men who left Compiègne at 10 a.m. on 2 July 1944, only 1,537 were still alive as the train pulled into Dachau at precisely 1.22 p.m. on 5 July. The other 984 had died of thirst, heat, and asphyxiation: in one coach containing 200 men, only three were still alive. In Dachau, the Spaniard Miguel Pórtoles, from Valencia, proved that his will to resist and organize resistance was unimpaired. But of the Spaniards deported from Eysses, only four would return from Germany.[26]

Preventing the Nazis from deporting Spaniards to Germany remained, as we shall see, the top priority of the Spanish Resistance until the last Germans had left the south-west. Their second priority was the general work of guerrilla warfare: impede the movement of the German forces by blowing up railway lines and bridges, by cutting telephone and power lines, and by setting up road blocks. The hour for lying in ambush had not yet struck. The hour for set-piece combat would never strike, but that is exactly the trap into which the Resistance fell in the first half of 1944, and not just once but twice. The Spanish *guerrilleros* were once again present in both engagements, and once again forgotten afterwards by the French.[27]

The battles of Glières and Vercors were similar actions, producing similar disasters: the destruction of the principal guerrilla bases, annihilation of most of the guerrilla force, and the dispersal of the survivors. Glières represented the first open battle of the Resistance. The purpose behind this tragic mistake was to group the local Resistance units into a zone where they could all be supplied from the air. The zone had to be suitable for parachute drops but difficult of access to the German and Italian occupation forces. The high plateau that overlooks Annecy to the south-west seemed ideal for the purpose: 10 kilometres square, it was set in the middle of a mountain range. No road led up to the plateau: all that existed were narrow, tortuous paths.

At that time, in January 1944, there was still no FFI to unite all Resistance forces under a single command, but the Gaullist Armée secrète and the communist FTP agreed to join in the operation, which was precipitated by the state of emergency in Haute-Savoie announced on 28 January by the Chief of Police at Annecy. On 31 January the first units began making the long climb up to the plateau. By 20 February, 545 *maquisards*, including sixty-five Spanish *guerrilleros* of whom fifty-six had escaped from the Groupes de travailleurs, were in position on the plateau. The force was commanded by Lieutenant Théodose Morel ('Tom') of the Armée secrète. The Spanish unit, known as the Ebro section, was commanded by Gabriel Vilches ('Antonio') and divided into three groups. A French survivor has described the Ebro section as 'one of the best, for its discipline and endurance'.[28] He adds that it was their policy not to fire on the French Milice: ' "We will be happy to attack the Germans and the Italians", they told us, "but we don't want to fire on the French. If you attack them though, we shall defend you".'[29]

Morel's men, though adequately supplied with arms, were ill-supplied with food, and were no match at all for the forces which the Germans now mustered. On 23 March, the German 157th Alpine Division, based in Grenoble and commanded by Generalleutnant Karl Pflaum, arrived in Annecy, its staff putting up at the Hôtel Imperial.[30] The total force of German, Italian, and Vichy troops is estimated at a minimum of 12,000.[31] Pflaum's forces at once began climbing the Massif while Stukas and artillery destroyed the mountain villages one by one. What followed three days later was the violation of every rule of guerrilla warfare. The *maquisards* met the German force on the plateau, and by the time the order to disband was given at 10 o'clock that night they had suffered casualties of 112 Frenchmen and nine Spaniards dead. Another seventy-five Frenchmen and five Spaniards were taken prisoner. One of the Spaniards, Francisco Rubino, managed to escape to fight another day. The others consisted of four brothers named Grenat, aged between 16 and 20. They were taken to Annecy, where they were interrogated by the police chief Lelong, then transported to Lyons and from there sent to Mauthausen, where all four died.[32] The remaining 293 Frenchmen and fifty-one Spaniards in Morel's force succeeded in breaking out of the encirclement. It is not certain that any of them reached safety. An exceptional authority, M. R. D. Foot, himself an agent of the SAS, refers to fifty Spaniards holding out on an isolated hillock, quite literally to the last man and the last round: 'Not one of the fifty was taken alive, and they had no ammunition left. This was magnificent, unforgettable, and tactically unsound.'[33]

Between the battles of Glières and Vercors, which were major guerrilla engagements, an operation of smaller scale resulted in a third disaster. In the area north-west of Alès, in the mining communities of La Grand'Combe and Collet-de-Dèze, a unit known as the 15th Brigade of Spanish Guerrilleros had been formed in late March 1943. Its commander from January 1944 was Miguel López, who in the new local guerrilla structure introduced that month took his orders from Cristino García Grandas, commanding the newly formed 3rd Division. The brigade, and indeed the division, drew many of its men from the nearby mining camps where Spaniards were employed in large numbers. The Spaniards also relied on the mining communities for their explosives. Here as elsewhere, the *guerrilleros* began without arms, so to equip themselves they raided the local gendarmeries, helping themselves not only to police weapons but also to the large stocks of hunting rifles that had been confiscated from the local farmers. It was only in late March 1944 that the Spaniards received a supply of arms from an Allied air drop, sharing the proceeds with the French *maquisards* and making their first acquintance with the British sub-machine-gun known as the Sten. A few weeks later, in April 1944, disaster struck both brigade and division. A certain Malatre Martínez, who was working for the Gestapo, succeeded in infiltrating the brigade. Some were arrested; the rest fled for their lives.

The survivors found a new refuge in the French Maquis group known as 'Bir Hakeim', named after the exploit of the French in Libya in 1942. The group, far from being communist, was a unit of the Gaullist Armée secrète, formed in Hérault, but its relations with the communist-dominated *guerrilleros* were so harmonious that the German reports later described their respective leaders, incorrectly, as regular officers. The group was commanded by Major Jean Capel ('Barot'), with the British Captain Fowler serving as his chief of staff. Barot had led most of his group into Lozère in order to prepare for an air drop to be made on the Causse Méjean 50 kilometres south of Mende. On 25 May the group had moved into position in the two hamlets La Parade and La Borie on either side of the approach road.

But the Germans were tipped off by an informer. In their reports they referred to the tip as the most useful they had ever received up to that time, precisely because the news it gave was up to the minute. The German force approaching them through the Meyrueis forest early on 28 May was made up of two companies belonging to the Freiwillige Stamm Regiment and provided by the Armenian Legion; they were supported by artillery and mortars. Barot's force consisted of only seventy men, made up of three elements: Armée secrète, the local MOI (most of them ex-International Brigaders), and twenty-six Spaniards of the 15th Brigade of Guerrilleros. Surprise was the key to the German attack. The motor-cyclist detailed to warn Barot of the Germans' arrival was taken prisoner. The five Spaniards guarding the road from Meyrueis were wiped out. Barot himself was cut to pieces by machine-gun fire, as he led his men in a counter-thrust, and Miguel López now moved into the command. The situation was bleak. The two hamlets together consisted of no more than half a dozen houses, together with the ruins of the castle of Lapeyre, which López made his command post. At nightfall the group was still holding out, but that night a Luftwaffe ground force of 120 men was dispatched from Millau to reinforce the Germans. By the time they arrived the next morning there was little left to do.

The Wehrmacht report on the action described it as a rarity, a total triumph for the occupying forces over a well-trained, well-armed, well-led guerrilla force composed, it said, mainly of Spaniards. It praised the soldiers of the Armenian Legion who had overcome an extreme deficiency in transportation (it lacked the means to transport a single company) in an operation which required a preliminary approach of 60 kilometres from the north and of 90 kilometres from the south, and without radio contact between the two groups. The report also noted the importance in the future of including artillery in such operations, since the French farmhouses in which the Maquis took cover were particularly solid and were impervious to grenade-launchers and in some cases even to anti-tank guns. The report took particular pride in the casualty figures. The Germans had lost only one German sergeant and eight Armenians, with five wounded. Even an all-German unit, it added, would not have done the job with fewer casualties.[34] As for the Maquis, it had lost thirty-two dead and twenty-seven taken prisoner, most of them wounded. The remainder had succeeded in breaking through the German lines. The prisoners, including Miguel López who was badly wounded, were then delivered to the Gestapo in Mende. López was among those they tortured, but he revealed nothing. The next day, 29 May, all twenty-seven prisoners were driven by truck along the road to the east of Mende, past the village of Badaroux. There they stopped, in the deserted ravine known as the Col de la Tourette. The men were lined up. But López was still not finished, despite the torture which had half paralysed him. He made one final attempt to escape, his body bounding forward in a hopeless rush as the Germans cut him down. The execution of all twenty-seven was completed. Of the fifty-nine men killed at La Parade or executed in Badaroux, twenty-three were Spanish. López was to receive the Croix de Guerre.[35]

Of the dozen men who had broken out of La Parade, three were Spaniards. One of them, Saturnino Gurumeta ('Antoine'), had actually been taken prisoner during the engagement but broke away, helped perhaps by the passivity of his Armenian guards—a lesson to all for the future. Another, Casimiro Camblor, was wounded, but was brought back to the 3rd Division's base at La Grand ' Combe by the third Spaniard, Manuel Zurita, riding a bicycle. Cristino García, as the 3rd Division's commander, decided to send Camblor to Dr Ruiz, a Spanish physician forced to work as a pit miner but ready enough at night to treat wounded partisans. Dr Ruiz lived in the hamlet of Larnac 10 miles to the east, and two other Spaniards, Zurita and Angel Suárez ('Polencho') were ordered to take him there, on bicycles. Meanwhile, from 8 May, a company under Leutnant Ernst Striefler of the raiding Brandenburg Division had requisitioned the Hôtel du Luxembourg in Alès. On the same morning that the three Spaniards set out from La Grand ' Combe on bicycles, two cars left the hotel in Alès, taking the road north to Langogne. The cars were disguised as partisan; so were their occupants, who all carried sub-machine-guns. By chance or by betrayal they reached the village of Affenadou in time to see the three Spaniards riding down the smaller road leading to Larnac and the home of Dr Ruiz. They gave chase, and caught the Spaniards just before they reached the château of La Plaine. Camblor was shot dead, Zurita was taken prisoner, but 'Polencho' escaped.

The incident served as a warning to the Spanish commander. The enemy was now travelling in disguise. A similar incident occurred shortly afterwards at Le Magistavol, north-west of Alès, where two carloads of well-dressed civilians, who were really Germans armed with sub-machine-guns, drew up at a house used by the Resistance. They announced that they were officers of the Armée secrète who had been sent to take command of the Maquis because of the danger it faced from criminal elements who had infiltrated it. The men spoke perfect French, but it was the presence of a Spaniard in the group that most reassured the partisans. This Spaniard was none other than Zurita, who had thus emerged either as a traitor or as a broken victim of the Gestapo. Zurita knew the house where the partisans met. The ruse finally failed, after more than one local partisan had been beguiled and quietly murdered, because the Germans, however carefully they had prepared their false identity as Gaullists, were unmasked on this occasion by their fellow Germans fighting in the MOI.[36]

Four months after the disaster at Glières, the Resistance took the equally unsound decision to engage the same German 157th Alpine Division, together with the 9th Panzerdivision, on the plateau of Vercors, to the south-west of Grenoble. The Vercors Maquis, numbering some 3,500, including eighty Spanish *guerrilleros*, was the largest in France. Serious thought had been given by Allied strategists to the idea of setting up a redoubt, prior to any invasion of the south of France, which could impede the German supply route down the Rhône valley. The project called for the preparation of a landing strip on the plateau for the purpose of a large airborne landing; the *maquisards'* mission would be to prevent the Germans from reaching the plateau for a certain number of hours. This project, however, had been shelved, and it was a different plan, or no real plan at all, that sent the *maquisards* into battle on 21 July with a force estimated at a minimum of 15,000. This force, again combining German, Italian, and French units, was once more commanded by General Pflaum. If the defenders hoped that the plateau, reached only by winding passes, might discourage the Germans, they were soon disabused. Again the German dive-bombers set about the destruction of the mountain villages, again their observer planes traced the movement of the *maquisard* units, and this time the attacking force included airborne SS. The *maquisards* held out for three days, until the order was given to disperse into the forests. Total Resistance casualties were 840 dead, including sixty-two Spaniards.[37] Among those taken prisoner was Manuel Correa Calderón, the founder and commander of a Spanish unit formed in Savoy in mid-1943. It was his distinction to be the only Spanish *guerrillero* known to have fallen into the hands of the Italians and deported to Italy.[38]

The action at Vercors left an even more bitter aftertaste than that at Glières, because the lesson of Glières had been ignored. Brave men had again been sacrificed to a hopeless mission, ordered by some unidentifiable official in Algiers or London, and no effort had been made to support them or extricate them. In the search for a meaning to it all, the rumour that never died had it that General de Gaulle was looking for a spectacular feat of arms that in time would leave the image of a France that had freed itself.

It would be difficult to imagine the reaction of a Spanish *guerrillero*, living in virtual isolation in some remote region of the Massif Central, to the kind of situation which might confront him now at any time. Six *guerrilleros* in a mountain hide-out: the sound of voices approaching in the still evening air: the *guerrilleros* freeze, straining for a glimpse of the uniforms or a clue to the language. Is it French, Spanish, or German? Are they comrades in the Resistance, local farmers, scouting Milice, or SS? What they hear and see leaves them dumbfounded. The two men approaching them are speaking English. They are Indians, and they are dressed in the uniform of the German Afrikakorps. Such an incident, repeated in different ways unnumbered times, reflects the complexities of the struggle between the camps in the summer of 1944.

We have seen that German Army Group. G covering the southern half of France included two armies and a headquarters force based in Toulouse. This headquarters force was remarkable by any standard, since it included the best and the worst of fighting troops. On the one hand, its LVIIIth Panzerkorps comprised three armoured divisions of distinction: 2nd SS-Panzer ('Das Reich'), 9th Panzer, and 11th Panzer.[39] On the other hand, alongside this Nazi élite stood a division made up of volunteers of many nationalities: Soviets from various southern republics, Poles, Czechs, Croats, even Indians. These Osttruppen were commonly lumped together by the Germans under the term Mongols, and by the Resistance under the name Vlasovs, after the Russian general who had fought in the Red Army, fallen into German hands, and offered his captors an army with which to fight Stalin. In 1943 fears of a mass betrayal resulted in the transfer of these troops to the south-western theatre (Italy) or the western (France and the Low Countries). Since these men had volunteered specifically to fight the communist regime, their transfer to the Western fronts dealt a severe blow to their morale, as was shown by the revolt, in September 1943, of a Croatian battalion stationed at Villefranche-de-Rouergue in Aveyron. After killing their German officers they fled north-west to the mountains, the Germans in deadly pursuit. Denounced to the Germans by the local inhabitants, approximately 200 were trapped and shot. But two companies managed to escape, and after wandering in the mountains they made contact with the local unit of Spanish *guerrilleros*: the 9th Brigade, led by Amadeo López ('Salvador'). López, and his senior officer Miguel Angel Sanz commanding the 4th Division, interviewed the leader whom the Croats had elected. The Spaniards agreed to incorporate the Croatian companies into their local forces, and the Croats were to fight with the Spaniards until the liberation of Aveyron.[40]

Such acts of treason up to 1944 were apparently rare. In the south-west of France, the Wehrmacht's Deputy Chief of Operations made a

1. Fleeing from Spain in the wake of the Casado coup, Pasionaria arrives at Gare de Lyon in Paris on 9 March 1939. From left to right: PCF *député* Jean Catelas, General Juan Modesto, Pasionaria, Irene Falcón. *Keystone.*

2. Spanish prisoners of the Germans in Stalag XVIIA (Kaisersteinbruck, near Vienna), 1940. Back row, third from right: Mariano Constante; middle row, second from left: Antonio García Alonso. *Wehrmacht photograph, by courtesy of Antonio García.*

3. Himmler and (at right) Kaltenbrunner on a visit to Mauthausen, 27 Apr. 1941. *SS photograph, by courtesy of Dr Přemysl Dobiáš*

4. Mauthausen: prisoners at roll-call in −10°C. *SS photograph, by courtesy of the Commission de l'Information historique de la paix, Paris*

5. Mauthausen: Lagerführer Ziereis with four of his staff, summer 1943. From left to right: Seidler, Beck, Ziereis, Bachmayer, Schütl. *SS photograph, by courtesy of the Bundesministerium für Inneres, Vienna*

6. Mauthausen. Clockwise from top left: Schulz, Bachmayer, Dr Krebsbach, Fassel. *SS photographs, by courtesy of Antonio García.*

7. SS General Lammerding with staff officers of *Das Reich* as the division leaves Montauban for the north, June 1944. From left to right: Major Helmut Kampfe, Major Ernst Krag, Colonel Albert Stückler, General Heinz Lammerding. *SS photograph, by courtesy of Max Hastings*

8. Toulouse, 26 Aug. 1944. the FFI Matabiau Group greets the first Allied units to reach Toulouse, in front of Matabiau station. Front centre: Major Anthony Brooks, of the British Special Air Service. *Yan/Jean Dieuzaide*

tour of inspection of 1st Army in February 1944 and noted in his report: 'Black, yellow and other auxiliaries are employed in the rein-forcement of the coastal defences. . . . The morale of the troops is high. That is equally true in the case of the Russian and Indian units incorporated.'[41] By June, in their desperate attempt to free all Ger-mans for combat duty, the Wehrmacht was relying on non-Germans for up to half of their garrisons and security guards. This reliance on non-Germans was the Achilles' heel of Army Group G, and the Re-sistance was aware of it.

Meanwhile, the French Resistance had been so deeply infiltrated by German agents that General de Gaulle was given the date of D-Day only two days in advance and General Koenig was informed only on 5 June.[42] That evening the BBC's coded messages to the south-west were picked up on wireless sets in Rieumes and Muret. '*Veronese était un peintre*' and '*Le père La Cerise est toujours verni*' were all the Resistance leaders needed to hear. Members quietly left their homes to join their groups. Some days would be spent in organizational matters before the groups would move into the work of setting up the ambushes. In Toulouse, the 160 men of the Saint-Lys Maquis, including a number of Spaniards, received their marching orders on 7 June. By the next day, travelling by bicycle or the Toulouse–Lombez milk train, they had assembled at their rendezvous in the wild, forested area 25 kilometres to the south-west of the city. The site was never intended as a base of operations; it consisted of two adjacent châteaux (Gagen and Candelé) well hidden in the forest, the site's only function being to serve as a centre for organization, assembly, and stores. The stores, however, consisted of very few arms; the arms were to arrive by parachute drop on 12 June. 'Das Reich' was not going to give them that much advantage. At 7 p.m. on the evening of 12 June, 600 SS troops silently closed in on Gagen, shutting off their engines as they came down the slope from Saint-Lys. The men belonged to the IIIrd Battalion (under SS-Sturmbannführer Schreiber) of the 3rd ('Deut-schland') Regiment. They included some Hungarians, Poles, Czechs, Russians, and Alsatians. All were heavily armed, against a resistance force that was barely armed at all. Abandoning Gagen for the slightly better protection of Candelé, the *maquisards* resisted as best they could, sustaining heavy casualties before dispersing into the forest. A few hours later, the Allied arms arrived as scheduled, into the arms of the Germans.[43]

The German situation in the Massif Central, however, was deterior-ating to the point that, on 8 June, von Rundstedt, as Supreme Com-mander West, ordered 'the immediate application of even more ruthless force'. To this end he ordered the 2nd SS-Panzerdivision to move at once into the Tulle–Limoges area, where strong guerrilla forces were in evidence. The orders to 'Das Reich' were thus to engage the guerrillas, not to make for Normandy, which disposes of the popular argument that 'Das Reich' was slowed down for a week or more by the Resistance. This is not to say that the division's commander, General Heinz Lammerding, considered the mission less important. On 10 June, the day of Oradour, Lammerding wrote a report to his corps commander which was marked by a sense of frustration, giving the impression of a man bent on a terror mission and little concerned whether those he massacred were *maquisards* or not. The report ran in part:

The area Figéac–Clermont-Ferrand–Limoges–Gourdon is firmly in the hands of the terrorists. The local German garrisons are encircled and for the most part besieged; here and there entire companies have been annihilated. The French administration services are paralysed. The helplessness of the German outposts is utterly scandalous. Unless the most determined, drastic and ruthless measures [*entschlossenes rücksichtloses Durchgreifen*] are taken, the situation in this area will become a danger of dimensions not yet imagined. In this area a new communist state is believed to be coming into being, a state which governs without accountability and which carries out methodical conscription.

Lammerding deplored only that the job of annihilating the Maquis was being given to Panzer divisions when it could be accomplished by local Wehrmacht units.[44]

The march of 'Das Reich' produced the two worst atrocities committed in France during the entire war, in Tulle on 7 June and in Oradour-sur-Glane on 10 June. In Tulle, ninety-nine of its inhabitants dangled from every balcony, lamp-post, and tree in the Place de Souillac. In Oradour, virtually the entire population was murdered in cold blood: a total of 642 inhabitants, including 241 women and 202 children.[45] Among these were at least eighteen Spaniards: three men, nine women, six children.[46] The slaughter was carried out by the 3rd Company (commanded by Otto Kahn) of the Ist Battalion (Otto Diekmann) of the 4th ('Der Führer') Panzergrenadier Regiment (Sylvester Stadler).[47] The blame was to be endlessly shifted.[48] No man went to trial. The presence of Alsatians in the 2nd SS-Panzerdivision helps to explain why.

The question remains, was the Wehrmacht also responsible to some degree for the behaviour of the Waffen SS? Can it be said that only the SS countenanced atrocities? In the theatre of operations of Army Group G, a number of directives were issued to its units, including 'Das Reich'—the only SS unit in its command—which suggest that 'Das Reich' was encouraged in such action by the orders it received.

On 12 June, two days after Oradour, the increase in the level of Resistance activities in the centre and south-west induced von Blaskowitz to take personal charge of the anti-guerrilla war and to ask OKW to make the south-west a combat zone.[49] This request was approved, but without waiting for Berlin's reply von Blaskowitz issued an order, bearing his personal signature and addressed to both his armies as well as his reserve mass (including therefore 'Das Reich'), in which the Commander-in-Chief exhorted his subordinates 'to apply the most drastic measures without the slightest remorse [*ich erwarte hierbei schärfstes Durchgreifen ohne jegliche Rücksichtnahme*].'[50] What more encouragement could an SS division commander want from his Commander-in-Chief? Nor did the army and army corps commanders fail their Commander-in-Chief when it came to issuing orders of their own. Von der Chevallerie, commanding 1st Army, appealed for drastic and ruthless action ('*rücksichtsloses Durchgreifen ist erforderlich*'),[51] and Krüger, commanding LVIIIth Panzerkorps, reminded his division commanders (including Lammerding) that 'human feelings have no place here at all [*menschliche Rücksichten dürfen hierbei nicht genommen werden*]'.[52]

Lammerding, despite his mission to Limoges, was on his way to the Battle of Normandy, and was now frantic for the three battalions he had been forced to leave behind in Toulouse. Von Blaskowitz, loath to lose his last Waffen-SS, delayed as long as he could, until the Supreme Commander West took the decision for him. The situation in Normandy, where von Rundstedt had failed to mount a successful counterattack, had deteriorated to the point that Hitler decided to make his first visit to France since 1940. His choice of venue for his temporary GHQ, known as Wolfsschlucht II,[53] was a spot near Margival, north-east of Soissons, where in May 1918 he had won his Iron Cross First Class, a very rare award for a soldier in the ranks. Not surprisingly, for this visit of 17 June 1944, Hitler chose to wear it. But nothing inspired von Rundstedt to hurl the Allies back into the sea, and on 2 July he found himself relieved of his command and replaced by Generalfeldmarschall Günther von Kluge.

Within seven days of assuming the supreme command in the west, von Kluge was informed by von Blaskowitz that communications between his 1st and 19th Armies were no longer assured. Despite that, von Kluge ordered the immediate transfer of the remnants of 2nd SS-Panzerdivision northwards to La Flèche, in Sarthe, where, with the main body of the division, it would be integrated into 7th Army.[54] The last orders transmitted by LVIIIth Panzerkorps to 'Das Reich' went out from the Toulouse area on 15 July.[55] In its own reports, 'Das Reich' kept to its script to the last: '*Keine besonderen Ereignisse*' ('Nothing

to report').[56] In fact, by that time the proud division had been hacked
to pieces. A report from LVIIIth Panzerkorps[57] gave the following stark
figures:

	Officers	Non-Commissioned Officers	Men
Original strength	164	1,242	6,904
Casualties	109	741	3,781
Remaining in action	55	501	4,439

No explanation was given, but the figures reveal that the deficiency
in men had been made good by inducting new troops, while the SS
officers and non-commissioned officers could not be replaced.

While the Wehrmacht's forces in the south-west remained overwhelmingly German, and still included two Panzer divisions, the
reliance on non-Germans cannot be ignored. As an illustration of this
dependence, the task force under Generalmajor Hans von Taeglichs-
beck, retreating between the Loire and the Burgundy Canal in September 1944, counted among its 10,000 men no fewer than 7,000
Soviets and Indians.[58] The loyalty of such forces was a factor in the
battle for the south-west.

Last and least, the confrontation most devoutly wished by all Spanish
Republicans in France was now theoretically possible: a replay of the
scene in Russia on the Leningrad front where Franco's Blue Division
faced the Spanish communists fighting in the Red Army. In September 1943 Franco had decided to recall the division. Though he left a
battalion-sized force in its place, this too was withdrawn in February
1944. In order not to attract attention the force returned to Spain
quietly and in small units. Even more quietly, volunteers now rallied
to the cause of one last throw for Hitler, who was more and more
desperate for men. General Edwin Hexel was sent to Madrid to enroll
Spanish veterans eager to return to combat. The Franco regime fore-
saw the danger, and in April 1944 announced that any Spaniard still
serving in the German forces would forfeit his allowances, his pen-
sion, and even his Spanish citizenship. While the Spanish authorities
kept a tight watch on the frontier, about 150 volunteers crossed the
border and regrouped at a base in Lourdes. This and similar bases
along the Pyrenees were commanded by Oberstleutnant Heyde, and
in Lourdes the Spaniards were given combat training by Hauptmann
Karl Tägert of Sonderverband F. Although they were dressed as peasants in order not to attract attention, their identity and their purpose
soon became known to the Spanish *guerrilleros* in the region. After
that the Spanish legionnaires dispensed with the peasant clothes. By
July 1944 they were serving under German officers as a company of

the Brandenburg Division in the region of Pamiers, where they were not only in reconnaissance but in combat against the *guerrilleros*. The Chief of Staff at Army Group headquarters, Generalmajor von Gyldenfeldt, ordered General Krüger, commanding LVIIIth Panzerkorps, to give every possible assistance to this Spanish fascist unit under his command.[59]

10

The Liberation of the South-West

*The strategic importance of the Atlantic–Mediterranean land-bridge—
The Germans intensify their anti-guerrilla activities—The Todt Or-
ganization and its defaulters—Escape from the camps and prisons—
The 'ghost train' to Dachau—The effect of D-Day on the south-west:
General Krüger's report of 20 June on the guerrilla threat—The
Wehrmacht's problem with morale: disloyalty in the foreign units—
Allied aid to the Resistance—The proliferation of atrocities—General
Krüger's report of 12 July—Arrival of three Allied officers: Hilaire,
Brooks, Fuller—Reprisals and counter-reprisals—Effect of the July Plot
on the Wehrmacht—The Franco-American landing at Saint-Tropez
and its effect on the land-bridge—Hitler orders the retreat of Army
Group G: the race to escape the trap—Running the guerrilla gaunt-
let—The Toulouse garrison ordered to withdraw—The liberation of
Toulouse—Retreat of the last German forces from the south—The
liberation of Paris*

> but they are fled—
> Gone are they, viewless as the buried dead:
> Where now?—Their sword is at the Foeman's heart!
> And thus from year to year his walk they thwart,
> And hang like dreams around his guilty bed.[1]

We have seen that the basic objective of German Army Group G was
to maintain the land-bridge between the Atlantic and the Mediterranean and to be prepared to repel an Allied invasion on either coast
or on both coasts together. The two coasts are linked by the Garonne
valley from Bordeaux to Toulouse and by the Canal du Midi from
Toulouse to the Mediterranean, while the two major road and rail
routes are Bordeaux–Toulouse–Narbonne and Bayonne–Toulouse–
Narbonne. In assigning responsibilities to his two armies, von
Blaskowitz allocated to 1st Army the protection of the northern route
as far east as Marmande, and the southern as far east as Tarbes. To
19th Army he gave the Narbonne road as far west as Carcassonne.
This left the central section (including *HVS 564* in Toulouse), over
which he took direct tactical control. Security for Toulouse itself he

entrusted to LvⅢth Panzerkorps. In his first orders after D-Day he made it clear that the most urgent task in Toulouse was to seize from the commercial sector everything that might be needed in the way of motor vehicles, battery generators, fuel depots, and even bicycles.[2]

The question very soon arose: what was the primary objective, to protect the coasts or to wage battle with the guerrillas? It was the 11th Panzerdivision, given the job of guarding the Bordeaux–Marmande road for 1st Army, which first raised it, but other units would quickly find themselves in a similar dilemma. The decision was taken on 16 June, by von Blaskowitz's Chief of Staff, Generalmajor Heinz von Gyldenfeldt, that priority was to be given to waging war on the guerrillas.[3]

Von Blaskowitz then set out the matter clearly: 'As long as no enemy action is launched from without, the struggle against the enemy within remains the primary objective.'[4] The extent to which this situation had deteriorated was evident in a report from the 111th Panzergrenadier Regiment in the area of Tulle, site of the recent atrocity. The regiment paid tribute to the enemy's tactics. The guerrillas, it said, had at their disposal a superbly organized intelligence service, which enabled them to launch surprise attacks with numerically far superior forces on small isolated German units and administration posts. They were setting up road blocks and demolishing installations, and their acts of sabotage were terrorizing the French authorities. Their tactics were to avoid all set-piece engagements and to move their camp continually. Units were moved singly, in most cases in motorized transport, only by night, and mostly by secondary roads. Their strength was constantly increasing as a result of 'forced recruitment'.[5]

It was not the Resistance that was busy in forced recruitment. The Spaniards had long given top priority to the task of thwarting the efforts of the Organisation Todt to recruit Spanish manpower for work in German factories. Its system of recruitment varied from payment to volunteers to the most brutal methods for defaulters. The Spaniards showed remarkable ingenuity in avoiding the draft, and it was a fundamental error on the part of the Germans to employ Spaniards in the recruitment offices.[6] After the Allied landings in Normandy, the head office of the Organisation Todt in Paris drew up plans to transfer to Germany all those Spaniards it had hitherto employed in the Southern Zone of France. The Wehrmacht registered its objections, on the grounds that neither the transportation nor the security personnel was available. In fact, its principal concern was that the Spaniards, if the plan reached their ears, would take to the hills and reinforce the *guerrilleros*.[7] The Germans were almost certainly aware of the call that issued from the AGE the moment that the Allied invasion was announced: 'The hour has struck to exterminate the enemy without the slightest pity, leaving neither a German nor a collaborator alive.'[8]

The Spaniards, for their part, had every reason to fear that the Germans would undertake an exactly similar operation, exterminating every last inmate of the detention camps, and they therefore decided upon a combined operation (AGE units with other FFI units) to free them. At the time of D-Day the camps and prisons were still guarded by the French, but on 9 June the Germans, anticipating such an action by the Resistance, took control of the camps at Le Vernet and Noé as well as the prison of Saint-Michel in Toulouse. The Jews at Le Vernet had already left a month earlier, when Pierre Marty, the Vichy superintendent of police, ordered their transfer to the Cafarelli barracks in Toulouse as the first step in their deportation to Germany. Le Vernet nevertheless still contained over a thousand inmates. On 30 June the Germans began organizing a new dispatch—it proved to be the last—of the remaining prisoners. Those at Le Vernet were particularly vulnerable. If they had not been deported earlier it was because they were elements useless to Germany: disabled veterans of the Spanish Civil War, the sick, and the aged.[9] They were joined by 240 Resistance members, including forty-five women, held in the Saint-Michel prison, together with prisoners from the camps at Noé and Saint-Sulpice and from the fortress-prisons of Perpignan and Eysses. Saint-Sulpice, which in mid-June held 1,400 prisoners, mostly Spaniards and Italians, was considered too large to evacuate.[10] This did not offer the inmates any better hope. Escape became progressively more difficult, at the same time that the food supplies diminished. The French guards were replaced by a Georgian battalion, and on 22 July, when Army Group G transferred the Georgians to Agen, the responsibility for the camp was given to no less a unit than the 11th Panzerdivision.[11]

Nazi Germany was resolved never to allow those in its grip, in France as elsewhere, to taste the fruit of liberation. Precisely because the Nazis were tightening that grip, the assault on the prison at Nontron (Dordogne), as early as 10 June, was regarded as a spectacular feat of arms. Once again the purpose was to prevent the dispatch of political prisoners to Germany. The assault force was placed under the command of Emilio Álvarez Canosa ('Pinocho'), who succeeded in liberating eighty prisoners, including five members of the Central Committee of the PCF.[12] But the most spectacular escape was an act of self-liberation, by prisoners whom the Nazis obviously wanted to kill by degrees. Two of the very last trains for Dachau started off on the same day, 2 July 1944, one leaving from the sorting centre at Compiègne, north of Paris, and the other from the Gare Raynal, the freight station in Toulouse.[13] Both convoys included many of the most resolute fighters in the Resistance, whom the Gestapo could so easily have executed if quick death were its purpose. Both convoys were formed from groups remaining in the camps and prisons, and both included Spaniards. Of the 2,166 men who left Compiègne, at least 536 were dead on arrival. The stifling heat—it was 34 °C on 2 July—the lack of air, the compact loading of the human cargo, the refusal for two days at a time to allow the prisoners food or even water, and not least, the taunting of the guards outside the bolted cars, crowing that where the prisoners were going they would have no need of either. In such conditions, average men went mad. There was the son who tried to kill his father, in the crazed belief that he was responsible for his suffering. But once again, those who could maintain social discipline had a chance to pull through. In one car there was not a single fatality: each inmate was given his turn, even if he had to be held up, to put his face beside the crack in the wall of the car.[14]

The convoy that left Toulouse on 2 July consisted of 610 prisoners (including sixty women) of several nationalities, but the majority were French and Spanish. Among them were men of distinction: the Spanish surgeon Vicente Parra Bordetas, the French philosopher Albert Lautmann, and the Italian socialist member of parliament Francesco Fausto Nitti.[15] The women included the Spanish Resistance heroine Conchita Ramos. Nitti, who was to survive the ordeal and publish an account of it, mentions that he found himself in the company of four Spanish Republican colonels, all of them either disabled or sick, who had been imprisoned in the fortress-prison in Perpignan.[16] Another survivor, the Frenchman Claude Lévy, would become a distinguished physician later, and would also write his account.[17] Equally distinguished in a different sense was Inspector Fournera of the Vichy police, who had tortured many a Spanish *guerrillero* and who now found himself a prisoner on the train. One could imagine his fate, once he was recognized. But fate was kind to him, and he was shot early in the journey by the guards.

The organizers of the Ghost Train to Dachau clearly anticipated more than the usual difficulties of transit, for the convoy was more than usually protected. A passenger-car filled with guards was intercalated between every two or three cattle-cars; the passenger-cars had multiple doors, and the guards would sit on the steps on each side of the car, their rifles on their knees. Look-outs kept watch on top. At the rear of the convoy, a flat-top carried a heavy machine-gun, for use also against aircraft, and a searchlight for use at night whenever an attempt at escape was suspected. The prisoners who were assembled that day at the Toulouse freight station included a group of Wehrmacht soldiers who had been court-martialled for indiscipline; they were kept apart from the rest, and would not be subjected to the same conditions. As for the main prisoners, their worst fears may well have been allayed for a moment on seeing the uniform of their guards. It was not that of the SS. A French military officer recognized it as that of a German infantry regiment.[18] They were thus the average men of the Wehrmacht, commanded by an Austrian officer of the Condor Legion of the Luftwaffe, Oberleutnant Schuster, and they had apparently volunteered for the operation at this period in the war because it entitled them to a cherished privilege: evacuation to Germany, with no services more onerous to perform than guard duty in a convoy such as this.

What gave the convoy its name of 'ghost train' was the itinerary it was forced to take. Its destination was Dachau, to the north-east. The direction it took was in fact north-west—to Bordeaux, evidence of the impossibility of using the rail routes from Toulouse to the north or east. The success of the Resistance in sabotaging the tracks is shown in the fact that no more than one train completed the run between Toulouse and Brive (on the main line to Paris) between 4 June and 15 August.[19] Besides, the Germans had to contend with more than sabotage. The constant exposure to strafing by Allied aircraft and ambush by the Resistance turned this journey into an odyssey. After dragging its way to Angoulême, the train was attacked from the air. In the confusion two prisoners escaped, and the train was forced to return to Bordeaux. There, in reprisal for the escape, ten prisoners were selected and taken to the Fort du Hâ, where they were executed with forty others in that prison. Among the ten were Albert Lautmann and the Spanish socialist engineer Peyre Vidal, who had been engaged in the escape network running from Foix through Tarascon to Andorra. The rest of the prisoners were interned, from 12 July to 8 August, in the main synagogue, now converted into a detention centre the better to profane it. The train then took them back to their starting point in Toulouse, then braved whatever lay in wait as it headed east for Carcassonne, Montpellier, and Nîmes. Sometimes the prisoners would wait for days in a station because the train could not proceed. At other times they would be ordered out and made to walk for miles in order to board another train sent from the other end. The Wehrmacht in the east, south, and west was frantic for supplies, but priority in rolling stock was to be given to the most important task of all: making sure that the worst enemies of the Reich did not live to see the Liberation, and died in protracted agony.

What of the prisoners? As everywhere else they were packed at least seventy to a car. At the time of their departure from Toulouse, the Quakers had been allowed to supply the prisoners with food, consisting of bread sufficient for five days. After that the Germans left it to the International Red Cross to provide the food at the stations where they stopped. Worse for the prisoners was the heat. Each car had four ventilators, each large enough for a horse or cow to stick its head through, but we have the word of a medical doctor who was there that the temperature in the cars, crammed with the living, the dying, and the dead, under a leaden sun, reached 60 °C.[20] What air there was was made more putrid by the many suffering from diarrhoea, while the lice added to the misery. Worst of all was the refusal of the guards to provide water. Whenever the sick and wounded asked the guards for help, the answer was the same: 'Where you're going, you won't need help.'

For days and nights inside the cars, men and women struggled to breathe, their eyes rolling with thirst. No one spoke; there was no saliva to spare. Some sought relief by licking the iron fixtures on the car walls, only to find the metal burning hot, causing the tongue to swell until it seemed to fill the mouth like a rubber slab. Collective panic began to tighten its fatal grip.

Survive. Survive by escape. Escape however slight the chances of survival. Such were the thoughts of those still capable of thought, for the lack of water and air was driving the prisoners to distraction. It is possible that some prisoners succeeded in escaping at those points where they were transferred, but there is no evidence except that the SS shot fifteen who tried. The only other means of escape was for the prisoners to claw their way to freedom while *en route*. The first prisoner to act on this conclusion was a Spaniard from Alès, Angel Álvarez.

Angel Álvarez was only 17 when his daring actions in the Resistance won him fame. In September 1943 he fell into the hands of the Milice, who tortured him, and on 13 March 1944 a Special Court set up by Vichy in Toulouse sentenced him to death. On 30 June, however, Álvarez was among those handed over to the Germans, and two days later he found himself with two friends inside the train bound for Dachau. No sooner had he climbed into his car than he proposed to his fellow prisoners that they rush the nearest guard, seize his sub-machine-gun, open fire, and trigger a mass break-out. Almost every one of the prisoners in the car responded that they did not want to die, and that if Álvarez made a move they would at once alert the guards. 'Captivity', concluded Álvarez, 'had reduced these men to servile and solitary animals. It made me the more determined to escape.' The three companions decided to make their break-out through one of the ventilators, which were all secured not only by barbed wire but by two planks nailed into the car wall in the form of a cross. One of Álvarez's friends, who knew the region between Toulouse and Bordeaux, proposed that they make their jump to the left of the train at a point where the rail track ran close to the Garonne river. Having selected their ventilator, they elbowed their way roughly through the crowd of bodies until the three stood below it. While his two comrades held him up, Álvarez began work on the barbed wire. They had the time. Such were the train's unscheduled stops at junctions and in *dépôts* that it took 3 days even to cover the 100 kilometres to Agen, halfway to Bordeaux. By that time Álvarez had succeeded, at frightful cost to his hands, in dislodging the barbed wire and the two crossed planks. Having passed Marmande, the train made a brief stop at the little station of Sainte-Bazeille. It was now the middle of the short summer night. The three men pulled straws to decide in what order they would jump. Álvarez was to go first. He had a second advantage: he was very thin, and lithe as a cat. Christian de Roquemaurel de L'Isle, close to him in the car, remembers seeing him at the ventilator one instant and gone the next. Unaccountably, the train now accelerated to about 50 kilometres an hour. On the outside of the train, Álvarez was making a careful calculation for his jump when he found himself caught in the flat-top's searchlight. Álvarez missed his jump, his head striking the steel rail of the track before he rolled to the bottom of a ditch. The alert sounded, the machine-guns opened up, and the brakes began to screech. He knew at once that his comrades had lost their chance, but he was determined to make the best of his. He was in great pain from the injury to his head, and he still had the main road to cross before he could make for the Garonne, but he struggled to his feet and staggered towards the river, pursued all the way by the machine-gun fire from the train and by a number of guards sent after him. Taking whatever cover he could, he reached the river bank and with his last strength swam across to freedom.[21]

The exploit of Álvarez, to any prisoner who saw it, was a summons to do the same. The Spaniards, who were not imprisoned together but strung out at random along the train, were almost all resolved to escape but in every car opinion was divided. One group believed, like Álvarez, in the survival of the fittest. Another group, supported in their respective cars by Nitti and Lévy, wanted to organize a collective escape for all members of the car. A third opinion was in favour of a mass, all-train breakout, methodically organized by a committee. A fourth group, too old or weakened to escape or too demoralized to care, preferred to stay in the cars in the hope of being rescued by the

Maquis. The third opinion was quickly dismissed as a waste of everyone's time and energy: there was no means of communicating between one boxcar and another except when the train stopped and the respective interpreters (prisoners appointed by the commandant to translate his orders) alighted and had a chance to talk. Each car thus reached its own conclusion, but in one car the animosity between the groups holding the first and second opinions was so intense that the Spaniards in each group, their reason no doubt affected by their suffering, nearly came to blows, or to what weak blows their remaining strength allowed. But reason and the Nitti–Lévy approach prevailed. The attempt would be collective. The means would be the removal of a plank, or more than one, from the boxcar floors, or sides.

In the course of the odyssey, those in Nitti's car managed to collect various pieces of metal and even several knives, but in Lévy's car, which followed immediately behind, the prisoners were forced to do their entire work with a single nail. Progress was annulled when the train stopped and they had to changed cars, and thus start the work all over again. Such was the case when the train, having passed Remoulins on 15 August, broke down at Roquemaure. What followed became known as the Long March. 'Alles 'raus!' ran the cry. The prisoners in their weakened state were ordered to carry the Germans' packs all the way to Sorgues, a distance of 17 kilometres. Claude Lévy, crazed with thirst like the rest, remembers carrying a German's cask of wine, and watching him while he drank from it *en route*. At Sorgues, on the eastern bank of the Rhône, the prisoners received some help before being forced into a new train. Starting, stopping, taking this track, then that, the train made its laborious way up the Rhône Valley towards Lyons under the constant harassment of Allied planes, now in direct support of the Allied landing in Provence. No fewer than fifty prisoners were killed or wounded by the strafing, which reached its height at Marcoule and Pierrelatte near Orange. Again the locomotive was disabled, and again a second locomotive was sent down from the north to pull both train and locomotive up the valley. Just north of Valence, an air attack had damaged the steel bridge across the Isère. The Commandant decided not to risk the crossing. Again the cry 'Alles 'raus!' and again the prisoners were made to carry the Germans' baggage. On the other side of the bridge they were forced into a new train, but the change gave them the priceless gift of a few minutes of fresh air.

The work of break-out resumed, more desperately than ever, and with varying progress. The prisoners did not mix freely during the periods of transfer; they remained in their groups, separated one from another, with only the interpreters meeting. Nitti and his companions had managed to hold on to the superior tools in their possession, while Lévy and his companions still held nothing but a nail. While Nitti's group was now able to loosen four of the planks, it was only with extreme difficulty that those in Lévy's car succeeded in removing one. By then time was running out. On the night of 24–5 August they were already in Haute-Marne. Fortunately, the train had had to slow down to a speed estimated at only 30 km. per hour, but when it reached Montigny-le-Roi it was only twenty minutes from Germany's new frontier in Lorraine.

The escape was finally ready, but not before one group of prisoners found to their horror that some of the guards had taken refuge from the constant air attacks by setting up plank beds under the floor of their cars. Some advice on falling was now passed along. The prisoners were told to fall on the track feet first, then roll their bodies back with their faces towards the locomotive and their arms above their heads, then move as close as possible to a rail in the same position and with their bodies straight, thus minimizing the chance that the guards on the rear flat-top would notice a shape on the track behind them. The SS knew that if the prisoners attempted to escape it would be by dint of removing the planks, and they had taken every precaution they could, with stops and searches, to prevent it. What the prisoners now feared most was that the SS had draped a chain across the rear wheels of the flat-top to enmesh any prisoner who dropped on to the track. But this the Germans had not done, perhaps because with the condition of the track it would have impeded the train. The first to drop was a dummy, to see if the SS fired. There was no fire, and the break-out began. The final precaution taken by the prisoners was to stuff rags into their mouths at the moment of the drop, and thus stifle any cry that could alert the guards.

The precaution was necessary. Five or six of the escaping prisoners had their heads or limbs severed by the wheels as they miscalculated the manœuvre. Others remembered seeing the heels of the boots of the SS guards just 50 cm. from where they lay on the track, while the noise of the wheels shattered their ears. Nitti remembered counting, one by one, the seventeen cars that he knew would follow his, but still they lay motionless on the track, watching the red light on the flat-top as it grew smaller and smaller and then flickered out in the darkness. What followed was delirium. One survivor remembers fleeing like a maddened horse, head back, nostrils flaring, until he stumbled headlong into a pond, which gave him new energy and a clearer head, and most of all, fresh, cool, water.

All together, about 100 prisoners escaped. Fortune had indeed turned for them: the armies of Patch and Patton were hard behind, and the prisoners were able to make their way back through the turmoil to Toulouse, and share in the joy of the city's liberation. The rest, the living and the dead—and more than half were dead—reached Dachau on 27 August; half the survivors remained there, while the other half were sent on to Mauthausen and Ravensbrück.[22] Even the inmates of Dachau, it was said, listened with pity to their story.[23]

Meanwhile, in June 1944, liberation was still only a fervent hope, but three other *départements* were already bubbling with revolt: Gers, Tarn, and Ariège. Ariège was strategically of secondary importance, but the deteriorating situation in Gers and Tarn threatened the escape routes which no German commander could any longer dismiss from his mind. In proposing counter-measures to this worsening state of affairs, General Krüger, commanding LVIIIth Panzerkorps, admitted to his commander-in-chief that the rapid and total liquidation of the guerrilla groups was not possible, since the area in question was too large and too difficult to survey. Nor was it likely, he said, that reconnaissance, however vigilantly maintained, would succeed in locating the guerrillas' ever-shifting camps. All that was possible, with the forces currently available, was to interdict their night manœuvres in specified areas and to choke their effectiveness by using the hostage system.

On 11 June, 1st Army gave orders that every reconnaissance patrol was to include an interpreter, who was responsible for making the civilian population fully aware of the benefits of collaboration: information leading to the arrest of terrorists, or the capture of terrorist equipment, would be rewarded by up to 20,000 francs, either in cash or in the form of natural produce—chocolate and coffee excepted.[24] Inevitably, some people responded. The incident in Buziet (Basses-Pyrénées) on 17 July is an example. The home of Emiliana Blasco de Quintián served as a safe house and a hospital for the Spanish *guerrilleros* of the 10th Brigade under Julio Vicuña. Two Frenchmen from Arudy informed the German authorities, who surrounded the house. One of the Spaniards escaped. Seventeen others, who had only two pistols among them, were overpowered and executed on the spot, with a bullet in the back of the head.[25] Emiliana Quintián, who served as the brigade's courier, was among the captured; after being forced to watch the massacre of her friends, she was then taken to the Sipo's offices in Pau, installed in the Villa Albert. Refusing to yield any information even under torture, she was shot dead. In August 1946 she was posthumously awarded the Croix de Guerre.[26]

In the Wehrmacht's volunteer units, the question of loyalty and morale was constantly under study. Again, reports were mixed. On

D-Day Army Group G reported that morale was generally high, but low where the volunteers had no arms or proper uniforms. The Indian Legion reported 350 men missing. The frequency with which military passwords were being intercepted by the Resistance was another thorn in the Wehrmacht's flesh. To counter this, lst Army gave orders that all passwords were to begin with the sound 'h' or 'ch', which the French pronounce badly, and the sentries would thus be alerted. Army Group considered the idea sound. The Spanish, however, were not so inconvenienced by the shibboleth as were the French; although they have the same difficulty with 'h' (unless they come from Andalusia or Estremadura, where 'h' is aspirate), they have no trouble at all with 'ch', and the *guerrilleros* found themselves at an advantage when it came to penetrating lst Army installations.

The guerrilla forces in the south were still under orders from General Koenig, commanding the FFI and executing the instructions of the Supreme Allied Command, not to engage in open battle. There was a political reason why the communist leaders in France would be only too ready to comply. The suspicions that Stalin harboured towards the West in 1941–2[27] had not left him in 1944. Nor was he less duplicitous than before. If the Comintern had been dissolved in June 1943 as a token of his goodwill towards the Western democracies, the word was passed on to the communist parties that 'everything would continue as before'.[28] The Commander-in-Chief of the communist-dominated FTP, Charles Tillon, insists that Stalin ordered the PCF in 1944 not to get too deeply engaged in the work of liberation in order to slow the pace of the Allied advance eastwards.[29] Whatever the command orders were, the actions undertaken by the guerrilla forces were now taking on larger dimensions, the result of improvement in their co-ordination and supply.

This improvement was essentially the work of three separate Allied-organizations, of which two were British (Special Operations Executive and Special Air Service) and one was American (Office of Strategic Services).[30] For all of them, the first business was to make contact, to find out what groups were fighting in what areas, and to see how their operations could be co-ordinated. Of all the Allied agents sent, the best known, both to the Maquis and to the Germans, was Lieutenant-Colonel George Starr, of SOE, who went by the name of Hilaire. His torso bore the indelible marks of the torture he had undergone when, in 1941, he had fallen into Nazi hands, but his demeanour remained one of calm concentration. Following his escape, he had taken up residence in Castelnau-sur-l'Auvignon, a remote hamlet in Gers, living as a gardener in the home of its mayor, Roger Larribeau, and passing himself off to the neighbours as a retired Belgian mining engineer who had fled south in 1940. His mission was now to organize the Resistance from Dordogne to Landes and from Gers to the Pyrenees.

Castelnau-sur-l'Auvignon thus became the command post for all of Gascony, serving as a centre for liaison officers, intelligence agents, radio transmissions, arms storage, and Allied airmen on their way to Spain. All this activity gave the Germans reason to believe that the Allies planned to air-drop a division in Gers near the border of Landes. Hilaire had apparently unlimited credit, and by the end of 1942 he commanded 700 men in a region where the Spanish *guerrilleros* outnumbered the French *maquisards*. By then a legend had developed around him. Between July 1943 and September 1944 Hilaire supervised the reception of no fewer than 147 parachute drops, amounting to some 500 tons of weapons and supplies.[31] By D-Day he found that in Gers he had more weapons than he had *maquisards* to arm, and it was at that moment that he turned to the *guerrilleros*.[32] On 6 June, wearing his uniform of colonel in the British Army, Hilaire began arming the 400 men under the command of Tomás Ortega Guerrero, known by the name of Camilo and also, because he had lost a leg, as Cojo Camilo.[33]

Ortega Guerrero had allegedly escaped in 1943, with the help of the MOI, from the concentration camp at Le Vernet, and had since won fame as a guerrilla leader. He also had the charisma to inspire others. Among these was Conchita González de Boix, 17 years of age and employed in a school in Montauban. The house at 7 rue Lasserre where she lived with her mother and sister Adela was on the same street as the local Kommandantur, but otherwise it was ideal for Guerrero's purpose: they lived on the ground floor, the building had an exit on the Grand Promenade, and the courtyard contained several outbuildings. The house became a key centre of resistance activities. Guerrero gave the orders as to where the supplies and propaganda material were to be taken, and never seemed to lack young women to assist him in the vital matter of liaison. In Toulouse, Conchita's contact was Maximina Losa, a girl no older than herself who never met her twice in the same place. Losa, and another young liaison woman, Celia Llaneza, who worked in Montauban for the Unitarian Service run by the American Quakers, were both to win the Croix de Guerre. Celia Llaneza recounts how their idol Guerrero, despite his handicap, could jump and run like a young goat. Escholier too describes how he 'drives like a maniac, swims like a porpoise, rides like a Red Indian—all nerves and hot blood', and a French colonel, Henri Monnet, referred to him as 'Colonel Hilaire's Hollywood section'. So many pistols and daggers hung from his waist and shoulder that they jangled whenever he swung around on his crutch. As Hilaire now handed Ortega's men their weapons, discipline was forgotten. 'Instead of waiting their turn, they jostled and grabbed. Their eyes darted fire. It was as if they were there to receive the Eucharist.'[34]

Within a fortnight of receiving their arms, the 35th Brigade of Spanish Guerrilleros launched an attack, on 20 June 1944, on a German convoy at Francescas, 20 kilometres south-west of Agen. The Spaniards were now armed with light machine-guns and even bazookas. The Germans suffered three dead and fifteen wounded, but five Spaniards fell into German hands, including the brigade commander José Antonio Mendizábal; they were executed and found horribly mutilated.[35] The next day a combined force of *guerrilleros* and *maquisards* was attacked in its turn by two columns of German troops in the area of La Romieu, 8 kilometres east of Condom. They converged on the defenders from the east and the south, but they were in well-prepared positions strung out like a spider's web, and thus caught the Germans in a devastating crossfire. After a six-hour battle the defenders pulled back to Castelnau, and when that position was no longer defensible, Hilaire and the Franco-Spanish force succeeded in breaking out, the Spanish women helping the wounded to walk; taking the Condom road, they regrouped in Lupiac, 35 kilometres to the south-west. The *maquisards* had lost seventeen dead (including eleven Spaniards) and twenty-nine were wounded. But the German losses were staggering: 238 dead and some 300 wounded. In Castelnau, Hilaire had prepared a deadly reception. Two tons of explosives had been stored in the belfry of the ancient church. A slow fuse was left burning. As the German troops assembled in the village square to toast their triumph, the tower suddenly exploded, hurling 800-year-old stones upon the soldiers below. The thunder of the falling stones continued for several minutes.[36] The escalation of atrocities that followed in that region was due in part to the Germans' frenzy for revenge.

Reprisal was answered by reprisal. On 12 July a German colonel from the Bayonne garrison was kidnapped in Sainte-Christie, a north-west suburb of Auch, by men of Ortega Guerrero's brigade. Since he was carrying coded Wehrmacht documents, these were transmitted to London. The colonel was handed over to the French, who shot him.[37] It has often been said that the Germans were safer in the hands of the Spanish. Four days later, on 16 July, it was the turn of Calmont, a village 35 kilometres south-east of Toulouse, where a unit of 'Das Reich' not yet called north to Normandy executed a number of hostages.[38]

If Hilaire was to become the most renowned of Allied agents in France,[39] two others also deserve mention, one belonging like Hilaire to SOE and the other to OSS. Anthony Morris Brooks, code-named Alphonse, was the youngest agent SOE ever sent into the field: he was just 20 when he landed by parachute, on the night of 1–2 July 1942, in the area of Bas-Soleil in Limousin. Brought up in Switzerland and perfectly bilingual, Major Brooks's mission was to make his way to Toulouse, with the help of his contact in Limousin, and there to construct the 'Pimento' network of CGT (communist) railwaymen throughout the Southern Zone, and especially on the routes linking Toulouse with Bordeaux, Marseilles, and Lyons. His mission was very successful. M. R. D. Foot, himself a former agent of SAS and the leading authority on the subject, affirms that 'main-line rail traffic in Southern France was brought to a standstill from D-Day onwards, quite as much by 'Pimento''s efforts as by anybody else's.'[40] Others who knew Brooks in 'Pimento', including André Moch, the son of Jules Moch, found him among the most tactful of agents.[41] He was also among the most self-effacing, to the point that he has effaced himself from the history books.[42]

The American officer was Lieutenant-Colonel Hod Fuller, code-named Kansul, of OSS. As head of a Jedburgh team,[43] code-named Bugatti, he landed in Tajan (Hautes-Pyrénées) at the end of June 1944. Like Hilaire, Fuller not only organized Allied supply drops but took an active part in the operations, first in the region of Saint-Gaudens, then in the liberation of Tarbes, then in the pursuit of the Germans up the Vallée de Luchon to the Spanish frontier. Finally, with the help of Major Grosby of the Gordon Highlanders, he formed the Bigorre Battalion which marched north to take part in the liberation of Jonzac and Rochefort in Charente-Maritime.[44] By that time an Allied military staff had been formed in the south-west, consisting of Hilaire, Fuller, three French colonels (Marceau, Terminion, Parisot), and the Spanish *guerrillero*, Lieutenant-Colonel Ortega Guerrero.[45]

It was not until 15 July, nearly six weeks after D-Day, that Eisenhower's Supreme Allied Headquarters officially announced that the FFI constituted 'a fighting force placed under the command of General Koenig and an integral part of the Allied expeditionary forces'. The announcement did not win any quick acknowledgment from the Germans, who were caught in a dilemma. To recognize French troops in Normandy in French uniform was one thing; to recognize the 'terrorists' behind their lines as their fellow-FFI, when all they wore for uniform might be an armband, was quite another. On the other hand, as long as the 'terrorists' were not recognized as combatants, they were not bound by the Geneva Convention. While that might encourage Wehrmacht soldiers to fight harder and not be taken prisoner by the Maquis, the idea that the Maquis was not bound by law was disconcerting to the German commanders. In mid-June the SS 'Deutschland'

Regiment had reported the situation in Betchat, where they had
liberated some Germans held prisoner by the Maquis. The released
Germans declared that discipline among their captors was so bad that
they broke the basic rules even in the presence of their prisoners. The
report added that the treatment of prisoners by the terrorists was
variable, while the food rations were plentiful.[46] This was not the case
in an incident in mid-July in an area north of Pau, where a German
force arrived to find the bodies of eight Germans (four Customs officers,
two railroad officials, and two soldiers) who had been murdered just
before the arrival of the troops. The corpses, it reported, had been
mutilated in the most bestial fashion, to the point that they were
no longer identifiable. Beside them lay sign-boards with the words
in French: 'In reprisal for the murders carried out by the German
Army in Portet-sur-Garonne.' General von Blaskowitz himself took
the matter up, with a general order to his troops:

I expect, in accordance with my order of 17 June, that innocent civilians,
especially women and children, will be spared. But against gangs which engage in criminal conduct of this kind, you are to proceed without remorse and
with the utmost severity. Captured terrorists are to be executed wherever
possible in groups on the very spot where the Germans were murdered. Sign-
boards are then to be affixed to the bodies with the words [in German]: 'Vile
murder will be thus requited'.[47]

The trend in Wehrmacht attitudes was in fact towards more, not
less, severity. Von Blaskowitz, moved no doubt by the horrors of
Tulle and Oradour, had seriously considered, if not actually offered,
a pledge of amnesty to 'repentant terrorists'. In mid-July, von Kluge,
as Supreme Commander West, decided that any pledge of amnesty
was at variance with the orders of the Führer, who had ruled that
terrorists were to be treated as irregulars (*Freischärler*). No military
district was to allow any special treatment without the approval of
OB-West. No German agency was to make any promise to any terrorist
gang, and no safe-conduct passes were to be issued to any terrorists.

The agreement of Hitler to the Allied proclamation of 15 July came
too late for the liberators of the south-west. A further exchange of
atrocities in August prolonged the Germans' bitter dilemma, since it
both postponed German action and focused German attention on the
need to take such action. The incident this time was in the south-
east. In reprisal for the execution of Resistance members in the Fort
de Montluc in Lyons, the FFI responded on 25 August by executing
eighty German soldiers captured at Annecy. It was not until 22
September that Hitler decided to grant the FFI the status of regular
combatants.[48]

The motive for Hitler's concession could be nothing but self-interest, for the Bomb Plot of 20 July made his direction of the war even more murderous. Only now was the Nazi salute imposed on the Wehrmacht, but the attempt on Hitler's life also gave local commanders an opportunity to express their support of the Führer in their own way.[49] While Karl-Heinrich von Stülpnagel, the MBH in Paris who was implicated in the plot, tried, unsuccessfully, to blow out his brains,[50] General Krüger in the south-west addressed his Panzertroops in the following bulletin:

Traitors have undertaken an attempt on the life of our beloved Führer Adolf Hitler. Thanks to the providence of fate, the German people have been spared an indelible shame and most tragic loss.

In an address from his headquarters around midnight last night, the Führer pledged the German people implacable revenge for the crime. The German people and their Wehrmacht are called upon to perform their duty unswervingly. The commanders-in-chief of the Wehrmachtteile, Reichsmarschall Göring and Grossadmiral Dönitz, have issued a call to all units to show their unshakeable loyalty to the Führer. Reichsführer-SS Himmler and Generalobersten Stumpff and Guderian have received special assignments from the Führer to guarantee security and order throughout the Reich.

For us, soldiers of LVIIIth Panzerkorps, there is only word: Fight, until final victory. Long live the Führer Adolf Hitler!

General Krüger added instructions that this announcement was to appear in all communiqués down to the level of company commanders. Company commanders were to arrange for their troops to muster and his address to be read out.[51] A new note of desperation was audible and visible. 'Sieg oder Sibirien!' (Victory or Siberia) became the slogan.

Operation *Anvil-Dragoon*,[52] the landing of General Patch's US 7th Army at Saint-Tropez on 15 August, succeeded as planned, but the Germans could hardly say that they were caught by surprise. The strategic advantage of an invasion in the south was clear to all, and its likelihood, even its imminence, was understood by the Maquis no less than by the Germans.

The security of Toulouse, and of the land-bridge connecting the Atlantic and the Mediterranean, had become more precarious week by week, and von Blaskowitz had already told von Kluge that contact between 1st and 19th Armies could no longer be assured.[53] On 27 July, all hope of maintaining the land-bridge vanished: LVIIIth Panzerkorps itself, including 9th Panzerdivision under Generalmajor Jolasse in Nîmes, was assigned to the Battle of Normandy, now entering its critical stage.[54] Just before leaving, General Krüger warned that the event of 20 July would bring with it an increase of terrorist activity

'by those who consider their moment has arrived'. He added that
there was no doubt, in the event of invasion in the southern part
of France, that the participation of guerrilla gangs, led by military
officers, amounted to a very serious handicap for the Wehrmacht.
Like the good soldier he was, he called upon his officers to use the
time down to the very moment of the invasion in the most profitable
way.[55]

The four weeks that followed the Allied invasion of the south were
to be a very severe strain on OB-West, and especially on Army Group
G which, unlike Army Group B, faced encirclement. Up until the
moment of the landing at Saint-Tropez, von Blaskowitz had kept his
headquarters astride the two coasts. He now decided to move to the
eastern side of the Rhône.[56] This meant leaving the collapsing land-
bridge to Generalleutnant Schmidt-Hartung, commanding the garrison
in Toulouse,[57] who had been ordered to create an assault force out of
the Ost-Stamm Battalion.[58]

Meanwhile, 19th Army in the south-east was under new command:
General von Sodenstern had been replaced on 2 July by General Wiese,
who in early August had taken the precaution of pulling his headquarters back from Marseilles to Villeneuve-lès-Avignon. Nothing,
however, worked for Wiese, and the beachhead at Saint-Tropez now
became an Allied advance west, east, and especially north up the
Rhône valley. The strategy was self-evident: General Patch's US 7th
Army driving north would link up with General Patton's US 3rd
Army driving south-east, and all German forces that had not passed
the gap would be caught in the trap.

Hitler was now torn between his instinct never to order a retreat
and his desire to save 1st Army, as well as half of 19th Army, before
they found themselves cut off from any way of escape. The very same
thing was happening at the very same time in Normandy, where
General Montgomery, commanding British 21st Army Group, was to
close the Falaise Gap on 19 August and end the Battle of Normandy.
On 17 August then, sickened by the thought that he was yielding
the spoils of war but mindful of the disaster he had inflicted on von
Paulus at Stalingrad, the Führer took two decisions. The first was
to fire his Supreme Commander West: Kluge was now replaced by
Generalfeldmarschall Walther Model, the third in the post since
D-Day. The second of Hitler's decisions eclipsed the first in the
Kriegstagebuch of Army Group G: at 11.15 that morning von Blaskowitz received the order to withdraw all German forces west of the
line Orleans–Clermont-Ferrand–Montpellier, whether Wehrmacht, SS,
or other, excepting only those units of 19th Army presently in combat

and those units assigned to the defence of Marseilles, Toulon, and the Atlantic pockets.[59] The remainder, numbering 209,000 men, were to make for Dijon and to take up a position alongside Army Group B, as the southern flank of the Kitzinger Line. This new defence line was fixed by the Führer on 22 August. Code-named 'Förderkorb', but commonly named after the Luftwaffe general Karl Kitzinger whom Hitler had chosen as his last Militärbefehlshaber in Frankreich, it ran from Abbéville along the Seine, Yonne, and Burgundy Canal through Dijon to Dole and the Swiss frontier. The two bases on the south coast had each been assigned one division, with orders to fight to the last man. The end for both was less dramatic. The Toulon garrison under Konteradmiral Heinrich Ruhfus, to which the 242nd Infantry Division was assigned, was soon overwhelmed by the French 1st Army under General de Lattre de Tassigny. The same fate befell the 244th Infantry Division under Generalleutnant Hans Schäfer in Marseilles, while Patch's American divisions drove the German 148th Infantry Division through Cannes and Nice into Italy.

More dramatic was the race, the gauntlet even, run by Army Group G to escape the trap now set. Guerrilla warfare had come into its own. Von Blaskowitz later described the experience as being stung by a swarm of wasps: 'They don't kill, but they make life very unpleasant.'[60] If the guerrilla attacks merely stung, it was because the Germans too had been learning about guerrilla warfare, and the best means to break through or out of an ambush.

The most affected by the order to withdraw was General Karl Sachs, whose LXIVth Army Corps was virtually isolated on the Biscay coast. Evacuation by rail was no longer possible: tracks had either been sabotaged already or were at the mercy of saboteurs. With the collapse of the land-bridge, the Germans no longer had safe use of the two main road routes linking the Atlantic with the Mediterranean: N 113, running from Bordeaux through Toulouse to Carcassonne and Béziers: and N 117/D 117, the meandering route through the foothills of the Pyrenees, running from Bayonne through Tarbes and Foix to Perpignan, before turning north to Narbonne. As a result, 1st Army, to which LXIVth Army Corps belonged, was transferred temporarily from Army Group G to Army Group B.[61] Sachs thus had to lead his army corps northwards and find the best route he could between the Massif Central and the Loire. He nevertheless reached Dijon in good order.

The first stage of the evacuation of the most southerly German bases on the Atlantic coat was covered in principle by the Kühnemann–Rougès agreement, under which the German troops were to have unhindered passage to the River Dordogne in exchange for the promise to destroy nothing in their wake. The agreement was not respected by the Resistance, perhaps because the agreement was not generally known. Nor was it always observed by the Germans, who blew up the road and rail bridges at Libourne at a time when they had little military importance to Germany. The German withdrawal from the Biscay coast in fact began too late. Bayonne was not evacuated until 27 August. It is unlikely that the German garrison, which passed through Mont-de-Marsan, could have succeeded in breaking through to the north or east, with or without the Kühnemann–Rougès agreement. On the other hand, the avoidance of a battle of Bordeaux may explain some unsavoury excesses at the moment of the city's liberation. From the windows of the German library, some patriots vented their feelings by hurling its bookshelves into the street. In the place Gambetta, paving stones sailed through the windows of the Café Régent, where the Wehrmacht officers had liked to sit. Members of the Milice, it was said, were hiding on the rooftops, justifying the bursts of machine-gun fire loosed in that direction by other patriots, new perhaps to the struggle but resolved not to be forgotten by posterity.[62]

Years later, while in Allied captivity, von Blaskowitz explained that the route taken by General Sachs involved forced marches chiefly at night, supply difficulties, and loss of time, but it would not have been easier for Sachs to fight his way through the Massif Central. The heavy concentration of guerrilla forces there and further south in the Cévennes made a detour highly advisable. The only other route was the coastal road through Béziers, Montpellier, and the narrow Rhône valley. This meant exposure to the Allies' superiority in the air, accentuated by the clear summer weather, but the retreating forces that took this route had the advantage of being protected (and their rearguard later reinforced) by those units of 19th Army still stationed west, south, and north of Narbonne.[63]

Even before the Germans started the evacuation, the liberation of the towns began. The Wehrmacht no longer had the strength to defend them all. On 13 August the Allied regional command in the south-west (Hilaire, Fuller, the three French colonels, and Tomás Ortega Guerrero) decided to assault Aire-sur-l'Adour, in the Landes, still under the control of General Sachs. Ortega Guerrero's 35th Brigade of Spanish Guerrilleros, based nearby at Lupiac, shared with the Armagnac Battalion the honour of liberating the town.[64] Moving east, the two units pursued the German force which left Auch on 19 August, stopping it at L'Isle-Jourdain.[65] Ortega Guerrero then swung south-west, pursuing another German force to Bedous, within 25 kilometres of the Spanish frontier, and after six hours of combat took two companies of Germans prisoner.[66] The *guerrilleros* then helped to liberate Basses-Pyrénées and Hautes-Pyrénées, including the chief towns of Pau and Tarbes. The German garrison in Tarbes under General Mayer set out eastwards to Toulouse on 19 August but got no further than the plateau of Lannemezan, where in a two-day battle it was cut to ribbons and Mayer taken prisoner.[67] Tarbes's two Gestapo chiefs, Pradel and Peter Blindauer, escaped the trap, but Blindauer was captured as he passed through Nîmes. Imprisoned first in Tarbes and then in Toulouse, he was persuaded to divulge the names of his several informers in Hautes-Pyrénées. Pradel succeeded in reaching Germany.[68]

Meanwhile, on 18 August—the day that Oberg and Knochen left Paris[69]—von Blaskowitz gave orders to General Schmidt-Hartung in Toulouse to evacuate the garrison, which numbered some 20,000 men, and to make for Dijon by the coastal route through Carcassonne and Béziers. The order was received at the Kommandantur at 3 a.m. on 19 August, and by 5 a.m. the first convoys were being assembled at the Raynal marshalling yards. But the railwaymen were ready. Every conceivable error was made in assembling the trains, and by 10 a.m. no train had left the station. Furious at the delay, the Germans abandoned the station to form road convoys instead. When the bulk of the force had left, the Resistance closed the exits, trapping the remainder. But all in all, the garrison evacuated the city in good order. Even the Gestapo chief Suhr, with his interminable motorcade,[70] was not obstructed. The urban Resistance simply lacked the means to prevent the evacuation: the arms it had stocked in 1942 had been handed over little by little to the Maquis in the surrounding area. It was now up to the *maquisards* and the *guerrilleros* to settle the score.[71] Four days later the column reached the comparative safety of Avignon, but the going was unquestionably hard.

The evacuation of Toulouse robbed the Resistance of the symbolic prize it craved: the military conquest of the capital of the south-west. It also created one of the enduring points of friction for the future: between those, like Pierre Bertaux, who stress the theme that since the Germans had left the city there was nothing to liberate, and those, like Jean Cassou, who oppose any attempt to reduce the role of the Resistance. This argument outlived the lives of both of these leading participants, dying as they did in 1986 and 1985 respectively, but numerically Cassou enjoyed the wider support and, at the conference held in Toulouse in 1985, Bertaux's enemies showed that they had still not forgiven anything: the former FTP leader Jean Carovis publicly insulted Bertaux,[72] and *La Dépêche du Midi*, still the leading journal of the south-west, persisted in its puerile policy of never spelling Bertaux's name correctly.[73]

In selecting the man to serve as regional commander of the FFI in the south-west, General de Gaulle's provisional government in Algiers decided on 4 June to appoint Serge Asher ('Ravanel') who had arrived in Toulouse from the Lyons region a few weeks earlier. The son of Czechoslovak immigrants, and a graduate of the prestigious Polytechnique in Paris, Ravanel (as he has been known ever since the war) was still only 24 years old. Guessing (correctly) that von Blaskowitz would give top priority to maintaining communications between Bordeaux and Narbonne, Ravanel drew up a plan to divide the territory into two zones north and south of the line of the Garonne valley and the Canal du Midi. The purpose of this was to force the Germans to run an organized gauntlet when the time came, and the time had now come, but it is uncertain to what extent the attacks on the Germans could be called truly co-ordinated, and it might have been beyond the power of the Resistance to mount such attacks in terrain that gave them little cover.

The same inferiority was visible in Toulouse itself: the Resistance forces could not have taken on the occupying troops in full-scale street battles. Ravanel had worked out a plan for an insurrection with Jean-Pierre Vernant ('Berthier'), who had been appointed the FFI leader for Haute-Garonne, but the Germans no doubt had wind of it, for on 12 August they took the precaution of disarming the police. On 17 August the call went out for a popular uprising; several units in the surrounding region received their orders to march on Toulouse. When, however, on the Saturday morning of 19 August the Germans suddenly began the evacuation of the city, having given no sign of preparing one, it caught Ravanel off balance, and he issued new orders that the surrounding Resistance units must be ready to enter the city by the morning of 21 August. The task of the Resistance would then be to mop up whatever units of the Milice had not left with the Germans, to seize all bridges, and to make certain that no German units fleeing eastwards should pass through the city.

In their evacuation, conducted in sweltering heat, the Germans did not blow up Toulouse any more than they blew up Paris, but they took care of the essentials. The telecommunications centres on boulevard Riquet and place Saint-Aubin were destroyed, thirty wagons loaded with munitions were blown up at Blagnac, and the archives of the German Consulate and the Gestapo were incinerated. The Gestapo's headquarters on the rue Maignac were partly destroyed. The Germans meanwhile appropriated every vehicle in sight, including bicycles, but it was still not enough for all their units, and the 'Mongols' in particular were given horse-drawn transport or forced to march.

Whatever the liberation of Toulouse amounted to, it was the jewel in the crown of the Spanish Resistance, and it was a Spanish unit that carried out the first assault within the city, at noon on 19 August. Again the fear that inspired it was that the Nazis would not walk away from their prisons without first slaughtering their prisoners. A group of *guerrilleros* launched an attack on the prison on the rue du Rempart-Saint-Étienne where several *guerrillero* leaders were being held. After a 2-hour engagement, all the prisoners were released un-hurt.[74] The next target, attacked shortly after noon, was the Saint-Michel Prison, which the Germans had left in the hands of the Vichy police. Using either force or threat, the assailants helped the prisoners to escape in small groups. Among those escaping was André Malraux ('Colonel Berger'), who had been captured in Lot and transferred to Saint-Michel on 2 August 1944. (Malraux's description of his release in his memoirs is one more example of his mythomania.[75]) There was still some danger: German convoys continued to pass along the road outside the prison. By the afternoon of 19 August the city erupted in its first street fighting. The FTP launched an attack on the Raynal marshalling yards and Matabiau Station, where a number of German soldiers and civilian workers were forced to surrender. Matabiau be-came the first building in the liberation of Toulouse to sport the Tricolour.[76] By the evening most of the city was liberated, but a number of bastions remained in the hands of Wehrmacht units or the Milice. The FTP had already issued an order to 'exterminate all the traitors and members of the Milice, without exception and without remorse'. On the evening of 19 August the FTP were distributing pamphlets whose underlying purpose was to be endlessly debated in the future: the pamphlets called for a national insurrection.[77]

That same evening, the senior leaders of the Resistance in the south-west met in a safe-house at 10 rue d'Orleans. Among those attending were Jean Cassou, the Commissaire of the Republic; Ravanel, the FFI leader for the south-west; his adjutant and FFI leader in Haute-Garonne, Jean-Pierre Vernant; and the future chief of police Antoine Poggioli. At about midnight Cassou and others were driving home along the rue Roquelaine when, at the moment they turned into the main boulevard, they were intercepted by a Wehrmacht unit. The unit, consisting of Vlasov troops under a German officer, was on its way out of the city and had dismounted to ascertain the route; for one reason or another it stopped for an identification check of the French-men in the car. The Commissaire of the Republic was showing his papers when he was suddenly struck on the head with the butt of a rifle. As he fell into the gutter his friends fled. The troops opened fire, some died, but the rest escaped.[78] The Resistance was alerted and

Cassou, with a fractured skull and broken ribs, was taken in a coma
to the Hospital Hôtel-Dieu. He survived, but it was obvious that he
was now incapable of serving as Commissaire of the Republic. It
would be months before he was released. The French authorities in
Algiers, however, had nominated a surrogate for an event such as this.
Their choice had fallen on Pierre Bertaux, the distinguished Germanist
at the University of Toulouse before the war. Even now he was only
37. We have seen the reputation he won as a leader of the Resistance
when resistance was hardest. He had been captured and imprisoned
together with Jean Cassou, and both had been released in 1943. But
while Cassou had returned to the Resistance, Bertaux had taken to a
quiet and secluded life in the Pyrenees village of Castelnau-Rivière-
Basse, looking forward to becoming editor-in-chief of the new Toulouse daily *La République*. It was precisely this detachment which
rankled with the communist elements of the Resistance, who now
insisted that they had not been consulted on any successor to Cassou.
This quarrel was to continue until Bertaux's death, forty-two years
later.

Toulouse, capital of the south-west and, for many, capital of the
Resistance, was free. Now came the moment for vainglory, as various
elements claimed the honour of having liberated it. The fact that
liberation implies battle, tied with the fact that the Germans evacuated
the city, explains the first painful confrontation between two schools
of historians. The second confrontation concerns the first Resistance
units to reach the city as 'liberators': who arrived there first? There
is a French answer and a Spanish answer. It is surely of significance
that the version given in *Jours de gloire, jours de honte*, attributing
this to Spaniards, was not contested by any Frenchman, either in
print or on television or at the 1985 conference in Toulouse on the
Liberation. The accepted version among the French historians is that
the first FFI troops to reach Toulouse were those of Colonel Georges
(né Robert Noireau), who arrived on the night of 20–1 August, having
first made Lot the first *département* in France (after Corsica) to be
liberated. Cahors had been freed on 17 August and Montauban on 18
August, when Ravanel called on Georges to continue his advance
southwards to Toulouse. The bridges into Toulouse were already in
the hands of the partisans from the morning of 20 August, and with
the departure of the last Germans the liberators found no one to fight
except the Milice, still firing from the roofs. The laurels are therefore light that crown the head of the liberators of Toulouse, but they
are disputed none the less, even among the Spaniards. Lieutenant
Colonel Luis Bermejo, commanding the 2nd Division of Spanish
Guerrilleros, emerged, in the Spanish communist version of history,

as liberator of the city. On 14 July 1946, he was awarded the Croix de Guerre by General Paul Bergeron, commanding the 17th Military Region (Toulouse). Awards continued to arrive. On 5 April 1976 the Minister of Defence conferred upon him the Médaille Militaire, and on the fortieth anniversary of the Liberation (19 August 1984) he received the Médaille de la Résistance from Dominique Baudis, Mayor of Toulouse. But another Spanish leader, Lieutenant-Colonel Vicente López Tovar, rejects the notion that Bermejo could ever be called the liberator of Toulouse. 'The most important operations in the Toulouse region', he says, 'were carried out by the anarchist leader Joaquín Ramos, in the early period, and in the weeks prior to the Liberation by Ortega Guerrero and the FTP-MOI.'[79] López Tovar's position is not politically biased: both men are communists, though López Tovar would later break free from the Party's restraints.

Whatever the rightful shares were in the common achievement, the achievement itself was considerable. The FFI in R4 (Toulouse) took 13,000 prisoners and captured 400,000 tons of equipment, plus 900,000 gallons of petrol.[80] Nor did it rest from its labours. The first regular French division raised in 1944 on the soil of metropolitan France was the division raised in Toulouse, its 8,000 men parading in the city on 3 September prior to their joining the army of General de Lattre de Tassigny in its advance towards Germany.[81]

Meanwhile, others were pursuing or lying in wait for the fleeing Germans. In what may have been the only intervention by the Allies (apart from the Jedburgh missions) in the liberation of the south-west, a squadron of RAF planes caught a German column at noon on 20 August as it entered Villenouvelle, on the main road eastwards to Carcassonne.[82] Another German column of 2,000 men stopped that same Sunday afternoon in the village of Villaudric, 25 kilometres due north of Toulouse. It included several German civilians, so that it presumably arrived from Toulouse. The local FFI force began negotiating the surrender of the column when, without warning and without any known reason, the Germans suddenly opened fire in all directions. In the Café Jambert, in the village centre, the Germans ordered everyone there to line up against a wall, then gunned them down. The massacre at Villaudric left nineteen dead, including a child.[83] Now that Toulouse could no longer be crossed, those German units arriving late had to make detours. A German column of over 3,000 men reached Toulouse from Cahors in the north on 22 August. It had to reverse to the north-east, passing through Gaillac where the Spanish *guerrilleros* were in the process of liberating the prison. On arriving in Albi the Germans found the bridges in the hands of the *guerrilleros* and the FTP. Forcing his way through the town under fierce fire, the German commander, after losing 200 men, decided not to continue along the logical route of retreat to Rodez and the north-east, but instead to strike south-east along a minor and mountainous road that required him to run the gauntlet of the guerrilla forces in both Tarn and Hérault. As the road wound into the mountains, the Spaniards lay in wait near the villages of Lacaune, La Salvetat, and Saint-Pons. The *guerrilleros* had already liberated Castres, and the Germans fleeing from there through Mazamet to Saint-Pons found more Spaniards waiting for them at Labastide-Rouairoux. Every action took its heavy toll of lives.[84]

To the south, in Ariège, the Spanish *guerrilleros* had received considerable supplies in a parachute drop on 8 August. With this help their participation was decisive in the liberation of Foix on 19 August. If Pamiers was evacuated on 18 August, in Foix not all the Germans had time to flee. Two hundred barricaded themselves in the town's Lycée. Since the telephone was still working, the negotiations were conducted by phone. The British Major Probert and the French customs officer Captain Gisquet (from Lorraine) both spoke German. The Germans were told: 'If you don't surrender, we can't answer for what the Spaniards intend to do to you.' The Germans agreed to surrender, but the German colonel insisted on surrendering to Probert. The 3rd Brigade of Spanish Guerrilleros under Pascual Jimeno ('Royo') then took over the Lycée. A detachment under Ramón Rubio Miranda, who lost his right arm the next day in Saint-Girons but who went on to replace Jimeno as brigade commander before the end of August, succeeded in capturing a Gestapo official. The Gestapo agent was immediately tried by a regular court and sentenced to death; on 24 August he was hanged in front of the town hall.[85] Other bloody encounters occurred at Prayols, just south of Foix, on 20 August, and especially in the area between Rimont and Castelnau on 21–2 August. In the latter case, the German garrison of Saint-Gaudens under Colonel Dreyer was attempting to break through on the road to Foix when it was stopped 15 kilometres to the east. One reason for this was that two-thirds of its vehicles had been tampered with, a mechanic named Marcel in Saint-Girons having poured sulphuric acid into the gasoline. The other reason was that the German force was intercepted by a joint force of FTP-MOI and Spanish *guerrilleros*. Although the German force was larger and better armed, the *maquisards* co-ordinated their actions to a high degree. The German force included a number of 'Mongols'. Their morale and discipline were both low, and several pointless atrocities were committed against the inhabitants of the village of Rimont. Colonel Dreyer died in the action, and when his staff took note of the impossibility of ever reaching the Mediterranean coast, with all roads now controlled by the Resistance, the Germans surrendered, after a 13-hour combat. German losses were 150 dead and 1,200 taken prisoner. Some 500 more wandered aimlessly for a time through the mountains before falling one by one into the hands of the Resistance.[86]

Wherever the German lines of retreat ran, through the Corbières, or the Massif Central, or the coastal roads northwards from Narbonne, there were the Spanish *guerrilleros* lying in ambush. The evacuation of the German bases on the Mediterranean coast proceeded without necessarily waiting for the forces further to the west to reach the coast. Perpignan, Béziers, and Sète were thus evacuated on the same day as Toulouse, 20 August. That afternoon, a train carrying 1,000 troops left the frontier town of Cerbère for Perpignan. When word reached the commanding officer on the train that Major Parthey, the German garrison commander in Perpignan, had already abandoned the city and that the railway station was in the hands of the FFI, the train stopped in open country and the troops were ordered to disembark. They scattered in the vineyards, some entering Spain through the Col de Perthus and others trying to make their way around Perpignan. Failing to break through the Resistance lines, they ended up surrendering.[87]

The evacuation of Montpellier followed on 21 August, and that of Nîmes the next day.[88] On 25 August a German report ran: 'Orders received to make contact with the remnants of the naval group stationed in the Agde-Sète sector cannot be carried out. All vehicles destroyed. Nîmes in the hands of the terrorists.'[89] On the same day, General Patch's forces reached Avignon. As a result of the impending loss of Nîmes and Avignon, retreating German columns had moved inland from Montpellier to make for Alès, on the edge of the Cévennes mountains. That same day, at Tornac near Anduze, to the south-west of Alès, a German column of some 500 men under General Konrad Nietzsche Martin[90] found the Madeleine bridge sabotaged. A group of eighteen Spanish *guerrilleros* under the command of Cristino García, who had turned the old château into their base, prevented the Germans from breaking through. By 6 o'clock in the evening an Allied air strike, called in by the Resistance, persuaded the Germans to surrender. Since the German losses were only six killed and about 175 wounded, the ignominy was understandably too much for someone who bore the name of Nietzsche, and the German commander, together with one of his officers, committed suicide. The remainder were taken prisoner by the Spaniards.[91]

In assessing the contribution of the Resistance to the liberation of the south-west, three factors require mention. First, the entire region was liberated without the help of any Allied army, but certainly with the help of the German decision to retreat. Secondly, the various elements making up the FFI were never properly unified, but their operations were co-ordinated reasonably well and political jealousies were submerged. Thirdly, an element of vainglory has impaired even some scholarly accounts. While some French historians have conceded that in German eyes the action of the FFI was not particularly effective, and that it was the weight and speed of Patch and Patton that the Germans feared most,[92] others have suggested that the FFI transformed the Germans' organized retreat into a semi-rout.[93] It would seem more correct to call the retreat of Army Group G a feat of arms. It was always a race against time, and the speed set by Patch explains why von Blaskowitz had to alter the escape route so that it passed not through Lyons,[94] which fell on 3 Septenber, but through Clermont-Ferrand and Moulins further to the north. On 12 September Patch linked up with Patton at Dijon, dooming those German forces which had not yet passed through the gap. These included the rearguard column of 19,800 men under Generalmajor Ester, made up for the most part of poorly armed civilians; worn out by the long march, they finally surrendered in the region of Nevers. But of the 209,000 men involved in the retreat, no fewer than 130,000 reached the safety of the Kitzinger Line, where they could regroup and, when necessary, plan a more orderly retreat to the Rhine. The heroic action and skill in retreat of the 11th Panzerdivision played no small part in that success, and perhaps 11th Panzer alone saved Army Group G from annihilation.[95]

If the contribution of the Spanish *guerrilleros* to the liberation of the south was belittled or ignored, despite the fact that they helped to liberate over 40 *départements*, their role in the liberation of Paris (25–6 August 1944) was oddly magnified. The Commander-in-Chief of the FTP, Charles Tillon, himself estimated the Spaniards present at the insurrection and liberation of the capital at 4,000.[96] The true figure is probably no more than 500, but in a region so far from their concentration, the figure is not negligible. Some of these were members of the Spanish communist underground. José Barón, leader of the PCE in Paris and Chief of Staff, Northern Zone, had been active in the summer of 1944 in the Bordeaux region (which, as an original part of Occupied France, remained in the 'Northern' Zone).[97] Ordered by the PCE leadership to return to Paris at the beginning of August 1944, he was mortally wounded on 21 August in the fighting in the place de la Concorde. But in Paris the Spaniards achieved a symbolic success greater than any in the Southern Zone. General Leclerc, commanding the French 2nd Armoured Division to which General Omar Bradley had granted the honour of liberating Paris, in turn granted a Spanish unit the honour of taking the van of that division.[98] The unit chosen was the 9th Company of the 3rd Battalion of the Chad Regiment which, despite its name, contained so many Spaniards that even the French called it 'la Nueve'. When the unit received its assignment of new armoured cars at its base in Hull, England, earlier that year, a delegation of Spaniards applied for permission to baptize some of the vehicles in their own way.[99] This was granted, and the result was that the four half-tracks and four other vehicles in the 9th Company bore the names *Belchite, Brunete, Ebro, Guadalajara, Guernica, Madrid,* and *Teruel,* with only *Don Quichotte* christened in French. The 9th Company fought in the liberation of Paris in some of the key combat zones: Opera, Chamber of Deputies, Hôtel Majestic, and place de la Concorde. But the crowning moment was their arrival at the city hall (Hôtel de Ville). An award of 1,000,000 francs had allegedly been announced, to be paid to the crew of the first tank to reach the venerable building. According to this rather dubious source, the prize was shared by two vehicles bearing Spanish names.[100] The fact that these were not tanks but half-tracks detracts from the story. The three light tanks that reached the Hôtel de Ville at the same time all bore French names.[101] As for the commander of the *Teruel,* an Aragonese named Valera who was one of the two putative prize-winners, he proferred the modest remark that his good fortune might have been the result of his 'not knowing Paris and getting lost in its streets'.[102] Coupled to this immortal piece of Spanish folklore is another, that it was a Spaniard who was the first to hoist the flag of the Free French on the roof of the Hôtel de Ville.[103] But verifiable feats of arms remain beyond dispute, as the French colonel Raymond Dronne attests,[104] and Staff Sergeant Martín Bernal was cited in the dispatches of General Leclerc for his leadership in the van of the division. Following the liberation of the capital, the Spaniards received a well-earned rest before proceeding, on 8 September, on the march towards Strasbourg and the liberation of the remaining territory of France.[105] Beyond that their advance brought them to a country they had come to look at, over nearly a decade, as something alien, vicious, and dark.

11

Survival and Liberation at Mauthausen

The Spanish communists take charge of organizing resistance—The quest for posts of privilege—The SS need of artisans and clerks—Juan de Diego becomes Lagerschreiber III—The visit of Himmler—The arrival of the first guerrilleros—*Creation of a Spanish national committee and of an international committee—The prisoners offered their freedom in exchange for service in the Wehrmacht—The Reds replace the Greens and Blacks—Himmler's instructions of May 1944 and April 1945—Other camps evacuated to Mauthausen—The uprising of Block 20—The International Red Cross intervenes—Mauthausen's Kommandos converge on Mauthausen—Mauthausen in the final weeks—The flight of the SS—The dawn of liberation—The arrival of the first Allied unit, and reactions of the inmates—Gusen and Ebensee liberated—Revenge on the Kapos—The hunt for the SS: retribution for a few, absolution for the rest*

> Poor naked wretches, whereso'er you are,
> That bide the pelting of this pitiless storm,
> How shall your houseless heads and unfed sides,
> Your looped and window'd raggedness, defend you
> From seasons such as these?[1]

We have said that the principal credit for giving an organized form to the resistance at Mauthausen goes to the Spaniards. It is important not to repeat the exaggerations of authors such as Razola and Constante, who would claim more for the resistance than was the case. For most of the time it was merely an organized attempt to maintain morale and save its members whenever possible. But even that much, in the context of Mauthausen, was a major achievement. A non-Spanish eyewitness, Michel de Boüard, has said of the Spanish 'collective' that it alone, up until 1943, had the character of a solid organization in which communists joined with anarchists, socialists, and republicans.[2]

Just as the Spaniards were in the forefront of the first stage of the resistance (the moral struggle), so were they in the van of the second, constructing what became known as the secret organization. Here the credit must go precisely to the Spanish communists, assisted by other communists. Communist and non-communist sources alike attest to the fact that, up to the beginning of 1944, there were very few organizations at all, in Mauthausen proper, that were not created by the communists. Even the iron discipline of the communists, who prided themselves on their ability to organize resistance however unfavourable the circumstances, was ineffectual at first in a situation such as this. The first Resistance committee was said to be formed by the Spanish communists on 21 June 1941,[3] when an order for a general disinfection[4] of the camp provided an opportunity for them to meet. The leading figure to emerge was Manuel Razola Romo, a peasant from Guadalajara province who had served in the French labour companies, participated in the retreat from the Maginot line to Belfort, crossed into Switzerland, returned to France, landed in German hands on 21 June 1940, and arrived at Mauthausen on 26 April 1941. Razola himself attests to (and takes pride in) the fact that the committee was a political directorate limited to the PCE and PSUC.[5] The committee defined as its first objective, essential to the Spanish group's survival, the removal of the Greens and Blacks from the subaltern positions and their replacement by the Blues and Reds; it was understood that this would require tenacity and patience. The Greens were still in control of the administration even at the end of 1942, and the systematic identification and liquidation of the communist leaders by the SS explains the continued weakness of the organization, as Arthur London admits.[6]

The resistance organization faced almost insuperable difficulties. Most prisoners spent whatever free time they had in seeking food and rest; few were attracted to the idea of resisting.[7] There was still no attempt to organize anything on the international level. Apart from the differences of language and culture, there were the dangers of betrayal by blabbermouths, by the fainthearted, and by outright traitors. Not all prisoners were antifascist. The Greens, most of them Germans or Poles, included some who, in the opinion of the Spanish communists Razola and Constante, were worse Nazis than the SS—an absurd remark, of course, for the worst Greens were merely cold-blooded gangsters. Others had been arrested for black-marketeering, or for no other reason than that they were netted in a police raid. Few of them had much stomach for the fight.[8]

The Spaniards persevered. Meetings of their committee were held in the latrine of Block 3, the latrines being the usual venue of all committee meetings at Mauthausen.[9] Since nothing in the camp was given away, and since the cigarette was the unit of currency, priority was given to stealing cigarettes, not for personal use, but as the means to buy privileges, and especially food.[10] Already in 1941 the Spaniards were entering the service Kommandos. While not all were qualified at first for the jobs they obtained, the Spaniards in general represented a vast pool of skilled labour[11] to which the SS turned more and more for help. They worked as masons, painters, carpenters, tailors, blacksmiths, electricians, and shoemakers; in the linen store and in the disinfection squad; in the quarry where many Spaniards were professional stone-cutters or pneumatic drillers; and in the kitchens where a large number of them were cooks.[12] Ester Borrás and Razola, for example, worked in the disinfection squad,[13] Luis Gil as a servant to the Lagerälteste, Marcel Rodríguez as a clockmaker, and Manuel Azaustre as a barber in Block 13 and cleaner in the office of Ziereis.[14] Eight barbers were assigned to the SS, and of these seven were Spaniards, to be known inevitably as the barbers of Seville.[15] A certain Espí, from Valencia, was in charge of the boilers in the *Effektenkammer*, where the Spanish network was now so finely woven that it was possible for a Spanish prisoner to recover in the showers something that he had lost moments earlier in that dreadful line where he had been stripped like a chicken.[16]

A prisoner from Aragon called Manuel ('El Maño') was probably the first Spaniard to obtain a post as Kapo, in the Kommando constructing the rampart; he then succeeded in placing other Blues as Kapos.[17] Another Spaniard called Cheka became a Kapo in the kitchens.[18] This allowed the Catalan Tarrago, leader of the PSUC group in Mauthausen, to find a job there too. He was a cobbler by trade, but he had once worked in a hotel, so on that basis the Spanish network turned him into a cook.[19] Mariano Constante had the singular experience of serving as orderly to SS-Oberscharführer Willy Weber, who was chief clerk to Ziereis himself. While some orderlies were forbidden to touch the uniforms of SS officers, they were all responsible for cleaning their latrines and handling their dirty laundry, which explains why the SS referred to them as *Klosettreiniger*. It was while carrying Weber's basket to the laundry that Constante fell foul of the Kommandoführer of the Siedlungsbau, or housing detail. The Spaniards had christened him 'la Niña' for his effeminate gait and manners. Effeminate or not, 'la Niña' ordered Constante to plunge into a tank of water, whereupon he held the prisoner's head below the water with his boot, laughing hysterically. But every time Constante managed to bring his head to the surface, 'la Niña' became more furious at his failure to drown him. Snatching a pick handle, he drove Constante to the centre of the tank so that he could not grab the sides. Constante succeeded anyway, whereupon 'la Niña' ran to where the Spaniard was clinging and stamped his boot on his fingers, turning his heel as if for all the world he were crushing a snake. Constante was to survive, but a deformed hand is his permanent reminder of the encounter with 'la Niña'.[20]

Few events, though, were more important to the Spaniards than the promotion of Juan de Diego Herranz to the *Lagerschreibstube*. De Diego, as we have seen, had arrived in Mauthausen on 6 August 1940 with the very first contingent of Spaniards; he received the number 3156.[21] A Catalan from Barcelona and member of the moderate leftist Ezquerra, he had served in the Civil War, on the Aragon front and later in Madrid, as secretary to Colonel Joaquín Blanco Valdés; he had then been transferred to the 26th ('Durruti') Division, where his responsibility had been to teach administrative skills to the anarchists. From his arrival in Mauthausen until 1 March 1941, he worked, like everyone else, in the quarry. His transfer to the *Lagerschreibstube* resulted from several chance factors. In 1940 Bachmayer had chosen as his Lagerschreiber I the Austrian Green Josef Leitzinger. Leitzinger thus began work in Block 1 under the Rapportführer Dostoevski, and as a *Prominenter* was free to bestow some favours. Some of them fell on Mario Arnijas, a Spanish amateur tenor whose voice Leitzinger liked to hear around the office. Arnijas was thus hired to amuse. He was saved from the work that killed, but he was fed no better than before, and he subsequently arranged his transfer to a service Kommando, where he ate more and ultimately survived the war. At the moment that Arnijas left the *Schreibstube*, in February 1941, he proposed that his friend Juan de Diego take his place. The latter presented himself to Leitzinger: he did not sing, but he did speak German, having learnt it from exchanges with German prisoners and by listening carefully to the SS; he would carry up a rock while conjugating the verb *haben*, reciting it like a prayer, which in fact it was. The office already had a Lagerschreiber II, the German Green Karl Weber,[22] but the SS were by then very conscious of the fact that they had made a great number of errors in recording Spanish names. The Germans were also intrigued by the 'de' in his name and assumed that it was the equivalent of 'von'. De Diego was thus employed in the new post of Lagerschreiber III, who was also made responsible for the *Todesmeldung*, or Register of Deaths. When in late 1942 Weber was transferred to an Aussenkommando, he was replaced by a Czech graduate in commerce and engineering, Kuneš Pany, who was not only a Red but a member of a group arrested in Czechoslovakia in the reprisals that followed the assassination, on 4 June 1942, of Himmler's deputy, SS-Obergruppenführer Reinhard

Heydrich. In such circumstances, Pany's survival was miraculous, the more so since Bachmayer was known for a special hatred of the Czechs,[23] but we must assume that the SS needed someone of his linguistic talent. While any open opposition was too dangerous, a Red and a Blue now vied with a Green in the influence they could exert in the appointment of the Kapos. Even before the removal of Leitzinger, the new balance gave the resistance a vital impetus. It was now a matter, through international co-operation, of driving the Greens from all the administrative posts they had monopolized until now.

Now that Juan de Diego worked in the *Lagerschreibstube*, he could see at first hand the way the camp functioned. The orderly room was the responsibility of SS-Hauptscharführer Johann Haider, whose office was with the rest outside the fortress. It was situated in Block 1, the first building to the left on entering the fortress through the main gates. Like every Block, it was divided into two parts, A and B. *Stube* A contained the brothel and Bachmayer's dog kennels; *Stube* B, the orderly room, and at the end the saddleries (responsible for the cords and whips) and the cobbler's shop. The *Lagerschreibstube* was therefore square in shape, with six windows, three opposite three. No pictures relieved the walls. As one entered the office, three desks stood in a line to the right, the three clerks sitting in order, their backs to the windows. Juan de Diego thus sat farthest from the door. Opposite the Lagerschreiber I was the occasional desk shared between Climent (on his visits from the Politische Abteilung) and George Streitwolf, a German Green responsible for delivering and collecting the mail (Arbeitskommando Poststelle); Streitwolf, far from being a criminal type, was a true musician and the conductor of the camp orchestra. Between the occasional desk and the chief clerk, against the wall, stood the SS library. Opposite the Lagerschreiber II was the massive card index, and opposite de Diego sat the *Buchbinder*, a German Green named Emil Rau, who bound the books for the library. Between de Diego and Rau, above their heads, ran a wooden beam no different from any other except in the horrors this particular one inspired. In the centre stood a charcoal-burning stove, and at the side of the card-index a small cupboard containing plates and other utensils for the four *Prominenten*; these ate in the office, but slept with the other *Prominenten* in the adjacent building, Block 2. While the life of a Lagerschreiber was bliss compared with that of the standard prisoner, these clerks went through their own ordeal, as when a new consignment of prisoners arrived and the clerks had to work non-stop for 24 or 30 hours in making out an index card for each. Worse experiences than that, however, awaited Juan de Diego as he began his life as a *Prominenter*.

No one entered the *Lagerschreibstube*, not even the SS, unless he was specifically authorized to do so. 'The SS would stand outside the door like little boys,' recalls de Diego. If ever an SS man was allowed in, he was never allowed to touch the records, which were sacrosanct. The office was at the same time a venue for each day's banal barbarities. A prisoner would be ordered to report there for an infringement of the regulations, and he would stand at attention outside the office until the Rapportführer, or Bachmayer, or Ziereis himself arrived. Sometimes the summons would be due not to an infringement but of some reason out of the black pit of their minds, or for no other reason than that it was something to do. Sometimes the glowing stove would serve them in the same way it served Schulz in the Politische Abteilung, the victim being forced to place his hands on it or sit. More usually, the SS officers would order the prisoner's wrists to be bound behind his back; his body was then hoisted on to the beam. Occasionally the feet would be tied to the wrists. This was the practice that the SS called the *'Pfahlbinden'*, and it invoked a numbing fear in every prisoner. The rumour ran that the worst agony came at the beginning, while the shoulders were in the process of dislocation. It was therefore recommended that the victim shake his body at the moment he was suspended in order to assist in the dislocation.[24] Poor wretches that they were to be thus reduced to this subhuman level of reasoning. The body was nevertheless left dangling in this position for up to an hour or even longer, while Juan de Diego, seated so close that he could have reached out and touched the victim, had no choice but to continue his clerical work at the table. Here in capsule was the essence of *KZ* life: a large part of the programmed degradation of the prisoners was to let them sit there, observers of the scene, powerless to intervene or express the slightest hint of humanity or compassion. After ten minutes of so, the pain was so intense that the victim invariably passed out. When he was eventually let down, the SS had not finished their sport. The prisoner had to find his own way out of the office, by opening the door. If he failed he could expect a further round of punishment, perhaps the stove. But opening the door meant turning the large enamel knob, and the prisoner was virtually unable to move his arms at all. It was here that de Diego was able to render a small but perhaps vital service. He arranged when he came in, or after the prisoner came in, that the knob was left in a way that, while the door appeared quite shut, it required only the smallest pressure to open. It may well have saved a life.[25]

Juan de Diego also had the singular experience of meeting the Reichsführer-SS himself. Heinrich Himmler, or 'Reichsheini' as the German prisoners called him (not to his face), made two visits to

Mauthausen after his initial visit in 1938. The first of the two took place on 27 April 1941, when he arrived with Dr Ernst Kaltenbrunner and Gauleiter August Eigruber. Unlike Kaltenbrunner, the 2-metre Austrian whose facial scar enhanced his savage image, Himmler struck de Diego as a mild-mannered bourgeois. 'The Reichsführer is banal,' was the impression he remembered. Moving about the camp with all the bland politeness of Edward VIII visiting an orphanage, Himmler remained calm and correct even when addressing the Lagerschreiber III. 'There was nothing striking about his eyes,' de Diego remembers. 'They were the eyes of a dull bureaucrat. His arrogance showed in the way he held back his head.'[26] Other reports suggest that there was nothing banal about this visit. Ziereis told his interrogators on his death-bed that Himmler was disappointed with him, since Mauthausen was killing only 3 per cent of its prisoners a day; the Reichsführer then set an example during his visit to the quarry by ordering a prisoner to turn and hurling a rock into his back.[27] The story may have been the Lagerführer's own invention: Ziereis may have been hoping to survive.[28] There is also evidence that although Mauthausen did not yet have a gas-chamber, Himmler used his visit to test the effect of Zyklon-B gas, selecting for the test a cell in the Bunker where the future gas-chamber would be installed. As for Himmler's last visit, on 31 May 1943, *KZ* business may not have been its primary purpose at all: the excavations at Gusen had unearthed the earliest human relics ever found in Austria, and Himmler wanted the best samples shipped to Nuremberg.[29]

Juan de Diego had the further distinction of being one of the very few Spanish prisoners in Mauthausen to catch the interest of the Spanish Embassy in Berlin. The matter began when Father Luis García, rector of San José de la Montaña, a convent for sick and abandoned children in the north of Barcelona, took an interest in his case. The two men were distant cousins but had never met. Knowing only that Juan de Diego had been taken prisoner by the Germans, Father García decided to send a letter, dated 16 September 1941, to the Count de Mayalde, Franco's Ambassador to Berlin. It is unlikely that Luis García knew the Count de Mayalde; his only motive seems to have been a sense of Christian duty. A letter of reply from the Spanish Embassy in Berlin duly reached him in Barcelona. The letter, dated 14 April 1942 and signed *per pro* by Alonso Caso, referred to information received by the Spanish Embassy from the competent German authorities (a euphemism for the Gestapo), according to which Juan de Diego was 'still' in *KL*-Mauthausen, 'in good health and fit to work'.[30] The letter has its importance, because if the Spanish Embassy in Berlin knew where Juan de Diego was, it demolishes the claim of Serrano

Súñer that no one in the Spanish Embassy in Berlin had any know-ledge of the fate of the Spaniards brought prisoner into Germany.[31]

The ways of the SS being virtually impenetrable to man, it may be useless to examine why, in 1943, the SS suddenly and briefly allowed the prisoners in Mauthausen to write home. Up until that year, no non-German in any SS camp was ever given the privilege. Only in very special cases was any news of a Spanish prisoner sent by the German authorities to his next-of-kin. The Spaniards were thus treated very much as if they were in the category of *Nacht und Nebel*, even though only thirty-three Spaniards were officially classified *NN*, these being *guerrilleros* or urban Resistance members captured in France.[32] Perhaps as a result of the International Red Cross increasing its pres-sure,[33] the prisoners now found themselves, at Christmas 1943, free to write home. Strict limitations were inevitably imposed. Prisoners were allowed to write only one letter every six weeks, and to receive only one reply every six weeks. The letter, which could not exceed twenty-five words, had to be written in German and restrict itself to personal and familial matters. The language requirement was not universally imposed: the Spaniards wrote in Spanish. Juan de Diego wrote twice: in December 1943 and in March 1944. Both letters ar-rived in Barcelona, and he received two replies. After that, no further correspondence was permitted.[34]

It was the proud boast of the Spanish organization that from the beginning of 1943 every single Spaniard entering Mauthausen could count upon its help.[35] Mid-1943 saw the arrival of the first Spaniards arrested in France for resistance activities; the very first was a miner turned *guerrillero* by the name of Felipe Martínez, who was sent to Ebensee, where he set to work organizing the resistance there.[36] Such men brought a new language to Mauthausen: that of sabotage, am-bush, derailment, but more than anything, of hope, survival, and lib-eration. Among the new arrivals arrested in the French Resistance were some very active members of the anarchist CNT. José Ester Borrás, for example, arrived at Mauthausen in the same contingent as the communists José Miret Musté and Luis Montero.[37] While Miret was dispatched to Floridsdorf,[38] Ester and Montero were both assigned in September 1943 to the internal Kommando attached to the SS armoury; this two-man Kommando was responsible for the hard cleaning work. Ester began to organize those Spaniards who, for ideo-logical reasons, had refused to join the communist-led organization, while Montero, described as 'an indefatigable organizer and exemplary man of action',[39] became the soul of the Spanish military formation.

With the arrival of the CNT *guerrilleros*, the old quarrels between

Spanish communists and non-communists began to subside. Ester and Montero, representing their respective committees, worked together not simply in the armoury but in the secret organization, and a Spanish 'committee of national union' was formed in the spring of 1944. This committee consisted of two communists (Sánchez and Fernando Fernández Lavín), two anarchists (Capdevilla and Ester), and two socialists or republicans whose names have not been recorded.[40]

On the same day that the Spanish national committee was formed an international committee was also constituted: not without difficulty, for certain German communists considered the enterprise too risky—among them Franz Dahlem, the former assistant to Dimitrov, who was especially familiar with the dangers.[41] The committee had a pronounced communist predominance, and all its leaders who survived were to have important roles in their respective countries after the Liberation. At the time of its creation the committee consisted of three Austrian communists (Josef Kohl, Hans Maršálek, and a certain Mayer) and one Czech (Arthur London).[42] The predominance of the Austrians was logical, since they were better equipped to make contact with the Austrian Resistance. As for London, after his arrest in Paris in August 1942[43] he had been sent, in September 1943, to the prison in Blois, then to the Neuebremme punishment camp near Saarbrücken for a month, and on 26 March 1944, he arrived in Mauthausen.[44] His arrival among so many Spanish communists and former members of the International Brigades—Dahlem had been a leading participant—must have seemed to him like a class reunion. The Spaniards now protected him by making him Blockschreiber in Block 6, which contained a large number of Spaniards.

The international committee proceeded to set up a highly ambitious—and partly impracticable—seven-point programme on the following basis: to complete the internal organization of each national section, with leadership and structure; to perfect the communist education of all militants; to work out a plan of international solidarity; to establish small combat units; to monitor Allied radio broadcasts and spread the news; to plan the escape of any militant threatened with execution (where an interval of time existed, and however slim the chance of escape), and to attempt, with the help of comrades in the Aussenkommandos, to make contact with sympathetic elements in the Austrian population.[45]

The work of radio monitoring was performed by Istvan Balogh, a Hungarian volunteer in the International Brigades and member of the Spanish Communist Party. Balogh had been assigned to the electrical workshop (Elektrikerkommando) in January 1941. His early attempts to monitor Allied broadcasts were unsatisfying, since the SS left him free to do so during only two or three short periods per week. He therefore decided to build his own set. But he faced the risk of betrayal by the prisoner in charge of the detail, an elderly Austrian Black named Franz-Joseph Steininger, who was said to be ready to sell information to anyone in exchange for tobacco. Every day Balogh sequestered some part or other from the workshop supplies, and by September 1941 the secret radio was in working order. The news he obtained was passed only to two Spaniards, Marcelo Rodríguez and Luis Gil, the former employed as a clockmaker and the latter as servant to the Lagerältester. It was just as well that the Allied broadcasts at that time were not made known to the prisoners in general, for the news, however mitigated by Allied propaganda, could only have served to demoralize the inmates, many of whom were already critically depressed. The triad was later joined by Razola, who worked in the disinfection detail, and through Razola the group entered the secret organization.[46] By then the thirst for news had increased. Up until the Battle of Stalingrad, the SS beamed Berlin's news bulletins to the extensions installed in every Block. When the tide of battle turned, the news relays stopped. The prisoners could guess why.

Austria was never to know the kind of sustained bombing that Germany underwent, but in 1944 Allied air raids on selected Austrian targets were considerably increased. Linz was the most natural target, for its Hermann Goering Works, but the Aussenkommandos at Melk, Steyr, and Gusen were also hit. As a result of these raids, Juan de Diego, and he alone—the other two Lagerschreiber were never sent on such a mission—was dispatched first to Linz and later to the other three Kommandos[47] to restore order to the ledgers, because when a Kommando's records were destroyed the SS depended entirely on the records maintained by de Diego in the *Mutterlager*. His assignment then was to determine the number and identity of the prisoners killed in the bombing and those left alive. Travelling in a Wehrmacht sidecar with an SS driver and an escort of four SS motorcyclists behind him, de Diego felt for all the world like a visiting head of state. On each trip he did his best to make confusion worse confounded, mislaying a paper here, a paper there, thus saving a prisoner a day or two of labour—and each day's work he saved could be a month of life. The trip to Melk was especially noteworthy. The Allied air raid on that town was more destructive to the prisoner population than any other in Austria—more than 500 died—and it was Bachmayer himself on that occasion, to de Diego's total bewilderment, who drove the sidecar in which he rode. The visit also happened to coincide with the July Plot. Fear transformed the faces of the SS through the hours in which they believed the Führer dead. The effect on Lagerführer Ludolf was particularly in evidence. Whether it was the Plot, or the disorder in his archives, or the presence of Bachmayer, Juan de Diego recalls the impact it all had on Ludolf, now reduced to such servility that he personally served not only Bachmayer but even de Diego, 'as though he were no better than a Bierkellermeister'. Meanwhile the orders from Ziereis were for Bachmayer and all SS on leave to report at once to the *Mutterlager*. None of this dismay on the part of the SS offered any comfort to the prisoners, for the SS knew well enough how to take their revenge.

Throughout the summer of 1944 the communist groups were busily engaged in persuading those non-communists in each national collective who had not yet organized themselves, to do so. The French were probably the first to respond to this appeal, and at the request of three leaders of the French communist group, Michel de Boüard established an executive committee representing a broad ideological range.[48] As a result of the new collaboration it was now possible to smuggle clothes out of the clothing store, linen from the laundry, food from the storehouse, and medicine from the SS infirmary. Several lives were thus saved.[49]

In August 1944 the Austrian communists Mayer and Leo Gabler were executed[50] at the same time that London fell gravely ill. The fate of Gabler dealt a particularly heavy blow to the resistance, since he was much admired. London was placed in the *Revier*, where he stayed for months, escaping transfer to the gas chamber only through the protection given to him by Professor Podlaha and the other inmate-doctors. Meanwhile, Mayer and London were replaced on the international committee by three new members: the Frenchman Octave Rabaté, the Spaniard Manuel Razola, and the Czech Leopold Hoffmann. Liaison with the Slav groups, mainly Poles and Russians, was entrusted to Hoffmann, while Razola, who had long experience with other national groups, was made responsible for liaison with the other Latin groups, French, Belgian, and Italian. A few serious ideological conflicts apparently remained, in the Spanish group as in others, and Razola often visited Arthur London to seek his political advice.[51]

It may well have been with the help of Arthur London that, in September 1944, the Spaniards formed the Frente nacional antifascista español. Juan de Diego calls it 'a retroactive organization, and a piece of theatre; its leader, the communist Ronda, was a non-entity'.[52] Its purpose was to give the impression of solidarity behind communist leadership, with every ideology expressing its trust in communist goodwill. Much was made of this Frente after the Liberation, but it was indeed a front, of the kind the communist parties would perfect a few years later.

In the midst of so much suffering, few acts of barbarism stood out. If they did, it was because the SS were changing the rules. We have seen that Mauthausen contained many thousands of Soviet prisoners of war, whose inclusion the SS would justify in terms of race. As Nazi Germany became more desperate, it began to treat certain prisoners of war from the Western Allies in the same way, especially if their prisoners were from élite units which were striking the hardest blows to Germany. In September 1944 an atrocity took place in Mauthausen to which the Spanish Lagerschreiber, Juan de Diego, was an important witness, his testimony later serving to close the case on some of the perpetrators. On the morning of 6 September forty-seven Allied officers, comprising thirty-nine Dutch, seven British, and one American, arrived in Mauthausen from prisons in Holland and France.[53] On the orders of Ziereis, the prisoners of war were taken straight to the *Bunker* without being registered. Instead, their numbers were inscribed on their chests. Ziereis personally shaved the head of a parachutist, leaving it covered in blood. Bachmayer loosed his hound Lord on to the right forearm of another young Allied officer, who lost consciousness. In the afternoon, the entire group was taken to the quarry. A crowd of SS lined the summit of the famous steps, keeping away from the cliff edge. Some had even brought their wives: Ziereis had promised them an extravaganza. At the base of the steps stood SS-Unterscharführer Johann Vinzenz Gogl. The Allied officers were ordered to pick up a rock, then mount the steps, then do so at a run. Six times in the course of the afternoon they climbed the staircase; each time the staircase took its toll. By evening only twenty-five were left alive. These were taken to the *Bunker*. When Juan de Diego visited it the next morning in order to try to identify those officers whose registration numbers on their chests had been erased in the course of the dreadful mutilation of their bodies, he found, crammed into cells designed for a single prisoner, no fewer than twelve in one and thirteen in another, in air that was unbreathable. That morning on the quarry steps the show's second act began. Not one of the officers had received any food or water from the moment they arrived. This time, as the prisoners neared the camp's perimeter with their rocks, all dropped their burden together and raced for the barbed wire. Like a conductor beckoning to the trumpet section of an orchestra, Ziereis signalled to the machine-guns in the towers, whose rapid staccato brought the carnival to an end. But that evening, as the other prisoners returned to the fortress, having witnessed the scene on the steps, thousands of wooden clogs beat a rhythm of protest in honour of the Allied dead.[54]

Once again, the role of the Spanish Lagerschreiber was crucial to the preservation of the evidence. For reasons unknown, the names of the forty-seven Allied officers were not entered and counter-signed in the *Todesmeldung*. Instead, some days later, some unranked SS were ordered to the *Lagerschreibstube* and told to type up a report listing the Allied officers and accusing them of having staged a rebellion. The carbon paper they used happened to be new. Juan de Diego waited for his chance, retrieved the carbon, held it against a mirror while he copied it, and hid the copy.

In the same month of September 1944, the international committee, as if inspired by the massacre of the Allied officers, established a military branch, responsible for the organization of combat groups and known by the acronym AMI, in its French version the Appareil militaire international. The Spanish group, which already had its own military organization headed by regular officers such as Luis Montero,[55] at once offered its services.

If we can believe the communists' claims, which choose to overlook the extreme fatigue under which the prisoners were operating, the AMI developed into a remarkable organization, with squads, platoons, companies, and battalions grouped into a brigade of some 4,000–5,000 men.[56] Each national unit had its distinct and precise assignments. Very careful training was given in gauging the distance to certain objectives such as sentry-boxes and watch-towers and the precise time required to reach them. Studies were made of variations in visibility and of areas safe from the SS arc of fire. All the time the national committees persevered in stealing and concealing knives, axes, picks, and whatever else could serve as a weapon on the day of reckoning.[57] Occasionally they did better: at least one pistol was stolen from the SS armoury by a Spaniard working in that Kommando,[58] and other Spaniards, employed in the garage Kommando, had made a duplicate key to a locker which they knew contained weapons and ammunition.[59] Their secret weapon was the fire extinguisher with the brand name Minimax. It was discovered that the foam it ejected had a range of 6 metres, and that anyone hit four-square in the face would be blinded. The weapon had the further advantage that it made no noise. A rehearsal was arranged: Block leaders found their way during evening soup to the wall that separated the quarantine Blocks from the rest, which was the only spot in the camp not in clear view of the SS watch-towers. There they were shown how the extinguisher could be dismantled from its casing and how it could be fired.[60] On the vital matter of security, no one apart from the committee members could identify more than his immediate superior and his immediate subordinate.[61]

To overcome the problem posed by the diversity of languages, it was agreed that the Soviet commander, Major Andreï Pirogov, who had been transferred to Mauthausen from Sachsenhausen, would be responsible also for the Czechs and Yugoslavs, while the Spanish commander, now Fernández Lavín,[62] was given charge of the French, Belgians, Italians—and the Poles, who clearly objected to being placed under a Soviet. Since the Spanish unit was the largest and the best of the national units, when the decision was taken to create an overall command it went to the same Spaniard Fernández Lavín. But Lavín had no military expertise, and he too was replaced (in early 1945) by Miguel Malle, a member of the PCE.[63] His staff consisted of a German, an Austrian, a Czech, and a Frenchman.[64] But the dominant figure seems to have been the Soviet major Pirogov. The Spanish commander maintained his liaison with the Soviet through Mariano Constante, who spoke Russian, and the official AMI report presented on 16 May 1945 before an assembly of Spanish survivors describes the AMI command as a Spanish–Soviet duumvirate.[65]

On 28 February 1945, the international committee was reinforced by the inclusion of several new members. Joining Kohl, Maršálek, Rabaté, Razola, and Hoffmann were the German Franz Dahlem, the Soviet Andreī Pirogov, the Italian communist Giuliano Pajetta, the Polish socialist Cyrankiewicz and the Austrian communist Dr Heinrich Dürmayer—the last two having arrived in Mauthausen the previous month as evacuees from Auschwitz.[66]

What gave the prisoners a new chance was the situation facing Nazi Germany, especially in the east. From the beginning of 1943, with the surrender of von Paulus at Stalingrad, the Wehrmacht faced a steadily increasing need for men, and the whole German economy a similar need for skilled labour. Many Greens and Blacks accepted the offer to serve in the Wehrmacht,[67] and some Green Kapos were transferred in late 1944 to other camps where the crimes they had committed in Mauthausen were unknown.[68] But the SS had another reason for removing the old Kapos, and especially the old Lagerschreiber: if they survived they could testify to the crimes committed.[69] This explains the secret order, which Ziereis divulged on his death-bed, calling for the liquidation of the current crematorium Kommando every three weeks.[70] It also explains in part the dismissal and subsequent execution of the Lagerschreiber I himself. Josef Leitzinger was cordially hated by his fellow-prisoners. He beat everyone, and he once hit his fellow-clerk Juan de Diego. The little Spaniard waited his moment, and when Leitzinger was about to hit him again de Diego drove his elbow into the Austrian's mid-section with all his force. Leitzinger did not trouble de Diego again, but the Spaniards and the Reds were determined to oust him, and since Leitzinger was a drug addict they knew how to trap him. With the help of Professor Podlaha, who obtained the wherewithal, Leitzinger was given a massive dose and was then found by Bachmayer, on 12 March 1944, in a total daze. The Schutzhaftlagerführer promptly removed him from his post—certainly not because he was a brutal sadist—and sent him to Gusen.[71] There he was shot on 16 January 1945, 'while attempting to escape'.[72]

With the removal of Leitzinger and the departure of so many Green and Black Kapos, the whole of Mauthausen's internal structure began to move into the control of the Reds. The Czech Kuneš Pany now moved up into the position of Lagerschreiber I, the Austrian Hans Maršálek became Lagerschreiber II and Juan de Diego remained as Lagerschreiber III.[73] The *Schreibstube* now became the centre of resistance, but these clerks had plenty to fear, not only that what had happened to Leitzinger could happen to them, but also that the Greens could still recover their control.[74]

The immediate result was that in Mauthausen and in certain of its Aussenkommandos, the Spaniards became the predominant group in the organization of the prisoners. The Spaniards in their turn were offered freedom in exchange for service in the Wehrmacht, the entire group being drawn up in the *Appellplatz* to hear the call from Ziereis for volunteers to step forward from the ranks; not a single Spaniard moved.[75] At the same time the continuous Allied bombing disrupted the work in the quarry and the adjacent factories, with the result that camp discipline was relaxed. Those SS sent to the eastern front were replaced by less fanatical elements, including some older Austrians; as the Nazi situation deteriorated further, these SS in turn were replaced, early in 1945, by Luftwaffe troops, anti-aircraft crews, and the Volksturm. The SS command was also aware of the homogeneity, solidarity, and organizational discipline of the Spanish group, to the extent that it tolerated towards the end what would never have been tolerated at an earlier time. As for the final stage that now approached, the Spaniards especially let it be known that they were on guard, prepared for the eventuality of a total extermination, and determined not to submit without a fight to the death.[76]

While certain factors were thus working to the advantage of the prisoners, others reduced even further their chances of survival. On 7 May 1944, Himmler wrote a terse four-line message, whose only recipients were Kaltenbrunner and Pohl, and which somehow survived destruction at the end. It ran: 'For reasons of security, I forbid the release of any prisoner from *KL*-Mauthausen for the duration of the war.'[77] After the failure of the attempt on Hitler on 20 July, there was many a hint from the SS at Mauthausen as elsewhere that if Nazi Germany were to lose the war there would be no prisoner in Nazi hands who would celebrate it.[78] The secret organization had worked hard to infiltrate its agents into some key areas of the camp. Ramón Bargueño, for example, made the beds and cleaned the boots of the SS; he was also responsible for taking meals to the SS on duty in the *Bunker* and to the occasional members of the SS who were themselves confined there as punishment for indiscipline.[79] The Catalan communist leader Tarrago succeeded, with the help of Boix, in getting himself assigned in early 1944 to the NCO's mess (*Unterführerheim*). Tarrago was in contact with the barber Manuel Azaustre, who was responsible for cleaning the *Kommandantur*.[80] Azaustre also had the privilege of shaving Ziereis, and it was he who heard the camp Commandant threaten to kill the prisoners *en masse* at the moment the Allies approached the camp. The international committee was thus informed, and the AMI was alerted.[81]

Mariano Constante, as orderly to Ziereis' chief clerk, was also in a good eavesdropping position, but his misfortunes were not ended. He was given a subsidiary assignment as orderly to a certain Keller, one of the newly arrived Romanian SS for whom the Germans could not conceal their contempt. As Keller's orderly, Constante found moments to consult his three dictionaries (German–Spanish, German–Russian, and French–Russian), important tools in the prisoners' struggle for better communications. One day Constante was caught by a German NCO, SS-Unterscharführer Hans Bruckner, while he was taking notes from an old copy of *Völkischer Beobachter*. (Bruckner was to become known to the Spaniards as 'el Capado', the eunuch, following the mishap that befell him on the Russian front.) Since no prisoner was allowed to read a Nazi journal, Bruckner marched Constante to the main gate, set him against the wall, and placed the chain on his wrists behind his back. The officer of the guard happened to be Keller. The Romanian approached the German and told him that no one was hanged at that gate without Bachmayer's permission. A violent discussion followed for a full minute, at the end of which Constante was released. Bruckner walked out through the main gate swearing, heading for Bachmayer's office. Constante waited for Bachmayer, and for death. Instead, he felt the gentle hand of Juan de Diego, who, lynx-eyed as always, had seen the incident from his office window; though it was forbidden for any prisoner to approach another at the *Klagemauer*, de Diego had taken the risk of making his way to the gate to see what he could do. When Constante told him the story, de Diego went back to the *Lagerschreibstube* to see his senior colleague Maršálek. They were at the gate together at the moment that Bachmayer arrived, with the still-raging Bruckner. Maršálek and de Diego explained their presence to Bachmayer. To the astonishment of everyone, Bachmayer merely ordered Constante to get back to work and told Bruckner, in front of the prisoner-clerks, that he was a blithering idiot.[82]

From that moment on, Constante lived in mortal terror of seeing Bruckner around the camp. It was agreed that his only hope of survival was to disappear into the *Sanitätslager*, or 'Russian camp', the huge hospital annex.[83] The international organization took the matter in hand, and Maršálek included Constante in a batch of sixty sick who were to be sent to the 'Russian camp' the next day. It was a bitter irony, as Constante passed through the careful check at the gate, that he should have felt such fear of being stopped from going in, when the fear of everyone else was of never getting out. It was indeed a desperate solution, for inside lay more than 5,000 prisoners in pitiful condition. Constante has described the scene: day and night the collective groaning of the dying, the screams of the wounded as gangrene spread across their limbs, the sobs of the starving begging for anything, from time to time the creaking of the death-cart dragged by the two Poles who collected the bodies, and over everything the fetid, perfervid smell of filth as the motionless living entwined with the dead. Almost everyone around him, he found, was injured in the feet or ankles, for almost all had been working in the quarry. It was the rocks that had caused their wounds, the steps their injuries, as their exhausted legs twisted under the weight of the rock. The denial of medical treatment had achieved the rest: the wounds became infected until the flesh rotted and came away from the bones.

Once again, the Spanish virtue of steadfastness in suffering triumphed over the worst the SS could do. Constante was visited several times every day by the Spanish doctors who were permitted to practise in the *Sanitätslager*. The day finally came when Bruckner was given a new posting. No sooner had he left Mauthausen than Constante got the Spanish doctors to give him a discharge to return to the main camp. De Diego nevertheless advised him to move for a while into the bricklayers' Kommando, which was the largest of its kind and under Spanish Kapos, in order to remain inconspicuous a little longer.[84]

From February 1945 the Wehrmacht was in rout, and this offered quite new perspectives, but it was also clear that the period before liberation was going to be the most dangerous of all. Three plans were worked out, to meet the three most likely situations: an attempt by the SS to poison the entire prisoner population by mixing some toxic product in the soup; an Allied parachute drop in the vicinity of the camp; and a mass evacuation of the prisoners by forced march. In the first eventuality, it was decided that a careful watch would be sufficient, and for the second, final plans were laid for an assault on the armoury. Block 2, close to the main gate, became the command post. It was the third eventuality that was considered the most likely. The prisoners knew, from the accounts of survivors now reaching Mauthausen, that in an evacuation from one camp to another, four out of every five prisoners died or were murdered on the road. The international committee concluded that Mauthausen's population would be driven either into the Austrian mountain redoubts or to Gusen, where all would be exterminated by gas in the underground tunnels of St Georgen. Its conclusion was perceptive. We now know that on 4 April 1945, Himmler instructed the commandants of *KL*-Flossenburg and *KL*-Dachau to evacuate their prisoners immediately, without allowing a single prisoner to fall alive into enemy hands.[85] On his death-bed Ziereis disclosed that he had received an order from Pohl in February to the effect that if the war were lost, every last prisoner was to be killed; Ziereis added that the Reichsführer subsequently ordered him to convey all his prisoners into the Kellerbau and Bergkristall tunnels in Gusen and to blow them up with dynamite.[86]

The international committee therefore decided that an attack on the SS would be launched no later than the afternoon of the first day's march, that is to say before the prisoners were too tired. 'Shock' details were to place themselves in the two ranks closest to the guards. The signal would be divulged at the moment the column left Mauthausen, and when the signal was given the 'shock' details were to hurl themselves on the guards, whatever the consequences might be.[87]

Any more distant evacuation was quite unlikely for those at Mauthausen, located as it was almost exactly in the centre of the invading Allied armies. It was, instead, the evacuation of so many other camps and Kommandos to Mauthausen that increased the danger, this time from mass starvation. In the last months of 1944, convoys had begun to arrive from Poland and France. While only a small fraction of the prisoners survived the journey, their arrival at Mauthausen increased the strain on the already dwindling food supplies.[88]

Although the general direction of evacuation was to the west, if all accounts are to be believed there was a certain confusion in the orders.[89] The first evacuees to reach Mauthausen were several hundred Poles who arrived from Warsaw in June 1944, followed by two convoys from Auschwitz on 28 September and 3 November. Another convoy from Auschwitz in January 1945, probably the last, took fourteen days to arrive, in temperatures of between −10 and −20 °C. When the train pulled in to Mauthausen station, it was found that half the wagons contained nothing but corpses.[90] The evacuees who survived these convoys from Auschwitz included at least 150 former members of the International Brigades.[91] If these early evacuations were by train rather than forced march, the wagons were often of the transporter (open platform) variety, with the SS guards mounted between watching to see if any head rose too high; if one did, they would shoot at it as if it were a revolving rabbit at a fairground.[92]

While the SS never left anything to chance, it had not been able to prevent some isolated escapes from Mauthausen's various Aussenkommandos. As far as the Spaniards were concerned, their most important attempt at escape was from the SS farm at Bretstein in the Tyrol, where a group of 150 Spaniards had been sent to build a road between two mountain villages. In July 1941 four of them (Velasco, Izquierdo, López, and Cerezo) managed to escape by night, walking along the bed of a mountain stream to throw off the SS dogs. They then struck out in what they hoped was a westerly direction. In fact they wasted several days before they found their bearings, by which time they realized that with neither money, nor information, nor knowledge of the language, and dressed in their prison garb, they were mad to have thought that escape was possible. But they continued west, hiding from the inhabitants and managing to steal some food and some peasant clothes. For a whole month they wandered over the mountains until their strength began to fail. At this point Izquierdo gave up, finding refuge with a group of French prisoners of war under Wehrmacht guard. The other three kept going until they were spotted, not far from the Swiss frontier, by an Austrian who struck Velasco a blow on the back of the head and took him prisoner. Cerezo and López were shortly afterwards picked up by the local police. All three were at once identified as prisoners from Mauthausen. They had succeeded in remaining at liberty for two months, but had travelled no farther than 150 kilometres. All three were returned to the *Mutterlager* (Velasco after treatment in hospital), and there, strangely enough, they were exempted from the standard punishment. Instead, they were merely hanged by their feet and whipped before being assigned to the *Strafkompanie* in the quarry, wearing the red circle on their new uniforms that denoted their special class. Despite dreadful sufferings all three survived, the other Spaniards succeeding in sending them extra spoonfuls of food. As for Izquierdo, his identity was similarly discovered and his journey ended in Dachau.[93]

If an escape from a Kommando in the mountains was theoretically possible, an escape from the *Mutterlager* was a different story. The attempt in July 1942 by the Austrian Green Hans Bonarewitz became the most celebrated, precisely because some of the photographs which the SS took of his return were among those that the Spaniards were able to save. Employed in the SS garage, Bonarewitz managed to construct a false bottom to a crate containing a motor, then hid in it as the SS loaded the crate on to a truck bound for Steyr. Since his family lived in the vicinity of Mauthausen and he knew the region, he had a better chance than most, but after three weeks on the run he found himself turned in by the local inhabitants. Looking for a punishment to fit the crime, Ziereis had him buried in his box, but he took care to exhume him before he suffocated, for nothing was to mark the festivity he had planned. On the evening of 29 July the prisoners paraded as usual on the *Appellplatz*. The roll-call was taken, but the prisoners were not dismissed. A wait, then the main gates of the fortress opened. The gypsy orchestra, led by Karl, came in playing an adagio. Two prisoners dragged the cart, normally used to convey corpses to the crematorium but now carrying the wretched Bonarewitz, who struggled to keep his balance. The procession stopped between the long rows of prisoners drawn up in formation on either side. The orchestra now attacked a livelier piece. All the while the Kapo who led it, dressed as for a carnival, strutted like a buffoon, one hand on his left hip, the other beating time with his baton. Everything had the appearance of a circus. For one hour the procession worked its way along the rows of prisoners, until it stopped in the centre. Over 10,000 men, of whom several hundred remain alive in 1992, were witnesses to the scene, as Bonarewitz was ordered to dismount and the SS surrounding him, after punching and kicking him, tied him to the wooden horse and administered the statutory 25 lashes. So ended the first day. On 30 July all the prisoners paraded again before a scaffold erected for the occasion. Bonarewitz was brought back on to the parade ground. Ziereis arrived, accompanied by 'King Kong'. The Lagerälteste attached the noose, climbed down, kicked away the support; the body dangled, shook; the rope snapped. The scene was repeated. Only on the third try was Bonarewitz dead. For two hours more the parade remained standing in front of the corpse. Then the prisoners, all 10,000 of them, were ordered to walk around it, one at a time, and look it in the face. The ceremony ended.[94] The temptation to escape, the SS wished to suggest, should be resisted wherever possible.

If one-man or small-scale attempts seemed doomed to failure, the revolt of Block 20 on the night of 2–3 February 1945 showed that large-scale concerted action could succeed, even against a machine as alert and ruthless as the SS. The revolt led to the only mass break-out ever known at Mauthausen *Mutterlager*, and one of only three ever known in the *KZ* universe. Of the other two, one was at Sobibor and the other, as we shall see, was launched from a Mauthausen Aussenkommando. The exploit of 2–3 February nevertheless remains a model for all time.

The plan was simplicity itself. If enough men accepted the principle that the objective be pursued regardless of how many died, some prisoner or other would finish up with his two thumbs pressing on some Nazi's gurgling windpipe. Block 20 at Mauthausen was isolated from the rest of the camp by a wall and an electrified fence, and was the most heavily guarded. From April 1944 it was reserved for Soviet officers and political commissars, especially those who had escaped from the prisoner-of-war camps, and for certain K prisoners. Since it was now normal for the Germans to shoot prisoners of war who escaped and always normal for the SS to execute K prisoners on arrival, the presence of 4,300 such prisoners in Mauthausen's Block 20 has only one explanation: it was intended that they slowly starve to death. The man responsible for Block 20, Josef Niedermayer, admitted as much at his trial in Dachau: 'The prisoners were to die slowly, from starvation or disease. The daily food ration consisted of half a litre of so-called soup, an eighth or a sixteenth of a kilo of bread, which frequently I didn't distribute, and a thin slice of cheese, salami, or margarine.' For good measure, the eight Green Kapos responsible for Block 20 would empty the dixies into wash-basins, forcing the prisoners to lap up the food with their hands. As a result, of the 4,300 prisoners interned there in April 1944, only 1,300 were still alive in November, and only 500 by February 1945.[95]

The idea of an attempt at mass escape came from a group of Soviet officers who had arrived in Mauthausen, following their escape and recapture elsewhere, at the end of January 1945. Still in reasonable physical condition, but aware that they were all very soon to die, they formed their plan. Mauthausen was, as usual in winter, under a heavy blanket of snow. In clearing the snow on 2 February, the prisoners were able to heap it up close to the wall, under the towers. That night, in the early hours, the order rang out: '*Alles raus!*' It was not unusual for the SS to arrive at a Block in the middle of the night and haul all the inmates outside for a general beating. No one therefore was surprised. But this time it was a ruse: it was the Soviets who barked the German orders, which were to provide the cover. In no time at all the Block Kapo and his seven acolytes were strangled to death by the Soviets, and the rebels then dressed in their clothes. Two groups then clambered up the two watch-towers and blinded the guards with fire extinguishers. Taking control of the machine-guns, they trained them on the adjacent towers. Meanwhile, others threw blankets over the electric wire, and men began to pour over. Out of some 400 who took part in the escape, only 14 died in the break-out. The rest dispersed in the countryside, not before staging an attack on a local anti-aircraft post where they helped themselves to small arms.

The manhunt that followed was pursued with a ferocity that knew no bounds. For four days, every available SS man and every dog in the region was mobilized. So too were the Austrian civilians in the surrounding areas, a reward being offered to them for every fugitive they killed. The extent of the mobilization was such that the work Kommandos were not able to leave the camp on 3 February for lack of guards to accompany them. For two days the disfigured corpses of the Russians continued to arrive in Mauthausen, over 300 in all, many of them dragged by a cord attached to their feet. Nevertheless, some prisoners eluded their pursuers. On 7 February a farmer named Langthaler discovered two famished, shivering Russians hiding in his stable. He knew where they were from, he knew exactly what it meant to him to return them or to hide them, and he chose to hide them, for three long months, until the day of Liberation.[96] Another dozen prisoners, perhaps several dozen,[97] succeeded in crossing the Yugoslav border and joining Tito's partisans. Those left behind in Block 20 were liquidated, with the single exception of a Russian Komsomol member named Ivan, from Leningrad, whom Juan de Diego saved by finding him a post in a group of electricians.[98]

The other mass break-out took place at Loibl-Pass, where some 5,000 prisoners were digging a tunnel between Austria and Yugoslavia. Several Spaniards were among those who attempted the escape, but only 150 prisoners, including two Spaniards, managed to avoid recapture. Making their way over a mountain range which none of them knew, without arms or provisions, they succeeded in reaching Tito's forces. The two surviving Spaniards are mentioned in the official Yugoslav history of the war. One of them arrived disguised as a herdsman leading a cow he had brought all the way from Austria. Neither of the Spaniards is recorded by name, but the Spaniard leading the cow was given the nickname *čika* (in Serb, uncle), a nickname bestowed in good humour to anyone of a certain age. The Spaniard was, in fact, still young; he simply looked old. All in all, seventeen Spaniards escaped from Mauthausen, but seven of these died in the process.[99]

After Mauthausen and Dachau, it was Buchenwald that contained the largest number of Spanish prisoners.[100] The first evacuation left for Mauthausen on 3 February 1945, arriving four days later. Of the 3,000 who set out, only 1,200 reached Mauthausen alive.[101] Altogether, half the population of Buchenwald was evacuated, and the vast majority died.[102] At Buchenwald's Aussenkommando at Ohrdruf, 8,000 prisoners stayed behind to work underground, excavating the tunnel shelter for Hitler's private train in accordance with a contingency plan to evacuate the Führer's headquarters from Berlin. Two days before the Kommando was overrun, on 5 April 1945, by the 4th Armored Division of the US 3rd Army, the 8,000 prisoners were massacred, each one shot in the back of the neck by members of the Hitler Jugend.[103]

Two more convoys of evacuated prisoners arrived in Mauthausen in mid-February and met an identical fate. The first arrived at noon on 15 February from Oranienburg. Of the 2,500 prisoners who set out, only 1,700 were still alive. The weakest 200, including General Dimitry Mikhailovich Karbychev of the Red Army, were made to stand at attention in the *Appellplatz*, naked in a temperature varying from −15 °C to −1 °C, for the rest of the day, through the night, and through the following day. For good measure, the firemen were ordered to douse them with their hoses. Some 150 died, in coffins of ice, including General Karbychev, who was determined to die on his feet. To finish off the last fifty, the SS, armed with cudgels and axes, waded in, bathing in gaping wounds. The next day, 17 February, another convoy arrived from Sachsenhausen, similar in the number who started out and the number who died *en route*. A survivor, Irène Gaucher, has described how some sank into cannibalism, deciding in advance of a comrade's death who was to have his arm and leg muscles; two other prisoners waited only for a comrade to die before opening his chest and eating, raw, the heart and liver.[104] On arrival at Mauthausen, it was Trum and a Blockführer who selected the weakest 500. These were ordered to strip and to form a line along the *Klagemauer*. Again the firemen played jets of ice-cold water on them throughout the night. In the morning Niedermayer, Bachmayer's driver and a few Blockführer finished off the survivors with bludgeons and iron bars. All except one. The French Lieutenant-Colonel de Dionne had buried himself under the bodies of the dead, from which he derived some warmth, and though a blow from an axe, intended as the *coup de grâce*, scarred him for life, he escaped a mortal wound. He was taken as dead to the crematorium, but there he was hidden and looked after, and at the Liberation would provide the Allied War Crimes Commission with eye-witness testimony. The scene was also witnessed by members of the kitchen staff, the kitchen block being less than fifty yards from the *Klagemauer*. Further evidence was provided by many other prisoners in the surrounding huts (including Juan de Diego in Block 2) who heard the shouts and screams all night long.[105] The evidence that appeared showed that this massacre had been planned in advance, no doubt in revenge for the mass escape, and that Schulz attended it in person.[106]

In the convoy from Sachsenhausen was a German Jew from Odessa by the name of Salomon Smolianov, who being stateless wore the Blue as well as the Yellow triangle. Before he became a prisoner his profession had been to renovate the works of great artists and to make facsimiles, an art which had gained him a certain celebrity. He had been sent to Sachsenhausen when Heydrich established there the centre of the Nazi counterfeit-sterling industry (Operation *Bernhard*),[107] and now the entire unit was to be set up in Austria. Juan de Diego was able to speak with Smolianov about his work, before the unit, now ordered to produce counterfeit documents and dollars, was sent off on 14 April 1945 to its new centre at Redl-Zipf, officially known as Schlier.[108]

On 2 March 1945, a convoy left Ravensbrück with 1,981 women and children. Five days later, in the middle of the night, they reached Mauthausen, where they were shown the full standard SS reception the whole distance from the station to the main gate; many spent the first night standing in the snow, chained to the wall. As a result, only 1,799 were still alive when registration was completed on 10 March; the 182 who had died included all the children, those surviving the journey being murdered on arrival. Among the survivors who were registered were 579 French and four Spanish women. The women were kept separate from the men by every possible barrier, but the news still moved, and many women experienced the emotional shock of finding that the camp contained a comrade, a family member, or even a husband, which was the case for two of the Spanish women: the wives of José Ester Borrás and Joaquín Olaso Piera. In the case of the first, Alfonsina Bueno de Ester, though she and her husband were to survive Mauthausen both her father and her brother perished. The women in general found themselves treated no better than the men. Alfonsina de Ester recalls how they too worked in the quarry and carried rocks of 40 kilos up the 186 steps, and how three exhausted women, unable to go further, were hurled to the bottom with their rocks.[109] Despite everything, the mere presence of the women galvanized the men, which in turn fortified the energies of both.[110]

Not all the women evacuated from Ravensbrück were directed to Mauthausen. A different fate befell Conchita Ramos Veleta who, as we have seen, had been taken prisoner in southern France and dispatched in the 'ghost train' from Toulouse to Dachau. From Dachau she reached Ravensbrück on 9 September 1944, finding it infinitely worse, with filth and stench beyond description. There she found herself among a group of Resistance women who had been arrested in the Hôtel Moderne in Figéac. One of them was a Spanish maid of 24 named Mimi Tapia, who had sunk into nervous depression; unable to work, she was sent to the gas chamber. Ramos and the others were sent to a Kommando on the River Spree south-east of Berlin, where a two-storey factory had been built of wood; inside, 500 women, divided into two shifts of 12 hours, laboured in the construction of aircraft. Gone was the German passion for cleanliness: all the women were suffering to some degree from dysentery, and there were only four toilets. Meanwhile the Allied bombing increased, and in April 1945 the factory was destroyed. The SS kept the women in an underground cell for three days, then transported them westwards across Berlin. It was 14 April. The day of the Spanish Republic would remain in their memory, as their eyes now perused the smoking ruins of Hitler's capital. However little their lives were worth, however much life hung by a thread, it was a point of infinite satisfaction to them all to see what Nazi Germany had come to. From Berlin, some, including Conchita's cousin, were sent to Bergen-Belsen; others, including Conchita, went to Oranienburg, where they found themselves face to face with the former Spanish Prime Minister Largo Caballero. They were now put to work with pick and shovel digging trenches and erecting fortifications as the Battle of Berlin moved towards its climax. With the approach of the Russians the last eighty-five women were ordered to join a convoy on the road towards Rostock. They pledged to one another that, whatever happened, they would not abandon anyone too weak to walk; it had an enormous impact on the morale of each. 'It will be over soon. Another small effort,' they told one another again and again. One night they arrived in a pine forest. The trees were young, the branches low. Ramos and twenty-one others darted into a copse. That night the SS opened up with machine-guns, killing all but the twenty-two who lay motionless in the copse. Conchita Ramos was to live and find her way home to Toulouse.[111]

Meanwhile in Mauthausen, the fears of the international committee were not unfounded. We have seen that Ziereis had received an order from Pohl, unquestionably endorsed by Himmler and Kaltenbrunner, to the effect that if the war were lost, not one prisoner was to survive. Ziereis, with responsibility for every camp in Austria, called a meeting in the *Kommandantur* of all his officers and informed them of the order from Berlin. The plan proposed was to assemble all the prisoners in the *Appellplatz* and, at a given moment, open fire with all the machine-guns in the watch-towers, at the same time firing anti-tank grenades into the Blocks to set them ablaze. The resistance got to know about the plan, but it also discovered that the SS were divided on the question of implementing the order, with one side fearing for their future. In their hesitation they were now overtaken by events. Outside Mauthausen, on all roads from the east, droves of deserters and scattered troops were making their way westwards, while SS generals strove to reorganize them and hurl them back into the inferno. Almost all the German and Austrian Greens in Mauthausen, and even some Polish Greens, had by now been incorporated, willy-nilly, into SS units. On 15 April the Red Army was already in Vienna. That morning August Eigruber, the Gauleiter of Oberdonau, was called to the headquarters of General Rendolitsch, Commander-in-Chief of the German forces in that sector. Eigruber was instructed to inform Ziereis that Himmler had agreed to the formation of an SS regiment from the Mauthausen garrison.[112] This unit, stuffed with prisoner volunteers, became known to the prisoners as the Afrikakorps, since the only German uniforms available to them were the old uniforms of Rommel's desert army.[113] Ziereis made a new attempt to enrol the Spaniards, this time with open threats: if they did not follow the example of the Blue Division and fight the Russians, they would forfeit their last chance to survive. The Spaniards again refused, and awaited the usual reprisal; but none came.[114]

Even Nazi Germany could be inconsistent. On 21 April the 490 French, Belgian, Dutch, and Luxemburger women prisoners were ordered to assemble by national groups. They were to be evacuated by the International Red Cross. Until now the IRC had only once been seen at Mauthausen, in 1943, when three trucks driven by Canadian prisoners of war arrived to evacuate 120 Norwegians.[115] When it was now discovered that the IRC still had space in their white trucks for seventy-two more, the places were filled by men of the same nationalities, and by some Canadians.[116] Two further evacuations of Frenchmen, Belgians, and Dutch followed before the end of April.[117] The reason these prisoners were liberated was that certain Nazi leaders, including Himmler, were now trying to negotiate a separate peace with the Western Allies.

Almost the entire French contingent, including Captain Olivier who commanded the seventy-five Frenchmen in the AMI, were thus evacuated. But by a secret arrangement with the International Red Cross, the evacuations proceeded without prejudice to the resistance organization. Precautions were thus taken to replace any evacuated leaders, and Olivier's place was now taken by Emile Valley. Besides, the Frenchmen who left were soon replaced by others transferred from Aussenkommandos in the east (especially Wiener-Neustadt,

Wiener-Neudorf, Schwechat, and Mödling-Hinterbrühl), mainly if not entirely by forced march.[118]

This transfer westwards was part of the general order given by Ziereis on 31 March for the evacuation to Mauthausen not only of Aussenkommandos in the Vienna area but also those at Melk and St Ägyd. The evacuation was entrusted to Streitwieser, who had been given command of several Kommandos in the Vienna area.[119] The inmates of these Kommandos were congregated at Hinterbrühl, south of Vienna, and on the following morning, Easter Sunday, Streitwieser was ready to march them to Mauthausen. Before leaving, on the Saturday night, he ordered a number of prisoner-physicians to administer benzene injections to the fifty-four prisoners who were unable to walk. Every one of them refused, but Streitwieser knew that there would always be willing hands at some lower level of humanity to do his bidding. Indeed, the German red-triangle Georg Goessl, who was Kapo of the *Revier*, did not refuse the order, while the male nurse Karl Sasko, a Green from Vienna, offered his assistance. The injections were supposed to be intracardiac, but Goessl and Sasko lacked experience: most of the time they injected the benzene into the lungs, causing the victim a long and atrocious agony. Goessl cleaned up his mess by strangling those who lingered.

The next morning, Streitwieser realized that he was desperately short of guards: he had just twelve SS left. He therefore decided to enrol German and Spanish Kapos and certain German and Spanish *Prominenten*. The Spaniards refused *en bloc*, whereupon Streitwieser ordered up two machine-guns, trained them on the Spaniards, and gave them ten minutes to decide. In the end the Spaniards yielded. A few were given rifles, the rest clubs. It was a perfect opportunity for a mass break-out, but for reasons not clearly known it was not tried, or at least did not succeed. The column set out, the doctors who had refused the order the night before serving as grave-diggers at the back, and the SS in strategic positions all around. Every day they had to cover some 30 kilometres, with Streitwieser, riding in a red car with his servant Max Ramón, deciding the stops. Two Frenchmen moved to the support of a third who could walk no further. The SS spotted them, ordered them out of the ranks, shot all three in the mouth, and threw the bodies in a ditch. So it continued. On the fourth and fifth days, a torrential downpour turned the road into a marsh. When they reached a bridge over the Danube a short distance from Mauthausen, some prisoners threw themselves into the river and drowned. The column reached Mauthausen at 4 p.m. on 7 April. In seven days of marching 160 prisoners had died, of whom 131 were shot.[120] In another, and longer, evacuation to Mauthausen which lasted eight days, the break-outs led on the second day to the elimination of the stops. From then on the prisoners were covering the 30-kilometre daily march without food or water.[121] In southern Austria, in the Graz region, the prisoners in the Hinterberg Kommando found on 2 April that they were not leaving as usual to excavate the tunnels. Their commandant, SS-Untersturmführer Mirov, issued each inmate with a loaf of bread and began marching them to the *Mutterlager*. The account of their journey is the replication of a theme. To hold a whole loaf in one's hand proved too much of a temptation. The prisoners ate too much too quickly; their stomachs churned, and they began leaving the column to squat on the edge of the road. Since any prisoner who stopped received a bullet, the SS guards made no exception for their condition and shot them as they squatted. This forced the rest to satisfy their physical needs as they marched.[122] Meanwhile, of the 403 prisoners in Floridsdorf on 13 April, 394 had been exterminated by 19 April; the nine survivors were transferred to Mauthausen, two on 15 April and seven on 19 April.[123]

Mauthausen continued to serve as the last depository of every abandoned camp. On the eve of Dachau's liberation on 29 April, a convoy of 4,800 prisoners set out with the same destination; only 180 arrived.[124] On 4 May, only 24 hours before Mauthausen was liberated, another 397 women arrived from the Freiberg Kommando, a subsidiary of *KL*-Flossenburg.[125]

The liquidations continued more frenetically than ever. Nazi Germany was going down, but it was resolved to take with it those who hated and despised it most. In the final days, most of those whose death sentences had been postponed, for one reason or another, were liquidated. Even after the Führer's death, those suspected of complicity in the July bomb plot were still being executed at Mauthausen.[126] However fast the prisoners were being liquidated, the Blocks were still insufficient to accommodate all those who were arriving from the outlying Kommandos, so the Kapos made them lie, head to tail, on straw thrown on the floor. As for the hospital camp, or *Sanitätslager*, it was now the scene of indescribable squalor, with 8,000 sick sleeping five to a bed and with occasional cases of cannibalism.[127] More than 3,000 of these men were transferred to the Blocks of Camp III, at the eastern end of the camp, where there was no water or sanitation at all. Jean Benech, the only French doctor to remain in the camp after the French inmates had been given the opportunity in April to be repatriated, has described the scene he faced: while the sluice no longer functioned, a volume of unregulated water ran into the latrines and carried the filth over the ground, for prisoners to splash through in their bare feet. Some 800 of those transferred to Camp III were led to the gas chamber and put to death. The remainder were left without palliasses and given no food at all. The collapse of discipline served to revive old hatreds among the various national groups. Once again it was the Spaniards who, in the view of a non-Spaniard, behaved the best and contributed the most to a reduction in the tension.[128]

The SS still hesitated to initiate a massacre, for fear of the reaction of the mass.[129] Nor were the officers entirely sure of their troops, since too many of them had only recently been inducted, and by force. This vital matter was known to the resistance: some SS were saying they were opposed to such inhuman action, others that if it occurred they would fight on the other side, and others promised the resistance that if the decision were taken they would at once make it known. While all this was reassuring, there were nevertheless reports that large quantities of gas had arrived in Mauthausen and that the SS had reinforced their night watch.

Starvation and exhaustion now took an unprecedented toll, since no more food supplies were delivered to the camp. No fewer than 4,147 prisoners died in the week before the Liberation.[130] In addition to the hundreds who died each day of 'natural' causes, some 500 or 600 exhausted prisoners were sent daily to the gas chamber.[131] Since the crematoria were incapable of handling such a quantity of corpses, the bodies piled up in pyramids, and enormous ditches had to be dug to bury them. At the same time, the Nazis could no longer conceal their own predicament, when thousands of prisoners were now assigned to digging fortifications around the village and camp of Mauthausen; a few days later these same fortifications would be manned by the prisoners themselves.[132] Their predicament was further seen in the way they began the destruction of the material evidence, first by murdering the prisoners they had employed in the gas chamber and the crematoria,[133] then throwing all the SS records into the crematoria—this order, originating from General Glücks, was passed down by Niedermayer to Ramón Bargueño and the other two Spaniards working under him in the *Bunker*[134]—and finally, by attempting to destroy the gas chamber and the crematoria themselves.[135]

It is probable that the SS would still have set about liquidating the entire camp population if they had not feared for their personal safety. No doubt they suspected that several prisoners were armed and resolute. In fact, the lack of arms was the prisoners' main concern: the Spaniards had only two pistols, some knives, and some cudgels.[136] Add to that the Minimax fire-extingushers—each Block had two—which could blind a sentry, together with an assortment of rubber gloves, wire-cutters, ladders, axes, ropes, and grappling hooks.[137] But the claim that they had much more seems to be an example of deliberate untruth.[138] In any event, the SS had received their orders to engage in what was to most of them a novel experience: military combat. For years they had lived the pretence of being *Übermenschen* among *Untermenschen*. Now came the chance to prove it.

There was little attempt to preserve such a fiction. Mauthausen had become virtually the last refuge for Nazi fugitives fleeing from east, west, north, and south. Elegant limousines arrived from Vienna, carrying Nazi officials and their women draped in sumptuous fur blankets.[139] On the night of 2–3 May, individual SS members began deserting the *Lager*, dressed in civilian clothes. Others followed on the morning of 3 May, in groups and in uniform, both in Mauthausen and in Gusen. Their pretext was that they were off to fight the Russians. In fact, it was only a very small part of the Mauthausen garrison that led its 'Afrikakorps' into line against the Red Army, and there is no evidence that it fought an actual engagement either with the Russians or with the Americans.[140] The rest, led by the senior officers, fled to the woods or mountains, either taking their families or abandoning them.

Ziereis stayed just long enough to hand over the command of *KL*-Mauthausen and Gusen, on 3 May, to Hauptmann Kern, who arrived at the head of a police formation of the Vienna fire department.[141] That afternoon, Ramón Bargueño and the other two Spaniards working in the *Bunker* were ordered to carry the suitcases of the SS officers to cars waiting outside the camp. The officers would now show the way. '*Meine Ehre heisst Treue*', the sacred motto of the SS, had entered oblivion.

For the last several months, Ziereis had neglected both his *Lager* and his family to live with August Eigruber, the Gauleiter of Oberdonau, quartered in Linz. It was the renewal of an old friendship: it was Eigruber who had proposed Ziereis for his last promotion and for the award of the Silver Cross. They had been travelling between Linz and Vienna, drinking and visiting brothels, in a vain attempt to escape the hell they had created. On the morning of 3 May,[142] Ziereis ordered his wife Ida to pack the bags. With her three children she got into their limousine and found Schulz and his mistress, the typist Neugebauer, already inside. Later, to her horror, Ida Ziereis also found, hidden under blankets, Schulz's prisoner-servant, the Czech Johan Krutis. They drove to the Phyrn Pass near Spittal, and stopped at Ziereis's hunting lodge. In the baskets they had brought there was enough food for several days. The next day Schulz announced that he intended to return to Mauthausen. His secretary and prisoner-servant disappeared a few days later. As for Ziereis, he appeared and disappeared without any explanation.[143]

Schulz's decision to return to Mauthausen might have been an expression of remorse. Whether he knew it or not, his flight had been a grievous disappointment to the subordinates who trusted him, and a portrait of him had been ripped from an office wall and smashed.[144] Alternatively, but less probably, he was concerned about his wife and children. In any event, when he arrived, he found the camp in American hands. He then made use of the uniform of a SS-Unterscharführer and false papers in the name of Kurt Müller. In the company of one of his maids he drove to a friend's house in Bad-Ischl. He was suffering from severe stomach cramps, but under his false identity he succeeded in getting treatment in an American hospital train which took him to Heidelberg. In Heidelberg, he entered a clinic and found a cure. The Bird of Death walked out a free man.[145]

In the case of Bachmayer, the collapse of Nazi Germany came as a shock. Walking into the *Schreibstube*, he put the pathetic question to Juan de Diego: 'What's going to happen to my wife?' De Diego did not reply. Bachmayer repeated his question, then broke down and cried on de Diego's shoulder. Bachmayer was prepared to shoot, but not at the Russians. He left the *Lager*, met his wife and two young daughters in the house near Schwertberg where they had taken refuge, and drove to Altenberg, near Perg. There, in the tradition set by Josef Goebbels, Bachmayer blew out the brains of his wife and children before turning the weapon on himself.[146] Dr Rudolf Lohnauer, the director of Hartheim, followed suit on 5 May.[147] The last victims of the *KZ* system were thus the innocent children of the assassins.

Meanwhile in the *Lager* on 3 May, it was a time of extreme ambiguity. When Bargueño and his two comrades returned to the *Bunker* after carrying the suitcases of the SS officers, they found a Wehrmacht captain left in charge. He was weeping and insisting that he was innocent of the crimes committed there. The Spaniards, who had picked up the keys of the cells left lying on the ground by the departing SS, disarmed him and told him to leave. The AMI was now poised to strike, but only in self-defence: there were still enough SS in the camp to make any confrontation suicidal for the prisoners.[148]

The departure of the remainder of the SS was conducted with such stealth that the fact was not known by the prisoners until the following morning, 4 May. The international committee at once delegated two of its members, the Austrians Dr Heinrich Dürmayer and Hans Maršálek, to win a promise from Hauptmann Kern to keep all guards outside the inner camp. At 2 p.m. that afternoon, the international committee formally took authority from Kern for the administration of the fortress and the outlying *Sanitätslager*.[149] Kern gave a further promise that he would defend the camp against any attempt by the

SS to force its way back inside. On this question the prisoners were not reassured, for it was known that SS guards had joined forces with Waffen-SS units, that they were in strength and not far off, along the Enns river on the right bank of the Danube. The SS units might well fall back in retreat, and with tanks and flame-throwers set about the final massacre. In such a situation the international committee could not trust in the good intentions of Hauptmann Kern, and if the police refused to hand over their arms the prisoners resolved to seize them.[150] A group of Catalans meanwhile lassoed the bronze eagle over the swastika above the garage gate and wrenched it to the ground. That night, at the main gate, from the tower above the orderly room, the Red Flag fluttered as the international symbol of resistance to fascism. But it was the Spaniards who carried off the finest prize. Muñoz, the camp painter, produced a long white cloth with the words, unapologetically in Spanish: '*Los españoles antifascistas saludan a las fuerzas liberadoras!*'[151] Were the liberators to come from the east or the west? Or from the south? Some 900 prisoners, forced to march from Loibl-Pass and Klagenfurt, were liberated at Freistritz, near Kärnten, by the Jugoslavs.[152]

No survivor was ever to forget, as long as he lived, the fifth of May. The morning dawned majestic upon the grey-silver Danube and its valley clothed in a misty veil. The spring sunshine, the mountain greenery, the dark pines, the snowy crests, all seemed in retrospect like the birth of a new life. On this magnificent morning, just before midday, a white car of the IRC, escorted by two US armoured scout-cars, arrived on the road from Linz, drove up the camp approach, and stopped at the *Sanitätslager*. The Americans could not believe their eyes. As from some mass grave reopened, the survivors stumbled towards them, living skeletons, half naked, quite naked, or in filthy rags. They clapped their hands without speaking. Their hands were so emaciated, thought one of the Americans, that it sounded like the clapping of seals.[153] The two half-tracks continued up to the fortress gates. There was no resistance from the Schutzpolizei or any other Austrian unit. On the contrary, the sight of the Americans was enough to disperse the Austrian police. The US patrol, which was under orders to reconnoitre more closely to the German lines, left five hours later. Meanwhile, the 4,200 prisoners of Linz III who were able to walk had set out that day at 7.30 a.m. on a march to the *Mutterlager*. That afternoon they were liberated by American troops near Urfahr.[154]

On the same afternoon of 5 May, the international committee held an open meeting and elected Dr Dürmayer as its president. The combat groups decided not to wait for the SS to return, but instead went off in hot pursuit. As many as 3,000 prisoners could now be equipped with the arms seized from the SS armoury. Under the command of the Austrian Colonel Heinrich Kodré and the Soviet Major Andreī Pirogov, they occupied Mauthausen village, seizing the Nazi Bürgermeister and replacing him with an anti-Nazi. But the nearby railway and road bridges were still in the hands of the SS, and since they were the last two Nazi-held bridges across the Danube, they were vital to any Nazi unit trying to make its way across to the right bank and the safety and opportunity of the so-called Alpen-Festung, the redoubt that never was. Emile Valley, who would later become president of the French survivors' association, asserts that the night of 5–6 May was the most anguished night of all they went through. Razola writes of battles raging 50–60 kilometres to the east and south-east, with strong SS units less than 10 kilometres away.[155] Indeed, the units in the immediate area included the lst SS-Panzerdivision ('Leibstandarte Adolf Hitler'), still capable of anything, including a retreat to the fortress of Mauthausen and the massacre of all its survivors.[156] An attack on Pirogov's force at Mauthausen village was beaten back, but among those who fell were two Spaniards, Badia and Juan Bisbal Costa, at the very moment of their liberation.[157]

At a meeting of the military staff held on the same day, Major Pirogov, who presided, reported that SS units were attempting to cross the Enns. He argued that it would be a mistake for the group to engage in open battle. Its strength would be better used in the pursuit of SS fugitives and in preparation for the defence of the fortress, which had to be held whatever the cost, until the first Allies arrived. In the late afternoon of 5 May, a unit under the command of Lieutenant-Colonel Richard R. Seibel, attached to the US llth Armored Division of Patton's 3rd Army, entered the gates, passing under the banner erected by the Spanish Republicans and through the frenzied cries of the survivors as they hugged one another, wept, and sang, the Spaniards that most joyous of anthems, the 'Himno de Riego', and everyone the single word, whether *Freiheit! Svoboda! Wolnosc! Szabadsag!* or *Libertad!* Some danced or hopped around, some screamed hysterically, some broke down in tears. As for the Vienna police, the wheel had turned full circle since the day when Nazi culture first arrived in Austria and Austrian policemen helped the Gestapo dispatch their victims to the camps. Without resisting they were now disarmed, the officers fleeing, and their men rather content to be excused from duty in this way.[158]

Not all the inmates laughed and sang. An inmate doctor has affirmed that at the time the SS left Mauthausen there was no water left at all.[159] Seven hundred corpses lay rotting in the alleys, awaiting burial or incineration. Among the living, many who had waited so long for this moment now lacked the emotional power either to laugh or weep, being instead barely conscious in their joy, while joy itself could be a cause of death, the sudden release from tension proving fatal to some prisoners.[160] More than 450 survivors continued to die every day until 10 May. According to the last roll-call taken by the SS, on 4 May 1945, Mauthausen's total prisoner population stood at 66,534, including 1,734 women.[161] At that time there were still 264 Green and 120 Black Kapos.[162] By 11 May the number of ex-prisoners evacuated from Mauthausen proper had far exceeded the number of ex-prisoners who had arrived, with the result that the camp then contained only 15,211 men and 2,079 women; of the men, 14,741 were Reds and 470 Greens—whether former Kapos or not, but surviving Green Kapos would be rare, now that retribution had begun.[163] We must add to these figures the populations of Mauthausen's various Aussenkommandos, especially Ebensee (with 13,000, including 2,500 critically ill, on 7 May) and Gusen (with 8,000, including 1,000 critically ill, on the same day).[164] As for the Spaniards, of the total of over 7,000 interned in Mauthausen and all its Kommandos, fewer than 2,400 were still alive.[165]

The two Aussenkommandos Gusen and Ebensee were special, not only because *KZ* life there, as we have seen, was the hardest trial of all, but because these two were so situated between the Soviet and the American advance that they were the very last to be liberated. Since their prisoner populations were now the largest, their experience in May 1945 was also the most dramatic.

Even in Gusen there was a resistance movement, and it was again the Spaniards, housed in Block 9, who were in the forefront of it. The groundwork was laid by Santiago Raga, until his transfer back to Mauthausen *Mutterlager* in February 1942. Others who helped to organize it were Amadeo Cinca Vendrell and Patricio Serrano. Despite the difficulties and the risks, prisoners succeeded in spiriting some weapons out of the workshops, removing them piece by piece and screw by screw.[166]

Any resistance movement at Gusen had to overcome, before anything else, the sense of impending doom, which was probably stronger there than anywhere but Ebensee. The vast tunnels seemed to beckon like enormous tombs. Whole camp populations could be buried alive. Add to that the squalor of Gusen I, where the *Muselmänner* were more in evidence than anywhere else in Austria. The SS figures for 27 March 1945 show a population for Gusen I of 10,415; Gusen II, 10,893; and Gusen III, 304.[167] Given the evacuation westwards of the Kommandos in eastern Austria, it is possible that Gusen contained at the end, as Pappalettera recount, a higher population than Mauthausen itself, and in a smaller space.[168] More than 37,000 prisoners died in the Gusen camps alone,[169] and the scene in April 1945 is described by Vilanova: the sick lying naked, three to a filthy bunk, on a mattress of straw and muck, suffering from typhus, dysentery, tuberculosis, pneumonia, and more diseases besides than can be listed, and each bunk sharing a single blanket stained with urine, soup, excrement, and blood.[170] Block 31, known as the 'Bahnhof' and used for those suffering from dysentery, was the worst of all: the victims lay on the ground where they were flung, covered in their own excrement and that of others, denied food, and left to die.[171]

From the evidence presented by the IRC delegate who spoke with Ziereis in April 1945, we know that Ziereis passed on an order to Seidler to liquidate the populations of Gusen I and II, estimated at some 40,000 people, by stacking twenty-four tons of dynamite in advance in the tunnels of the underground factories, herding the prisoners inside, and then blowing up the entrances.[172] We may suppose, though proof is lacking, that Seidler intended to carry out this massacre when he invited the prison population to take refuge in the tunnels at Kellerbau (Gusen I) and Bergkristall (Gusen II). The prisoners certainly did not comply. In any event, the prisoners were in control at the time the first Allied vehicle, a US tank, reached St Georgen from Linz. Before returning to Linz, the Americans asked the prisoners to stay in place. But the situation was already out of hand. There was nothing similar at Gusen to the AMI in Mauthausen. Some 20,000 prisoners, with the Poles being the most numerous, were under no authority. Led by their Kapos they appropriated the arms abandoned by the fleeing SS and terrorized the camp. Fights broke out among ex-prisoners that left several dead, at the very moment of their liberation. The food depots and supplies were pillaged. Some of the Kapos responsible for crimes under the SS barricaded themselves in Block 32, before deciding to kill themselves; others were torn apart by the prisoners they had tormented. Most of the prisoners made for Mauthausen, but others like Amadeo Cinca Vendrell preferred to flee, changing their rags for civilian clothes and making their way to Linz, and from there to Innsbruck. As for Seidler, Ziereis on his death-bed branded him a coward, claiming that when Seidler left Gusen with his force of SS he watched the unit through his field glasses, and instead of fighting the Americans he let his men surrender without firing a shot. Seidler himself chose to emulate Goebbels, Bachmayer, and Dr Lohnauer, by murdering his wife and children before putting a bullet through his own brain.[173]

At Ebensee, the population had also swollen with the arrival of those evacuated from other Kommandos, especially Melk,[174] and the total in April 1945 had passed 18,000. The mortality rate, on the other hand, was rising commensurately: from 705 in January 1945, it rose to 1,852 in February and to 4,587 in April.[175] The bread ration at that time had been cut by half for those working, and by two-thirds for those too sick to work. As a result, men working in the tunnels were reduced to chewing the pitch used for the manufacture of synthetic fuel,[176] and cannibalism broke out in Block 26. Cannibalism was the one inmate reaction that caused the SS to worry, since it told them they were losing control. In the closing weeks, the death toll reached and even exceeded 300 a day.[177] But with no reduction in the influx, the population of Ebensee on the day of liberation stood between 16,400[178] and 16, 650, including 7,566 sick.[179]

The liberation of Ebensee, like that of Mauthausen and Gusen, was virtually self-accomplished. A rudimentary resistance organization had been established. A Spanish committee was headed by Felipe Martínez, and an international committee was composed of the German Konrad Wegner, the Frenchman Jean Laffitte (representing also the Spaniards and Belgians), the Jugoslav Hrvoje Macanovic (representing also the Poles), and the Czech Drahomir Barta (representing also the Soviets). The Spaniard Augusto Havez, evacuated from Melk, was later added to the committee, giving the Spaniards direct representation.[180] The committee members succeeded in listening in to Allied wireless bulletins. They also succeeded in pilfering some dynamite and seven pistols. Some 200 volunteers still in a fit state to fight were organized into two combat groups, under Soviet, French, and Spanish officers; one of the groups was exclusively communist and all the pistols were in their hands.[181]

What had been offered to the Spaniards elsewhere was now repeated at Ebensee. Lagerführer Julius Anton Ganz ordered them to assemble on the *Appellplatz* and offered them their freedom if they agreed to enrol in the Waffen-SS and fight the Russians. There was a long pause. 'Well, I'm waiting', cried Ganz. A Spaniard finally stepped forward: '¡Todos!' At once, all the Spaniards joined him. It was undoubtedly a spontaneous, unthinking gesture of solidarity and defiance, and it served to infuriate Ganz. 'I don't want all of you!' he yelled, and ordered the SS to select 92. The action placed the Spaniards in a most unwanted position and led to bitter recriminations, but it seems clear that they never intended to wear a Nazi uniform, and they soon enough found a way out of their predicament.[182]

The prisoners of Ebensee now faced the same prospect that confronted those at Gusen. The committee had already sent an anonymous warning to the SS, through the *Prominenten* in the *Schreibstube* and the barber's shop, suggesting the advantages to the SS of forgoing either an evacuation or a final bloodbath. At this point in the war there was nowhere left to which the SS could evacuate Ebensee, but the use to which the SS might put the tunnels was not lost on any inmate. On 3 May, after the evening muster, a member of the committee was approached by a certain Josef Poltrum, an Austrian non-commissioned officer who headed an anti-Nazi group in the Wehrmacht unit to which he belonged.[183] Poltrum informed him that a locomotive loaded with 40 kilos of dynamite had been placed at the entrance to one of the tunnels used for shelter from air attack.[184]

The fateful day arrived.[185] By 4 a.m. on 4 May the international committee had been informed of the plan to exterminate the camp. The message went out from the committee not to follow any SS order. At 8 a.m., Ganz, his voice breaking with rage, announced to a general muster that the SS staff had decided to fight to the end against the Americans. To save themselves from the crossfire, Ganz added, all the prisoners were to take shelter inside Tunnel 5. This tunnel, designed for the production of synthetic fuel, was indeed so enormous that the entire population of Ebensee could fit inside. The order in itself was not unusual: there had been many air-raid warnings at Ebensee, as many as seven in a single day, and the prison population had regularly taken refuge in the tunnels, though usually in Tunnel 6.[186] But this day was different, and Ganz was answered by a massive refusal to move. A sudden eerie silence hung over the field, broken only by the sound of the twenty SS guards surrounding Ganz as they cocked their sub-machine-guns. Hundreds more watched from the towers or waited outside the camp. Ganz walked up and down the ranks, the SS guards around him levelling their guns at the prisoners. Then, suddenly, Ganz and his escort withdrew; the SS was never to enter the camp again. The Kapos, now unprotected by the SS, walked nervously in groups, looking desperately for an escape. The SS were still in the towers and the Kapos were strong, their dogs powerful, but they were surrounded by famished wolves. They were now in cold panic. The lynchings began that evening. Starving men, consumed with the rage for vengeance, found the strength to hurl themselves on their tormentors, gouging out their eyes, crushing their skulls, opening their bellies.[187] The following morning the SS still encircled the camp, but inside the camp the prisoners were in full control. Both sides feared the strength of the other. But now the SS guards were replaced by old Wehrmacht soldiers and men of the Vienna *Volksturm*, albeit in SS uniforms. The day of 5 May was to see the last muster within the *KZ* archipelago. At noon the next day, the first Allied troops were sighted on the road at the end of the valley. As the last SS guards abandoned the towers and made for the hills, a US Army unit entered Ebensee on Sunday, 6 May at 2.45 p.m.[188]

The very last *Lager* in the *KZ* archipelago had been liberated. But again, not all who had survived to the day of liberation would reap the benefit: 700 were beyond help and died in the days that followed. The rest could be grateful: Tunnel 5 had indeed been designated as their tomb. A Spaniard known only by the name of Antonio, while scouring the area, found a locomotive at the tunnel's entrance packed with 5 tons of dynamite ready to be detonated; the charge was considered ten times the amount necessary to seal the tunnel.[189] As for Ganz, it was widely believed by the prisoners that he was dead, killed in the mountains by his own SS.[190] Instead, he escaped, and it would be twenty years before he was uncovered. Of his 400 Kapos, fifty-two were killed, many of them in the same brutal style in which they lived. The Oberkapo Otto was grabbed by the Spaniards in the *Revier* and cut into ribbons.[191] The Kapo they knew as 'el Gitano' had his eyes torn out and his legs broken; whimpering for mercy he found none, and a young Russian lifted a 20-kilo rock, positioned it over the Kapo's head, then let it drop; it cracked his skull like a nut.[192] Colonel Seibel, commanding the US Army unit, set out to restore order, but he also ordered the villagers of Ebensee to walk through the camp and view the evidence, and as elsewhere he set them to work burying the dead.[193]

While the ex-inmates of Mauthausen were delighted to see the local villagers ordered by Colonel Seibel to clean up the camps,[194] there was resentment over Seibel's statement that Mauthausen had been 'uncovered in the course of a military action, which explains why nothing had been prepared'. It was not forgotten that in the early afternoon of 15 April 1945, Allied reconnaissance planes had flown over the *Mutterlager* at an altitude so low that those on the ground could see the men in the cockpit.[195] Even more invidious was the spectacle of American officers walking around with cameras taking photos of the dying.[196] While the Allied services worked valiantly to save lives, the suspicion remained that more would have been saved if the necessary preparations had been made. According to a doctor, the Americans fed the prisoners high-fat soups, oblivious to the danger of allowing starving men to decide how much to eat at a time. Glucose serum was tried, but the supplies arrived too late.[197] On 7 June 1945, after all the Soviet prisoners had been repatriated, the population had fallen to 5,200 (including 850 women) of whom 1,621 were still under medical care; of these, some 4,000 were Poles, Italians, or Germans.[198] The Spaniards had by then returned to France via Switzerland, travelling either to Paris or to Lyons and Toulouse.[199] While joy was unconfined, there were some psychological problems ahead for many of the Kapos and *Prominenten* who survived. As for the worthy villagers of Mauthausen, in whose taverns the SS had been carousing every night for years, they had a single refrain: all that had happened on the hill came as a dreadful shock to them.[200]

From the moment that Mauthausen and its last Kommandos were liberated, the hunt began for the SS and the Kapos who had fled or hidden. The Kapos did less well, since they lacked the means of escape, especially 'King Kong', whose physical bulk would stand out even in the Tyrol. 'King Kong' had escaped being lynched at Ebensee by fleeing in time; he now saved his neck by turning witness for the prosecution at the Dachau trial.[201] At first the international committee was hard put to prevent the lynching not only of Kapos but also of collaborators and suspected informers.[202] Chony, the quarry Kapo, and Marion, the Baukommando Kapo, were seized and executed on the night of 5–6 May. Karl the Kapellmeister and 'Popeye' were beaten to death. The Oberkapo Lorenz was shot. Others were dragged to the *Appellplatz* where the prisoners jumped on their bodies with their clogs, or used their clogs to beat them senseless.[203] The Spaniard Tomás was also executed. It is worth noting that the Spaniards were the only national group to pursue, immediately after the Liberation, those of their fellow-countrymen who had collaborated with the SS; those who had murdered or who were accomplices to murder were brought before special courts, and if found guilty, sentenced to death and executed.[204] But most of the criminal Kapos slipped away as the craving for food tugged harder on the pursuers than the thirst for revenge,[205] and Vilanova estimates that fewer than a tenth of the 530 Kapos guilty of murder paid for their crimes.[206]

Only a small number of SS were captured in the manhunt, but to the joy of all those still in the camp they included Standartenführer Franz Ziereis. On the evening of 23 May, a US Army patrol, with a Spanish and a Czech ex-prisoner serving as auxiliaries, was crossing open country in the Spittal area when they spotted a man who tried to hide when he saw them coming. He was arrested as a suspect. Although wearing civilian clothes and a beard, he was recognized at once by the ex-prisoners. The Americans took him back to Mauthausen, where Maršálek and Boix assisted at his interrogation, the former serving as German–English interpreter.[207] Ziereis cavilled and whimpered that it was not his fault, that he had merely carried out orders. The ex-prisoners began to suspect that this argument might just possibly impress the Americans, that they would detain him for a long time to extract information, but that in the end they would set him free. As a result, Ziereis was deliberately given a chance to escape, and took it. The Americans opened fire on him, but only to warn him. The Spaniards and Czechs, on the other hand, aimed directly at him, and hit him, once in the left arm and once in the back, the bullet passing through his body. He was rushed to the US military hospital at Gusen, but it was no use: the bullet had perforated his intestines. The next day he was dead, but not before leaving behind a signed final statement in which he admitted that Himmler had given the order, through Kaltenbrunner, to wall up three of the four exits in one of Gusen's tunnels and then exterminate the populations of Gusen I and II. Ziereis made no reference to the other camps, and claimed he had refused to execute Himmler's order.[208] His death was painless compared with those he caused, and it denied justice its due process, but post-war events suggest that Ziereis might well have retained or regained his freedom had he escaped and hidden. Hans Killermann, for example, who had been promoted to Rapportführer at Gusen for his skill on the gong at Mauthausen, was never found.[209]

SS-Standartenführer Walter Rauff, the inventor of the mobile gas chamber, was indeed found, but he certainly was not held. Rauff was arrested in Milan by US troops on 30 April 1945, and interned in the detention camp in Rimini. What happened after that is still in dispute. Rauff himself revealed (in a deposition addressed to the Supreme Court of Chile in December 1962) that he escaped from the camp in Rimini at the end of 1946 with the help of a German prioress who then hid him in a Franciscan monastery. With her help he made his way to Naples, and there received further help from the Church to get to Rome. He then spent the next eighteen months as a refugee in the Vatican City, living in convents and teaching French and mathematics in the Via Pia orphanage in Rome. Meanwhile the Vatican made arrangements for Rauff's wife and two children, then in the Soviet Zone of Germany, to join him. It should be remembered that by then the Nuremberg Tribunal had not only sentenced Rauff *in absentia* to death but had turned him into a figure of world-class infamy. From Rome, again with the help of the Vatican, the Rauff family moved to Damascus, where Rauff worked variously for a Syrian family and as military adviser to the Syrian Government. In 1949 the family moved to Ecuador, and in 1958 to Chile. There, under his own name, he ran the profitable Sara Braun canned-fish factory in Punta Arenas.[210] On 13 March 1961 a warrant for his arrest was issued by the magistrates' court in Hanover, and France, the Federal Republic of Germany, and Israel all appealed for his extradition. The Supreme Court of Chile, having received Rauff's deposition, responded that Chile's fifteen-year period of limitations had now expired. In May

1984 Rauff died a natural death in Santiago, but three months before he died a top-secret US State Department report, dated 1947, was obtained by the American historian Charles R. Allen Jr. The report, whose authenticity was at once confirmed by the US National Archives, had been compiled by Vincent La Vista, a US Foreign Service officer in Rome. The report referred to Opera San Raffaelle, the Vatican's organization of emigration aid, as 'the largest single organization involved in the illegal movement of emigrants, including Nazis'. The only prerequisites fixed by the Vatican, the report concluded, were that the applicant be anti-communist and able to prove himself a Catholic. Three months after this report was revealed, and only days after the death of Rauff, a very different account was made public by John Loftus, a former investigator for the US Department of Justice who had specialized in tracking down Nazi criminals. According to Loftus, Rauff had been approached even before the war had ended by Allen Dulles, then head of the Geneva branch of the OSS (and later first head of the CIA). Quoting what he said were also top-secret documents, Loftus reported that Rauff in Milan had agreed to surrender all SS forces under his control in return for a promise from Dulles that he and other SS officers would not be prosecuted as war criminals. Rauff was duly released from Allied custody in April 1945, and in return worked for Dulles in anti-communist operations in Italy, an area in which the former Sipo-SD officer was supremely qualified. While the Vatican provided Rauff with food, shelter, and identity cards, concluded Loftus, it did the same for all refugees; 'its contribution to helping Nazis was minimal, since the work of smuggling them across national frontiers was handled by Dulles and his contacts'.[211]

Justice came to some others among Mauthausen's killers in the form of two trials, the first at Dachau in 1946 and the second in Cologne in 1966–7. The former was conducted while the United States held jurisdiction in Bavaria; the second, after the creation of the Federal Republic of Germany. In the former case, it should be noted that the United States courts limited their jurisdiction to crimes committed from 1 January 1942, insisting on their lack of competence to examine events preceding the entry of the United States into the war. Thus all crimes committed at Mauthausen from August 1938 up to 31 December 1941 lay outside the purview of the trial. This was particularly galling to the Spaniards, since most of those who died succumbed in the period between August 1940 and the end of 1941. Francesc Boix, who provided the court with the photographs, asked that Constante appear as a witness. Constante took all the necessary steps to do so, and was supported by Frédéric Ricol, the current president of the Association des déportés français. The United States authorities everywhere received him politely, but they were adamant: no Spaniard was permitted to enter the American Zone of Germany. It was a blunder of the worst kind, and it would not be forgotten.[212]

Of the sixty-one SS members tried at Dachau and found guilty, fifty-eight were sentenced to hanging and three to life imprisonment; of those, nine were pardoned and the remainder hanged in May and June 1947. A distinguishing feature of the trial was that not one of the accused—including Grimm, Niedermayer, Trum, the three senior SS doctors of Mauthausen, and Vetter of Gusen, all of whom were hanged—had the courage of a true Nazi to defend his actions on ideological grounds. The only motives revealed were those of self-advancement, self-aggrandizement,[213] and self-preservation. Nor for that matter did the condemned men, with one single exception,[214] show any sign of remorse before mounting the gallows.[215]

Of the sixty or more Lagerführer in the Mauthausen complex, only two—Julius Ludolf of Melk and Heinrich Haeger of Gunskirchen—found themselves in the dock at Dachau. Chmielewski and Ganz were conspicuously absent. So were Schulz and Streitwieser, and it was many years before justice caught up with these four. Streitwieser had escaped from Mauthausen on 5 May on a motor-cycle driven by his subordinate SS-Scharführer Hans Bühner. Bühner was discovered when, after going to the trouble of excising the SS tattoo in his armpit, he was recognized in 1946 by a Mauthausen survivor while travelling in a train in the French Zone of Germany; he was promptly arrested by the French military police.[216] As for Streitwieser, he made his way to his parents' home near Laufen, where American troops discovered and arrested him. He was interned in the concentration camp at Auerbach, in Bavaria, where some prisoners, for reasons unknown, wore US Army uniforms. Streitwieser appropriated one of the uniforms, added to it the insignia of an American officer, and walked out of the main gate past the American guards, who saluted him. He rejoined his wife Kate and, with false papers taken out in Kate's maiden name, Klaus Werner Krug became one of the most successful taxi-rank owners in Cologne. Only as a result of denunciations was he finally identified and arrested, on 6 July 1956. He remained in prison until 21 November 1966 when he found himself on trial in Cologne in the company of an old friend, Karl Schulz, the Bird of Death.[217]

After he walked out of the clinic in Heidelberg under the name of Kurt Müller, Schulz had continued with that identity, mainly as porter at the Hotel Nuenzig in Cologne, until the day in 1946 when he thought he could benefit from an amnesty and gave himself up. It was a serious miscalculation: he was arrested, and remained in prison for twenty years, awaiting his trial.[218]

As for Chmielewski and Ganz, the former had not fared so well after his transfer from Gusen to Holland. He was accused of embezzling military equipment and was expelled from the SS. After the war he managed to live in Austria under a false identity until his discovery and arrest in 1956. Brought to trial at Ansbach in 1961, he was sentenced to life imprisonment.[219] The same sentence was handed down to his henchman Jentzsch, the 'Bademeister' of Gusen; arrested in Berlin, where he had set himself up as a building entrepreneur, he was brought to trial in Hagen in 1967.[220] As for Ganz of Ebensee, the world long believed him dead, shot by his own men in the Tyrolean mountains, until in April 1966 he was recognized by a Czech survivor. He was then in Stuttgart, at the head of a large transport company, living under a false name. He was denounced and quickly arrested, just as the Cologne trial was beginning, but too late to be included in it.[221]

The two Spanish *Prominenten*, Climent Sarrion and Juan de Diego, both attended the Cologne trial as witnesses. They heard Schulz deplore in court 'the senseless hatred of the former prisoners who would like to bring ruin on any of the SS of Mauthausen who are still alive'. The trial, he added, was a staged production: 'At least 80 per cent of Germany repudiates these trials'. Neither Schulz nor Streitwieser showed the slightest remorse, and Kate Streitwieser was even found to have suborned some of the German and Austrian witnesses. In the end, Streitwieser was sentenced to life imprisonment, and Schulz to fifteen years. Both were then provisionally released, 'for reasons of health'.[222] Schulz and Streitwieser were the grand beneficiaries of the changing times, the 'new dangers', the desire to forget the old,[223] and that particular fuzziness of mind that claims it does no good to rake the ashes of the past: the Nazis have suffered more than enough.[224] And so it came to pass that of the 15,000 SS of Mauthausen who murdered up to 200,000 prisoners[225] in the most ignominious of ways, fewer than 200 paid for it with their lives.

EPILOGUE
Rendezvous in Toulouse

I know how men in exile feed on barren hope.[1] . . .

From Mauthausen, from Mexico, from Moscow, from all the points elsewhere, Spanish exiles converged on France, a country they had known only in adversity and suffering, but still the country known for the rights of man, and the country closest to where they most wanted to be: Spain—but a Spain free of Franco and Falange. Many an amnesty would be offered by Franco from 1945 to his death in 1975, but few were the exiles who returned.

Most of the Nazi concentration camps where the Spaniards had been held were situated either in the southern half of Germany or in Austria, and they were liberated therefore by the Americans. The language barrier between the liberators and the liberated created problems, but in Dachau the US forces included some Mexican-Americans with whom the Spaniards could converse. The Mexicans, thought the Spaniards, knew next to nothing about fascism or democracy, but they learned about it all soon enough by seeing the reality of the camps. Other Spaniards were struck by what they considered the liberators' excessive concern for hygiene. It was one thing, they thought, to spray them with DDT before they climbed into the trucks, but it was another to issue some of them with SS uniforms (with only the insignia removed) on the grounds that their *Drillich* had to be burned and there were no other clothes to give them. At least one Spaniard who could find no clothes in his size was forced to wear his SS uniform all the way to Toulouse.[2] Lack of transportation or the zeal of bureaucrats explains why prisoners liberated in April did not arrive back in France until as late as 5 June. The Spaniards were also conscious of being treated differently on arrival. For the returning Frenchmen and Frenchwomen there were ceremonies and festivals, but no Spanish political organization paid any tribute to the Spanish survivors. On the contrary, in some places they were received like carriers of some deadly plague. Such treatment made them the more grateful to General Leclerc, who met at least one convoy of Spanish survivors on their arrival in Paris. He had known Spaniards in every campaign, in the Battle of France, in Chad, in Libya, in Tunis, and in the liberation of Paris: 'Everywhere I go,' he told them, 'I seem to meet you.' Meeting them there, in that pathetic state, a battle-hardened general was moved to tears.[3]

While some returning survivors passed through Mulhouse or Lyons on a direct route to Toulouse, most passed through Paris. They were directed to the Hôtel Lutétia, which had only recently served the Gestapo and now served as a sorting centre for all returning deportees. Captain Robert Dubois, a French Army officer who had been a prisoner of war in Germany, was selected by the Prefect of Seine to take charge of the Spanish survivors, and was assisted in this by Madame Riquelme, the wife of the general, and vice-president of the Spanish Republican Red Cross.[4] The reception at the Lutétia was the subject of further grievance, even among the French who were no doubt treated the best. After a shower and disinfection, wrote one, they dressed again in the same costume they had worn from Mauthausen, which was still damp from the disinfection. A cup of hot chocolate, some croissants, a parade in front of innumerable desks, answering endless questions, with files checked and cross-checked, and several hours later, a free travel pass and permission to return home.[5]

For the Spaniards in the Lutétia, home meant one of the two centres which Madame Riquelme administered and kept open until 1948. One of these was the Centre Gallet, a former garage at 165 rue de Vaugirard in Paris; the other was the Centre Montrouge, in the suburbs to the south. A Spanish medical centre was also set up at 47 rue Monge. Some 1,500 Spaniards were looked after, the French Government paying for their lodging, food, and clothing, and Pablo Picasso the salaries of the twelve workers in the centres.[6] The hope that the centres would enable Spanish families to be reunited was not fulfilled: only six families were reintegrated, all at Montrouge.[7]

The seat of the Spanish Republican Red Cross was in Toulouse, its president, Dr José Martí Feced, having delegated the authority in Paris to Madame Riquelme. Its premises, on the rue Pargaminières, were similarly provided by the French Government, but the French Government was reluctant to entitle the Spaniards to the pensions and other benefits which were given to the French survivors. As a result, the Spaniards were denied even the modest parcel issued to the returning French deportees, and dependent as they were upon public charity some of them were still walking around the streets of Toulouse in their *Drillich* five or six days after their return to the city. Pierre Bertaux, as Commissaire of the Republic, took the matter in hand. He had already appointed Lieutenant-Colonel Angel Hernández del Castillo, a Spanish officer of renown,[8] to the post of Delegate for

Spanish Refugees and Chief Spokesman for Spanish Affairs. He now appointed the Catalan Anne Marie Berta (of no political persuasion) as Delegate of the Spanish Red Cross responsible for all Spanish deportees returning from Germany. Berta set herself up in the Hôtel Victoria opposite Matabiau Station, presiding over a committee composed of one representative of the PCE, one of the libertarian CNT, and one of the socialist PSOE.[9]

Across the Canal and in front of the station, Toulouse opened its heart to the survivors, French or Spanish. The bands played 'La Marseillaise' and the mournful but resolute hymn of the Resistance. Children clutching bunches of flowers ran to fathers (and mothers) they could still recognize (approaching with nervous steps those they could not), parents hugged their returning children, while other deportees came out of the station in a daze, welcomed by the city at large but by no one they knew by name, and others, mere skin and bones, too weak to walk, were carried to the ambulances lined up outside, and thence to the hospitals Purpan and Hôtel-Dieu. Little was known at the time of survivor's syndrome. No one would be more likely to experience it than a *Prominenter* from Mauthausen, and Juan de Diego was among those who suffered a nervous collapse on realizing that they had survived when so many of their friends had succumbed. When he arrived back in France in mid-1945, at a time when there were hardly any facilities or funds for psychiatric aid, the French authorities considered his case serious enough for him to be sent to a clinic in the Pyrenees at Bagnères-de-Luchon.

Now given the funds with which to handle the responsibility, Pierre Bertaux proceeded to convert the former detention camp at Récébédou, near Portet-sur-Garonne, into a hospitable village, and the red, yellow, and purple flag of the Spanish Republic flying over it could be seen for miles around. Originally named Blasco Ibáñez, after Spain's greatest historical novelist, the village was soon renamed the New Republic of Don Quijote, or Villa Don Quijote. The change of name did nothing to please the communists, who refused to be housed in it if it meant sharing it with non-communists, even if they were their fellow-survivors of the Nazi camps.[10]

That attitude was an illustration of the sudden turn in politics. In the Nazi camps, all antifascists had worked together. In a ceremony held in the place Wilson in Toulouse on 10 June 1945 to pay homage to the returning deportees, and chaired by the city's new socialist mayor Raymond Badiou, the speakers included a communist from Buchenwald (Jaime Nieto), an anarchist from Mauthausen (José Ester Borrás), and the anarchist leader Federica Montseny. Merely to have taken part in the ceremony could have sealed the fate of Jaime Nieto, for PCE leaders, now gathering in Toulouse, began a systematic investigation into the activities of all Party members. Joan Martorell, a survivor of Dachau, has described how he thought it natural that the Party would interrogate all of them as to the reasons for their being deported. His opinion radically changed when, at a meeting in Toulouse chaired by Pasionaria in person, he and other communists were treated with suspicion for no other reason than that they had been taken prisoner. Equally galling to Martorell was the rebuke they received for their behaviour in Dachau. There they had kept aside a little portion of the tiny ration of bread and margarine that they received because they worked. This portion was kept for those who were disabled and could not work, and who hence received from the SS only half their ration. But Martorell and his group faced a dilemma: to save any, it was necessary to sacrifice others. Those who were going to die anyway, they concluded, could not be helped; they would help only those who had a chance. This required their applying certain criteria of selection which caused them deep problems of conscience, but they came away gratified that they had succeeded in saving many a sick comrade. What they hardly expected to hear on their return to freedom was the reproach of the Party leaders accusing them of behaviour 'both inhuman and sectarian'.[11] It was a lesson in doublespeak that opened their eyes.

The disaster of the Arán Valley in October 1944 offered a different lesson.[12] To every clear-sighted observer, it was a mistake to imagine that the Resistance in France could serve as a model for the Resistance in Spain, and that the Spanish people burned with desire to rise against their oppressors. When newspapers with references to the invasion first reached the inmates of Dachau or Mauthausen, at the moment of their liberation, the prisoners' first reaction was to spread the news and thus give strength to those most in need of moral uplift; when they learned the invasion had failed, the story was suppressed, for fear that it would be fatal to those in very weak condition.[13] Then, on their return to France, came the shock of finding Party leaders and Republican generals whom no one had ever seen in action in the bleak years 1940–2, or even later. The true heroes, men like Cristino García and José Vitini, were to be sent on suicide missions to Spain. As for Monzón, the man who had headed both the Party and the front in whose name the invasion was launched, held political and military control over a sizeable guerrilla force in France, and built contacts with other parties and even embassies in Spain—without even being a member of the Party's Central Committee—was so massive an embarrassment to the Party's leadership that more than his physical elimination would be necessary.

There is every reason to suppose that the fiasco in the Arán Valley caught the PCE leaders in Moscow by surprise. It was André Marty of the PCF, from his base in Algiers in September 1944, who first informed them of the plan.[14] They were horrified to hear that Monzón, or any other PCE leader in France, had acquired a prestige and an authority sufficient to take such an initiative by himself. Pasionaria promptly decided that the PCE leaders in exile in the Union of Soviet Socialist Republics or in the Americas were to return immediately to France. Enrique Líster and Juan Modesto reached Paris in late February 1945, after staying for some months in Belgrade to discuss guerrilla strategy and tactics with Tito.[15] Pasionaria joined them in April 1945, after receiving a farewell blessing from Stalin on 23 February and travelling via Cairo in the company of Ignacio Gallego and José Antonio Uribes. All three reached Toulouse on 24 April.[16] Among those returning from the Americas were Antonio Mije, Vicente Uribe, and Francisco Antón.[17]

The rank-and-file were not so privileged. Of the Spaniards in the Soviet Union, only 2,500 returned home.[18] The remainder were integrated into Soviet life, but as late as 1985 some 1,500 Spaniards were reported to be eager to leave but unable to do so because they had not received their Soviet retirement pensions.[19] Even in the 1980s there were reports of Spaniards still imprisoned in the Gulag.[20] It was a question that King Juan Carlos and Queen Sofía raised during their state visit to the Soviet Union in May 1984.[21] In their subsequent state visit to Mexico in January 1990, the King was more expansive: Mexico's readiness throughout the Franco era to shelter thousands of Spanish exiles, he said, deserved 'the everlasting gratitude of Spain'.[22]

The Spanish communists in exile thus entered the post-war period in a mixture of jubilation and frustration. They were very much aware that even their enemies, in France as elsewhere, recognized them as second to none in their contribution to the antifascist struggle. The communists never tired of repeating it, resorting to any lie or evasion when the subject of the Molotov–Ribbentrop pact was raised. The respect in which the Soviet Union was held added to their sense of well-being. On the other hand was the bitterness that followed the failure of the invasion of Spain, made worse by the general opinion among Spanish Republicans that it was the fault of the bad leadership and bad planning of the communists. Spanish communists, like the rest of the Republican camp, continued to look at Franco's Spain with undiluted venom, but the post-war period of harmony among the victors was among the very shortest in all history. Within two years the Cold War had been declared on both sides, and while the Spanish

Republicans remained united in their hatred of Franco, the Republican camp was as deeply divided on the rest as were the wartime Allies. In the course of that new struggle, the truth about Soviet life and Stalin's crimes would little by little become apparent to every communist willing to distinguish between the reality and the dream. The dream still lingered on. The author of this work has received his share of threats and abuse, of hate-letters and false accusations, but the impression which has left the deepest mark is the sadness of those many communists he has known who look back to that struggle against fascism, whether it was in the Resistance in France, or in the prisons of the Gestapo, or in the hell of Mauthausen, and think of the comradeship and the hope that inspired them. Even those like López Tovar who left or were driven out of the Party cannot bear to think that their struggle to build a better world was all in vain. No one put it better than Mississippi's Richard Wright, who left Stalin's temple like so many others when the credibility gap became too wide to leap, but knowing in his heart that he 'should never be able to feel with the same sharpness about life, should never again express such passionate hope, should never again make so total a commitment of faith'.

NOTES

PREFACE

1. Private conversation, Toulouse, 7 June 1985.
2. A rare example of this is Sanz, *Luchando*, 147–8.
3. Cf. International Committee for the History of the Second World War, *News Bulletin*, 22 (summer 1985), 10.
4. The theses compiled by Marie-Conchita Alonso and the partnership of Dominique Billes and José García Villar illustrate the point. The first, directed by Manuel Tuñón de Lara, recounts (p. 6) that of 150 or more questionnaires distributed, only 34 Spaniards responded. The authors of the second thesis report (p. 6) that of the large number of *guerrilleros* whom they approached, only one (a boy of 17 in 1944) agreed to provide his testimony.
5. I am grateful to Dr Claude Lévy (letter of 3 Jan. 1985) for revealing to me how the same Vichy police officers who arrested members of the Resistance, imprisoned and maltreated them, and handed them over to the Gestapo were, after all, secretly, all the time—bona fide members of the Resistance! One of them sought to establish his credentials by slipping a copy of a Resistance journal into Dr Lévy's prison cell. 'Why', he asks, 'did he not just open the door?'
6. William Manchester, *International Herald Tribune*, 22 Oct. 1985.
7. *Le Monde*, 23–4 Aug. 1987. The Soviet archives face another danger: the quality of the paper is so poor—many documents are merely third or fourth carbons—that unless they are microfilmed in the next few years their value will be seriously impaired.
8. *Daily Worker* (London), 6 Mar. 1953.

INTRODUCTION

1. Although I have added much to *Vae Victis* in subsequent writings, I must acknowledge here the omission of the camp at Rivesaltes (Pyrénées-Orientales), which was the sixth of those large inland centres ordered by General Ménard in Feb. 1939 to reduce the population in the camps on the Mediterranean shore. Each of these six camps had its particularity: Gurs was for Basques and International Brigaders, Agde and Rivesaltes for Catalans, Septfonds and Vernet for skilled workers (to be incorporated into French industry), and Bram for the aged (Laharie, 22–3; Macdonald, 98–9). Cf. Soriano, 222–4.
2. To commemorate the 50th anniversary of the Spanish refugees' arrival in

France, a meeting was held on 22 May 1989 at the Biblioteca Española in Paris, with the Spanish ambassador attending. Professor Emeritus Pierre Vilar, the distinguished Catalanist, had the chair. Jean–Claude Villegas presented his *Plages d'exil*, a collective work which had just appeared. Villegas spoke of the passivity shown by the Spaniards to the appalling conditions of the French camps. The remark galvanized a large part of the audience. If the Spaniards had said little at the time, they retorted, it was because any complainant would be playing into Franco's hands. Now, 50 years later, they were ready to speak out, in France and in French. If the soldiers maltreating them were ignorant Senegalese, they went on, their officers nevertheless were French, and the French had never faced up to the truth about the camps. María Ángeles Volait, née Mellado, living in Paris, told a startled audience what it was like to be in the group of 30 children, aged 6 to 14, who had been evacuated from Madrid to Barcelona during the Civil War and had then been forced to leave Barcelona for the French frontier on the eve of the city's surrender to Franco. 'We were placed in a truck, given nothing to eat, and bombed all the way to the frontier. At Le Perthus, in the Pyrenees, the French authorities refused to let us cross. For ten days we had to stay in the château in Cantallops [on the Spanish side], where we literally starved. Finally we were told we could walk across. Some of the children were crippled. The snow came up to our thighs. Behind us we had the wolves. We reached Le Perthus. At last we were fed—a mouthful each of cod and a spoonful each of condensed milk. Nothing else. It was an abomination.' Other Spaniards present at the meeting insisted that what the French felt towards them was pure hatred, and that it was high time the truth were told.

Among the most recent testimonies is that of Juan Segobrigano, who writes that the Spaniards interned at Bram were so filled with rage and frustration that some hurled themselves in a final gesture against the barbed wire that enclosed them (Milza and Peschanski, 603). In the film documentary *Otro futuro* (1989), directed by Richard Prost, a woman survivor recounts how, in Feb.–Mar. 1939, women prisoners on a beach lost their young children when the tide came in at night, and how the male prisoners leaped into the water to try to save the children, where-upon the Senegalese went in after the men with their cudgels, dragging them back to the beach.

3. Laharie, 23. Great effort has been expended, especially by Javier Rubio, in assessing the Spanish refugee population in France in the aftermath of the Civil War. The recent estimate that 'More than 300,000 Spaniards remained in France during the [Second World] war and beyond' (Sweets, 112) finds no authoritative support.

4. *Journal officiel*, 16 Apr. 1939.

5. 'Rapport général sur les activités des Républicains espagnols dans la libération de la France et dans la lutte contre l'armée d'occupation', Amicale des Anciens FFI et Résistants espagnols, Conseil national, 2.

6. Rubio, *Guerra civil*, 415.

7. Barthonnat, 141.

8. Soriano, 29, reports that 1,400 Spaniards volunteered from the detention camp in Gurs, leaving for the Legion's basic training centre at Sathonay (Rhône) prior to being sent to Sidi-Bel-Abbès in Algeria. Cf. Pike, *Français*, 388–9.
9. Rubio, *Guerra civil*, 205. Cf. Vilanova, 87; Razola and Constante, 31; Alfaya, 98; Sanz, *Luchando*, 20; Arasa, 22. Gordon, 435–6, gives the exaggerated figure of 30,000 for total volunteers in the two branches, Legion and Bataillons de marche.
10. Soriano, 124.
11. Laharie, 128–9.
12. Gamelin, ii. 407. Avakoumovitch ('Résistance', 92) refers to 4,000 labourers of various nationalities, but mostly Spaniards and Italians, working on the Bricy airfield near Orleans.
13. Some 12,000 were assigned to the Maginot Line, 30,000 to the area between the Maginot Line and the Loire, and 8,000 south of the Loire (Sanz, *Luchando*, 22; Arasa, 22).
14. Gordon, 435.
15. Cf. Pike, *Français*, 363–6.
16. Marty, 20–1. Cf. Carr, 82.
17. Barthonnat, 140.
18. Rubio, *Guerra civil*, 896–7.
19. Ibid. 901; Laharie, 128.
20. In Nov. 1939, the Minister of Labour adopted the same position as his colleagues in the Ministry of National Defence and War, requesting Sarraut to keep the Spanish refugees in France.
21. Sanz, *Luchando*, 19; based on a study by Arturo Escoriguel commissioned by the French Ministry of National Defence and War.
22. Montagnana, ii. 194.
23. Trempé, 65.
24. Gordon, 436; Laharie, 124, who both cite the *Journal officiel*, 14 Dec. 1939; but cf. ch. 2, n. 44. Although deported later to Dachau by the Gestapo, Ybarnegaray was automatically sentenced, on 18 Mar. 1946, to loss of civil rights for his role in the Vichy Government; he was immediately reprieved (Novick, 283).
25. Rubio, *Guerra civil*, 205, 392; Crémieux–Brilhac, 510, who gives a figure of only 6,000 Spaniards in the Foreign Legion and the Bataillons de marche together. All 104,000 veterans of the Spanish Republican Army in France were thus accounted for.
26. Of these, about 1,000 died in French uniform, out of 3,500 who wore it. Some 500 Spaniards were incorporated into the 13th Semi-Brigade of the Foreign Legion, a unit which would provide the Free French with their first shock troops, but in the opening and closing stages of the war the Spaniards proved intractable. At their base in Larzac (Tarn) in March 1940, 30 of them deserted, allegedly in response to communist orders. The unit took part in the Narvik expedition and the Battle of France, the remaining 1,600 men (including 300 Spaniards) being evacuated from Brest to Plymouth on 18 June 1940. At their new base in Trentham Park,

Surrey, the Spaniards refused to follow orders; in the end, half of them rallied to the forces of de Gaulle. Reconstructed, the unit took part in the unsuccessful expedition to Dakar, then fought the Italians in Abyssinia before being transferred to Palestine. Other Spaniards reached Palestine by deserting *en masse* from the Vichy-controlled forces in Syria and crossing the desert. In Palestine they served in the British Army, forming a battalion of the Queen's Regiment and a commando unit which took part in the final stage of the defence of Crete. Other Spaniards deserted from the Vichy-controlled Legion in Algeria and Morocco, a few crossing the Sahara to Lake Chad and enlisting in the French 2nd Armoured Division of General Leclerc which crossed to Libya and fought at Bir Hakeim, while others took advantage of the Allied landings of Nov. 1942 to join General Juin's army in the Italian campaign or General de Lattre de Tassigny's army in the drive from Provence. Cf. Crémieux-Brilhac, 510–17.

The account of the Narvik expedition by M. J. Torris (*Narvik*, Paris: Arthème Fayard, 1946) exemplifies the pattern of denying the Spaniards any credit for their contribution: Torris does not mention a single Spaniard. Cf. Vilanova, 327, and Stein, 113–14, who argue the contrary. As for the experiences of Spanish soldiers evacuated to England, hardly any account exists, but Joaquín Zurita Castañer, who was evacuated from Dunkirk and spent a week in Dover, Exeter, and Bournemouth before returning in June 1940 to the Battle of France, was amazed by the warmth of the reception. 'They treated us as victors rather than as vanquished. I now think that living those moments almost compensates for all the misery we had undergone' (Zurita, 109–10).

27. For the activities of these two organizations, see Pike, *Vae*, 80–8; Fagen, 35–8, 106–7; Rubio, *Emigración española*, 224–9, and *Guerra civil*, 129–50; Powell, 150–9; Estruch, 14.

28. Castro, *Hombres*, 659, refers to him as a communist puppet.

29. Inspecteur de police mobile René Félix, to Commissaire divisionnaire chef de la Ire Section, Inspecteur général des Services de Police criminelle: Paris, 18 Sept. 1939. This credit was discovered by French intelligence on 12 June 1939, but the date that the funds were deposited was not indicated in the report, and the transaction might have taken place months earlier.

30. F7 14809 (Archives nationales, Paris). The report was prepared by a Commissariat Spécial for the Military Governor of the Paris region, but bears no date; from its position in the papers (which proves nothing) it was compiled in Jan. 1940.

31. PA 10. 914/1: Paris, 11 Sept. 1939 (Archives nationales).

32. Powell, 151.

33. PA 11. 114/1: Paris, 14 Sept. 1939 (Archives nationales).

34. Cf. Rolland, 'Aperçus', 57. After the war Ossorio returned to Paris to work for UNESCO.

35. Cf. Pike, *Vae*, 105.

36. The head of the Mexican Legation in France was Narciso Bassols, who was pro-communist (cf. ibid. 83–4). He later served as Mexico's ambassador to Moscow.

37. 17th Military Region (Vichy), 69717S, dated 24 Aug. 1940 (Archives de la Haute-Garonne).
38. Vichy Government to Vichy Prefects: telegram 094444 75/1/74, 20 July 1940, Secret (Archives de la Haute-Garonne).
39. Powell, 153.
40. Negrín arrived in England aboard a Royal Navy vessel on 25 June. Spain's last prime minister then settled into a pleasant country house at Bovington, not far from London, to which he invited the Soviet Ambassador and his wife for weekends (Maisky, 117–18). In 1942 Negrín founded a Republican organization called El Hogar Español, which he installed at 22 Inverness Terrace, W2. The man to whom Negrín gave its presidency was Colonel Rodrigo Gil, an artillery officer who had served as under-secretary of war in the Largo Caballero Government of Sept. 1936. Under Gil's presidency, the Hogar soon fell into the hands of the communists.
41. Alvarez del Vayo, 308.
42. Paselli, 402–6; Soriano, 142; Rivas, 12–30, *passim*.
43. Cf. Pike, *Vae*, 108 n.
44. Cf. ibid., 41 n., 106 n. Aguirre managed to reach Belgium, from where he left in disguise for South America (Legarreta, 228). At the Pétain–Franco meeting in Montpellier in Feb. 1941, Franco reportedly asked for the extradition of 2,000 Spanish Republicans, including that of Portela Valladares, requested on 10 Feb. 1941 and supposedly carried out on 15 Sept. 1941 (Rolland, *Vichy*, 148, and 'Aperçus', 93). Cf. ibid. 61–8; Grynberg, 644–6. However, at the time of the Liberation, Blanco, 569, reports that he found Portela Valladares in prison on the outskirts of Marseilles.
45. Commissaire Pierre Mace, Paris: 9 Mar. 1939 (fragment: Archives nationales).
46. Pierdona, Mémoire, 216.
47. *La Dépêche*, 5 Feb. 1939.
48. Cf. Pike, *Français*, 394.
49. Largo Caballero published two accounts of his arrest by the Gestapo which are fundamentally different. The first, which appeared in his Paris newspaper *Renovación*, implies that he was arrested by the Gestapo only after the German occupation of Vichy France. I have followed the version in his memoirs, on the assumption that he would have given the matter more thought. In Oranienburg he was given a red triangle (Political) instead of the blue (Stateless) given to virtually all Spanish prisoners.
50. Wilebaldo Solano has pointed out that Prieto's dislike of her never matched her hatred for him, and that his opposition to the communists never went beyond public criticism. In her second autobiography, Pasionaria claims that, politics aside, she felt esteem for his talent and fighting spirit (Ibarruri, *Memorias*, 629).
51. Smith, 255; Marrus and Paxton, 14; Falcoff and Pike, 81–5; Rolland, 'Vichy' 68–70. Franco had no objection to the French–Mexican agreement, except in the case of 800 Spaniards who were wanted in Spain (Rolland, *Vichy*, 145). The number of Spanish Republicans who actually entered Mexico is contested. According to the meticulous Spanish historian Javier Rubio

(*Guerra civil*, 180, 454), their total in the period 1940–2 is only some 7,000, including 2,055 arriving in 1940 and 1,917 in 1941. Vicente Llorens, in Abellán, i. 126–7, writes that by 1 July 1940 there were already 8,625 Spanish Republican refugees in Mexico; by 31 Mar. 1941 a total of 9,695 Spaniards had left France for Mexico, and a further 2,534 arrived in 1942. Others arrived later (some of them relocating in Mexico from other countries in Latin America), so that Llorens calculates the total at over 15,000. Cf. Jaume Sobrequés, *El País*, 10 Apr. 1984.

CHAPTER 1

1. The PSUC was not a branch or offshoot of the PCE but a purely Catalan creation which came into being after the Civil War began, as a result of the fusion of two Catalan socialist groups, one led by Comorera and the other by Vidiella.

2. The exact whereabouts are in question. Heine, 86, gives the town-hall of Ivry, the suburb to the south-east held by the PCF; Estruch, 8, gives the Château de Glatigny, near Versailles.

3. His real name was Stoian Minev Ivanov. He was now going under the name of Moreno (Heine, 86; Morán, 646; Ibarruri, *Memorias*, 477).

4. Estruch, 7–10; Heine, 85–92. The report of the Antwerp Conference was drawn up by José del Barrio and Josep Miret. Against the advice of Comorera, Codovila took it upon himself to 'correct' the report (José del Barrio, in Milza and Peschanski, 613).

5. Pasionaria was accompanied by Stepanov, Jesús Monzón, her secretary Irene Falcón, and the PCF *député* Jean Catelas, whom the Party had sent to Spain to ensure her safe evacuation. Two other communist leaders, Francisco Romero Marín and Ramón Soliva, also joined Pasionaria in Oran, but since they were officers in the Republican Army they were interned in the fortress of Mers el-Kébir (Camino, 168; Tillon, *On chantait*, 249; Heine, 61; Ibarruri, *Memorias*, 477–8, 569). Both Romero and Soliva had achieved very early success: neither had turned 25 when they were made division commanders in Spain.

6. *Guerra*, 301, cited by Estruch, 11. In Spain, meetings of the PCE's Politburo had always been attended by Togliatti and Stepanov. At the Politburo's meeting in Toulouse on 12 Mar. 1939, neither Togliatti nor Checa was present. This limited the scope of the resolutions (Morán, 22).

7. London, *Aveu*, 93–5.

8. Barthonnat, 130.

9. Among the very few exceptions, Jesús Hernández was interned in a prison in Oran in May 1939. But Hernández was not among the PCE leaders who left Spain in early March: he, Checa, and Togliatti were ordered to remain behind in Spain long enough to organize the evacuation of the maximum number of communist militants and to establish a clandestine party with the remainder.

10. Rubio, *Guerra civil*, 339.

11. Líster would presumably have found himself in the company of President Azaña and ex-prime minister Largo Caballero (Pierdona, 'Réfugiés', 216).
12. The lady could hardly have been Carrillo's wife Consuelo, if Carrillo is to be believed. In the interview he gave to María Eugenia Yagüe, 37, he declared that he left Consuelo (whom he had married in 1936 when they were both 20) and his little daughter behind in Spain: 'the Party did not let him go back for them. It was too great a risk for him to run'. María Llena, who knew the communist leaders, refers to the lady as Carmen (interview).
13. Líster, *Memorias*, 411–12.
14. Líster, *Basta*, 117. Líster may have been quite wrong about Carrillo: according to a report that is poorly substantiated, Carrillo returned to Madrid and was then the last communist leader to leave, on 27 Mar. (Thomas, 913). Thomas gives as his source Hermet, *Espagnols*, 168, but there is no such reference in Hermet. Carrillo's biographer, Fernando Claudín, makes no mention of Carrillo returning to Spain, reporting only that at the time of Casado's coup d'état on 5 Mar. Carrillo was still in Toulouse, 'waiting his turn to move to the central-southern zone' (Claudín, *Santiago*, 59). Carrillo himself avoids the issue, saying only that he was suffering, like so many others, from scabies and that he left for Paris (Carrillo, *Demain*, 73). Bolloten, 1010, 1180, states that Carrillo did not return to Spain. Cf. Morán, 68.
15. Líster, *Memorias*, 413, 439.
16. Ibid. 439–41.
17. Heine, 94; Morán, 29. There is doubt as to when Martínez Cartón arrived in Mexico. One version has it that he was in the Soviet Union for some weeks or months after the German attack of June 1941, but reached Mexico before the end of that year. There is also support for the version (initiated by Julián Gorkin) that Martínez Cartón reached Mexico, albeit from the USSR, in Aug. 1939, and that he was chosen to direct the team sent to assassinate Trotsky and the other targeted victims.
18. Comín, *República*, 210. Cf. Général 'el Campesino', *Vie*, 181; *Yo escogí*, 229. Although el Campesino was an eyewitness, his version of the matter is less convincing. How very different from all this is Pasionaria's recollection of the role of the PCE leaders in France. The PCE leaders, she told her interviewer in 1977, encouraged the return to Spain of all those Spanish families who had nothing to fear from Franco, while they themselves remained in France 'to do everything possible to make life easier for all the exiles who remained and to arrange the transit to America of those who wished to leave' (Camino, 169–70).
19. Gros, 22–4; Heine, 92. Cf. el Campesino, *Yo escogí*, 230. For some weeks in April–May 1939, Pasionaria had reassembled the PCE Politburo in Paris. Responsibility for finance was given to Vicente Uribe; contracts and publishing to Manuel Delicado; *Mundo obrero* and relations with other parties to Antonio Mije; organization and refugee aid to Luis Cabo Giorla; liaison with the PCE in Spain to Francisco Antón; and organization within the detention camps in France to Juan José Manso. Jesús Monzón and Irene Falcón served as secretaries to Pasionaria (Morán, 21).

20. Hernández, *En el pais*, 21.
21. Ibid. 18–21.
22. Wide disparities are to be found in the estimates of the number of Spanish children sent to the Soviet Union. The author with best access to the truth is Jesús Hernández, since he was both a leader of the PCE and the Minister of Education in the Spanish Republican Government of that time, but his estimate of 5,000 (*Grand*, 183) is at least 1,000 too high. The estimates of Comín and Ruiz, both with 3,500, prove more accurate. Rafael Miralles, 206–13, a Cuban diplomat in Moscow in 1944–5, gives 4,000. Further support for this estimate comes from Estruch, 59, with 3,000 plus 122 teachers and nurses arriving in the USSR in 1937; and Legarreta, 166, with 3–5,000 (not just Basques). The most recent estimate, that of Zafra *et al.*, is the most authoritative: 2,895 (pp. 20, 38)—they even provide a list of names (pp. 187–221)—but they admit that their total is limited to the number of children that they have been able to identify. There have been several higher (and unacceptable) estimates (cf. Pike, *Jours*, 97–8 n.). Pedro Conde, 197–200, who was in Moscow at the time, gives the figure of 6,000, comprising 1,500 Basques, 1,500 from Levante, and 3,000 from other parts, especially Asturias and Catalonia. The disparity in the figures may be due to conflicting interpretations of the term 'children': some writers may have defined it as anyone under the age of 18.

     The first 21 children to leave Spain sailed from Cartagena on the *Gran Canarias* on 17 Mar. 1937, bound for Odessa; they were the sons and daughters of Republican pilots and PCE officials in the Madrid area, including Pasionaria's daughter Amaya (Legarreta, 157). Cf. Rubio, *Guerra civil*, 108, for the sailings in 1937 of the *Kooperatsia* and the *Felix Dzerzhinski*.
23. El Campesino (*Vie*, 184) gives the figure of 5,973; Gorkin, 262, gives 'some 6,000', including 3,961 communist militants and International Brigaders. Cf. Rubio, *Guerra civil*, 201, 442; Estruch, 49; Morán, 28; and Fundación Pablo Iglesias, 191, which gives 6,000.
24. Fernando Claudín, report to the PCE plenary meeting held in Toulouse in 1945; cited by Borrás [Cascarosa], 149.
25. Comín, *República*, 207.
26. The order to transport the archives had been given to Mije by Pedro Checa, the PCE's secretary of organization, just before the collapse of Catalonia. They were to be carried in a bulk liquid conveyance in order to escape detection by the French authorities at the frontier. The French customs officials, however, uncovered the cargo, which included the complete dossiers with photographs of every Party official in both the PCE and the PSUC. The entire material was then passed over to the French police (Heine, 91). The loss of the files was so disastrous to the Party that its leaders suspected betrayal. While Checa was equally responsible, the blame fell on Mije, who did all he could to shift it, sending a letter to Moscow from Paris in which he accused Miquel Serra i Pàmies of the PSUC of working for French intelligence and of informing the French

police of the operation (Estruch, 52). Other leaders who were implicated in the disgrace were Victorio Sala, who was sent to Mexico City, and Luis Cabo Giorla, who was dispatched to Buenos Aires (Morán, 29).

27. Rubio ('Parti', 95) refers to the appearance from Apr. 1939 of *Juventud de España* and *Treball*, 'among others', but their circulation must have been limited in the extreme. Apart from *Treball*, the Catalan press in exile also included the weekly *Catalunya* (see below, Ch. 5, n. 83).

28. Tagüeña, 349–59; Carrillo, *Demain*, 74–5; Yagüe, 37–8; Estruch, 17–18; Claudín, *Santiago*, 59–60, 63–7.

29. Estruch, 12.

30. Cf. Pike, *Jours*, pp. xli–xlii.

31. Razola and Constante, 30.

32. Miguel Celma, letter of 7 Jan. 1980.

CHAPTER 2

1. Rossi, *Communistes*, 17. There is some confusion over this author's identity. Angelo Tasca, a disciple of Bukharin and leader of the right-wing faction of the PCI, broke with the Party and became its arch-enemy. He went under the name of Serra and wrote under the name of A. Rossi, and earlier, during the Spanish Civil War, under that of André Leroux in *Le Midi Socialiste* (cf. Pike, *Français, passim*).

2. The state of Stalin's apologists, in France as elsewhere, was already one of despair some time before the cataclysm of 1989–91. To judge from a recent attempt, that of Roger Martelli ('Stratégie'), the communist intellectuals have simply given up on the question.

3. *Nuestra bandera*, 28 (June–July 1948).

4. Carrillo, *Demain*, 75. Carrillo's Stalinist viewpoint is shared by Sixto Agudo, 24: 'The communists approved the Pact without reservation.' It was Agudo who was given responsibility for setting up a political indoctrination school for the Resistance (ibid. 54).

5. Tagüeña, 360.

6. Estruch, 35. They included Miquel Ferrer, Miquel Serra Pàmies, Víctor Colomer, and Avel·li Artís Gener. The interviews that Carrillo later gave to Lilly Marcou appeared in 1984. Having published a work on the Cominform in 1977 without even mentioning the PCE, the Romanian communist Marcou now made amends by devoting a whole book to Carrillo. The PCE leader could hardly have found a more agreeable interviewer: no question was put that might trouble Carrillo's conscience. 'The Pact went down with us like a letter down the chute!', was again Carrillo's answer to her perfumed question; 'it was all for the sake of peace'. After Marcou had expressed her agreement with Carrillo that the Pact was in the interests of the USSR, she asked Carrillo if, at the moment he arrived in Russia (a few months after its signing), he was aware of the 'adverse effects' of the Pact within the Soviet Union: the prohibition of all antifascist activity, the banishment of the word fascism in any

pejorative sense, the order forbidding Ehrenburg to write. 'No', replied Carrillo, 'we knew nothing about that' (Carrillo, *Communisme*, 23–5).

7. *L'Humanité*, 28 Aug. 1939. In the original, the words 'les communistes au premier rang' are in italics.

8. P.-L. Darnar, *L'Humanité*, 26 Aug. 1939.

9. *La Voz de los españoles*, 26 Aug. 1939; cited by Estruch, 34. Despite the law requiring that a copy of every issue be deposited in the Bibliothèque nationale, this issue is not to be found in that library, nor in any library in France.

10. *Catalunya*, 4 (26 Aug. 1939); cited by Estruch, 34.

11. *L'Humanité's* issue of 26 Aug. was the last to be authorized and the last to appear in its normal format. Its first underground issue (in smaller format) appeared on 28 Aug., followed by its second on 26 Oct., the latter bearing the number 1. In the last issue of *Ce Soir*, that of 25 Aug., Louis Aragon wrote in the editorial: 'If France, in accordance with its treaty obligations (to Poland, for example), goes to the help of a country that falls victim to aggression, the USSR will necessarily come to the aid of France. . . . [The Pact] contains no provisions detrimental to the interests of a third party' (cited in *Dossiers*, 41).

12. F7 14809 (Archives nationales, Paris).

13. The calculations regarding the exact number of PCF *députés* who left the Party at this time are so varied that Jean-Paul Brunet, in his authoritative study (*Histoire*, 65), prefers to leave it at 'about one-third' by January 1940. It seems that the total included 1 senator and 21 *députés*, reducing the parliamentary group from 74 to 52 (Amouroux, i. 138; Wall, 20). Cf. Robrieux, 504, who gives 27 *députés* defecting out of a group of 72.

14. *Catalunya* 4 (26 Aug. 1939); cited by Estruch, 34.

15. Rieber, 4; Estruch, 31.

16. Daix, 138, then a member of the PCF, now among its fiercest critics, considers that Daladier's actions came down like manna.

17. F7 14810 (Archives nationales, Paris).

18. Ibarruri, *Social-democracia*; cited by Estruch, 46; and by Rubio, 'Parti', 96–7. Morán, 32, shows that the same diatribe appeared in *España popular*, 18 Feb. 1940.

19. 'España hoy', Editorial Problemas, Buenos Aires, 1940; cited by Rubio, 'Parti', 98. Cf. Heine, 96.

20. Mije, *Refugiados*, 5; cited by Rubio, *Guerra civil*, 506.

21. 'Manifiesto de la Internacional Comunista del primero de mayo de 1940', *España popular*, 19 May 1940; cited by Heine, 97.

22. Heine, 99.

23. *Nuestra bandera*, 1 (June 1940); cited by Estruch, 44–6.

24. His wife Jeannette Vermeersch picked him up at Chauny in a car driven by a Party chauffeur, a Spaniard by the name of Pelayo. The operation was well prepared. The car that took Thorez across the Belgian frontier carried the flag of a South American republic (Robrieux, 502).

25. Cf. Pike, *Jours*, 22.

26. For a denial of this by Thorez, cf. *La Défense de la liberté: Cahiers du*

bolchevisme, 2e semestre 1939 – janvier 1940. The original edition of this book is not to be found in any library in France, and may well have been published in Nazi Germany.

27. There is doubt only about the route that Thorez took and the time it took him. According to Borkenau, 300, Thorez continued to direct anti-war propaganda in Belgium until the end of 1939, and, after a stay in Switzerland, reached Moscow, perhaps through Germany, in the summer of 1940. According to Moch (*Communisme*, 51), it is certain that Thorez went through Germany: 'He was seen'. The most recent statement on the subject by a scholar is that of Jean-Jacques Becker (in Azéma *et al.*, 285), who affirms that Thorez left Belgium soon after arriving, 'either on a Sabena flight to a Scandinavian city or in making a detour to London'.

28. *L'Humanité*, 15 May 1940.

29. Cf. Pike, *Vae*, 100; *Français*, 319 n.

30. Ministre de l'Intérieur, Paris: File 9647, 13 Sept. 1939, Secret.

31. F7 14809 (Archives nationales, Paris).

32. Inspecteur général des services de Police administrative, Directeur général de la Sûreté nationale, to Prefect of Ariège: PA 585/5, 11 Jan. 1940, Confidential.

33. Commissaire divisionnaire de Police spéciale, to Prefect of Haute-Garonne: no. 413, 23 Jan. 1940, Secret and Reliable.

34. Inspecteur principal de Police spéciale, to Subprefect, Saint-Gaudens (Haute-Garonne): Luchon, 6 Feb. 1940.

35. Major-General Michel (Toulouse), 70–1870D, 5 Mar. 1940, Top Secret.

36. Ministre de Intérieur: telegram, 2 Oct. 1939, confirmed in circular letter, 9 Oct. 1939.

37. Inspecteur général des services de Police criminelle, Directeur général de la Sûreté nationale: circular letter no. 39, 29 Feb. 1940.

38. Although still popularly known by the name Farman, the plant belonged by this time to the Société nationale de constructions aéronautiques du Centre. Farman was easier to pronounce than SNCAC.

39. *España popular* 7 (28 Mar. 1940); cited by Estruch, 38.

40. F7 14830–1 (Archives nationales, Paris). Cf. Borkenau, 304; Noguères, i. 449; Pfister, 'Georges Marchais'. One of the 3 communists sentenced to death was under 18. Investigators observed him as he sabotaged 17 engines out of 20 (Tandler, 51–2).

41. Ros, 421–2.

42. Madariaga, 735; Rubio, *Guerra civil*, 420.

43. Carrillo, *Eurocomunismo*, 163.

44. Arasa, 22, quotes Enric Adroher ('Gironella'), then a member of the POUM and detained in the camp of Le Vernet: 'Loudspeakers inside the camp relayed the war reports. In June 1940 we heard the news that the Germans were advancing on Paris. At the thought of the German victory the communists in the camp broke out every day in applause.'

45. Commissaire divisionnaire de Police spéciale, Toulouse, to Prefect of Haute-Garonne: no. 509, 2 Feb. 1940.

46. Ibid. no. 197, 21 Feb. 1941.

47. Cf. Avakoumovitch, 'Résistance', 51, 74, 95, citing Micro. T-501/143, National Archives, Washington, DC; Azéma *et al.*, 153–4; Pike, 'Between'.
48. *Nuestra bandera* 4–5 (Oct. 1940), cited by Claudín, *Santiago*, 68.
49. Estruch, 41.
50. The communist-controlled SERE and the socialist-controlled JARE (see above, Intro.).
51. Minister of the Interior, Vichy, to Prefect of Haute-Garonne: DJT/43134, 8 Jan. 1941, Secret.
52. Cf. Smith, 217.
53. Rolland, 256. Cf. Pike, *Jours*, 32–3.
54. Burnett Bolloten, letter of 19 Mar. 1984.
55. Vichy Government to Prefect of Haute-Garonne: file PA 11/S, 2 Jan. 1941, Secret; Commissaire divisionnaire de Police spéciale, Toulouse, to Prefect of Haute-Garonne: no. 197, 21 Feb. 1941.
56. Cf. Bolloten, 614. This secret police organization was created by Indalecio Prieto in 1937 at the request of the Soviets, shortly after the May Days in Barcelona. The SIM soon fell under the control of Soviet agents, who made its principal activity the hunt for Trotskyists and members of the POUM.
57. Cf. Pike, *Jours*, 29. Following the invasion of 22 June 1941, *La Vérité* did not hesitate to rally to the cause of the Red Army.
58. The heaviest sentence of 20 years was given to the journalist Wilebaldo Solano. Andrade received 5 years, for no other reason than that he was a party member. On 14 Mar. 1942, he was transferred to the Eysses penitentiary near Villeneuve-sur-Lot, thence in June 1943 to the military prison in Mauzac (Haute-Garonne), and finally, on 24 Feb. 1944, to the military prison in Bergerac, where he remained until his liberation on 24 Aug. (Andrade, 187–8).
59. López Tovar (interview). Agudo's account includes only one reference to López Tovar (p. 57), saying that he was then expelled from the group.
60. Those who attended the meeting inside the camp at Argelès included several future leaders of the Spanish Resistance in France. Pelayo Tortajada, the former political commissar of the xxth Army Corps in Spain during the Civil War, became the first overall leader. Manolo Sánchez Esteban was made responsible for organization, and was later given regional responsibility for south-eastern France. Jaime Nieto ('Bolados') took control of the Toulouse region, and Angel Celadas ('Paco') that of Perpignan. Manuel Gimeno was given the responsibility for the JSU youth organization, formerly headed by Carrillo. Other future leaders attending the meeting included Jesús Carreras and Sixto Agudo (Agudo, 37).

CHAPTER 3

1. An earlier attempt at biography, that by Teresa Pàmies in 1975, was equally uncritical.
2. In compiling his 1977 work, Camino reveals that he shares Pasionaria's ideology and never comes close to asking a hard question. No doubt he

feels that the woman whose cries of defiance in 1936 won her the admiration of half the world ('Better to die on your feet than live on your knees!' 'Better to be the widow of a hero than the husband of a coward!') is beyond the reach of criticism. In this dulcet dialogue, attended by her lifelong secretary Irene Falcón, Pasionaria recalls with difficulty that she had already visited the USSR twice, the first time in 1933 when she represented Spain in the plenum of the Comintern. She later remembered that the youngest of her children, her son Rubén, had arrived in Russia in 1931 at the age of 11, presumably without her. He had returned to Spain in 1938, aged 18, to fight under Modesto in the Battle of the Ebro (Camino, 170–9).

3. Carrillo, *Demain*, 76–8; Carrillo, *Communisme*, cover, 8, 20–1, 25–6, 33–4, 152. Claude Durand, director of the series that published *Demain l'Espagne*, is no doubt the first publisher in the world to misspell, on cover, spine, and title-page, the name of his author.

4. Comín *República*, 211–30, *passim*.

5. Ruiz, 71. He is also proud to have written his history in less than 8 months, even if the rush to press entailed, e.g., placing the capital of Georgia in the Crimea.

6. *Habla un aviador* centres on the author's role in the Spanish Civil War; only on p. 335 does he enter the period from Jan. 1939.

7. His political affiliation is less clear. Miralles was a socialist in Spain in 1931 but then joined the Communist Party. He presumably left it, since at the time he wrote his book (*Españoles en Rusia*) he was strongly Catholic. The book itself is a curious hash. Despite the title, there is no reference to a Spaniard until p. 149, in the last third of the book. Its first two-thirds are concerned only with sex, night life, black marketeering, and smuggling.

8. Rico, 259–60. The book received the distinction of a review by José Vasconcelos in *Novedades*, 20 July 1951.

9. See above, Ch. 1, nn. 22–3.

10. To these must be added 3 other categories of Spaniards who arrived later: the men of the Blue Division, of whom 321 were taken prisoner; an unknown number of Spanish workers who were deported from France to Germany and who were captured by the Red Army in its advance; and another unknown number of Spaniards who, having been interned in Nazi concentration camps, fell into Soviet hands. As Estruch, 59–60, points out, all prisoners of the Nazis were suspect in Stalin's eyes, which explains the arrest of those in the last two categories.

11. According to most accounts, the other two Spanish members on the committee were Modesto and Líster, but Morán, 28, gives Checa and Hernández (later replaced by Antón).

12. Gros, 25–8. Gros himself was selected, from among the 60,000 workers in his factory in Moscow, as 'the best Stakhanovite' (*Lluita*, 14 Feb. 1945). It was the 10th anniversary of the feat of Aleksei Stakhanov in Kadiyevka, later Stakhanov, where according to legend he mined 102 tons of coal in a single shift, or 14 times the norm. It was a case of Bolshevik *pokazukha*,

or boasting of non-existent achievements, for the truth that emerged in the age of *glasnost*, from among those who knew him, was that Stakhanov was not so much a hero as an alcoholic and a womanizer.

13. Morán, 24–5. José del Barrio reports that in Moscow it took 36 meetings to resolve the differences (Milza and Peschanski, 613).

14. Morán, 63, reports that Díaz was hospitalized in the USSR as early as Sept. 1937 after already undergoing an operation in Paris, and that he underwent 2 further operations in the Soviet Union, in 1937 and 1939. Ibarruri, *Memorias*, 487, says that when she arrived in Moscow in 1939 and rejoined her children, they settled into an apartment on Kislovski Pereulok, in the centre of the city, in a building in which José Díaz and his family were also living.

15. Saña, 271; Thomas, 703.

16. Estruch, 51. Estruch adds that of the PCE leaders only Díaz, Pasionaria, Hernández, and Antón came out of the inquest with their prestige enhanced. In regard to Díaz, I lean here towards the contrary opinion of Morán, 25. Cf. Moreno, 400–1.

17. Alexander, 33; Morán, 25. Again, Estruch, 55, differs, saying that Pasionaria wanted parity with Díaz and demanded a redistribution of their spheres of authority, giving Central America and India to Díaz and South America to her, and that the secretariat of the Comintern agreed to this. Although Morán does not reveal his source, it appears to be primary.

18. Norman L. Jones, in Preston, 244, 323; Estruch, 7; Morán, 72. Cf. Alba, *Partido*, 291, who maintains the opposite.

19. Members of the PSUC in the USSR were, in point of fact, integrated into the PCE (Estruch, 55).

20. Miralles, 206–7; Zafra *et al.*, 50.

21. Legarreta, 158. The post of first secretary of Komsomol's Central Committee was held by Nicolai Aleksandrovich Mikhailov, who played a key role in the fate of the Spanish children,

22. Conde, 200. Legarreta, 266, is of the opinion that the change did not come until Hitler's invasion in June 1941. Probably some children were luckier than others.

23. 'El Campesino', *Vie*, 190.

24. Vilanova, 466; Pons, *Republicanos*, 503. For a map of their centres drawn by a child survivor, cf. Zafra *et al.*, 96.

25. Cf. Legarreta, 230, for the attempt by Leizaola, the Basque Minister of Justice and Culture, to arrange the exchange of the Basque children for a group of 150 Soviet sailors interned in Majorca by Franco; Franco agreed instead to exchange the sailors for a consignment of Soviet oil.

26. Hernández, *En el pais*, 111.

27. Tagüeña, 408.

28. Ibid. 541.

29. Vilanova, 466.

30. 'El Campesino', *Vie*, 185. Cf. Vanni, 48–77. Vanni's identity is unclear. According to Comín, *Españoles*, 17, Ettore Vanni was merely the *nom*

de guerre of Andrés Familiari, but that name has been given by others as Andrea Famillioni. A former editor of the Valencia journal *La Verdad*, Vanni worked in the USSR as a schoolmaster of the Spanish children and remained there until 1947.

31. Tagüeña, 400.
32. Hernández, *Yo fui*, 279–91; *Grande*, 223–4; *En el pais*, 108.
33. Of 14 Spanish children born in Kramatorsk (Ukraine), 12 died of hunger within a year (Castro, *Mi fe*, 104).
34. Miralles, 208.
35. 'El Campesino' also affirms (hyperbolically) that 'thousands' of Spaniards were liquidated as a result of the accusations which had been presented to the NKVD by PCE leaders. These included not only Pasionaria, Martínez Cartón, Enrique Líster, Juan Modesto, Vicente Uribe, Nemesio Pozuelo, and Rafael Vidiella—from whom such behaviour might be expected—but also Jesús Hernández and Manuel Tagüeña ('El Campesino', *Vie*, 38, 189–92; 'El Campesino', *Yo escogí*, 243).
36. Cf. Estruch, 55. The Comintern's executive committee was made up of Dimitrov and Manuilski (CPSU), André Marty (PCF), Gottwald (Czechoslovak Communist Party), Florin and Pieck (KPD), and Díaz and Ibarruri (PCE). Tolstoy, 111, asserts that even high-ranking officials of the Comintern were treated with contempt by the plain-clothes NKVD guards outside the Comintern's headquarters.
37. Thomas, 121; Morán, 18.
38. Castro *Mi fe*, 85; Thomas, 9.
39. Cf. Hernández, 'Besteiro', 1010–4.
40. Hernández, *En el pais*, 224–5; Morán, 23.
41. Castro, *Mi fe*, 21; Morán, 27.
42. Yagüe, 39; Claudín, 64.
43. The academy was named after the Soviet hero Mikhaïl Frunze, who had succeeded Trotsky as People's Commissar of Defence. It was currently directed by General Ivan Koniev, who as Colonel 'Paulito' in Spain had got to know the Spanish communist leaders as well as the leaders of the International Brigades (González, *Comunista*, 83).
44. El Campesino claims, unconvincingly, that he was admitted to the Frunze Academy with the rank of major-general (ibid. 109). He should have said 'major'. Cf. Moreno, 135, 321; Vilanova, 471.
45. Antonov-Ovseyenko, 63. According to Stalinist legend, the 14-year-old Morozov, after denouncing his parents as enemies of the state, was murdered in 1932 by kulaks ('wealthy landowners' in Stalinese) who wanted revenge. The cult of Morozov as a model of communist morality and revolutionary devotion ended in March 1988 when Vladimir Amlinsky, a Soviet novelist and historian, wrote in the literary monthly *Yunost* that Morozov stands only 'as a symbol of legalized and romanticized treachery'.
46. The name was probably Lisytin. Miralles, 180–1, gives it as Lisitski. But Miralles is a careless writer: on p. 205 he spells the name Lisetski; he says that Líster retained his rank of general; and twice he gives Líster's

first name as Eduardo. Miralles adds that although he and Líster had met on the battlefield in 1939, Líster deliberately avoided greeting him when they saw each other again in Moscow. In other name-changes for the Spanish leaders, Vice-Admiral Pedro Prados became Patapof, Col. Antonio Cordón became Korsakov, and Ramón Soliva Vidal (whom Miralles describes as Líster's adjutant, wearing the insignia of a Soviet colonel) became Soloviov (180–1, 205). Cf. Moreno, 135.

47. González, *Comunista*, 81.
48. Ibid. 110.
49. Ibid. 80–1.
50. Tagüeña, 391.
51. The authors of *Comunista en España*, 13, warn that a pirated edition of *La Vie et la mort en URSS, 1939–1949* (Paris: Plon, 1950) was published in Mexico (*sic*), that it was an atrocious translation from the French, and that they disowned it. The edition in question was presumably *Vida y muerte en la URSS* (Buenos Aires: Editorial Bell, 1951). This explains the new title (*Yo escogí la esclavitud*) given to the edition published by Plaza and Janes in Barcelona in 1977. While the structure of the chapters in the 1977 edition is completely changed, the text is exactly the same except for the omission of Gorkin's introduction.
52. His legend ran differently. The anarchist authors of *Karaganda*, 26, for example, write that el Campesino was no less ferocious than Líster. But Julio Carrasco ('Renard') who also knew him well, bears out the opinion of Gorkin (interview). Both sides are right, attesting to his cyclothymic personality.
53. 'El Campesino', *Vie*, 7–17, *passim*; González, *Comunista*, 20.
54. González, *Comunista*, 48–51. Gorkin's own comments on first meeting Stalin, which so incensed Margarita Nelken, 15, are similar in content: 'I had the occasion to observe him at close hand. He made a very poor impression upon me. A physique that was commonplace, almost coarse. A face that was devoid of intelligence, with its narrow forehead and hard, motionless features. He spoke with difficulty, like an ungifted orator. How could anyone imagine that such a mediocrity could transform himself into a monster?' Nelken, 27, 29, offers her own contribution to the perpetuation of the Stalin cult: 'The whole cult of Stalin in the USSR is carried out against his wishes, and even in defiance of his oft repeated instructions.... On one occasion Stalin was so upset by this cult that he cried out: "Are you Bolsheviks or are you sycophants?"'
55. González, *Comunista*, 40–1, 69, 71.
56. Ibid. 41.
57. Miralles, 192–3. Miralles bases his account on several interviews he had with el Campesino's wife in 1945. He gives the date of birth of their first child as 1939, which is impossible: el Campesino did not leave France until May 1939, and his meeting with his future bride was not immediate.
58. Cf. Comín, *República*, 229; Pike, *Jours*, 103 n.
59. Estruch, 56.

60. Tagüeña, 411.
61. Comín, *República*, 228. Cf. *Martínez*, 317.
62. Castro, *Mi fe*, 85, 88; Morán, 24. Cf. Montagnana, 194–5. It is uncertain whether Antón reached the USSR by plane or by train.
63. Comín, *Españoles*, 25; Hernández, *Yo fui*, 253; Tagüeña, 356, 399, 440. Pasionaria, her two children, and Antón had moved into a dacha in the town of Pushkin, 32 kilometres from the city centre. Hernández had his own dacha close by (Jesús Hernández, *Horizontes*, 7 (June 1947); reproduced in *La Batalla*, 28 Feb. 1948). That Pasionaria and Antón were lovers is not seriously questioned by anyone in the closed circuit of the Spanish colony in Moscow. In Pasionaria's wider entourage, and even more so among her mass following, the notion is dismissed as fascist propaganda ('Pasionaria la puta'). María Llena (interview), who knew Pasionaria in Paris after the war and remained faithful to her to her life's end, scoffed at the idea; she added that Antón had a wife, Carmen, and that they had a Mongol daughter. María Llena's background mirrored Pasionaria's, that of the fervent Catholic who found a better church; once she had found Pasionaria, her break with Catholicism was final. As for Pasionaria, it is significant that her autobiography makes no mention of Antón, not even in *Memorias*, 552, where she lists the young leaders of the PCE and includes even the renegade Fernando Claudín.
64. Ruiz, 67; Tagüeña, 582.
65. Morán, 71, asserts that her father was a Yugoslav Jew who died when she was only 5. Hitherto, it was assumed that Levi was the name of the Comintern official who became her second husband, who was Jewish but of no precise nationality. In any event, she chose to retain the name of her first husband, the Peruvian journalist Falcón.
66. Castro, *Mi fe*, 239, reveals that his wife came to realize, before he did, that the USSR was 'an immense concentration camp complete with metro, trams, and trolley-buses'.
67. Líster had arrived in France with his wife Carmina and their daughter.
68. Castro, *Mi fe*, 280–1; Morán, 76. Moreno, 146, recounts that the Politburo member Luis Cabo Giorla, who had been governor of Murcia at the end of 1936, had, in Moscow, abandoned his wife María Carrasco (who was also a Party member) and his two young daughters in order to marry a nurse. Castro, 347, writes of María Carrasco that her wedding gift from Cabo had been the transmission of syphilis; the gift and the betrayal had turned her into a woman who hated everyone, and in her life of seclusion she had given herself up to a savage fanaticism.
69. Morán, 71.
70. Tagüeña, 391.
71. Ibid. 345, 391, 469.
72. Nollau, 128. Manuilski's adjutant was the Hungarian Ernö Gerö, who had been given control of the communists in Catalonia.
    Santiago Carrillo claims the opposite, that it was Dimitrov who made all the decisions. 'There was no Sovietization of the secretariat?', Marcou meekly asked Carrillo in her interview. 'No, no', replied Carrillo. 'In that

case', she responded, 'it was truly an international organism' (Carrillo, *Communisme*, 28).

73. Líster, *Basta*, 125, attributes his information to what he heard from Vicente Uribe in 1961. He adds that both the Comintern secretariat and the PCE's Politburo felt revulsion towards Carrillo 'not only for his Trotsky-leaning past but also for certain shady aspects in his behaviour', and provides details.
74. Ibid. 113–14.
75. Tagüeña, 359. For an attempt to re-establish Carrillo's filial piety, cf. Yagüe, 34–6.
76. Carrillo, *Libertad*, 155.
77. Apart from Uruguay, Mexico was the only country in Latin America where its Communist Party was legal. In Argentina it was tolerated.
78. Estruch, 44.
79. Hernández, *Yo fui*, 234.
80. José del Barrio and Serra Pàmies thus landed in Chile without passing through Mexico. Del Barrio had been accused by the Comintern in June 1939 of being a Trotskyist and a Catalan nationalist. Although he had succeeded in clearing himself of these charges, he was still suspect in the eyes of the PCE, and both he and Serra Pàmies arrived in Chile as simple and unpaid party members in a country where the PSUC membership barely amounted to 50 (Estruch, 52–3; José del Barrio, in Milza and Peschanski, 613).
81. Estruch, 46–7; Heine, 114–16.
82. Estruch, 35–6, who cites *Catalunya*, 18 (24 Jan. 1941).
83. The leadership of the PCE in Cuba was entrusted to Santiago Alvarez, who was assisted by Luis Delage (the political commissar of Modesto's army during the Civil War), Wenceslao Roces and Félix Montiel. Cf. Alba, *Historia*, 135–6; Ruiz, 52, 67, 102; Rubio, *Guerra civil*, 504–12. Estruch, 46, considers that the Spanish communists in Cuba contributed to the shaping of the Cuban Communist Party.
84. Morán, 69, who cites *Correspondance internationale*, 3 June 1939.
85. Yagüe, 38–9; Claudín, 64.
86. Claudín, 67; Morán, 70. Browder was to be expelled from the Party in 1948. Carrillo attributes Browder's decline to the fact that in 1942, at the time the Germans were advancing on Stalingrad, he gave instructions to prepare for the defeat of the Soviet Union (*Communisme*, 40).
87. Cf. Morán, 66–7.
88. Codovila had the responsibility for all the Southern Cone, but his actual control was limited to Argentina (Claudín, *Santiago*, 75).
89. Carrillo, *Demain*, 78–80.
90. Claudín, *Santiago*, 75.
91. Vidali had previously lived in Mexico, 1927–32, under the name of Arturo Sormenti (Alexander, 37). Cf. Gorkin, 262–5; Thomas, 323 n. Shortly after the opening of the Spanish Civil War, Vidali, as chief political commissar in Madrid, took command of the militia in the capital.
92. Ruiz, 58, based on the testimony of Julián Gorkin.

93. 'El Campesino', *Vie*, 197; *Yo escogí*, 253. Cf. the detailed account in Saña, 274–80, who even suggests (p. 275) that Puentes directed the operation.
94. Heine, 94–5. See above, Ch. 1.
95. Estruch, 62.
96. Ruiz, 58–9.
97. Morán, 29, tells us that Martínez Cartón did not arrive in Mexico before 1941.
98. Born in Valencia in 1901 under the name García Gómez, Gorkin entered politics at the age of 16. In the 1920s he was one of the leaders of the young PCE, but his refusal to serve in Morocco during the dictatorship of Primo de Rivera led to his exile from Spain. He went to Russia where, as a member of the Comintern, he moved in the company of Stalin, Zinoviev, Bukharin, and other members of the top Soviet leadership. But in 1929 he broke with Stalin and returned to Spain, founding the POUM in 1934 with Andrés Nin. During the Civil War he was editor of the POUM's central organ, *La Batalla*, but the May Days in 1937 led to his arrest. Given the unusual opportunity of a trial, Gorkin was able to mobilize his considerable support in Europe and the Americas with the result that he avoided execution, and though dragged from secret prison to secret prison he had the good fortune in 1939 to be released by his last jailers just before the arrival of Franco's forces. He reached Mexico in 1940, where with Victor Serge he founded the review *Análisis*.
99. These included his 2 sons Leon and Sergei Sedov, the first being murdered in Paris in Feb. 1938 and the second dying in a Soviet camp following his arrest in Jan. 1937; his two daughters Nathalia and Zeila Bronstein; and 6 of his secretaries, including Rudolf Klement and Erwin Wolf.
100. Conquest, 445–6. Since the first attempt to assassinate Trotsky in Mexico was bungled, it is probable that the mastermind was replaced for the second attempt. Eitingon may have been responsible for only one attempt, probably the second.
101. Gorkin, 34–5, raises the question of why Harte, against all the regulations, had opened the door to strangers, and he wonders if Harte might have been an accomplice; cf. Broué, 129–31. Victor Serge, 9, suggests instead that Harte opened the door precisely because he recognized a voice; then when he saw the gunmen and realized their intentions, they had to kill him to protect their identity. The memorial plaque which was later attached to a wall in Trotsky's garden reads: 'In memory of Robert Sheldon Harte. 1915–1940. Murdered by Stalin.'
102. 'Un Stalinien type'; Conquest, 446–7; Saña, 274–80; Broué, 123–9. Ricardo Paseyro reports, in Montaldo, 248, that as a result of this the Popular Front government of Chile, which had the proof of Neruda's complicity and of his relations with the NKVD, expelled him from the diplomatic service.
103. Conquest, 447.
104. Serge, 9.
105. James M. Markham, *New York Times*, 28 Oct. 1978.

106. There was no mention at all of Trotsky's death in the clandestine issues of *L'Humanité*. Yuri Paporov, the cultural attaché at the Soviet Embassy in Mexico City during Stalin's last years, retired from the diplomatic corps in the 1980s to devote himself to an investigation of Trotsky's death. Paporov has said that his research proves beyond doubt that Mercader was sent by Stalin, and that Mercader's body lies in Kuntsevo Cemetery in Moscow under a gravestone that reads: 'Lopez, Ramón Ivanovich, Hero of the Soviet Union' (Mark A. Uhlig, *International Herald Tribune*, 21 Dec. 1990).

107. Pivert *et al.*, 34–5. The brochure includes (p. 54) an open letter to President Avila, drawn up in New York on 9 Feb. 1942 and signed by an impressive number of celebrities. The letter defended the 4 anti–Stalinists against the hate campaign directed at them by the Comintern. Among the signatures were John Dewey, John Dos Passos, James T. Farrell, Frank P. Graham (president, University of North Carolina), Sidney Hook, Mary McCarthy, Thomas Mann, Reinhold Niebuhr, Culbert L. Olson (Governor of California), Katherine Anne Porter, Vincent Shean, Dorothy Thompson, and Edmund Wilson.

108. Settling in Paris, Gorkin moved into line with the PSOE, the Spanish socialist party. In March 1953 he launched the first issue of his Paris quarterly *Cuadernos*, organ of the Congrès pour la liberté des peuples et de la culture, which he served (until 1966) as secretary for Latin America. The Congress was anticommunist, and its very creation was the work of some American conservatives, but the masthead of *Cuadernos* ran like a *Who's Who* in Western philosophy and literature. The 7 honorary presidents were Benedetto Croce, John Dewey, Karl Jaspers, Salvador de Madariaga, Jacques Maritain, Bertrand Russell, and Reinhold Niebuhr. Its secretary-general was Nicolas Nabokov, and its first issue included articles by Victor Serge, Benedetto Croce, Fernando Valera, Ignazio Silone, André Malraux, Norman Mailer, Lionel Trilling, Upton Sinclair, Jean Cassou, Stephen Spender, and Herbert Read. Its last issue (no. 69, Feb. 1963) shows that its editorial board had become Hispanic, but again it was replete with leaders, this time in Spanish and Spanish-American letters. In 1970 Gorkin received the *Prix Voltaire*, and died in Paris on 20 Aug. 1987.

Gorkin's experiences made him reluctant to let even his friends know his address, but in his last years his home at 48 avenue Philippe-Auguste in Paris was open even to strangers. His astonishing memory and command of detail did not decline with the years. Bukharin, he would tell his guests, was his favourite among the followers of Lenin, 'the most human, the most open and decent'. As for Stalin, he found in him no redeeming features. 'His left arm was slightly shorter than his right. His left hand was slightly paralysed, and he would keep it close to his heart while he pummelled the table with his right. His whole profile was that of a monster. His face, when not wreathed in a smile for the required public image, was an expression of hatred and fury.' For two hours at a time Gorkin would reminisce without a pause, with such honesty and candour that it would have sickened his detractors to hear it. He readily admitted that he had friends in the American AFL-CIO who arranged his passage to New York in 1939 before he left for Mexico, but he was furious with Carrillo for his insinuation that he had been financed by the US intelligence services. In the course of several meetings I had with Gorkin, he ended one (on 21 Jan. 1984) with a curious confession: 'If I may speak candidly of this, I was the lover of Thorez's wife, a most beautiful woman. Thorez never touched her'.

Few men were more vilified than Gorkin. My personal impression never changed, that here was a scrupulously honest man, and that those who claimed the opposite found in him a massive hindrance to their hopes of falsifying the historical record.

109. *La Batalla*, 29 Nov. 1948; 'El Campesino', *Vie*, 197–8; Rienffer, 125–39; Gorkin, 273, who adds: 'I publicly accuse Contreras of this murder'; Macdonald, 112. According to Rienffer, 18, the Comintern also sent to America in 1941 its old agent Felipe García Guerrero, known in Spain during the Civil War under the pseudonym Santiago Matas. But the guilt of the Stalinists is no more proved in the murder of Tresca than it is in that of Berneri, because the finger of suspicion has also been pointed at Vito Genovese, an associate of Charles ('Lucky') Luciano. Genovese had already provided Mussolini with $250,000 for the construction of the Fascist Party's headquarters in Rome, and to do him another favour (at a time when Luciano was co-operating with the US Government) Genovese allegedly arranged the killing of Tresca.

110. In Jan. 1947 Vidali left Mexico for Moscow, and within a few weeks he was Stalin's choice for a very special mission: to take command of the Party in the Free Territory of Trieste, and to counter Tito. In a speech he gave in Nov. 1948, he declared: 'The battle against Tito must be waged to the very end.' Tito, of course, was not the same easy target as Tresca.

111. Gerö won a certain world fame on 23 Oct. 1956 when, as leader of the Hungarian Communist Party, he sought to discourage the growing anti-Soviet feeling in Budapest by ordering police to fire into a group of demonstrators, thus triggering the Hungarian uprising. He died in Budapest in Mar. 1980, aged 81.

112. See above, Ch. 1, n. 26.

113. *'Un stalinien type.'*

114. Thomas, 702.

115. Claudín, *Santiago*, 72.

116. Ibid. 78. Checa died in Mexico on 6 Aug. 1942 (Heine, 230).

CHAPTER 4

1. SS advice to every *Zugang*.

2. 'Rapport général sur les activités des Républicains espagnols dans la libération de la France et dans la lutte contre l'armée d'occupation', Amicale des Anciens FFI et Résistants espagnols, Conseil national, 2;

Gordon, 437; Weill, 112–13, who cites the report of Maurice Dubois, of the Secours Suisse aux Enfants, according to which the number of those detained in Argelès on 20 Nov. 1940 amounted to 15,500, including 13,000 Spaniards and 1,300 International Brigaders, but excluding the 3,000 Spaniards who arrived from Bram. The figures provided by Rubio, *Guerra civil*, 319–20, 334, differ starkly from those of Dr Weill. According to Rubio, whose source is Dr Cramer's report to the International Red Cross, there were no more than 3,024 Spaniards in Argelès in Nov. 1940, and only 4,651 Spaniards interned in the whole of France. Rubio (ibid. 320) refers to a 'probable error' in Dr Cramer's report in respect to Argelès, which he corrects without explaining the substance of the error.

3. Rubio, ibid. 924. The GTE in 1941 numbered 60,000, of whom 20,000 were Jews and most of the rest were Spanish (Marrus and Paxton, 171).

4. Vilanova, 199. They included some Spaniards taken prisoner in the Compagnies de travailleurs.

5. Stein, 125–6. Stein adds that the Spaniards were in possession of German safe-conduct passes as they left Perpignan.

6. Dalmau, 7–13; Wood, 124; Soriano, 35. Dalmau tells us that his killing of Schultz was an act of personal revenge.

7. The Soviets were the second group to enter. Another convoy of Spaniards arrived on 22 Feb. 1942, and the Jews from Drancy on 12 Aug. 1943. There were 1,500 prisoners in the camp in May 1944 when orders were given to begin the evacuation in preparation for the expected Allied invasion. The evacuation was completed on 25 June (Iselin, 59).

8. Dalmau, 16.

9. Angel [Sanz], *Guerrilleros*, 51. During the Civil War, *Acero* had been the name of the journal of Líster's vth Army Corps of Modesto's Army of the Ebro.

10. Dalmau, 24; Pantcheff, *passim*; Steckoll, 26, 84–9; Soriano, 35. After the Liberation, Adler and Evers were tried as war criminals by a French court and were sentenced to long periods of imprisonment (Pantcheff, 77).

11. Vilanova, 147, 198, gives the figure of 46,000, broken down as follows: Captured in 1940 in the French Compagnies de travailleurs, Bataillons de marche, and French Foreign Legion, 30,000; Forced or voluntary workers, 15,000; Arrested Resistance members and captured guerrilleros, 1,000. Rolland, *Vichy*, 144, gives a total of 40,000.

12. Vilanova, 147. Vilanova tends to inflate his figures.

13. Cinca, 14–51, *passim*; Juan de Diego Herranz (interviews).

14. Vilanova, 198; Stein, 242. Stein gives the figure of 10,350 Spaniards entering Mauthausen from a single camp (Stalag xi-b, at Fallingbostel, north of Hanover) during the period from 6 Aug. 1940 to 20 Dec. 1941, using the official German record which, Stein adds, contains gaps. These figures, however, are disputed by Juan de Diego, whose lower figures (7,288 for the entire period from 6 Aug. 1940 to 16 Apr. 1945) are given in Fabréguet, 'Groupe', 35. Cf. Borrás [Lluch], 89, 363–7.

15. Cf. Pike, *Jours*, 13 n.; and Fabréguet, 'Groupe', 34–5, who points out that

over 1,000 Spaniards had arrived in Mauthausen even before Serrano Súñer arrived in Berlin. Serrano's visit to Berlin on 15–25 Sept. 1940 was memorable for more than his talks with the Nazi leaders. A group of Spanish Republicans then in Berlin were assembled in the Olympic Stadium, where they were inspected by Serrano and his SS hosts and ordered to give the Nazi salute. An eyewitness, Enrique Ruiz, has described the scene. (Ruiz was only 16 when he served in the Civil War as lieutenant escort to General Vicente Rojo, the Republican chief of staff, and he was only 17 now.) The Republicans remonstrated, whereupon Serrano lunged at them with his baton, drawing blood from Ruiz's nose, and all the while calling them Red cowards (*Hispania*, 66, 2nd series (Feb. 1980)).

16. Vilanova, 200–1; Climent Sarrión, *Hispania*, 54, 2nd series (Apr.–May 1976). Cf. J. Bailina, *Hispania*, 42, 2nd series (July 1972), whose figures are close to those of Climent.

17. Vilanova, 199. Constante's performance on Spanish television on 17 Jan. 1976, and the information he presented in *Vanguardia*, on 21 Jan. 1976, drew an angry response from Climent. Climent, who worked in Mauthausen's Politische Abteilung from the day he arrived (25 Nov. 1940), described Constante, who was employed in the Disinfection squad, as a novelist who recounts war stories that never happened and a participant who claims ranks and responsibilities he never held. As for Constante's ever more inflated figures, added Climente, 'they all come straight off the top of his egocentric head' (*Hispania*, 54, 2nd series (Apr.–May 1976)).

18. Borrás [Lluch], 185. Borrás, no less than Juan de Diego and Razola, was an inmate of Mauthausen, entering the camp on 23 July 1941 at the age of 24 (ibid. 127).

19. Including 3,839 in Gusen and 499 in Schloss Hartheim.

20. Including 4,200 in Gusen. In their 1979 Spanish edition, which is merely a translation from the French except for the addition of 2 appendices (pp. 193–330) listing the dead, the authors scale down their estimate to a total of 4,074.

21. Rovan, 68.

22. Alfaya, 102.

23. Rubio, *Guerra civil*, 406 n.

24. Vilanova, 98.

25. Through some administrative error 17 non-Jewish Spaniards were transferred from Dachau and Maidanek to Auschwitz. One of them, José Guerrero Pérez, survived (Vilanova, 98, 176). Still alive and well in Paris in 1992, he refuses to speak of the past (interview).

26. The astonishing figures given above by the survivor John Dalmau are omitted from this tableau, because no figures at all for Alderney appear anywhere else. Even the detailed account by Pantcheff virtually ignores the presence of Spaniards on the island.

27. The equally astonishing figures given by the survivor Largo Caballero to Pasionaria: '5,000 Spaniards interned, of whom 500 survived' (Ibarruri, *Memorias*, 611), are also omitted for lack of corroboration.

28. Vilanova, 200–1. No one else has produced an estimate of Spanish fatalities in SS camps other than Mauthausen, but it seems, in the light of the above, that the total is considerably higher.
29. Ibid. 201.
30. Ibid. 98.
31. Rubio, *Guerra civil*, 406.
32. Razola and Constante, 76.
33. Vilanova, 196.
34. Ibid. 200–1; Rubio, *Guerra civil*, 410.
35. Boüard, 'Mauthausen', 41; Vilanova, 96–7. The latter claims that Himmler took this decision earlier, on 28 Aug. 1940.
36. Le Chêne, 64.
37. Busson, 176.
38. This list is by no means complete.
39. Vilanova, 182.
40. Ibid. 184.
41. Maršálek, *Geschichte*, 286.
42. So called from the pronunciation in German of *KZ*, one of the two abbreviations of *Konzentrationslager*; hence, a concentration camp inmate.
43. This category included supporters of Ernst Röhm as well as Germans taken prisoner while serving in the French Foreign Legion and sentenced as traitors to Germany.
44. A green triangle pointing in the opposite direction (upwards) indicated that the holder was given to uncontrollably violent behaviour; in most cases he had been released from a mental institution to which he had been confined for murder, incest, or rape.
45. Mauthausen had only 40 (Tillard, 30).
46. While the majority of these were German Jehovah's Witnesses, any German refusing to serve Hitler on the basis of religious beliefs could be given the purple triangle. Catholic priests were referred to by the SS as *Kanzeljuden*, and monks as *Kuttenscheisse*.
47. The yellow triangle, pointing upwards, was placed under a second triangle, pointing downwards, forming a Star of David. The second triangle could be red, green, or black, depending on the prisoner's status.
48. This category consisted of those who had refused the work or workplace assigned to them.
49. Tillard, 30, tells us, from his own experience in Mauthausen, that black triangles were never made Block Kapos, since the job required an ability to speak, write, and count, and they lacked it.
50. Vilanova, 135–6; Le Chêne, 40–1; Alfaya, 107.
51. Pappalettera, 221.
52. Cf. Borrás [Lluch], 264, for a table of the 160 Spaniards who attained these posts. Among the rarer forms of employment was that given at Buchenwald to 3 German communists, who were appointed by 2 SS officers, who were doctoral candidates, to write the officers' dissertations (Kühn and Weber, 78).
53. Pappalettera, 41–2. Even survivors from the same camp can fundamentally

contradict one another in their testimony. Jean Laffitte, 242–3, presents an inmate hierarchy in which the *Prominenten* are the most privileged class. Juan de Diego and Lázaro Nates, on the other hand, point out that where privilege is concerned, the only one that any prisoner really cared about was eating more. The *Prominenten* ate a little better than the mass, but not all that much better, while the Kapos ate well (interviews).

54. Glücks, headquartered at Oranienburg, thereafter answered both to Pohl and to Heydrich.
55. Pappalettera, 31, 38; Iselin, 77–8; Borrás [Lluch], 169–70. Even the total of 91 Mauthausen Aussenkommandos compiled by Borrás, 263, is not complete; cf. Iselin's list and the International Tracing Service, *Catalogue*.
56. Pappalettera, 143.
57. Kruger was employed at Mauthausen first as a sentry and later in the Politische Abteilung.
58. Boüard, 'Mauthausen', 56; Pappalettera, 28–33, 79. Gœring and Kaltenbrunner attested to this at the Nuremberg Tribunal (Borrás [Lluch], 175).
59. *Mauthausen*, 17.
60. Vilanova, 116, 144.
61. Debrise, 48; Boüard, 'Mauthausen', 59.
62. Debrise, 35.
63. At the barbers, nothing was wasted. Vilanova, 119, refers to 7 tons of women's hair used by the Raeski firm to make carpets and slippers for U-boat crews.
64. Aldebert, 22; Delfieu, 68, 103; Iselin, 95–6.
65. Boüard, 'Mauthausen', 59.
66. Juan de Diego, interview. The lights could not be seen beyond 500 m., nor above a height of 100 m. (Horwitz, 15–16).
67. Pappalettera, 122, 127.
68. Tillard, 43, 61.
69. Le Caër, 19.
70. Cinca, 117; Razola and Constante, 41–2; Vilanova, 141–2; Maršálek, *Geschichte*, 30.
71. Aldebert, 56.
72. Pappalettera, 25.
73. Maršálek, *Geschichte*, 285.
74. Mauthausen being different from the normal, the prisoner there had the right to rest only every other Sunday, except at Ebensee, where there was no rest at all (Laffitte, 256). On the other hand, once the decision was taken to reduce the death rate, those working in Mauthausen's quarry were excused work from Saturday afternoon to Monday morning. The purpose, writes the survivor Tillard, (p. 51), was only to prolong the agony, to prevent any prisoner from dying too fast.
75. Maršálek, *Geschichte*, 200.
76. 'J'attendrai, toujours, jour et nuit, ton retour...'
77. Vilanova, 176–7; Maršálek, *Geschichte*, 197.
78. Maršálek, *Mauthausen*, 18. Even in hanging, the SS worked out some refinements. At *KL*-Buchenwald and elsewhere, victims were hanged from

the mouth instead of the throat in order to prolong the agony. Again, at *KL*-Flossenburg and elsewhere, those waiting to be hanged were gagged up to the last moment to deprive them of the chance to call out last appeals for courage and defiance.

79. Vilanova, 101, 139–40. Maršálek, *Geschichte*, 292, considers that the SS were the first to adopt it, as an alternative to their other terms, *Kretiner* and *Schwimmer*. The term derives from the bodily movements of these prisoners, especially in the use of their hands and the forward fall of their bodies, reminiscent of a Muslim at prayer.

80. Juan de Diego (interview).

81. Boüard, 'Mauthausen', 68, 79.

82. Roig, 'Generación', 36.

83. Razola and Constante, 65. Whoever was unattached, or had no family left, may well have held an advantage. 'If a man broke down and cried for his family, as some men did, he was doomed. We said he had 10 days left to live' (Dobias, interview).

84. Gouffault, 42.

85. Primo Levi, *The Drowned and the Saved* (New York: Summit, 1987).

86. Gaucher, 3.

87. Arrested at 19 by the Gestapo near Auxerre, when he operated under the name of Gérard, Semprún had been sent to the sorting centre at Compiègne and had then undergone the 5-day nightmare journey, with 120 to a cattle-car, in the train to Buchenwald. For his poem, written at Buchenwald on 17 Feb. 1945 and entitled 'Le rêve ancien', see Pouzol, 109–10. Cf. Jorge Semprún, *Le Grand Voyage* (Paris: Gallimard, 1972), 119.

88. Hénoque, 46–8.

89. Vilanova, 131.

90. Ibid. 105–6. Juan de Diego (interview), denies this: 'The lights were not kept on all night.' The truth, apparently, is that some were, but were not visible to aircraft (see above, n. 66).

91. Boüard, 'Mauthausen', 40, contends that this action was taken 'at the beginning of 1938', presumably before the *Anschluss*. This is not possible.

92. Maršálek, *Mauthausen*, 32; Alfaya, 104.

93. Vilanova, 133.

94. Inmate no. 1 was a Jewish doctor who had served as a surgeon in the International Brigades in Spain; he died on the barbed wire (Macdonald, 299).

95. Boüard, 'Mauthausen', 41.

96. Alfaya, 102.

97. Pappalettera, 38.

98. Alfaya, 102, estimates the number of K prisoners at 25,000.

99. Maršálek, *Mauthausen*, 1.

100. Vilanova, 108; he suggests that all these were registered, which is surely untrue. Vilanova, 116, subsequently adds 30,000 who were executed without being registered.

101. Pappalettera, 38. Cf. Borrás [Lluch], 183–4.
102. Maršálek, *Geschichte*, 30.
103. Cf. Vilanova, 121.
104. Maršálek, *Geschichte*, 103, reproducing an official WVHA chart. Only Buchenwald and Gross-Rosen had more, and only because of the large number of women in these two camps.
105. Pappalettera, 38, citing SS documents. The figures given by Vilanova, 121, and Razola and Constante, 149, are inaccurate guesses.
106. Pappalettera, 38.
107. Ibid. 50; Juan de Diego (interview).
108. Le Chêne, 172. The Totenkopfverbände was that part of the Allgemeine-SS which was consigned to guarding the concentration camps, and is not to be confused with the 3rd SS-Panzerdivision ('Totenkopf') which was Waffen-SS.
109. Boüard, 'Mauthausen', 68. Christopher Burney, 156, who was interned in Buchenwald, presents a different picture of the communists he observed in that camp: 'The communists were merely Nazis painted red, neither better nor worse, pawning their souls and their fellows' lives for a mock abstract power.'
110. Michelet, 154–6. Cf. the memoirs of Charles Renaud, a survivor of Ebensee, who combines a chauvinism with a dislike of both Jews and Spaniards (56, 125).
111. José Amat Piniella nevertheless held the distinction, while a prisoner in Mauthausen, of surviving a sentence of 3 months in the punishment company, as is shown in the surviving German records (Borrás [Lluch], 369).
112. Juan de Diego, who is not anticommunist, considers Razola and Constante shameless manipulators (interview). Constante later produced a more detailed account (*Yo fui ordenanza*), but the question must be asked if he could really trust his memory after waiting 30 years to write it. Constante was nevertheless among the best placed of prisoners to compile a useful memoir: taken prisoner in France on 21 June 1940 and given the early Mauthausen registration number 4584, he was assigned to the office of the camp commandant Ziereis as orderly to SS-Oberscharführer Willy Weber.
113. Boüard, 'Mauthausen', 80.
114. Ibid. 74.
115. Razola and Constante, 161.
116. Cf. Vilanova, 85, 197.
117. Ibid. 215. Vilanova, 197, refers to Casimiro Climent and Manuel Razola as the two Spaniards holding the key positions in the camp, without mentioning Juan de Diego. Vilanova interviewed the first two but not the third. Razola, however, is not in the same class as the other two: although he was a leader of the resistance organization and is an important witness to that, he was not employed as the others were in the camp archives.
118. Le Chêne, 153, writes that they even had to wear SS uniform. Juan de Diego (interview) emphatically disagrees.

119. Vilanova, 215; Pons, *Republicanos*, 42.
120. Vilanova, 197, 215–16.
121. At least another 50 Spaniards died between 2 May and the liberation of the camp a few days later. Juan de Diego, keeping his own secret record while working in the *Lagerschreibstube*, produced a total of 4,854.
122. Ferencz, 53. Ferencz is now Senior Special Fellow at the United Nations Institute for Training and Research, and a professor of international law at Pace University, New York.
123. Juan de Diego (interview).
124. Le Chêne, 109–10, who interviewed Climent, writes that he managed to hide no less than 14 kilos of prisoners' files behind a cabinet placed there to conceal a former window in the wall. Since there are 3 separate surviving collections involved here, it seems that Le Chêne has confused Climent's testimony: the largest of the 3 collections, weighing the 14 kilos to which she refers, was in fact hidden in the boxes.
125. The copies were distributed to the International Red Cross, the Ministère des Anciens combattants et victimes de guerre in Paris, the Asociación de Deportados Españoles Antifascistas (which later became the Amicale de Mauthausen) also in Paris, and the leaders of the 5 Spanish political parties or labour unions represented in Mauthausen (Vilanova, 216; Rubio, *Guerra civil*, 410 n.).
126. Juan de Diego Herranz to Herr Ohren, Magistrates' Court, Cologne: Luchon, 21 Dec. 1962.
127. Michael S. Bernstein, Office of Special Investigations, US Department of Justice, Washington, DC, to Juan de Diego Herranz: 23 June 1987.
128. Boix, in turn, agreed to develop and print the private photos of an Obersturmführer in exchange for his help in assigning a Spaniard, who was a cook, to the SS kitchen (Constante, *Yo fui*, 109).
129. Juan de Diego (interview).
130. Cf. García (interview): 'Bargueño hid them briefly in the *Arrest*.'
131. Frau Pointner was a communist and member of the local resistance who kept close contact with the Spanish boys. Constante, 268–9, writes that, even if she had been arrested, the treasures that they entrusted to her would have been safe, so carefully did she hide them.
132. Razola and Constante, 12, 103–4; Vilanova, 214–15; Roig, 'Generación', 37. Boix took the material with him to France, and the collection first appeared in the two works, both published in 1969, of Vilanova and Razola-Constante. Alfaya, 120, mentions that the curator of the museum at Mauthausen (in 1976) was a former Spanish prisoner, Manolo García.

CHAPTER 5

1. Such was the contemptuous remark of an Arab chronicler in reference to Don Pelayo, who from a cave at Covadonga sallied forth to launch guerrilla warfare (the first of its kind) against the occupation forces of Islam.

2. Tillon, *On chantait*, 339.
3. Cf. Pike, *Jours*, 34–5. Even in 1986, Goubet and Debauges' *Histoire* covers the contribution of the Spaniards in less than 3 pages; their bibliography contains not a single item by a Spanish author. Stein, 292, would make an exception in the case of Chambard on the grounds that he has 'many favourable comments on the Spaniards'. But Chambard's French edition does not even mention a Spaniard; his American edition mentions Spaniards only in reference to the 'Ebro' platoon at Glières, and gives the names of two sentries (105, 122–4).
4. Bravo-Tellado, 266, 353. Trempé, 66, refers to a contingent of forced labourers assembled in Aude in June 1943 in which 200 were Spaniards and only 69 were French. All together, in the period 1943–4, 40,000 Spaniards, or over half the remaining Spanish refugee population in France, were sent to Germany as forced labourers (Rolland, *Vichy*, 144, 157).

   One of the rare accounts by a Spaniard of life in Germany as a foreign volunteer is that of Vicente Fillol, 44–5. Fillol was apparently not a communist; if he had been, his later contribution to the Resistance would have qualified him for the rank of hero, in which case he would have been eligible for a suicide mission to Spain. The Germans had announced that, for every 5 workers who volunteered to work in Germany, 1 French prisoner of war would be allowed to return to France. Fillol did not actually volunteer. Instead he was caught in a round-up, probably in late 1941, and he and those with him (3 Catalans, the rest French) were simply shanghaied. They were sent to Berlin, where they were well treated. Their barracks were heated and comfortable, with hot showers, blankets and sheets, good and abundant food, and coffee at all times. In exchange for the clothing they arrived in, which was burnt, they were given new, including shoes, overcoat, and gloves. They even received money to spend in the free time they were allowed every day to get to know Berlin. They were then sent to Russia, and in Feb. 1942 they found themselves in the area between Estonia and Leningrad. Their work consisted of driving and operating tip-trucks used by the Wehrmacht for the repair of the roads; the sand they carried was loaded and unloaded by Soviet prisoners of war. It was not long before the group's working conditions deteriorated to the point that they may as well have been forced labourers. When their assignment was completed—it was still 1942—they returned to Berlin and thence to Paris, being astonished in both cities to receive a heroes' welcome. In both cases it was due to administrative error: they were mistaken for members of the Blue Division, a mistake which of course they silently resented.
5. Maury alias Frank, *Maquis*, 152.
6. In his review of my *Jours de gloire*, Hervé Coutau-Bégarie writes that I am wrong to give the credit to the Spaniards, since their first rally did not convene until Oct. 1940, while the French Resistance was already at work in July (*Politique étrangère*, 2184 (1984), 448). The problem is how

to define active resistance. I submit that the guerrilla unit organized by Jesús Monzón in late 1940 was the earliest of its kind. The first French Maquis was not formed before the end of 1942, and the earliest engagements were not undertaken until July 1943, as the French historians Henri Michel and Henri Noguères confirm, while a *guerrillero* unit was in action in the Alps from the beginning of that year (see below, n. 49).

7. Cf. Pike, *Jours*, 32–3. Riquelme was now working with other Spanish Republicans in the Mexican Legation in Vichy. None of them held diplomatic immunity, and the authorities took advantage of the temporary absence of General Aguilar, the Mexican minister, to enter the Legation on 13 May 1942 and arrest Riquelme. This led Mexico to withdraw its minister (Rolland, 146, 148, 152, 258, 323). Although Riquelme subsequently regained his freedom, he played no role of any consequence in the Resistance.

8. Cf. Pike, *Jours*, 32 n.

9. The first call, in *L'Humanité*, 2 July 1941, invited communist railway workers to make 'mistakes', whereby munitions trains *en route* to Germany would take the wrong direction.

10. *L'Humanité*, July 1941, special issue.

11. *L'Humanité*, 7 Aug. 1941. It was an example of that *pokazukha* (boasting about non-existent achievements) that became a household word—and strictly within the household—in the Soviet Union.

12. Cf. Amouroux, ii. 415–61.

13. No intimidation could be effective for long, added Keitel on 7 Dec. 1941, just before the *Nacht und Nebel* decree was introduced, unless the victim's relatives and friends and the population in general were left in total ignorance of the victim's fate; for this purpose, the victims were to be taken to Germany for execution. The name '*Nacht und Nebel*' derives from a passage in Wagner's *Rheingold*, in which Fafner tells the dwarfs to disperse like the night and mist. In Gestapo practice, it meant that the victim literally disappeared in the middle of the night, with no word ever heard from him or of him again.

14. Defrasne, *Occupation*, 71.

15. Estruch, 69.

16. Heine, 102.

17. Morán, 80, notes that only Pasionaria or Uribe could have taken the initiative to offer peace to the socialists, and surmises that the 'open letter' carries the stamp of Pasionaria, her style being more fluid than the turgid and tautological prose of Uribe.

18. Heine, 104–6, who cites *Nuestra bandera*, Aug.–Sept. 1941; Morán, 80.

19. Anarchists also took part, but in autonomous units and without co-ordination. The socialists either fought with the anarchists or, more frequently, were swallowed up in the communist organization.

20. Amouroux, i. 437.

21. Trempé, 65.

22. Goubet and Debauges, 17.

23. Trempé, 65.
24. A former professor of law at the University of Padua and socialist member of parliament, Trentin had lived in France as a refugee since 1926, opening his bookshop in 1934. He returned to his home in Treviso after the fall of Mussolini, but prematurely, for he was arrested by the fascists and died in detention on 12 Mar. 1944.
25. Goubet and Debauges, 18, 118.
26. Ibid. 116.
27. This lacuna was finally filled by *Les Juifs dans la résistance et la libération: Histoire, témoignages, débats* (Paris: Scribe, 1985).
28. Kriegel, 138.
29. Robrieux, ii. 316–17.
30. Faligot and Kauffer, 64. Grojnowski writes under the name of Gronowski-Brunot.
31. Noguères, i. 161.
32. Arthur London admitted that before the invasion of the USSR neither the Travail Allemand nor *Der Soldat im Westen* was in existence: 'Only pamphlets were printed, and unfortunately these were not conserved' (interview).
33. The Travail Allemand published, more or less regularly, 9 underground journals and some 200 pamphlets, printing a total of some 5m. copies. Among the journals was *Der Soldat am Mittelmeer*, produced in the Southern Zone (Sentis, thesis, 65). A German soldier working as a telephone switchboard operator in Albi was won over to the Resistance in June 1944 and assisted the Resistance in this work (ibid. 213).
34. Mercedes de la Iglesia, in Catalá, 171.
35. Arthur London, French television Channel 2, 18 Mar. 1984.
36. Noguères, i. 89; Trempé, 72–3; Goubet and Debauges, 93.
37. Wood and charcoal were the commodities which the French were allowed to use as fuel, whether for heating or for running their cars. This explains the new importance of the charcoal workers, whose role in the Resistance is reminiscent of that of the *carbonari* in Italy in the early 19th c.
38. Cassou, 57.
39. e.g. by inserting a cow's horn into the rail, creating a false point (Cossías, 53).
40. Heine, 209.
41. Goubet and Debauges, 22. This branch of the Resistance did nevertheless attract certain Spanish anarchist leaders, notably Paco Ponzán and José Ester Borrás.
42. As a survivor; the Gestapo had dismantled the 'Musée de l'homme' Resistance network in Paris.
43. Cassou, 'La Résistance en Languedoc', *Résistance R4*, 1, p. 65. Cassou himself admits to the extreme difficulty of presenting a comprehensive account of the Resistance in Toulouse and its surrounding region.
44. At their trial in July 1942, Bertaux, Cassou, and Nitti received sentences

of 1–3 years' imprisonment, Bernard was given 20, but no one was executed.

45. Goubet and Debauges, 23–4.
46. Artís-Gener, 167; Francesc Parramón, in Milza and Peschanski, 607. François Mongelard passed through several *KL*, but apparently not Mauthausen. He died in *KL*-Nordhausen on 6 Mar. 1943. His wife survived and returned to Toulouse, but died soon afterwards (Pons, *Republicanos*, 305–6).
47. Cf. Weill, 114.
48. Arasa, 34.
49. Formed near Villards-sur-Thônes in Haute-Savoie, it began with 15 men, including Miguel Vera and several other Spaniards, under the command of a Frenchman (Pons, *Republicanos*, 252).
50. Goubet and Debauges, 95.
51. In Greffeil (Aude) on 15 May 1942, *guerrilleros* made off with 200 kilos of dynamite from the mines of La Caunette (Agudo, 50). Dynamite from mines was also obtained by *guerrilleros* in Haute-Garonne, in the area around Alès in Gard, and especially in Carmaux in Tarn (Fernández, *Emigración*, 28). It was in the mines of Grand-Combe (Gard) that Cristino García organized a passive resistance, perhaps as early as July 1940 (Billes and García-Villar, 135).
52. Fernández, *España*, 28; Agudo, 49–50; Trempé, 68–9. The unit included several anarchists employed as charcoal workers in Montfort and Mérial— sites of atrocities committed by communists against anarchists in the wake of the Libération (cf. Pike, *Jours*, 80–2).
53. *Reconquista de España*, 16 Sept. 1944.
54. Fernández, *España* (1967), 18.
55. Ibid.
56. Antonio Ferriz, in *Conferencia de Unión Nacional Española*, 45.
57. Pilar Claver, in Català, 111–12.
58. A notable exception was Francisco Perramón (Heine, 86). Under the name 'Dupuis', Perramón headed the PCE in the south-west from May 1940 until June 1942, when he moved to Paris to reorganize the Party after the massive round-up in that month (Z6 NL 13717, Archives nationales, Paris).
59. Sanz, *Luchando*, 68.
60. Alff, 6.
61. Claudín, 64; Arasa, 24; Morán, 84. Antón, adds Morán, considered Carmen de Pedro more reliable than Monzón, but Monzón had the advantage that Pasionaria found him appealing.
62. Estruch, 95; Morán, 87–8.
63. Azcárate was in charge of the JSU at the time of his arrival in France, but had then moved into the PCE administration, leaving the responsibility for the JSU to Gimeno.
64. The subject is so hard to elucidate that every account should be considered, even that of the Francoist chronicler Tomás Cossías, who should be approached with caution if only because Angel Ruiz Ayúcar, who

shares his ideology, rarely follows his lead. (Cossías refers, e.g., to Luis Fernández as 'Evaristo', which he never was, and as chief of the AGE, which he could not have been before the AGE was created—in 1944). Be that is it may, Cossías presents the Delegation as Mariano (secretary-general), Gimeno (secretary of organization), and Carmen de Pedro (secretary of Agitprop). Cossías is the only writer to mention a woman known both as Raquel and Rebeca, who served as secretary-general of the JSU, and another, known as Elena, who served as Mariano's mistress (Cossías, 51, 56). Cossías also tells us that the PCE's controlling committee divided the Southern Zone into 3 organic sectors. One of these consisted of Basses-Pyrénées, Hautes-Pyrénées, and Gers, and was entrusted to Francisco Mera ('Julio), a nephew of the fiercely anticommunist Cipriano Mera of the anarchist CNT. A second sector comprised Haute-Garonne, Ariège, and Pyrénées-Orientales, under the control of Agustín Cortés. The third, covering Tarn, Aude, and Hérault, was commanded by Francisco Bas Aguado ('Pedro'), who later became the information chief at AGE headquarters (Cossías, 53; Arasa, 80).

For another version of how the Delegation developed, see Morán, 84. Unfortunately, this author provides no bibliography and almost never reveals his sources.

65. Also in the 'first circle' was Adela Collado ('Anita'), who became the wife of Gimeno (Arasa, 25), and Esperanza Rodríguez, who became the wife of Ignacio Gallego (Cossías, 56; cf. Sanz, *Luchando*, 128).

66. Cf. Pike, *Jours*, 191 n.

67. Sanz, *Luchando*, 43; Heine, 193; Arasa, 26; Morán, 85. It was in Marseilles that the PCE moved into close contact with the PCI, which at that time had greater experience in clandestine operations. It was the PCI that gave Monzón the duplicating machine with which he published, in Aug. 1941, the first issue of *Reconquista de España*.

68. Sanz, *Luchando*, 43, and Heine, 192, deny it; Sanz states that the Delegation came into existence only after the German invasion of Russia. Arasa, 25, writing after Sanz but before Heine, strongly believes that the Delegation was already formed before October 1940. Arasa, a Catalan journalist, has written a useful work of investigation, but unfortunately in an unscientific form. As this important matter now stands, no conclusive evidence has been presented either way.

69. Arasa, 26.

70. Heine, 193. Agudo, 54, writes that he himself was given charge of a school of political education, named 'Cara a España', which was set up in the forests of the Montagne Noire.

71. Sanz, *Luchando*, 30. Cf. Agudo, 37.

72. Arasa, 26. Radio España Independiente was indeed heard in France. Neus Català, who was arrested and sent to Ravensbrück in 1943, attests to this, having listened to it while living in Dordogne. It was relayed, she believes, from Algiers or Andorra (interview).

73. Ibid. 46. Cf. Morán, 86, who attributes their move to Switzerland in 1943 to the pressure of the Gestapo.

74. Sanz, *Luchando*, 46; Heine, 193; Arasa, 27.
75. Sanz, *Luchando*, 46, based on the testimony of Sánchez Vizcaino. María Llena has told how *Mundo obrero* was printed in the Paris suburb of Saint-Denis, and how she received orders to pick up a batch of 50 at a time and distribute them (interview).
76. Sanz, *Luchando*, 46. Sanz adds that Arthur London and Lise Ricol served as intermediaries, but in my interview with the two Londons the only Spaniards in the Resistance whose names they recognized were Azcárate and Miret Musté.
77. Its commanding officer was Domingo Ungría, and its political commissar Peregrín Pérez. The idea for such a guerrilla force in Spain was formed as early as 1937, and its organization went into effect in Feb. 1938. The modest guerrilla operations which it mounted were disrupted in Mar. 1939 by the Casado rebellion, and the xivth Army Corps quickly disintegrated (Arasa, 18). Ungría and Pérez were in Russia by 1940.
78. Sanz, *Luchando*, 112; Agudo, 49.
79. They included Angel Celadas, Julio Lucas, Cristino García, and Jesús Ríos. Most of the 12 were employed as charcoal workers in Aude (Agudo, 49).
80. Courtois *et al.*, 141, 180. The raid, which became known to the French police as the '1st affair of the Spaniards', was ordered by Paul Martz, Commissaire de Police à la Direction générale des Renseignements généraux. Martz entrusted the operation to Buisson, Inspecteur principal adjoint à la 3ème Section, and his deputy, Inspecteur Eugène Raymond Bijeau, who in 1945 would find himself on trial for collaboration with the enemy. Even the police described the operation as a monster round-up: no fewer than 150 inspectors were assigned to it. Buisson attributed the success of the operation to the arrest of some Spaniards a few days earlier (implying that they broke under torture), and to the help of one of these, a woman identified only as 'Paquita', who, for one reason or another, had denounced one or more of her comrades (Buisson to Commissaire principal, chef de la 3ème Section: Paris, 30 Nov. 1942. Z6 NL 13717, Archives nationales, Paris).
81. María Llena (interview). This account fundamentally contradicts the testimony given in her name by Català, 195–7; suffice it to say that María Llena had never seen Català's book before I showed it to her. She remains a most loyal admirer of Pasionaria, whom she met several times in Paris and whose giant portrait hangs in her foyer. Her daughter still lives in the apartment on the rue Quincampoix that served as their resistance centre.
82. Sanz, *Luchando*, 40, 52, 56. Sanz is the only author to describe the PCE leadership in Paris, but he contradicts himself on Juan Montero: after writing (pp. 56–7) that Montero was arrested in Nov. 1942 and sent to Mauthausen in 1943, he states (p. 92) that Montero was arrested in Rennes in 1944 soon after he had arrived in Paris to head the movement.
83. The weekly but ephemeral *Catalunya* first appeared on 5 Aug. 1939, under the direction of Raymond Legrand whose editorial office was at 50 rue de Paradis. Its fifth issue of 2 Sept. was its last (following the law

suppressing the communist press) until its rebirth in the Liberation. *Catalunya* in 1939 was conciliatory: it paid tribute not only to the USSR, André Marty, the PSUC, and Comorera, but also to the former Catalan president, Lluis Companys.

84. Courtois *et al.*, 182. In spelling the cover name of this Catalan communist leader, French police reports alternate between 'Regnier' and 'Reignier' (Z6 NL 13717, Archives nationales, Paris).

85. The role of Olaso Piera remains obscure. Early in the Spanish Civil War he had been appointed inspector-general of public order in his native Catalonia, taking his orders directly from Ernö Gerö ('Pedro'), head of the Soviet services in that region. The post enabled Olaso to spread the communist network throughout the Catalan police organization (cf. Bolloten, 614). At the end of the Civil War he fled to France with his companion Dolores García, and the two then set themselves up, first in Bordeaux and then in Paris, under the name of Martin. At the urging of Olaso, and under the name of Charlotte Jeantet née Martin, she obtained a post in the Chilean Embassy as personal secretary to Pablo Neruda, who in the absence of the Ambassador served as Minister Plenipotentiary. Her real function was to keep watch on all Spanish refugees and to report to the NKVD. With the arrival of the Germans, Olaso, now known as 'Emmanuel', became the third man in the leadership of the FTP-MOI, responsible for the acquisition, storage, and distribution of arms and explosives. In early December 1942, the network's no. 2, the Czech Karel Stepka, fell into a police trap and broke down under torture, giving away Olaso's address at 7 rue du Colonel-Oudot. Early in the evening of 5 Dec., the police pounced. Olaso was taken away, and whether or not under torture gave away in turn the address of Boris Holban, chief of the network. Meanwhile, a trap was set in Olaso's apartment which resulted in the capture of several of his Spanish comrades (Courtois *et al.*, 146, 174, 180–1).

86. Pau Cirera, in *Lluita*, 23 June 1945; Sanz, *Luchando*, 50; Estruch, 39–40; Heine, 115, 122. Josep Miret had entered Aussenkommando Schwechat on 10 Sept. 1943, and Floridsdorf on 14 July 1944 (Josep Bailina, *Hispania*, 22 (Apr. 1967)).

87. Arthur G. London (interview). Estruch, 39, gives a rather different version, based on the testimony of General Juan Blásquez: in 1940 Conrad Miret organized the first group of foreign Francs-Tireurs, and was captured and shot by the Germans.

88. Another victim of the round-up in Paris of 30 November 1942 ('2nd affair of the Spaniards') was Francisco Perramón, the PCE's secretary of organization. On 30 Nov., Perramón arrived at a café to meet the two PCE provincial leaders. Noticing a suspicious character coming out of the phone booth, they paid and left as quickly as they could, but a car suddenly drew up in front of them and police surrounded them. Among the few at the top to escape was Josep Miret's companion Elisa Uriz, who managed to get out through the window when the police called at her house (Sanz, *Luchando*, 47, 57, 89; Arasa, 27). Miret's 20-year-old

French wife, Colette Regnier (or Reignier), née Julienne Brumeshurst, was not so lucky: she was arrested with him (Z6 NL 13717, Archives nationales, Paris).

89. Sanz, *Luchando*, 47.
90. Ibid. 46–8, 57; Arasa, 27.
91. *'Ami si tu tombes*
    Un ami sort de l'ombre
    A ta place'.
92. Pons, *Republicanos*, 273; Sanz, *Luchando*, 90.
93. Pons, *Republicanos*, 272; Sanz, *Luchando*, 91–2; Faligot and Kauffer, 234. As stated above, Sanz includes Montero among the Spanish leaders caught at this time.
94. Fillol, 155.
95. In this capacity Barón became, in May 1944, Chief of Staff of the 24th Division of Spanish Guerrilleros, in action in Gironde.
96. According to Courtois *et al.*, 458, Ilic used a second pseudonym, Major Brunetto.
97. Barón took part in the liberation of the capital, receiving a mortal wound on 21 Aug. in the place de la Concorde. A plaque, alongside others, now commemorates him at the spot where he fell.
98. Sanz, *Luchando*, 48–9.
99. Pons, *Republicanos*, 150.
100. Michel, *Histoire*, 91, 98.
101. Brunet, 76.
102. Pons, *Republicanos*, 138.
103. Goubet and Debauges, 95.
104. Such is also the conclusion of Arasa, 35.
105. Brunet, 76.
106. Laborie, 'Partis', 25.
107. Estruch, 73, gives their strength at 21,000, which is surely an exaggeration.
108. As we have seen, they were employed in road-building, quarries, and lumber-yards. Cf. Pons, *Republicanos*, 250; Sanz, *Luchando*, 199.
109. The STO thus replaced the GTE, from which so many enlisted Spaniards had deserted that two Spanish companies had to be disbanded (Pons, *Republicanos*, 250). In more general terms, the decree of 4 Sept. 1942 was an admission of Germany's failure to recruit a sufficient number of volunteer workers, even though Vichy stressed that each volunteer meant the return home of a French prisoner of war in Germany—the bargain known as *la relève*.

CHAPTER 6

1. SS caveat posted in the *Appellplatz* at Gusen.
2. SS expression for 'Get moving!'
3. The moment of entering any of the *KL* was an unforgettable experience. It was normal to enter Mauthausen's fortress through this main gate,

but some survivors (Tillard, 14; and Navarro, in Razola and Constante, 48–9) remember passing through the garage gate, surmounted by the German eagle.

On 7 Apr. 1941, of 348 Spaniards who arrived at the station, 48 'disappeared' between the station and the camp (Fabréguet, 'Républicains', 37). It is certain that they did not escape.

4. *Maricones*, Spanish colloquialism for 'faggots'.

5. 'Enriquito', known also to the Spaniards as 'Manolita', was Mauthausen's official German–Spanish interpreter. Despite his effeminate manner, he was sufficiently Nazi to have been selected for a mission to Spain before the Civil War began. His atrocious Spanish could not have helped him in his mission. He was arrested in Barcelona in 1937 and remained in prison until liberated by the Nationalists after the fall of Barcelona. On his return to Germany his superiors considered that he had failed in his mission and he was sent to Mauthausen, but with a red, not a pink, triangle, and—most importantly—as a Kapo. He was assigned to Block 13 (Juan de Portado [Antonio García Alonso], *Hispania*, 73 (Jan. 1982); 74, (Apr. 1982)).

6. This practice of itemizing the personal possessions of *KZ* prisoners continued, throughout the Mauthausen complex, up to 1942 (Juan de Diego, interview).

7. The showers at Mauthausen were not installed until the end of 1942 (Le Chêne, 60). The temperature of these showers would change, by design, from scalding hot to freezing cold (Sheppard, interview; Renaud, 18).

8. Cf. Delfieu, 106: 'I was never once sick, or even indisposed by the slightest cold.' Many survivors have reported the same.

9. These include the published accounts of Tillard, 14–20; Aldebert, 22; Marcelino Bilbao and Patricio Serrano, in Razola and Constante, 36, 38, 41–2; Vilanova, 115, 132–3; Juan de Portado, *Hispania*, 73 (Jan. 1982), and 74 (Apr. 1982); and various oral accounts by survivors at reunions in Paris and Mauthausen.

10. Bernadac, 68.

11. Razola and Constante, 38.

12. Vilanova, 129–30. A survivor of Ebensee writes of the fear felt by the incoming prisoner of dropping in the snow and being unable to rise, there to freeze to death in some grotesque position (Debrise, 158).

13. Renaud, 17.

14. Wetterwald, 35. Tillard, 13, remarks, on the arrival of his own convoy at Mauthausen station, that the villagers in their Tyrolean hats showed a certain pity towards them. Other survivors, Riquet (interview) and Renaud, 16, remember the villagers watching them from behind their curtains as they passed. Dobias (interview) recounts how, in May 1942, his little group passed through first Linz and then Mauthausen village: 'The Austrians spat at us.'

15. Le Chêne, 59.

16. Juan de Diego (interview); Vilanova, 193, 211.

17. Ziereis's widow told the court that their marriage was so unhappy that she wanted to divorce him. She claimed that she opposed her husband's activities. This is refuted by the eyewitness Mariano Constante, *Yo fui*, 224, who affirms that Ida Ziereis shared fully in her husband's work, and that the leading figures in the SS were received in her home. Le Chêne, 35, is surely in error in calling Ziereis 'a model husband and a devoted father'. The description does fit Bachmayer, however. Vilém Stašek, who was Ziereis' orderly, saw Ida only twice (in the tailor's shop) and never spoke with her (letter from Mariánské Lázně of 4 Nov. 92).
18. Constante, *Yo fui*, 221, 224, 237.
19. Pappalettera, 149.
20. Juan de Diego (interview).
21. *Bulletin de l'Amicale de Mauthausen*, 123 (June 1965).
22. Le Chêne, 175.
23. Juan de Diego (interview).
24. Constante, *Yo fui*, 222–3.
25. Pappalettera, 86–7.
26. Despite his aristocratic origin, Prellberg, up to his entry into the SS, was the owner of a laundry in Braunschweig (Bernadac, 189).
27. Juan de Diego (interview); *Bulletin de l'Amicale de Mauthausen*, 136 (Sept. 1967); Pappalettera, 62, 72–9, 215–21. At his trial, Werner Fassel admitted to the use of the stove, but gave his opinion that no one intended to inflict physical pain on the victim (Pappalettera, 82).
28. Bernadac, 190.
29. Constante, *Yo fui*, 141. Eisenhöfer was tried and hanged at Dachau in 1947.
30. *Bulletin de l'Amicale de Mauthausen*, 136 (Sept. 1967).
31. Maršálek, *Geschichte*, 276. Pappalettera, 206, and Constante, *Yo fui*, 250, confuse Asta with Schulz's hound Hasso.
32. Pappalettera, 204–6, 210–11.
33. Juan de Diego (interview); Vilanova, 175.
34. Razola and Constante, 65.
35. Pappalettera, 140–1.
36. Marcelino Bilbao, in Razola and Constante, 65.
37. Tillard, 20.
38. Pappalettera, 140.
39. Boüard, 'Mauthausen', 65.
40. Ibid. 59.
41. Maršálek and others give his name as Trumm. I follow Pappalettera, since these Italian authors have consulted the trial proceedings.
42. It should be remembered that, proportionate to population, there were more Austrians both in the Nazi Party and in the Allgemeine SS than there were Germans. While Austrians made up only 8% of the population of Germany after the *Anschluss*, about one-third of all those enlisted in the Allgemeine SS, from Himmler's deputy Ernst Kaltenbrunner downwards, were Austrians (Horwitz, 182).
43. Boüard, 'Mauthausen', 56.
44. Niedermayer's own estimate, presented at his trial (Pappalettera, 94).

45. Pappalettera, 91.
46. Notably the 47 Dutch, British, and American parachutists who were 'shot while attempting to escape' in June–July 1944 (see Ch. 11).
47. They included Nicolas Horthy, son of the Regent of Hungary, code-named 'Maus' by the SS, and placed in Cell 1 from the end of 1944; and the son of Marshal Badoglio, code-named 'Brauswetter' (*Bulletin de l'Amicale de Mauthausen*, 23 (Oct. 1955); Le Chêne, 125, 141–2, 145).
48. Maršálek, *Mauthausen*, 6.
49. Pappalettera, 94.
50. Juan de Diego (interview); Pappalettera, 188; Vilanova 177. Ziereis, on his death-bed, gave Killermann's first name as Michael.
51. Constante, *Yo fui*, 188, 190; Borrás [Lluch], 379. Sir Robert Sheppard adds that Müller much resembled the German heavyweight champion Max Schmelling (letter of 26 Sept. 1989).
52. The brothel at Mauthausen was housed in Block 1, at the other end of the administration building. The women took their exercise in an enclosure behind the Block, and were seldom if ever seen by the ordinary prisoners. As elsewhere, the brothel provided the SS with a means of gleaning information on the camp's black market or the organization of resistance. At Gusen, where the brothel opened its doors in Oct. or Nov. 1942, the primary purpose was to put an end to the pederasty into which certain Kapos, mainly Green, were forcing Polish and Russian youths (Boüard, 'Gusen', 59; Le Chêne, 87).
53. It would seem that the Kapos, without exception, were drunkards: if they had nothing else, they would drink raw alcohol mixed with jam. The survivor Charles Renaud, claims (p. 57) they would bargain with the SS guards for the gold in the prisoners' teeth, and that they would even tear out the teeth of the living with pincers.
54. Pappalettera, 40–1. The cudgels carried by the Kapos were hose-pipes braided with iron wire, 80 cm. in length (Tillard, 16).
55. Pappalettera, 169. This was part of Zoller's scheme to save his own life. It failed: he was hanged.
56. Ibid. 81, 98. The matter is not without significance, for it reveals what was necessary for National Socialism to operate. Draw up the regulations that prohibit you from doing the thing you intend to do, then do it. Before liquidating millions, proscribe the use of violence. Legislation forbids it, therefore it did not happen.
57. Boüard, 'Mauthausen', 59; Le Chêne, 76.
58. Vilanova, 136, is in error in making a distinction between Magnus Keller and 'King Kong', whose real name he gives as Hermann. Hermann was another Kapo, who was bayonetted to death by an SS (Pappalettera, 231).
59. Laffitte, 293, who was himself with Keller at Ebensee, denies this, as do others, saying that Keller preferred to order a killing than to kill with his own hands. Keller may have changed his style in the course of his long *KZ* career.
60. Debrise, 125; Wetterwald, 92; Pappalettera, 228–9; Maršálek, *Geschichte*, 257–8. Gilbert Debrise was a French doctor permitted to practice both in Mauthausen and Ebensee.

61. Vilanova, 136. There may well have been more than one Kapo known to the Spaniards as el Gitano; one of the Kapos in the quarry at Gusen was also known by that name (Laffitte, 294). The name el Gitano did not necessarily refer to a brown-triangle gipsy, who was little more eligible than a Jew for a Kapo post; like el Negro, el Gitano was a favourite nickname for dark-skinned Spaniards from Andalusia.

62. Tillard, 20.

63. Boüard, 'Mauthausen', 65; Maršálek, *Geschichte*, 40.

64. Pappalettera, 145, 156.

65. Debrise, 158; Wetterwald, 94, 99; Laffitte, 166. Among Karl's victims were the Spaniards Alonso and Rodríguez. The latter may have been Enrique Rodríguez, who had previously been kicked in the stomach by an SS with such force that it crushed a kidney and the next day he was urinating blood (Vilanova, 175).

66. Pappalettera, 14. Indalecio González and three other Spaniards (Moisés Fernández, Félix Domingo, and Laureano Navas) were arrested as war criminals in 1945 by the US 511th CIC Detachment and were put on trial at Dachau on 23 July 1947. Charged with murdering two fellow-prisoners by plunging their heads into a cesspit, González was sentenced to death (*Bulletin de l'Amicale de Mauthausen*, 8–9 (May–Sept. 1947); Pappalettera, 187; Le Chêne, 175, 266). See Ch. 11.

    As for el Negro, that nickname, like that of el Gitano, was given to more than one Kapo. It was given, e.g., to a German gipsy Kapo at Mauthausen *Mutterlager* who especially hated Jews (Le Chêne, 74).

67. El Negus has been wrongly identified by several writers as el Negro. El Negus wanted revenge on the French for the months he had spent in 1939 interned at Argelès-sur-mer (Tillard, 20).

68. The case of Palleja was heard by the court on 11 Mar. 1947. He was sentenced to death.

69. The date of 6 Aug. 1940 is confirmed by Juan de Diego, who arrived in the first contingent. Cinca Vendrell, 63, Vilanova, 131, and Alfaya, in Abellán, ii. 106, are in error. So are Razola and Constante, 38, in assuming it arrived from Angoulême.

    Juan de Diego recounts that his group arrived in French uniform. At the moment of their arrival, the new station was being constructed by the prisoners, who were busy putting up the wall. The road to the camp, he adds, was not paved at that time (interview).

70. Pappalettera, 66.

71. José Escobedo, in Razola and Constante, 38–9. Delfieu, 42, reports that his group arrived at Mauthausen after 57 hours in the train; they were thrown on to the platform naked.

72. Aldebert, 12.

73. Constante, *Yo fui*, 290. He adds that only 32 of them were still alive in May 1945.

74. Heim, 12.

75. Aldebert, 20, writes that his group arrived at 5 p.m., at a time when many Austrians were waiting for trains; they were all witnesses to the scene.

76. The steps could not therefore have been built by the Spaniards. But since the Spaniards built the ramparts, the road, and so much else of Mauthausen, it would explain why Tillard, 33, despite his personal experience as an inmate, would write that it was the Spaniards who built the steps.

77. Razola and Constante, 38–9, 46–7; Le Chêne, 110.

78. Juan de Diego (interview); Cinca, 74; Razola and Constante, 38; Vilanova, 132; Le Chêne, 110; Pilar Claver, in Català, 104–5. Several authors have stated that some of the women and children were sent to Ravensbrück. While Spanish women and children were indeed sent to Ravensbrück, on this particular occasion, reports the eyewitness Lázaro Nates, all the women, with their daughters and under-aged sons, were sent back to Spain (interview).

79. Lázaro Nates is adamant on this point, in an article he wrote under the pseudonym of el Pua: 'España, Anguleme, Mauthausen', *Hispania*, 55, 2nd series (Nov. 1976).

80. Vilanova, 110.

81. Roig, 'Generación', 36.

82. Vilanova, 110. Cf. Heim, 14. Tillard, 44, recounts that 30 men from each national group, all working in the quarry, were assigned to an experiment to test the difference in working capacity among the various national groups. The SS proudly announced that the competition had been won by the Germans.

83. Roig, 'Generación', 36.

84. Tillard, 17.

85. Anton Poschacher, the owner of the stone works, was an enthusiastic supporter of the Nazi Party; even in the little village of Mauthausen, the party's local chapter in the year of the *Anschluss* claimed 130 members (Horwitz, 24). The Poschacher company is still in existence, but it has moved out of the quarry business into the manufacture of bricks.

86. Some authors have written that these Poschacher boys were assigned to work in Mauthausen village and the surrounding farms. Lázaro Nates, a former Poschacher youth, denies this, saying that a few only worked in the camp farm (interview).

87. Vilanova, 214–15; Roig, 'Generación', 37.

88. Nates (interview).

89. Razola and Constante, 85.

90. Alfaya, 106. Mariano Constante arrived on 7 Apr. 1941 and Manuel Razola on 26 Apr. 1941 (Razola and Constante, 57).

91. Boüard, 'Gusen', 50; cited in Le Chêne, 213.

92. This situation was not, of course, peculiar to Mauthausen. At Dachau as elsewhere, relations among the national groups were equally poor; cf. Rovan, 65–96.

93. Razola and Constante, 105. Cf. Debrise, 65: 'The French in Mauthausen were looked upon as traitors by the Spaniards, Czechs and others.'

94. Laffitte, 173. The matter runs much deeper than mere politics. The account by the Briton Christopher Burney, 67, 97–104, of the behaviour

of the French in Buchenwald is a terrible indictment, but it is written with pain and reluctance by one 'who had known France intimately and loved her before the war and loved her and worked for her during it'. Burney arrived in Buchenwald in a convoy of 2,000 Frenchmen. 'The French', he writes, 'were slovenly, greedy, lazy and succumbed both physically and morally more readily than any other people.... They were cowed by the enemy's show of force and had too little faith in themselves to make the necessary moral come-back to join us.... We had no wish to appear condescending, we only wanted to see a flicker of real spirit. But it never came, and we went our separate ways, ourselves to freedom, even in honourable death, and they to a life of bitter bickering or a death of misery, and in either case of shame before themselves and before others. What right had Frenchmen so to behave, so to betray themselves and each other that uncouth savages hailing from countries still plunged in the Dark Ages scorned them and said to them: '*Franzas scheisse!*' ... Their minds seemed to foment eternally, but some missing function of their spirit rendered them impotent either for action or for compassion with each other.... Those who should have taken the command, and who had in fact the opportunity to help—the many senior and junior officers of the Army and Air Force—shrank from responsibility....'

The Frenchman Maurice Delfieu, interned in Mauthausen, corroborates this sad portrait of his countrymen: 'Far from bringing us together, misfortune drove us apart. Far from kindling feelings of nationhood, of overcoming the causes of disagreement based on class difference, political opinion or religious persuasion, far from softening the hard edges of our characters, exile made us intolerant, sectarian, irascible and pitiless' (Delfieu, 210–11). Another French survivor of Mauthausen, Charles Renaud, a chauvinist who cannot conceal his dislike of Spaniards and Jews, admits that a French group was badly demoralized even at the moment it entered the camp (Renaud, 65). Against this sombre portrait one should set the model of indomitable courage which other Frenchmen provided, especially, in Mauthausen, the French doctors and Père Michel Riquet, and in Buchenwald and Dachau, the abbé Georges Hénocque. In fact, the Spaniards speak highly of the French in Mauthausen; their only criticism, stronger in 1992 than before, is aimed at the chauvinism evident at their reunions and in their historiography.

95. Cf. above, n. 67. Nevertheless, this Kapo was not in the top class where brutality was concerned. He was shocked by the savagery of his superiors: the SS officer known as the 'blonde young lady' and the Kapo known as Hans the Killer. These two were responsible for a frenzied attack, witnessed by the Spanish prisoners under el Negus, on a group of 87 Dutch Jews who had just arrived at Mauthausen. Several of them had Spanish names, and spoke an antiquated form of Castilian. They were all working on the granite face of the quarry when the SS officer and the Kapo waded into them, raining blows on their heads. The Dutchmen thought that if they worked harder they would be spared. No

one was spared. El Negus went on telling his group: '*No miréis, trabajad!*' (Don't look, get on with your work!) By 11.30 a.m. the two tormentors had beaten to death 47 of the 87 Jews, but they were tired, so they stopped for lunch. After lunch they resumed. At the end of the day there were only 3 Dutchmen left alive (Tillard, 22).

96. Razola and Constante, 105.
97. Alfaya, 115.
98. Boüard, 'Mauthausen', 57.
99. Tillard, 34.
100. Riquet, 292.
101. Razola and Constante, 57.
102. Cinca, 154.
103. Boüard, 'Mauthausen', 57.
104. Juan de Diego is of the opinion that at Mauthausen all the prostitutes were gypsies (interview). At least one was a gypsy; none were Jews. When the gypsy, who was exceptionally beautiful, fell sick, it was a Spaniard, Ginestá, working in the Bahnhof Kommando, who saved her life, giving his blood to Professor Podlaha in the *Revier*. Ginestá is still alive and living in Paris in 1992 (Juan de Diego, interview).
105. These *Bordellscheine* were known to the inmates as '*Sprungkarten*'.
106. Tillard, 40, writes that the winning of this privilege reflected the growing prestige of the Spaniards in the camp.
107. Cf. Alfaya, 116–17, which is based on a misreading of his source.
108. Tillard, 40.
109. Razola and Constante, 105.
110. Juan de Diego, interview.
111. Boüard, 'Mauthausen', 57.
112. Tillard, 33; Boüard, 'Mauthausen', 57.
113. Maršálek, *Geschichte*, 299.
114. Ibid. 249.
115. Burney, 113.
116. Rovan, 93. For a negative and totally biased appraisal, cf. Renaud, 56.
117. Maršálek, *Geschichte*, 286. The Spaniards' use of the word '*agua*' (water) as a warning signal became adopted by all prisoners in Mauthausen.
118. Arthur London, in Razola and Constante, 122; Vilanova, 197; Rubio *Guerra civil*, 409.
119. Maršálek, *Geschichte*, 250.
120. Jean Benech, 'Le Revier', *Bulletin de l'Amicale de Mauthausen*, 37 (May 1954).
121. Suppl., *Bulletin de l'Amicale de Mauthausen*, 210 (June 1982).
122. Wetterwald, 137.
123. R. P. Riquet, 'L'Europe à Mauthausen', *Études*, June 1945; cited in Alfaya, 116. Interviewed in 1992 at the age of 93, Père Riquet, whose mind and memory remain very alert, expressed again his admiration for the cohesion of the Spanish community 'and its readiness to help the French'.
124. Laffitte, 268–9.
125. *Hispania*, 73 (Jan. 1982).

126. Laffitte, 180.
127. Sheppard (interview). The Catalans and masonry have been long associated. Not for nothing was St Eulalia, the patron saint of masons, chosen as the patron saint of Barcelona.
128. Riquet, 299; Boüard, 'Mauthausen', 57.
129. Riquet, 293–4. The show was obviously sponsored by Bachmayer as a means of entertaining the SS, but the Spaniards readily agreed to arrange everything: décor, costumes, orchestra, and artistes, who included an opera singer from the Capitole in Toulouse. The show even ran for a week, and the prisoners' morale rocketed (Riquet, interview).
130. Tillard, 54.
131. Le Chêne, 137–8; Maršálek, *Geschichte*, 294; Borrás [Lluch], 264.
132. Indeed a list compiled by the survivor-author José Borrás Lluch, 264, gives the membership of these protected classes: 13 footballers, 8 boxers, 4 entertainers, 2 musicians, 1 sculptor.
133. Luis Gil, in Razola and Constante, 54.
134. Pappalettera, 107.
135. Tillard, 60.
136. Pappalettera, 116–17.
137. Constante, *Yo fui*, 194.
138. There, on 6 Aug. 1944, Krebsbach gave lethal injections to all Jewish prisoners unable to march west to escape the Soviet advance (Pappalettera, 107).
139. The injections were administered by Sanitätsunterscharführer Otto Kleingünter, of Vienna (Bernadac, 48). The Czech Dr Premysl Dobias, who worked as Blockschreiber 3 in the *Sanitätslager*, testifies that Kleingünter used to enter a Block, select two dozen of the weakest inmates, and order the Blockschreiber to send them to the *Revier*, where he murdered them one by one (interview).
140. 'Ziereis parle', *Bulletin de l'Amicale de Mauthausen*, 14 (Mar. 1950), *et seq.*
141. Roig, 'Generación', 36.
142. Marcelino Bilbao, in Razola and Constante, 64.
143. Gaucher, 36; Busson, 169–70; Ellen Lentz, *New York Times*, 14 June 1979; Wiesenthal, 133–5.
144. Dobias (interview); Maršálek, *Geschichte*, 139. The testimony of Tillard, 59–60, though he was a survivor, contains several serious errors.
145. Nates (interview).
146. Ibid. Juan Gil survived and became president of the FEDIP.
147. Pappalettera, 97, 107–8; Maršálek, *Geschichte*, 143. Pappalettera, presumably in error, refer to the chemist as Wasicky. Since the gas chamber was fitted out, as elsewhere, in the exact form of a shower-room, with the gas entering through the shower-heads, victims were issued with a small towel and piece of soap, with the result that the operation was faster and more efficient.
148. Vilanova, 178. Executions by shooting into the back of the neck were carried out in a tiny cell adjacent to the gas-chamber and known as the

'portrait studio'. The prisoner was told to stand up facing the wall while his photograph was taken; through an opening in the wall opposite, an SS fired the *Genickschuss*.

149. More precisely, from Schulz's aide, SS-Hauptscharführer Krüger, who in civilian life had been a postage-stamp-dealer in Constance (Bernadac, 189).

150. Tillard, 41.

151. Juan de Diego (interview); Amat Piniella, in Roig, 'Generacion', 37. Albert Speer was among those immune to Mauthausen's mephitic odour. The sweet and sickening smell of burning human flesh did not spoil his visit to the camp in late March 1943. On the contrary, wrote Hitler's Minister of Armaments in his memoirs, the camp produced on him 'an almost romantic impression'. Everything was clean and orderly. As for cachexia, he saw no evidence of it: 'I saw no emaciated inmates. They were probably at the infamous stone quarry at the time.' Nor were the Reichsführer-SS and his deputy any better informed than he, continues Speer, despite their visits to Mauthausen, because 'the camp directors disguised the true situation . . . even from Himmler and Kaltenbrunner' (Speer, 41–2).

152. Vilanova, 181. Vilanova's account of how a kitchen Kapo, to stoke up his fires, might step outside to the mound of corpses and select one which was especially thin, 'because it burned better than one which still contained some fat, and of course better than the wood' (ibid.) could be a fabrication. The kitchens at Mauthausen were equipped with ultra-modern electric pressure-cookers that did not burn wood (Juan de Diego, interview). If, however, Vilanova meant to refer to one of Mauthausen's Aussenkommandos, the account could still be accurate. Since Vilanova was not himself a former *KZ* inmate, it is possible that he simply confused his material. His account is certainly authentic in another context, because it is supported by an unimpeachable authority, Dr Wetterwald, 48. The Kapo 'Al Capone' of Block 18 (one of the Spanish Blocks) would go out with an axe and cut the corpses into logs, which he would use to fuel his cooking-stove and fry his sausages.

How the crematorium functioned is described in the deposition of two Polish prisoners, Ignacy Bukowski and Tadeusz Lewicki, who worked there under the crematorium Kapo, the Austrian Hans Kanduth. The two Poles escaped liquidation only by being transferred, in Mar. 1944, to another work Kommando (deposition in the possession of the author).

153. Tillard, 19.

154. The analogy of the 186 steps to the Via Dolorosa trod by Jesus has occurred to others, including the designer of the stained-glass window installed in the Votivkirche in Vienna; it carries a reference to St Paul's Epistle to the Colossians, 1: 24.

155. Boüard, 'Mauthausen', 40.

156. Juan de Diego (interview); Sebastián Mena, in Razola and Constante, 75. Cf. Delfieu, 60.

157. Not that the SS knew it, but the myth of Sisyphus carried a meaning

for them, since his punishment was retribution for a crime identical to theirs: laying heaps of stones on those whom he had plundered, and allowing them to die in the most agonizing torments.

158. Charles Renaud, 26, describes the fate of those who cheated. The SS forced them to attempt the impossible, carrying up a rock of 50 kilos, on their knees. As their strength gave out the SS shot each one in the head.

159. Delfieu, 60, who gives the weight of the rocks as between 15 and 25 kilos.

160. Juan de Diego (interview).

161. Le Chêne, 70–1.

162. Wetterwald, 45.

163. Morel (interview).

164. Vilanova, 160.

165. Maršálek, *Geschichte*, 297.

166. Ibid. 287. ('Who is responsible for our misfortune?' 'The Jews.')

167. Vilanova, 170. The big intake of Hungarian Jews was yet to come, as was the evacuation of other camps to Mauthausen.

168. Le Chêne, 69–70; Maršálek, *Mauthausen*, 11.

169. It is not entirely certain that Jo Attia witnessed the event, since Juan de Diego remembers Attia being sent to Loibl-Pass, though he is not sure on what date (interview). Prof. Dr Léon Schwarzenberg, the distinguished cancerologist and former French Minister of Health, who has heard every account of this event, discounts (interview) the version of the quartet ('they would have been too weak, and too frightened of the revenge which the SS would take on the camp inmates afterwards'). On the other hand, collective hallucination has been recognized by medical science at least since 23 Aug. 1914, when the Angel of Mons, observed in the sky by entire units, entered the histories of the British and French Armies.

170. Razola and Constante, 47, 59, 64.

171. Juan de Diego (interview); Nates (interview).

172. Juan de Diego (interview); Esteban Balogh, in Razola and Constante, 73–4.

173. *Mauthausen*, 40.

174. Razola and Constante, 175.

175. Ibid. 88.

176. Ibid. 46.

177. Cinca, 105.

178. Razola and Constante, 187.

179. Heim, 22–3.

180. Le Chêne, 172.

181. Cinca, 158–63, offers some interesting lists, but they contain serious errors, and his work lacks authority.

182. Boüard, 'Gusen', 49.

183. Patricio Serrano *et al.*, in Razola and Constante, 179.

184. Pappalettera, 14.

185. Alfaya, 111.

186. Boüard, 'Mauthausen', 50.
187. Patricio Serrano *et al.*, in Razola and Constante, 180.
188. Ibid. 179.
189. Cinca, 118, 121; Pappalettera, 190–1; Razola and Constante, 182; Vilanova, 177.
190. Razola and Constante, 183; Vilanova, 175. Aldebert, 40, writes of Tomás that he rarely used his cudgel, preferring to use his boot.
191. *Mauthausen*, 50.
192. Alfaya, 112.
193. Pappalettera, 188.
194. Vilanova, 184–5; Alfaya, 111.
195. Pappalettera, 187; Razola and Constante, 186–9; Vilanova, 170; Alfaya, 110–11.
196. Boüard, 'Gusen', 58.
197. Heim, 22–3.
198. Maršálek, *Mauthausen*, 3.
199. Razola and Constante, 83, 91; Patricio Cruz, ibid. 176.
200. José Borrás Lluch, the communist author of *Histoire de Mauthausen*, was himself a prisoner in Steyr. His experience was apparently limited to that Kommando.
201. Razola and Constante, 88.
202. *Mauthausen*, 56. It was at Loibl-Pass that Louis Brieux, a captured member of the French Resistance, served as a Kapo and won such a reputation for cruelty to his fellow-prisoners that in 1947 he was sentenced to death by a French court and hanged (Pappalettera, 14, 51).
203. Sanz, *Luchando*, 50. SS-Scharführer Hans Bühner, the Rapportführer of Floridsdorf, and later of Mödling and Hinterbrühl, was brought to trial in 1949 in Rastatt, W. Germany, charged with, among other crimes, murdering those wounded in the air raid on Floridsdorf. Bühner admitted only to giving, 'for humanitarian reasons', the *coup de grâce* to Miret. He was sentenced to death on 7 Sept. 1949 and hanged in Jan. 1950 (*Bulletin de l'Amicale de Mauthausen*, 14 (Mar. 1950); Pappalettera, 203; Maršálek, *Geschichte*, 231).
204. The Spanish survivor Amadeo López Arias attests to this (Le Caër, 14).
205. Le Caër, 8–60, *passim*.
206. The first of these was totally deranged (Le Chêne, 224). The second, SS-Hauptsturmführer Otto Riemer, was removed after a celebrated incident. On the evening of 23 May 1944, Riemer, while drunk, mounted a horse, seized a sub-machine-gun, and led a hunting party in pursuit of any prisoner found in the open. The party killed 15, while 12 more were brought, in grave condition, to the *Revier*, where they were treated by the French surgeons Wetterwald and Quenouille. While there was nothing unusual about the killings, word of a manhunting party leaked out to the villagers of Ebensee, a serious matter indeed (Wetterwald, 84–5; Laffitte, 290–1; Le Chêne, 228; Maršálek, *Geschichte*, 179, 197; Pappalettera—who spell his name Reimer, almost certainly in error—135, 137–9, 230).

207. Le Chêne, 231, describes Ganz as a former night–club bouncer, and others have called him semi–literate, but the description given by the French surgeon Dr Wetterwald, working at Ebensee, must take priority, however much it is at variance: 'He was small, slim, elegant in his high boots, and spent much of his time fondling a ridiculously small lapdog' (Wetterwald, 103). Renaud, 130, refers to him as Gango, perhaps a nickname given to him by the Spaniards.

208. Vilanova, 136, selects Ganz and Chmielewski as the worst of all the camp commandants in Austria. Ganz is particularly remembered for an incident in December 1944. A Christmas tree had been planted on Ebensee's *Appellplatz*. Ganz celebrated the birth in Bethlehem by hanging a small Italian boy of 17 by the wrists in front of it, his feet a metre from the ground. Ganz then let loose his dogs. '*Pietà, commandante, pietà!*' cried the boy, as the dogs tore off his feet (Tillard, 68; *Bulletin de l'Amicale de Mauthausen*, 130 (July 1966)). Renaud, 127, describes a similar scene when his group arrived at Ebensee and saw men hanging with their lower legs torn off by the mastiffs.

209. Gouffault, 35.

210. Le Chêne, 224.

211. Wetterwald, 155–6.

212. Laffitte, 269, 323. An official report after the Liberation (compiled on 17 May 1945) shows 240 Spaniards still alive at Ebensee (Le Chêne, 241).

213. Laffitte, 269.

214. Gouffault, 31.

215. Ibid. 20–2.

216. *Mauthausen*, 59–61; Pappalettera, 230; Gouffault, 6–16, 20–2, 25–40. Gouffault, 31, also describes how one night in the winter of 1944–5, when the detail set out for the overnight shift in the tunnels, Ganz ordered the sick to be rounded up, then made them stamp down the snow in their bare feet, and finally forced them to run in a circle until they dropped.

217. Le Chêne, 243.

218. *Mauthausen*, 58. Renaud, 42, writes that 5,000 prisoners were sent from Mauthausen *Mutterlager* to build one such underground factory at Melk; within a few months this number had been almost entirely used up, but the *Mutterlager's* inexhaustible stock continued to replenish Melk's losses with a new supply every fortnight.

219. Le Chêne, 104.

220. But not entirely: some of the buildings standing today within 400 m. of the château were built before the war.

221. Le Chêne, 106.

222. Lohnauer's second-in-command was SS-Obersturmführer Christian Wirth, who was reassigned in 1941 and his place taken by SS-Obersturmführer Franz Paul Stangl; Stangl, who was Austrian, would soon leave to become the infamous Commandant of Sobibor, and (in 1942) of Treblinka. It was while Wirth was at Hartheim that gas was first used to kill the victims, their death agony being precisely timed and photographed, and

the reports and prints sent to Berlin (Maršálek, *Geschichte*, 162; Wiesenthal, 96).

223. Juan de Diego, letter to Herr Ohren, Public Prosecutor, Cologne Magistrates' Court: Luchon, 21 Dec. 1962.

224. Alfaya, 110.

225. One of them, a Spaniard, escaped death by feigning it, and gave an account of his experience during the 40th anniversary celebration of the liberation of Mauthausen.

226. Le Chêne, 106; Billig, 121–3; *Mauthausen*, 62. In the reconstruction of Hartheim into a school, there was space in 1945 for 400 children (International Tracing Service, *Catalogue*, 31). Despite the Nazis' attempt to destroy all the evidence, the Allies found the remains of the experimental laboratories and of the crematoria, while a group of Poles, employed in the subsequent excavations, unearthed, in 26 tons of human ash, the identifiable remains of women's and children's clothing (Gaucher, 36; Busson, 179).

227. Rauff had served as a regular navy officer from 1924 to 1937, when his friend Heydrich invited him to join the RSHA. In 1941–2, when his work brought him to Mauthausen, he served as head of Amt II-D, the section responsible for organizing the SS Einsatzgruppen, or extermination Kommandos, and for fitting them out with the best possible equipment. After leaving this post Rauff served as Gestapo chief in Tunisia, and then in Rome. After the Italian surrender Rauff became head of the Sipo-SD in German-occupied Italy, using Milan as his base.

228. Juan de Diego (interview); Pappalettera, 104; Vilanova, 179; Le Chêne, 80–2; Billig, 122.

229. Rauff's 'Black Ravens' required 20 mins. to kill 50 prisoners. Even so, Rauff could report on 5 July 1942 that, counting all camps in which his invention had been used since its introduction in Dec. 1941, '97,000 [had] been processed'.

CHAPTER 7

1. Castro, *Mi fe*, 140–1.

2. Pons, *Republicanos*, 510.

3. Villalón was killed in the Ukraine (ibid. 561). The pilot Manuel Rodrigo was among those who were allowed to fly, but only after he had fought as a guerrilla. He was given a Mosca, and later the latest-model fighter, in which he took part in various battles including Kursk in July 1943 (Soriano, 98). Another prominent Spanish pilot was Juan Lario Sánchez, who fought as a squadron leader in the Battle of Stalingrad; he survived the war, and published his memoirs.

4. Vilanova, 481; Pons, *Republicanos*, 504–10.

5. At their closest point, the Germans penetrated to within 23 km. of the capital; a monument was erected at that point in July 1988.

6. Vilanova, 472, 475. The incident is an example of how a story, true in

essence, could be built into a myth. The legend that the defence of the Kremlin was entrusted solely to units made up of Spaniards is scorned by Agustí Vilella, the former commander (when only 26) of the 72nd Division in Spain. During the retreat of 1939, he had quarrelled with a Comintern agent and was summoned to Moscow, sailing from Le Havre on 4 June. From Moscow he had been sent to the Crimea to teach the children, but with the German invasion he was able to take part in the defence of Moscow. During the evacuation of the capital in October 1941, Vilella found himself in the group guarding the Kremlin and Red Square, but the group, he says, was part of a larger unit made up mainly of Soviets (Soriano, 121–2). At the end of the war he held the rank of lieutenant, and he subsequently became Professor of Spanish Language and Literature at the University of Moscow. He returned to Catalonia in 1980 (Agustí Vilella, in Milza and Peschanski, 614). Cf. Moreno, 203.

7. Vilanova, 466–7; Pons, *Republicanos*, 505, 565–6.
8. Castro, *Mi fe*, 153. He adds (p. 226) that in the second winter of the war he lost 30 kilos; to enable him and his wife to eat, he sold her Spanish coat, the only thing they had to sell.
9. Morán, 99.
10. Ibid.; Soriano, 97.
11. If this brigade came under the command of an Aleksandr Orlov, it was certainly not the famous general (Pike, *Jours*, 101), who had already defected (in 1938) to the United States.
12. Morán, 99.
13. Ruiz, 65. Ungría survived the war only to die in Spain at the end of 1945 while trying to cross the frontier illegally (Arasa, 284; Soriano, 97).
14. Tagüeña, 449–53; Pons, *Republicanos*, 511; Ruiz, 63–5.
15. Pons, *Republicanos*, 535; Morán, 98. Cf. Ibarruri, *Memorias*, 532, who admits to the participation of Fusimaña in the engagement but gives the group leader as Miguel Boixó. This could be significant, since Pasionaria in her memoirs gives credit only to those who remain in her good graces.
16. Pons, *Republicanos*, 516, 533. Gros also received, in a later ceremony in the Kremlin, and this time from Nikolai Svernik, Vice-President of the Supreme Soviet, the Order of the Red Flag and the Guerrilla Medal, 1st Class (*Lluita*, 14 Feb. 1945).
17. She also received the Guerrilla Medal, 1st Class (Pons, *Republicanos*, 516, 528, 532–3).
18. Vilanova, 488–9; Tagüeña, 463–4; Pons, *Republicanos*, 534–40; Ruiz, 64; *Moscow News*, 19 (11–17 May 1990).
19. Ibarruri, *Memorias*, 530. Jakov Stalin was born to the leader's first wife, the pianist Caterina, who committed suicide. His father's declaration that any Soviet in German hands was a traitor to his country apparently depressed him, despite the fact that no fewer than 5,700,000 Red Army troops were taken prisoner, of whom 3m. died in captivity. In *KL-Sachsenhausen*, relations between Soviet and British prisoners of war grew increasingly tense in the oppressive atmosphere of the camp. On 14 Apr. 1943, the tension reached its peak when the British prisoners

accused the Russians, specifically Jakov Stalin, of purposely defacing the latrine and defecating on the ground. A fist fight broke out. Stalin asked to see the camp commandant. This was refused, whereupon Stalin began acting like a man berserk, running straight towards the electrified wire. British Staff Sergeant Thomas Cushing remembers seeing a huge blue flash and all the searchlights suddenly turned on. Stalin stood still for a moment, with his right leg back and his chest pushed out, then shouted to an SS guard, Konrad Harfich, to shoot him. Harfich fired a single shot into Stalin's head, killing him instantly. Following the liberation of the camp in 1945, the decision was taken by the British Foreign Office, with the agreement of the US State Department, not to tell Josef Stalin that his son had ended his life in the same way as his first wife.

20. Morán, 98, without disclosing his source, gives the total number of Spaniards serving in the Red Army as 749, of whom 204 were killed. Cf. Ibarruri, *Memorias*, 530.

21. Pasionaria also refers to her nephew, Alberto Rejas Ibarruri, who served in the ranks of the Red Army all the way to Berlin (Ibarruri, *Memorias*, 529). Palacios, 226, refers to her sister, María Ibarruri, living in the Moscow residence to which the Spanish airmen were sent (see below) with her daughter and a niece, and in conditions very close to poverty.

22. Pelayo de Hungría has described how Rubén Ruiz, at the time in 1942 when his unit, the 35th Guards division, was being transferred to the Stalingrad front, spent 5 days in his home at 28 Bolshaya Kalujskaya Ulitza in Moscow. Such was his resentment over the treatment of his father and over the neglect of the Spanish children—for both of which he held his mother responsible—that he spent the whole time drinking (Moreno, 145).

23. Pasionaria received the news from Nikita Khruschchev, who was then a member of the war council on the Stalingrad front and who had just lost a son of his own in battle (Ibarruri, *Memorias*, 541). The body of Rubén Ruiz was reinterred in Stalingrad on 2 Nov. 1948 in a great ceremony attended by the Soviet leaders. Pasionaria's claim that he also received the award of Hero of the Soviet Union (Ibarruri, *Memorias*, 543; Zafra *et al.*, 72) is nevertheless contested by several writers.

Pasionaria suffered much within her family. By the time she returned to Spain in 1977, Amaya was the only one of her 6 children still alive (Pàmies, *Española*, 12).

24. Margarita Nelken had switched to the PCE at the beginning of the Civil War, but in Oct. 1942, while she was already in Mexico, she was expelled from the Party on charges of discrediting and sabotaging the policy of Unión nacional. Her memoirs, *Las Torres del Kremlin*, were published in Mexico City in 1943. This desultory and rather pretentious account of the events of the last 12 years contains not one mention of the PCE, of Pasionaria, or of the Spaniards in Russia, but it nevertheless contributes to the cult of Stalin by its stress on Stalin's innate modesty and by its diatribes against the Western democracies, especially Britain, which she holds responsible for the war. Her memoirs did not serve, however, to

reinstate her in the Party's graces, for the Party continued to accuse her of harbouring bitterness and lacking trust (Morán, 67).

25. Camino, 176–7. Cf. Pike, *Jours*, 102–3. Comín, *Españoles*, 22, refers to Santiago de Paúl Nelken as a trained Soviet agent. Pasionaria, who devotes pages to the death of her son, says almost nothing of Santiago's, and in fact contradicts herself on the matter (Ibarruri, *Memorias*, 529, 532).

26. Conde, 208. Cf. Zafra *et al.*, 68–9. The original *besprizorni* were the homeless, wandering children left parentless by the October Revolution. The problem had supposedly been solved in the 1920s, but a new outbreak of 'hooliganism' among Soviet children in 1935 led to a decree by the Central Committee and the *Sovnarkhoz* (regional economic councils), on 2 June of that year, to improve the health and morals of the young.

27. Miralles, 207–8. Cf. Zafra *et al.*, 70.

28. Castro, *Mi fe*, 287; Vilanova, 473; Rubio, *Guerra civil*, 444 n.

29. One of them was Lieutenant-Colonel Sánchez, who spoke Russian and was known as Semionov.

30. *Procès*, 178. Cf. the comment at this time of el Campesino to Pelayo de Hungría: 'Even Indians in the Amazon live better than workers in the USSR' (Moreno, 321).

31. *Solidaridad obrera*, 10 Apr. 1948; Miralles, 196–7; Conde, 269–72.

32. Pasionaria recounts that the crowd at Kazan station was such that she lost both her children in the mêlée and had to travel alone, but they managed to find their own way to Ufa. Trains left with no posted destination. In the train in which she travelled, she adds, she found to her astonishment—and to that of her readers—that she was sitting in the same compartment as her secretary Irene Falcón. Her travelling companions also included Dimitrov's secretary Stepanov and political aide Boris Ponamariev, together with Ilya Ehrenburg and even Sir Walter Citrine, Secretary-General of the British Transport Workers' Union (Ibarruri, *Memorias*, 536).

33. Hernández set up home on the outskirts of the city, supporting himself by writing for the Argentine journal *Crítica* (Morán, 72).

34. Pasionaria claims that she directed the radio station herself, with the help of Rafael Vidiella, Francisco Antón, Irene Falcón, and others, and makes no mention at all of Castro (Ibarruri, *Memorias*, 526–7, 633). Such omissions are typical of Pasionaria.

35. Hernández, *Horizontes*, 7 (June 1947), reproduced in *La Batalla*, 28 Feb. 1948; Hernández, *Yo fui*, 227; Castro, *Mi fe*, 222; Tagüeña, 468; Heine, 109. Pasionaria's Catholic radio programme was called 'La Virgen del Pilar'. Its impact, she claims, was such that Radio Vatican had to announce that the two stations were not connected (Ibarruri, *Memorias*, 527). Pasionaria was later allowed the use of Radio Moscow to beam programmes to Spain under the curious pseudonym of Antonio de Guevara (ibid. 557).

36. Morán, 26. Stalin did not waste his time in such visits. His own mother lived in Tbilisi from 1918 until her death in 1938, but Stalin visited her only 3 times, never staying more than 15 mins. On the last occasion, in

1938, as he was getting up to go, his mother, whose lean face, high cheek-bones, and rimless spectacles gave her the appearance of a stern nun, made the remark: 'It is a pity you did not make it as a priest' (Colonel-General Dimitry Volkogonov, to Nicholas Beeston, *The Times*, 11 Mar. 1989).

37. Vanni, 125–6; el Campesino, *Vie*, 181, 194–6; 'José Diaz', *Nuestra bandera*, 5 Apr. 1950, 227–43; Borkenau, 191; Moreno, 143–4; Comín, *República*, 228–30; Thomas, 950. Margarete Buber-Neumann, an authority on the workings of the Comintern, supports the view that Díaz killed himself (*Révolution*, 329). Julio Carrasco, an intimate friend of el Campesino, came to the opposite conclusion: 'Díaz had this fixed idea about social justice, about the need to fight against hunger. It was necessary to kill him' (interview).

38. Castro, *Mi fe*, 207–8.

39. Semprún (interview).

40. González, *Comunista*, 95.

41. Cf. Pike, *Jours*, 160.

42. Castro, *Mi fe*, 205, 207; Ibarruri, *Memorias*, 545–7. Pasionaria does not mention Díaz's fall from the window. She writes that she and Irene Falcón flew from Ufa in a military plane to attend the funeral.

43. Alba, *Partido*, 267. Pasionaria claims she spoke at the funeral in front of his tomb, which she describes as crowned by a fine statue by a Georgian sculptor commissioned by the people of Tbilisi (ibid.). Both tomb and statue may have been erected later, but Pasionaria does not give the location.

44. As the PCE's representative on the Comintern, Hernández found himself occasionally in the presence of the Vozhd, but he describes the care that Stalin took to protect himself. The first occasion was in Nov. 1941, when Hernández received an invitation, at exactly 5 minutes' notice, to attend the 24th Anniversary of the October Revolution; a limousine appeared at the precise minute to whisk him to the Bolshoi Theatre. It was Stalin's fashion, as he found out again on another night at the Bolshoi, to be the last to arrive and the first to leave. The chances of assassinating him, Hernández concluded, were nil (Hernández, *En el pais*, 152–3).

45. Stalin had already decided that Svetlana would marry Zhdanov's son Yuri. She did, briefly, in 1949.

46. Ibarruri, *Memorias*, 555–6, insists that she did not seek the post, telling Dimitrov that she would be glad to see it go to some other comrade. Hernández on the other hand, she adds, wanted it badly enough to engage in various manœuvres, and in Mexico tried a little *coup d'état* that failed. In any event, she concludes, it was all legitimized when she was demo-cratically elected secretary–general at the 5th Congress of the PCE in 1954.

47. Hernández, *En el pais*, 177.

48. Ibid. 202. The decision to dissolve the Comintern had been taken a week earlier, on 15 May 1943. Ibarruri, *Memorias*, 564, writes that from a practical point of view the activities of the Comintern had to be sus-pended as early as July 1941.

49. Castro, *Mi fe*, 235.
50. Ibid. 150.
51. Ibid. 246–7. And no doubt Manuilski's secretary Gerö ('the statue of bronze', ibid. 354) and Dimitrov's secretary Stepanov.
52. Ibid. 248.
53. Hernández, *Yo fui*, 354; *En el pais*, 219. Hernández's posthumous 1974 edn. is fuller than his 1953 account, and no doubt includes some corrections, but his recollection of events could not have improved in the intervening years. In neither version does he describe the experiences of his travelling companion Francisco Antón.
54. Tagüeña, 440, 467.
55. Morán, 66.
56. Hernández, *En el pais*, 218–19; Claudín, *Santiago*, 72; Morán, 99.
57. Hermet, 53. Hernández was not alone. Within the PSUC, José del Barrio criticized both Pasionaria and the USSR, with the result that he was drummed out of the Party in October 1943.
58. Cf. Ibarruri, *Memorias*, 555–6.
59. Hernández, *En el pais*, 216, mentions his abandoned mother and sister. Tagüeña refers to his abandoned wife and daughter.
60. Castro, *Mi fe*, 264, 267. The recollections of Hernández throw a different light on their parting. 'Castro was certainly no coward', he writes, 'but in Moscow I saw him turn pale and even fall sick as the date of my departure approached. . . . What caused it was his realization that he would have to face Pasionaria on the Soviets' home ground, where whoever loses loses all there is to lose' (Hernández, *En el pais*, 90).
61. Castro, *Mi fe*, 265.
62. Castro Delgado was the first—with el Campesino in his 1950 French edition—to publish his memoirs: first in Madrid in 1950 (*La vida secreta de la Komintern*) and then in Mexico City in 1960 (*Hombres made in Moscú*). In Sept. 1963 he returned to Spain, to die 2 years later in Madrid, virtually forgotten. Hernández's memoirs first appeared in typewritten form under the title 'Yo ministro de Stalín en España'. Its preface, by the Argentine fascist Mauricio Carlavilla, was dropped when the memoirs were published in Mexico City in 1953 under the title *Yo fui un ministro de Stalín*. It was there in Mexico City that he remarried, this time with a Mexican, and ran a coffee shop until his death in 1971. Both Hernández and Castro tried to re-enter political life. The only success they had was due to the Cold War and the use that others, especially Franco, could make of their first-hand experience of Soviet life (cf. Morán, 78).
63. Tagüeña, 476; Morán, 74. Castro makes little mention of this in his memoirs. He refers instead to the rise of José Antonio Uribes, who was his colleague in the PCE delegation to the Comintern but who rarely spoke to him, or if he did he spoke about trivia (*Mi fe*, 293). In the reorganization of the leadership, Uribes and Gallego were to be the PCE's delegates to the Comintern, with Uribes still in charge of all matters of emigration (ibid. 265–6).
64. Tagüeña, 510. Pasionaria did all she could to prevent his leaving, writing

to Dimitrov on 8 June 1944 ('It is my opinion that Castro should not leave the Soviet Union') and to another Soviet official 2 days later ('I am convinced that, far from making amends, Castro intends to continue his struggle against the Party and against our common cause'). For reasons unknown, the Soviets ignored her plea (Morán, 77).

65. Cf. Pike, 'Républicains', 102–3.
66. A noteworthy exception here was Rómulo Negrín, a son of the Republic's last prime minister, who was a trainee-pilot in Russia until his father called for his return (Rico, 346); cf. Moreno, 141. Comín, *Españoles*, 22, refers to him (as he does to Nelken's son) as a trained Soviet agent.
67. Most of the Spanish airmen who arrived in the USSR in 1937 returned of course to Spain in time to take a further part in the war. This was the case of the pilot Pablo Salén, who had left Spain in the very first group, of some 200, which arrived in Russia in Feb. or Mar. 1937 and returned to Spain the following Sept. Salén went back qualified to fly Mosca fighters (Soriano, 89). The last expedition of Spanish pilots still in Republican service left Rouen for Leningrad on 8 Jan. 1939 aboard the *Kooperatsia* (Rubio, *Guerra civil*, 108), but at least one such group left after hostilities had ended. Juan Lario Sánchez was one of a group of 50 pilots, observers, and technicians who had served in Spain in the Gloriosa Squadron; released from French camps, they were sent, on 28 May 1939, from Pau to Paris and Le Havre and thence to Leningrad (Lario, 379).
68. Estruch, 61, who cites Blasco, 22.
69. Rico, 300, gives mid-May 1939; Comín, *Españoles*, 22, gives Sept. 1939.
70. El Campesino, *Yo escogí*, 237.
71. At the residence the airmen found themselves in the company of María Ibarruri, Dr Juan Boté García, and the future communist leader of Romania Anna Pauker, whom they described as semi-hysterical (Palacios, 226).
72. José Ester Borrás, *Solidaridad obrera*, 20 Mar. 1948. This raid on the airmen's residence in Moscow was carried out by the NKVD on the night of 24–5 Jan. 1940. Among the 12 arrested Spaniards were José Girones Llop, from Reus, who had expressed his wish to leave for Mexico, and Vicente Monclus Guallar, from Abriego, who had said he wanted to return to France (*Conférence de Presse*, 1–2). El Campesino later admitted taking part in this action, telling Pelayo de Hungría in 1954 how deeply he regretted striking the Spanish airmen (Moreno, 142).
73. These survivors entered Novosibirsk's pestilential prison on 22 July 1941. The temperature in Novosibirsk the following winter fell to –50 °C, but the prisoners were given no winter clothing, and even their underwear was confiscated on their arrival (*Conférence de Presse*, 2).
74. *La Batalla*, 53 (10 Feb. 1948); Palacios, 221–7. Cf. Comín, *Españoles*, 23, who writes that the airmen were given sentences of 15 years, most of them being sent to Siberia but others to Archangel or Pechoraliev.
75. Palacios, 215, and Vilanova, 467, list 9 vessels anchored in Soviet waters at the time the Civil War ended: the *Cabo San Agustín*, in Feodosiya (Crimea); the *Cabo Quilates* and the *Marzo*, in Murmansk; the *Ciudad de Tarragona*, the *Ciudad de Ibiza*, the *Mar Blanco*, the *Isla de Gran*

Canaria, and the *Inocencio Figueredo*, in Odessa; and the *Juan Sebastián Elcano*. Moreno, 140, adds a tenth vessel: the *Aldecoa*. Some naval officers from the Republican warship *Jaime Primero* (blown up in June 1937) were also reported at that time in Odessa (*La Batalla*, 53 (10 Feb. 1948)).

76. Rico, 356, 372, 423–5; Palacios, 214–21; cf. Vilanova, 467–8. Both Rico and Palacios provide lists of the crew members; Rico adds a promise to write a sequel entitled *Amanecer en Estocolmo*, describing the odyssey of the Spanish captives; the work never appeared. Comín, *Españoles*, 22–3, adds that the Russian and Spanish girls with whom they had associated shared their fate.

77. Castro, *Mi fe*, 102, 210.

78. Jesús Hernández and Castro Delgado, as members of the Spanish delegation to the Comintern, served on an inspection team visiting the camps (ibid. 98). Neither mentions Karaganda in his accounts.

79. *La Batalla*, 71 (5 Mar. 1949). Cf. Conquest, 349.

80. *Kazakhstanskaya Pravda*, 24 July 1988.

81. These Jews had fled their homeland to take refuge from Hitler in the Baltic States, only to be arrested by the NKVD and made slave workers.

82. J. E. Borrás, *Solidaridad obrera*, 31 Jan. 1948.

83. Ibid. Born in Alcuéscar (Cáceres) in 1898, Dr Boté had worked for 5 years in Spanish Guinea as director of the Santa Isabel Laboratory and the San Carlos Hospital, and during the Civil War as director of the Workers' Institute in Sabadell. José Antonio Rico knew Dr Boté in a recuperation centre in Opaliya, before the doctor was sent to Karaganda—as Rico puts it (p. 402), for teaching the children notions of freedom and democracy.

84. *La Batalla*, 71 (5 Mar. 1949).

85. Commission internationale contre le régime concentrationnaire, 52–3.

86. Written deposition of Col. Andreiev, Commission internationale contre le régime concentrationnaire, 121. Margarete Buber-Neumann, *Déportée*, 96–7, recounts that the 5 sectors of the camp that she knew were spaced about 48 kilometres apart. Each sector was divided into subsectors, which were mainly groups of cattle sheds and miserable hovels. In the whole of Karaganda there was not a single paved road; footpaths served in their place.

87. Solzhenitsyn, i. 86; iii. 51; cited by Legarreta, 172.

88. Commission internationale contre le régime concentrationnaire, 79.

89. Jouvenel, 230–1.

CHAPTER 8

1. William Wordsworth, 'The French and the Spanish Guerrillas' (1810 or 1811).

2. Von Rundstedt had set up his headquarters at Saint-Germain-en-Laye, in the château once used by the exiled King James II of England.

3. Rommel had established his headquarters on the Seine at La Roche-Guyon, some 64 kilometres downstream from Paris, in the former château

of the Dukes of La Rochefoucauld. His command consisted of General Dollmann's 7th Army, responsible for Normandy; General Salmuth's 15th Army, responsible for Somme, Pas-de-Calais, and the Low Countries; and General Geyr von Schweppenberg's Panzer Group West.

4. Steinberg, *Allemands*, 312; Defrasne, *Occupation*, 123.
5. When lst Army first arrived in the south-west of France (in Nov. 1942), it had its base in Toulouse, moving to Bordeaux in May 1944, when von der Chevallerie established his headquarters in the Château Lafage. The German commander of the Bordeaux garrison, General von Faber du Faur, like his counterparts elsewhere, set up his own quarters in the seat of the former French commandant of the local Military Region; in Bordeaux, seat of the 18th Military Region, this was on the rue Vital-Carles. Like his superior von der Chevallerie, the garrison commander found in the Bordeaux region his French and Protestant roots (Bécamps, 17, 50; Goubet and Debauges, 45).
6. *Kriegstagebuch*, 281.
7. Ibid. 286.
8. Ibid. 285.
9. Maurin, in Trempé, 22.
10. *Kriegstagebuch*, 286.
11. In recent years Paris has set out to remove the few remaining mementoes of the German occupation. One might cite the pillbox at the entrance to the catacombs at Denfert-Rochereau, and the plinth on the south side of Les Invalides. The latter had once borne the statue of General Mangin, but Hitler would not enter the Invalides during his 1940 visit to Paris until the statue was demolished. After the war the French Government had kept that memory alive by inscribing on the plinth: 'démoli par les envahisseurs allemands'. Now that too has been demolished.
12. Michel, *Paris*, 78.
13. Ibid. 77.
14. Knochen's area of responsibility included Belgium (Avakoumovitch, 'Résistance', 53).
15. Eychenne, *Pyrénées*, 123; Defrasne, *Occupation*, 74. The total of RSHA personnel in France was given by Himmler in autumn 1943 as 2,200, and by Kaltenbrunner in July 1944 as 2,400 (Bourderon and Avakoumovich, 39).
16. Becamps, 113. In Lyons Klaus Barbie headed a team of 78 SS and 149 French collaborators. Gestapo records for Saint-Étienne show 15 SS and over 300 French agents, and for Marseilles, some 50 SS and over 1,000 French agents, many of them recruited after D-Day (Dank, 222).
17. The Demarcation Line was not abolished until Feb. 1943.
18. Eychenne, *Pyrénées*, 123.
19. Cf. Pike, *Jours*, 65 n.
20. There was nothing secret about the code numbers. In Toulouse, e.g., the sign HVS 564 was displayed outside the requisitioned Grand Hôtel de la Poste on the rue Alsace-Lorraine. Room 132, on the 4th floor, was used for interrogations (Monsieur Paul, janitor, interview).

21. Noguères, v. 424.
22. Defrasne, *Occupation*, 15.
23. Among them, 9 allées Frédéric-Mistral; 1 and 9 Boulingrin; 36 rue des Chalets; the Maison Lahana at 23 rue d'Aubuisson; the École Normale; and an unidentified building on the rue Raymond IV.
24. Goubet and Debauges, 47, claim the change occurred earlier, in Feb. 1943.
25. Steinberg, *Allemands*, 250–1, 257.
26. Defrasne, *Occupation*, 84.
27. The Italo-German demarcation line ran along a line from La Ciotat northwards through Aubagne to Avignon (German), Valence (Italian), and Nantua (German).
28. Italy in Nov. 1942 was given 8 *départements*: Alpes-Maritimes, Var, Basses-Alpes, Hautes-Alpes, Drôme, Isère, Savoie, Haute-Savoie. The German commission was installed at Bourges, the Italian at Gap. So great was French resentment over the presence of the Italians that Laval even asked General von Neubronn, who was liaison officer between Pétain and von Rundstedt, if it might be possible to station German troops among the Italians in the coastal towns (Marrus and Paxton, 315).
29. Goubet and Debauges, 46, 225.
30. Eychenne, *Montagnes*, 115–16; Maurin, in Trempé, 22.
31. Goubet and Debauges, 232.
32. Colonel Berthier [Jean-Paul Vernant], *Résistance R4*, 6 (Dec. 1978), 3.
33. These units were the 3rd Brigade (Ariège), under José Oria from Apr. 1942; the 2nd Brigade (Haute-Garonne), under Joachim Ramos from July 1942; the 27th Division (Cantal), under Silvestre Gómez from Oct. 1942; and the 5th Brigade (Aude), under Antonio Molina from Oct. 1942 (Pons, *Republicanos*, 72, 91, 135, 197).
34. The 2nd Division covered only 2 (cf. Pike, *Jours*, 55). The period when this reorganisation went into effect is in dispute; Goubet and Debauges, 95, give spring 1942, while Heine, 210, gives the end of 1943.
35. Maury, *Résistance*, ii. 167; Goubet, 'République', 30.
36. Cf. Pike, *Jours*, 45 n.
37. Maury, *Résistance*, ii. 169.
38. Fareng, 123, 373; Eychenne, *Pyrénées*, 122.
39. Delpla (interview).
40. Sanz, *Luchando*, 116. In a letter to the author, 6 May 1980, Sanz contradicts himself, saying that Ríos was arrested for carrying false papers.
41. Sanz, ibid., adds that Ríos escaped from the train 'with his friend Ramos'. Sanz neither identifies Ramos nor explains how he came into possession of this dubious information.
42. Ibid.
43. Testimony of Conchita Ramos Veleta ('Grange'), in Català, 231–2; *Train*, 32–3, 201. Cf Pike, *Jours*, 48n.; and Maury, *Résistance*, ii. 169, who reports that Ríos died in the hospital at Foix at the beginning of 1944. If Maury found Ríos's death certificate, then everything else—the transfer north, the escape, the re-enlistment, and death in the home of Veleta—is an elaborate invention, the purpose of which is unfathomable.

44. Laurens, 33.
45. Sanz, *Luchando*, 117.
46. The Sipo in Tarbes was installed in the Hôtel Family. Its staff of 10 members was commanded by SS-Obersturmbannführer Pradel, who was assisted by SS-Sturmbannführer Peter Blindauer, both of the Gestapo. Pradel was responsible for all Hautes-Pyrénées, Blindauer for the Tarbes region (Pottier, 71–2; Eychenne, *Pyrénées*, 121–2).
47. Cf. Pike, *Jours*, 49n. The property seems to have belonged to Germaine Claudín, wife of the Spanish communist youth leader Fernando Claudín (cf. Sanz, *Luchando*, 176).
48. Angel [Sanz], *Guerrilleros*, 89. It is of interest that in his subsequent memoirs (*Luchando*, 125) Sanz avoids this embarrassing problem by omitting the reason for Gómez's departure.
49. Segriá Doménech, in Català, 259.
50. Rubio Miranda, in Català, 248–50.
51. Castro, *Mi fe*, 223–5. Morán, 81, refers to a manifesto signed by the PCE Central Committee and published on 16 Sept. 1942; Morán adds that Pasionaria wrote the whole of it, and most probably later than Sept. 1942.
52. Rubio, *Guerra civil*, 945.
53. Two similar organizations, the Unión democrática española and the Aliança nacional de Catalunya, already existed in Mexico (Heine, 200).
54. Arasa, 30, was told by Manuel Gimeno that he first heard of the UNE by listening to Radio Moscow. Manuel Azcárate also admitted to Arasa that the UNE was at first more an idea than a real organization.
55. Perhaps Théodore Cros, described by Goubet and Debauges, 120, as one of the very earliest members of the Resistance in Haute-Garonne.
56. Heine, 205, 441, writes that the meeting was held earlier (in the summer of 1942), that it was organized by Tomás Tortajada (whom Heine interviewed), and that some 20 delegates from all over France attended.
57. Cf. Pike, *Jours*, 64 n.
58. The machine had belonged to the PCI's underground bureau in Marseilles; the PCE had transported it to Vaucluse (Heine, 193). Cf. Arasa, 30.
59. Copies of the earliest issues are extremely rare. The Bibliothèque nationale holds a copy of only 3 of the underground issues. All are typeset and the earliest is dated Nov.–Dec. 1942; it carries the subtitle, *Órgano de Unión Nacional de todos los Españoles*. Cf. Arasa, 31.
60. Miguel Sánchez Boxa, letter of 28 Apr. 1981, containing the testimony of Antonio Pomares, then president of the Haute-Garonne committee of the Amicale des Anciens FFI et Résistants Espagnols.
61. Antonio Ferriz, in *Conferencia de Unión nacional española*, 44.
62. Fernández, *España*, 47.
63. Cf. Pike, *Jours*, 66.
64. A journal called *España popular*, published by the PCE, also appeared in Algiers.
65. A copy of an 8-page typeset issue of *Mundo obrero*, published in Ariège

in June 1943, can be seen in the Bibliothèque nationale. According to Sanz (*Luchando*, 46, 108), *Mundo obrero* published an issue in Marseilles on Nov. 7, 1940.

66. Antonio Ferriz, in *Conferencia de Unión nacional española*, 46.

67. Ippécourt, 49.

68. Estruch, 78, points out that the PCE did not begin to speak of the JSUN until the beginning of 1944. Castro (*Mi fe*, 288–90) says that news of its constitution reached Moscow in 1944 in a report in French sent by André Marty in Algiers. Marty had persuaded Dimitrov to let him leave the USSR and had persuaded de Gaulle to let him enter Algeria. Dimitrov's purpose was to persuade the Western Allies that the PCE was a team player, opposed only to fascism, and Marty's mission was to launch the news of the birth of the JSUN, claiming that he had translated it into French in order to relay it to the PCF. Morán, 76, writes that the constitution itself was written in French, Trilla having drawn it up in France before he left for Spain. Arasa, 41–4, on the other hand, accepts the Party's version on the basis of his interviews with Gimeno and other PCE leaders. According to Gimeno, the constitution, written in Spain in Spanish, had to be sent to France and reproduced in the printing shop in Cavaillon (which would explain the missing Spanish accents and other characters), after which the copies were carried into Spain and distributed.

69. According to Alba (*Historia de la Segunda*, 291), the UNE looked for converts even among members of the Falange. Cf. Gallo, 132.

70. Laurens, 33.

71. Agudo, 54–5, reports that it was as a result of this raid on the Udaves' home that Jesús Ríos, the *guerrillero* commander in chief, had fled for his life from Aude into Ariège, assuming a new identity (see above). A bicycle that the police found in searching the house carried a licence plate in the name of Jesús Ríos. The police then raided his home in Carcassonne, where only the intervention of his wife enabled him to escape.

72. Among the witnesses to this was Claude Lévy, who met both Nieto and Celadas, and many other Spanish *guerrilleros*, when he too was thrown into Saint-Michel Prison in Dec. 1943; the Spaniard in the next cell to his had a face 'swollen out of human shape' (Dr Claude Lévy, interview).

73. Cf. Agudo, 55, who states that the names were found in Bermejo's home.

74. Angel [Sanz], *Guerrilleros*, 64, 75 n., 247; Sanz, *Luchando*, 108–9; Heine, 196; Arasa, 47; Agudo, 54–5.

75. Angel [Sanz], *Guerrilleros*, 110.

76. Cossías, 50.

77. Cf. Pike, *Jours*, 119, 131.

78. Rubio, *Guerra civil*, 422–25.

79. Trempé, 68.

80. Arthur London (interview).

81. Pons, *Republicanos*, 67.

82. Anniversary of the proclamation in 1931 of Spain's 2nd Republic.

83. Cf. Goubet and Debauges, 229.
84. Pierdona, Mémoire, 282.
85. But Dupont, by his own admission, did not arrive in Toulouse before 1942 (*Trempé*, 202–3; Goubet and Debauges, 89–90). If Goubet and Debauges have failed to uncover the story, it is most unlikely that anyone else can, unless Dupont himself chooses to reveal it before he dies.
86. *Aspects*, 70; Marcelle Strickler, letter, 25 Feb. 1985; Goubet and Debauges, 36, 147, 152; Goubet, 127.
87. Pichon served as his political commissar, and Rojo as his chief of staff (Goubet and Debauges, 96).
88. Ibid. 95.
89. Ibid. 93.
90. Pierdona, Mémoire, 191.
91. Apart from the Hôtel de Paris mentioned earlier, the Hôtel-Restaurant Casimir, also in the centre of the city, provided another rendezvous. Its proprietor, Monsieur Bastide, an airman in the First World War, could be relied upon, but its location, on the rue Austerlitz right opposite the Hôtel de l'Ours Blanc, was less than ideal when the Germans arrived and requisitioned the Ours Blanc. Other rendezvous included the shop of the Ros brothers on the rue Matabiau, the Bibliothèque municipale (thanks to its director, Mlle Dobelman), the Bibliothèque universitaire on the rue du Taur (thanks to its librarian, the Catalan poet Miquel Serra i Baldó), and especially the back room of a restaurant on the rue des Potiers, owned by the Catalan Joan Clot. The restaurant was chosen because it had a rear exit. Clot had two children who agreed to serve as look-outs. But Ravanel, who sometimes used the restaurant as a rendezvous, states that Clot himself was not in the Resistance and did not know that his restaurant was being used—or that his children were serving in the Resistance (Ravanel, interview; Francesc Parramón, in Milza and Peschanski, 607; Horacio Doménech, ibid.). Cf. Araza, 32.
92. Sanz, letter, 6 May 1980; Sanz, *Luchando*, 124.
93. Pons, *Republicanos*, 158; Pilar Claver, in Català, 106, 117.
94. Goubet and Debauges, 76. So many small acts of courage and ingenuity have gone unrewarded and even unrecognized. There was the case in Toulouse, for example, of the German Jewish tailor Paul Ullmann, who employed his whole family in manufacturing false French uniforms. They were caught and deported (Pons, *Republicanos*, 306).
95. In 1983, when my *Jours de gloire, jours de honte* was already at press, I interviewed Chief Inspector Maurice Espitalier in Toulouse. He and his wife Juliette, a survivor of Ravensbrück, convinced me of the innocence of Caussié who, they said, not only played no part in the torture of Langer but did his utmost to save him, and if Caussié's efforts failed, it was because there was no one in the police headquarters to help him. Since Caussié survived the post-Liberation hunt for collaborators, and was still in his job in 1950, I assumed this version to be true and made the last-minute amendment that appears in *Jours*, xxxi n. I am now convinced to the contrary, and express my apologies to Dr Claude Lévy

whose testimony I unwisely refuted. Interviews with Dr Lévy (who was Langer's comrade in the 35th Brigade and an inmate of both the Toulouse prisons only a few weeks after Langer's execution), Claude Urman (Langer's successor as commander of that brigade), and Jaime Amorós Vidal (the Toulouse bookseller whose contacts are exceptional) persuade me that Vichy's 8th Brigade was in the business of torture; that Caussié controlled its business; and that there was no conceivable reason for Caussié to make an exception for a leader of the enemy he was fighting. Add to that the evidence given by Maître Arnal, the attorney who defended both Langer and Lévy, who has attested to the 'unspeakable cruelties' inflicted on Langer.

What is probably true in Maurice Espitalier's testimony is that, at the moment Langer arrived at the 8th Brigade's headquarters, and just before his first interrogation, he said to a policeman: 'If you're a Frenchman, help me.' This, added Espitalier, was in vain: 'the policeman thought he was doing his duty by refusing'. The policeman, of course, was handpicked, like Caussié, to serve the collaborationist cause of Vichy, and neither he nor anyone else in the building would have offered any shrift to any prisoner—until 1944, when the Vichy police began to worry about their own survival.

If further evidence were needed, the transcript of Langer's interrogation survives. Dr Lévy has had access to it, and still retains a copy of a part of it. A report signed by Caussié describes how Langer tried to escape, 'which compelled the police to use force'. So ends Caussié's claim—a successful claim, since he was honoured after the war as a Resistance hero—to have tried to help Langer to escape.

96. On the eve of his execution, Langer wrote a letter, which has been preserved, to the wife and child he had left behind in Spain, and which is most touching in its affection for them. Only in 1984 did they hear of his fate and visit the cemetery of Terre-Cabade in Toulouse where he is buried (*Résistance R4*, 3. (Mar. 1978), 41; *Mauthausen: Bulletin Intérieur de l'Amicale des Déportés et Familles de Mauthausen*, 220 (Dec. 1984)).

97. *La Dépêche*, 10 Oct. 1943.

98. *Aspects*, 58; Goubet and Debauges, 94–5, 148–53.

99. This documentary, entitled 'Les terroristes à la retraite' and produced by the Romanian exile Serge Mosco, was to have been shown in Feb. 1984, but it was a bad time for such an exposé: the French Government included four communist ministers. Following their resignation from the Cabinet, the film was scheduled to be shown on 2 June 1985, but the furious opposition of Albert Ouzoulias and other leaders of the PCF blocked the showing until 2 July. Cf. *International Herald Tribune*, 31 May 1985 and 7 June 1985.

100. Holban had been given another assignment, away from Paris.

101. The name of Alfonso has been given to a street in the Paris suburb of Ivry-sur-Seine.

102. This account, narrated in the Mosco documentary by a member of the

Manouchian group who was covering Alfonso in the park and was an eyewitness to the assassination, fundamentally contradicts the version given by Michel-Antoine Burnier and Luis González-Mata, who describe the Nazi as a certain Dr Wallenher and the incident as a bungled attempt at assassination.

103. This again totally contradicts the account given by Burnier and González-Mata, which carries an entirely different set of details. The account I have given is that by Boris Holban, presented in the Mosco documentary.

104. Pons, *Republicanos*, 287–90; Steinberg, *Allemands*, 167, 327; Sanz, *Luchando*, 54–5, 59–61. The staff officer was finally identified (by von Boinelburg-Langsfeld himself), as Lieutenant-Colonel Moritz von Ratibor und Corvey (Holban, 163–8; Courtois *et al.*, 319).

105. No transcript of the trial has survived (Denis Peschansky, private information).

106. *Paris-Soir*, 21 Feb. 1944; cited by Courtois *et al.*, 361. Victoria Kent, 172, found a different account in the same press: 'Of all the accused, the only one to remain perfectly calm was Alonso.'

107. Courtois *et al.*, 368. Again Alonso was singled out. A press account ran: 'He alone remained calm, and even smiled' (Kent, 172).

108. The letter to Mélinée was among the papers confiscated by the Soviet authorities when she accepted an invitation in 1945 to visit Armenia. She was able to return to France in 1964 only through the intercession of President Charles de Gaulle, and able to recover her letters only as a result of further pressure by the French Government.

109. Robert Amouroux, French television channel 2, 'Dossiers de l'écran', 2 July 1985. Charles Lederman, the communist senator from Val-de-Marne, who was also on the panel and who threatened to take legal action against the film's producer, ended a 3-hour debate by claiming that the betrayer to whom Manouchian referred was none other than Vichy. 'The transcript proves it', he added, mindful of the fact that no transcript exists.

110. Jérôme, whose real name was Michel Feintuch, was of Polish origin. He had served in Spain as comptroller of the International Brigades.

111. Cf. the article by Burnier and González-Mata, which includes the sworn and signed testimony of Joseph Tomasina regarding his conversation with Manouchian when the two men shared a prison cell in Jan. 1944. Tomasina was not among those selected for execution; he was deported to Germany instead, but survived. In his deposition, he recounts that Manouchian saw the political commissar Albert signal at the station to the plain-clothes police nearby.

CHAPTER 9

1. George Gordon Lord Byron, *Child Harold's Pilgrimage*, LXXXVI. Byron is referring to Palafox's answer to the French general at the siege of Saragossa: '¡La guerra! ¡La guerra aunque sea a cuchillo!'

For a more detailed account of the operation of the Wehrmacht forces in south–west France in the summer of 1944, which are discussed briefly in this chapter and Ch. 10, see my articles in *Guerres mondiales et conflits contemporains*, Oct. 1988 and Oct. 1991.

2. This reflected a change of policy on the part of the British Government that ran the risk of offending Franco.

3. In July 1944 Colonel Sanz was appointed the AGE's delegate at FFI general headquarters in Toulouse (Goubet and Debauges, 228). His post as chief of staff AGE was taken by Colonel José García Acevedo. The question must still be asked whether, for those few weeks, Colonel Sanz really was chief of staff to General Fernández. Sanz has insisted to me that he was. Fernández has insisted to me equally strongly that he was not (cf. Pike, *Jours*, 49). Colonel López Tovar has since added his voice to the debate, insisting that Sanz never was chief of staff (interview).

4. Paz was assisted in the work of liaison by Carmen Royo, the wife of Miguel Angel Sanz. Royo had previously served as liaison agent in her husband's 4th Division, and following the Liberation she was awarded the Croix de Guerre (Cossías, 56; Sanz, *Luchando*, 177).

5. Interviewed in the communist press after the Liberation, Fernández stated that he had fought during the Civil War on the Basque front, assigned to an anti–aircraft battery in the 3rd Brigade (*Juventud*, 1 (28 Sept. 1944)).

6. His first command post was in the forest near the village of Crampagna, a few kilometres north of Foix. It was there that two other Spaniards settled who were to play a major role in later events: the Valledor brothers, José Antonio and Modesto, both hardened veterans from the Asturias.

7. Little is known of Luis Fernández's sojourn in Toulouse, except that he lived there with his young wife and a group of Basques. With a fishmonger called Pozuelo they began producing an edition of *Mundo obrero*. Pozuelo was dynamic but indiscreet, and was soon caught in a police raid on a restaurant. Cf. Teresa Moratilla, in Català, 214–16.

8. *Juventud*, 1 (28 Sept. 1944).

9. Serge Ravanel (interview).

10. General Chevance-Bertin (interview).

11. Jean-Pierre Vernant (interview); Dr Claude Lévy (interview).

12. Carmen de Pedro (interview).

13. Claude Urman (interview).

14. The 4th Division was commanded, successively, by Manuel Castro, Miguel Angel Sanz, and José Vitini (Pons, *Republicanos*, 68; Sanz, *Luchando*, 127).

15. López Tovar had commanded the 46th Division and the 42nd Division of the Republican Army, serving under General Tagüeña in the Battle of Catalonia.

16. Vicente López Tovar (interview). Cf. Arasa, 36.

17. López Tovar, unpub. 'Memoires', 4.

18. López Tovar (interview).

19. The Romanians were Mîchai Florescu and Pavel Cristescu. Cristescu, under the name of 'Major Octave', then built a MOI group in Corrèze, which was joined by several Spaniards in that area. He later commanded

the MOI forces in the Limoges region, and after the war became Minister of Science and Technology in his home country.

20. In an interview published after the Liberation in the communist *Juventud* 2 (5 Oct. 1944), Blázquez was presented (curiously) only by his *nom de guerre* 'César' and without the title of general; it described him as a member of the middle class ('not the bourgeoisie') who had served in the Civil War as commissar first of a battalion, then of a brigade, and finally of a division.

21. This numbering system derived from the organization of the Gaullist Armée secrète.

22. In the successful action in Feb. 1944 against the Central Prison in Nîmes, some 20 FTP leaders were liberated. The PCE would later bestow the laurels for the action on the head of its favourite *guerrillero*, Cristino García Grandas. But however important his role may have been in subsequent events, his part in the break-out in Nîmes was an embarrassment. García, who was then fighting in the MOI, began the operation by accidentally firing his revolver into his right leg, shattering his tibia. He had to be carried by two Spanish comrades to Dr Fayot, a surgeon in the Resistance. He was then hidden for 3 weeks in the Protestant Maison de Santé, and then in a succession of homes until he had recovered sufficiently to rejoin a MOI group in the forest of Goudargues. After taking part in various actions he won the credit, this time rightly, for leading the engagement at La Madeleine, but for the operation in Nîmes the honour goes to the Catalan anarchist leader Miguel Arcas ('Victor') and the Montaigne brigade (Vielzeuf, *On les appelait*, 125, 143–6; Brès, 128–9, 161).

23. According to Joan Martorell, in Soriano, 128, there were as many as 170 Spaniards.

24. General Jean de Bermond de Vaulx, 185, refers nevertheless to the help given by Hilaire in the evacuation to Spain of 15 prisoners who escaped from Eysses on 3 Jan. 1944.

25. Sanz, *Luchando*, 96.

26. *L'Insurrection*, 72; Fernández, *España*, 1971 edn., 87–91; Pons, 164–77; Soriano, 128–9.

27. e.g. Claude Chambard, cited above.

28. Pierre Golliet, in Jourdan *et al.*, 88.

29. Ibid. Cf. Hernando, 127, for the role of Antonio Jurado and José Mari.

30. Sanz (*Luchando*, 202) reports that even Oberg and Knochen of the SS arrived from Paris to take part.

31. Dreyfus, 100; Friang gives the figure of 20,000, perhaps by counting those held in reserve.

32. *Bulletin de l'Amicale de Mauthausen*, special issue, Aug. 1962.

33. Foot, 373. Foot's figures may be inflated: his estimate of 700 for the strength of the force at Glières is higher than others. Cf. Jourdan *et al.*, 88, who add that the Spanish survivors regrouped under Miguel Vera; Pons, *Republicanos*, 257–8; Sanz, *Luchando*, 200–2.

34. Vielzeuf, 201–9, provides the full German report in French translation.

35. Fernández, *España*, 92–3; Pons, *Republicanos*, 116–18; Sanz, *Luchando*, 161–7; Brès, 214–16, 251–2; Hernando, 122–3.

36. Brès, 253–61. The unit belonged to the Streifkorps Südfrankreich (Feldpost 15727). Even one of the German partisans, Paul Huber, fell for the ruse and allowed himself to be taken away, the presence of the Spaniard in the SS unit dispelling whatever doubts he might have had.

37. Pons, *Republicanos*, 268. Sanz, *Luchando*, 206, gives the much lower figure of 14 Spaniards killed and 4 taken prisoner, but his research on this subject is weak. The account by Dreyfus does not include a single reference to a Spaniard; nor does the official account published in 1984 by the French Ministry of Defence. The Resistance lost only 140 combatants. The remaining 700 killed were civilians: doctors and nurses, teachers and children, peasants and shepherds.

38. Pons, *Republicanos*, 261; Sanz, *Luchando*, 206, who gives his name as Manuel Correa Granados.

39. 'Das Reich' and 11th Panzer had been withdrawn from the Russian front for refitting in early 1944, and had then been attached to 1st Army, in the Bordeaux area. 'Das Reich' arrived in the Toulouse area in the last week of Apr. 1944.

40. Pons, *Republicanos*, 88; Sentis, 96. The claim that Capdenac-Gare, southeast of Figéac, was liberated on D-Day itself is highly implausible, and Sanz, *Luchando*, 191–3, makes no reference to it in his account.

41. Schramm, 284.

42. Henri Michel, summing up the Colloque sur les Maquis, Paris, 22–3 Nov. 1984. '*Philémon réclame six bouteilles de Sauternes*', the signal of alert, was issued on 2 June (Bécamps, 49). But there was more than one alert signal. The one received by Hilaire on 5 June ran: '*Il a une voix de faussette*'.

43. Goubet and Debauges, 157–8, 163.

44. LVIII Pz. K., *KTB* Anlage 32*b*, 10 June 1944 (microfilm 173, SHAT, Vincennes).

45. Cf. Amouroux, viii. 179 n.

46. Vilanova, 224, who gives the names of the 12 adults; his list does not include, however, the name of the Lafuente family to which Montseny, 6, refers. Oradour was socialist and hospitable towards refugees, and Spanish exiles of 1939 had found a welcome in the little town (Amouroux, viii. 168). Hastings, 185, refers to 30 Spaniards working there as labourers.

47. Diekmann was present in person (Amouroux, viii. 167), and it is certain that, if 200 troops were involved, more than the 3rd Company took part. The name of Fritz von Brodowsky has also been associated with these operations. Von Brodowsky had for 3 months (Mar.–June 1944) been in command of *HVS* 588 (Clermont-Ferrand), where the German forces included many Ost Legion troops (Noguères, v. 138). According to Defrasne, *Occupation*, 123, von Brodowski was selected in June 1944 to head a special staff (perhaps an *Einsatzgruppe*) to fight the Resistance. He was not, however, involved in the Oradour massacre, since he mentioned in his own report that he had received his information about this from a French source (Amouroux, viii. 162–3).

48. Hastings, 244, argues that the order emanated from no higher than Diekmann. Diekmann was blown to pieces in Normandy on 30 June 1944, and Kahn was never found. Lammerding lived out his life in ease as a building constructor in Düsseldorf, not far from the famous Schmoller Restaurant on Graf-Adolf Platz where Kurt Franz, the deputy commandant of Treblinka, now a chef, regaled the guests with his French cuisine. In a letter published after his death in 1971, Lammerding described Oradour as a Resistance nest which the SS had to wipe out, but he insisted that Diekmann had received the order not from him but from Stadler—a frivolous remark, if the brigade commander had received it from the division commander. On the other hand, Lammerding did not argue, as others have argued, that the SS confused Oradour-sur-Glane with Oradour-sur-Vayres, the one north-west, the other south-west of Limoges; cf. Amouroux, viii. 160–1. As for Stadler, in 1992 he remains an active Nazi. He was to preside at a reunion of Austrian Waffen-SS veterans, to be held in Styria on 23–4 May, but a public outcry forced its cancellation.

    For a revisionist approach, see the work of the former SS officer Herbert Taege, who in *Wo ist Kain?* presents the following scenario: Spanish *guerrilleros* hiding in the church belfry had stored explosives behind the altar; when the Germans, in self-defence, opened fire, the stores exploded, causing casualties to the unfortunate women and children whom the Germans had placed inside the church out of concern for their safety.
49. Hastings, 182.
50. LVIII Pz. K., *KTB* Anlage 52, 12 June 1944.
51. Ibid. 85, 20 June 1944.
52. Ibid. 111*a*, n.d.
53. *Wolfsschlucht I*, the GHQ used by Hitler in June 1940, had been established near Givet in the Ardennes. *Wolfsschlucht* is not to be confused with *Wolfsschanze*, Hitler's permanent headquarters near Rastenburg, in East Prussia.
54. LVIII Pz. K., *KTB* Anlage 208*a* and Anlage 209*b*, 11–12 July 1944.
55. Ibid. 222, 15 July 1944.
56. Ibid. 202, 10 July 1944.
57. Ibid. (reference illegible; perhaps 21 June 1944). Hastings, 239, estimates Das Reich''s losses at only 35 dead, out of some 15,000 men, but cites no sources.
58. Extraits du journal de marche du Groupe d'Armées G, 8 June 1944, 14.
59. LVIII Pz. K., *KTB* Anlage 190*b*, 5 July 1944.

CHAPTER 10

1. William Wordsworth, 'The French and the Spanish Guerrillas' (1810 or 1811).
2. LVIII Pz. K., *KTB* Anlage 52, 12 June 1944 (microfilm 173, SHAT, Vincennes).
3. Ibid. 67, 16 June 1944.

4. Oberkommando Armeegruppe G, 593/44, 17 June 1944; LVIII Pz. K., *KTB* 10, 26 June 1944 (microfilm 34, SHAT).
5. LVIII Pz. K., *KTB* Anlage 88a, 20 June 1944 (microfilm 173, SHAT).
6. The success of the Spanish Resistance can be gauged by the situation in Dec. 1943 in the *départements* of Hérault and Aveyron, where 3,750 Spaniards were ordered to report; only 150 were actually enlisted, most of them in Aveyron (Antonio Gardó, in *Conferencia de UNE*, 47; cf. Pike, *Français*, 391).
7. Alff, 'Tätigkeitsbericht vom 1. bis 31. VII 1944 des Oberkommandos der Armeegruppe G', in 'Gutachten', 27.
8. *Reconquista de España*, special issue 32 (June 1944). According to this school of thought, the proper role of the Resistance, the urban no less than the Maquis, was to treat all Germans as 'the vermin in grey-green' and to exterminate them wherever the opportunity arose: in the street, in dark alleys, in the Métro. This would provoke a massive German retaliation, which would in turn force the general public to abandon its wait-and-see attitude. The contending school of thought argued against such tactics, urging the Resistance to concentrate on the leaders of the Milice and members of the Sipo-SD.
9. Agudo, 133, writes of 403 people, of whom half were Spanish and some were women, leaving Le Vernet on 30 June and entering the Cafarelli barracks in Toulouse that evening. Cf. Hernando, 84.
10. Such was the conclusion reached on 12 June by the senior intelligence officer of LVIIIth Panzerkorps, after a meeting in Toulouse with the SD commander and the *HVS* garrison commander.
11. LVIII Pz. K., *KTB* Anlage 262, 23 July 1944.
12. Vilanova, 260–4; Pons, *Republicanos*, 182–4.
13. At least one train left Toulouse for Germany after 2 July; cf. *Train*, 155, for the departure of the last convoy, not specifically for Dachau, on 31 July 1944.
14. *Le Monde*, 29 June 1984; 13 July 1984; 10 Aug. 1984.
15. Dr Parra was widely respected: for three years he had served as head of the medical services in the detention camp at Le Vernet. Throughout the voyage of the 'ghost train', Dr Parra continued to tend the sick; in Pierrelatte he had the chance to escape, but he refused to abandon his companions (*Train*, 18). He nevertheless survived both the journey and Dachau. Professor Lautmann, Jewish and a friend of Bertaux, was a leader of the Resistance who had been taken prisoner and escaped, only to be denounced by a Frenchman in June 1944. The parliamentarian Nitti had been imprisoned by Mussolini, but escaped and took part in the Spanish Civil War. In France he had entered the Bertaux Resistance network, and had been arrested with Bertaux and Cassou in Dec. 1941. But while Bertaux and Cassou were eventually released, Nitti had remained in prison.
16. The four colonels were Eleuterio Díaz Tendero, Vicente Redondo, César Blasco Sasero, and Jesús Velasco. Among the Spaniards who had been dispatched from Le Vernet was the former Republican fighter pilot Manolo

Morató Arias. After escaping from the 422nd Group of MOE (cf. Pike, *Français*, 391) and serving in the 5th Brigade of Guerrilleros (Aude), Morató had been arrested on 5 May 1944 (Pons, *Republicanos*, 97, 102, 234).

17. Dr Lévy was a member of a Jewish family which had left Paris in June 1940 for Lyons. Originally with a Gaullist Resistance group, he left it to join the FTP, which he found 'much more ready to engage in combat'. He also found that in his FTP unit not everyone was communist: 'most of the youth cared little for politics'. Promoted in 1943 to platoon leader, Lévy was arrested in Toulouse on 7 Dec. and taken to the police head-quarters on the rue du Rempart-Saint-Étienne. Under the Resistance code it was his duty to hold out under torture for 2 days in order to give his comrades time to escape. He nearly succeeded, but the treatment he underwent at the hands of the Vichy police wrung from him his address, and with that they found evidence of his connections. Lévy was sent to Saint-Michel Prison, and later to Furgole Military Prison.

18. Christian de Roquemaurel de L'Isle (interview). This was probably the same unit that evacuated Le Vernet: 3rd Company, 726th Inf. Btn. That battalion belonged to the 716th Inf. Div. which had been shattered in the Cotentin peninsula and sent to recover in the Perpignan area, as part of ɪvth Lw. K.

19. Michel, *Histoire*, 114.

20. Dr Claude Lévy (interview); corroborated by another surviving witness, de Roquemaurel (interview).

21. When the manhunt was called off and Alvarez had recovered a little strength, he made his way to the Sainte-Bazeille station, which had already been checked by two German patrols. Fortunately for Alvarez, the station-master and the head railroadsman were in the Resistance. The latter, the Basque Gabriel Bereza, gave him a railwayman's uniform and a two-handed hammer, then took him home and hid him for several days until the authorities had ended their inquiries and Alvarez had recuperated. He then rejoined the Resistance in a group based in Saint-Vivien (Angel Alvarez, deposition; Jacques Bellay, interview; de Roque-maurel, interview).

22. Conchita Ramos, a survivor, reports (in Català, 232) that the authorities at Dachau would not accept the women, and they were sent on to Ravensbrück on 9 Sept. while the rest of the men reached Mauthausen-Ebensee on 19 Sept. (*Train*, 196).

23. Dr Claude Lévy (interviews); Nitti, *passim*; Debrise, 34; Lévy, *Parias*, 215–34; Lévy, 'L'autre train du 2 juillet 1944', *Le Monde*, 29 Aug. 1984; Agudo, 134, 139; Goubet and Debauges, 119, 169, 228; Soriano, 32; *Train*, *passim*. Dr Lévy returned part of the way in a US Army vehicle, reach-ing Toulouse with a captain's commission in late Sept. He was now a member of the PCF and mixed in the company of the Spanish *guerrillero* leaders, especially Luis Fernández and José García Acevedo. As for travelling by train, it would be 15 years before he could bring himself to step aboard again.

24. ʟvɪɪɪ Pz. K., *KTB* Anlage 98, 22 June 1944.

25. Pons, *Republicanos*, 132; Carrasco, 222. Carrasco attributes this action to 'Das Reich'; this is not likely, since the units it had left behind in the south-west were by then rejoining General Lammerding in Normandy.

26. Eychenne, *Pyrénées*, 122. Pons, *Republicanos*, 132–3; Vitorio Vicuña ('Oria'), in Català, 273–8.

27. Cf. Heine, 111.

28. Brunet, 81.

29. Ibid.

30. 'The FTP relied on SOE for arms and equipment', writes Beevor, 153; 'resistance in France was made possible only by SOE, the RAF, the Gaullist movement, with the OSS and USAAF in the final year.'

31. Escholier, 27; Bertaux, 88–9; Bermond de Vaulx, 103, 185–6. Hastings, 77, writes that Hilaire eschewed all sexual activity for the entire time he was in France: it was not worth the risk.

32. Colonel Henri Monnet, 'Propos', *Résistance R4*, 3 (Mar. 1978), 3.

33. Ortega has adopted his matronymic, Guerrero, which has caused some confusion.

34. Escholier, 66, 121; Bermond de Vaulx, 104; Concha González de Boix, in Català, 161–2; Celia Llaneza, in Català, 190–3. Cf. Hernando, 114–15.

35. Pons, *Republicanos*, 121, gives the names of the Spanish dead, but locates the engagement 50 kilometres to the west. I have followed the official records of the brigade, compiled by Tomás Ortega Guerrero, who replaced Mendizábal as its commander.

36. Pons, *Republicanos*, 121–3; Trempé, 77, who mentions the participation in the engagement of the MOI and the Armagnac Battalion of Captain Parisot.

37. Ortega Guerrero, 'Historique de la 35ème Brigade de Guérilleros espagnols', 1.

38. Goubet and Debauges, 172.

39. This is partly due to his celebrated quarrel in Toulouse with General de Gaulle (cf. Pike, 'La retraite', 118 n.). On this matter the best authority is not M. R. D. Foot but Sir Brooks Richards, to whom Hilaire confided the story the morning after it happened. 'The conversation took place in the Préfecture *in French*. The General opened by asking Hilaire what he was doing in France, to which Hilaire replied with a brief description of his work in arming, training, and leading the *maquisards*. The General replied that he, a British officer, had no right to be doing such things and that he must leave French territory within the next 24 hours, to which Hilaire's response was, "*Mon Général, je vous connais comme chef de la France Combattante, mais je ne vous connais pas comme un officier supérieur; et je vous emmerde*". De Gaulle replied: "*Il y a une chose de vraie dans ce qu'ils m'ont dit à votre sujet,—c'est que vous savez dire 'Merde'.*" ' (Sir Brooks Richards, letter of 30 Oct. 1988).

Pierre Bertaux (interview) considered that the cause of the quarrel was Hilaire's arrogance, but Jean-Pierre Vernant (interview) did not find him arrogant at all: 'The heart of the matter was that de Gaulle was determined to show that he had undisputed control of the south-west.'

40. Foot, 218–19. On 21 July 1944 Hitler ordered the appointment on all

vital communications routes of 'section chiefs', to whom the normal railway employees would be subordinate. The General Director of Transport of OB West opposed the measure, which left Army Group G pleading with OB West to decide the matter one way or the other ('Extraits du journal de marche du Groupe d'Armées G', 49).

41. Jean-Pierre Pignot, 'Aspects', Mémoire, 81.
42. It was apparently Brooks who directed the two French girls, aged only 14 and 16, in the sabotage of the motors of *Das Reich's* tanks (Mackness, 72–3; cf. Pike, 'Forces', 11).
43. Under its agreement with the British Secret Intelligence Service, OSS was not permitted to launch independent operations from the UK, but in early 1944 OSS had joined with the British SOE in a joint enterprise known as Special Force Headquarters. Its purpose was to co-ordinate all guerrilla resistance in France in support of the Normandy invasion. Its method was to launch 3-man teams known as Jedburghs. These teams, 103 in number and named Jedburgh after the village on the Scottish side of the Border where they trained, each consisted of a Briton, an American, and a Frenchman, Belgian, or Dutchman, and comprised 2 officers and a sergeant radio-operator, but in any combination. The teams provided arms and food supplies to the Maquis while also taking part in small- and medium-scale guerrilla operations (Colby and Forbath, 57–8). Foltz, 57–8, shows that US and British arms were parachuted to the Spanish *guerrilleros* in the Pyrenees region as well as to the Maquis. Beevor, 270, refers to Spaniards fighting during the liberation of France in the British Special Service Brigade, but he provides no details. Cf. Drew Middleton, *New York Times*, 2 June 1984, for a 1984 reunion in Paris of some 200 Jedburgh veterans.
44. Guy Labedan, in Trempé, 44; Goubet and Debauges, 133, 139–40, 176, 233; Goubet, 145.
45. Ortega Guerrero, 'Historique de la 35ème Brigade de Guérilleros espagnols', n.p. Hod Fuller was another who never spoke of his wartime experiences, even to his close friends.
46. LVIII Pz. K., *KTB* Anlage 59b, 14 June 1944.
47. Ibid. 251, 20 July 1944.
48. Steinberg, *Allemands*, 314.
49. Von Blaskowitz was not involved in the Plot, but some former members of his staff were (Snyder, 29).
50. At the moment of firing, von Stülpnagel had the barrel of the gun too far forward. As a result, the bullet missed his brain but passed through his eyes, blinding him totally. Hitler had him brought to Germany, nursed him back to health, and then, at Ploetzensee on 30 Aug. 1944, had him strangled to death. Jäckel, 485, confuses the two von Stülpnagels. It was Karl Heinrich's cousin Otto who hanged himself in a French prison on 6 Feb. 1948.
51. LVIII Pz. K., *KTB* Anlage 245, 21 July 1944.
52. Originally *Anvil*, it was renamed *Dragoon*.
53. See above, p. 205.
54. LVIII Pz. K., Ic, Tätigkeits-Bericht, 27 July 1944.

55. LVIII Pz. K., *KTB* Anlage 263*a*, 23 July 1944. On 29 July, 150 Spanish *guerrilleros* and 50 FTP *maquisards* launched an assault on the town of Prades, their main target being the Gestapo centre in the Villa Marguerite. After 5 hours of bitter fighting, the partisans held only its ground floor. The approach of German reinforcements from Perpignan induced the partisans to break off the engagement and to withdraw to Valmanya and La Bastide in the nearly mountains. Valmanya proved to be accessible to their enemy, and on 4 Aug. a force of Germans and French Milice arrived and destroyed the village (Grando *et al.*, 208).

56. By 19 Aug. von Blaskowitz had set up his general headquarters in Pierrelatte on the Rhône, between Avignon and Valence. Two days later, with the situation worsening, he fell back to Lyons, and by 23 Aug. he was in Dijon.

57. Schmidt-Hartung had replaced Schubert as officer commanding *HVS* 564 (Toulouse).

58. LVIII Pz. K., *KTB* Anlage 209*b*, 11 July 1944.

59. South of the Loire, these pockets consisted of La Rochelle–La Pallice and the two positions controlling the estuary of the Gironde: Royan and Pointe-de-Grave.

60. Steinberg, *Allemands*, 326.

61. 1st Army returned to von Blaskowitz's command, but with a new commander: on 6 Sept., von der Chevallerie was replaced by General Otto von Knobelsdorff.

62. Bécamps, 12–13.

63. MSS A-868 and B-800, Militärgeschichtliches Forschungsamt, Freiburg-im-Breisgau. The second of these documents suggests that this was the route taken by von Blaskowitz himself.

64. Ortega Guerrero, 'Historique de la 35ème Brigade de Gúerilleros espagnols', n.p.

65. In Auch the Gestapo had been headed by SS-Hauptsturmführer Jaeger, assisted by SS-Obersturmführer Enne Gerdes, the latter falling prisoner to the Maquis.

66. Ortega Guerrero, 'Historique de la 35éme Brigade de Gúerilleros espagnols', n.p. Cf. Goubet and Debauges, 177, who refer to a separate action under Colonel Fuller further east in the Luchon valley, where 200 Germans were captured before they could cross into Spain.

67. Chambard, 496.

68. Pottier, 71–2.

69. Cf. Dronne, 341; Michel, *Paris*, 127.

70. Steinberg, *Allemands*, 256.

71. The French historian Henri Noguères described to me how he was taken hostage at that moment by Germans in panic. They made him ride on his motorcycle at the head of the column, telling him, 'that way, the terrorists will get you first'. They drove all night, arriving in Béziers the next morning.

72. For a bowdlerized account of this debate, see Trempé, 182.

73. Bertaux explained to me the resentment he had expressed, ever since 1944, that a great European newspaper—the *Dépêche* of Clement Attlee,

Julien Benda, Yvon Delbos, Guglielmo Ferrero, Salvador de Madariaga, Herbert Samuel, Count Sforza, Albert Thibaudet, Emile Vandervelde, and especially Heinrich and Thomas Mann—should have fallen into the hands of a family that had made a fortune not in publishing but in road construction. For earlier attacks on Bertaux, see *La Dépêche du Midi*, 19 Feb. 1967 and 5 Mar. 1974.

74. Precisely because this was the first combat inside the city, the laurels are strongly contested. The lore of the Communist Party holds that the attack was led by the Commander-in-Chief, Luis Fernández, in person. This is denied by Colonel López Tovar, who insists that at that time General Fernández was in his headquarters at Isle-en-Dodon, south-west of Toulouse. The leader of the assault force, adds López Tovar, was Major Luis Bermejo. López Tovar is not a friend of Luis Fernández, but his relations with Bermejo are much worse: he has accused him publicly of desertion in the field of battle, imposture, and embezzlement, so his position on this particular question is disinterested. It is nevertheless wrong, says Claude Urman, Commander of the MOI's 35th Brigade: López Tovar could not know at first hand, because he was at the time in Dordogne. Urman's account puts the matter to rest, because his wife Pauline was among those liberated from the prison, and she reports that the assault force was under the direct command of General Fernández, even though Fernández did not take a personal part. Pauline Urman ('Paulette') provides an example of how close the surviving prisoners were to death. She had been arrested in Toulouse on 8 Aug. 1944 by the Marty Brigade, the police unit commanded by Pierre Marty, which served as Vichy's own roving Gestapo. She was picked up in an arms depot of the MOI's 35th Brigade on the second floor of 6 rue de la Pomme; the location was known only to her and to Lazare Frydman ('Pierrot'). When the latter was arrested and tortured he revealed the secret of the depot, and Pauline Urman happened to be there at that moment. Taken to the prison on the rue du Rempart-Saint-Étienne, she too was tortured and was sentenced to be executed on 20 Aug. (Interviews with Vicente López Tovar, Claude Urman, Pauline Urman.) Cf. Hernando, 82–7.

75. 'It was impossible ever to get the truth from Malraux', Pierre Bertaux once told me; 'I never knew any man so given to mythomania.' Julien Segnaire, who had served in the Spanish Civil War as political commissar of the Escadrille España and who knew Malraux as well as anyone could know him, told me that the reason why Malraux waited until the summer of 1944 before joining the Resistance was that 'he wanted to know that his action, his participation would be decisive'. Or, in Malraux's terminology, an action, not a gesture.

76. *Le Jeune Combattant*, 1 (1 Sept. 1944).

77. Trempé, 43; Goubet and Debauges, 182–7.

78. Including Marcel Ségaud, the future prefect of Hautes-Pyrénées, who was wounded.

79. Interview. Ramos had commanded the 2nd Brigade of Spanish Guerrilleros between July 1942 and May 1944.

80. Col. Ravanel, in Trempé, 52.

81. Goubet and Debauges, 206.
82. Guy Labedan, in Trempé, 44.
83. Goubet and Debauges, 171–2; Goubet, 149.
84. Carrasco, 200; Col. Ravanel, in Trempé, 50.
85. Carrasco, 198, provides a photograph of the Gestapo official being led in handcuffs to the place of execution by *guerrilleros* of the 3rd Brigade. Cf. Fareng, 353; Bertaux, 64, who gives the man's name as Grosle; Ramón Rubio Miranda, in Català, 247.
86. Pons, *Republicanos*, 79–83; Sanz, *Luchando*, 150; Guy Labedan, in Trempé, 38; Casimir Lucibello, in Trempé, 58; and Trempé, 77. Pons makes the interesting point that the prisoners taken included former officers and men of the Blue Division, but provides no names.
87. Sentis, *Communistes*, 132, 137.
88. Bouladou, 76; Jules Maurin, in Trempé, 28.
89. RH 20–19/90, fo. 50 (Bundesarchiv-Militärarchiv, Freiburg-im-Breisgau).
90. Cf. Pike, *Jours*, 58; Bounin, 158.
91. Bouladou, 78; letters from Aimé Vielzeuf dated 12 Mar. 1981 and 22 Feb. 1983; Jules Maurin, in Trempé, 28. The Battle of the Madeleine, as the PCE's propaganda machine now restyled this worthy but relatively modest engagement, became the most famous exploit of the Spaniards' most famous hero. A veteran not only of the Civil War (where he fought in the xivth Corps of Guerrilleros) but even of the 1934 rebellion in his native Asturias, Cristino, as he was known to all, was the model of the miner-turned-revolutionary: tall, slim, tempestuous, and never shaken. Such was the force of the Madeleine myth that even scholarly accounts refer to German losses as 600 dead and wounded, with 1,500 taken prisoner (Morán, 103).
92. 'For the Germans', writes Jules Maurin in Trempé, 29, 'the FFI were numerically strong but of no great effectiveness in combat.'
93. Trempé, 405.
94. The first German columns in retreat from the south-west reached Lyons on 26 Aug. (Bouladou, 76).
95. MS A-868, Militärgeschichtliches Forschungsamt, Freiburg-im-Breisgau; 'Extraits du journal de marche du Groupe d'Armées G', 42–74, *passim*; Jäckel, 488–90; Noguères, v. 424; Steinberg, *Allemands*, 325–6.

    Praise of 11th Panzerdivision came from the highest authority of all, General der Panzertruppen Freiherr Leo Geyr von Schweppenburg, who commanded Panzer Group West. Interviewed after the war (probably at Altendorf in 1947, but the document does not so specify), Schweppenburg classified all his Panzer divisions according to their 'fighting worth'. Although 'Das Reich' included 'the best tank battalion in the West' (the battalion was not specified), Wietersheim's 11th was placed in front of it, subordinate only to 2nd Panzer, 9th SS-Panzer ('Hohenstaufen'), 12th SS-Panzer ('Hitlerjugend'), and Panzerlehr (MS B-466, Service historique de l'armée de Terre, Vincennes).
96. Tillon, *FTPF*, 541; Tuñón de Lara, 'Españoles', 62; Estruch, 73.
97. He had served as chief of staff of the 24th Division in the Gironde region.

98. Gordon, 438, who cites Olivé, who cites General Leclerc.
99. Pons, 'Españoles', 11–12.
100. Fillol, *Perdedores*, 172. Fillol was a participant who, after the war, went to live in Venezuela, where he published the first edition of his book in 1971. He gives the names of the two vehicles as *Teruel* and *Farlete*. Pons (*Republicanos*, 394) gives the honours to the *Ebro* and the *Guadalajara*.
101. Chambard, 373.
102. Fillol, *Perdedores*, 172.
103. Gordon, 438.
104. Dronne, as a captain, commanded the 'Nueve', with the Spanish lieutenant Amadeo Granell as his adjutant. In his 1970 work *La Libération de Paris*, Dronne refers to Spaniards only on pp. 281 and 285, and then only briefly, Nothing supports the claim of Stein, 292, that Dronne, in *Le Serment de Koufra* and *La Libération de Paris*, 'speaks with admiration of the Spaniards'. Where Dronne does indeed write a glowing tribute to the Spaniards is in a long section inserted by Vilanova into his *Olvidados*, 371–450. Vilanova explains that he has translated the section from French with Dronne's permission and describes the text as a manuscript (p. 374 n.). What is curious is that Dronne chose to omit the tribute to the Spaniards in writing his book for the French public. That was enough to galvanize Santiago Blanco, pp. 39–40, 548–50, who presents his own fiction, that of the 'liberation of Paris by the Spaniards', among whom Amadeo Granell, 'in command of a section of tanks, truly deserved the title of the liberator of Paris'. The self-effacing Granell would have winced at the hyperbole.
105. Pons, *Republicanos*, 384–95.

CHAPTER 11

1. Shakespeare, *King Lear*.
2. Boüard, 'Mauthausen', 68; cf. Arthur London, in Razola and Constante, 123. Razola and Constante, 127, consider this situation continued until spring 1944.
3. Razola and Constante, 87, 121; Rubio, *Guerra civil*, 409 n. The date, one day before the German attack, is just possibly contrived. Juan de Diego warns against the ideological bias of Razola and his co-authors.
4. The poster displayed in every Block: '*Eine Laus dein Tod!*' ('One louse spells your death!'), was not the usual hate-filled type of SS warning, but reflected instead the terror of the SS of being contaminated by plague or other epidemic. The *Lauskontrolle* was held in the evenings, several times a month.
5. The committee was composed of Manuel Razola, José Perlado, Santiago Bonaque, Mariano Constante, and a certain Bonet, all of the PCE, with Juan Pagès representing the PSUC. Santiago Raga was added to the committee in 1942 (Razola and Constante, 87; Vilanova, 204).

6. Boüard, 'Mauthausen', 68; Arthur London, in Razola and Constante, 122–3.
7. Vilanova, 197.
8. Razola and Constante, 149.
9. Vilanova, 206.
10. Luis Gil, in Razola and Constante, 80. The *valuta*, or exchange rate, was: one slice of bread for 10 or 15 cigarettes; a dead cat, 20 cigarettes; a small dead dog, 30 cigarettes (Maršálek, *Geschichte*, 304).
11. Fabréguet shows that 1 in every 5 of the Spaniards was an artisan by profession ('Groupe', 38).
12. Razola and Constante, 133; Vilanova, 196.
13. Razola, who was to become the senior political leader of the Spaniards in Mauthausen, had previously worked for a number of years in the quarry (Constante, *Yo fui*, 79), presumably as a machinist or a mason.
14. Esteban Balogh, in Razola and Constante, 139; Constante, *Yo fui*, 74, 152.
15. The eighth was a German Red, who being German inevitably served as Kapo (Constante, *Yo fui*, 47).
16. Ibid. 144, 206.
17. Razola and Constante, 57–8.
18. Vilanova, 196.
19. Constante, *Yo fui*, 108.
20. Ibid. 38, 40, 53, 62–3.
21. This did not mean that only 3,155 prisoners had preceded him, as Juan de Diego himself quickly discovered in his new job. The names of prisoners were entered in the register in pencil. When a prisoner died, his name was erased and replaced by that of the new holder of the number. Thus in the early years the total prisoner population did not officially exceed 3,000. The purpose was to conceal the truth (Macdonald, 301).
22. Weber was merely a swindler; he was a good type, and spoke good French.
23. Le Chêne, 67.
24. Bernadac, 210.
25. Juan de Diego, (interview).
26. Ibid.
27. Pappalettera, 151.
28. The account of what Ziereis actually said is itself open to question; see below, n. 208. The figure of 3% is incongruous: we have seen that until 1944 Himmler railed against the high mortality rates at Mauthausen, which prevented *KL*-M from reaching the population he wanted it to have (see above, Ch. 4).
29. Le Chêne, 207. Cf. Wormser-Migot, 288, for other SS interest in Neolithic remains.
30. A copy of the letter is in the author's possession.
31. An earlier case involved the Spanish prisoner Bautista Nos Fibla, who was released from Mauthausen on 22 Aug. 1941 through the intervention of the Spanish Embassy in Berlin ('Resumen Audición de los días

14 y 15 de septiembre de 1962 ante el juez de la Instancia de Colonia (proceso Schulz)ᵖ.1).

32. Vilanova, 84 n.

33. Migot-Wormser, 143, refers to an Austrian prince working for the IRC whom she calls simply 'S'. He succeeded in getting packages delivered to Buchenwald and Dachau but never to Mauthausen.

34. Juan de Diego (interview). He still holds the two letters he wrote. Other survivors report that their letters were never mailed, and were handed back to them weeks later at the precise moment they had been told that mail from home would be distributed. The Nazis thus kept their promise.

35. Razola and Constante, 96.

36. Vilanova, 203; Alfaya, 117.

37. In France, Ester had joined Paco Ponzán in the small group that rallied to Britain and de Gaulle from the very beginning of the Occupation. Montero, a former CGT leader in Spain, is said to have organized communist shock troops against the Germans in the Paris area. Both arrived in Mauthausen in the *Nacht und Nebel* category (Constante, *Yo fui*, 215).

38. On 17 Nov. 1944 this *Aussenlager* north-west of Vienna was attacked by Allied aircraft and Miret was wounded; the SS guards finished him off.

39. Razola and Constante, 151.

40. Ibid. 126; Rubio, *Guerra civil*, 409 n.

41. A former communist member of the Reichstag, Dahlem had taken refuge in France. After fighting in the Spanish Civil War he was interned in 1939 in Le Vernet, and after June 1940 the Vichy authorities handed him over to the Gestapo. After the war he became Minister of Education in the German Democratic Republic.

42. Boüard, 'Mauthausen', 68–71; Alfaya, 117. Both Arthur London, in Razola and Constante, 124, and Vilanova, 204, give the Austrian Leo Gabler as the leader; neither mentions Mayer, and Vilanova puts Razola in the committee from the beginning, which is not the case in Razola and Constante's own account.

43. London was not recognized either as Gérard or as Singer, but as a foreign suspect he was imprisoned and deported anyway (interview).

44. Boüard, 'Mauthausen', 68; Arthur London, in Razola and Constante, 117.

45. Boüard, 'Mauthausen', 71.

46. Istvan Balogh, 'La radio au service de l'organisation internationale', *Bulletin de l'Amicale de Mauthausen*, 123 (June 1965); Esteban Balogh, in Razola and Constante, 137–9. The suspicion in which the Spanish communists held Steininger may have been unjustified and even spurious. It was, after all, to Steininger that Hans Kanduth went when the crematorium Kapo hit upon the idea of adapting the wireless of his Kommandoführer, Martin Roth, so that it could pick up foreign channels. Steininger succeeded, and Kanduth was able to pick up Allied broadcasts, until one day Roth switched on, tuned the set, and found a foreign

channel. Suspecting nothing, Roth told Kanduth that the wireless was out of order. Kanduth replied that he would take it in to Steininger. Steininger 'repaired' it, but also constructed a tiny amplifier which could be inserted into a device he added to the back of the wireless. The device, no bigger than a matchbox, could be hidden when not in use in a crevice in the crematorium. But Steininger was betrayed to the SS: on 3 Nov. 1944 they found listening devices hidden in his bed and marched him to the *Klagemauer*. Fearing what he might divulge under torture, the secret organization made contact with him and persuaded him to commit suicide ('Témoignage de Ignacy Bukowski et Tadeusz Lewicki', 6–7).

47. Macdonald, 305. Even Salzburg was bombed, on 16 Oct. 1944.
48. The committee consisted of Boüard, Georges Savourey, Dr Fichez, and Jean Guillon (Boüard, 'Mauthausen', 71).
49. Ibid.
50. Gabler was given the mission, while in an Aussenkommando, of making contact with the Austrian Resistance. He actually succeeded in escaping from the Kommando, but was caught and guillotined in Vienna (Juan de Diego, interview; Vilanova, 204). Cf. Arthur London, in Razola and Constante, 125.
51. Razola and Constante, 128; Vilanova, 204; Alfaya, 118.
52. Juan de Diego (interview). Only Vilanova, 204, refers to it; he adds that its other leaders were the anarchist Prat, the socialist Antonio, and the republican Calmarza—none of them of any political significance.
53. The Dutch had been held since the catastrophic failure of the 'North Pole' intelligence mission in Dec. 1941; the British, since the successful raid on Saint-Nazaire in Mar. 1942.
54. Juan de Diego (interview); Pappalettera, 144–7; transcript in German of the sworn testimony of Juan de Diego Herranz given to US authorities on 17 May 1945, in Le Chêne, 122–3; Juan de Diego, *Hispania*, 51 (May 1975), 7–8; Wiesenthal, 321. The SS could not be faulted in the care they took to destroy the evidence. The two prisoners in the crematorium Kommando who survived report that the bodies of Allied officers could only be burnt at night. They included the Soviet General Boms Dworkin, and a number of US Army Air Force officers who had been shot down in raids on Linz and Steyr ('Témoignages de Ignacy Bukowski et Tadeusz Lewicki', 4, 6).
55. The Spanish unit included, besides Montero, 3 infantry majors, 1 naval lieutenant-commander, 9 infantry captains, 18 lieutenants, and 36 sergeants. Its approximate strength was 3 companies, with the lowest unit, the squad, varying in size from 5 to 15 men (Razola and Constante, 151).
56. *Mauthausen*, 44. Sir Robert Sheppard (interview) disputes this, as do others. Although he left Mauthausen for Dachau in 1943, Sir Robert strongly doubts that there were ever that many men in Mauthausen fit enough to take part.
57. Vilanova, 203.
58. This was the work of José Ester Borrás (Constante, *Yo fui*, 214), but it

is significant that Constante does not claim, as others have, that several pistols and hand-grenades were stolen.

59. Boüard, 'Mauthausen', 75.
60. Constante, *Yo fui*, 212.
61. Razola and Constante, 151.
62. No author has explained, or even mentioned, the removal of Luis Montero as commander of the Spanish group. Montero, in fact, had problems with the Communist Party (Juan de Diego, interview). He survived the war, returned to France in 1945, and then 'disappeared tragically during a secret mission to Spain', in the words of Ramón Bargueño (Razola and Constante, 142), by which we may understand that he died on another suicide mission.
63. Malle, from Jaca, had served in the Civil War with Constante in the 43rd Division, and in France, up to his capture, he had fought as a major commanding guerrilla groups in Landes and Basses-Pyrénées (Constante, *Yo fui*, 210).
64. Razola and Constante, 128, 153; Vilanova, 204. The Frenchman was Capt. Olivier; the Austrian, Col. Heinrich Kodre (Maršálek, *Geschichte*, 266).
65. Razola and Constante, 151.
66. Boüard, 'Mauthausen', 71; Baum, 116; Razola and Constante, 134; Vilanova, 205; Alfaya, 117.
67. Vilanova, 201.
68. Razola and Constante, 136. Maršálek mentions the case of Johann Zaremba, guilty of multiple murder in the quarry, who was transferred on 10 Feb. 1944 to *KL*-Kauen (*Geschichte*, 40).
69. Pappalettera, 230.
70. Baum, 133.
71. Pappalettera, 230; Maršálek, *Geschichte*, 40, 258.
72. Hans Maršálek, letter to Juan de Diego Herranz, Vienna, dated 8 Nov. 1969; quoting from the official Gusen register of deaths, the original copy of which is in his personal possession.
73. The Czech Jan Pstros has been mentioned by some authors as a Lagerschreiber IV. Juan de Diego (interview) denies this, explaining that Pstros was merely a Hilfsschreiber, protected by Maršálek.
74. Boüard, 'Mauthausen', 58; Arthur London, in Razola and Constante, 125; ibid. 193.
75. Razola and Constante, 136.
76. Ibid. 134–6; Vilanova, 201–3.
77. Maršálek, *Geschichte*, 188.
78. Razola and Constante, 152.
79. Ramón Bargueño, ibid. 140. Bargueño became known to the SS as 'Marmeladeding' after an incident in which he was caught stealing a 3-kilo container of jam. He was forced to eat the entire container in a single sitting (Maršálek, *Geschichte*, 292; Borrás [Lluch], 381).
80. Razola and Constante, 106.
81. Ibid. 140; Alfaya, 118.

82. The present author has gone over Constante's account very carefully with the eyewitness whom he cites, Juan de Diego. De Diego, who has gone out of his way to maintain friendly relations with the Party stalwart Constante (as indeed he has with all who fought fascism), warns nevertheless against the exaggerations of a man he calls 'frantic to be acclaimed a hero'. Constante, says de Diego, was not, as he claims in his memoirs, hanged at the gate in the '*Pfahlbinden*' position or in any other position, and his arms were not paralysed as a result. On the other hand, Constante omits in his account the fate of Bruckner, who was foolish enough to rebuke Bachmayer, and in public, saying that Bachmayer had 'sided with a prisoner against an officer of the SS'. Bachmayer listened without saying a word, then had him dispatched immediately to the Russian front. There Bruckner was badly wounded—an exchange of fire left him emasculated—and he was consequently sent back to guard duty at Mauthausen (Juan de Diego, interview). Bruckner later appeared before the Dachau tribunal (see below) and was hanged.

83. The *Sanitätslager*, less officially known as the *Krankenlager*, was originally called the *Russenlager* since it was built by the Soviet prisoners in 1942–3. Those entering the *Sanitätslager*, which was outside the fortress and down the hill, retained their *KL*-M number but had *SL* prefixed to it.

84. Constante, *Yo fui*, 272–84, *passim*.

85. Pappalettera, 34.

86. Ibid. 34, 138. Vilanova, 193, refers to a message from Kaltenbrunner to Bachmayer in words identical to those above from Pohl to Ziereis. Vilanova provides no date, or reference, and he is probably wrong, unless Ziereis's memory failed him on his death-bed.

87. Boüard, 'Mauthausen', 75–6; Razola and Constante, 130, 153; Vilanova, 210.

88. Razola and Constante, 131. The stocks, however, were in no way depleted. The US Army reported that at the time of the liberation it found considerable supplies of food, especially potatoes (Pappalettera, 121).

89. Cf. Vilanova, 212.

90. Boüard, 'Mauthausen', 52–3. This evacuation to Mauthausen in Jan. 1945 included 60,000 Hungarian Jews. A study, admittedly incomplete, of the death marches, shows a mortality rate of 59% (*The Liberation of the Nazi Concentration Camps*, 91).

91. Maršálek, *Geschichte*, 250.

92. F. Ricol, *Bulletin intérieur d'information et de liaison de l'Amicale des déportés politiques de Mauthausen*, 4 (Feb. 1946).

93. Constante, *Yo fui*, 162–8, *passim*; Borrás [Lluch], 286.

94. Juan de Diego, deposition signed in Paris on 5 Dec. 1978, and countersigned by four leading officials of the Amicale de Mauthausen. De Diego affirms that he saw the photographs being taken by an SS NCO attached to the *Erkennungsdienst*, and that four Spaniards (three of whom survived) are identifiable in the photos which were saved. Cf. Constante, *Yo fui*, 162–8; Borrás [Lluch], 202–3.

95. Pappalettera, 93; Ramón Bargueño, in Razola and Constante, 141; Maršálek, *Mauthausen*, 4.
96. Wormser-Migot, 130–1.
97. Maršálek, *Mauthausen*, 6, gives the figure of 13, out of 500 who escaped; Vilanova, 225, gives 72 out of 700.
98. Boüard, 'Mauthausen', 57, 76; Pappalettera, 67; Razola and Constante, 94; Vilanova, 225; Le Chêne, 152; *Mauthausen*, 42.
99. Vilanova, 112; based on a report issued by the Legation of the Spanish Republic in Belgrade on 1 Oct. 1965.
100. Buchenwald's Gustloff Werke arms factory had been the target of a heavy Allied air raid on 24 Aug. 1944, following which the factory never re-entered production. The resistance network in this camp, which up until 1943 had been purely German, was by now in the hands of an international committee composed of three Germans and one member representing all other nationalities. By March 1945 Buchenwald had its International Military Organization, in which the Spanish section, comprising 9 groups under the command of Ramón Bertolini, formed part of the 'Blau' sector headed by Erich Kurschinski (*Konzentrationslager Buchenwald*, 136).
101. Wiesenthal, 25. Among the survivors was Simon Wiesenthal himself.
102. The evacuation from Buchenwald of its remaining 47,000 prisoners was ordered by Lagerführer Hermann Pister on 5 Apr. 1945. This was not completed, and those still in the camp rose in revolt some hours before the arrival of General Patton's units on 11 April. On 19 Apr. the leaders of the communist parties represented in Buchenwald signed a resolution, with Jaime Nieto ('Bolados') signing on behalf of the PCE (*Konzentrationslager Buchenwald*, 167). The resolution read in part: 'Thus we swear in front of the whole world on this roll-call square, this place of fascist cruelty, that we will give up the fight only when the last guilty parties stand before the people's judges.'
103. Burney, 37–8, 120–34; Abzug, 21–30.
104. Gaucher, 35.
105. Gaucher, 33–4; Vilanova, 178; Pappalettera, 92; Le Chêne, 120; Maršálek, *Geschichte*, 182; Wormser-Migot, 137; Expo Mauthausen, Galerie Daguerre, Paris (2–30 Apr. 1985). Cf. F. Ricol, *Bulletin intérieur d'information et de liaison de l'Amicale des déportés politiques de Mauthausen*, 4 (Feb. 1946), which paints an even grimmer picture.
106. Boüard, 'Mauthausen', 65. Another crime involving Schulz would have vanished with the mass were it not for the evidence provided by the Spanish *Prominenten* at Schulz's trial at Dachau. John Kennedy was a young Englishman from Manchester whose mother was Polish. He had been parachuted into Germany on special mission and arrested. Sent to Mauthausen, he was assigned to Baukommando *II*. On the evening of 3 Apr. 1945, as the Kommando was passing Schulz's office on its return to the fortress, Schulz happened to notice a slight figure trailing behind the rest, whom he at once recognized (from their introductory meeting in the Politische Abteilung) as Kennedy. Schulz called to Climent to

bring him Kennedy's file. Immediately after roll-call that evening Kennedy was summoned to the *Lagerschreibstube*, and from there escorted by an SS to the *Bunker*. The next morning his body was lying in the morgue: his life had ended in the 'portrait studio'. The appropriate falsification was then made in the register ('Resumen Audición de los días 14 y 15 de septiembre 1962 ante el juez de la Instancia de Colonia (proceso Schulz)', 3–4).

107. Thanks to the files of Interpol—in Germany's possession from the moment that the RSHA seized its headquarters in Vienna in 1938— Heydrich was able to round up all the top counterfeiters in German-occupied Europe and set them to work for him. The quality of the forgery was thus the highest, especially of British pound notes, in accordance with Heydrich's plan to ruin the British economy by flooding Britain with counterfeit money. The design of the false note was perfect; the only mistake made was to use new cotton, when the Bank of England used only worn cotton.

108. Juan de Diego (interview); Le Chêne, 136–7; Maršálek, *Mauthausen*, 3, 22. The counterfeit project was housed near Schachting, at the northern end of Lake Attersee.

109. Testimony of Alfonsina Bueno Ester, signed in Toulouse, Dec. 1975, in Català, 93.

110. Vilanova, 114, 146; *Mauthausen*, 38; Català, 93. Cf. Razola and Constante, 134, and 140–5 for Ramón Bargueño's account. Bargueño's work in the *Bunker* certainly gave him the opportunity to witness many an atrocity. According to Bargueño, 144, even Niedermayer, whom Michel de Boüard describes as one of the four most brutal men in Mauthausen, now broke down and cried at the sight of his superior officer smashing the head of a child against the wall of the crematorium. No doubt some women were taken to the *Bunker* in April 1945, undressed, and axed to death (ibid.), but his account lacks corroboration.

111. Conchita Ramos Veleta, in Català, 232–7; in *Train*, 198–9.

112. Pappalettera, 165. On his arrival at Mauthausen at 2 a.m. on 16 Apr., Eigruber began drinking with Ziereis, Schulz, Niedermayer, Roth, Trum, and 2 others. At 4 a.m. they decided to end the party with a massacre and went to the Bunker, where they shot 2 Americans, 6 Kapos who had directed the crematorium at Auschwitz, and 4 others.

113. Maršálek, *Geschichte*, 275.

114. Razola and Constante, 160–1; Vilanova, 193.

115. Juan de Diego (interview).

116. Le Chêne, 154.

117. Boüard, 'Mauthausen', 74–5; Germaneau, 27. With the third convoy of 27 Apr., all French inmates of Mauthausen proper, other than those too sick to walk, had been evacuated.

118. Boüard, 'Mauthausen', 77; Razola and Constante, 154–5. Such was the experience of Antonio García, whose group marched from Klein Bodunke (Vilanova, 189).

119. Streitwieser served briefly as Kommandoführer of Melk in the spring of

1944. He was subsequently Kommandoführer of Schwechat, Floridsdorf, and Mödling-Hinterbrühl, among other Kommandos. An incident occurred at Floridsdorf in late Feb. 1945 that was particularly remembered. During roll-call, some prisoners unable to stand were lying in long rows in front of the laundry, waiting to be counted with those who could still stand. Streitwieser was overheard discussing with another SS whether these 'beggars' could be sent to the next world with a single kick. The two took a bet. Twice Streitwieser took a short run and drove his boot into a prisoner's side with all his force. Then the other SS took his turn. The bet was interrupted by the order to proceed with the roll-call (Pappalettera, 206; Vilanova, 171). The other SS might have been Scharführer Hans Bühner, who seems to have accompanied Streitwieser in his various assignments.

120. *Bulletin de l'Amicale de Mauthausen*, 136 (Sept. 1967); Pappalettera, 193–5, 210.
121. Wormser and Michel, 477.
122. Germaneau, 22–3.
123. Josep Bailina, *Hispania*, 22 (Apr. 1967).
124. These figures are attributed to Ziereis in his death-bed confession (Tillard, 78). Soriano's account of the liberation of Dachau contains a number of errors (41, 130, 133). Sir Robert Sheppard, who was earlier in Mauthausen, was in Dachau at the moment of its liberation. If the Catalan Lluis Sunyer in the tailor's shop sewed the flags of the Spanish Republic and the Austrian International Brigade, Sir Robert writes (letter dated 26 Sept. 1989), they were certainly not flying over the main gate when the Americans arrived, nor did Dachau (or Buchenwald) liberate itself by the armed insurrection of the Spaniards and International Brigaders (or by any other insurrection). It is another sad instance of survivors rewriting history in line with their dreams.
125. Borrás [Lluch], 172.
126. Wormser-Migot, 216.
127. Tillard, 36; Busson, 178–9; Maršálek, *Mauthausen*, 10, 139.
128. Jean Benech, *Bulletin de l'Amicale de Mauthausen*, 37 (May 1954).
129. Maršálek, *Mauthausen*, 6, is of the opinion that the remainder of Camp III were saved only by the determined action of the international movement.
130. Vilanova, 210.
131. The last gassing was carried out on 28 Apr. The gas chamber was dismantled on the night of 29–30 Apr. (Maršálek, *Geschichte*, 243, 267).
132. Razola and Constante, 160–1.
133. Ziereis admitted on his death-bed that Bachmayer had ordered their execution (Tillard, 78). The last execution took place on 2 May, when 8 prisoners who had worked in the Gusen crematorium were shot (Maršálek, *Geschichte*, 243).
134. The SS records at Mauthausen ended on 2 May. The order to destroy all records in Mauthausen and all its remaining Kommandos went into effect on the same day (Maršálek, *Geschichte*, 267). Bargueño was one

of the very few among those so employed not to have been sent to the gas chamber after this work was completed (Borrás [Lluch], 381).

135. Ramón Bargueño, in Razola and Constante, 144.
136. Juan de Diego (interview); Vilanova, 210.
137. Razola and Constante, 155.
138. Razola and Constante, 155, claim that the AMI held 1 machine-gun, 20 pistols, 34 grenades, and 47 Molotov cocktails. Juan de Diego, who is not anticommunist, scorns this communist boast, adding that if Razola were a serious author he would tell his readers where the weapons were hidden. Cf. Alfaya, 114.
139. Jean Benech, *Bulletin de l'Amicale de Mauthausen*, 37 (May 1954).
140. Maršálek, *Geschichte*, 268.
141. Ibid.
142. Ziereis's widow, in an official deposition, gave 5 May as the date of their departure (Pappalettera, 150; cf. ibid. 74). Boüard, 'Mauthausen', 77, gives the last days of April. 3 May is the only date which conforms with the surrounding events, and is supported by Maršálek, *Geschichte*, 267.
143. Pappalettera, 150; Borrás [Lluch], 138.
144. Pappalettera, 216, 218.
145. Pappalettera, 75; Maršálek, *Geschichte*, 149.
146. Juan de Diego (interview); Pappalettera, 86–7; Le Chêne, 174. The US authorities exhumed his body to identify him, then reburied it in the same place.
147. Maršálek, *Geschichte*, 162.
148. Ramón Bargueño, in Razola and Constante, 145.
149. Maršálek, *Geschichte*, 268.
150. Boüard, 'Mauthausen', 77; Razola and Constante, 146, 162. It was at this moment that Juan de Diego received a phone call at the central switchboard from a German Panzer commander who asked to speak to Lagerführer Ziereis. Realizing at once the importance of the call, but unable to pass himself off as a German, de Diego quickly obtained the agreement of his new assistant, the Czech Premysl Dobias, a graduate in law whose German was excellent, to pose as Ziereis. The Panzer commander then told Dobias that for tactical reasons he wanted to move his tanks into Mauthausen, but he wanted to be sure that Mauthausen was not already in American or Soviet hands. He therefore had to take every precaution. 'Natürlich,' replied Dobias. The Panzer commander proceeded to question 'Ziereis' on his identity: his age, his rank, his appearance. Scrambling but ready (for this information was well enough known) and still maintaining the necessary composure, Dobias may have satisfied the Panzer commander with the answers, but when the Panzer commander asked 'Ziereis' about his SS decorations, Dobias and de Diego broke down, the Panzer commander hung up, and the tanks—which presumably were not on their way to massacre the prisoners—never arrived in Mauthausen (Juan de Diego, interview; Dobias, interview).
151. The famous photograph of the Spanish banner over the main gate has been reproduced in certain books, including some published in France,

in a falsified form, with the banner deleted. The Spanish survivors' association protested against this falsification of history (*Hispania* 84, (May–June 1985)).

152. Maršálek, *Geschichte*, 269. Constante, in his grandiloquent style, writes that the prisoners of Mauthausen won their freedom with their own weapons (*Yo fui*, 288). He makes no mention of the fact that the SS had already left, leaving the inner camp to itself.

153. *The Liberation of the Nazi Concentration Camps*, 42.

154. Maršálek, *Geschichte*, 269. These troops, belonging to General Dager's 11th Armored Division, had been halted in compliance with the International Restraining Line (Lt.-Col. Richard R. Seibel, deposition dated 20 May 1980).

155. Razola and Constante, 162.

156. Baum, 102. It was this division which, on 17 Dec. 1944, had murdered 71 American prisoners of war at Malmédy. Also not far off was the 2nd SS-Panzerdivision ('Das Reich'), beaten back from Vienna by the Red Army; most of its surviving units surrendered to United States forces on 5 May 1945.

157. Boüard, 'Mauthausen', 77; Vilanova, 210; Alfaya, 119.

158. Boüard, 'Mauthausen', 77; Razola and Constante, 147, 162; Vilanova, 211; Maršálek, *Geschichte*, 268–9; *Mauthausen*, 45–6. Constante recounts that he and Miguel Malle led Colonel Seibel to the *Bunker* where they had imprisoned the SS they had captured (*Yo fui*, 288). No other account mentions SS personnel captured inside Mauthausen except that of Renaud, 367, who was at Ebensee, not in the *Mutterlager*, at that time. Col. Seibel refers instead to a confrontation he had, on the day of his arrival, with the Soviet Major Pirogov, who had installed himself at the Lagerführer's desk. Pirogov told Seibel that he, not Seibel, was in command of the camp and that he and the Soviets intended to remain in command. Since he refused to leave the office, Seibel had to point a pistol at him and order his men to escort Pirogov and his subordinates to the Soviet compound (Seibel, deposition).

159. Jean Benech, *Bulletin de l'Amicale de Mauthausen*, 37 (May 1954).

160. Le Chêne, 169.

161. *Mauthausen*, 35; cf. Borrás [Lluch], 183. An earlier SS report, drawn up on 31 Mar. 1945, showed the total prisoner population as 78,547, including 2,187 Spaniards. The report was broken down into the following age groups (Le Chêne, 240A; *Mauthausen*, 34):

	All	Spaniards
under 20	19.2%	0.2%
20–29	38.4	53.0
30–39	26.6	38.5
40–49	13.0	8.0
50–59	3.0	0.13
60–69	0.38	0.09
70–79	0.006	0.000

162. Vilanova, 122. As almost always, Vilanova provides no source reference, and his figures must be treated with reserve, but there are no others on this question.
163. Boüard, 'Mauthausen', 78.
164. Ibid.
165. Maršálek, *Geschichte*, 120. Cf. Alfaya, 119.
166. Vilanova, 203, 205.
167. Alfaya, 111.
168. Pappalettera, 187.
169. Ibid.
170. Vilanova, 185.
171. Le Chêne, 209.
172. Tillard, 78; Wormser-Gigot, 231; Vilanova, 213; Le Chêne, 156. According to Patricio Serrano *et al.*, in Razola and Constante, 187, two Spaniards working in the kitchen Kommando at Gusen II heard that the explosives had been placed in the tunnel.
173. Pappalettera, 88; Razola and Constante, 165, 171; Vilanova, 209; Le Chêne, 173.
174. The evacuation of Melk, on 11 Apr. 1945, was among the last: 5,839 prisoners set out—many others were too sick to move—and the survivors reached Ebensee on 19 Apr. (Le Chêne, 243). The last Kommando to be evacuated was Schlier, at Redl-Zipf, which a little earlier had been reinforced by the arrival of some 250 Spaniards evacuated from the Kommando at Ternberg. About 100 Spaniards were subsequently transferred to Gusen II, but at the time that Schlier was evacuated (and then burnt) on 3 May 1945, the camp population consisted of 60 Spaniards, 20 Italians, 9 Frenchmen, 1 Belgian, and an unknown number of Germans. The evacuation of Schlier meant the end of the great counterfeit project. On 3 May some 80 cases of counterfeit sterling and dollars were loaded into trucks and taken to the Zipfer brewery where they were hidden in its caves or dropped in Lake Attersee. The tiny subsection of Kommando Schlier then left on foot for Ebensee. Meanwhile, the rest of the Kommando was marched along the road toward Schachting. The prisoners knew they were close to the counterfeit Kommando and knew all about their work. They strongly suspected that every one of the prisoner-counterfeiters would be murdered, not evacuated. Fearful of sharing their fate, they took the unusual step of increasing the pace of march, passing through Schachting on 4 May and following the road running south along the eastern side of the lake. As it turned out, the counterfeit Kommando was not exterminated. It arrived intact at Ebensee on 6 May. So did all the Spaniards in the rest of the Kommando, except for López Arias, who escaped from the convoy on 4 May (Paul Le Caër, interview); Le Caër, *Bulletin de l'Amicale de Mauthausen*, 27 (July 1952); Le Caër, 56–60.
175. Laffitte, 351; *Mauthausen*, 61.
176. Wormser-Gigot, 232.
177. Wetterwald, 167–8; Laffitte, 371, 374.

178. Maršálek, *Geschichte*, 268.
179. Laffitte, 401; *Mauthausen*, 61. Le Chêne's figure here of 30,000 (p. 235) is unlikely.
180. Vilanova, 205; Maršálek, *Geschichte*, 262; Wormser-Migot, 232.
181. Laffitte, 379.
182. Ibid. 361–2.
183. Maršálek, *Geschichte*, 262. Earlier that day another Austrian, a civilian who headed one of the tunnel workshops, had been hanged for sabotage and fraternizing with prisoners (Gouffault, 44). Poltrum was much admired by the survivors, and 20 years later the *Bulletin de l'Amicale de Mauthausen* paid honour to him at his death.
184. Tillard, 69.
185. Vilanova presents two separate, unco-ordinated versions, 208–9, 212–13, of unclear chronology. Laffitte's version, 376–9, is his eyewitness account, but its chronology is not clear either. I have followed the chronology of Tillard, 69, and Gouffault, 44.
186. Tillard, 72; Laffitte, 350.
187. Renaud, 131–2.
188. Debrise, 182; Laffitte, 376–80; Vilanova, 208–9, 212–13; Renaud, 131–3; Maršálek, *Geschichte*, 268–9. Cf. Le Chêne, 235, who gives the date of arrival of the first Americans as 8 May, presumably in error.
189. Laffitte, 404–5; *Mauthausen*, 61. Gouffault, 44, refers to only 40 kilos of explosive, which might not have been sufficient for the task.
190. Laffitte, 400.
191. Debrise, 182.
192. Tillard, 30; Laffitte, 381–2.
193. Laffitte, 407.
194. Jean Benech, *Bulletin de l'Amicale de Mauthausen*, 37 (May 1954); Le Chêne, 166.
195. Boüard, 'Mauthausen', 78.
196. Debrise, 185. For the photographers at work in the liberated camps, see Abzug.
197. Jean Benech, *Bulletin de l'Amicale de Mauthausen*, 37 (May 1954). A survivor of Dachau, the Spanish communist Francisco García Mochales, who was employed in the camp's porcelain Kommando producing *objets d'art* for sale by the SS, has a similarly bitter memory of his first post-liberation experience: 'The American soldiers gave us nothing, or nothing we could eat' (interview). At Mauthausen, Col. Seibel denied this, insisting that the first food distributed was weak potato soup and a small piece of oat bread (deposition).
198. Boüard, 'Mauthausen', 78. The Soviet evacuation was carried out in a way that astonished Col. Seibel. An entire Soviet army was in place opposite the US forces, but no food, medical care, or transport was provided to the Soviet survivors. The sick and crippled were left behind; the rest were made to march (Seibel, deposition).
199. Cinca, 183.
200. Jean Benech, *Bulletin de l'Amicale de Mauthausen*, 37 (May 1954).

201. Pappalettera, 230.
202. Alfaya, 119.
203. Bernadac, 367. Col. Seibel attests to the continuing tension. Four Kapos in custody had their throats cut during the night. At 8 a.m. on 6 May, 18,000 prisoners gathered in the Appellplatz. Seibel ordered the US troops to form a phalanx and fix bayonets. The ex-prisoners were then forced off the alleys and into their Blocks. All their weapons were collected and destroyed (Seibel, deposition).
204. Maršálek, *Geschichte*, 250.
205. Inevitably, some ex-prisoners, maddened by hunger and avid for revenge, formed groups and went out to satisfy both desires, helping themselves to whatever they found in the surrounding farms (Maršálek, *Geschichte*, 269).
206. Vilanova, 209.
207. Le Chêne, 170–1. After the Liberation Maršálek became a police inspector in criminal investigation in Vienna.
208. The accounts of Ziereis's death and his death-bed testimony are many and varied: Tillard, 76–8; 'Ziereis parle', *Bulletin de l'Amicale de Mauthausen*, 14 (Mar. 1950); 15 (May 1950); 16 (July 1950); 17 (Oct. 1950); 18 (Dec. 1950); 20 (Mar. 1951); 23 (Oct. 1951); Boüard, 'Mauthausen', 78; Baum, 129–36; Razola and Constante, 148; Vilanova, 211; Le Chêne, 171–4, 282; Borrás [Lluch], 138. Razola and Constante claim that Ziereis was executed by an American officer of Cuban origin, who took it upon himself to prevent his compatriots from ever releasing Ziereis. As for the Lagerführer's signed statement, Baum and Le Chêne produce widely differing versions; common to both is the incoherence and vindictiveness of the statement. Among Ziereis's more precise recollections is his account (in 'Ziereis parle') of sending to the Gunskirchen Kommando the SS doctor SS-Obersturmführer Hermann Richter, with instructions to 'look after' that camp's inmates. 'Inspired by no other motive than the desire to further science', Richter performed operations on several hundred inmates requiring surgery to the brain, stomach, intestines, or liver.
209. Cinca, 125; Pappalettera, 188.
210. Cf. Pike, *Latin*, iii. 83, 100, 148.
211. Beate and Serge Klarsfeld, private information; John Loftus, *Boston Globe*, 29 May 1984. Wiesenthal, 74–75, cites the importance to Rauff, in his escape from the camp at Rimini, of the Austrian bishop in Rome Alois Hudal.
212. Constante, *Yo fui*, 293. Premysl Dobias was equally embittered by his experience at the Dachau trial. When he discovered that Otto Kleingünter was among those in custody awaiting trial, he asked and obtained permission to confront him in his cell. The two men recognized each other at once. Kleingünter winked, imagining that Dobias would help him. When that approach failed, Kleingünter declared that he had never set foot in Mauthausen. Dobias, who was witness to over 100 murders committed by Kleingünter in the *Revier*, then found that, without a corroborating

witness and without the details required in any trial under common law, his testimony was insufficient and Kleingünter was acquitted (Dobias, interview).

213. For some time after the war it was common for the villagers of Mauthausen to discover in the local woods the elaborate hiding places used by the SS to store their stolen treasures, and it was known that the same SS, if still at large, came back to recover them. Some Kapos too had amassed fortunes. Karl, the Oberkapo in the *Revier* at Ebensee, had 3 kilos of gold in his bags when they were seized on 6 May 1945; the gold had been extracted from the teeth of the dead (Tillard, 63).

214. That of SS-Hauptsturmführer Hans Altfuldisch, who had served under Bachmayer.

215. Pappalettera, 45, 48, 88, 235–6.

216. Ibid. 51, 200–3.

217. Ibid. 202–4.

218. Ibid. 75; Maršálek, *Geschichte*, 149.

219. Pappalettera, 189. Wormser-Gigot, 255, is in error.

220. Jentzsch was sentenced in 1968 to be hanged, but the sentence was commuted to life imprisonment (Pappalettera, 191; Maršálek, *Geschichte*, 277).

221. Paul Tillard, *Bulletin de l'Amicale de Mauthausen*, 130 (July 1966); Pappalettera, 231.

222. Pappalettera, 82, 84, 211, 222.

223. Not even Schloss Hartheim was exempted from the resolve in certain quarters to forget. As early as 20 Aug. 1949, a group of 60 visitors from France wanted to honour the Nazis' victims by a few minutes of silent prayer, only to find their ceremony blasted by the noise of a wedding party that had booked the castle (Horwitz, 171).

224. The case of SS-Unterscharführer Johann Gogl, who played a leading part in the murder of the 47 Allied officers, seems not to have much excited the Allied and Austrian authorities. It was not until 1965 that Gogl was uncovered—by Wiesenthal—having travelled no further than Linz, and it was not until mid-1971 that he was arrested. At his trial in Linz in April 1972 Gogl faced 23 charges. The evidence adduced by the prosecution was not challenged by the defendant. The jury of 8 nevertheless acquitted him unanimously on every count. On the other hand, the preservation, thanks to Juan de Diego, of the *Unnatürliches Todesfalles*, enabled the US Department of Justice to strip two former SS guards at Mauthausen of their US citizenship. The second of these cases, involving the Romanian-born SS-Schütze Martin Bartesch who had served at Mauthausen in 1943–4, became a *cause célèbre*. Bartesch had emigrated to the United States in 1955 and had been granted citizenship in 1966. In May 1987 Bartesch, then 61, was working as a janitor in Chicago when the US authorities denaturalized him but allowed him to avoid legal proceedings by returning to Austria. The Austrian authorities expressed their indignation that Bartesch should be returned to Austria, but no one spoke of putting Bartesch on trial.

The dwindling list of hunted Nazi criminals had by 1990 moved Dr Heribert ('Aribert') Ferdinand Heim to virtually its top position. Heim, of Schloss Hartheim infamy, now aged 76, owns a house in Berlin, at 28 Tile-Wardenbergstrasse, which he rents out. Since Heim never appears on the premises, the rent is collected every month by his sister, Frau Hilde Barthe, who lives in Buchschlag near Frankfurt-am-Main. When the German internal revenue service intercepted a payment to Frau Barthe and demanded to know if she was the beneficiary of the rent and hence liable to taxes on the revenue, a lawyer appeared on the scene with a tape-recording of the voice of Dr Heim declaring he was the sole beneficiary. Wiesenthal's Dokumentationszentrum in Vienna subsequently asked the West German Minister of Justice Dr Vogel how it was possible for a man convicted of mass murder on 13 June 1979 by a Berlin court, with two separate warrants out for his arrest, to hide from justice and at the same time collect the profits from his estate.

225. The total of 102,876 given by Borrás [Lluch], 183, is based on officially recorded deaths; of this total, 36,295 prisoners (or more than a third) died in the first 4 months of 1945. Juan de Diego (responsible for the register of deaths) emphatically rejects this estimate (and another cited elsewhere of 127,000), insisting that if all deaths are included, especially those of prisoners who were sent to Mauthausen for immediate execution or who were evacuated there in 1944–5 without, in either case, receiving *KL*-M matriculation, the total runs up to 200,000; 'the only precise records were those of the crematorium Kommando, and those records were all destroyed by the SS' (interview).

EPILOGUE

1. Aeschylus, *Agamemnon*.
2. This could have created problems for the returning prisoner, who could easily have been mistaken for a returning veteran of the Blue Division. Even Spaniards who had been employed in German factories—almost all of whom were conscripts in the STO—were subjected to severe physical assault in the course of their repatriation across France, so intense was the antipathy to the Franco regime in France in 1945 (Payne, 344).
3. Soriano, 130–4.
4. Its Paris premises, originally at 11 rue Gerbier, were transferred to the home occupied by Madame Riquelme up to her death in 1988.
5. Renaud, 136; Macdonald, 307–8.
6. Picasso's painting, 'Monument to Spaniards Who Died for France', produced in 1946–7, was presented in 1991 to the Reina Sofía art gallery in Madrid by the survivor of Buchenwald—and now Spanish Minister of Culture—Jorge Semprún.
7. Pérez, 92–6; Macdonald, 307–8.
8. Hernández del Castillo had served in the First World War as a foreign guest at the headquarters of Marshal Foch. In the Second World War, he

had been active in France in recruiting volunteers for General de Gaulle, until in Nov. 1941 he was arrested in Castelsarrasin by Vichy's notorious 8th Brigade of Security Police. He succeeded in May 1943 in making his escape (DST Secteur de CE de Toulouse, 10 Mar. 1947; Archives de la Haute-Garonne). Cf. Pierre Bertaux, preface to Pike, *Jours*, xxii; ibid. 205.

9. There were several other aid organizations operating in Toulouse, notably the Universalist Unitarian Service Committee on the nearby rue Riquet, run by Persis Miller of California (cf. Pike, *Jours*, 175, 177).

10. Renseignements généraux, Toulouse: 9097 (30 May 1945); Archives de la Haute-Garonne.

11. Soriano, 134–5.

12. For the story of the invasion, see Pike, *Jours*, ch. 10; and Arasa, 121–241.

13. Soriano, 132.

14. Ruiz, 82.

15. Antonio Cordón accompanied them to Belgrade and stayed there a year longer (Arasa, 255).

16. Morán, 108. Morán, 104, points out that Pasionaria in her memoirs cannot even give the correct date of her arrival.

17. Others included Fernando Claudín, Joan Comorera, Julián Grimau, Josep Moix, and Félix Montiel.

18. Zafra *et al.*, 81–4.

19. Macdonald, 334.

20. Estruch, 64–5.

21. *Pravda* of 12 May 1984 reported that the King spoke in the most courteous terms of the treatment the Spaniards had received, but it failed to mention that some Spaniards who were presented to the King had raised the question of their return.

22. *International Herald Tribune*, 13 Jan. 1990.

A GLOSSARY OF THE PRINCIPAL
SPANISH CHARACTERS

ANTÓN, FRANCISCO: favourite of Pasionaria, member of the PCE Politburo.

AZAÑA, MANUEL: second president of the Second Spanish Republic (1936–9).

BLÁZQUEZ, Juan: chief of staff of the Agrupación de Guerrilleros españoles.

CARRILLO, SANTIAGO: member of the PCE Politburo, leader of the JSU.

CASTRO DELGADO, ENRIQUE: former general secretary of the political commissariat of the Spanish Republican Army, member of the PCE Central Committee, member of the executive committee of the Comintern.

COMORERA, JOAN: General Secretary of the PSUC.

CORDÓN, General ANTONIO, former under-secretary of war in the Spanish Republican Government, member of the PCE Politburo.

DÍAZ, JOSÉ: General Secretary of the PCE (1933–42).

FERNÁNDEZ, LUIS: Commander-in-Chief of the Agrupación de Guerrilleros españoles.

FERNÁNDEZ CHECA, PEDRO: member of the PCE Politburo.

GONZÁLEZ, General VALENTÍN ('El Campesino'): former division commander in the Spanish Republican Army, member of the PCE Central Committee.

HERNÁNDEZ, JESÚS: former commissar general of the Spanish Republican Army, member of the PCE Politburo, member of the executive committee of the Comintern.

HIDALGO DE CISNEROS, General IGNACIO: former commander-in-chief of the Spanish Republican Air Forces, member of the PCE Central Committee.

IBARRURI, DOLORES ('Pasionaria'): General Secretary of the PCE (1942–60).

LARGO CABALLERO, FRANCISCO: former prime minister of the Spanish Republic, left-wing socialist.

LÍSTER, General ENRIQUE: former corps commander in the Spanish Republican Army, member of the PCE Politburo.

MARTÍNEZ CARTÓN, Colonel Pedro: member of the PCE Politburo, assigned to the NKVD.

MIJE, ANTONIO: member of the PCE Politburo, head of the PCE in Mexico.

MODESTO, General JUAN: former commander-in-chief of the Spanish Republic's Army of the Ebro, member of the PCE Politburo.

MONZÓN, JESÚS ('Mariano'): head of the 'Delegation of the PCE Central Committee in France'.

NEGRÍN, JUAN: last prime minister of the Spanish Republic, left-wing socialist.

PRIETO, INDALECIO: former minister of defence in the Spanish Republican Government, moderate socialist.

RIQUELME, General JOSÉ: former commander-in-chief of the Spanish Republic's Army of the Centre.

URIBE, VICENTE: member of the PCE Politburo.

BIBLIOGRAPHY

The Bibliography is arranged as follows:

1. Primary Sources
   A. Documents
      1. *Official*
         a. unpublished
         b. published
      2. *Non-official*
   B. Communiqués, proceedings, posters, leaflets, pamphlets, brochures
   C. The communist press
   D. Interviews
   E. Memoirs: While memoirs properly belong among primary sources, many of the memoirs included in this work rely in greater or lesser degree upon the testimony of other people. For the purpose of simplification, all memoirs are incorporated into Section 2.
2. Secondary Sources

NOTES ON SOURCES

Of the four component themes of this book (the Spanish Communist Party, exile in Russia and America, Mauthausen, and the Spanish Resistance in France), none lends itself to a standard scientific investigation. The communist archives which are available are best described as useless. In Moscow, the Comintern and the NKVD archives will presumably be open one day, but the wait could still be long. Mauthausen has provided us with many published memoirs and offers even now the chance of further testimony from many thousands of survivors, but the SS left few records behind and scholarly research started at least twenty years too late. Only the events in France allow for a standard approach to the evidence, whether from French or German sources. Gaining access to official French documents of this period that are of any value to the historian remains very much a matter of luck. The files F7 14722, 14738, and 14809 listed in the Bibliography were, as I was informed by letter, not to be shown to me *in toto*. As far as the Spanish Resistance is concerned, the surviving German records remain the soundest base on which to construct the account. Remarkably, these German records have lain all this time unlooked at, whether in Freiburg-im-Breisgau or Vincennes. While several American historians, notably Arthur Funk, have examined the US–French advance up the Rhône Valley in 1944, no one except Jörg Staiger has covered the campaign from the German side, and no one at all has written a book on the situation in the other third of France, the south-west. The

German archives have so far been examined only at army group level, with General de Nanteuil producing a 46-page typewritten abstract in 1974. The present work expands on this by examining the surviving records down to the level of army and army corps.

Hitler ordered that all records be destroyed, of course. The three branches of the Wehrmacht (*Wehrmachtteile*) did not respond uniformly to the order. Doenitz ordered the Kriegsmarine not to destroy the navy records, on the grounds that the navy had done no wrong and had nothing to hide; as a result they are almost intact. The records of Goering's Luftwaffe, on the other hand, were almost totally destroyed. As for the Heereswehr, a copy of every *Kriegstagebuch* down to division level was deposited in the Wehrmacht's archives in Potsdam, but these were destroyed by Allied air action in April 1945. In the field, it seems that most army units executed the order to destroy their records, and this is generally true in the case of Army Group G in southern France. Not only are its *Kriegstagebücher* fragmentary, but the documents listing the destruction of the documents are also fragmentary. Despite this, the survival—intact—of the LVIIIth Panzerkorps' records, at least for the key months of June–July 1944, is a historiographical bonanza. It should nevertheless be noted that the traditional Wehrmacht standards of clean typed copy were no longer maintained in that time of crisis: the reports show various typographical errors, overstrikes and messy alterations. Worse for the researcher, who has to examine the documents in microfilm, is the fact that the paper used recto-verso by the German typists was not always opaque; and sometimes all that the Allies found was a carbon copy, which, when micro-filmed, is barely legible. Another disappointment for the researcher is the absence of any records of the Ost Legion, whose use of Soviet and Indian troops makes it of special interest to the history of the Resistance in France.

Army Group G's commander-in-chief, Generaloberst Johannes von Blaskowitz, remained in command of an army group (a considerable achievement) and survived the war. Before committing suicide in 1948, he participated with other high-ranking Wehrmacht officers in captivity in providing the Allied military authorities with detailed information on the military situation in southern France in 1944. This information, together with carefully drawn maps signed by von Blaskowitz, is available in the Militärgeschichtliches Forschungsamt in Freiburg-im-Breisgau. As for pursuing the investigation by questioning those who served him as cooks and maids in his residence at Rouffiac-Tolosan outside Toulouse, and in the various other administration centres in the city, the attempt ran into the same obstacle that has discouraged anyone from writing a book on Toulouse under the occupation. Not that Toulouse is unique; but in the era when M. le Doyen Jacques Godechot directed research in contemporary history in Toulouse, he would explain to his students that the attempt could be fruitless, because people were still afraid to speak for fear of being branded as collaborators. Unfortunately, it may now be too late.

1. PRIMARY SOURCES

A. Documents

1. Official

a. *Unpublished*

Material pertaining to events in France

Archives nationales (Paris)
F7 14721
F7 14722
F7 14738
F7 14740
F7 14755
F7 14809
F7 14810
F7 14830
F7 14831
Z6 NL 13717

Archives de la Haute-Garonne (Toulouse)
M 1912 (4)
M 1913 (6)
M 1940 (11)
M 1941 (9)
M 2186
M 2187
1020 W 22–31

Service historique de l'armée de Terre (Vincennes)
microf. 34 Kriegstagebuch des LVIII Pz. K.
microf. 35 Kriegstagebuch des LXVI AK Res.
microf. 105 Kriegstagebuch der 1 Armee
microf. 173 Kriegstagebuch des LVIII Pz. K.
MS B-466 Gen. d. Panzertruppen Freiherr Leo Geyr von Schweppenburg

Bundesarchiv-Militärarchiv (Freiburg-im-Breisgau)
RH20–1, MSg 2/3158 Kriegstagebuch der 1 Armee

Militärgeschichtliches Forschungsamt (Freiburg-im-Breisgau)
A-868 Die deutsche Reaktion zur Invasion in Südfrankreich
B-800 Kampf der Armeegruppe G in Südfrankreich bis Mitte Sept. 1944;
    Generaloberst Johannes von Blaskowitz, Allendorf, 16 May 1947

National Archives (NNR-CG: Washington, DC)
A-868 v. Blaskowitz: Aug. 1944
A-880 v. Wietersheim (11 Pz. Div.)
A-888 Gruppe Kniess
A-911 1 AOK
B-157 Krüger: 22 Aug.–6 Sept. 1944
B-421 v. Blaskowitz: Aug. 1944

B-422 Verbindungsstab 659 (Tarbes)
B-423 159. Inf. Div.
B-440 v. Gyldenfeldt: May–July 1944
B-445 Krüger: 24 July–15 Sept. 1944
B-471 Oberkommando Südwest
B-486 Krüger: 6 Jun.–24 July 1944
B-488 v. Gyldenfeldt
B-552 v. Gyldenfeldt: May–July 1944
B-557 198 Inf. Div.
B-588 v. Gyldenfeldt: May–July 1944
B-742 v. Wietersheim: 12 Aug.–2 Sept. 1944
B-800 v. Blaskowitz: May–Sept. 1944
B-805 11 Pz. Div.

Material pertaining to events in the USSR

Hoover Institution on War, Revolution, and Peace (Stanford, Calif.) Nicolaevsky Collection: Box 278, folder 22

Material pertaining to events in Austria

Amicale des Déportés et Familles de Mauthausen, 31 boulevard Saint-Germain, Paris

Dokumentationsarchiv des österreichischen Widerstandkampfes, Wipplingerstrasse 6–8 (Altes Rathaus), Vienna

Dokumentationszentrum des Bundes judischer Verfolgter des Naziregimes, Salztorgasse 6, Vienna

Mauthausen Museum, Bundesministerium für Inneres, Abt. IV/4, Herbststrasse 57, Vienna

b. *Published*

'Extraits du journal de marche (26 avril 1944–10 september 1944) du Groupe d'Armées G (de la Wehrmacht).' Selected, annotated, and translated by General de Nanteuil and Major Even of the SHAT. Vincennes: Service historique, État-major de l'Armée de Terre, Ministre de la Défense, 1974.

Kriegstagebuch des Oberkommandos der Wehrmacht (Wehrmachtführungsstab), iv. 1 Jan. 1944–22 May 1945. Introduced and annotated by Percy Ernst Schramm. Frankfurt-am-Main: Bernard & Graefe Verlag für Wehrwesen, 1961.

40ᵉ anniversaire des combats des Glières, ed. Serge Barcellini. Paris: Secrétariat d'État auprès du ministère de la Défense chargé des Anciens combattants, 1984.

40ᵉ anniversaire des combats du Vercors, ed. Serge Barcellini. Paris: Secrétariat d'État auprès du ministère de la Défense chargé des Anciens combattants, 1984.

2. Non-official

AGUDO, SIXTO, Recueil de témoignages et de documents concernant les FFI de la R. 4 (Aubervilliers, 15 Apr. 1976). Toulouse: Collection Daniel Latapie, vi.

ÁLVAREZ, ANGEL, Deposition recounting his escape from the 'ghost train' (1944), n.p., n.d., 3 pp.

Amicale des Anciens FFI et Résistants espagnols, Conseil national. 'Rapport général sur les activités des Républicains espagnols dans la libération de la France et dans la lutte contre l'armée d'occupation', n.p., roneotyped, n.d.

BERMEJO, LUIS, Recueil de témoignages et de documents concernant les FFI de la R. 4 (Toulouse, n.d.). Toulouse: Collection Daniel Latapie, vi.

Bulletin de l'Amicale de Mauthausen. Title changes to *Mauthausen: Bulletin intérieur [et de liaison] de l'Amicale des déportés et familles de Mauthausen*. Paris, irregular (1946 onwards).

Bulletin municipal, Ville de Toulouse. Special issue dedicated to the liberation of Toulouse. Oct. 1944.

Catalogue des périodiques clandestins diffusés en France de 1939 à 1945. Paris: Bibliothèque nationale, 1954.

DIEGO HERRANZ, JUAN DE, Deposition signed in Paris on 4 Dec. 1978 and countersigned on 5 Dec. 1978 by the following officials of the Amicale de Mauthausen: M. Hacq, Directeur Central Honoraire de la Police Judiciaire au Ministère de l'Intérieur (Vice-President); A. Petchot-Bacque, Médecin-Général Inspecteur (Deputy Vice-President); E. Valley (Secretary-General); J. Gavard, Inspecteur de l'Administration au Ministère de l'Education Nationale (Secretary), 3 pp.

'La France résistante: les Républicains espagnols en France'. Papers of General Buttet, 2 dossiers (Paris: Institut d'histoire du Temps présent).

International Tracing Service, *Catalogue of camps and prisons in Germany and German-occupied Territories, September 1939–May 1945*. Arolsen: July 1949.

LÓPEZ TOVAR, VICENTE, 'Mémoires de guerre et de résistance'. Toulouse: 5 Sept. 1972.

ORTEGA GUERRERO, TOMÁS, 'Historique de la 35ème Brigade de Guérilleros espagnols', n.p., n.d., 4 pp.

Résistance R4. Quarterly, 1–12 (Sept. 1977–June 1980). Toulouse: Comité des résistants pour l'histoire de la libération de Toulouse et de sa région.

'Resumen Audición de los días 14 y 15 de Septiembre 1962 ante el juez de la Instancia de Colonia (proceso Schulz)', unsigned, n.p., n.d., 4 pp.

SANZ, MIGUEL ANGEL, and GARCÍA ACEVEDO, JOSÉ, Témoignage, n.p., n.d. With a rebuttal by Maurice Bénézech, Tarbes, 19 Sept. 1978. Paris: Institut d'histoire du Temps présent.

'Témoignages de Ignacy Bukowski et Tadeusz Lewicki' (formerly of the crematorium Kommando in Mauthausen), tape-recorded in St Georgen, Austria, on 10 May 1980 and translated by P. S. Choumoff in the presence of J. Gavard, 7 pp.

B. *Communiqués, Proceedings, Posters, Leaflets, Pamphlets, Brochures*

CODOVILLA, VICTORIO [Vittorio Codovila], *Unidos para aplastar al monstruo fascista*. Buenos Aires: Editorial Problemas, 1941. 3 arts.

Conférence de presse au sujet des Républicains espagnols internés au camp de concentration de Karaganda (URSS). Paris: FNDIR-FEDIP, Apr. 1948. 28 pp.

Conferencia de Unión Nacional Española, celebrada en Toulouse los días 2, 3 y 4 Noviembre 1944, n.p.: Servicios de Propaganda del Secretariado de U.N.E., en Francia, n.d.

España hoy. PCE manifesto. Mexico City: no pub., n.d. (1939). Same manifesto published under the title *España y la guerra imperialista,* Buenos Aires: Editorial Problemas, 1940.

HERNÁNDEZ, JESÚS, 'The Besteiro Trial', *The Communist International,* xvi, 9 (Sept. 1939), 1010–14.

IBARRURI, DOLORES, *¡Guerra implacable al nazismo!* Havana; Ediciones Sociales, 1941. 18 pp.

—— *Implacable War Against Fascism.* Moscow: Foreign Languages Publication House, 1941. 24 pp.

—— *La social-democracia y la actual guerra imperialista.* Mexico City: Editorial Popular, 1940. 12 pp.

—— *Women Against Hitler.* London: Communist Party of Great Britain, n.d. 16 pp.

—— *The Women Want a People's Peace,* introduced by Elizabeth Gurley Flynn. New York: Workers' Library Publishers, 1941.

Jesús Hernández y Negrín contra Unión Nacional Española. Toulouse: Secretaría de propaganda del PSOE en Francia, Apr. 1945. 36 pp.

¡Karaganda! La tragedia del antifascismo español. Toulouse: Ediciones del MLE-CNT, Mar. 1948. 32 pp.

MARTY, ANDRÉ, *Une Solution humaine et française: Comment en finir avec les camps de républicains espagnols.* Address given at the international conference held in Paris on 15–16 July 1939. Paris: Bureau d'Éditions, n.d. (1939?). 32 pp.

MIJE, ANTONIO, *La democracia y la Unión Nacional.* Mexico City: Ediciones España Popular, 1944.

—— *España y el segundo frente.* Address given at the Palacio de mármol, Mexico City, on 10 Sept. 1942. Mexico City: no pub., 1942. 30 pp.

—— *Los refugiados republicanos españoles en Francia y la solidaridad americana.* Mexico City: Editorial Morelos, 1940. 16 pp.

—— *Unidad de combate y victoria.* N.p. (Mexico City?): Ediciones *España popular,* n.d.

¡Mujeres españolas! Unión Nacional Española llama, España os necesita. Toulouse: El Comité départemental de la Haute-Garonne, Unión Nacional Española, Aug. 1944.

PIVERT, MARCEAU, SERGE, VICTOR, REGLER, GUSTAVO, and GORKIN, JULIAN, *La GPU prepara un nuevo crimen.* Mexico City: Ediciones de *Analisis,* Apr.–May, 1942.

La social democracia y la actual guerra imperialista. PCE manifesto, 1 Nov. 1939. Mexico City: Editorial Popular, 1940.

C. The Communist Press

L'Internationale Communiste: Organe du Comité exécutif de l'Internationale communiste. Fortnightly, then monthly; last issue July 1939. Paris: Librairie de *L'Humanité.* 1919–39.

La Vie du Parti. Bulletin bi-mensuel réservé aux sections et cellules du Parti communiste français. 1938–56.

For a list of the Spanish and French communist journals and periodicials, see Pike, *Jours,* 263–6.

D. Interviews

ANDRADE, JUAN (Paris), 21 Sept. 1974.

ARCANGUES, Gen. CLAUDE (Paris), 3 Apr. 1992.

ARQUER, JORDI (Perpignan), 10 Sept. 1978.

BELLAY, JACQUES (Montrouge), 3 Apr. 1992.

BERMEJO, Lt. Col. LUIS (Toulouse), 12 Sept. 1978.

BERTAUX, PIERRE (Sèvres), various.

BONIFACI, Dr JOSEP (Barcelona), 14 Sept. 1979.

CARRASCO, JULIO (Lavardac), 11–12 Nov. 1983.

CASSOU, JEAN (Paris), 13 June 1979.

CATALÀ, NEUS (Paris), 29 Nov. 1991.

CHEVANCE-BERTIN, Gen. MAURICE (Toulouse), 6 June 1985.

DIEGO HERRANZ, JUAN DE, various.

DOBIAS, PREMYSL J., Dr Jur. (London), 17, 19 July 1992.

ESPITALIER, MME MAURICE (wife of the Commissaire principal de Police, Toulouse), 13 Nov. 1983.

ESTER BORRAS, Mme JOSÉ (Odette) (Paris), 5 Jan. 1981.

GARCÍA ALONSO, ANTONIO (Paris), various.

GARCÍA MOCHALES, FRANCISCO (Paris), 22 Apr., 26 June, 2 July 1991.

GARDÓ CANTERO, ANTONIO (Paris), 14 Nov. 1979.

GAVARD, JEAN (Paris), 16 June 1992.

GORKIN, JULIÁN (Paris), various.

ILIC, Gen. LJUBOMIR (Paris), 18 Oct. 1986.

IRUJO, MANUEL DE (Paris), 5 Mar. 1974.

KOHN, PHILIPPE (Paris), 3 Apr. 1992.

LE CAËR, Dr PAUL (Deauville), 11 Aug. 1989.

LÉVY, Dr CLAUDE (Paris), various.

LLENA, MARÍA (Paris), 8, 23 July 1989.

LONDON, Arthur and Lise (Paris), 29 Oct. 1979, 2 Mar. 1980.

LÓPEZ TOVAR, Col. VICENTE (Toulouse), various.

MACDONALD, NANCY (New York), 10 Sept. 1981.

MARQUÈS, PIERRE (Paris), 20 Feb. 1992.

MILLER, PERSIS (Toulouse), 15 July 1966.

MOCH, JULES (Paris), 24 Nov. 1973.

MONTSENY, FEDERICA (Toulouse), 16 July 1966; (Barcelona), 21 Apr. 1979.

NATES, LÁZARO (Paris), 24 Oct., 28 Nov. 1986.
NICOLETIS, Col. JOHN (Paris), various.
NOGUÈRES, HENRI (Toulouse), 6 Jun. 1985.
NOIREAU, ROBERT ('Col. Georges'), 21 Nov. 1981 (Le Perray en Yvelines).
ORTEGA GUERRERO, Lt. Col. TOMÁS (Aignan), 18 May 1985.
PEDRO, CARMEN DE (Paris), 31 May 1985.
PEIRATS, JOSÉ (Toulouse), 1 Nov. 1964; (Béziers), 5 Jan. 1981.
RAVANEL, SERGE (Paris), 20 Jun. 1984.
RIQUELME, Mme la générale (Paris), various.
RIQUET, Père MICHEL, SJ (Paris), 2 June 1992.
ROQUEMAUREL DE L'ISLE, Col. CHRISTIAN DE (Paris), 3 Apr. 1992.
SAINT-MACARY, Gen. PIERRE (Paris), 16 June 1992.
SANZ, Col. MIGUEL ANGEL (Paris), various.
SCHWARZENBERG, Prof. Dr. LÉON (Paris), 22 June 1992.
SEGNAIRE, JULES (Paris), 11 Dec. 1989.
SEMPRÚN, JORGE (Paris), various.
SHEPPARD, Sir ROBERT (Hermanville), various.
SOLANO, WILEBALDO (Paris), 16 Feb. 1985.
TILLON, CHARLES (Paris), various.
URMAN, CLAUDE and PAULINE (Paris), 18 Oct. 1986.
VALERA, FERNANDO (Paris), 7 Feb. 1974; 1 Aug. 1979.
VERNANT, JEAN-PIERRE (Paris), 21 May 1992.

2.   SECONDARY SOURCES

ABELLÁN, JOSÉ LUIS (ed.), *El exilio español de 1939*, i. La emigración republicana; ii. *Guerra y política*. Madrid: Taurus, 1976.
ABZUG, ROBERT H., *Inside the Vicious Heart: Americans and the Liberation of Nazi Concentration Camps*. New York and Oxford: Oxford University Press, 1985.
AGUDO 'BLANCO', SIXTO, *En la 'Resistencia' francesa*. Saragossa: Ámbar, 1985.
ALBA, VICTOR, *The Communist Party in Spain*, trans. Vincent Smith. New Brunswick, NJ: Transatlantic Books, 1983.
—— *Historia de la resistencia antifranquista (1939–1955)*. Barcelona: Planeta, 1978.
—— *Historia de la Segunda República española*. Mexico City: Libro Mex Editores, 1960.
—— *El Partido Comunista en España*. Barcelona: Planeta, 1979.
ALDEBERT, BERNARD, *Chemin de croix en 50 stations: De Compiègne à Gusen II en passant par Buchenwald, Mauthausen, Gusen I*. Paris: F. Brouty, J. Fayard, 1946.
ALEXANDER, ROBERT J., *Communism in Latin America*. New Brunswick, NJ: Rutgers University Press, 1957.
ALFAYA, JAVIER, 'Españoles en los campos de concentración nazis', in Abellán, ii. 89–120.
ALFF, Dr WILHELM, 'Gutachten zur Frage der republikanischen spanishen

Flüchtlinge ("Rotspanier")'. Munich: Institut für Zeitgeschichte, 26 Nov. 1964.

ALLAUX, JULIEN, 'Libération du département de l'Aude: 6 juin–15 septembre 1944'. Carcassonne: offset, 1974.

ALONSO, MARIE-CONCHITA, 'La emigración política española en Francia, 1939–1945'. Mémoire de maîtrise, université de Pau, 1973.

ÁLVAREZ DEL VAYO, J[ULIO], *The Last Optimist*. London: Putnam, 1950.

AMOUROUX, HENRI, *La Grande histoire des Français sous l'occupation, 1939–1945*, 10 vols. Paris: Robert Laffont, 1976–92.

ANDRADE, JUAN, *Recuerdos personales*. Barcelona: Ediciones del Serbal, 1983.

ANGEL, MIGUEL (see also SANZ), *Los guerrilleros españoles en Francia (1940–1945)*. Preface by Rol-Tanguy, introduction by Serge Ravanel, postface by Santiago Carrillo. Havana: Editorial de Ciencias Sociales, Instituto Cubano del Libro, 1971.

ANTONOV-OVSEYENKO, ANTON V., *The Time of Stalin: Portrait of a Tyranny*. New York: Harper & Row, 1981.

ARAQUISTAIN, LUIS, *Sobre la guerra civil y en la emigración*, preface by Javier Tusell. Madrid: Espasa-Calpe, 1983.

ARASA, DANIEL, *Años 40: Los maquis y el PCE*. Barcelona: Argos Vergara, 1984.

ARON, ROBERT, *Histoire de la Libération de France, juin 1944–mai 1945*, 2 vols. Paris: Arthème Fayard, 1959.

ARTÍS-GENER, AVEL-LÍ, *La diáspora republicana*. Barcelona: Euros, 1975.

Aspects de la Résistance en Haute-Garonne. Paris: Secrétariat d'État auprès du ministère de la Défense chargé des Anciens combattants, 1984.

AVAKOUMOVITCH, IVAN, 'La Résistance du PCF vue par l'occupant (juillet 40–juin 41)', *Cahiers d'histoire de l'Institut de recherches marxistes*, special issue 14 (Sept. 1983), 47–110.

AZÉMA, JEAN-PIERRE, PROST, ANTOINE, and RIOUX, JEAN-PIERRE (eds.), *Le Parti communiste français des années sombres, 1938–1941*. Proceedings of the conference held in Paris in Oct. 1983. Paris: Le Seuil, 1986.

—— 'L'Attitude du PCF par rapport aux réfugiés espagnols durant l'année 1939'. Mémoire de maîtrise, université de Paris I (Paris-Sorbonne), 1977.

BARTHONNAT, JEAN-PIERRE, 'Le Parti communiste français et les réfugiés d'Espagne en 1939', *Mouvement social*, 103 (Apr.–June 1978), 123–41.

BAUM, BRUNO, *Die letzten Tage von Mauthausen*. Berlin: Deutscher Militärverlag, 1965.

BÉCAMPS, PIERRE, *Libération de Bordeaux*, preface by Jacques Chaban-Delmas. Paris: Hachette, 1974.

BEEVOR, JOHN G., *SOE: Recollections and Reflections 1940–1945*. London: The Bodley Head, 1981.

BERMOND DE VAULX, Général JEAN DE ('Colonel Grave'), *Souvenirs de Résistance (1940–1944)*, introduction, notes, and presentations of the Annexes by Pierre Couétard. Nîmes: Presses de ICSA, 1984.

BERNADAC, CHRISTIAN, *Les 186 marches: Mauthausen*. Paris: Éditions France-Empire, 1974.

BERTAUX, PIERRE, *Libération de Toulouse et de sa région*. Paris: Hachette, 1973.

BILLES, DOMINIQUE, and GARCÍA-VILLAR, JOSÉ, 'Le Parti communiste espagnol dans la guérilla, ou de la lutte armée à l'action de masses'. Mémoire de maîtrise, université de Toulouse II (Le Mirail), 1975.

BILLIG, J., 'Sur la déportation: les chambres à gaz dans les camps', *Revue d'histoire de la Deuxième Guerre mondiale*, 101 (Jan. 1976), 121–3.

BLANCO, SANTIAGO, *El inmenso placer de matar un gendarme: Memorias de guerra y exilio*. Madrid: Cuadernos para el diálogo, 1977.

BLASCO LOBO, JUAN, *Un piloto español en la URSS*. Madrid: Antorcha, 1960.

BOLLOTEN, BURNETT, *La guerra civil española: Revolución y contrarrevolución*, trans. Belén Urrutia. Madrid: Alianza, 1989.

BONET, PEDRO, 'Un nouveau crime du GPU: soixante Espagnols antifascistes séquestrés dans le camp de Karaganda (URSS)', *La Révolution prolétarienne*, 12 (Mar. 1948), 10/366.

BORKENAU, FRANZ, *European Communism*. London: Faber & Faber, 1953.

BORRÁS [CASCAROSA], JOSÉ, *Políticas de los exiliados españoles, 1944–1950*. Paris: Ruedo ibérico, 1976.

BORRÁS [LLUCH], JOSÉ, *Histoire de Mauthausen: Les cinq années de déportation des républicains espagnols*. Chatillon-sous-Bagneux: Imprimerie SEG, 1989.

BOÜARD, MICHEL DE, 'Gusen', *Revue d'histoire de la Deuxième Guerre mondiale*, 45 (Jan. 1962), 45–70.

—— 'Mauthausen', *Revue d'histoire de la Deuxième Guerre mondiale*, 15–16 (July–Sep. 1954), 39–80.

BOULADOU, G[ÉRARD] 'Les Maquis du Languedoc dans la Libération', *Revue d'histoire de la Deuxième Guerre mondiale*, 55 (July 1964), 55–80.

BOUNIN, JACQUES, *Beaucoup d'imprudences*. Paris: Stock, 1974.

BOURDERON, ROGER, and AVAKOUMOVITCH, YVAN, *Détruire le PCF: Archives de l'État français et de l'occupant hitlérien 1940–1944*. Paris: Messidor/Éditions Sociales, 1988.

BRAVO-TELLADO, A. A., *El peso de la derrota, 1939–1944: la tragedia de medio millón de españoles en el exilio*. Madrid: Francisco M. Sedeño, Edifrans, 1974.

BRÈS, EVELINE and YVAN, *Un Maquis d'antifascistes allemands en France (1942–1944)*. Montpellier: Les Presses du Languedoc/Max Chaleil, 1987.

BROUÉ, PIERRE, *L'Assassinat de Trotsky*. Paris: Éditions Complexe, 1980.

BRUNET, JEAN-PAUL, *Histoire du PCF*. Paris: Presses Universitaires de France, 1985.

BUBER-NEUMANN, MARGARETE, *Déportée en Sibérie*, trans. Anise Postel-Vinay, postface by Albert Béguin. Paris: Le Seuil, 1949.

—— *La Révolution mondiale: L'Histoire du Komintern (1919–1943) racontée par l'un de ses principaux témoins*, trans. Hervé Savon. Paris: Casterman, 1971.

BURNEY, CHRISTOPHER, *The Dungeon Democracy*. New York: Duell, Sloan & Pearce, 1946.

BURNIER, MICHEL-ANTOINE, and GONZÁLEZ-MATA, LUIS, 'Manouchian: La Vérité cachée depuis 40 ans', *Actuel*, 68 (June 1985), 186–211.

BUSSON, SUZANNE, *Dans les griffes nazies*. Le Mans: Pierre Belon, 1948.

CAMINO, JAIME, *Íntimas conversaciones con la Pasionaria*. Barcelona: Dopesa, 1977.

CARR, E. H., *The Comintern and the Spanish Civil War*, ed. Tamara Deutscher. London: Macmillan, 1984.

CARRASCO, JUAN, *La odisea de los republicanos en Francia. Album-Souvenir de l'exil républicain espagnol en France (1939–1945)*, prologue by Eliseo Bayo. Barcelona: Edicions Nova Lletra, 1980.

CARRILLO, SANTIAGO, *Le Communisme malgré tout: Entretiens avec Lilly Marcou*. Paris: Presses Universitaires de France, 1984.

—— *Demain l'Espagne: Entretiens avec Régis Debray et Max Gallo*. Paris: Éditions du Seuil, 1974.

—— *'Eurocomunismo' y Estado*. Barcelona: Crítica, 1977.

—— *Libertad y Socialismo*. Paris: Éditions Sociales, 1971.

CASSOU, JEAN, *La Mémoire courte*. Paris: Éditions de Minuit, 1963.

CASTRO DELGADO, Enrique, *Hombres made in Moscú*. Barcelona: Luis de Caralt, 1965.

—— *J'ai perdu la foi à Moscou*, trans. Jean Talbot. Paris: Gallimard, 1950.

—— *Mi fe se perdió en Moscú*. Barcelona: Luis de Caralt, 1964.

—— *La vida secreta de la Komintern: Como perdí la fe en Moscú*. Madrid: Ediciones y publicaciones españolas, 1950.

CATALÀ, NEUS, *De la resistencia y la deportatión: 50 testimonios de mujeres españolas*. Barcelona: Adgena, n.d. (1987?).

CHAMBERLAIN, BREWSTER, and FELDMAN, MARCIA (eds.), *The Liberation of the Nazi Concentration Camps, 1945*, introduction by Robert H. Abzug. Washington, DC: US Holocaust Memorial Council, 1987.

CHOUMOFF, PIERRE-SERGE, *Les Chambres à gaz de Mauthausen: La Vérité historique, rétablie par P. S. Choumoff, à la demande de l'Amicale de Mauthausen*. Paris: Amicale des déportés et familles de disparus du camp de concentration de Mauthausen, 1972.

CINCA VENDRELL, AMADEO, *Lo que Dante no pudo imaginar: Mauthausen-Gusen, 1940–1945*. Saint-Girons (Ariège): Imprimerie Descoins, n.d. (1946?).

CLAUDÍN, FERNANDO, *The Communist Movement: From Comintern to Cominform*, 2 vols. New York and London: Monthly Review Press, 1975.

—— *La Crise du mouvement communiste: Du Komintern au Kominform*, 2 vols, trans. Carlos Semprún, preface by Jorge Semprún. Paris: François Masperó, 1972.

—— *La crisis del movimiento comunista, i. De la Komintern al Kominform*, preface by Jorge Semprún. Paris: Ruedo ibérico, 1970.

—— *Santiago Carrillo: Crónica de un secretario general*. Barcelona: Planeta, 1983.

COLBY, WILLIAM, and FORBATH, PETER, *Honorable Men: My Life in the CIA*. New York: Simon & Schuster, 1978.

COMÍN COLOMER, EDUARDO, *Españoles esclavos en Rusia*. Madrid: Temas Españoles 14, Publicaciones Españolas, 1952.

—— *La República en el exilio*. Barcelona: Editorial AHR, 1957.

Commission internationale contre le régime concentrationnaire, *L'Institution concentrationnaire en Russie (1930–1957) par Paul Barton que précède Le Sens de notre combat par David Rousset*. Paris: Plon, 1959.

—— *Livre blanc sur les camps de concentration soviétiques*. Paris: Le Pavois, 1951.

CONDE MAGDALENO, PEDRO, *En busca de la verdad soviética: ¿Por qué huyen en baúles los asilados españoles en la URSS? Los asilados españoles en la URSS.* Buenos Aires: Nandubay/Penitenciaria Nacional (U.l), 1951.

CONQUEST, ROBERT, *The Great Terror: Stalin's Purges of the Thirties.* London: Macmillan, 1968.

—— *Kolyma: The Arctic Death Camps.* London: Macmillan, 1978.

CONSTANTE, MARIANO, *Les Années rouges: De Guernica à Mauthausen.* Paris: Mercure de France, 1971.

—— *Los años rojos: Españoles en los campos nazis.* Barcelona: Martínez Roca, 1974.

—— *Yo fui ordenanza de los SS.* Barcelona: Martínez Roca, 1976.

CORMOR, ANDRÉ-PAUL, 'La 13ème DBLE pendant la Seconde Guerre mondiale, 1940–1945.' Thèse pour le doctorat de 3ème cycle, université de Montpellier (Paul Valéry), 1985.

COSSÍAS, TOMÁS, *La lucha contra el 'Maquis' en España*, prologue by Eduardo Comín Colomer. Madrid: Editora Nacional, 1956.

COURTOIS, STÉPHANE, *Le PCF dans la guerre.* Paris: Ramsay, 1980.

—— PESCHANSKI, DENIS, and RAYSKI, ADAM, *Le Sang de l'étranger: Les Immigrés de la MOI dans la Résistance.* Paris: Arthème Fayard, 1989.

COZAR, MARÍA, 'Les Réfugiés espagnols dans le département de l'Ariège'. Mémoire de maîtrise, université de Toulouse II (Le Mirail), 1971.

CRÉHANGE, Dr PIERRE-ANDRÉ, *La Gestapo aux fesses.* Paris: Rabelais, 1974.

CRÉMIEUX-BRILHAC, JEAN-LOUIS, 'L'Engagement militaire des Italiens et des Espagnols dans les armées françaises de 1939 à 1945', in Milza and Peschanski, 505–17.

CRUZ GOYENOLA, LAURO, *Rusia por dentro, apuntes.* Montevideo: Ediciones Universo, 1946.

DAIX, PIERRE, *Les Hérétiques du PCF.* Paris: Robert Laffont, 1980.

DALMAU, JOHN, *Slave Worker in the Channel Islands*, foreword by HE Air Marshal Sir Thomas Elmshirst, Lieutenant-Governor of Guernsey. Printed by the Guernsey Press Co., n.p., n.d.

DANK, MILTON, *The French Against the French.* London: Cassell, 1978.

DEBRISE, [Dr] GILBERT, *Cimetières sans tombeaux*, preface by [Louis] Aragon. Paris: La Bibliothèque française, 1946.

La Défense de la liberté: Cahiers du Bolchevisme, 2e semestre 1939–janvier 1940. N.p. (Germany?): n. pub., n.d.

DEFRASNE, JEAN, *Histoire de la collaboration.* Paris: Presses Universitaires de France, 1982.

—— *L'Occupation allemande en France.* Paris: Presses Universitaires de France, 1985.

DELFIEU, MAURICE, *Récits d'un revenant: Mauthausen-Ebensee (1944–1945).* Paris: Indicateur Universel des PTT, 1947.

DENNIS, NIGEL, *José Bergamín: A Critical Introduction, 1920–1936.* Toronto: University of Toronto Press, 1986.

La Deuxième Guerre mondiale, special double-issue. *Recherches internationales à la lumière du marxisme*, 9–10 (Sept.–Dec. 1958).

DE ZAYAS, ALFRED M., *Wehrmacht War Crimes Bureau, 1939–1945.* Lincoln: University of Nebraska Press, 1989.

Les Dossiers noirs d'une certaine Résistance, 1944: Trajectoires du fascisme rouge. Dossier assembled by the Puig Antich group of the Fédération anarchiste de Perpignan. Perpignan: Édition du CES, 1984.

DREYFUS, PAUL, *Histoire de la Résistance en Vercors.* Paris: Arthaud, 1980.

DRONNE, RAYMOND, *La Libération de Paris.* Paris: Éditions Presses de la Cité, 1970.

—— *Le Serment de Koufra.* Paris: Éditions du Temps, 1965.

'EL CAMPESINO' (General Valentín González), *Vida y muerte en la URSS.* Buenos Aires: Bell, 1951.

—— *La Vie et la mort en URSS (1939–1949)*, trans. Jean Talbot, transcription and introduction by Julián Gorkin. Paris: Les Îles d'Or, Plon, 1950.

—— *Yo escogí la esclavitud*, prologue by José María Garzón. Barcelona: Plaza & Janes, 1977.

See also González, Valentín.

ESCHOLIER, RAYMOND, *Maquis de Gascogne.* Geneva: Éditions du Milieu du Monde, 1945.

Españoles en Francia 1936–1946, proceedings of the international conference held in Salamanca on 2–4 May 1991. Salamanca: Universidad de Salamanca, 1991.

ESTRUCH TOBELLA, JOAN, *El PCE en la clandestinidad, 1939–1956.* Madrid: Siglo Veintiuno de España Editores, 1982.

El exilio español de 1939, see *Abellan, José Luis (ed.).

EYCHENNE, EMILIENNE, *Montagnes de la peur et de l'espérance: Le Franchissement de la frontière espagnole pendant la Seconde Guerre mondiale, dans le département des Hautes-Pyrénées.* Toulouse: Privat, 1980.

—— *Les Pyrénées de la liberté, 1939–1945: Le Franchissement clandestin des Pyrénées pendant la Seconde Guerre mondiale.* Paris: Éditions France-Empire, 1983.

FABRÉGUET, MICHEL, 'Les "Espagnols rouges" à Mauthausen (1940–1945)', *Guerres mondiales et conflits contemporains*, 162 (Apr. 1991), 77–98.

—— 'Un groupe de réfugiés politiques: les Républicains espagnols des camps d'internement français aux camps de concentration nationaux-socialistes (1939–1941)', *Revue d'histoire de la Deuxième Guerre mondiale*, 144 (Oct. 1986), 19–38.

FAGEN, PATRICIA, *Exiles and Citizens: Spanish Republicans in Mexico.* Austin: University of Texas Press, 1973.

FALIGOT, ROGER, and KAUFFER, RÉMI, *Service B.* Paris: Arthème Fayard, 1985.

FARENG, ROBERT, 'La Libération de l'Ariège (1940–1944)'. Thèse DES, Faculté des Lettres et Sciences humaines de Toulouse, 1946.

FERENCZ, BENJAMIN B., *Less Than Slaves: Jewish Forced Labor and the Quest for Compensation.* Cambridge, Mass.: Harvard University Press, 1979.

FERNÁNDEZ, ALBERTO [E.], *Emigración republicana española (1939–1945).* Algorta: Zero, 1972; Madrid: Zyx, 1972.

—— *La España de los Maquis.* N.p. (Paris?): Ediciones 'Avance', 1967.

—— *La España de los Maquis*, preface by Julio Alvarez del Vayo. Mexico City: Editorial Era, 1971.

—— *Españoles en la resistencia.* Bilbao: Zero, 1973; Madrid: Zyx, 1973.

FERNÁNDEZ, JOSÉ, *Mi infancia en Moscú.* Madrid: Ed. del Museo Universal, 1988.

FILLOL, VICENTE, *Los perdedores: Memorias de un exiliado español*. Madrid: Ediciones 'Gaceta ilustrada', 1973.

—— *Underdog: Los perdedores; crónica de un refugiado español de la Segunda Guerra Mundial*. Caracas: CASUZ Editores, 1971.

FOLTZ, CHARLES, jun., *The Masquerade in Spain*. Boston: Houghton Mifflin, 1948.

FOOT, M. R. D., *SOE in France: An Account of the Work of the British Special Operations Executive in France, 1940–1944*. London: Her Majesty's Stationery Office, 1966.

FRANK, PIERRE, *Histoire de l'Internationale communiste (1919–1943)*, 2 vols. Paris: La Brèche, 1979.

FRIANG, BRIGITTE, *Les Glières: Histoire secrète des maquis*. Geneva: Éditions de Crémille, 1971.

Fundación Pablo Iglesias, *50 aniversario del exilio español*. Madrid: Editorial Pablo Iglesias, 1989.

GALLO, MAX, *Histoire de l'Espagne franquiste*, i. *De la prise du pouvoir à 1950*. Paris: Robert Laffont, 1970.

GAMELIN, Général, *Servir*, ii. *Le Prologue du drame: 1930–août 1939*. Paris: Plon, 1946.

GARCÍA, MAURICE, 'L'Exode de la Catalogne de 1939'. Mémoire de maîtrise, université de Clermont-Ferrand II. 1979.

GARRIDO, LUIS, *Los niños que perdimos la guerra*. Madrid: Edimundo, 3rd edn., 1987.

GAUCHER, IRÈNE, *Camps de mort*, preface by Vercors. Paris: Julien Wolff, 1946.

'GEORGES, Colonel' (Robert Noireau), *Le Temps des partisans*, preface by Pierre Clostermann. Paris: Flammarion, 1978.

GERMANEAU, JEAN, *Mauthausen: Kommando de Hinterberg bei Peggau*. Paris: L'Amicale de Mauthausen, 1982.

GIRAL, FRANCISCO, 'Actividad de los gobiernos y de los partidos republicanos (1939–1976)', in Abellán, ii. 179–225.

GONZÁLEZ, VALENTÍN ('El Campesino'), *Comunista en España y antistalinista en la URSS (nuevas revelaciones)*, transcription by Julián Gorkin. Mexico City: Guaranía, 1952.

See also 'el Campesino'.

GORDON, RICHARD ALAN, *France and the Spanish Civil War*. Ann Arbor, Mich.: University Microfilms, 1974.

GORKIN, JULIÁN, *L'Assassinat de Trotsky*. Paris: René Julliard, 1970.

GOUBET, M[ICHEL], 'Une "République rouge" à Toulouse à la Libération: mythe ou réalité?', *Revue d'histoire de la Deuxième Guerre mondiale et conflits contemporains*, 131 (July 1983), 25–40.

—— 'La Résistance toulousaine: structures, objectifs (printemps–été 1944)', *Revue d'histoire de la Deuxième Guerre mondiale*, 99 (July 1975), 25–44.

—— *Toulouse et la Haute-Garonne dans la Guerre*. Le Coteau: Horvath, 1987.

—— and DEBAUGES, PAUL, *Histoire de la Résistance dans la Haute-Garonne*. Toulouse: Milan, 1986.

GOUFFAULT, ROGER, *Ebensee: Kommando de Mauthausen*. Paris: L'Amicale de Mauthausen, n.d.

GRANADOS, MARIANO, *La extradición de los refugiados españoles*. Mexico City: Agrupación de Universitarios Españoles, n.d.

GRANDO, RENÉ, QUERALT, JACQUES, and FEBRÉS, XAVIER, *Camp du mépris: Des chemins de l'exil à ceux de la Résistance (1939–1945)*, preface by Bartolomé Bennassar. Perpignan: El Trabucaire, 1991.

—— *Vous avez la mémoire courte . . .*, preface by Claude Marti. Marcevol (Pyrénées-Orientales): Éditions du Chiendent, 1981.

GRIÑO, MARIE-CARMEN, and CABAL, MARIJOE, 'Les Réfugiés espagnols dans le Tarn, de 1936 à 1940'. Mémoire de maîtrise, université de Toulouse II (Le Mirail), 1976.

GROS, JOSÉ, *Abriendo camino: Relatos de un guerrillero comunista español*, prologue by Dolores Ibarruri. Paris: Colección Ebro, Librairie du Globe, 1971.

GRYNBERG, ANNE, 'Les Camps en France', in Milza and Peschanski, 637–46.

Guerra y revolución en España, 1936–1939. Moscow: Progreso, 1966–71.

HAGNAUER, ROGER, 'Le Crime de Karaganda: de Franco à Staline!', *La Révolution prolétarienne*, 14, (May 1948), 23/443.

HASTINGS, MAX, *Das Reich: Resistance and the March of the 2nd SS Panzer Division through France, June 1944*. London: Michael Joseph, 1981; Pan Books, 1981.

HEIM, ROGER, *La Sombre Route*. Paris: José Corti, 1947.

HEINE, HARTMUT, *La oposición política al franquismo: De 1939 a 1952*, prologue by Angel Viñas. Barcelona: Editorial Crítica, 1983.

HÉNOCQUE, Abbé G., *Les Antres de la bête: Fresnes, Buchenwald, Dachau*. Paris: G. Durassié, 1947.

HERNANDEZ, JESUS, *En el pais de la gran mentira*. Madrid: G. del Toro, 1974.

—— *La grande trahison*, trans. Pierre Berthelin. Paris: Fasquelle, 1953.

—— *Yo fui un ministro de Stalin*. Mexico City: Editorial América, 1953.

HERNANDO VILLACAMPA, FORTUNATO. *Amical de Guerrilleros españoles: Su historia, 1947–1984*. Toulouse: no pub., n.d. (1991?).

HOLBAN, BORIS, *Testament: Après quarante-cinq ans de silence, le chef militaire des FTP-MOI de Paris parle*. Paris: Calmann-Lévy, 1989.

HORWITZ, GORDON, J., *In the Shadow of Death: Living Outside the Gates of Mauthausen*. London: I. B. Tauris, 1991.

IBARRURI, DOLORES, *Memorias de Pasionaria: La lucha y la vida*. Part 1: *El único camino*. Part 2: *Me faltaba España, 1939–1977*. Barcelona: Planeta, 1985.

L'Insurrection d'Eysses (19–23 février 1944): Une prison dans la Résistance. Paris: Éditions Sociales, 1957.

IPPÉCOURT, PIERRE VUILLET, *Les Chemins d'Espagne: Mémoires et documents sur la Guerre Secrète à travers les Pyrénées, 1940–1945*. Paris: Gaucher, 1948.

ISELIN, BERNARD, 'La déportation', *Les Dossiers de l'histoire*, 67 (Dec. 1988–Jan. 1989), 23–123.

Italiens et Espagnols en France, 1938–1946, see *Milza and Peschanski (eds).

JÄCKEL, EBERHARD, *La France dans l'Europe d'Hitler*, trans. Denise Meunier, preface by Alfred Grosser. Paris: Fayard, 1968.

JIMENO, ARSENIO, *Francisco Largo Caballero: Unos apuntes biográficos y tres conferencias*. Paris: Ediciones Acción, n.d.

JOURDAN, LOUIS, HELFGOTT, JULIEN, and GOLLIET, PIERRE, *Glières, Haute-Savoie, 31 janvier–26 mars 1944: Première bataille de la Résistance.* Geneva: L'Association des Rescapés des Glières, n.d. (1957).

JOUVENEL, BERTRAND DE, in collaboration with Jeannie Malige, *Un Voyageur dans le siècle, 1903–1945* Paris: Robert Laffont, 1979.

KENT, VICTORIA, *Quatre ans à Paris.* Trans. from the Catalan by Pierre Darmangeat. Paris: Le Livre du Jour, 1947.

Konzentrationslager Buchenwald Post Weimar/Thür. Buchenwald: Nationale Mahn- und Gedenkstätte, 1990.

KRIEGEL, ANNIE, in collaboration with Guillaume Bourgeois, *Les Communistes français, 1920–1970.* Paris: Le Seuil, 1985.

KÜHN, GÜNTER, and WEBER, WOLFGANG, *Stärker als die Wölfe.* Berlin: Militär-verlag der Deutschen Demokratischen Republik, 1976.

LABEDAN, GUY, 'La Libération en R4', in Trempé, 33–47.

LABORIE, PIERRE, 'Opinion et représentations: la Libération et l'image de la Résistance', *Revue d'histoire de la Deuxième Guerre mondiale et conflits contemporains,* 131 (July 1983), 65–91.

—— 'Les Partis politiques et la Résistance dans le Lot', *Revue d'histoire de la Deuxième Guerre mondiale,* 85 (Jan. 1972), 3–32.

LAFFITTE, JEAN, *Ceux qui vivent.* Paris: Éditions Hier et Aujourd'hui, 1947; Les Éditeurs Français Réunis, 1958.

LAHARIE, CLAUDE, *Le Camp de Gurs, 1939–1945.* Pau: Info-Camp, 1984.

LARIO SANCHEZ, JUAN, *Habla un aviador de la República.* Madrid: G. del Toro, 1973.

LAROCHE, Colonel GASTON [Colonel FTPF Boris Matline], *On les nommait des étrangers: Les Immigrés dans la Résistance.* Paris: Les Éditeurs Français Réunis, 1965.

LAURENS, A[NDRÉ], 'Statistique de la répression à la Libération: département de l'Ariège', *Bulletin du Comité d'histoire de la 2ᵉ Guerre mondiale,* 239 (Jan.–Mar. 1980), 32–9.

LE CAËR, PAUL, *KL Mauthausen: Schlier/Redl-Zipf, 1943–1945.* Paris: Amicale de Mauthausen, 1984.

LE CHÊNE, EVELYN, *Mauthausen: The History of a Death Camp.* London: Methuen, 1971.

LEGARRETA, DOROTHY, *The Guernica Generation: Basque Refugee Children of the Spanish Civil War.* Reno: University of Nevada Press, 1984.

LEGRIS, MICHEL, 'Les Espagnols en deçà des Pyrénées', *Le Monde,* 8–12 Jan. 1964.

LÉVY, [Dr] CLAUDE, *Les Parias de la Résistance.* Paris: Calmann-Lévy, 1970.

LÉVY, [Général] GILLES, and CORDET, FRANCIS, *A nous, Auvergne! La vérité sur la Résistance en Auvergne (1940–1944).* Paris: Presses de la Cité, 1982.

La Libération dans le Languedoc, proceedings of the conference in Montpellier. Toulouse: Eché, 1989.

La Libération dans le midi de la France, see *Trempé, Rolande (ed.).

La Libération de la France, proceedings of a conference held in 1974. Paris: Éditions du Centre national de la recherche scientifique, 1976.

The Liberation of the Nazi Concentration Camps, 1945, ed. Brewster

Chamberlain and Marcia Feldman, introduction by Robert H. Abzug. Washington, DC: US Holocaust Memorial Council, 1987.

LINDQUIST, ELIZABETH ANN MARIE, 'The Experience of the Spanish Republicans in the Auvergne, 1936–1946'. Ph.D. dissertation, University of Kansas, 1984.

LISTER, ENRIQUE, *¡Basta! Una aportación a la lucha por la recuperación del Partido*. N.p.: n. pub., n.d.

—— *Cómo destruyó Carrillo el PCE*. Barcelona: Planeta, 1983.

—— *Memorias de un luchador*. Madrid: G. del Toro, 1977.

LLORENS, VICENTE, 'La emigración republicana de 1939', in Abellán, i. 95–200.

MACDONALD, NANCY, *Homage to the Spanish Exiles: Voices from the Spanish Civil War*. New York: Human Sciences Press, 1987.

MACKNESS, ROBIN, *Oradour, l'or des SS*. Geneva: Alpen, 1989.

MADARIAGA, SALVADOR DE, *España*. Buenos Aires: Editorial Sudamericana, 1944.

MARRUS, MICHAEL R., and PAXTON, Robert O., *Vichy France and the Jews*. New York: Basic Books, 1981.

MARSÁLEK, HANS, *Die Geschichte des Konzentrationslager Mauthausen: Dokumentation*. Vienna: Österreichische Lagergemeinschaft Mauthausen, 1974.

—— *Giftgas im KZ-Mauthausen: Die Vergasungsaktionen im Konzentrationslager Mauthausen (Gaskammer, Gaswagen, Vergasungsanstalt Hartheim, Tarnnamen)*. Vienna: Österreichische Lagergemeinschaft Mauthausen, 1988.

—— *Mauthausen: 8. 8. 1938–5. 5. 1945*. Vienna: Steindl-Druck, n.d.

MARTELLI, ROGER, 'La Stratégie communiste de Munich au Front national', *Cahiers d'histoire de l'Institut de recherches marxistes*, special issue 14 (Sept. 1983), 9–46.

MARTÍN CRISTINA, *Éxodo de los republicanos españoles*. Mexico City: Colección Malaga, 1972.

MARTÍN, MARCOS, *Reportajes desde la Unión Soviética*. Moscow: Agencia de Prensa Novosti, 1981.

MARTÍNEZ, CARLOS, *Crónica de una emigración: La de los republicanos españoles en 1939*. Mexico City: Libro Mex Editores, 1959.

MARTÍNEZ, REGULO, *Republicanos en el exilio*. Barcelona: Editorial Personas, 1976.

MAURIN, JULES, 'La Situation militaire à la Libération dans la R3', in Trempé, 21–31.

MAURY, LUCIEN, alias Frank, *Le Maquis de Picaussel: De l'Aude au Danube*. Quillan: Imprimerie T. Tinena, 1975.

—— *La Résistance audoise (1940–1944)*, 2 vols. Quillan: Comité d'histoire de la Résistance du département de l'Aude, 1980.

Mauthausen: Des pierres qui parlent. Paris: Amicale des déportés et familles de Mauthausen, 1985.

MICHEL, HENRI, *Histoire de la Résistance en France (1940–1944)*. Paris: Presses Universitaires de France, 1950.

—— *Paris allemand*. Paris: Albin Michel, 1981 .

MICHELET, EDMOND, *Rue de la liberté: Dachau, 1943–1945*. Paris: Le Seuil, 1955.

MILZA, PIERRE, and PESCHANSKI, DENIS (eds.), *Italiens et Espagnols en France*,

1938–1946, proceedings of the international conference held in Paris on 28–9 Nov. 1991. Paris: Institut d'histoire du Temps présent, 1991.

MIRALLES [BRAVO], RAFAEL, *Españoles en Rusia*. Madrid: Ediciones y publicaciones españolas, 1947.

MOCH, JULES, *Le Communisme, jamais!* Paris: Plon, 1978.

MONTAGNANA, MARIO, *Ricordi di un operaio torinese*, ii. *Sotto la guida di Togliatti*. Rome: Rinascità, 1949.

MONTSENY, FEDERICA, *Pasión y muerte de los españoles en Francia*. Toulouse: Éditions Espoir, 1969.

MORÁN, GREGORIO, *Miseria y grandeza del Partido Comunista de España, 1939–1985*. Barcelona: Planeta, 1986.

MORENO HERNÁNDEZ, RAMÓN, *Rusia al desnudo: Revelaciones del Comisario comunista español Rafael Pelayo de Hungría, comandante del Ejército ruso*, prologue by Guillermo Alonso del Real. Madrid: Actualidad mundial, 1956.

MUSARD, FRANÇOIS, *Les Glières (26 mars 1944)*, preface by Colonel H. Romans-Petit. Paris: Robert Laffont, 1965.

NELKEN, MARGARITA, *Las torres del Kremlin*. Mexico City: Industrial y distribuidora, 1943 (3rd edn.).

NITTI, FRANCESCO FAUSTO, *Chevaux 8, hommes 70*, preface by Jean Cassou. Toulouse: Chantal, 1945.

NOGUÈRES, HENRI, *Histoire de la Résistance en France*, with the collaboration of Marcel Degliame-Fouché (i–v) and of Jean-Louis Vigier (i–ii). Paris: Robert Laffont, i (June 1940–June 1941), 1967; ii (July 1941–Oct. 1942), 1969; iii (Nov. 1942–Sept. 1943), 1972; iv (Oct. 1943–May 1944), 1976; v (June 1944–May 1945), 1981.

NOLLAU, GÜNTHER, *International Communism and World Revolution: History and Methods*, trans. Victor Andersen, foreword by Leonard Schapiro. New York: Frederick A. Praeger, 1961.

NOVICK, PETER, *The Resistance versus Vichy: The Purge of Collaborators in Liberated France*. New York: Columbia University Press, 1968.

OLIVÉ, FRANÇOIS, 'Les Réfugiés espagnols'. Unpublished article by an official of the Paris bureau of the Spanish Refugee Aid, Inc., New York, n.d.

PALACIOS CUETO, TEODORO, and LUCA DE TENA, TORQUATO, *Embajador en el infierno, memorias del capitán Palacios, once años de cautiverio en Rusia*. Madrid: Rivadeneyra/LUYVE, 1955.

PÀMIES [BERTRÁN], TERESA, *Una española llamada Dolores Ibarruri*. Mexico City: Ediciones Roca, 1975.

—— *Los que se fueron. Los que no volverán. Los que vuelven*. Barcelona: Martinez Roca, 1976.

—— *Quan érem refugiats: Memories d'un exili*. Barcelona: Dopesa, 1975.

PANTCHEFF, T. X. H., *Alderney, Fortress Island: The Germans in Alderney, 1940–1945*. Chichester: Phillimore, 1981.

PAPPALETTERA, VINCENZO and LUIGI, *La parola agli aguzzini: Le SS e i Kapò di Mauthausen svelano le leggi del Lager*. Milan: Arnoldo Mondadori, 1969.

PASELLI, LUIGI, *Azaña e la guerra di Spagna*. Florence: Le Monnier, n.d.

PAYNE, STANLEY G., *The Franco Regime, 1936–1975*. Madison: The University of Wisconsin Press, 1987.

Le PCF, 1938–1941: Front populaire, antifascisme, résistance. Special issue, *Cahiers d'histoire de l'Institut de recherches marxistes*, 14 (Sept. 1983).

PÉREZ, LÉONARD, [*Léonard Pérez*] *raconte ses mauvais souvenirs de Mauthausen Gusen.* Toulouse: n. pub., 1981.

PERO, MANUEL, *Cristino le guérillero.* Paris: Éditions France d'abord, 1946.

PFISTER, THIERRY, 'Ce que Georges Marchais ne peut pas dire', *Le Nouvel Observateur*, 17–23 Mar. 1980.

PIERDONA, CHRISTIAN, 'Les Guérilleros espagnols dans le Gers', *Résistance R4* (Toulouse), 3 (Mar. 1978), 21–4.

—— 'Les Réfugiés espagnols dans le département du Gers'. Mémoire de maîtrise, université de Toulouse II (Le Mirail), 1973.

PIGNOT, JEAN-PIERRE, 'Aspects de la Resistance à Toulouse et dans sa région: "Libérer et Fédérer".' Mémoire de maîtrise, université de Toulouse II (Le Mirail), 1976.

PIKE, DAVID WINGEATE, 'Between the Junes: The French Communists from the Collapse of France to the Invasion of Russia', *Journal of Contemporary History*, forthcoming, 28, 3, July 1993.

—— 'Les Forces allemandes dans le sud-ouest de la France, mai–juillet 1944', *Guerres mondiales et conflits contemporains*, 152 (Oct. 1988), 3–24.

—— *Les Français et la guerre d'Espagne, 1936–1939*, preface by Pierre Renouvin. Paris: Publications de la Sorbonne/Presses Universitaires de France, 1975.

—— *Jours de gloire, jours de honte: Le Parti communiste d'Espagne en France, depuis son arrivée en 1939 jusqu'à son départ en 1950*, preface by Pierre Bertaux. Paris: Sedes, 1984. (Contains list of *manuscrits inédits*, pp. 268–9).

—— (ed.), *Latin America in Nixon's Second Term.* Paris: ACP Publications, 1982.

—— 'La Retraite des forces allemandes du sud-ouest de la France, août 1944', *Guerres mondiales et conflits contemporains*, 164 (Oct. 1991), 49–73.

—— *Vae Victis! Los republicanos españoles refugiados en Francia, 1939–1944.* Paris: Ruedo ibérico, 1969.

Plages d'exil: Les camps de réfugiés espagnols en France, 1939, see Villegas, Jean-Claude (ed.).

PONS PRADES, EDUARDO, 'Españoles en la liberación de París', *Historia 16*, 111 (July 1985), 11–21.

—— *Guerrillas españolas, 1936–1960.* Barcelona: Planeta, 1977.

—— *Republicanos españoles en la 2a guerra mundial.* Barcelona: Planeta, 1975.

POTTIER, General FRANCIS ('Quasimodo'), *Le Commando Hispano: Episodes de la Résistance en Bigorre.* Pau: Imprimerie Marrimpouey, 1975.

POUZOL, HENRI, *La Poésie concentrationnaire: Visage de l'homme dans les camps hitlériens, 1940–1945*, preface by Pierre Seghers. Paris: Seghers, 1975.

POWELL, T[HOMAS] G., *Mexico and the Spanish Civil War.* Albuquerque: University of New Mexico Press, 1981.

PRESTON, PAUL (ed.), *Spain in Crisis: The Evolution and Decline of the Franco Regime.* Hassocks: Harvester Press, 1976.

Le Procès concentrationnaire pour la vérité sur les camps: Extraits des débats. Paris: Le Pavois, 1951.

RAZOLA, MANUEL, and CONSTANTE, MARIANO, in collaboration with Patricio Serrano, *Triangle bleu: Les Républicains espagnols à Mauthausen, 1940–1945*, preface by Pierre Daix. Paris: Gallimard, 1969.

—— and C[ONSTANTE] CAMPO, Mariano, in collaboration with Patricio Serrano, *Triángulo azul: los republicanos españoles en Mauthausen, 1940–1945*, preface by Pierre Daix; trans. by Janine Muls de Liarás. Barcelona: Ediciones Peninsula, 1979.

RENAUD, CHARLES, *Matricule 63037*. Dunkirk: Imprimerie Pierre Landais, n.d. (1973).

RICO, JOSÉ ANTONIO. *En los dominios del Kremlin: Ocho años y medio en Rusia*. Mexico City: Editorial Atlantico, 1952.

RIEBER, ALFRED J., *Stalin and the French Communist Party, 1941–1947*. New York and London: Columbia University Press, 1962.

RIENFFER, KARL (pseudonym), *Comunistas españoles en América*. Madrid: Editora Nacional, 1953.

RIQUET, MICHEL, SJ, *Chrétiens de France dans l'Europe enchaînée: Genèse du Secours catholique*. Paris: Editions S.O.S., 1972.

—— L'Europe à Mauthausen: souvenir de la maison des morts', *Études*, Apr.–June 1945, 289–304.

RIVAS, ENRIQUE DE, 'Azaña en Montauban: del asilo político al confinamiento a perpetuidad', *Historia 16*, 178 (Feb. 1991), 12–30.

ROBRIEUX, PHILIPPE, *Histoire intérieur du Parti communiste*, i. *1920–1945*. Paris: Arthème Fayard, 1980.

ROIG, MONTSERRAT, *Els Catalans als camps nazis*, prologue by Arthur London. Barcelona: Edicions 62, 1977.

—— 'Una generación romántica: Españoles en los campos nazis', *Triunfo*, 532 (9 Dec. 1972), 34–7.

ROLLAND, DENIS, 'Aperçus sur la réémigration vers l'Amérique latine des réfugiés espagnols en France pendant les années de guerre: politique des États et profil de réémigrants', in Milza and Peschanski, 51–94.

—— *Vichy et la France Libre au Mexique: Guerres, cultures et propagande pendant la Seconde Guerre mondiale*, foreword by François Bédarida, preface by François-Xavier Guerra. Paris: L'Harmattan, 1990.

—— 'Vichy et les réfugiés espagnols', *Vingtième siècle*, July–Sept. 1986, 67–74.

ROS, ANTONIO, *Diario de un refugiado republicano*, prologue by José María Pemán. Barcelona: Grijalbo, 1976.

ROSSI, A. (pseudonym of Angelo Tasca), *A Communist Party in Action: An Account of the Organization and Operations in France*. New Haven, Conn.: Yale University Press, 1949.

ROVAN, JOSEPH, *Contes de Dachau*. Paris: René Julliard, 1987.

RUBIO, JAVIER, *La emigración de la guerra civil de 1936–1939*, 3 vols. Madrid: San Martín, 1977.

—— *La emigración española a Francia*. Barcelona: Ariel, 1974.

—— 'Nuevas precisiones sobre la inmediata postguerra civil: el exilio en 1939–

1940'. Paper presented at the International Conference on the Spanish Civil War held in Barcelona on 19–21 Apr. 1979.

—— 'Le Parti communiste d'Espagne en exil dans l'immédiate après-guerre civile (1939–1941)', *Matériaux pour l'histoire de notre temps*, 3–4 (July–Dec. 1985), 93–9.

RUIZ AYÚCAR, ANGEL, *El Partido Comunista: 37 años de clandestinidad*. Madrid: San Martín, 1976.

SALAS LARRAZABAL, Ramón, *Pérdidas de la guerra*. Barcelona: Planeta, 1977.

SAÑA [ALCÓN], HELENO, *La internacional comunista: 1919–1945*. Madrid: Zero, 1972.

SANZ, MIGUEL ANGEL (see also ANGEL), *Luchando en tierras de Francia: La participación de los españoles en la Resistencia*, prologue by Jean Cassou. Madrid: Ediciones de la Torre, 1981.

SCHRAMM, HANNA, and VORMEIER, BARBARA, *Vivre à Gurs: Un camp de concentration français, 1940–1941*, trans. Irène Petit. Paris: François Masperó, 1979.

SENTIS, GEORGES, 'Les Communistes des Bassins houillers de l'Avignon et du Tarn à la Libération', 4 vols. Thèse pour le doctorat de 3ème cycle, université de Lille, III, 1980.

—— 'Les Communistes du Tarn et de l'Aveyron à la Libération', *Cahiers d'histoire de l'Institut de Recherches marxistes*, 5 (39) (2nd trimester 1981), 95–120.

—— *Les Communistes et la Résistance dans les Pyrénées-Orientales*, 2 vols. Paris: Institut des recherches marxistes, Comité d'histoire de la Résistance catalane, 1983.

SERGE, VICTOR, 'L'Assassinat de Léon Trotsky', *La Révolution prolétarienne*, Apr. 1947, 9–12.

SMITH, LOIS ELWYN, *Mexico and the Spanish Republicans*. Berkeley, Calif., and Los Angeles: University of California Press, 1955.

SNYDER, LOUIS L., *Encyclopedia of the Third Reich*. New York: Paragon House, 1989.

SOLZHENITSYN, ALEKSANDR ISAEVICH, *The Gulag Archipelago, 1918–1956: An Experiment in Literary Investigation*, 3 vols. New York: Harper & Row, 1974–8.

SORIANO, ANTONIO, *Éxodos: Historia oral del exilio republicano en Francia, 1939–1945*, prologue by Roberto Mesa. Barcelona: Crítica (Grupo editorial Grijalbo), 1989.

—— 'Itinéraire des exilés espagnols en France dans Toulouse et sa région: Témoignages', in Milza and Peschanski, 601–14.

SOULA, SYLVIE, 'Ceux qui vivent . . . Les Résistants en Haute-Garonne. Histoire, organisation et sociologie'. Mémoire de maîtrise, université de Toulouse II (Le Mirail), 1987.

Spain in Crisis: The Evolution and Decline of the Franco Regime, see *Preston, Paul, (ed.).

SPEER, ALBERT, *Infiltration*, trans. Joachim Neugroschel. New York: Macmillan, 1981.

STECKOLL, SOLOMON H., *The Alderney Death Camp*. London: Granada, 1982.

STEIN, LOUIS, *Beyond Death and Exile: The Spanish Republicans in France, 1939–1955*. Cambridge, Mass.: Harvard University Press, 1979.

STEINBERG, LUCIEN, *Les autorités allemandes en France occupée: Inventaire commenté de la collection de documents conservés au Centre de Documentation juive contemporaine*, foreword by Isaac Schneersohn, preface by Jacques Delarue. Paris: CDJC, 1966.

—— in collaboration with Jean-Marie Fitère, *Les Allemands en France, 1940–1944*. Paris: Albin Michel, 1980.

SWEETS, JOHN F., *Choices in Vichy France: The French under Nazi Occupation*. New York and Oxford: Oxford University Press, 1986.

TAEGE, HERBERT, *Wo ist Abel? Weiterer Enthüllungen und Dokumente zum Komplex Tulle-Oradour*. Lindhorst: Askania, 1985.

—— *Wo ist Kain? Enthüllungen und Dokumente zum Komplex Tulle-Oradour*. Lindhorst: Askania, 1981.

TAGÜEÑA LACORTE, MANUEL, *Testimonio de dos guerras*. Mexico City: Oasis, 1973.

TANDLER, NICHOLAS, *L'Impossible Biographie de Georges Marchais*. Paris: Albatros, 1980.

TESSIN, GEORG, *Verbände und Truppen der deutschen Wehrmacht und Waffen SS im Zweiten Weltkrieg 1939–1945*, ii: *Die Landstreitkräfte 1–5*. Frankfurt-am-Main: E. S. Mittler, 1965.

THOMAS, HUGH, *The Spanish Civil War*. London: Hamish Hamilton, 1977.

THOUREL, MARCEL, *Itinéraire d'un cadre communiste, 1935–1950: Du stalinisme au trotskysme*, preface by Rolande Trempé, introduction and notes by Dominique Porté. Toulouse: Privat, 1980.

TILLARD, PAUL, *Mauthausen*, preface by Jean-Richard Bloch. Paris: Éditions Sociales, 1945.

TILLON, CHARLES, *Les FTPF: Témoignage pour servir à l'histoire de la Résistance*. Paris: René Julliard, 1962.

—— *On chantait rouge*. Paris: Robert Laffont, 1977.

Le Train fantôme: Toulouse–Bordeaux–Sorgues–Dachau, preface by Jean Garcin, President of the General Council of Vaucluse. Sorgues: Études Sorguaises, 1991.

TREMPÉ, ROLANDE (ed.) *La Libération dans le midi de la France*, proceedings of the conference organized by the universities of Toulouse-Le Mirail and Paul Valéry de Montpellier and held in Toulouse on 7–8 June 1985. Toulouse: Eché, 1986.

TUÑÓN DE LARA, MANUEL, 'Los españoles en la II guerra mundial y su participación en la resistencia francesa', in Abellan, 11–87.

VANNI, ETTORE, *Io, comunista in Russia*. Bologna: Cappelli, 1949.

VEGA, BERNARDO, *La migración española de 1939 y los inicios del marxismo-leninismo en la República Dominicana*. Santo Domingo: Fundación Cultural Dominicana, 1984, 1989.

VIELZEUF, AIMÉ, *Et la Cévenne s'embrasa*. Nîmes: Louis Salle, 1965.

—— *On les appelait 'les bandits'*, preface by André Chamson. Uzès: Ateliers H. Peladan, 1967.

VILANOVA, ANTONIO. *Los olvidados*. Paris: Ruedo ibérico, 1969.

VILLEGAS, JEAN-CLAUDE (ed.), *Plages d'exil: Les Camps de réfugiés espagnols en France, 1939*, preface by Jorge Semprún, introduction by Pierre Vilar. Nanterre: Bibliothèque de Documentation Internationale Contemporaine, 1989.

WALL, IRWIN M., *French Communism in the Era of Stalin: The Quest for Unity and Integration, 1945–1962*. Westport, Conn.: Greenwood, 1983.

WATT, GEORGE, *The Comet Connection: Escape from Hitler's Europe*. Lexington: The University Press of Kentucky, 1990.

WEILL, Dr JOSEPH, *Contribution à l'histoire des camps d'internement dans l'Anti-France*. Paris: Éditions du Centre de documentation juive contemporaine, 1946.

WETTERWALD, Dr FRANÇOIS, *Les Morts inutiles*. Paris: Éditions de Minuit, 1946.

WIESENTHAL, SIMON, *Justice n'est pas vengeance: Une autobiographie*, trans. Odile Demange. Paris: Robert Laffont, 1989.

WOOD, ALAN and MARY, *Islands in Danger*. Morley, Yorks.: Elmfield Press, 1975.

WORMSER-MIGOT, OLGA, *Le Retour des déportés: Quand les alliés ouvrirent les portes*. Brussels: Éditions Complexe, 1985.

—— and MICHEL, HENRI, *Tragédie de la déportation, 1940–1945: Témoignages de survivants des camps de concentration allemands*. Paris: Hachette, 1954.

YAGÜE, MARÍA EUGENIA, *Santiago Carrillo*. Madrid: Editorial Cambio 16, 1977.

ZAFRA, ENRIQUE, CREGO, ROSALÍA, and HEREDA, CARMEN, *Los niños españoles evacuados a la URSS (1937)*, prologue by Angel Galán Sánchez. Madrid: Ediciones de la Torre, 1989.

ZURITA CASTAÑER, JOAQUÍN, *Los círculos del exilio español en Europa (1939–1975)*. Saragossa: self-pub., 1985.

INDEX